CENTURY 21®

Computer Applications and Keyboarding 9E

COMPREHENSIVE, Lessons 1-170

JACK P. HOGGATT, ED.D.

Professor of Business Communication
University of Wisconsin
Eau Claire (WI)

JON A. SHANK, ED.D.

Professor of Education
Robert Morris University
Moon Township (PA)

SOUTH-WESTERN
CENGAGE Learning™

Australia • Brazil • Canada • Mexico • Singapore • Spain • United Kingdom • United States

Century 21® Computer Applications and Keyboarding, Comprehensive, Lessons 1-170, Ninth Edition
Jack Hoggatt, Jon Shank

Vice President of Editorial, Business: Jack W. Calhoun

Vice President/Editor-in-Chief: Karen Schmohe

Acquisitions Editor: Jane Congdon

Sr. Developmental Editor: Dave Lafferty

Consulting Editor: Jean Findley, Custom Editorial Productions, Inc.

Marketing Manager: Valerie Lauer

Sr. Content Project Manager: Martha Conway

Manager of Technology, Editorial: Liz Wilkes

Media Editor: Sally Nieman

Technical Reviewers: Gayle Statman, Amy Cole

Sr. Manufacturing Buyer: Charlene Taylor

Production Service: GGS Book Services

Copyeditor: Gary Morris

Sr. Art Director: Tippy McIntosh

Cover and Internal Designer: Grannan Graphic Design Ltd.

Cover Image: Grannan Graphic Design Ltd.

Photography Manager: Deanna Ettinger

Photo Researcher: Darren Wright

For product information and technology assistance, contact us at
Cengage Learning Customer & Sales Support, 1-800-354-9706

For permission to use material from this text or product, submit all requests online at www.cengage.com/permissions Further permissions questions can be emailed to **permissionrequest@cengage.com**

Microsoft and Windows are registered trademarks of Microsoft Corporation in the U.S. and/or other countries.

The names of all products mentioned herein are used for identification purposes only and may be trademarks or registered trademarks of their respective owners. South-Western disclaims any affiliation, association, connection with, sponsorship, or endorsement by such owners.

ISBN-13: 978-0-538-44906-9
ISBN-10: 0-538-44906-3

South-Western Cengage Learning
5191 Natorp Boulevard
Mason, OH 45040
USA

Cengage Learning products are represented in Canada by Nelson Education, Ltd.

For your course and learning solutions, visit **school.cengage.com**

Printed in the United States of America
2 3 4 5 6 7 13 12 11 10

A Century of Innovation

Century 21® Computer Applications and Keyboarding, 9E Hoggatt and Shank

Provide students with the best in keyboarding education from the proven leader in Business Education. The latest edition of *Century 21® Computer Applications and Keyboarding* prepares students for a lifetime of keyboarding success with innovative technology solutions that reflect today's business needs. Students tap into the latest keyboarding technology, learn to master computer applications, and increase their math and communication skills with this best-selling text.

Unparalleled Enhancements

- **NEW! Twenty additional lessons** provide a more complete integration of computer applications throughout the text.
- **NEW for Office 2007!** Integrates new document formats that support the defaults in Microsoft Office 2007 and still covers traditional document formats.
- *Century 21* works with the new *MicroType 5 with CheckPro™*—the all-in-one software solution for new-key learning and review, skill building, and document checking.

Proven Cycle Approach — *Learn. Improve. Enhance. Build.*

No other text does a better job of ensuring that your students understand and effectively use what they've learned. *Century 21's* **unique cross-curricular cycle approach** reflects a strong instructional design based on decades of learning success. Instruction is broken into two cycles each semester. Students begin with a foundation in the **basics**, and then revisit content to **improve** skills. Students return to content again to **enhance** abilities, and finally learn to **build** upon the knowledge already developed.

Interactive Innovation

Integrated computer applications effectively prepare students for the business world by bringing technology into each instructional cycle. **Current technologies** including the Internet, e-mail, database, electronic presentations, spreadsheets, and advanced word processing are addressed to prepare students for tomorrow's business environment. **Coverage of input technologies** equips students to integrate the power of PCs and PDAs. Includes emerging technologies such as speech recognition.

Accurate Assessment with Triple Controls

Only *Century 21* uses **Triple Control** guidelines for timed writings and skill building. Three factors—syllabic intensity, average word length, percentage of high-frequency words—are combined for the most accurate evaluation of students' keying skills.

Exceptional Resources

The online companion site at www.cengage.com/school/keyboarding/c21 offers a stimulating, interactive learning environment. Students can find links for Internet research, online simulations, Career Cluster information, and more. Instructors will have immediate access to all necessary course materials including lesson plans, tests, and software ancillaries.

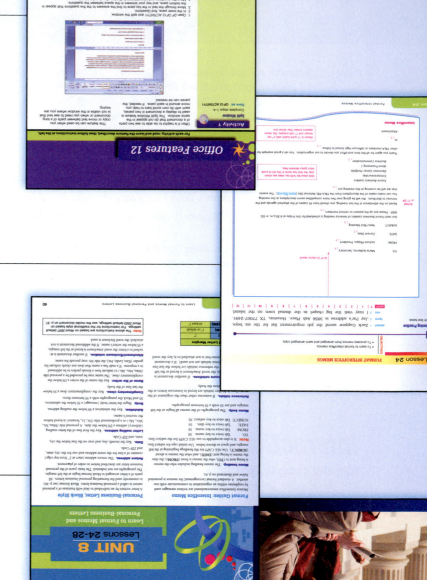

New for Office 2007

- **Office Features** offer specific instruction on Microsoft Office 2007 applications—Word, Excel, PowerPoint, and Access.

Lesson Opener

- **Model documents** show correct formatting and illustrate cross-curricular themes.
- **Scales** identify gross words a minute (*gwam*) to measure keying productivity.
- **Lesson Objectives** identify key areas of learning material.
- **Warm-up drills** prepare students to key lesson throughout.

Unit Opener

- **Format Guides** provide overviews of document formats.

Established Cycle Approach

- **Cycle approach with cross-curricular themes** reinforces skills and enhances learning in other disciplines. Each cycle emphasizes a unique subject throughout—from source document to Internet activities.
  - **Cycle 1:** Arts & Literature
  - **Cycle 2:** Social Studies
  - **Cycle 3:** Science & Math
  - **Cycle 4:** Environment & Health

New-Key Learning and Review

- **New-key learning** provides the basic skills for success.
- **New-key review** lessons provide an alternative for experienced students.
- **Correct keyboarding techniques** are emphasized visually. Keyboards help students with correct hand and finger positions.
- **Instructions** appear at left of page with **source copy** at right.
- **Balanced-hand drills** ensure equal use of right and left hand for maximum proficiency.

Timed Writings

- **Triple Controls** provide the most accurate evaluation of students' skills.
- **Lesson activities** are clearly labeled.
- **Icons** identify timings checked in *MicroPace* and indicate the difficulty of each timing.

Proofreading Practice

- **Script and rough-draft copy** provide real-world keying experience.

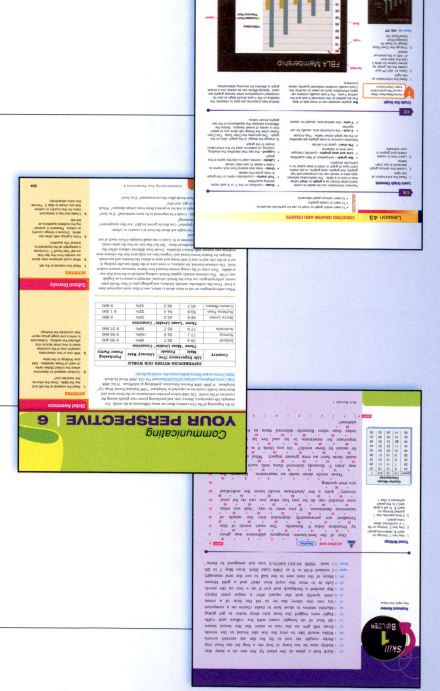

Strengthen Skills

- **Skill Builders** reinforce speed and accuracy for keyboarding success. The activities help students improve keying techniques and productivity.

Exciting Features

- **Communicating Your Perspective** activities focus on timely topics such as global awareness, cultural diversity, and ethics.
- **Special pages** invite individual and group participation.
- **Activities** combine keying practice with research and critical thinking.

Software Success

- **Computer applications** are integrated throughout the text to better prepare students for using these important skills.
- **Influential technology** such as PDAs, Internet, e-mail, database, electronic presentations, and spreadsheets are emphasized.

Innovative Instruction

- **Application Icons and Paths**—tab/group/command—provide clear directions on the ribbon to guide students to the commands within each application.

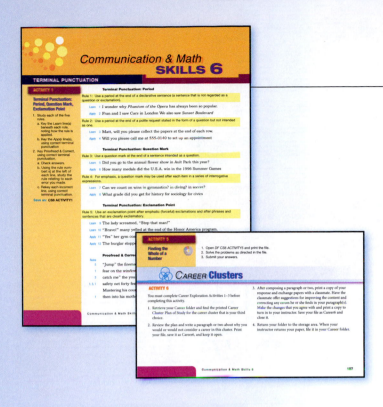

Cross-Curricular Reinforcement

- **Communication Skills,** such as grammar and punctuation, strengthen students' knowledge. Students complete exercises to apply rules given in the activity.
- **NEW! Math skills activities** reinforce the cross-curricular approach.
- **Career Clusters** reinforce the core standards and help students make a real-world connection.

Additional Features

- **Language skills** are incorporated into lessons.
- **Internet activities** enhance lessons and follow cross-curricular themes.
- Optional **word processing activities** introduce commands and provide additional practice.

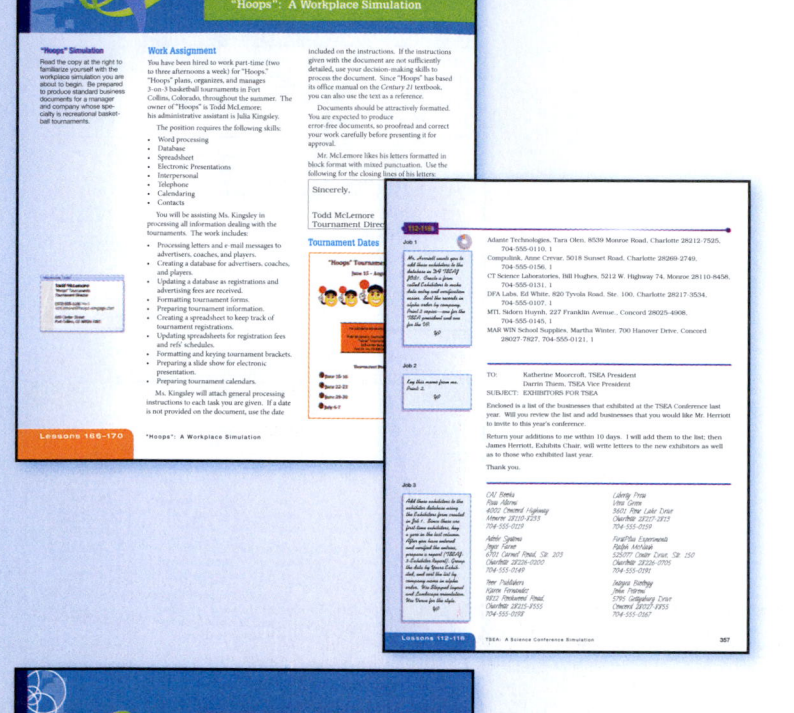

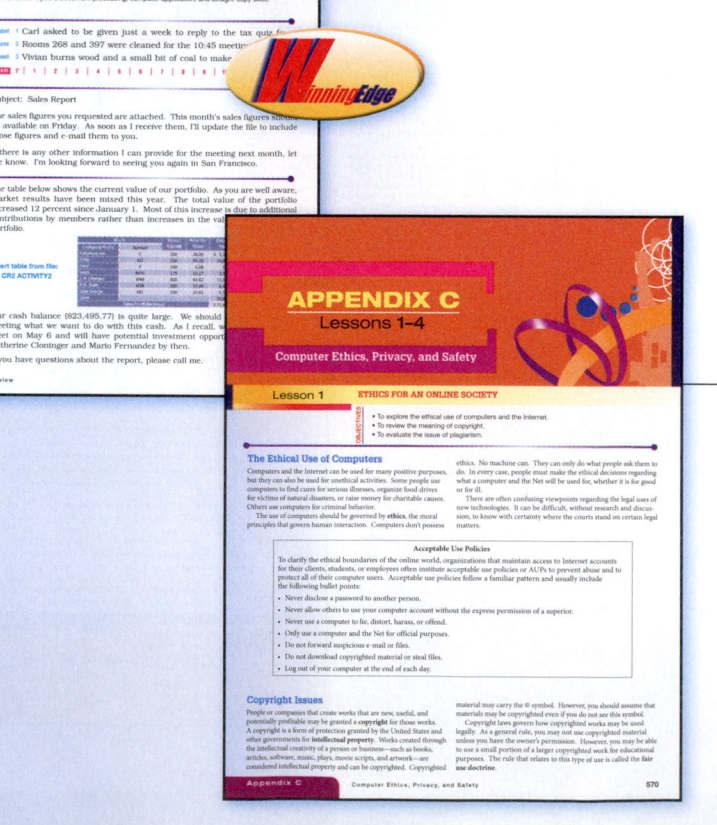

- **CD Icons** throughout the text identify data files.

- Updated **Integrated Workplace Simulations** reflect new business topics, current technology, and actual job situations.

- The **Capstone Project**—Hoops—reflects current technology and actual job situations.

Winning Edge activities and performance indicators throughout the Cycle Reviews and Assessments prepare students for competitive BPA and FBLA events.

Appendices provide in-depth information about current career and technology issues.

- Career Development and Employment Readiness

- Leadership

- Computer Ethics, Privacy, and Safety

Everything You and Your Students Need for *Success*

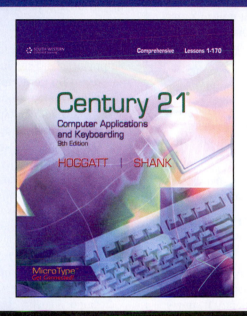

Century 21 Computer Applications and Keyboarding 9E

Item	ISBN
Text, Century 21 Computer Applications and Keyboarding Comprehensive, Lessons 1–170	978-0-538-44906-9
Comprehensive Text, Lessons 1–170/eBook Bundle	978-0-324-67238-1
Workplace Enrichment Activities	978-0-538-44921-2
Spanish Language Supplement	978-0-538-44915-1
Style Manual	978-0-538-44916-8
Placement/Performance Tests	978-0-538-44922-9
Wraparound Instructor's Edition, Comprehensive, Lessons 1–170	978-0-538-44917-5
Instructor's Manual and Solutions Key	978-0-538-44919-9
PC Keyboard Wall Poster	978-0-538-44923-6
Instructor's Resource CD	978-0-538-44913-7
ExamView	978-0-538-44920-5
Instructor's Resource Kit	978-0-538-44944-1
MicroType 5 Network/Site License Package	978-0-538-44977-9
MicroType 5 with CheckPro Network/Site License Package	978-0-538-44983-0
MicroType 5 with CheckPro Demo CD	978-0-538-44986-1
Century 21 9E Sampler	978-0-538-44953-3

Preface

The ninth edition of *Century 21 Computer Applications & Keyboarding* provides a high degree of flexibility for moving between traditional and new content areas. This flexibility permits the structuring of courses to meet the needs of students, school districts, and the community. Instructors can determine where students will begin—with refresher lessons for those who have had prior touch keyboarding instruction, or with new-key lessons designed for true beginners. A placement test is available.

The 9th Edition presents choices in word processing, database, spreadsheet, and electronic presentation software features. It offers units on "Using Help," "Personal Information Management," and "Creating Web Pages," as well as workplace simulations that can be incorporated in your course as needed.

For this edition, South-Western/Cengage Learning surveyed business teachers, employed content reviewers, and met with focus groups to determine the needs of today's keyboarding students and instructors. The features of *Century 21 Computer Applications & Keyboarding, 9th Edition*, address those needs.

The *Century 21* family includes a full range of high-quality supplementary items to enhance your courses, including a Web site at www.cengage.com/school/keyboarding/c21. Thank you for choosing *Century 21*. Whether you are a new instructor, new to *Century 21*, or simply updating your C21 materials, we know that you will find this edition an exciting solution for your classes.

ABOUT THE AUTHORS

Dr. Jon A. Shank is a Professor of Education at Robert Morris University in Moon Township, Pennsylvania. For more than 20 years, he served as Dean of the School of Applied Sciences and Education at Robert Morris. Dr. Shank retired as Dean in 1998 to return to full-time teaching. He currently teaches methods courses to students who are studying to become business education teachers. Dr. Shank holds memberships in regional, state, and national business education organizations. He has received many honors during his career, including Outstanding Post-Secondary Business Educator in Pennsylvania.

Dr. Jack P. Hoggatt is Department Chair for the Department of Business Communications at the University of Wisconsin-Eau Claire. He has taught courses in Business Writing, Advanced Business Communications, and the communication component of the university's Masters in Business Administration (MBA) program. Dr. Hoggatt has held offices in several professional organizations, including the Wisconsin Business Education Association. He has served as an advisor to local and state business organizations.

Dr. Jon Shank (left) and Dr. Jack Hoggatt

REVIEWERS

Karl Gussow
Fairfax High School
Fairfax, VA

Penny Guthrie
High Plains Technology Center
Woodward OK

Linda Inman
Pasco Middle School
Dade City, FL

Bonnie Lillibridge
Wickliffe High School
Wickliffe, OH

Karen Bean May
Blinn College
Brenham, TX

Billie Miller, Ph.D.
Consumnes River College
Sacramento, CA

Kitty Olson
Blue Ridge High School
Greer, SC

Tracy Sanders
South Carolina Virtual School Program
Columbia, SC

Mary Williamson
Peabody Magnet High School
Alexandria, LA

Robin M. Albrecht
Osbourn High School
Manassas, VA

Brenda Albright-Barnhart
Bolton High School
Alexandria, LA

Maureen Anderson
City Charter School
Pittsburgh, PA

Jeff Aronsky
La Mesa Junior High School
Santa Clarita, CA

Barbara Beasley
Taylor High School
Pierson, FL

Carla Bradley
Burlington High School
Burlington, WI

Ruby Calhoun
Consumnes River College
Sacramento, CA

Marie N. Coleman
Sam Houston High School
Lake Charles, LA

Kathy Dunaway
Lloyd High School
Erlanger, KY

Peggy Eaton
Columbia Central High School
Brooklyn, MI

CONTENTS

CYCLE 2 Social Studies

CYCLE 3 Science & Math

CYCLE 4 Environment & Health

NEW KEY LEARNING

APPENDICES

RESOURCES

COMPUTER CONCEPTS

A **computer** is a machine that processes data and performs tasks according to a set of instructions. To do anything, computers must be given specific directions to follow. They get these directions from software. **Software**, such as that used for word processing, is a set of step-by-step instructions for the computer, written by computer programmers in a programming language like C++.

Computers also get instructions from you, the user. When you use the mouse (more in a moment about this tool) or the keyboard, you are giving instructions, or *input*, to your computer. That is why the mouse and keyboard are sometimes referred to as **input devices**.

Hardware is computer equipment. It carries out the software instructions. Hardware includes the central processing unit (CPU) as well as the monitor, keyboard, mouse, printer, and other *peripherals*. **Peripheral** is the name used for a piece of hardware that works with the CPU.

USING YOUR COMPUTER SAFELY

Follow these guidelines to use your computer safely:

1. Keep air vents unobstructed to prevent the computer from overheating.
2. Keep food and liquids away from your computer. If something does spill, unplug the computer and notify your instructor immediately.
3. Do not expose disks to excessive heat, cold, or moisture or to magnets, x-ray devices, or direct sunlight.
4. Use a felt-tip marker, not a ballpoint pen or a pencil, to write on disk labels.
5. Do not remove a disk from the drive when the in-use light is on.

STARTING YOUR COMPUTER

Follow these steps to start your computer:

1. Remove any disks from the disk drives.
2. Turn on the power. You may need to flip a switch or press a button on the CPU or press a button or key on the keyboard. You may also have to turn on the monitor separately.

Your computer may take a few moments to power up. The computer will execute a series of automatic steps that will load the **operating system**. The operating system—Windows® Vista, for example—is the program that manages other programs on the computer.[1] It will prepare the computer to receive your instructions and run software.

GETTING AROUND THE DESKTOP

The screen on your monitor is your **desktop**. Like the desk where you are sitting, your computer desktop is your main work area. It likely contains **icons** (picture symbols) for programs and documents, some resembling file folders that contain programs and documents. You probably have a taskbar or menu bar at the top or bottom of the screen (more about these in a moment). From here, you can start programs, find files, get information about your computer, and shut down the computer when you are finished.

A **mouse** is a tool for getting around the desktop. The same mouse actions are used in any software, though the results may vary depending on the software and version. Here are the basic ways to use a mouse:

- **Point**. Move the mouse (roll it on the work surface) so that the **pointer** (the arrow that represents the mouse's position on the screen) points to an item.
- **Click**. Press the left mouse button once and let go.
- **Double-click**. Press the left mouse button twice quickly and let go.
- **Drag**. Press and hold down the left mouse button and move the pointer to another location.

WHAT IS APPLICATION SOFTWARE?

You have probably heard the terms *application*, *application software*, and *application program*. They all mean the same thing. **Application software** is a computer program designed to perform a specific task directly for the user or for another application. Some common types of application software are word processing, spreadsheet, database, presentation, and Internet software.

---

[1] Windows® is a registered trademark of Microsoft Corporation in the United States and/or other countries.

STARTING SOFTWARE

Your computer gives you several different ways of starting programs, depending on the operating system and version. Here are two ways:

- If you have the Microsoft® Windows® operating system, click the *Start* button on the taskbar, point to *All Programs*, and click the name of the program you want to open. Your program may be inside a folder. If so, open the folder (by pointing to it) to get to the program.

- With Microsoft® Windows® operating system and Macintosh® computers, double-click the program icon on the desktop. Your program may be inside a folder. If so, open the folder (by double-clicking it) to get to the program.

Application software is displayed in a **window** on the monitor. The features of all windows are the same. At the top is the **title bar**. The title bar displays the name of the file you are working on and, for some programs, the name of the software (such as *Microsoft® Word*). If you haven't yet saved the document with a filename, the title bar will say something like *Document* or *unmodified*, along with the name of the software. Under the title bar, you may see a menu bar and one or more toolbars or button bars. These bars allow you to choose commands in your software. We'll talk more about them in the next section.

The title bar contains boxes that allow you to resize and close the window. At the bottom and right sides of the window are **scroll bars**. You can click or drag these bars with the mouse to navigate (move around in) your document. To learn more about resizing and navigating a window, go to the Windows® Tutorial on pages R5–R7.

CHOOSING COMMANDS

Most software gives you several different ways to choose commands. As you work with a program, you will find the ways that are easiest for you.

The Ribbon. If you are using the applications in the 2007 Microsoft Office System (such as *Word, Excel,* or *PowerPoint*), you will see a Ribbon at the top of your application window. The ribbon is comprised of tabs, groups, and commands.

Microsoft® Word 2007 Home Ribbon[2]

The tabs are located at the top of the Ribbon. When you click on a tab, the commands available in that tab are shown beneath the tab. The commands are grouped by purpose. The groups are shown below the commands. For example, the Microsoft Word ribbon shown above illustrates what happens when the Home tab is clicked. The Home tab contains five groups:

- Clipboard
- Font
- Paragraph
- Styles
- Editing

The first group, Clipboard, has four commands that are related: Cut, Copy, Paste, and Format Painter. To use a command, click it's icon. Notice the next group is Font. All of the actions you can perform related to fonts are contained in this group.

The tabs of the Ribbon are **context-sensitive**, which means that they vary depending on what you are working on in your program. For example, the Picture Tools tab will only appear when you have selected a picture in your document, and the Table Tools tab only appears when you have selected a table.

Menus. A **menu bar** may appear at the top of your application window, just under the title bar. Like a menu in a restaurant, a menu bar offers you choices. From the menu bar, you can open a document, spell-check it, and so on. To open a menu and see its options, click the menu name in the menu bar. For example, to open the File menu, click *File*. For some software, you have to hold the mouse button down to keep the menu displayed. To choose a command, click it (Windows®) or drag down to it (Macintosh®). In some software, you can also open menus by tapping ALT plus the underlined letter in the menu name. For example, ALT + F opens the File menu. Menu names vary a little but are much the same across application software.

Toolbars. **Toolbars** let you choose commands quickly and easily. Most applications have toolbars. They have different names, such as *button bars*, in different software; but all toolbars are similar. They consist of icons or buttons that represent commands; some of the same commands found on menus. The standard toolbar contains icons for basic, often-used commands, such as saving and printing. Toolbars also exist for certain tasks, like formatting text or creating tables. In most software, pointing to a toolbar icon displays the name of the command. Clicking the icon executes the command.

Microsoft® Word 2003 Standard Toolbar

Keyboard shortcuts. Each application has its own set of **keyboard shortcuts** for opening menus and executing commands. Keyboard shortcuts usually consist of tapping a function key (e.g., F1, F2, F3) or tapping the ALT, CTRL, or COMMAND key plus some other key. For example, to open a file in *Microsoft® Word* for PCs, you would key CTRL + O. These shortcuts are often displayed on the menus and can also be found in the software's Help feature.

STARTING A NEW DOCUMENT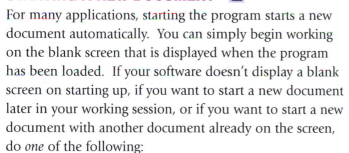

For many applications, starting the program starts a new document automatically. You can simply begin working on the blank screen that is displayed when the program has been loaded. If your software doesn't display a blank screen on starting up, if you want to start a new document later in your working session, or if you want to start a new document with another document already on the screen, do *one* of the following:

- Select the *New* command on the File menu or from the Office Button.
- Click the *New* icon, usually the first icon to the left on the standard toolbar.
- Use the keyboard shortcut for the *New* command.

A new document window will display. In some software, you may first see a **dialog box** that gives you setup options for your document. Tapping ENTER or RETURN or clicking *New* or *OK* will take you from the dialog box to a blank document window.

KEYING TEXT

Keying text in a new word processing document is easy. Simply begin keying. Text is entered to the left of the **insertion point** (the flashing line). You will use many features of your word processing software in the special Word Processing pages of this book.

SAVING A DOCUMENT

Saving a document places a copy of it on a disk in one of the computer's disk drives. This may be the hard (internal) disk of the computer or some kind of removable **medium**, such as a CD-ROM or thumb drive. This copy will not be erased when your computer is shut down. It is permanent until you delete or modify it.

Save any documents that you think you will need later. You can save a document anytime the document is on the screen—just after starting it, while you are working on it, or when you are done. Save often as you work on a document so that you will not lose your changes in case of a power failure or other problem. Follow these steps to save a document:

1. Select the *Save* command from the File menu, click the *Save* icon on the standard toolbar or Quick Access toolbar, or use the keyboard shortcut for the *Save* command.
2. If you did not save the document before, the software will display the Save As dialog box. In this dialog box, look at the *Save in, ___ Folder* box, or something similar. If the drive and/or folder where you want to save the file does not show, click the down arrow and double-click drives and folders until the box shows the correct location. The computer's hard drive is most often (C:); the drive that takes removable disks, (D:).
3. If you are saving the file to any kind of removable medium, insert that disk into the disk drive.
4. Key a name for the document in the box that says *File name, Name,* or something similar. Click *Save* or *OK* or tap ENTER or RETURN.

If you modify a document after saving it, resave the document by selecting the Save command (Step 1). The Save As dialog box will not appear this time because you already named the file.

window. The Close button in applications based on the Microsoft® Windows® operating system is the button containing an *x* at the far right of the title or menu bar. Each document window has a Close button, as does the software window.

- Use the keyboard shortcut for the Close command.

OPENING A DOCUMENT

Opening a document means retrieving it from wherever it is stored and displaying it on the screen. Follow these steps to open a document:

1. Select *Open* from the File menu or Office Button, click the *Open* icon on the standard toolbar, or use the keyboard shortcut for the Open command.
2. Choose or key the filename of the document. If you don't see the filename displayed in the Open dialog box, navigate with the mouse to where the file is stored by choosing the appropriate disk drive (and folder, if any), just as you do when saving a document. If you are retrieving a file from a CD-ROM or other external media, you will need to insert that disk into the disk drive to get the file.

CLOSING THE SOFTWARE

Choose one of these options for closing the application software:

- Select the *Exit* or *Quit* command from the File menu or Office Button.
- Click the *Close* button or *Close* box.

If you still have a file open and have not saved it, or if you have made changes to the file since your last save, you will be *prompted* to save the file. The computer is programmed to remind you of certain steps. These reminders are called **prompts**.

TURNING OFF THE COMPUTER

Follow these steps to turn off your computer:

1. Close all application software.
2. Remove any media from the disk drives.
3. Select *Shut Down* from the Start menu (Microsoft® Windows® operating system), Apple menu (Macintosh® computers), or Special menu (Macintosh® computers). On some Macintosh® computers, you can press the on/off key instead.

PRINTING A DOCUMENT

Follow these steps to print a document:

1. Turn on the printer. Make sure it is loaded with paper.
2. Display the document on the screen.
3. Select the *Print* command from the File menu or Office Button, click the *Print* icon on the standard toolbar, or use the keyboard shortcut for the *Print* command.
4. In the Print dialog box, select the print settings you want or use the settings that are already there (the **default settings**). In most software, the default settings print one copy of the document. When you are ready to print, click OK or *Print* or tap ENTER or RETURN.

CLOSING A DOCUMENT

Closing a document removes it from the window. If you have not yet saved the document, or if you have made changes to it that you haven't saved, you will be asked when you choose the **Close** command whether you first want to save the document. Choosing *No* will erase a document that has not yet been saved. For a document that has been saved, choosing *No* will erase any changes you have made to the document since last saving it. You can close a document in any of these ways:

- Select the *Close* command from the File menu or Office Button.
- Click the *Close* icon on the standard toolbar.
- Click the *Close* box or *Close* button. In Macintosh® applications, the Close box is at the top left of the

The Microsoft® Word 2007 Save As Dialog Box³

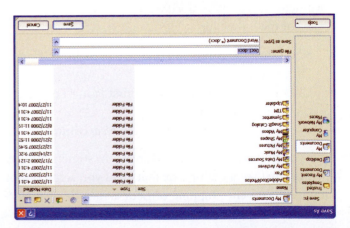

³Microsoft® is a registered trademark of Microsoft Corporation.

CYCLE 1

Computers are not just for business anymore—they are for *every*one, *every*where!

In our world of fast-paced communication, almost everything we see on TV and the Internet, hear at rap concerts and Broadway musicals, or read in books and newspapers began as keystrokes entered into a computer by a keyboard operator.

To get the most value from high-speed computers, users must be competent at the input end—the keyboard. A computer processes data and text at the same speed for everyone. But a person who keys 50 words a minute produces twice as much work as a person who keys 25 words a minute for the same amount of time.

Lessons in Cycle 1 *reinforce* your keying skills. E-mail, reports, letters, and tables are some of the ways you then apply those skills, using the features of your word processing software. The Internet activities in these lessons represent an increasingly important use of keyboarding. A series of Communication and Math Skills activities can help you do error-free work. Activities focusing on Office Features aid in refining your software skills. You'll begin looking at career options in Career Clusters activities.

Here you have an opportunity to develop skills for traveling the Information Superhighway. Take it—straightaway!

Arts & Literature

- Shoulders and upper arms should be relaxed.
- Elbows should be close to the body, bent between 90 and 120 degrees.
- Feet should be fully supported on the floor or a footrest.
- Back should be fully supported by your chair, and you should be sitting up straight or leaning back slightly.
- Thighs and hips should be parallel to the floor, with knees about the same height as the hips and feet slightly forward.

Working in the same posture or sitting still for too long is not healthy. You should change your working position frequently throughout the day by stretching your fingers, hands, and arms and by standing up and walking around occasionally.

The Department of Labor and the Workplace

In the United States, there are a number of agencies, laws, regulations, and guidelines that apply to the workplace, all designed to protect employee safety, comfort, and accessibility. Some agencies within the Department of Labor (DOL) have responsibility for administering the laws enacted to protect worker safety and health.

The Occupational Safety and Health Act is administered by the Occupational Safety and Health Administration (OSHA). Safety and health conditions in most private industries are regulated by OSHA or OSHA-approved state systems. Nearly all employees come under OSHA's jurisdiction with some exceptions such as miners, some transportation workers, some public employees, and the self-employed. Small employers (with ten or fewer employees) don't have to report injuries and illnesses, but they still must follow OSHA regulations. In addition to the specific OSHA requirements for various industries, every business has to comply with general industry standards, which cover things like safety exits, ventilation, hazardous materials, personal protective equipment like goggles and gloves, sanitation, first aid, and fire safety.

The Fair Labor Standards Act (FLSA) contains rules for the employment of young workers under the age of 18. It is administered and enforced by the Employment Standards Administration's Wage and Hour Division within the DOL. Intended to protect the health and well-being of young workers, the FLSA contains minimum age restrictions for employment, as well as restrictions on the times of day young people may work and the jobs they may perform.

The DOL also has a program called Working Partners for an Alcohol- and Drug-Free Workplace that helps employers develop guidelines for drug-free workplaces. Although such programs are not required under any laws or regulations, they help ensure safe and healthy workplaces.

Safety Policies for the Workplace

Besides having an ethical responsibility toward their employees, employers know that workplace accidents cost both money and time. OSHA's penalty for violation of safety rules that could result in death or serious physical harm is $5,000 to $70,000.

Once a safety policy is developed, it should be put it in writing. The safety policy should explain what to do in the event of a fire, explosion, natural disaster, or any other catastrophe the business may face. Fire extinguishers and first-aid kits should be provided at convenient locations, and employees should know where these are located and how to use them. In addition to emergency procedures, a safety manual should explain proper procedures for performing any routine tasks that could be hazardous.

Sample Safety Policy

It is the intent of [organization name] to provide a safe environment for all employees. It is also our intent to properly manage any accidents that occur in a way that minimizes injury and other forms of loss. In order for [organization name] to achieve our goals, we have developed a workplace safety program outlining the policies and procedures regarding employee health and safety.

While management is responsible for developing and organizing this program, its success depends on the involvement of each employee. We look forward to your cooperation and active participation.

There are established policies and laws governing what happens when a workplace accident does occur. Within the DOL, the Office of Workers' Compensation administers disability compensation programs that provide wage replacement benefits, medical treatment, vocational rehabilitation, and other benefits to workers who experience work-related injury or occupational disease.

The Americans with Disabilities Act

President George H. W. Bush signed the Americans with Disabilities Act (ADA) into law on July 26, 1990. The ADA prohibits discrimination and ensures equal opportunity for persons with disabilities in employment, state and local government services, public accommodations, commercial facilities, and transportation.

The purpose of the ADA is to ensure that people with disabilities can perform everyday activities, such as shopping, going to the movies, eating at a restaurant, or exercising at a health club. To meet the goals of the ADA, the law established requirements for businesses of all sizes. Businesses that meet these requirements recognize the importance and value of doing business with the 50 million Americans with disabilities.

Businesses that serve the public must make changes to any policies and practices that discriminate against people with disabilities; comply with accessible design standards when constructing or altering facilities; remove barriers in existing facilities; and provide auxiliary aids and services when needed to ensure effective communication with people who have hearing, vision, or speech impairments. And all businesses, even those that do not serve the public, must comply with accessible design standards for their employees.

UNIT 1
Lessons 1-8

Review Letter Keys

This unit is an 8-lesson review of the letter keys. For 16 traditional new key lessons, see New Key Learning, pages 505–545.

Lesson 1   REVIEW HOME KEYS (fdsa jkl;)

OBJECTIVE

• To review control of home keys (**fdsa jkl;**), **Space Bar**, and **Enter**.

1A

Review Work Area Arrangement

Arrange work area as shown.

- keyboard directly in front of chair
- front edge of keyboard even with edge of desk
- monitor placed for easy viewing
- book at right of keyboard

© CENGAGE LEARNING

Properly arranged work area

1B

Review Keying Position

Proper keying position includes:

- fingers curved and up-right over home keys
- wrists low but not touch-ing keyboard
- forearms parallel to slant of keyboard
- body erect, sitting back in chair
- feet on floor for balance
- eyes on copy

© franksiteman.com 2007

Proper position at computer

To protect yourself, never give your full name, personal address, phone number, school address, or other private information to individuals you do not know personally. This cannot be emphasized strongly enough. For example, never send your picture to someone you meet online that you do not know. Never agree to a face-to-face meeting with a person you have met online unless you have taken the time to run a security check on this person and have friends, peers, and parents present when you meet. Never meet a stranger in private. Do not take a chance with your personal information.

E-Harassment

Online harassment is a crime. In the workplace as well as in schools, people are obligated to cultivate an atmosphere where harassment is not tolerated. The same is true for the online community. Harassment of any kind, especially regarding race, color, religion, sex, national origin, age, or disability, may be grounds for immediate dismissal on the job, possible expulsion from school, or exclusion from using the services of an Internet service provider.

Unlawful harassment is characterized by unwelcome or unsolicited verbal or physical conduct that creates an intimidating, hostile, or offensive environment. It must be reported immediately to supervisors, human resource personnel, or Internet service providers. Companies and schools are required to investigate each allegation of harassment promptly and to act accordingly. To the extent possible, all complaints and related information should remain confidential.

ACTIVITY 3B SEARCH FOR PROBLEM-SOLVING SOLUTIONS

1. Visit two of the largest and most popular software security companies online. As you do so, take notes on the current virus threats and learn what services the companies offer for virus protection, spyware protection, firewalls, and spam blockers.
   - http://www.norton.com
   - http://www.mcafee.com/us/
2. Using Google or some other search tool, find websites for other virus protection services and companies. Take notes on what you find. For people without a lot of money, are there free or inexpensive software security solutions? How many of the sites would you trust with your computer's data?

3. There are many terms related to fraudulent activity and Internet attacks on networks and personal computers. If you don't already know the meaning of the following terms, look them up online:

Adware	Spam
Backdoor	Spyware
Cookies	Virus
Encryption	Web bugs
Hacker	Worm
Malware	Zombie PC
Phishing	

4. Prepare a briefing in the form of a press release assuming the role of a network administrator informing your network's users of the various threats to their data. Explain how they should protect themselves from malicious attacks to their digital data.

5. Form groups and discuss spam, viruses, phishes, scams, and online illegal activity. What experience has each team member had with scams, phishes, and other illegal activities? Have they heard any stories that can be researched and validated about ways people have been scanned and cheated?

> ### Tip
>
> The manufacturers of Web browsers offer secure data connections. After a secure data connection is made, you will see a little icon in the shape of a lock on the status bar of your browser. Also, the appearance of _https_ rather than _http_ in the address indicates a secure connection.

Corporate Responsibility

Companies have a responsibility to secure the privacy of their customers. To assist in this, many companies post a privacy policy on their websites. A privacy policy states how personal data will be stored, used, and deleted. Links such as _Privacy Statement_ or _Privacy Policy_ are often shown at the bottom of a site's welcome page.

Lesson 4   WORKPLACE SAFETY

OBJECTIVES
- To review proper setup of a computer workstation.
- To learn about OSHA standards and the role of the Department of Labor.
- To explore the issue of safety in the workplace.
- To learn about the ADA.

Your Computer Workstation

As you learned in Unit 1, it is important to set up your computer workstation so that you will be in a comfortable working posture. This reduces stress and strain on the muscles, tendons, and skeletal system and reduces your risk of developing a musculoskeletal disorder (MSD). Think about your computer workstation with the following points in mind:

- Arrange your desk to minimize glare from overhead lights, desk lamps, and windows to avoid eye strain.
- Hands, wrists, and forearms should be straight, in line, and parallel to the floor.
- Head should be level or bent slightly forward; you should not have to look up at your monitor.

1C

Review Home-Key Position

1. Locate and place your fingers on the home keys (**a s d f j k l ;**) with your fingers well curved and upright (not slanting).

2. Remove your fingers from the keyboard; then place them in home-key position again, curving and holding them lightly on the keys.

Left Fingers   Right Fingers

1D

Review Techniques: Keystroking and Spacing

1. Read the hints and study the illustrations at the right.

2. Place your fingers in home-key position.

3. Key the line beneath the illustration, tapping the Space Bar once at the point of each arrow.

4. Review proper position at the keyboard (1B); key the line again.

Technique Hints

Keystroking: Lightly tap each key with the tip of the finger. Keep your fingers curved.

Spacing: Tap the Space Bar with the right thumb; use a quick down-and-in motion (toward the palm). Avoid pauses before or after spacing.

© CENGAGE LEARNING

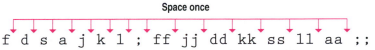

Space once

f d s a j k l ; ff jj dd kk ss ll aa ;;

1E

Review Technique: Hard Return

Read the information and study the illustration at the right.

Hard Return

`This is called a **hard return**. Use a hard return at the end of all drill lines. Use two hard returns when directed to double-space.

Hard Return Technique

Reach the little finger of the right hand to the **ENTER** key, tap the key, and return the finger quickly to home-key position.

Practice the **ENTER** key reach several times.

© CENGAGE LEARNING

criminals will find out as much as possible about a victim. They may be able to acquire bank account numbers, social security numbers, job information, loan information, family information, and spending records. Personal information may also come from stolen purses or wallets. Information can also be derived by stealing mail from trash cans!

Once a criminal has this type of information, he or she can pretend to be the victim. This is called **identity theft**. Money may be moved out of the victim's bank account, purchases made on their credit cards, loans taken out using the victim's name, and charges made on phone cards. Vacations, cars, and other expensive items may be charged to the victim.

When bills are not paid, the overdue accounts are reported on the victim's **credit report**. Credit reports keep track of a person's financial history and award them a score that is used to predict their financial integrity and ability to pay debts. A positive credit report is necessary in order to take out a loan or to make a major purchase. The victim may then be turned down for loans or not hired for jobs because of a negative credit report. The victim may not know at first what is happening or that a credit report has gone negative.

Matters can go from bad to worse. An identity thief may give the victim's name to the police during an arrest. If the person is released from police custody but does not show up for a court date, an arrest warrant may be issued for the victim!

Millions of Americans have been victims of identity theft. Businesses and victims have lost billions of dollars due to this type of crime. The U.S. Federal Trade Commission and other government and private financial institutions provide resources to help victims of identity theft. To reduce the chance of becoming a victim, read and follow the *Ten Rules to Help Avoid Identity Theft*.

ACTIVITY 3A LEARN HOW TO OBTAIN A CREDIT CARD REPORT

1. A friend of yours is concerned about her credit. Prepare an e-mail to her explaining how she can check her credit report online. Prepare to write your message by researching the following:

- Visit the FTC site at http://www.consumer.gov/idtheft/ and read what they suggest to do if you suspect identity theft. Take notes on what you learn, and include the main points in your e-mail.
- Visit the FTC site that will guide you to more information about obtaining free credit reports at http://www.ftc.gov/bcp/menus/consumer/credit/rights.shtm.
- Visit an industry site that can help you learn more about viewing your credit report on a yearly basis: point your Web browser to http://annualcreditreport.com.
- In your e-mail, explain that there are three major credit card reporting agencies. Visit each and learn how your friend can

obtain credit reports from each of them. Include information on the services they provide.

- http://www.Equifax.com
- http://www.Experian.com
- http://www.TransUnion.com

2. Prepare an e-mail message based on what you have learned and recorded in your notes.

Going Phishing?

Criminals are using increasingly sophisticated ways to steal identities. One scam is called **phishing**. Criminals may mock up an e-mail message, complete with company logos and seemingly proper information, to fool customers into thinking the e-mail is legitimate. Criminals out phishing are only looking for a few victims to take their bait.

Here is an example of an actual phish that was sent out over the Net through e-mail. We have removed the name of the bank because they are also victims of this scam.

Dear [name of bank] customer,

Fraudulent activity has been registered on your account. Please visit the following webpage [http://www.linktofakewebsite.com].

Once you have confirmed your account records you will be able to continue using your [name of bank] Internet Banking account.

Copyright © 2009 [name of bank]. All Rights Reserved [name of bank] Bank, Member FDIC.

online-banking-representative@name_of_bank.com

Phishers have become more and more creative. One infamous phish proclaimed that the recipient's personal Internet account was about to expire due to a credit card reporting error. Unless the victim clicked a hypertext link, then entered and verified his or her personal information, Internet service would be cut off within 24 hours! Naïve Internet users would take the bait, hand over all of their personal information, and then have to deal with the consequences of identity theft.

Protect Yourself

Most people online are honest and trustworthy. However, there are also people online who *will* cheat or harm you. For this reason, computer users must consider their personal security, even safety.

People online often assume imaginary identities—sometimes for fun but sometimes with malicious intent. Someone may say they are a woman when they are really a man. A person may pretend to be interested in the things that interest you in order to gain your trust. The real motive may be to deceive, scam, or even harm you.

Home-Key and Space Bar Review

Key each line twice single-spaced (SS); double-space (DS) between 2-line groups. Do not key numbers.

1 a aa j jj s ss k kk d dd l ll f ff ; ;; asdf jkl;

2 a aa j jj s ss k kk d dd l ll f ff ; ;; asdf jkl;
Tap the ENTER key twice to double-space (DS).

Spacing Cue

Tap the **ENTER** key twice to insert a DS between 2-line groups.

3 k kk a aa l ll f ff ; ;; d dd j jj s ss jkl; asdf

4 k kk a aa l ll f ff ; ;; d dd j jj s ss jkl; asdf
DS

5 la la jf jf ks ks ;d ;d ls ls aj aj kf kf d; d; k

6 la la jf jf ks ks ;d ;d ls ls aj aj kf kf d; d; k
Tap the ENTER key 3 times to triple-space (TS).

Review Technique: ENTER (Return) Key

Key each line twice SS; DS between 2-line groups.

1 js fk ld a; kj f;

2 ds af lk ;j aj sl jd f;

3 fa sd j; kl f; dj ka ls al fk

4 js ;d fj d; sk al sj d; jf ;d ks la

5 dd ;; jj ss ff kk aa ll as df jk l; la df

> Reach out with little finger; tap the ENTER key quickly; return finger to home key.

Keyboard Reinforcement

Key each line twice SS; DS between 2-line groups.

1 as; as;|lad lad|jak jak|adds adds|ask ask|sad sad;

2 dad dad|fall fall|fad; fad;|salad salad|lass lass;

3 as a fall fad; add a jak salad; as a sad lad falls

4 ask a lad; ask a lad; all jaks fall; all jaks fall

5 as a fad; as a dad; ask a lad; as a lass; all lads

6 add a jak; a fall ad; all fall ads; ask a sad lass

7 a sad lad; ask a dad; all jaks; ask a jak; sad dad

8 ask dad; as a lass falls; a fall ad; ask a sad lad

For additional practice:
MicroType 5
New Key Review, Alphabetic Lesson 1

The scammers contacted the Nebraska-based e-business, fooling them into believing they represented a legitimate import-export business. Orders were placed for thousands of dollars against the card. But a sales manager in Nebraska was suspicious and blocked the order at the last second, stopping shipment in Hong Kong, the last transit point before the goods arrived at their final destination. She checked with the bank and found that the owners of the credit card lived in neighboring Kansas, not in a country on the other side of the planet. The case was turned over to law enforcement.

The story had a happy ending and may seem like an isolated incident. Far from it. Security breaches have compromised millions of credit card numbers. For example, *CNN/Money* reported on August 6, 2008, that eleven persons were charged in the theft of over 40 million credit card accounts. The accounts were compromised by **hackers**. A hacker accesses computers and networks without proper permission. The criminals gained access to the computers of a Tucson, Arizona company that processes credit card transactions for businesses and banks. In total, more than 40 million credit and debit card accounts were compromised by the hacker's **virus**, which is a form of malicious computer code. This particular virus was designed to search out certain types of credit card transactions and steal vital information. This case may be the largest hacking and identity theft case ever prosecuted by the Department of Justice.

Computer-related crime can take many forms. For example, malicious computer viruses can hijack information, destroy data, shut down computers, or disrupt entire computer networks. Any computer that has received a virus is said to be **infected**. Some viruses can steal e-mail names from your computer without you even knowing about it, and hit your friends, colleagues, and coworkers with viruses and **spam** (unwanted and unsolicited advertising).

Individuals, governments, schools, and businesses all can become victims of high-tech crime. Even charitable organizations must take care of private information. During the Hurricane Katrina disaster, criminals posing as representatives of the American Red Cross created and sent fake e-mail messages with links to web sites that looked exactly like the real thing. Many well-meaning people were conned into giving their credit card numbers and other personal information to these criminals.

In the sections to follow, you will learn more about protecting yourself and the organizations you work with against criminal activity.

Identity Theft

Sometimes criminals may take more than a credit card number or a few e-mail addresses. They may steal a person's entire identity. The

	TEN RULES TO HELP AVOID IDENTITY THEFT	
1.	Avoid giving out personal information on the phone, through the mail, or over the Internet unless the company is reputable and provides guaranteed service warranties and consumer protection. Never give out financial information like credit card, social security, or account numbers unless you know exactly with whom you're doing business.
2.	Use strong passwords on credit card, bank, and phone accounts. Never share your ATM PIN or your passwords for your bank accounts, Internet service provider, or other Internet access point.
3.	Ask about information security procedures in your workplace and security measures provided by your Internet service provider.
4.	Install software to protect your data. For example, install any security updates to your e-mail and Web browser software. Use virus and **spyware** protection software and other tools, such as **firewalls**, to protect personal information. A firewall can include a combination of hardware and software security tools to block and filter out intrusions made by a hacker. Spyware can be installed on a computer by a hacker to gather data about the computer user.
5.	Secure personal information in the home and office. Shred charge receipts, credit records, checks, bank statements, invoices, and bills before they are thrown away. Shred any documents that may contain personal account and credit card information.
6.	Keep your social security card, driver's license, and passport in a safe place.
7.	Protect access to home computers and guard against computer viruses and hackers.
8.	Notify your bank or credit union of any suspicious e-mail messages, text messages, or phone calls asking you to verify financial information.
9.	Make sure your bank or credit union and companies with which you do business have privacy policies that they enforce. Make sure they use **encryption**, which is a set of software security tools that converts information to secure, unbreakable code.
10.	Order an annual copy of your credit report in order to look for any potential problems.

Lesson 2 — REVIEW LETTER KEYS (h, e, i, AND r)

OBJECTIVE

• To review reach technique for **h**, **e**, **i**, and **r**.

2A

H and E Review

Key each line twice (SS); DS between 2-line groups.

Review h

1 j jh j jh│ha ha│had had│has has│ash ash│hash hash;

2 had had│hall hall│half half│dash dash│flash flash;

3 ha ha; had had; has has; a hall; a hall; sash sash

Review e

4 d de d de│seed seed│deal deal│feed feed│sale sale;

5 fade fade│keel keel│sake sake│lead lead│lake lake;

6 feel safe; a lake; a leak; a jade; a desk; a deed;

2B   Skill Building

Keyboard Reinforcement

Key each line twice SS; DS between 2-line groups.

home row

1 sad sad│jak jak│salad salad│lass lass│flask flask;

2 a sad lad; a sad lad; a dad; a dad; a fall a fall;

h/e

3 heed heed│shed shed│lead lead│held held│jell jell;

4 he has a shed; half ash; he feeds; a shelf; he has

all keys learned

5 jak jak│lake lake│held held│desks desks│half half;

6 a lake sale; she has half; he held a flask; a jade

all keys learned

7 held a; he has; a jak ad; a jade seal; a sled fell

8 he fell; ask a lad; he has a jak; all fall; a shed

all keys learned

9 a jade; she fell; a lake; see dad; she fed a seal;

10 he fell│has had│he had a jade desk│she held a sash

- Do not use ALL CAPITAL LETTERS for whole words. Using ALL CAPS is viewed as shouting at the reader and is considered rude.
- Proofread your messages before you send them.
- Do not send private or personal information.
- Remember that e-mail and instant messages are not private forms of communication. Always assume that someone besides the person to whom you're writing may see the message.
- Do not forward inappropriate or private correspondence.

Netiquette

When communicating online—via voice, video, graphics, or text—apply the rules of polite behavior to whatever situation you're in. On the Internet, these implied rules of behavior are called **netiquette**. The word is formed by merging the words **etiquette** (the requirements for proper social behavior) and **Net**.

To be an effective online communicator, you must learn the nuances of netiquette. Some rules are a bit obscure, such as the non-use of UPPERCASE letters in e-mail, text messages, and instant messages. Uppercase letters imply shouting, agitation, or extreme excitement. Uppercase words can be used to add EMPHASIS, but they must be used sparingly, if at all.

Often, particularly in e-mail and other text formats, humor sometimes comes across with a big thud. Some humor relies on facial expressions, body language, and verbal inflections to project the witticism, cheeky comment, or sarcasm. All are difficult to achieve in a text format. Therefore, **emoticons** and abbreviations are used to signal those inflections, such as :-) to mean a smile or <grin> to signal humor or sarcasm, or LOL to mean *laughing out loud*.

Many communication conflicts are the result of unedited messages. People should proofread and review their e-mail, instant messages, blogs, and podcasts to make sure they are grammatically correct and ethically appropriate. Sometimes, after a bit of reflection, effective communicators will revise what they wish to share with others. Careful editing is the highest form of netiquette.

ACTIVITY 2A LEGAL DEFINITIONS

1. Use your Internet search tools to define the following legal terms:
   - libel
   - slander
   - aspersion
   - defamation
   - harassment
2. Which term or terms above do not apply to a blogger? to a podcast? to e-mail?
3. Imagine you're working for a company and amending the AUP. As a team, write a one-paragraph explanation for each of the unethical behaviors listed in step 1. Attempt to explain to employees why libel, slander, aspersion, defamation, and harassment cannot be tolerated in the workplace.

ACTIVITY 2B FIRST AMENDMENT PROTECTIONS

1. Using a search tool, locate a copy of the First Amendment to the Constitution of the United States. Read and review it.
2. As a group, address the following question:

   While libel, slander, aspersion, defamation, and harassment are clearly out of bounds, what First Amendment protections do bloggers and podcasters have in regard to freedom of speech?

3. Research the question posed in step 2, looking for citable sources on the topic of freedom of speech as it relates to blogging and podcasting.
4. Have each member of the team prepare individual position papers, of roughly 1,500 words, on the topic.
5. Debate within the group various position papers explaining freedom of speech in regard to the use of these new technologies.

Lesson 3 — FIGHTING ONLINE CRIME

OBJECTIVES
- To study cyber crimes and scams.
- To learn ways that hackers, phishers, and identity thieves operate.
- To research viruses, spyware, firewalls, and other potential online security solutions.
- To learn how to protect yourself from identity theft and other online crime.

Clearly a Crime

While the Internet and e-commerce created new opportunities for business, they also opened up new ways for criminals to cheat consumers. The CEO of a Nebraska-based online business described this **scam**, or con game, that almost cost the company thousands of dollars.

A vacationing Kansas couple took a cruise from Seattle to Alaska. A member of the crew stole their credit card number and e-mailed it to criminals in another hemisphere. The cyber-criminals then scoured websites from all over the world looking for products that could be purchased online and shipped quickly using the stolen credit card number. Speed was essential. The card number had to be used quickly before the victims returned home and found the problem. The products purchased with the stolen credit card number could be sold for a profit on the black market.

2C

I and R Review

Key each line twice SS; DS between 2-line groups.

Review i

1 k i ki ki|did did|dial dial|side side|likes likes;
2 is is|if if|his his|file file|hail hail|hide hide;
3 filed his lease; a field; if she did; she did like

Review r

4 f r fr fr|free free|ride ride|rake rake|fear fear;
5 rare rare|hear hear|read read|real real|dark dark;
6 hear her read; red jars; hear her; dark red dress;

2D — Skill Building

Keyboard Reinforcement

Key each line twice SS; DS between 2-line groups.

Technique Cue

- fingers deeply curved
- wrists low but not resting on keyboard
- eyes on copy

reach review
1 jh de ki fr hj ed ik rf jh de ki fr hj ed ik rf jh
2 his his|are are|jar jar|risk risk|if if; |shed shed

h/e
3 hear hear|she she|held held|heir heir|share share;
4 he held; had jak; hear her; had a shed; he has her

i/r
5 hair hair|risk risk|hire hire|iris iris|ride rides
6 a fair; hire a ride; a raid; a fire risk; her hair

all keys learned
7 is is|her her|jak jak|did did|fire fire|lake lake;
8 a lake; her jar; she did fall; hear a lark; see if

2E

Technique: ENTER

Key each line twice SS; DS between 2-line groups.

1 hear her;
2 ask if she is;
3 she had a real jar;
4 if she has a fair share;
5 ask if she likes red dresses;
6 ask dad if he has had a real sale;
7 he has real dark hair; she held a sale;
8 has a red shed; he hired her; he feels safe;

> At the end of the line, tap ENTER quickly and begin the next line without pausing.

For additional practice:
MicroType 5
New Key Review, Alphabetic
Lesson 2

Avoiding Plagiarism

The fair use doctrine does not apply to plagiarism. Plagiarism is an all-too-common online activity that is clearly unethical. Plagiarism is the unauthorized use of someone else's words, ideas, music, or writing without acknowledgment. When you use someone else's material in your document, you must give that person credit for his or her work. It is unethical, unprofessional, and possibly illegal to quote online work that is not your own without citing it. Plagiarism is best explained with examples:

- Copying text, graphics, music, video, or other content
- Paraphrasing without referencing the source
- Buying a research paper online and presenting it as your own
- Having others prepare your work

Finding a report on the Internet that just fits your assignment and turning it in with your name as the author is plagiarism. Plagiarism in academic work may result in serious punishment.

Much of the information found on Web pages online is copyrighted. This means that it may be illegal to reprint, post, download, and republish without permission. For example, suppose you see a picture you like on a website. You decide to download the picture and display it on the desktop of your computer. You also send it to friends. If the picture has been copyrighted, you may be breaking the law by copying and sharing it without the owner's permission. Look for copyright statements and links such as legal notices on the websites you visit. These notices will help you determine whether the material is legally protected or not. They may even provide the exact wording that must be used for a citation.

If you take an image, a quote, or information from online sources, you must create a proper citation. There are many different style guides governing how citations should be written. Review the information on textual citations in the Language and Writing Reference section of the Resources at the end of this book.

Lesson 2 — PERSONAL DIGITAL RESPONSIBILITY

OBJECTIVES

- To explore the concepts of libel, slander, aspersion, harassment, and defamation.
- To evaluate First Amendment protections in regard to the use of new technologies.
- To review e-mail and instant messaging guidelines.
- To study the role of online netiquette.

The First Amendment vs. Libel, Slander, Aspersion, Harassment, and Defamation

The Web continues to present us with new technologies for sharing digital communication. With each new creation, old ethical issues resurface and need to be reevaluated, reinvented, or reinforced. Ethical principles regarding **libel**, **slander**, **aspersion**, **harassment**, and **defamation**—long applied to print and broadcast journalism—must be reconsidered.

E-mail was one of the first new technologies to bring up these ethical issues. Sometimes people say things in an e-mail message that they regret later. The same is true for instant messaging on a computer and text messages from cell phones, which allow instantaneous responses between people online. E-mail, text messages, and instant messages have been available for years, so rules have been established for their ethical use.

E-mail is usually stored on a server and can be retrieved months, years, even decades later. Oftentimes, old e-mail messages are subpoenaed by courts in order to help law enforcement determine if crimes have been committed.

A relatively new form of communication is called a **blog**. The origin of the word is from the term *Weblog*, which is an online personal journal or log. Someone who keeps a blog is called a **blogger**. The world of blogs is called the **blogosphere**.

The first blogs started as personal weblogs or journals written by individuals. Bloggers typically update their blogs daily or weekly.

Because blogs are considered personal journals, bloggers tend to write what they think and bring their opinions to the forefront for all to read.

Similar to blogging is a relatively new phenomenon called **podcasting**. Podcasts are audio transmissions. Because podcasts are audio files, they can be downloaded through peer-to-peer technologies the way MP3 music files can so listeners may hear a favorite podcast whenever they feel like it. Individuals can create podcasts of their own or subscribe to the podcasts of others.

The First Amendment to the U.S. Constitution guarantees freedom of speech, but there are areas where bloggers, podcasters, e-mailers, and instant messengers may go too far and actually break laws. While all of these technologies are positive tools expanding free speech, they can also resurrect traditional legal and ethical issues related to libel, slander, harassment, defamation, and aspersion.

E-mail, Text Messaging, and IM Guidelines

Follow these guidelines for writing e-mail, sending text messages, or using your instant messaging software (IM) on your computer:

- Be courteous to others in your messages.
- Keep your messages short and to the point, but include all the needed information.
- Place the most important points of the message in the first few words or lines of text.

Lesson 3   REVIEW LETTER KEYS (o, t, n, AND g)

OBJECTIVE

- To review reach technique for **o**, **t**, **n**, and **g**.

3A

Conditioning Practice

Key each line twice SS; DS between 2-line groups.

h/e   1 held a sale; he has a shed; he has a desk; she has

i/re   2 fire risk; hire a; her side; like air; a fire; sir

all keys learned   3 as he fell; he sells fir desks; she had half a jar

3B

O and T Review

Key each line twice SS; DS between 2-line groups.

Review o

1 l o|lo lo|fold fold|doll doll|joke joke|load load;

2 also also|sold sold|road road|look look|hold hold;

3 a hoe; a joke; old oak door; load of sod; old oil;

Review t

4 f t|ft ft|fast fast|tied tied|heat heat|tilt tilt;

5 took took|feet feet|tear tear|date date|take take;

6 a tree; three kites; a fast jet; tree forts; a hit

3C   Skill Building

Keyboard Reinforcement

Key each line twice SS; DS between 2-line groups.

Technique Goals

- curved, upright fingers
- wrists low but not resting on keyboard

reach review   1 ki fr jh ft lo de ik rf hj tf ol ed took ride deer

2 if led for hit old fit let kit rod kid dot jak sit

h/e   3 hero hero|held held|heir heir|here here|hike hike;

4 he led|ask her|she held|has fled|had jade|he leads

i/t   5 its its|fits fits|kite kite|site site|first first;

6 a kit|a fit|a tie|lit it|it fits|it sits|it is fit

o/r   7 road road|fort fort|sort sort|rode rode|soar soar;

8 a rod|a door|a rose|or for|her or|he rode|or a rod

space bar   9 of he or it is to if do el odd off too for she the

10 it is|if it|do so|if he|to do|or the|she is|of all

APPENDIX C
Lessons 1–4

Computer Ethics, Privacy, and Safety

OBJECTIVES

- To explore the ethical use of computers and the Internet.
- To review the meaning of copyright.
- To evaluate the issue of plagiarism.

The Ethical Use of Computers

Computers and the Internet can be used for many positive purposes, but they can also be used for unethical activities. Some people use computers to find cures for serious illnesses, organize food drives for victims of natural disasters, or raise money for charitable causes. Others use computers for criminal behavior.

The use of computers should be governed by **ethics**, the moral principles that govern human interaction. Computers don't possess ethics. No machine can. They can only do what people ask them to do. In every case, people must make the ethical decisions regarding what a computer and the Net will be used for, whether it is for good or for ill.

There are often confusing viewpoints regarding the legal uses of new technologies. It can be difficult, without research and discussion, to know with certainty where the courts stand on certain legal matters.

Acceptable Use Policies

To clarify the ethical boundaries of the online world, organizations that maintain access to Internet accounts for their clients, students, or employees often institute acceptable use policies or AUPs to prevent abuse and to protect all of their computer users. Acceptable use policies follow a familiar pattern and usually include the following bullet points:

- Never disclose a password to another person.
- Never allow others to use your computer account without the express permission of a superior.
- Never use a computer to lie, distort, harass, or offend.
- Only use a computer and the Net for official purposes.
- Do not forward suspicious e-mail or files.
- Do not download copyrighted material or steal files.
- Log out of your computer at the end of each day.

Copyright Issues

People or companies that create works that are new, useful, and potentially profitable may be granted a **copyright** for those works. A copyright is a form of protection granted by the United States and other governments for **intellectual property**. Works created through the intellectual creativity of a person or business—such as books, articles, software, music, plays, movie scripts, and artwork—are considered intellectual property and can be copyrighted. Copyrighted material may carry the © symbol. However, you should assume that materials may be copyrighted even if you do not see this symbol.

Copyright laws govern how copyrighted works may be used legally. As a general rule, you may not use copyrighted material unless you have the owner's permission. However, you may be able to use a small portion of a larger copyrighted work for educational purposes. The rule that relates to this type of use is called the **fair use doctrine**.

3D

N and G Review

Key each line twice SS; DS between 2-line groups.

Review n

1 j n jn jn|nine nine|torn torn|hand hand|noon noon;

2 neat neat|none none|land land|into into|dent dent;

3 no end; an ant; near land; nine nails; one to ten;

Review g

4 f g fg fg|go go|gone gone|ring ring|garage garage;

5 gift gift|golf golf|glad glad|goat goat|dogs dogs;

6 to go; he got; to jog; to jig; the fog; is to golf

3E   Skill Building

Keyboard Reinforcement

Key each line twice SS; DS between 2-line groups.

Technique Goals
- down-and-in spacing
- eyes on copy

reach review

1 feet feet|kind kind|roof roof|high high|toil toil;

2 his jet; an old fort; do a long skit; she left the

n/g

3 song song|sink sink|long long|sing sing|fang fang;

4 log on; sign it; and golf; fine song; right angle;

space bar

5 do do|go go|of of|or or|he he|it it|is is|and and;

6 if it is|is to go|he or she|to do this|of the sign

all keys learned

7 she had a fine old oak desk; a jet is right there;

8 he told a joke; need for; she goes there at eight;

all keys learned

9 he took the jar along; she said he did it for her;

10 the list on the desk; go right after the jet goes;

3F

Technique: ENTER

Key each line twice SS; DS between 2-line groups.

1 she is fine;

2 take a jet to go;

3 he is going to tattle;

4 she is the old song leader;

5 he took the song off of her desk;

6 he took the green dress to the store;

> Return quickly at the end of the line and begin the next line without pausing.

For additional practice:

MicroType 5
New Key Review, Alphabetic
Lesson 3

Leadership Opportunities in Professional Associations

Nearly every profession has an association to serve its members. Many professions have national, regional, state, and local associations. Each provides services to the profession and the members of the association. The associations, regardless of level, also provide opportunities for members to assume leadership positions.

For example, if you are a business education teacher in the Eastern Region of Illinois, there are several professional associations you might want to join. You could join the National Business Education Association (national level), the North-Central Business Education Association (regional level), the Illinois Business Education Association (state level), and/or the Eastern Illinois Business Education Association (local level).

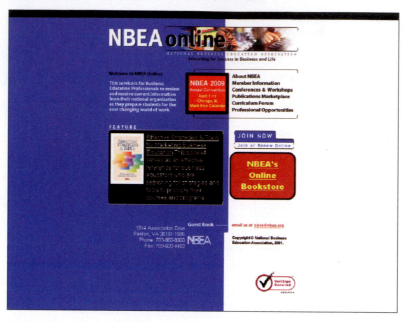

Figure B.4 NBEA Home Page

If you are an architect in the Cleveland, Ohio, area, you may want to join The American Institute of Architects (national level). You could also be a member of the American Institute of Architects Ohio (state level) and/or the American Institute of Architects Cleveland (local level).

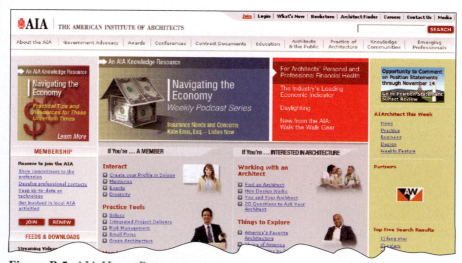

Figure B.5 AIA Home Page

Identify a profession you want to learn more about. Search the Internet to find associations related to the profession you choose. Look for national, regional, state, and local associations. Many professional organizations provide a wealth of information for students on their websites.

OBJECTIVE

• To review reach technique for **Left Shift**, . (period), **u**, and **c**.

4A

Conditioning Practice

Key each line twice SS; DS between 2-line group.

o/t   1   told lost sort took toad toll fort foot tore forth

n/g   2   long gone sang gang rang grand signs grain negate;

all keys learned   3   front door; the lake; so little; large jet; had to

4B

Left Shift and . (Period) Review

Key each line twice SS (slowly, then faster); DS between 2-line groups.

Spacing Cue

• Do not space after . (period) within abbreviations.

• Space once after . (period) following abbreviations and initials.

• Space twice after . (period) at end of a sentence.

Review Left Shift key

1   j a Jan Jan|Kent Kent|Lane Lane|Nate Nate|Ida Ida;

2   Jake left; Kate said; Hans has a jet; Jane is here

3   I see that Jan; Jett and Hank Kent; Oak Lake Lane;

Review . (period)

4   l .|l. l.|fl. fl.|ed. ed.|ft. ft.|rd. rd.|hr. hrs.

5   .l .l|fl. fl.|hr. hr.|e.g. e.g.|i.e. i.e.|in. ins.

6   fl. ft. hr. ed. rd. rt. off. fed. ord. alt. asstd.

4C   Skill Building

Keyboard Reinforcement

Key each line twice SS; DS between 2-line groups.

Technique Goals

• quick keystrokes
• eyes on copy

h/e   1   heir here then held shoe shed hide heat hear death

2   Heidi had a good lead at the end of the first set.

i/r   3   iris iron ring rifle right ridge rinse irate first

4   Kier is taking a high risk if he rides that horse.

o/t   5   took told lots oath notes those other joist hotel;

6   Olga has lost the list she took to the food store.

n/g   7   song sing gone long gang night signs grand ringing

8   Lang and she are going to sing nine songs at noon.

9   Lake Iris; Lila Lane; Lt. Jan Heredia; Lara Logan;

left shift/.   10   Ken Ladd is going to Illinois to see Irene Lanier.

Figure B.2 Kiwanis Home Page

Figure B.3 Rotary International Home Page

4D

U and C Review

Key each line twice SS; DS between 2-line groups.

Review u

1 j u | ju ju | just just | undo undo | rust rust | dust dust;

2 use use | hunt hunt | turn turn | hush hush | usual usual;

3 full sun; four fuses; a fungus; our used furniture

Review c

4 d c | dc dc | clock clock | cocoa cocoa | classic classic;

5 cute cute | dock dock | care care | luck luck | cost cost;

6 school dress code; ice chest; coat racks; a clock;

4E   Skill Building

Keyboard Reinforcement

Key each line twice SS; DS between 2-line groups.

Technique Goals

• Reach up without moving hands away from your body.

• Reach down without moving hands toward your body.

3rd/1st

1 ice curt none north current notice council conceit

2 Nan is cute; he is curt; turn a cog; he can use it

left shift/.

3 Jan had taken a lead. Kate then cut ahead of her.

4 I said to use Kan. for Kansas and Ore. for Oregon.

key words

5 and cue for jut end kit led old fit just golf coed

6 an due cut such fuss rich lack turn dock turf curl

key phrases

7 left turn | could go | to the | can use | such as | for free

8 just in | code it | turn on | cure it | as such | is in luck

all keys learned

9 Joe can use the truck to get the desk for Lucille.

10 Jason hired Luke; Jeff and Jack did not get hired.

4F

Technique: ENTER

Key each line twice SS; DS between 2-line groups.

Practice Cue

At the end of each line, quickly tap the **ENTER** key and begin the next line without pausing.

For additional practice:

MicroType 5
New Key Review, Alphabetic Lesson 4

1 Jake took the fruit.

2 Hank has her old journal.

3 He found the file on the desk.

4 I think Lane took her to the ocean.

5 Janet said she can take us to the dance.

6 Jane and Nick can take the car to the garage.

> Keep eyes on copy before and after tapping the ENTER key.

Students who are successful in these competitions bring favorable recognition to themselves, their teachers, and their schools.

ACTIVITY 2A FBLA RESEARCH

1. Access the FBLA-PBL website at http://www.fbla-pbl.org (see Figure B-1) to locate information about FBLA and how it is organized to serve middle school, high school, and college/university students and alumni.

2. Print at least one page of the information you find.

3. On the FBLA-PBL website at http://www.fbla-pbl.org, or if you prefer, on your state's FBLA-PBL website, explore to learn how FBLA provides leadership opportunities for high school students. Write a short description of your findings.

4. Save and print your file and print one or more pages from the website to support your description.

Leadership Opportunities Through Community Service Organizations

There are several organizations for service- and community-minded individuals. Among these are Kiwanis International and Rotary International, both of which sponsor organizations for high school students. Choose one of these organizations and access its website. Explore the site you selected to learn how the organization provides opportunities for high school students to develop leadership skills.

Figure B.1 FBLA-PBL Home Page

OBJECTIVE

• To review reach technique for **w**, **Right Shift**, **b**, and **y**.

5A

Conditioning Practice

Key each line twice SS; DS between 2-line groups.

left shift/. 1 Lt. Jakes or Lt. Haas can take us to Jackson Hole.

u/c 2 just rice clue cone used curl duck luck such uncle

all letters learned 3 Hugh has just taken a lead in a race for a record.

5B

W and Right Shift Review

Key each line twice SS; DS between 2-line groups.

Review w

1 s w|ws ws|who who|show show|wait wait|whole whole;

2 saw saw|two two|wear wear|aware aware|sweat sweat;

3 where will; we wish; wear a sweater; I walked down

Review Right Shift key

4 A; A;|R; R;|C; C;|Al Al|Dan Dan|Sue Sue|Rick Rick;

5 Frank Ford called Carlos Garcia and Rosa Callahan.

6 Stan left for Chicago; Sue left for San Francisco.

5C

Keyboard Reinforcement

Key each line twice SS; DS between 2-line groups.

Practice Cue

Key at a steady pace; space quickly after each word; keep insertion point moving.

w/right shift 1 Dr. Woodward is in Austin; Dr. Choi will see Dawn.

2 Will and Wes left with Wanda Wilson two hours ago.

n/g 3 Gail sang|turn right|long ago|cotton gin|ten signs

4 Eugene sang a long song; Angela sang a short song.

key words 5 dig hair held soak risk shelf sick then wish world

6 oak land half down dial coal disk rock forks aisle

key phrases 7 we did|work with|send her the|take it to|and those

8 we should|to own the|she is to go|when he has gone

all letters learned 9 Jack and Sarah will go to the fair without Glenda.

10 Jake Wilson could not take it; Heather Fong could.

4. A successful leader has great people skills. Leaders are open enough so that everyone around them can get to know and trust them. Great leaders have a genuine concern for those whom they lead. People expect their leader to safeguard their future.

5. A successful leader builds momentum and takes action. To be appointed or elected to a leadership position is not sufficient to make you a leader. You must, after being appointed or elected, take charge and begin leading. Leaders must have strong personal energy to get a project up and running. They must also maintain that energy to see the projects through to completion. Remember, effective leaders perform for results, not recognition.

6. A successful leader sets high standards and expectations. Leaders expect excellence of themselves and the people they lead, because they realize that for the most part leaders get what they expect. If they have low expectations, they are likely to get low performance. Conversely, if they have high expectations, they are likely to get high performance.

7. A successful leader can be trusted and is loyal to his or her followers. Trust is the single most important factor in building personal and professional relationships. Trust implies accountability, predictability, and reliability. More than anything else, followers want to believe in and trust their leaders. Only then will people follow them. Trust must be earned day by day. It calls for consistency. Some of the ways a leader can betray trust include breaking promises, gossiping, withholding information, or being duplicitous.

8. A successful leader delegates tasks. The question leaders must ask themselves is whether a task can be done by someone else. If so, it should probably be delegated. Good leaders focus on performing tasks that no one can do as well. Oftentimes these tasks relate to long-term planning and strategic thinking.

9. A successful leader makes decisions. Successful leaders do not agonize over a decision because they're afraid of making a mistake. They know mistakes are likely to happen, and they are willing to live with the consequences of their decisions. Also, leaders do not second-guess decisions they have already made. Rather, effective leaders focus their attention on doing the best thing in the present moment and planning for a better future.

10. A successful leader is friendly, teachable, and can control his or her ego. Leaders put empathy ahead of authority. Leaders are not arrogant or egotistical. They are friendly with all kinds of people regardless of their position or status. Successful leaders don't have fragile egos. They recognize that no single person can have all of the correct answers all of the time and that they can always learn from others. Leaders don't let their ego get in the way.

These attributes of leadership apply in all settings. They apply while attending school, playing with friends, participating in sports or other extracurricular activities, working with others, governing others, and being a family and community member.

ACTIVITY 1A A CLASSMATE AS A LEADER

1. Think of a student in your school whom you consider to be an effective leader. It doesn't matter whether he or she is a leader of a student club, in athletics, in student government, or in the community. What matters is that you believe this person is an effective leader.
2. Open *DF App B Activity1A* and print the file.
3. As you read each of the ten attributes of a successful leader listed above, use the four-point scale to rate the student you consider to be a leader. If desired, use the space at the bottom to explain your ratings.
4. Write any additional comments you have in the space provided on the rating form.
5. Submit your rating to your teacher.

Lesson 2   LEADERSHIP OPPORTUNITIES

OBJECTIVE

- To explore leadership opportunities in school, in the community, and in a profession.

Leadership Opportunities Through High School Student Organizations

One school organization that is popular with students who study business and computers is FBLA. FBLA stands for Future Business Leaders of America. It exists primarily to provide students with opportunities to learn and apply leadership and competitive skills. Members of FBLA have opportunities to become leaders by holding office at the local, regional, state, and national levels. In addition, you will have many opportunities to use leadership skills while serving on committees and participating in activities. FBLA sponsors numerous conferences to help students develop specific leadership skills.

Another aspect of participating in FBLA is the opportunity to take part in competitions at the local, regional, state, and national levels. These competitions are centered around business and computer subjects commonly completed in high school. Students who do well at the local level advance to the regional level. Those who do well at the regional level advance to the state level, and likewise those who do well at the state level can compete at the national level.

5D

B and Y Review

Key each line twice SS; DS between 2-line groups.

Review b

1 f b|fb fb|bead bead|cabs cabs|bush bush|bath bath;

2 blue blue|debt debt|jobs jobs|both both|book book;

3 big brown rabbits; before he bats; big rubber bats

Review y

4 j y|jy jy|eye eye|oily oily|cyst cyst|daily daily;

5 dry dry|cry cry|tiny tiny|daisy daisy|enjoy enjoy;

6 early day; baby boy; really dirty; forty or fifty;

5E

Keyboard Reinforcement

Key each line twice SS; DS between 2-line groups.

Technique Goals

- Reach up without moving hands away from your body.
- Reach down without moving hands toward your body.

reach review

1 jn tf ki jh bf ol ed yj ws ik rf hj cd nj tf .l uj

2 swish den free kick look cedar fifth golf injured;

3rd/1st rows

3 no in bow any tub yen cut sub coy ran bin cow deck

4 Cody wants to buy this baby cub for the young boy.

key words

5 by and for the got all did but cut now say jut ask

6 work just such hand this goal boys held furl eight

key phrases

7 to do|can go|to bow|for all|did jet|ask her|to buy

8 if she|to work|and such|the goal|for this|held the

all letters learned

9 Corky has auburn hair and wide eyes of light jade.

10 Darby left Juan at the dog show near our ice rink.

| gwam | 1' | 1 | 2 | 3 | 4 | 5 | 6 | 7 | 8 | 9 | 10 |

5F

Technique: ENTER

Key each line twice SS; DS between 2-line groups.

....

For additional practice:

MicroType 5
New Key Review, Alphabetic
Lesson 5

Jo can take a train.

He has three large tents.

Orlando is at San Diego State.

I wish Sheila would take the class.

Juan has to work on Friday and Saturday.

Dr. Chen scheduled our test for the last day.

> At the end of each line, quickly tap the ENTER key and begin the next line without pausing.

| gwam | 30" | 2 | 4 | 6 | 8 | 10 | 12 | 14 | 16 | 18 |

APPENDIX B
Lessons 1–2

Leadership Development

OBJECTIVES

- To learn about the need for effective leaders.
- To learn the attributes of effective leaders.

The Characteristics of Leadership

Leadership is an important foundation for our society. Effective leadership is needed in our schools, homes, government, and places of worship, work, and play. Therefore, much has been written about the attributes that many believe are essential for effective leadership.

Leadership Can Be Learned

It is a popular opinion that leaders are born, not made. However, in reality, leadership is a set of characteristics that can be learned. You will have many opportunities during your school years to develop leadership qualities. You may have opportunities to be a leader in student government, a student club or other extracurricular activity, and in your community or church. If you work, you will have opportunities to develop leadership qualities for the workplace.

Leadership Defined

Leadership can be defined as getting other people to follow you toward a common goal. For example, imagine that 12 students from your class, including yourself, were asked to move to the front of the room. Once there, the group is directed to line up in the order of their ages from the youngest to the oldest by year, month, and day. Also, the group is told they have five minutes to do this. No further instructions are given.

Consider whether this group of students could perform this simple task without one of them assuming a leadership role. Would you be the one who assumes that role? If so, would you do so immediately or would you wait to see if someone else was willing to step forward to lead the group?

If you assumed the role as leader, would you show any signs of frustration if you could not get others to follow your directions? If you did not assume leadership responsibilities, would you resent being "bossed" around by someone who assumed those responsibilities? Or would you willingly follow the leader's directions and

help the group meet its goal? If so, you would be demonstrating an equally important set of qualities—being a good follower or team player.

Attributes of a Successful Leader

1. A successful leader accepts responsibility and accountability for results. True leadership involves not only the exercise of authority, but also full acceptance of responsibility and accountability. Leaders accept responsibility for those whom they lead. The leader is accountable for everything that occurs, even the errors. Don't fault others; just accept the blame when things go wrong. On the other hand, good leaders always share credit for their successes. Leaders always try to exhibit an attitude of sharing, except when things go wrong.

2. A successful leader has self-discipline, good character, and is committed to personal development. The best leaders commit themselves to a life of ongoing personal development. An effective leader understands his or her own shortcomings and seeks improvement from within. The great leaders also give others the opportunity and encouragement to develop. The best leaders love to read. Most subscribe to a lot of different magazines, many of which are outside their area of expertise or current knowledge. They also read books about strategies for leading and biographies or autobiographies about respected leaders.

3. A successful leader is a great communicator. What separates many great leaders from others is that they have truly mastered the art of listening. They ask questions, and they really listen to the answers. They have learned the power of silence and remember the wise saying, "You can't learn with your mouth open!" Leaders follow up verbal communications with written communications to lessen misunderstandings.

Lesson 6   REVIEW LETTER KEYS (m, x, p, AND v)

- To review reach technique for **m**, **x**, **p**, and **v**.

6A

Conditioning Practice

Key each line twice SS;
DS between 2-line groups.

w/right shift   1   Wendy went with Wade to Walla Walla in Washington.

b/y   2   boy jury cynic tabby hybrid bylaw eyebrow syllable

all letters learned   3   Roberto Cain always fought with Jed on key issues.

6B

M and X Review

Key each line twice SS;
DS between 2-line groups.

Review m

1   j m|jm jm|man man|name name|game game|comic comic;

2   form form|came came|maid maid|harm harm|memo memo;

3   mimic the man; minimum amount; money market rates;

Review x

4   s x|six six|fix fix|box box|next next|exact exact;

5   axle axle|exit exit|axle axle|next next|oxen oxen;

6   next six exits; six extra boxes; the extra exhibit

6C

Keyboard Reinforcement

Key each line twice SS;
DS between 2-line groups.

Technique Goals

- Reach up without moving hands away from your body.
- Reach down without moving hands toward your body.

3rd/1st rows   1   buy amend fix men box hem but six now cut gem ribs

2   mint oxen buoy dent cube rant form went club fined

space bar   3   we it no of me do am if us or is by go ma so in ox

4   go to jet buy fan jam can any tan may rob ham lake

key words   5   if us me do an job the cut big jam was oak lax boy

6   also work cash born kind flex just done many right

key phrases   7   just a minute|if she could|is too big|make it work

8   to fix it|what if she|for our work|next day|to the

all letters learned   9   Jacki is now at the gym; Lex is due there by four.

10   Juan saw that he could fix my old bike for Glenda.

Application for Employment
Regency Insurance Company

An Equal Opportunity Employer

PERSONAL INFORMATION

NAME (LAST FIRST)		SOCIAL SECURITY NO.	CURRENT DATE	PHONE NUMBER
Ruckert, Douglas H.		368-56-2890	5/22/06	(713) 555-0121

ADDRESS (NUMBER, STREET, CITY, STATE, ZIP CODE)	U.S. CITIZEN	DATE YOU CAN START
8503 Kirby Dr., Houston, TX 77054-8220	☒ YES ☐ NO	6/10/06

ARE YOU EMPLOYED NOW? ☒ YES ☐ NO	IF YES, MAY WE INQUIRE OF YOUR PRESENT EMPLOYER? ☒ YES ☐ NO	IF YES, GIVE NAME AND NUMBER OF PERSON TO CALL James Veloski, Manager (713) 555-0182
POSITION DESIRED Customer Service	SALARY DESIRED Open	STATE HOW YOU LEARNED OF POSITION From Ms. Anne D. Salgado Eisenhower Business Technology Instructor

HAVE YOU EVER BEEN CONVICTED OF A FELONY?

☐ YES ☒ NO   IF YES, EXPLAIN.

EDUCATION

	NAME AND LOCATION OF SCHOOL	YEARS ATTENDED	DID YOU GRADUATE?	SUBJECTS STUDIED
COLLEGE				
HIGH SCHOOL	Eisenhower Technical High School Houston, TX	2002 to 2006	Will graduate 06/06	Business Technology
GRADE SCHOOL				
OTHER				

SUBJECTS OF SPECIAL STUDY/RESEARCH WORK OR SPECIAL TRAINING/SKILLS DIRECTLY RELATED TO POSITION DESIRED

Windows and Office Suite, including Word, Excel, Access, PowerPoint, and FrontPage

Office Procedures course with telephone training and interpersonal skills role playing

FORMER EMPLOYERS (LIST LAST POSITION FIRST)

FROM - TO (MTH & YEAR)	NAME AND ADDRESS	SALARY	POSITION	REASON FOR LEAVING
9/05 to present	Hinton's Family Restaurant, 1204 S. Wayside Avenue, Houston, TX 77023-8841	$6.85/hr.	Server	Want full-time position in my field
6/04 to 9/05	Tuma's Landscape and Garden Center 10155 East Freeway, Houston, TX 77029-4419	$5.75/hr.	Sales	Employed at Hinton's

REFERENCES (LIST THREE PERSONS NOT RELATED TO YOU, WHOM YOU HAVE KNOWN AT LEAST ONE YEAR)

NAME	BUSINESS ADDRESS	PHONE NUMBER	TITLE	YEARS KNOWN
Ms. Anne D. Salgado	Eisenhower Technical High School, 100 W. Cavalcade, Houston, TX 77009-2451	(713) 555-0134	Business Technology Instructor	Four
Mr. James R. Veloski	Hinton's Family Restaurant, 1204 S. Wayside Avenue, Houston, TX 77023-8841	(713) 555-0182	Manager	One
Mrs. Helen T. Landis	Tuma's Landscape and Garden Center, 10155 East Freeway, Houston, TX 77029-4419	(713) 555-0149	Owner	Three

I UNDERSTAND THAT I SHALL NOT BECOME AN EMPLOYEE UNTIL I HAVE SIGNED AN EMPLOYMENT AGREEMENT WITH THE FINAL APPROVAL OF THE EMPLOYER AND THAT SUCH EMPLOYMENT WILL BE SUBJECT TO VERIFICATION OF PREVIOUS EMPLOYMENT DATA PROVIDED IN THIS APPLICATION, ANY RELATED DOCUMENTS, OR DATA SHEET. I KNOW THAT A REPORT MAY BE MADE THAT WILL INCLUDE INFORMATION CONCERNING ANY FACTOR THE EMPLOYER MIGHT FIND	RELEVANT TO THE POSITION FOR WHICH I AM APPLYING, AND THAT I CAN MAKE A WRITTEN REQUEST FOR ADDITIONAL INFORMATION AS TO THE NATURE AND SCOPE OF THE REPORT IF ONE IS MADE. *Douglas H. Ruckert* SIGNATURE OF APPLICANT

Employment Application Form

Figure A.8 Sample Application Form

6D

P and V Review

Key each line twice SS;
DS between 2-line groups.

Review p

1 ; p ;p p;p|paed paid|open open|page page|cope cope
2 peak peak|plan plan|poem poem|plus plus|apex apex;
3 a pen; a cap; apt to pay; pick it up; plan to keep

Review v

4 f v|fv fv|five five|vote vote|have have|view view;
5 vast vast|even even|move move|cove cove|vase vase;
6 five jovial elves; vote for seven; view every move

6E

Keyboard Reinforcement

Key each line twice SS;
DS between 2-line groups.

Practice Cue

- Use quick keystrokes.
- Eyes on copy as you key.

reach review
1 sw jn xs ;p fv jm de yj fr ki ft ol cd hj gf ju fb
2 jet jet club kick owned maybe sixth vacant shelter

3rd/1st rows
3 six view north maybe pencil number western mention
4 byway button known cute sent enjoy gems five gripe

key words
5 like each work kept turn made duty check just have
6 begin where jury down vote exist came eight except

key phrases
7 if they go|they kept it|without them|on their farm
8 to leave it|please expect|to review it|so much fun

all letters learned
9 Kevin does a top job on your flax farm with Craig.
10 Dixon flew blue jets eight times over a city park.

6F

Technique: Spacing with Punctuation

Key each line twice SS;
DS between 2-line groups.

Spacing Cue

Do not space after an internal period in an abbreviation, such as Ed.D.

For additional practice:
MicroType 5
New Key Review, Alphabetic Lesson 6

1 Dr. Cabrera has a Ph.D.; Dr. Wesenber has an Ed.D.
2 Lynn may send a box c.o.d. to Ms. Fox in St. Paul.
3 J. R. and Tim will go by boat to St. Louis in May.
4 Lexi keyed ect. for etc. and lost the match to me.
5 Mr. and Mrs. D. J. Vargas set sail for the island.
6 Ms. Franco may take her Ed.D. exam early in March.

Reference List

When your resume indicates that references will be furnished upon request, you should prepare a reference list to take with you to interviews. If you prefer, references may be listed on the resume, at the end of the page. The reference list should contain the name, address, telephone number, and e-mail address (if the person uses e-mail) of three to six people (not relatives) who know you well. Teachers, clergy, and current or previous employers usually make good references. Ask each person in advance for permission to list her or his name as a reference, and describe the job for which you are applying. Be sure all names are spelled correctly and that addresses and telephone numbers are accurate. Include each person's organization and job title. To format a reference list, use a 2" top margin and default or 1" side margins. Include a centered title, such as *REFERENCES FOR* (insert your name) in bold, 14-pt. font. DS below the title; list the references SS with a DS between them.

Application Letter

An application letter should always accompany a resume. This personal-business letter should be limited to one page. The application letter should include three topics—generally in three to five paragraphs. The first topic (one paragraph) should specify the position for which you are applying and may state how you learned of the opening and something positive about the company. The second topic (one to three paragraphs) should include evidence that you qualify for the position. This is the place to interpret information presented in your resume and to show how your qualifications relate to the job for which you are applying. The last paragraph should request an interview and give precise information for contacting you to arrange it.

Application Form

Many companies require an applicant to complete an application form even though a resume and application letter have been received. Figure A.8 shows a sample application form. Applicants often fill in forms at the company, using a pen to write on a printed form or keying information into an online form. Sometimes applicants may take an application form home, complete it, and return it by mail or in person. In this case, the information should be printed in blue or black ink on the form. You should strive to provide information that is accurate, complete, legible, and neat. To lessen the chance of error on an application, make a copy of the blank form to complete as a rough draft.

Interview Follow-up Letter

The follow-up letter is a thank-you for the time given and courtesies extended to you during a job interview. This personal-business letter lets the interviewer know that you are still interested in the job, and it reminds him or her of your application and qualifications. This letter should be mailed within 24 hours after the interview to increase the likelihood that it is received before an applicant is selected for the job.

Lifelong Career Planning and Learning

Choosing a career is a journey, not a destination. As you learn more about your career, you may decide you have greater interest in one part of your job over another. New technology may change how you complete your work, causing you to focus on a different aspect of your job. You may decide to continue your education to get a better promotion or increase your value to your company. In any case, it is important to always learn on the job, to keep on top of the trends in your business, and to continue your education so you can be the best at what you do.

You should also take the time to update your resume every few years. Make sure it accurately reflects your current skill set. Examine current trends to determine how to keep on top of your career. There will always be new technology and new ways of doing things—make sure you take the time to advance your career and skills along with the times. The competition is tough. Invest the time in your skills and education to make sure you can compete with the best.

Lesson 7

REVIEW LETTER KEYS (q, comma, z, AND colon)

• To review reach technique for **q**, **comma**, **z**, and **colon**.

7A

Conditioning Practice

Key each line twice SS;
DS between 2-line groups.
If time permits, rekey the
lines.

m/x 1 extra room; exact amount; exciting menu; six exams

p/v 2 every paper; very poor; vivid picture; vital part;

all letters
learned 3 Jane Oka will place my bid for the ugly vase next.

7B

Q and , (Comma) Review

Key each line twice SS;
DS between 2-line groups.

🔶 **Spacing Cue**

Space once after , (comma)
used as punctuation.

Learn q

1 a q|aqua aqua|quiet quiet|quake quake|equal equal;

2 equip equip|query query|quote quote|equity equity;

3 require a quote; quite a sequel; requested a quote

Learn , (comma)

4 k ,|k, k,|Jill, Mary, Dick, and Juan rode the bus.

5 Javier hit a single, double, triple, and home run.

6 Three, four, five, and eight are my lucky numbers.

7C

Keyboard Reinforcement

Key each line twice SS;
DS between 2-line groups.

🔶 **Technique Goals**

• Reach up without
moving hands away
from your body.
• Reach down without
moving hands toward
your body.

reach
review 1 rf mj nj tf p; xs ,k ol cd ik vf ed hj bf qu .l ws

2 yj gf hj for vow got quote cute known mixer invite

3rd/1st
rows 3 cute muck just pick sixty maybe coyote wince turns

4 to win|to give|my voice|a peck|come back|next time

key
words 5 got sit man for fix jam via oak the wash bark code

6 buy lay apt mix pay when rope give just stub quick

key
phrases 7 of all|golf game|if he is|it is due next|to pay us

8 if we pay|is of age|up to you|so we own|she saw me

all letters
learned 9 Jevon will fix my pool deck if the big rain quits.

10 Rex did fly quick jets to map the seven big towns.

Douglas H. Ruckert

8503 Kirby Drive
Houston TX 77054-8220
(713) 555-0121

dougr@suresend.com

OBJECTIVE: To use my computer, Internet, communication, and interpersonal skills in a challenging customer service position.

EDUCATION: Will graduate from Eisenhower Technical High School in June 2006, with a high school diploma and business technology emphasis. Grade point average is 3.75.

Relevant Skills and Courses:

❑ Proficient with most recent versions of Windows and Office, including Word, Excel, Access, PowerPoint, and FrontPage.

❑ Excelled in the following courses: Keyboarding, Computer Applications, Business Communications, and Office Technology.

Major Accomplishments:

❑ Future Business Leaders of America: Member for four years, vice president for one year. Won second place in Public Speaking at the District Competition; competed (same event) at state level.

❑ Varsity soccer: Lettered three years and served as captain during senior year.

❑ Recognition: Named one of Eisenhower's Top Ten Community Service Providers at end of junior year.

WORK EXPERIENCE: Hinton's Family Restaurant, Server (2005-present): Served customers in culturally diverse area, oriented new part-time employees, and resolved routine customer service issues.

Tuma's Landscape and Garden Center, Sales (2004-2005): Assisted customers with plant selection and responsible for stocking and arranging display areas.

REFERENCES: Will be furnished upon request.

Print Resume (Resume 2)

Figure A.7 Print Resume

7D

Z and : (Colon) Review

Key each line twice SS; DS between 2-line groups.

Language Skill Cue

- Space twice after : (colon) used as punctuation.
- Capitalize the first word of a complete sentence following a colon.
- Do not capitalize a sentence fragment following a colon.

Review z

1 a z|az az|zone zone|raze raze|lazy lazy|zone zone;

2 ozone ozone|razor razor|amaze amaze|fizzle fizzle;

3 too lazy; a dozen zigzags; dozen sizes; he quizzed

Review : (colon)

4 ; :|;:|:; Date: Time: Name: Room: From: File:

5 Subject: File: Reply to: Dear Sue: Shift for :

6 Dear Mr. Smith: Dear Mr. Perez: Dear Mr. Mendez:

7E

Keyboard Reinforcement

Key each line twice SS; DS between 2-line groups.

Technique Goals

- curved, upright fingers
- steady keystroking pace

q/z

1 zinc quiz zero quota kazoo dazzle inquire equalize

2 Zelda and Quinn amazed us all on the zoology quiz.

p/x

3 except expect expel export explore explain express

4 Expect Roxanne to fix pizza for the next six days.

v/m

5 Vim man van dim have move vamp more dive time five

6 Val drove them to the mall in my vivid maroon van.

easy

7 Their sick dog slept by the oak chair in the hall.

8 Nancy may go with us to the city; Jane may go too.

alphabet

9 Nate will vex the judge if he bucks my quiz group.

10 Quig just fixed prize vases he won at my key club.

7F

Block Paragraphs

1. Read the note at the right below the paragraphs (¶s).
2. Key each ¶ twice (slowly, then faster).
3. If your instructor directs, key a 1' writing on each ¶; determine your *gwam*.

For additional practice:

MicroType 5

New Key Review, Alphabetic Lesson 7

Paragraph 1	**gwam**	1'

The space bar is a vital tool, for every fifth or   10

sixth stroke is a space when you key. If you use   20

it with good form, it will aid you to build speed.   30

Paragraph 2

Just keep the thumb low over the space bar. Move   10

the thumb down and in quickly toward your palm to   20

get the prized stroke you need to build top skill.   30

gwam 1' | 1 | 2 | 3 | 4 | 5 | 6 | 7 | 8 | 9 | 10 |

Note: At the end of a full line, the insertion point goes to the next line automatically. This is called **wordwrap.** Use wordwrap when you key a ¶. At the end of a ¶, tap the **ENTER** key twice to place a DS between the ¶s.

Douglas H. Ruckert
8503 Kirby Drive
Houston TX 77054-8220
(713) 555-0121
dougr@suresend.com

SUMMARY

Strong communication and telephone skills; excellent keyboarding, computer, and Internet skills; and good organizational and interpersonal skills.

EDUCATION

Will graduate from Eisenhower Technical High School in June 2006, with a high school diploma and business technology emphasis. Grade point average is 3.75.

Relevant Skills and Courses:

Proficient with most recent versions of Windows and Office, including Word, Excel, Access, PowerPoint, and FrontPage.

Excelled in the following courses: Keyboarding, Computer Applications, Business Communications, and Office Technology.

Major Accomplishments:

Future Business Leaders of America: Member for four years, vice president for one year. Won second place in Public Speaking at District Competition; competed (same event) at state level.

Varsity soccer: Lettered three years and served as captain during senior year.

Recognition: Named one of Eisenhower's Top Ten Community Service Providers at end of junior year.

WORK EXPERIENCE

Hinton's Family Restaurant, Server (2005-present): Served customers in culturally diverse area, oriented new part-time employees, and resolved routine customer service issues.

Tuma's Landscape and Garden Center, Sales (2004-2005): Assisted customers with plant selection and responsible for stocking and arranging display areas.

REFERENCES

Will be furnished upon request.

Electronic Resume (Resume 1)

Figure A.6 Electronic Resume

Lesson 8   REVIEW LETTER KEYS (CAPS LOCK, ?, TAB, ', -, AND ")

OBJECTIVE

- To review reach technique for **CAPS LOCK, ?** (question mark), **TAB** key, **'** (apostrophe), **-** (hyphen), and **"** (quotation mark).

8A

Conditioning Practice

Key each line twice SS; then key a 1' timing on line 3. Determine *gwam* using the scale below line 3.

alphabet	1	Gus Javon quickly baked extra pizza for the women.
z/:	2	To: Ms. Zachary Zeman; From: Dr. Liza J. Zitzer.
easy	3	Rick kept busy with the work he did on the mantle.

gwam 1' | 1 | 2 | 3 | 4 | 5 | 6 | 7 | 8 | 9 | 10 |

Note: Your *gwam* (gross words a minute) is the figure under the last letter keyed. If you keyed more than a line, add 10 for each additional line keyed.

8B

Review CAPS LOCK and ? (Question Mark)

Key each line twice SS; DS between 2-line groups.

Note: To key a series of capital letters, tap CAPS LOCK using the left little finger. To release CAPS LOCK, tap it again.

Spacing Cue

Space twice after a ? at the end of a sentence.

Review CAPS LOCK

1 The book, A NEW START, was written by JACK SPENCE.
2 JEFFERSON drafted THE DECLARATION OF INDEPENDENCE.
3 INDEPENDENCE HALL is situated in PHILADELPHIA, PA.

Review ? (question mark)

4 ; ? ;? ;? Who? What? When? Where? Why? Is it?
5 Where is it? When is it? Did he stay? May I go?
6 Do I space twice? Did you key all the lines once?

8C

Review TAB

Indent and key each ¶ once SS; DS between ¶s.

Note: To indent the first line of a ¶, tap TAB using the left little finger. Tabs are usually set every .5" to the right of the left margin.

Tab ⟶ The Tab key is used to indent lines of copy such as these. It can also be used for tables to arrange data quickly and neatly into columns.

Tab ⟶ Learn now to use the Tab key by touch. Tap the Tab key firmly and release it very quickly. Begin the line without a pause.

Tab ⟶ If you hold the Tab key down, the insertion point will move from tab to tab across the line.

8D

Review TAB

Key each line twice SS; DS between 2-line groups.

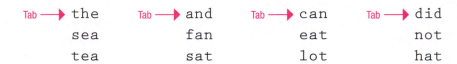

Tab ⟶ the	Tab ⟶ and	Tab ⟶ can	Tab ⟶ did
sea	fan	eat	not
tea	sat	lot	hat

```
┌─────────────────────────────────────────────────────────────┐
│                  Common Interview Questions                   │
│                                                               │
│   • How would you describe yourself?                          │
│                                                               │
│   • What do you consider your greatest strengths?             │
│                                                               │
│   • What do you consider your greatest weaknesses?            │
│                                                               │
│   • What are your favorite classes and why?                   │
│                                                               │
│   • What are your least favorite classes and why?             │
│                                                               │
│   • What are your hobbies and interests outside of school?    │
│                                                               │
│   • What are your favorite extracurricular activities and why?│
│                                                               │
│   • Have you ever been fired from a job?  Explain why.        │
│                                                               │
│   • Why do you want to work for this company?                 │
│                                                               │
│   • Explain your long-term goals and how you plan to achieve them. │
│                                                               │
│   • Why do you want this job?                                 │
│                                                               │
│   • Why should we hire you?                                   │
│                                                               │
│   • What do you look for in a job?                            │
│                                                               │
│   • How would your friends, classmates, or coworkers describe you? │
│                                                               │
│   • Explain a situation where you worked with a team to solve a problem. │
│                                                               │
└─────────────────────────────────────────────────────────────┘
```

Figure A.5 Common Interview Questions

Print versus electronic resumes. Print resumes are those printed on paper and mailed to prospective employers. Electronic resumes are those attached to e-mail or posted to a Web page. (See model electronic and print resumes on pp. 561 and 562, respectively.)

Resume scanning. Many companies scan both print and electronic resumes into database files and then search each file for specific information. They may search for education level, work experience, or keywords that are closely related to the position being filled. When you believe an employer is not likely to scan it, your print resume may contain format features, such as indentations and columns; and text enhancements, such as bold, bullets, several font designs and sizes, and underlines. These types of features and enhancements can cause errors or disappear entirely or partially when a resume is scanned, attached to an e-mail, or posted to a Web page. Therefore they should be omitted from an electronic resume—and from a print resume that may be scanned. To increase the likelihood that their resume will be selected in a database search, many people replace the Objective section with a Summary section (see the electronic resume on p. 561). The summary contains keywords describing education, positions held, skills, and/or accomplishments that relate to the position being sought.

Note: Some large corporations offer a Web page on which job applicants can post electronic resumes. Applicants also can post electronic resumes at career-oriented websites such as Monster (http://www.monster.com) or CareerBuilder (http://www.CareerBuilder.com).

Resume do's and don'ts. Follow these guidelines when creating your resume.

- Do use a simple format. Default top, bottom, and side margins are acceptable but may vary slightly depending on the amount of information presented.
- Do key your name at the top of the page on a line by itself. Key your address (standard, not USPS style) below your name, and list each telephone number on a separate line.
- Do arrange the resume parts attractively on the page. The arrangement may vary with personal preference and the purpose of the resume.
- Do use a basic font, such as Times New Roman or Courier, 12 pt.
- Do use white, ivory, or light-colored (gray or tan) paper, standard size (8.5" × 11"), for a print resume.
- On an electronic resume or print resume that may be scanned, don't use font effects, such as engrave and outline; apply borders or shading; or insert clip art, horizontal lines, or photographs.

EXERCISE A7 CREATING A RESUME

1. Compose a resume for yourself.
2. Edit the rough draft; then format the final draft as an electronic resume. Save as *App A Exercise A7a* and close the file.
3. Open *App A Exercise A7a*—your electronic resume.
4. Reformat as a print resume. Save as *App A Exercise A7b*.

Review ' (apostrophe), - (hyphen), and " (quotation mark)

Key each line twice SS; DS between 2-line groups.

Note: On your screen, apostrophes and quotation marks may look different from those shown in these lines.

Review ' (apostrophe)

1 ;' ;' ;' '; I didn't say Jen's keys weren't taken.
2 Didn't Jack's friend Mary say she'll be here soon?
3 I've been told she'll quit; I'm not sure how soon.

Review - (hyphen)

4 ; - ;- ;- up-to-date computer; hit-or-miss effort;
5 sister-in-law; do-or-die effort; first-rate report
6 Their high-priced player had a do-or-die attitude.

Review " (quotation mark)

7 ;" '" "They won." "I can't believe it." "I did."
8 "John Adams," he said, "was the second President."
9 "James Monroe," I said, "was the fifth President."

Keyboard Reinforcement

1. Key lines twice SS; DS between 2-line groups.
2. Key a 1' writing on lines 10–12.

Reach review (Keep on home keys the fingers not used for reaching.)

1 sixth jay bark wren quit truck open give team zero
2 pro quo|is just|my firm|was then|may grow|must try
3 Olga sews aqua and red silk to make six big kites.

Space Bar emphasis (Think, say, and key the words.)

4 to and but the men pay with land field visit girls
5 She may|on the|go to the|by the man|on a lake|I do
6 He is to go to the city hall for the forms for us.

Shift key emphasis (Reach up and reach down without moving the hands.)

7 Jan and I are to see Ms. Cey. May Lana come, too?
8 Denver, Colorado; Chicago, Illinois; New York City
9 Oates and Co. has a branch office in Boise, Idaho.

Easy sentences (Think, say, and key the words at a steady pace.)

10 Jake paid the six firms for all the work they did.
11 Chris is to pay the six men for the work they did.
12 Keith is to work with us to fix the big dock sign.

| gwam | 1' | 1 | 2 | 3 | 4 | 5 | 6 | 7 | 8 | 9 | 10 |

For additional practice:
MicroType 5
New Key Review, Alphabetic Lesson 8

always the everyday work attire for an organization, recruiters expect candidates to look their most professional during a job interview.

In an interview, you want to impress with your skills, accomplishments, and potential. First impressions are lasting impressions. You may never have a second opportunity to prove yourself capable of performing the job.

It is always better to look too conservative than too casual. Your clothing and accessories should not attract so much attention that they are distractions to the true purpose of the interview. You do not want the recruiter to remember you for the fact that you wore white socks or too much perfume.

Generally, purchase the highest-quality outfit and accessories you can afford, and make sure your clothing fits and is comfortable for both walking and sitting. Do not bring beverages to the interview, and do not chew gum. If you have your cell phone with you, turn off the ringtones and alarms. Avoid flashy colors, bold prints, scarves that come untied, and clanking jewelry.

It is difficult to describe the perfect interview attire that will match all occasions. You should always research a company to learn more about its dress code. However, below are some general tips for interview attire for men and women.

Interview Attire for Women

- Conservative pant or skirt suit. Navy or charcoal gray are the preferred suit colors, but other dark colors such as black or hunter green may be acceptable in certain industries.
- White, off-white, or light-colored cotton or silk blouse with conservative neckline.
- Leather shoes with closed toe and low to medium heel.
- Neutral hosiery.
- Moderate amount of jewelry or accessories. No more than one ring on each hand.
- Professional briefcase or portfolio; no backpack or purse.
- Minimal makeup and perfume.
- Trimmed fingernails with conservative polish color, if any.
- Neat hairstyle.
- Remove body piercings, except for one conservative earring in each ear. Cover tattoos.

Interview Attire for Men

- Single-breasted navy or charcoal gray two-piece suit.
- White or light-colored long-sleeved cotton shirt.
- Tie with small, conservative pattern.
- Dark socks that will remain above the pants cuff when you are seated.
- Well-polished shoes and matching belt, typically in black or cordovan.
- Professional briefcase or portfolio; no backpack.
- Minimal cologne.
- Neat hairstyle.
- No more than one ring on each hand.

- Professional (not sport) watch.
- Trimmed and clean fingernails.
- Remove body piercings, including earrings, and cover tattoos.

Source: http://www.ulm.edu/careerservices/dress.html

Interviewing Skills

Like many other aspects of your career, developing your interviewing skills is critical to your success. Without these skills, you may never get the chance to realize your career dreams. To prepare for an interview, you need to know your skills and you need to practice answering typical interview questions (see Figure A.5).

EXERCISE A6 EXPLORING INTERVIEW SKILLS

1. Review the Common Interview Questions presented in Figure A.5. In a word processing document, key the questions and a few sentences to answer each question.

2. Save as *App A Exercise A6*.

3. With a classmate, trade the roles of interviewer and interviewee and practice answering these questions with self-confidence and conviction.

Employment Documents

Employment documents provide applicants an opportunity to present their best qualities to prospective employers. These qualities are represented by the content of the documents as well as by their accuracy, format, and neatness. The care with which you prepare your documents suggests to employers how carefully you would work if hired. Therefore, give special attention to preparing your employment documents. In addition to a data sheet, or resume (pronounced REZ oo MAY), common types of employment documents are an application letter, application form, reference list, and interview follow-up letter.

Resume

In most cases, a resume should be limited to one page. The information presented usually covers six major areas: personal information (your name, home address, e-mail address, and telephone number[s]); objective (clear definition of the position desired); education (courses and/or program taken, skills acquired, grade point average [and grades earned in courses directly related to job competence], and graduation date); school and/or community activities or accomplishments (organizations, leadership positions, and honors and awards); work experience (position name, name and location of employer, and brief description of responsibilities); and a notation that references (names of people familiar with your character, personality, and work habits) will be provided upon request.

In general, the most important information is presented first, which means that most people who have recently graduated from high school will list educational background before work experience. The reference section is usually last on the page.

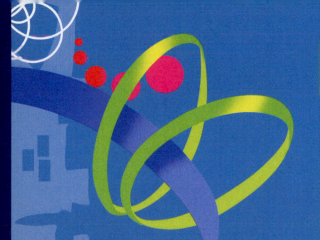

UNIT 2
Lessons 9-12

Build Keyboarding Skill

Lesson 9 · SKILL BUILDING

OBJECTIVE

- To learn proper response patterns to gain speed.

9A

Conditioning Practice

Key each line twice SS; then key a 1' timing on line 3. Determine *gwam*.

alphabet	1	Wusov amazed them by jumping quickly from the box.
spacing	2	am to | is an | by it | of us | an oak | is to pay | all of us
easy	3	The sorority may do the work for the city auditor.

| gwam | 1' \| | 1 \| | 2 \| | 3 \| | 4 \| | 5 \| | 6 \| | 7 \| | 8 \| | 9 \| | 10 \| |

9B

Speed Check: Sentences

Key each line three times SS at the speed level (see blue box at the right); DS between 3-line groups.

1 She has three more games left.

2 When will he make the payment?

3 Felipe left for school an hour ago.

4 Mary has four more puppies to sell.

5 The girls won the game by eleven points.

6 Taisho finished the report on Wednesday.

7 Their runner fell with less than a lap to go.

8 Inez will finish the project by the deadline.

9 You can register for classes starting next Friday.

10 Jessica was elected president by just three votes.

Technique Cue

- After keying the last letter of a word, quickly tap the Space Bar and immediately begin keying the next word.
- After keying the period or question mark at the end of each line, quickly tap **ENTER** and immediately begin keying the next line.

Speed Level of Practice

When the purpose of practice is to reach a new speed, use the **speed level**. Take the brakes off your fingers and experiment with new stroking patterns and new speeds. Do this by:

- reading two or three letters ahead of your keying to foresee stroking patterns;

- getting the fingers ready for the combinations of letters to be keyed;

- keeping your eyes on the copy in the book;

- keying at the word level rather than letter by letter.

---

necessary for your career choice. Many times, your ultimate career may mean higher-education requirements, industry certifications, or prior on-the-job experience. Developing a career plan will help you outline the steps needed to reach your career goals. For example, if your career goal is to become a computer software engineer, your first step would be to determine if you have the personality traits required for that type of career (e.g., analytical, detail-oriented, math and computer science skills). Your second step would be to study hard in your math, science, and computer science courses in school. A third step would be to obtain a bachelor's degree in computer science as well as important certifications in the field. All of these steps would need to be accomplished before actually applying for a job.

EXERCISE A5 DEVELOPING A CAREER PLAN

1. There are websites that offer additional information on developing a career plan. Search for sites you think might be useful. Some sites you might want to visit include the U.S. Department of Labor (http://www.bls.gov), America's Career InfoNet (http://www.acinet.org/acinet/), or Mapping Your Future (http://www.mappingyourfuture.biz/planyourcareer/). Figure A.4 shows the Career Planning tool available on the Mapping Your Future website. Review the career plan information provided.

2. Print a page or two of information from the most useful sites.

3. Using a career of your choice, develop a sample plan of your own.

4. Save as *App A Exercise A5*.

Portfolio

A *career portfolio* is a place to store items that show off your best work abilities. For example, if you want to be a photographer, you should store your best photos. If you want to be an architect, you should show samples of blueprints from your best designs. When you create a portfolio, the items you include should be neat, clean, and something to be proud of. Your portfolio should contain evidence of your skills, such as awards, certificates, letters of recommendation, samples of your work, and a flawless resume. Visit America's Career InfoNet (http://www.acinet.org/acinet/) for more information on building your portfolio.

Proper Business Attire

All of your research, exploration, and preparations are rewarded once you have applied for a job and been contacted for an interview. You can be the best, most qualified person for a position. You can have the highest grades, know the most in your career area, and have the fanciest suit. However, if you don't interview well, you won't get the job.

Different companies and industries have different expectations in regard to business dress. For example, a financial analyst or lawyer may not wear the same type of clothing as a computer programmer at a small start-up Internet company. A fashion designer's work clothing is far different from that of a hospital administrator. Most organizations in all industries, however, have similar expectations when it comes to interview attire. The standard protocol is professional dress, which means a conservative suit. Although a business suit is not

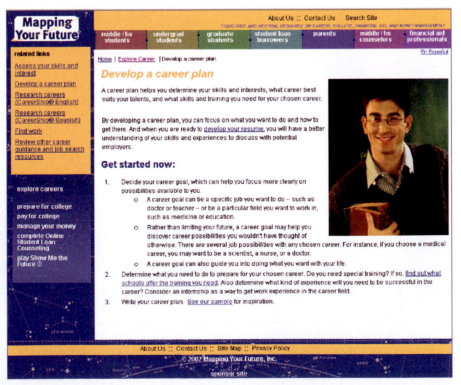

Figure A.4 Career Planning Information on the Mapping Your Future Website
Source: Mapping Your Future (http://www.mappingyourfuture.biz/planyourcareer/), November 4, 2008.

9C

Technique: Response Patterns

1. Key each line twice SS; DS between 2-line groups.
2. Key 1' timings on lines 10–12; determine *gwam* on each timing.

Technique Cues

Word response: Key easy (balanced-hand) words as words.

Letter response: Key letters of one-hand words steadily and evenly, letter by letter.

Balanced-hand words

1 us so an by is or it do of go he if to me of ox am
2 an box air wig the and sir map pen men row fix jam
3 girl kept quay town auto busy firm dock held makes

One-hand words

4 be my up we on at no as oh as ax in at my up be we
5 no cat act red tax was you pin oil hip ear fat few
6 milk fast oily hymn base card safe draw pink gates

Balanced-hand phrases

7 to go|it is due|to the end|if it is|to do so|he is
8 pay the|for us|may do the|did he|make a|paid for a
9 he may|when did they|so do they|make a turn|to the

Balanced-hand sentences

10 I am to pay the six men if they do the work right.
11 Title to all of the lake land is held by the city.
12 The small ornament on their door is an ivory duck.

gwam 1' | 1 | 2 | 3 | 4 | 5 | 6 | 7 | 8 | 9 | 10 |

9D Skill Building

Speed Building

1. Key a 1' timing on each ¶; determine *gwam*.
2. Key two 2' timings on ¶s 1–2 combined; determine *gwam*.

 E   all letters used   **MicroPace**   gwam 2'

To risk your own life for the good of others   5
has always been seen as an admirable thing to do.   10
Harriet Tubman was a slave in the South. She became   16
a free woman when she was able to run away to the   21
North. This freedom just did not mean much to her   26
while so many others were still slaves.   30

She quickly put her own life at risk by going   35
back to the South. She did this to help others get   41
free. She was able to help several hundred. This is   46
a large number. During the Civil War she continued   51
to exhibit the traits of an amazing hero. She served   57
the Union as a spy and as a scout.   60

gwam 2' | 1 | 2 | 3 | 4 | 5 |

For additional practice:
MicroType 5
New Key Review, Alphabetic
Lesson 9

Monthly Expenses Table	
Monthly Income	
Job	
Other	
Monthly Expenses	
Housing/rent	
Utilities	
o Phone	
o Cell phone	
o Gas & electric	
o Sewer & water	
o Cable	
o Other	
Food	
o Groceries	
o Lunch/eating out	
Car expenses	
o Car payment	
o Gas	
o Maintenance & repairs	
Entertainment	
Savings	
Miscellaneous	

Figure A.3 Sample Monthly Expenses Table

Lesson 2   APPLYING FOR A JOB

- To create a career plan.
- To explore proper interview attire and learn interviewing skills.
- To create employment documents.

Developing the Tools for Success

As you begin thinking about your career choices, you need to understand the tools that will help you successfully land your dream job. There are steps to take now, while you are in school, to ensure you are on the right path for your career. Developing a career plan will help you take the right direction in your schoolwork and professional development. Keeping a portfolio of your work will enable you to provide proof of your skills to employers. And, of course, building a top-notch resume is essential for landing an interview.

Career Plan

Attaining the perfect career takes careful planning. You need to thoroughly research the skills, education requirements, and experience

OBJECTIVES

- To build straight-copy speed and accuracy.
- To enhance keying technique.

10A

Conditioning Practice

Key each line twice SS; then key a 1' timing on line 3. Determine *gwam*.

alphabet	1	Levi Lentz packed my bag with six quarts of juice.
CAPS LOCK	2	KANSAS is KS; TEXAS is TX; IDAHO is ID; IOWA is IA
easy	3	Jan may name a tutor to work with the eight girls.

gwam 1' | 1 | 2 | 3 | 4 | 5 | 6 | 7 | 8 | 9 | 10 |

10B

Technique: Response Patterns

1. Key each line twice SS; DS between 2-line groups.
2. Key a 1' timing on lines 3, 6, 9, and 12.

	1	pink safe tree face hill look only fact date start
letter response	2	red dress|extra milk|union awards|pink car|you are
	3	Jim Carter started a car in my garage in Honolulu.
	4	with work dock half coal hair both busy city civic
word response	5	when they|fix their|pay the|did she|cut down|to it
	6	Diana and Jan may go to the island to do the work.
	7	big cat air act did fat due joy got pin rug was us
combination response	8	pink bowl|city street|their jump|extra chair|is at
	9	Ed Burns was with Steve when we started the feast.
letter	10	Jim saw a fat cat in a cab as we sat in my garage.
combination	11	Jay was the man you saw up at the lake in the bus.
word	12	I may go to the lake with the men to fix the door.

gwam 1' | 1 | 2 | 3 | 4 | 5 | 6 | 7 | 8 | 9 | 10 |

10C

Speed Check: Sentences

Key two 30" timings on each line. Try to increase your keying speed the second time you key the line. Determine *gwam* for the faster timing of each line.

1 Ben will be ready before noon.
2 Sam will bring his dog to the lake.
3 Jack did not fill the two cars with gas.
4 Jon will take the next test when he is ready.
5 Susan is to bring two or three copies of the play.
6 This may be the last time you will have to take a test.

gwam 30" | 2 | 4 | 6 | 8 | 10 | 12 | 14 | 16 | 18 | 20 | 22 |

Teamwork Skills

Read the following statements to determine if you are an effective team member.

_____ I enjoy working with others to solve problems.

_____ I always let others finish talking before I give my views.

_____ I listen carefully to what others have to say and never prejudge their ideas.

_____ When I have a problem to solve, I seek others' opinions before I make a decision.

_____ I consider myself a good leader.

_____ If others disagree with me, I always listen to their opinions before I answer.

_____ I enjoy debating issues and listening to others' opinions.

_____ I am careful not to hurt others' feelings when I offer my views.

_____ I set goals for myself and I usually achieve them.

_____ I like to help my family and friends work out their differences.

Figure A.2 Teamwork Skills

Employability Skills

There are certain skills that *every* employer is looking for. Do you know what they are? To be the perfect employee, you will need to have certain skills that will benefit any employer. You need to have excellent communication skills and the ability to talk with customers. You must work well with a team and be able to take the lead on group projects. You should be able to adapt to new situations. You should be willing to continue learning to be better at your job. You must be responsible, honest, and dependable. You should be able to prioritize your work to meet important deadlines. And, of course, you need to have the technical skills necessary for your job.

Personal Finance Skills

As you plan for the job of your dreams, you should also understand how that job will financially support your future. Some careers will be attainable after high school. Other careers require additional education, which may mean student loan payments. Usually, the more education you need for a career, the more money you will earn as income. You should be aware of what type of income to expect from your career. Knowing your expected income will allow you to estimate your living expenses and determine if you can pay your bills on your expected salary. Some websites to visit that offer expected salaries are the U.S. Department of Labor (http://www.bls.gov) and CollegeBoard.com (http://www.collegeboard.com).

EXERCISE A4 EXPLORING PERSONAL FINANCE SKILLS

1. The table in Figure A.3 shows a personal monthly budget. Visit either the Department of Labor (http://www.bls.gov) or CollegeBoard.com (http://www.collegeboard.com) and look up the salary of a career of your choice.

2. Use the table in Figure A.3 to help you determine your possible monthly income minus expenses. Ask an adult to help you estimate monthly expenses.

3. Create the table in a spreadsheet document. Then fill out the table to establish your monthly budget. *Tip*: Be sure to include formulas to deduct total expenses from total income.

4. Save as *App A Exercise A4*.

Ethics and Your Career

Successful companies practice business fairly and honestly. They strive to build trust with their customers, employees, other businesses, and the general public. In turn, companies expect their employees to be fair and honest in the workplace.

Many companies will establish a Code of Ethics or a Code of Conduct by which they expect their employees to act. For example, a company may establish guidelines for using the computer or Internet for non-company work while on the job. There may be standards for how to deal with angry customers on the phone or how to behave when representing the company at a meeting.

If an employee violates a code of ethics, the company may give a warning or suspend an employee without pay. In extreme cases, an employee may even be fired from the job. As an example, if a company discovers an employee lied about an important fact on his or her resume or application, that employee may be dismissed.

In order to be a successful, valued, and trusted employee, always act with integrity and honesty. If you are unsure how to act in a certain situation, discuss the situation with your supervisor or human resources director.

Quarter-Minute Checkpoints				
gwam	1/4'	1/2'	3/4'	Time
16	4	8	12	16
20	5	10	15	20
24	6	12	18	24
28	7	14	21	28
32	8	16	24	32
36	9	18	27	36
40	10	20	30	40

Guided (Paced) Timing Procedure

Establish a goal rate

1. Key a 1' timing on ¶ 1 of a set of ¶s that contain superior figures for guided timings, as in 10D below.

2. Using the *gwam* as a base, add 4 *gwam* to set your goal rate.

3. From column 1 of the table at the left, choose the speed nearest your goal rate. In the quarter-minute columns beside that speed, note the points in the copy you must reach to attain your goal rate.

4. Determine the checkpoint for each quarter minute from the word count above the lines in ¶ 1. (*Example:* Checkpoints for 24 *gwam* are 6, 12, 18, and 24.)

Practice procedure

1. Key two 1' timings on ¶ 1 at your goal rate guided by the quarter-minute calls (1/4, 1/2, 3/4, time). Try to reach each checkpoint before the guide is called.

2. Key two 1' timings on ¶ 2 of a set of ¶s in the same way.

3. If time permits, key a 2' writing on the set of ¶s combined, without the guides.

10D

Speed Check: Paragraphs

1. Key a 1' timing on each ¶; determine *gwam* on each timing.

2. Using your better *gwam* as a base rate, set a goal rate and key two 1' guided timings on each ¶ as directed above.

3. Key two 2' unguided timings on ¶s 1–2 combined; determine *gwam*.

LA   all letters used   MicroPace   gwam 2'

```
          •       2       •       4       •       6       •       8       •
     Is it possible for a mouse to make an individual        5
10      •      12       •      14       •      16       •      18       •      20
quite wealthy?  Yes, of course it is.  If you do not        11
         •     22       •      24       •      26       •      28       •      30
believe it, consider Walt Disney.  This individual          16
        •     32       •      34       •      36       •      38       •      40       •
came from a very humble beginning.  But in the end,         21
       42      •      44       •      46       •      48       •      50       •
he was a very wealthy person.  He was a person whose        26
     52      •      54       •      56       •      58       •      60       •
work brought great enjoyment to the lives of many           31
     62      •
people.                                                     31

          •       2       •       4       •       6       •       8       •
     A mouse, duck, and dog are just a few of the           36
     10      •      12       •      14       •      16       •      18       •
exquisite personalities he brought to life.  After          41
     20      •      22       •      24       •      26       •      28       •
all these years, his work is still a part of our            46
     30      •      32       •      34       •      36       •      38       •
lives.  People travel miles to step into the amazing        51
     40      •      42       •      44       •      46       •      48       •      50
world of Disney.  It would be impossible to picture         56
        •     52       •      54       •
this world without his work.                                59
```

gwam 2' | 1 | 2 | 3 | 4 | 5 |

10E

Technique

Key each line twice SS; DS between 2-line groups.

For additional practice:

MicroType 5
New Key Review, Alphabetic Lesson 10

Double letters

1 took yell meet carrot need cross spoon little loop
2 Dianna has lived in Massachusetts and Mississippi.

Shift keys

3 New Jersey, South Dakota, New Mexico, North Dakota
4 The Padres play the Cubs on Tuesday and Wednesday.

Lesson 10   *Skill Building*   **22**

Understanding Your Strengths and Passions

Everyone has their own set of strengths and weaknesses. There are things you excel at and other things that you would rather not do. You have special skills and abilities that make you more likely to succeed in a career than someone who has different skills. The trick is understanding how to identify your skills, passions, and personality traits so you can choose a career that will be right for you.

Identifying Personal Strengths and Passions

There are plenty of ways to help identify your skills and passions. You can begin by making a list of the things you enjoy best, such as working alone or as part of a team, working with numbers and money or working with words, caring for people or working with machines. You can search the many career websites for information on careers and the skills necessary to succeed in those careers. There are also websites with skills profiles to help you identify which type of career will be best suited to you. Some sites you may wish to explore include:

- U.S. Department of Labor (http://www.bls.gov)
- America's Career InfoNet (http://www.acinet.org/acinet/)

Personality Traits and Aptitude Tests

Another way to identify your strengths and weaknesses is to take a personality test or an aptitude test. Your career counselor may have these tools available at your school. There are also websites that offer personality tests online. Some tests are free and others may require a fee. These tests are designed to help you identify certain career choices that will fit your personality better than others. The tests offer a bank of questions that you answer honestly. At the end of the test, you are provided with scores that describe how you would best fit into the workplace. You can search for online personality tests in your favorite search engine.

EXERCISE A2 EXPLORING PERSONALITY TRAITS

1. With your teacher's permission, visit LiveCareer.com and take their free Career Interest Test (http://www.livecareer.com).
2. Print out your test results (if applicable). According to the tests, what type of career would best suit you? Open a new *Word* document and describe whether you were surprised by the results of the tests. How closely do the results align with your current career interests?
3. Save as *App A Exercise A2*.

Developing the Skills for Success

A company that is hiring a new employee will look for certain skills and traits. Some traits may be basic, such as "Does this person appear to take care of his health and personal appearance?" Other skills may be more difficult to identify, such as "Does this person have the ability to work as part of a team?" You may already have many of the skills necessary to be successful in the workplace. The information below is a sample of the skills and qualities that companies look for in their employees. No matter what path you take, these are skills and traits you will need for your personal development and success.

Leadership Skills

Do you know what it takes to be a good leader? Not everyone has the skills, or desire, to lead a group. However, if you have ever been part of a team that had a good leader, or a bad one, you know how the leader's skills affect the success of the team. Appendix B will guide you through specific information on leadership skills.

Teamwork Skills

What does it mean to be a team player? In the world of work, a *team* is a group of employees working together to achieve a common goal. People working as a team can usually accomplish more than people working alone. In fact, job success often depends on your ability to work well with others. Here are some things to remember when working with a team:

- **Be part of the team.** Work hard to get along with others, be cooperative, and always do your share of the work.
- **Be considerate.** Be respectful of others by admitting when you are wrong, apologizing if you hurt someone's feelings, and not acting like a know-it-all. In other words, treat others the way you want to be treated.
- **Be helpful.** Help others with their work, give compliments, listen to what others have to say, offer helpful and sincere feedback, and stay focused on the team goal.

EXERCISE A3 EXPLORING TEAMWORK SKILLS

Take the Teamwork Skills quiz in Figure A.2 to determine if you have what it takes to be an effective team member. If you can place a check mark by most of the statements, you could be an effective team member. Take note of items where you might need improvement.

Customer Service Skills

Many successful companies place great importance on customer satisfaction. Using good customer service skills means that you put the needs of your customer first. It also means that you are always concerned about how your actions and decisions will affect your customers. Companies with a customer service-based culture will often conduct surveys to make sure they are meeting the goals and standards their customers expect of them. Based on their findings, they may change the way they do business to better serve their customers.

Communication Skills

Most people assume they have good communication skills. However, good communication skills take practice and may be more difficult than you think. For example, as a good communicator, you need to speak clearly when giving instructions to others. When taking orders, you need to listen closely and follow directions without mistakes. When writing letters or e-mail, you need to use clear language with error-free grammar and spelling. When talking with customers, you need to convince others to do or buy something. If you can do all of this well, you can consider yourself a good communicator.

Lesson 11

OBJECTIVES
- To build straight-copy speed and control.
- To introduce rough-draft copy.

11A

Conditioning Practice

Key each line twice SS; then a 1' timing on line 3; determine *gwam*.

alphabet	1	J. Fox made five quick plays to win the big prize.
?	2	Where is Helen? Did she call? Is she to go, too?
easy	3	Pam owns the big dock, but they own the lake land.

gwam	1'	1	2	3	4	5	6	7	8	9	10

11B

Speed Building

Key each line twice SS with a DS between 2-line groups.

Technique Cue
- Reach up without moving hands away from your body.
- Reach down without moving hands toward your body.

za/az	1	zap lazy lizard pizza hazard bazaar frazzle dazzle
	2	Zack and Hazel zapped the lazy lizard in the maze.
ol/lo	3	old load olive look fold lost bold loan allow told
	4	Olympia told the lonely man to load the long logs.
ws/sw	5	swing cows sweet glows swept mows sword knows swap
	6	He swung the sword over the sweaty cows and swine.
ju/ft	7	often jury draft judge left just hefty juice after
	8	Jud, the fifth juror on my left, just wants juice.
ed/de	9	deal need debit edit deed edge deli used dent desk
	10	Jed needed to edit the deed made by the defendant.
ik/ki	11	kick like kind bike kiln hike kids strike king ski
	12	I like the kind of kids who like to hike and bike.

11C

Rough Draft (Edited Copy)

1. Study the proofreaders' marks shown below.
2. Key each sentence twice SS; DS between 2-line groups. Make all editing (handwritten) changes.

∧ = insert

= add space

∼ = transpose

⌿ = delete

⌒ = close up

≡ = capitalize

1 A first draft is a preliminary orr tentative one.

2 It is where the creator gets his thoughts on paper.

3 After the draft is created, it will be looked over.

4 Reviewing is the step where a person refines copy.

5 Proof readers' marks are used edit the original copy.

6 The edting changes will be then be made to the copy.

7 After the change have been made read the copy agian.

8 more changes still may need to be made to the copy.

9 Edting proof reading does take a lot time and effort.

10 error free copy is worth the trouble, however.

Top 30 Fastest-Growing Occupations
2006–2016 National Projections

1. Network systems and data communications analysts
2. Personal and home care aides
3. Home health aides
4. Computer software engineers, applications
5. Veterinary technologists and technicians
6. Personal financial advisors
7. Makeup artists, theatrical and performance
8. Medical assistants
9. Veterinarians
10. Substance abuse and behavioral disorder counselors
11. Skin care specialists
12. Financial analysts
13. Social and human service assistants
14. Gaming surveillance officers and gaming investigators
15. Physical therapist assistants
16. Pharmacy technicians
17. Forensic science technicians
18. Dental hygienists
19. Mental health counselors
20. Mental health and substance abuse social workers
21. Marriage and family therapists
22. Dental assistants
23. Computer systems analysts
24. Database administrators
25. Computer software engineers, systems software
26. Gaming and sports book writers and runners
27. Environmental science and protection technicians
28. Manicurists and pedicurists
29. Physical therapists
30. Physician assistants

Figure A.1 Top 30 Fastest-Growing Careers

Source: U.S. Department of Labor (http://www.bls.gov/news.release/ecopro.t06.htm), November 4, 2008.

Speed Check: Straight Copy

1. Key one 1' unguided and two 1' guided timings on ¶ 1 and then on ¶ 2, as directed on p. 22.
2. Key two 2' unguided timings on ¶s 1–2 combined; determine *gwam*.

LA   all letters used   MicroPace   gwam 2'

```
         •    2    •        4    •        6    •        8
     His mother signed her name with an X.  His        5
     •   10  •       12   •      14   •     16   •    18
 father had no schooling.  Could a President come      10
    •    20   •      22   •      24   •     26   •   28
 from such a humble background?  President Lincoln     14
    •    30    •     32   •      34   •     36   •   38
 did.  Lincoln was not just a President, he is often   20
    •    40   •      42   •     44   •      46   •   48
 recognized as one of the best to ever hold the office. 25
                •    2    •       4    •      6    •   8
     Honest Abe, as he was often called, always gave   30
    10    •      12   •      14   •      16   •    18    •   20
 the extra effort needed to be a success.  Whether the 35
     •    22   •      24   •      26   •     28   •   30
 job was splitting logs, being a lawyer, or being      40
     •   32    •     34   •      36   •     38   •   40
 President, he always gave it his best.  Dealing with  45
  •    42   •       44   •      46   •      48   •   50
 the Civil War required a man who gave his best.       50
```

gwam 2' | 1 | 2 | 3 | 4 | 5 |

Skill Transfer: Straight Copy and Rough Draft

1. Key each ¶ once SS; DS between ¶s.
2. Key two 1' timings on each ¶; determine *gwam* on each timing.

Straight copy

                                                        gwam 1'

```
     Documents free of errors make a good impression.   10
When a document has no errors, readers can focus on     20
the content.  Errors distract readers and can cause     31
them to think less of the message.                      38

     Therefore, it is important to proofread the        10
final copy of a document several times to make sure     20
it contains no errors before it leaves your desk.       29
Readers of error-free documents form a positive image   40
of the person who wrote the message.                    47
```

Rough draft

```
     When a negative image of the person who wrote the the   10
                  (positive)
messge is formed the message is less likely to succeed.      22
   (a)                  more (second)
remembre, you never get a another chance to make a good      34
                                    #        (first)
impression.                                                  36
```

For additional practice:
MicroType 5
New Key Review, Alphabetic
Lesson 11

APPENDIX A
Lessons 1-2

Career Development and Employment Readiness

Choosing a career is one of the most important decisions you will make about your future. Your choice will take you down a specific road in your education, training, and personal development. That is why it is so important to plan your career options carefully. You need to explore your talents and passions. You need to develop tools to help in your career search. You need to understand your options so you choose a path that will be rewarding both now and in the future.

In this Appendix you will learn how your personality traits can help you choose a career you will enjoy. You will explore writing a resume and learn how to apply for a job. You will identify the skills that employers want so that you can be successful in your professional life. You will discover how ethical behavior relates to employability. And you will read about the importance of lifelong learning and career planning.

Lesson 1   CAREER OPTIONS

OBJECTIVES
- To explore career options.
- To learn how your personality traits can help you choose a career.
- To identify skills employers want.
- To discover the importance of lifelong learning and career planning.

Understanding Career Options

Did you know that you currently have many skills that employers look for in an employee? The skills you are learning in this course will be important in your future job. Many companies require employees to have advanced computer skills. They expect you to come to the job knowing how to prepare a spreadsheet, format a letter, and develop a presentation. The word processing and database skills you are learning are necessary for careers in customer service, commercial art, and medical assisting. Excellent verbal and written communication skills are important in careers in sales, teaching, and magazine publishing. Spreadsheet, desktop publishing, and presentation skills are necessary for careers in newspapers, office management, and public relations. Most companies are dependent on computers, and they need skilled employees to help them do business.

As you begin to explore careers, you will find countless options to choose from. In fact, the number of career opportunities doubles every few years. New and exciting careers are available in sports marketing, international banking, health and medicine, hospitality and tourism, and the fast food industry. You have the opportunity to choose a career that is just right for you and to be wildly successful at it! Examine the table in Figure A.1 to see a list of the Top 30 Fastest-Growing Occupations as identified by the U.S. Department of Labor.

EXERCISE A1 THINKING ABOUT CAREER OPTIONS

1. Go to the site http://www.careerclusters.org/ and find the chart showing the 16 career clusters. Identify the clusters or careers in the table that interest you.

2. Choose two careers from the table and find out more about them by going to two of these sites:
   - Occupational Outlook Handbook on the U.S. Department of Labor website (http://www.bls.gov/oco/)
   - Careers.Org (http://www.careers.org/)
   - Science Careers (http://sciencecareers.sciencemag.org/)
   - Health Careers (http://www.explorehealthcareers.org/)
   - Computer Careers (http://www.computer.org/)

3. Open a blank *Word* document and summarize any information you find about working conditions, special skills or traits, training and education requirements, earnings potential, and related occupations for your chosen careers.

4. Save as *App A Exercise A1.*

OBJECTIVES
- To build straight-copy speed and control.
- To enhance keying technique.

12A

Conditioning Practice

Key each line twice SS; then key a 1' timing on line 3. Determine *gwam*.

alphabet 1 Kevin can fix the unique jade owl as my big prize.

spacing 2 She will be able to see the dogs in a week or two.

easy 3 A box with the form is on the chair by the mantle.

| gwam | 1' | 1 | 2 | 3 | 4 | 5 | 6 | 7 | 8 | 9 | 10 |

12B

Difficult-Reach Mastery

Key each line twice SS; DS between 2-line groups.

Adjacent keys

1 Her posh party on their new patio was a real bash.

2 Robert knew that we had to pool our points to win.

3 Juan will try to stop a fast break down the court.

4 Bart saw her buy a red suit at a new shop in town.

Long direct reaches

5 Betty is expected to excel in this next long race.

6 My fervor for gym events was once my unique trait.

7 Music as a unique force is no myth in any country.

8 Lynda has since found many facts we must now face.

Reaches with 3rd and 4th fingers

9 Nick said the cash price for gas was up last week.

10 My squad set a quarter quota to equal our request.

11 Zane played a zany tune that amazed the jazz band.

12 The poet will opt for a top spot in our port town.

12C

Speed Check: Sentences

Key two 30" timings on each line. Try to increase your keying speed the second time you key the line. Determine *gwam* for the faster timing of each line.

1 Yizel will take the test soon.

2 Nick will take his turn on Tuesday.

3 Felipe will apply for a job at the bank.

4 Marsha took both computers in to be repaired.

5 Their next ballgame will be in two or three weeks.

6 The repairs ended up costing much more than he thought.

| gwam | 30" | 2 | 4 | 6 | 8 | 10 | 12 | 14 | 16 | 18 | 20 | 22 |

APPENDICES

Technique: Response Patterns

1. Key each line twice SS; DS between 2-line groups.
2. Key a 1' timing on lines 10–12; determine *gwam* on each line.

For additional practice:
MicroType 5
New Key Review, Alphabetic
Lesson 12

One-hand words (Think and key by letter response.)

1 bear aware data gave edge states race great street
2 ink pin you hook milk moon only join union million
3 were you | up on | are in fact | my taxes are | star gazed

Balanced-hand words (Think and key by word response.)

4 oak box land sign make busy kept foal handle gowns
5 chair disown mantle right world theme towns theory
6 go to the | it may work | did he make | she is | he may go

One-hand sentences (Think and key by letter response.)

7 Jim gazed at a radar gadget we gave him in a case.
8 Dave saved a dazed polo pony as we sat on a knoll.
9 Carter gave him a minimum rate on state oil taxes.

Balanced-hand sentences (Think and key by word response.)

10 Rick may make them turn by the lake by their sign.
11 Jane may go to the city to work for the six firms.
12 Ken may make the girl pay for the keys to the bus.

gwam 1' | 1 | 2 | 3 | 4 | 5 | 6 | 7 | 8 | 9 | 10 |

Speed Building: Guided Writing

1. Key one 1' unguided and two 1' guided timings on each ¶.
2. Key two 2' unguided timings on ¶s 1–2 combined; determine *gwam*.

Quarter-Minute Checkpoints				
gwam	1/4'	1/2'	3/4'	1'
20	5	10	15	20
24	6	12	18	24
28	7	14	21	28
32	8	16	24	32
36	9	18	27	36
40	10	20	30	40
44	11	22	33	44
48	12	24	36	48
52	13	26	39	52
56	14	28	42	56

LA   **all letters used**   gwam 2'

Laura Ingalls Wilder is a beloved writer of books for   5
children. Most of her books are based on her own experiences   12
as a youth. Her first book was about her life in Wisconsin.   18
From just reading such a book, children fantasize about what   24
it would have been like to live with the pioneers during this   30
time period of our nation.   33

Besides writing about her own life and the lives of her   38
family members, she also wrote about the life of her husband,   45
Almanzo, and his family. Her second book was about the early   51
years of his life growing up on a farm near the Canadian bor-   57
der in the state of New York. Through these exquisite books,   63
this period of time in our history is preserved forever.   69

gwam 2' | 1 | 2 | 3 | 4 | 5 | 6 |

Lesson 5 DIVISION & MATH CALCULATIONS

- To learn division on numeric keypad.
- To learn to complete math calculations on numeric keypad.

5A

Keypad Review

Calculate the totals for the problems at the right.

A	B	C	D	E	F
20	92	872	613		
65	−43	−115	+716	438	704.9
39	+20	+178	−690	× 4.8	× 5.03
124	69	935	639	2,102.4	3,545.65

5B

Division

Learn Reach to / (Division Key)

1. Locate / (division key) on the numeric keypad.
2. Practice tapping the / key a few times as you watch the middle finger move up to the / and back to the 5 key.
3. With eyes on copy, key the data in Drills 1–3.
4. Verify your answer with those shown.

Drill 1

A	B	C	D	E
51.17	42	179	106	91
6/307	10/420	5/895	7/742	9/819

Drill 2

A	B	C	D	E
32.25	75.52	229.13	96.42	159.04
12/387	66/4,984	32/7,332	52/5,014	56/8,906

Drill 3

A	B	C	D	E
44.20	7.94	98.27	173.37	90.74
6.9/305	47.6/378	12.7/1,248	31.2/5,409	95/8,620

5C

Math Calculations

Use the numeric keypad to solve the math problems at the right.

1. Ken opened a checking account with $100. He wrote checks for $12.88, $15.67, $8.37, and $5.25. He made one deposit of $26.80 and had a service charge of $1.75. What is his current balance?

2. Jan purchased six tickets for the Utah Jazz basketball game. Four of the tickets cost $29.50; the other two cost $35.00. The service charge for each ticket was $1.50. What was the total cost of the six tickets?

3. Four friends went out for dinner. The cost of the dinner came to $47.88. They left a 15 percent tip and split the cost of the dinner equally among them. How much did each person have to pay?

4. Jay filled his car up with gas. The odometer reading was 45,688 miles. Jay drove to New York to see a Yankees game. When he got there he filled the car up again. It took 15.7 gallons. The odometer now read 45,933. How many miles per gallon did Jay get on the trip?

5. Mary bowled six games this week. Her scores were 138, 151, 198, 147, 156, and 173. What was her average for those six games?

6. There are 800 points available in the history class. Roberto wants an A in the class. To get an A, he needs to achieve 95 percent or better. What is the minimum number of points he will need to earn the A?

Communication & Math
SKILLS 1

SENTENCES

ACTIVITY 1

Simple Sentences

1. Study each of the guides for simple sentences shown below.
2. Key *Learn* lines 1–8, noting the subjects and predicates.
3. For *Apply* lines 9–11, combine the two sentences into one simple sentence with two nouns as the subject and one verb as the predicate.
4. Revise sentence 12 by combining the two sentences into one simple sentence with two nouns as the subject and two verbs as the predicate.

Save as: CS1 ACTIVITY1

A simple sentence consists of one independent clause that contains a subject (noun or pronoun) and a predicate (verb).

Learn   1   Stan is at the game.

Learn   2   Felipe went to the game.

Learn   3   Rebecca likes to play computer games.

Learn   4   Laura tried out for the basketball team.

A simple sentence may have as its subject more than one noun or pronoun (compound subject) and as its predicate more than one verb (compound predicate).

Learn   5   He painted the house.   (single subject/single predicate)

Learn   6   Steve and I won an award.   (compound subject/single predicate)

Learn   7   Jenny washed and polished her car.   (single subject/compound predicate)

Learn   8   Jay and I wrote and edited the paper.   (compound subject and predicate)

Apply   9   Juan read the book. Juanita read it, also.

Apply   10   Jason keyed his own paper. So did Keith.

Apply   11   Taji rode to the game with Monica. Alisha rode with her, also.

Apply   12   Mary washes and dries her hair every day. Jan also washes and dries hers.

ACTIVITY 2

Compound Sentences

1. Study each of the guides for compound sentences shown below.
2. Key *Learn* lines 13–20, noting the words that make up the subjects and predicates of each sentence.
3. For *Apply* lines 21–24, combine the two sentences into a compound sentence. Choose carefully from the coordinating conjunctions *and, but, for, or, nor, yet, and so.*

Save as: CS1 ACTIVITY2

A compound sentence contains two or more independent clauses connected by a coordinating conjunction (*and, but, for, or, nor, yet, so*).

Learn   13   Rhea likes to play softball, and Tara likes to play basketball.

Learn   14   The blue car is sold, but the red one is still available.

Learn   15   You may go with us, or you may stay at home.

Learn   16   Erika plays the flute, Joan plays the drums, and Tim plays the trumpet.

Each clause of a compound sentence may have as its subject more than one noun/pronoun and as its predicate more than one verb.

Learn   17   Jon came and stayed for the entire game, and Jay and Ty left at the half.

Learn   18   Don took biology and chemistry, but the others took only biology.

Learn   19   You can cook dinner, or you and Maria can go out to dinner.

Learn   20   Roberto finished the exam, but Alex and Karl needed more time to finish.

Apply   21   Sasha played video games. Mark read a book.

Apply   22   You may watch television. You and Lynda may go to a movie.

Apply   23   Jorge may play golf or tennis. He may not play both.

Apply   24   Karla went to the University of Iowa. Glen went to the University of Utah.

SUBTRACTION & MULTIPLICATION

OBJECTIVES

• To learn subtraction on numeric keypad.
• To learn multiplication on numeric keypad.

4A

Keypad Review

Calculate the totals for the problems at the right.

A	B	C	D	E	F
17	49	672	513	371	109
+83	+60	+ 415	+ 724	+ 564	+ 357
+52	+93	+ 808	+ 690	+ 289	+ 620
152	202	1,895	1,927	1,224	1,086

4B

Subtraction

Learn Reach to – (Minus Key)

1. Locate – (minus key) on the numeric keypad above the + (plus key).

2. Practice tapping the – key a few times as you watch the little finger move up to the – and back to the +.

3. With eyes on copy, key the data in Drills 1–3.

4. Verify your answers with those shown below the column.

5. Tap ESC on the main keyboard to clear the calculator; then key numbers in the next column.

Drill 1

A	B	C	D	E	F
27	50	893	798	523	401
−14	−26	−406	−235	−178	−300
13	24	487	563	345	101

Drill 2

A	B	C	D	E	F
84	56	996	829	759	83.6
−17	−38	−476	−514	−420	−41.5
67	18	520	315	339	42.1

Drill 3

A	B	C	D	E	F
99	89	505	807	978	63.4
−16	−10	−264	−234	−220	+37.5
−23	− 8	− 45	− 65	+461	− 8.9
−33	−17	− 87	−104	+309	−46.5
− 9	−24	−156	− 57	−218	+70.1
18	30	−47	347	1,310	115.6

4C

Multiplication

Learn Reach to * (Multiplication Key)

1. Locate the * (multiplication key) on the numeric keypad above the 9.

2. Practice tapping the * key a few times as you watch your ring finger move up to the * key and back to the 6 key.

3. With eyes on copy, key the data in Drills 1–3.

4. Verify your answers with those shown.

Drill 1

A	B	C	D	E
28	54	43	145	68.8
×13	×60	×89	×271	×19.3
364	3,240	3,827	39,295	1,327.84

Drill 2

A	B	C	D	E
603	109	837	468	219
× 24	× 72	× 55	× 90	× 34
14,472	7,848	46,035	42,120	7,446

Drill 3

A $3 \times 5 \times 6 = 90$

B $8 \times 7 \times 2 = 112$

C $2 \times 9 \times 4 = 72$

D $4 \times 10 \times 3 = 120$

E $67 \times 13 + 89 = 960$

F $7 \times 70 - 34 = 456$

ACTIVITY 3

Complex Sentences

1. Study the guides for complex sentences shown below.
2. Key *Learn* lines 25–32, noting the subject and predicate of the independent clause and of the dependent clause for each sentence.
3. For *Apply* lines 33–36, combine the two sentences into a complex sentence.

Save as: CS1 ACTIVITY3

A complex sentence contains only one independent clause but one or more dependent clauses.

Learn 25 The music that you bought for Ashley at the mall is excellent.

Learn 26 If I go on the trip, I will ask Marge to take care of your pets.

Learn 27 Ms. Moore, who chaired the committee last year, took a new job.

Learn 28 Students who do not procrastinate are generally successful.

The subject of a complex sentence may consist of more than one noun or pronoun; the predicate may consist of more than one verb.

Learn 29 All who attended the seminar received a free book and had lunch.

Learn 30 If you are going on the tour, you should call Tim and let him know.

Learn 31 After Jay and I left for the game, Joe and Barb washed and dried the dishes.

Learn 32 Even though they thought they would win, Nick and Phil were not sure.

Apply 33 My interview went really well. I may not get the job.

Apply 34 They attended the game. They went to the party.

Apply 35 Frank is going to take the CPS exam. He should register now.

Apply 36 You are buying the camera. You should also get a memory card.

ACTIVITY 4

Composing

Key each line once
(do not key the figure).
In place of the blank line,
key the word(s) that correctly
complete(s) the sentence.

Save as: CS1 ACTIVITY4

1. A small mass of land surrounded by water is a(n) _____.
2. A large mass of land surrounded by water is a(n) _____.
3. The earth rotates on what is called its _____.
4. When the sun comes up over the horizon, we say it _____.
5. When the sun goes down over the horizon, we say it _____.
6. A device used to display temperature is a(n) _____.
7. A device used to display atmospheric pressure is a(n) _____.

ACTIVITY 5

Math: Adding and Subtracting Numbers

1. Open *DF CS1 ACTIVITY5* and print the file.
2. Solve the problems as directed in the file.
3. Submit your answers.

CAREER Clusters

ACTIVITY 1

There are many different career opportunities available to you once you graduate from high school. Some careers require no additional education, while others require many years of additional education. The 14 career exploration activities will help you understand the requirements for some of the careers in which you may have an interest. Begin your exploration by completing the following steps.

1. Access http://www.careerclusters.org.

2. Complete the Career Clusters Interest Survey Activity. Your instructor will provide you with a copy of the survey or you can click on Free Career Clusters Interest Survey Activity and then click on View/Print Now. Print a copy of the survey and the Sixteen Career Clusters pages that follow the Interest Survey.

3. Obtain a folder for your Career Exploration Portfolio from your instructor, write your name and class period on it, place your completed Interest Survey and descriptions of the career clusters in the folder, and file the folder as instructed.

OBJECTIVE

• To learn reachstrokes for **1**, **2**, and **3**.

3A

Keypad Review

Calculate the totals for the problems at the right.

A	B	C	D	E	F	G
45	74	740	996	704	990	477
56	85	850	885	805	880	588
67	96	960	774	906	770	699
168	255	2,550	2,655	2,415	2,640	1,764

3B

New Keys: 1, 2, and 3

Learn Reach to 1

1. Locate 1 (below 4) on the numeric keypad.
2. Watch your index finger move down to 1 and back to 4 a few times.
3. Key 14 a few times as you watch the finger.
4. With eyes on copy, key the data in Drills 1A and 1B.

Learn Reach to 2

1. Learn the middle-finger reach to 2 (below 5) as directed in steps 1–3 above.
2. With eyes on copy, key the data in Drills 1C and 1D.

Learn Reach to 3

1. Learn the ring-finger reach to 3 (below 6) as directed above.
2. With eyes on copy, key the data in Drills 1E–1G.

Drills 2–4

1. Calculate the totals for each problem and check your answers.

Learn Reach to . (Decimal)

1. Learn the ring-finger reach to the decimal point (.) located below the 3.
2. Calculate the totals for each problem in Drill 5.
3. Repeat Drills 2–5 to increase your speed.

For additional practice:

MicroType 5
Numeric Keypad
Lesson 3

Drill 1

A	B	C	D	E	F	G
144	114	525	252	353	636	120
141	414	252	552	363	366	285
414	141	225	525	336	636	396
699	669	1,002	1,329	1,052	1,638	801

Drill 2

A	B	C	D	E	F	G
411	552	663	571	514	481	963
144	255	366	482	425	672	852
414	525	636	539	563	953	471
969	1,332	1,665	1,592	1,502	2,106	2,286

Drill 3

A	B	C	D	E	F	G
471	582	693	303	939	396	417
41	802	963	220	822	285	508
14	825	936	101	717	174	639
526	2,209	2,592	624	2,478	855	1,564

Drill 4

A	B	C	D	E	F	G
75	128	167	102	853	549	180
189	34	258	368	264	367	475
3	591	349	549	971	102	396
267	753	774	1,019	2,088	1,018	1,051

Drill 5

A	B	C	D	E	F	G
1.30	2.58	23.87	90.37	16.89	47.01	59.28
4.17	6.90	14.65	4.25	3.25	28.36	1.76
5.47	9.48	38.52	94.62	20.14	75.37	61.04

UNIT 3
Lessons 13-14

Learn/Review Figure-Key Technique

LEARN/REVIEW FIGURE KEYS (8, 1, 9, 4, AND 0)

OBJECTIVES

- To review reach technique for **8, 1, 9, 4,** and **0**.
- To improve skill on script and rough-draft copy.

13A

Conditioning Practice
Key each line twice SS.

alphabet	1	Jackie and Zelda's next big purchase may require two favors.
spacing	2	When you get to the game, save two seats for Rob and Felipe.
easy	3	Jan may make a big profit if she owns the title to the land.
gwam	1'	1 │ 2 │ 3 │ 4 │ 5 │ 6 │ 7 │ 8 │ 9 │ 10 │ 11 │ 12 │

13B

Learn/Review 8 and 1
Key each line twice.

Learn/Review 8

1 k k 8k 8k kk 88 k8k k8k 88k 88k Reach up for 8, 88, and 888.
2 Key the figures 8, 88, and 888. Please open Room 88 or 888.

Learn/Review 1

3 a a 1a 1a aa 11 a1a a1a 11a 11a Reach up for 1, 11, and 111.
4 Add the figures 1, 11, and 111. Only 1 out of 111 finished.

Combine 8 and 1

5 Key 11, 18, 81, and 88. Just 11 of the 18 skiers have left.
6 Reach with the fingers to key 18 and 188 as well as 1 and 8.
7 The stock person counted 11 coats, 18 slacks, and 88 shirts.

OBJECTIVE

• To learn reachstrokes for **7**, **8**, and **9**.

2A

Home-Key Review

Calculate the totals for the problems at the right.

A	B	C	D	E	F
4	44	400	404	440	450
5	55	500	505	550	560
6	66	600	606	660	456
15	165	1,500	1,515	1,650	1,466

2B

New Keys: 7, 8, and 9

Learn Reach to 7

1. Locate 7 (above 4) on the numeric keypad.
2. Watch your index finger move up to 7 and back to 4 a few times without tapping keys.
3. Practice tapping 74 a few times as you watch the finger.
4. With eyes on copy, key the data in Drills 1A and 1B.

Learn Reach to 8

1. Learn the middle-finger reach to 8 (above 5) as directed in steps 1–3 above.
2. With eyes on copy, key the data in Drills 1C and 1D.

Learn Reach to 9

1. Learn the ring-finger reach to 9 (above 6) as directed above.
2. With eyes on copy, key the data in Drills 1E and 1F.

Drills 2–5

1. Calculate the totals for each problem in Drills 2–5. Check your answers.
2. Repeat Drills 2–5 to increase your speed.

For additional practice:

MicroType 5
Numeric Keypad
Lesson 2

Drill 1

A	B	C	D	E	F
474	747	585	858	696	969
747	477	858	588	969	966
777	474	888	585	999	696
1,998	1,698	2,331	2,031	2,664	2,631

Drill 2

A	B	C	D	E	F
774	885	996	745	475	754
474	585	696	854	584	846
747	858	969	965	695	956
1,995	2,328	2,661	2,564	1,754	2,556

Drill 3

A	B	C	D	E	F
470	580	690	770	707	407
740	850	960	880	808	508
705	805	906	990	909	609
1,915	2,235	2,556	2,640	2,424	1,524

Drill 4

A	B	C	D	E	F
456	407	508	609	804	905
789	408	509	704	805	906
654	409	607	705	806	907
987	410	608	706	904	908
2,886	1,634	2,232	2,724	3,319	3,626

Drill 5

A	B	C	D	E	F
8	786	4	804	76	86
795	69	705	45	556	564
78	575	59	6	5	78
60	4	446	556	666	504
941	1,434	1,214	1,411	1,303	1,232

Keyboard Reinforcement

Key each line twice.

Figures

1 May 1-8, May 11-18, June 1-8, and June 11-18 are open dates.
2 The quiz on the 18th will be on pages 11 to 18 and 81 to 88.
3 He said only 11 of us got No. 81 right; 88 got No. 81 wrong.

Home/1st

4 ax jab van gab man call back land calf jazz hack cabana Jack
5 small man|can mask|lava can|jazz band|lack cash|a small lamb
6 Ms. Maas can call a cab, and Jan can call a small black van.

Learn/Review 9, 4, and 0

Key each line twice.

Review 9

1 l l 9l 9l ll 99 l9l l9l 99l 99l Reach up for 9, 99, and 999.
2 The social security number was 919-99-9191, not 191-99-1919.

Review 4

3 f f 4f 4f ff 44 f4f f4f 44f 44f Reach up for 4, 44, and 444.
4 Add the figures 4, 44, and 444. Please study pages 4 to 44.

Review 0

5 ; ; 0; 0; ;; 00 ;0; ;0; 00; 00; Reach up for 0, 00, and 000.
6 Snap the finger off the 0. I used 0, 00, and 000 sandpaper.

Combine 9, 4, and 0

7 Flights 904 and 490 left after Flights 409A, 400Z, and 940X.
8 My ZIP Code is 40099, not 44099. Kim keyed 0909, not 09094.

Speed Check

1. Key three 30" timings on each line. Try to go faster on each timing.
2. Key a 2' timing on 12E, p. 26.

1 The firm kept half of us busy.
2 The girls work for the island firm.
3 Diane may blame the girls for the fight.
4 Pay the man for the work he did on the autos.
5 The social for the maid is to be held in the city.
6 Jake may sign the form if they do an audit of the firm.

30" | 2 | 4 | 6 | 8 | 10 | 12 | 14 | 16 | 18 | 20 | 22 |

New Keys: 4, 5, 6, and 0 (Home Keys)

Use the calculator accessory to complete the drills.

1. Enter each number: Key the number and enter by tapping the + key with the little finger of the right hand.

2. After entering each number in the column, verify your answer with the answer shown below the column.

3. Tap ESC on the main keyboard to clear the calculator; then key numbers in the next column.

4. Repeat steps 1–3 for Drills 1–6.

Technique Cue

Tap each key with a quick, sharp stroke with the *tip* of the finger; release the key quickly. Keep the fingers curved and upright.

Tap the 0 with the side of the right thumb, similar to the way you tap the Space Bar.

Drill 1

A	B	C	D	E	F
4	5	6	4	5	6
4	5	6	4	5	6
8	10	12	8	10	12

Drill 2

A	B	C	D	E	F
44	55	66	44	55	66
44	55	66	44	55	66
88	110	132	88	110	132

Drill 3

A	B	C	D	E	F
44	45	54	44	55	66
55	56	46	45	54	65
66	64	65	46	56	64
165	165	165	135	165	195

Drill 4

A	B	C	D	E	F
40	50	60	400	500	600
50	60	40	506	604	405
60	40	50	650	460	504
150	150	150	1,556	1,564	1,509

Drill 5

A	B	C	D	E	F
45	404	404	406	450	650
55	405	505	506	540	560
65	406	606	606	405	605
165	1,215	1,515	1,518	1,395	1,815

Drill 6

A	B	C	D	E	F
40	606	444	554	646	456
50	505	445	555	656	654
60	404	446	556	666	504
150	1,515	1,335	1,665	1,968	1,614

For additional practice:

MicroType 5
Numeric Keypad
Lesson 1

13F

Speed Building

1. Key a 1' timing on ¶ 1; key three more 1' timings on ¶ 1, trying to go faster each time.
2. Repeat the procedure for ¶ 2.
3. Key a 2' timing on ¶s 1 and 2 combined.

For additional practice:
MicroType 5
New Key Review, Number & Symbol Lesson 1

LA all letters used (MicroPace)   gwam 2'

					gwam 2'
How did music come about? If you enjoy music, you may					6
have thought about this query previously. It is extremely					11
doubtful that any of us has the answer to why, when, where,					17
or how it got its start. It is plausible that the people who					24
started music did not even realize they were creating music.					30
Today music adds a great deal to our lives and defines					35
who we are. Different types of music exist to please each					41
of our personal tastes. Some people think that classical					47
music is the only music worth hearing. Others would vote					53
for country, rap, rock, or another form of music. There is					59
one thing, though, that nearly all of us agree on; music					64
enriches our lives.					66

gwam 2' | 1 | 2 | 3 | 4 | 5 | 6 |

Lesson 14   LEARN/REVIEW FIGURE KEYS (5, 7, 3, 6, AND 2)

OBJECTIVES
- To review reach technique for **5**, **7**, **3**, **6**, and **2**.
- To improve skill transfer and build speed.

14A

Conditioning Practice

Key each line twice.

alphabet 1 Many expect Frank Valdez to quit working on all of the jobs.
spacing 2 Did they say when they will be able to do the work for Stan?
easy 3 Rick and the girls may go downtown to pay for the six signs.

gwam 1' | 1 | 2 | 3 | 4 | 5 | 6 | 7 | 8 | 9 | 10 | 11 | 12 |

14B

Learn/Review 5 and 7

Key each line twice.

Review 5

1 f f 5f 5f ff 55 f5f f5f 55f 55f Reach up for 5, 55, and 555.
2 Reach up to 5 and back to f. Did he say to order 55 or 555?

Review 7

3 j j 7j 7j jj 77 j7j j7j 77j 77j Reach up for 7, 77, and 777.
4 Key the figures 7, 77, and 777. She checked Rooms 7 and 77.

Lessons 1–5

Learn Numeric Keypad Operation

OBJECTIVE

• To learn reachstrokes for **4**, **5**, **6**, and **0**

1A

Numeric Keypad Operating Position

Follow the instructions given at the right for positioning yourself to effectively use the numeric keypad.

© franksiteman.com 2007

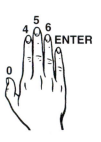

Curve the fingers of the right hand and place them on the keypad:

• index finger on 4
• middle finger on 5
• ring finger on 6
• thumb on 0

Sit in front of the keyboard with the book at the right—body erect, both feet on floor.

1B

Access the Calculator

Follow the instructions given at the right to access the calculator on your computer.

1. Click on Start.
2. Click on All Programs.
3. Click on Accessories.
4. Click on Calculator.
5. Activate the Num (number) Lock located above the 7 on the numeric keypad.

14c

Script and Rough-Draft Copy

Key each line twice.

☰ = capitalize

∧ = insert

∼ = transpose

⌇# = delete space

= add space

⌇ℓc = lowercase

◠ = close up

Script

1 Proofread: Compare copy word for word with the original.
2 Compare all figures digit by digit with your source copy.
3 Be sure to check for spacing and punctuation marks, also.
4 Copy in script or rough draft may not show exact spacing.
5 It is your job to insert correct spacing as you key copy.
6 Soon you will learn how to correct your errors on screen.

Rough draft

7 cap the first word an**d** all proper nouns in **each** ~~every~~ sentence.

8 For example: pablo Mendez is from San juan,Puerto rico.

9 Ami Qwan and **her** parents will return to Taipie this **fall** summer.

10 our coffee **comes** is from **Brazil** ~~Columbia~~; tea, from England or china.

11 How many of you have Ethnic origins in a foreign country?

12 **Do** did you know which of **our** the states once were part of mexico?

14d

Learn/Review 3, 6, and 2

Key each line twice.

Review 3

1 d d 3d 3d dd 33 d3d d3d 33d 33d Reach up for 3, 33, and 333.
2 Add the figures 3, 33, and 333. Read pages 3 to 33 tonight.

Review 6

3 j j 6j 6j jj 66 j6j j6j 66j 66j Reach up for 6, 66, and 666.
4 Key the figures 6, 66, and 666. Did just 6 of 66 finish it?

Review 2

5 s s 2s 2s ss 22 s2s s2s 22s 22s Reach up for 2, 22, and 222.
6 Reach up to 2 and back to s. Ashley reviewed pages 2 to 22.

Combine 3, 6, and 2

7 Only 263 of the 362 flights left on time on Monday, July 26.
8 Read Chapter 26, pages 263 to 326, for the exam on April 23.

21C

Speed Check: Sentences

Key two 30" timings on each line. Your rate in *gwam* is shown word-for-word below the lines.

	gwam	30"
1 When do you think you will go?		12
2 Tara just finished taking her exam.		14
3 Nancy told the man to fix the car brake.		16
4 Val could see that he was angry with the boy.		18
5 Karen may not be able to afford college next year.		20
6 Jay took three hours to complete the chemistry project.		22

30" | 2 | 4 | 6 | 8 | 10 | 12 | 14 | 16 | 18 | 20 | 22 |

If you finish a line before time is called and start over, your *gwam* is the figure at the end of the line PLUS the figure above or below the point at which you stopped.

21D

Speed Building

1. Key each line twice SS; DS between 2-line groups.
2. Key a 1' writing on each line; determine *gwam* on each timing.

Key the words at a brisk, steady pace.

1 Pamela may make a profit off the land by the lake.
2 Eight of the firms may handle the work for Rodney.

3 Vivian may make a map of the city for the six men.
4 Helen held a formal social for eight of the girls.

5 He may work with the men on the city turn signals.
6 The dog and the girl slept in a chair in the hall.

7 Dianna may cycle to the city dock by the big lake.
8 Half of them may be kept busy with the sick girls.

gwam 1' | 1 | 2 | 3 | 4 | 5 | 6 | 7 | 8 | 9 | 10 |

21E

Speed Check: Paragraphs

Key two 1' timings on each ¶; determine *gwam* on each writing.

 EA all letters used **MicroPace**

	gwam	2'
. 2 . 4 . 6 . 8 .		
Are you one of the people who often look from		5
10 . 12 . 14 . 16 . 18 .		
the copy to the screen and down at your hands? If		10
20 . 22 . 24 . 26 . 28 .		
you are, you can be sure that you will not build a		15
30 . 32 . 34 . 36 . 38 .		
speed to prize. Make eyes on copy your next goal.		20
. 2 . 4 . 6 . 8 .		
When you move the eyes from the copy to check		24
10 . 12 . 14 . 16 . 18 .		
the screen, you may lose your place and waste time		30
20 . 22 . 24 . 26 . 28 .		
trying to find it. Lost time can lower your speed		35
30 . 32 . 34 . 36 . 38 .		
quickly and in a major way, so do not look away.		39

New Key Learning   Lesson 21: apostrophe (') and hyphen (-)

545

Figure-Key Mastery

Key each line twice.

Straight Copy

1 She moved from 819 Briar Lane to 4057 Park Avenue on May 15.

2 The 50-point quiz on May 17 covers pages 88-94, 97, and 100.

3 The meeting will be held in Room 87 on March 19 at 5:40 p.m.

Script

4 The 495 representatives met from 7:00 to 8:40 p.m. on May 1.

5 Social Security Nos. 519-88-7504 and 798-05-4199 were found.

6 My office is at 157 Main, and my home is at 4081 9th Avenue.

Rough draft

7 Numbers *Runners* 180, # 190, *495,* and 5077 were schedule*d* for August 15.

8 her telephone number was change*d* to ~~807~~ *708*-194-5009 on July 1 *0*.

9 Review Rules 1-*9* on pages 89-90 and rules 15-19 *no* page 174.

14F

Speed Building

1. Key a 1' timing on ¶ 1; key three more 1' timings on ¶ 1, trying to go faster each time.
2. Repeat the procedure for ¶ 2.
3. Key a 2' timing on ¶s 1 and 2 combined.

For additional practice:

MicroType 5
New Key Review,
Number & Symbol
Lesson 2

LA all letters used **MicroPace** | gwam 2'

							gwam 2'
As you work for higher skill, remember that how well you | 6

key fast is just as important as how fast you key. How well | 12

you key at any speed depends in major ways upon the technique | 18

or form you use. Bouncing hands and flying fingers lower the | 24

speed, while quiet hands and low finger reaches increase speed. | 31

Few of us ever reach what the experts believe is perfect | 36

technique, but all of us should try to approach it. We must | 42

realize that good form is the secret to higher speed with | 48

fewer errors. We can then focus our practice on the improve- | 54

ment of the features of good form that will bring success. | 60

gwam 2' | 1 | 2 | 3 | 4 | 5 | 6 |

Lesson 21   NEW KEYS: APOSTROPHE (') AND HYPHEN (-)

OBJECTIVES

- To learn reach technique for ' (apostrophe) and - (hyphen).
- To improve and check keying speed.

21A

Conditioning Practice

Key each line twice SS; then take a 1' timing on line 3; determine *gwam*.

alphabet	1	Glenn saw a quick red fox jump over the lazy cubs.
CAPS LOCK	2	STACY works for HPJ, Inc.; SAMANTHA, for JPH Corp.
easy	3	Kamela may work with the city auditor on the form.

gwam 1' | 1 | 2 | 3 | 4 | 5 | 6 | 7 | 8 | 9 | 10 |

21B

New Keys: ' (Apostrophe) and - (Hyphen)

Key each line twice SS; DS between 2-line groups.

Note: On your screen, apostrophes may look different from those shown in these lines.

Apostrophe *Right little* finger

Hyphen Reach *up* to hyphen with *right little* finger

Learn ' (apostrophe)

1 ;' ;' ;' '; '; I've told you it's hers, haven't I.
2 I'm sure it's Ray's. I'll return it if he's home.
3 I've been told it isn't up to us; it's up to them.

Learn - (hyphen)

4 ;- ;- ;- -; -; -;- -;- Did she say 2-ply or 3-ply?
5 We have 1-, 2-, and 3-bedroom condos for purchase.
6 He rated each as a 1-star, 2-star, or 3-star film.

Combine ' and -

7 ;' ;' ;- ;- ;-' ;-' -'; -'; up-to-date list; x-ray
8 Didn't he say it couldn't be done? I don't agree.
9 I told him the off-the-cuff comment wasn't needed.

10 That isn't a cause-and-effect relationship, is it?
11 The well-known guest is a hard-hitting outfielder.
12 Put an apostrophe in let's, it's, isn't, and don't.

UNIT 4
Lessons 15-16
Build Keyboarding Skill

Lesson 15   SKILL BUILDING

OBJECTIVES
- To improve technique on individual letters.
- To improve keying speed on 1' and 2' writings.

15A

Conditioning Practice

Key each line twice SS.

alphabet	1	The exquisite prize, a framed clock, was to be given to Jay.
spacing	2	it has | it will be | to your | by then | in our | it may be | to do the
easy	3	The maid was with the dog and six girls by the field of hay.

gwam 1' | 1 | 2 | 3 | 4 | 5 | 6 | 7 | 8 | 9 | 10 | 11 | 12 |

15B   Skill Building

Technique: Response Patterns

Key each line twice SS.

Technique Cue

Keep keystroking movement limited to the fingers.

Emphasize continuity and rhythm with curved, upright fingers.

A 1 Katrina Karrigan ate the meal of apples, bananas, and pears.
B 2 Bobby bought a beach ball and big balloons for the big bash.
C 3 Cody can serve cake and coffee to the cold campers at lunch.
D 4 David did all he could to dazzle the crowd with wild dances.
E 5 Elaine left her new sled in an old shed near the gray house.

F 6 Frank found a file folder his father had left in the office.
G 7 Gloria got the giggles when the juggler gave Glen his glove.
H 8 Hugh helped his big brother haul in the fishing net for her.
I 9 Inez sings in a trio that is part of a big choir at college.
J 10 Jason just joined the jury to judge the major jazz festival.

K 11 Nikki McKay kept the black kayaks at the dock for Kay Kintz.
L 12 Lola left her doll collection for a village gallery to sell.
M 13 Mona asked her mom to make more malted milk for the mission.

gwam 1' | 1 | 2 | 3 | 4 | 5 | 6 | 7 | 8 | 9 | 10 | 11 | 12 |

For additional practice:
MicroType 5
New Key Review,
Number & Symbol
Lesson 3

New Key: TAB Key

The TAB key is used to indent the first line of ¶s. Word processing software has preset tabs called *default* tabs. Usually, the first default tab is set 0.5" to the right of the left margin and is used to indent ¶s (see copy at right).

1. Locate the TAB key on your keyboard (usually to the left of the letter *q*).
2. Reach up to the TAB key with the left little finger; tap the key firmly and release it quickly. The insertion point will move 0.5" to the right.

3. Key each ¶ once SS. DS between ¶s. As you key, tap the TAB key to indent the first line of each ¶. Use the backspace key to correct errors as you key.
4. If time permits, key the ¶s again to master TAB key technique.

Tab key *Left little* finger

Tab ⟶ The tab key is used to indent blocks of copy such as these.

Tab ⟶ It should also be used for tables to arrange data quickly and neatly into columns.

Tab ⟶ Learn now to use the tab key by touch; doing so will add to your keying skill.

Tab ⟶ Tap the tab key firmly and release it very quickly. Begin the line without a pause.

Tab ⟶ If you hold the tab key down, the insertion point will move from tab to tab across the line.

Speed Check: Paragraphs

Key two 1' timings on each ¶; determine *gwam* on each timing.

 E all letters used   **MicroPace**

```
           •    2    •    4    •    6    •    8    •
     Keep in home position all of the fingers not
  10    •    12    •    14    •    16    •    18    •
being used to tap a key.  Do not let them move out
  20    •    22    •    24    •    26    •    28
of position for the next letters in your copy.
           •    2    •    4    •    6    •    8    •
     Prize the control you have over the fingers.
  10    •    12    •    14    •    16    •    18    •
See how quickly speed goes up when you learn that
  20    •    22    •    24    •    26    •    28    •
you can make them do just what you expect of them.
```

For additional practice:

MicroType 5
Alphabetic Keyboarding
Lesson 20

Technique: TAB Key

Key the title, the author, and the first line(s) of the stories shown at the right. DS after keying the first line of each entry.

Key the copy again at a faster pace.

Save as: 15C TITLES for use in Lesson 25.

"Farmer Boy" by Laura Ingalls Wilder

Tab ⟶ It was January in northern New York State, sixty-seven years ago. Snow lay deep everywhere.

"The Scotty Who Knew Too Much" by James Thurber

Tab ⟶ Several summers ago there was a Scotty who went to the country for a visit.

"Roughing It" by Mark Twain

Tab ⟶ After leaving the Sink, we traveled along the Humboldt River a little way.

"The Chrysanthemums" by John Steinbeck

Tab ⟶ The high grey-flannel fog of winter closed off the Salinas Valley from the sky and from all the rest of the world.

"The Story of My Life" by Helen Keller

Tab ⟶ The most important day I remember in all my life is the one on which my teacher, Anne Mansfield Sullivan, came to me.

Speed Building

1. Key one 1' unguided and two 1' guided timings on each ¶.
2. Key two 2' unguided timings on ¶s 1–2 combined; determine *gwam*.

A all letters used **MicroPace**

gwam 2'

Austria is a rather small country, about three times the size of Vermont, located between Germany and Italy. The best known of the cities in this country is Vienna. Over the years this city has been known for its contributions to the culture in the region, particularly in the area of performing arts. Another place that has played an important part in the exquisite culture of the area is the city of Salzburg.

Salzburg is recognized as a great city for the performing arts, particularly music. Just as important, however, is that the city is the birthplace of Wolfgang Amadeus Mozart, one of the greatest composers of all time. Perhaps no other composer had an earlier start at his professional endeavors than did Mozart. It is thought that he began playing at the age of four and began composing at the age of five.

| gwam | 2' | 1 | 2 | 3 | 4 | 5 | 6 |

Quarter-Minute Checkpoints

gwam	1/4'	1/2'	3/4'	1'
20	5	10	15	20
24	6	12	18	24
28	7	14	21	28
32	8	16	24	32
36	9	18	27	36
40	10	20	30	40
44	11	22	33	44
48	12	24	36	48
52	13	26	39	52
56	14	28	42	56

20C

New Key: Quotation Marks

Key each line twice SS; DS between 2-line groups.

Note: On your screen, quotation marks may look different from those shown in these lines.

Quotation Mark: Press left shift and tap " (shift of ') with the *right little* finger.

1 ;; "; "; ";" ";" "I believe," she said, "you won."

2 "John Adams," he said, "was the second President."

3 "James Monroe," I said, "was the fifth President,"

4 Alison said "attitude" determines your "altitude."

20D

Speed Check: Sentences

1. Key a 30" timing on each line.
2. Key another 30" timing on each line. Try to increase your keying speed.

1 Karl did not make the ski team.

2 Jay shared his poem with all of us.

3 Doris played several video games online.

4 Their next game will be played in four weeks.

5 She will register today for next semester classes.

6 She quit the team so she would have more time to study.

20E

Keyboard Reinforcement

1. Key each line twice SS; DS between 2-line groups.
2. Key a 1' timing on lines 4–6.

Technique cue

- fingers curved and upright
- forearms parallel to slant of keyboard
- body erect, sitting back in chair

SHIFT key emphasis (Reach *up* and reach *down* without moving the hands.)

1 Jan and I are to see Ms. Han. May Lana come, too?

2 Bob Epps lives in Rome; Vic Copa is in Rome, also.

3 Oates and Co. has a branch office in Boise, Idaho.

Easy sentences (*Think*, *say*, and *key* the words at a steady pace.)

4 Eight of the girls may go to the social with them.

5 Corla is to work with us to fix the big dock sign.

6 Keith is to pay the six men for the work they did.

gwam	1'	1	2	3	4	5	6	7	8	9	10

Lesson 16

SKILL BUILDING

- To improve technique on individual letters.
- To improve keying speed on 1' and 2' writings.

16A

Conditioning Practice

Key each line twice.

alphabet	1	Zelda might fix the job growth plans very quickly on Monday.
spacing	2	did go | to the | you can go | has been able | if you can | to see the
easy	3	The six men with the problems may wish to visit the tax man.

gwam 1' | 1 | 2 | 3 | 4 | 5 | 6 | 7 | 8 | 9 | 10 | 11 | 12 |

16B

Technique: Response Patterns

Key each line twice.

Technique Cue

Keep keystroking movement limited to the fingers.

Emphasize continuity and rhythm with curved, upright fingers.

N	1	Nadine knew her aunt made lemonade and sun tea this morning.
O	2	Owen took the book from the shelf to copy his favorite poem.
P	3	Pamela added a pinch of pepper and paprika to a pot of soup.
Q	4	Quent posed quick quiz questions to his quiet croquet squad.
R	5	Risa used a rubber raft to rescue four girls from the river.
S	6	Silas said his sister has won six medals in just four meets.
T	7	Trisha told a tall tale about three little kittens in a tub.
U	8	Ursula asked the usual questions about four issues you face.
V	9	Vinny voted for five very vital issues of value to everyone.
W	10	Wilt wants to walk in the walkathon next week and show well.
X	11	Xania next expects them to fix the extra fax machine by six.
Y	12	Yuri said your yellow yacht was the envy of every yachtsman.
Z	13	Zoella and a zany friend ate a sizzling pizza in the piazza.

gwam 1' | 1 | 2 | 3 | 4 | 5 | 6 | 7 | 8 | 9 | 10 | 11 | 12 |

16C

Skill Building

Key each line twice.

Space Bar

1 and the see was you she can run ask took turn they were next

2 I will be able to fix the desk and chair for you next month.

Word response

3 the pay and pen make city rush lake both did dock half field

4 I may make a big sign to hang by the door of the civic hall.

For additional practice:

MicroType 5
New Key Review,
Number & Symbol
Lesson 4

Double letters

5 book grass arrow jelly little dollar illness vaccine collect

6 Kelly Pizzaro was a little foolish at the football assembly.

gwam 1' | 1 | 2 | 3 | 4 | 5 | 6 | 7 | 8 | 9 | 10 | 11 | 12 |

NEW KEYS: BACKSPACE, QUOTATION MARK ("), AND TAB

OBJECTIVES
- To learn reach technique for the **BACKSPACE key** and **TAB key**.
- To improve and check keying speed.

20A

Conditioning Practice

Key each line twice SS; then key a 1' timing on line 3; determine *gwam*.

alphabet	1	Jacky can now give six big tips from the old quiz.
CAPS LOCK	2	Find the ZIP Codes for the cities in IOWA and OHIO.
easy	3	It may be a problem if both girls go to the docks.

gwam | 1' | 1 | 2 | 3 | 4 | 5 | 6 | 7 | 8 | 9 | 10 |

20B

New Key: BACKSPACE Key

The BACKSPACE key is used to delete text to the left of the insertion point.

1. Locate the BACKSPACE key on your keyboard.
2. Reach up to the BACK-SPACE key with the right little finger (keep the index finger anchored to the *j* finger); tap the BACKSPACE key once for each letter you want deleted; return the finger to the ; key.

Note: When you hold down the BACKSPACE key, letters to the left of the insertion point will be deleted continuously until the BACKSPACE key is released.

This symbol means to delete.

Learn Backspace

1. Key the following.

   The delete

2. Use the BACKSPACE key to make the changes shown below.

   The ~~delete~~ backspace

3. Continue keying the sentence as shown below.

   The backspace key can be

4. Use the BACKSPACE key to make the change shown below.

   The backspace key ~~can be~~ is

5. Continue keying the sentence as shown below.

   The backspace key is used to fix

6. Use the BACKSPACE key to make the change shown below.

   The backspace key is used to ~~fix~~ make

7. Continue keying the sentence shown below.

   The backspace key is used to make changes.

Backspace Key
Right little finger; keep right index finger anchored to *j* key.

16D

Skill Building

1. Key three 1' timings on the ¶; determine *gwam*.
2. Key two 2' timings on ¶; determine *gwam*.

D all letters used MicroPace gwam 2'

| •   2   •   4   •   6   •   8   •   10 | |
Thomas Jefferson was an excellent persuasive writer. — 6
•   12   •   14   •   16   •   18   •   20   •   22
Conceivably his most persuasive piece of writing was the — 12
•   24   •   26   •   28   •   30   •   32   •
Declaration of Independence, on which he was asked to col- — 18
34   •   36   •   38   •   40   •   42   •   44   •
laborate with John Adams and Benjamin Franklin to justify — 23
•   46   •   48   •   50   •   52   •   54   •   56
the necessity for independence.   We all should recognize — 29
•   58   •   60   •   62   •   64   •   66   •   68
elements of that document.   For example, "We hold these — 35
•   70   •   72   •   74   •   76   •   78   •
truths to be self-evident, that all men are created equal, — 41
80   •   82   •   84   •   86   •   88   •   90   •   92
that they are endowed by their Creator with certain unalienable — 47
•   94   •   96   •   98   •   100   •   102   •   104   •
Rights, that among these are Life, Liberty and the pursuit of — 53
106   •
Happiness." — 54

gwam 2' | 1 | 2 | 3 | 4 | 5 | 6 |

16E

Skill Building

1. Key one 1' unguided and two 1' guided timings on each ¶; determine *gwam*.
2. Key two 2' unguided timings on ¶s 1–2 combined; determine *gwam*.

Quarter-Minute Checkpoints				
gwam	1/4'	1/2'	3/4'	1'
20	5	10	15	20
24	6	12	18	24
28	7	14	21	28
32	8	16	24	32
36	9	18	27	36
40	10	20	30	40
44	11	22	33	44
48	12	24	36	48
52	13	26	39	52
56	14	28	42	56

A all letters used MicroPace gwam 2'

•   2   •   4   •   6   •   8   •   10   •
Who was Shakespeare?   Few would question that he was the — 6
12   •   14   •   16   •   18   •   20   •   22   •
greatest individual, or one of the greatest individuals, ever — 12
24   •   26   •   28   •   30   •   32   •   34   •
to write a play.   His works have endured the test of time. — 18
36   •   38   •   40   •   42   •   44   •   46   •   48
Productions of his plays continue to take place on the stages — 24
•   50   •   52   •   54   •   56   •   58   •
of theaters all over the world.   Shakespeare was an expert — 30
60   •   62   •   64   •   66   •   68   •   70   •   72
at creating comedies and tragedies, both of which often leave — 36
•   74   •   76
the audience in tears. — 38

•   2   •   4   •   6   •   8   •   10   •
Few of those who put pen to paper have been as successful — 44
12   •   14   •   16   •   18   •   20   •   22   •
at creating prized images for their readers as Shakespeare. — 50
24   •   26   •   28   •   30   •   32   •   34
Every character he created has a life of its own.   It is — 56
•   36   •   38   •   40   •   42   •   44   •   46
entirely possible that more middle school and high school — 62
•   48   •   50   •   52   •   54   •   56   •   58
students know about the tragedy that Romeo and Juliet experi- — 68
•   60   •   62   •   64   •   66   •   68   •   70
enced than know about the one that took place at Pearl Harbor. — 74

gwam 2' | 1 | 2 | 3 | 4 | 5 | 6 |

New-Key Mastery

1. Key each line twice SS; DS between 2-line groups.
2. Key a 1' writing on line 11 and then on line 12.

> **To find 1' gwam:**
> Add 10 for each line you completed to the scale figure beneath the point at which you stopped in a partial line.

Goal: finger-action keystrokes; quiet hands and arms

CAPS LOCK/?
1 UTAH is the BEEHIVE state.   What is HAWAII called?
2 Who did Mark select to play CASSIE in CHORUS LINE?

z/v
3 Vince Perez and Zarko Vujacic wore velvet jackets.
4 Zurich, Zeist, Venice, and Pskov were on the quiz.

q/p
5 Paula, Pepe, and Peja took the quiz quite quickly.
6 Quincy Pappas and Enrique Quin were both preppies.

key words
7 very exam calf none disk quip wash give just zebra
8 lazy give busy stop fish down junk mark quit exact

key phrases
9 if you can|see the|when will you|it may be|when he
10 where will|and the|as a rule|who is the|to be able

alphabet
11 A complex theory was rejected by Frank G. Vizquel.

easy
12 Lock may join the squad if we have six big prizes.

gwam 1' | 1 | 2 | 3 | 4 | 5 | 6 | 7 | 8 | 9 | 10 |

Block Paragraphs

1. Key each ¶ once.
2. If time permits, key a 1' timing on each ¶.

Paragraph 1

gwam 1'

Dance can be a form of art or it can be thought of   10
as a form of recreation.   Dance can be utilized to   20
express ideas and emotions as well as moods.   29

Paragraph 2

One form of dance that is quite common is known as   10
ballet.   The earliest forms of ballet are believed   20
to have taken place in Western Europe.   30

Paragraph 3

To excel at ballet, you must take lessons when you   10
are very young.   It is not uncommon to see a three   20
year old in a dance studio taking ballet lessons.   30

Paragraph 4

In addition to starting at a very young age, hours   10
and hours of practice are also required to develop   20
into a skilled performer of ballet.   30

gwam 1' | 1 | 2 | 3 | 4 | 5 | 6 | 7 | 8 | 9 | 10 |

For additional practice:
MicroType 5
Alphabetic Keyboarding
Lesson 19

Office Features 1

For each activity, read and learn the feature described, then follow instructions at the left.

Activity 1

Insert, Typeover, Auto-Correct, Underline, Italic, and Bold

WP • Home/Font/Select Feature

1. Read the information at the right; learn to use the features described.
2. Key lines 1–10. Note how the errors in line 1 are corrected automatically.
3. After keying the lines, make the following changes:

line 2
Change *January* to *October.*

line 9
Insert *new* before *car.*
Insert *for college* after *left.*

line 10
Insert *not* before *know.*
Insert *the* after *know.*

Save as: OF1 ACTIVITY1

Note: In lines 8 and 10, the punctuation after a formatted word should NOT be formatted (underlined, bolded, or italicized).

Insert

The **Insert** feature is active when you open a software program. Move the insertion point to where you want to insert text; key the new text.

Typeover

Typeover allows you to replace current text with newly keyed text.

AutoCorrect

The **AutoCorrect** feature detects and corrects *some* typing, spelling, and capitalization errors for you automatically.

Underline

The **Underline** feature underlines text as it is keyed.

Italic

The **Italic** feature prints letters that slope up toward the right.

Bold

The **Bold** feature prints text darker than other copy as it is keyed.

> **Note:** When keying the numbers, key <number> <period> <space> <space> <text>.

1. would it help if rebecca johnson and i made the boxx for you?
2. His credit card bill for the month of January was $3,988.76.
3. Rebecca read *Little Women* by Louisa May Alcott for the test.
4. Yes, it is acceptable to *italicize* or <u>underline</u> book titles.
5. Patricia used the **bold** feature to **emphasize** her main points.
6. Their cell number was **698 388 0054**, not 698 388 9954.
7. I have read both *The Firm* and *The Rainmaker* by John Grisham.
8. She overemphasized by <u>*underlining*</u>, <u>*bolding*</u>, and <u>*italicizing.*</u>
9. I believe James bought a car before he left.
10. Sarah did know difference between <u>affect</u> and <u>effect</u>.

Activity 2

Select Text/ Select All

1. Read the copy at the right.
2. Learn how to select text.
3. Open *DF OF1 ACTIVITY2.*
4. Use the select text feature to select and change the copy as shown at the right.

Save as: OF1 ACTIVITY2

The **Select Text** feature allows you to select (highlight) text to apply formatting changes to after copy has been keyed. Text can be selected by using the mouse or by using the keyboard. As little as one letter of text or as much as the entire document (**Select All**) may be selected.

Once selected, the text can be bolded, italicized, underlined, deleted, copied, moved, printed, saved, etc.

John F. Kennedy: *"And so, my fellow Americans: ask not what your country can do for you—ask what you can do for your country."*

Dwight D. Eisenhower: *"Love of liberty means the guarding of every resource that makes freedom possible—from the sanctity of our families and the wealth of our soil to the genius of our scientists."*

Franklin D. Roosevelt: *"I see a great nation, upon a great continent, blessed with a great wealth of natural resources."*

Abraham Lincoln: *"Both parties deprecated war, but one of them would make war rather than let the nation survive, and the other would accept war rather than let it perish, and the war came."*

Lesson 19   NEW KEYS: CAPS LOCK AND QUESTION MARK (?)

• To learn reach technique for **caps lock** and **?** (question mark).

19A

Conditioning Practice

Key each line twice SS; then key a 1' timing on line 3; determine *gwam*.

alphabet   1   Zosha was quick to dive into my big pool for Jinx.

z/:   2   To: Ms. Lizza Guzzo From: Dr. Beatriz K. Vasquez

easy   3   The firms paid for both of the signs by city hall.

gwam 1' | 1 | 2 | 3 | 4 | 5 | 6 | 7 | 8 | 9 | 10 |

19B

New Keys: CAPS LOCK and ? (Question Mark)

Key each line twice SS; DS between 2-line groups.

Tap the CAPS LOCK to key a series of capital letters. To release the CAPS LOCK to key lowercase letters, tap it again.

Caps Lock
Left little finger

? (question mark)
Left Shift; then *right little* finger

Learn Caps Lock

1 The CARDINALS will play the PHILLIES on Wednesday.
2 Use SLC for SALT LAKE CITY and BTV for BURLINGTON.
3 THE GRAPES OF WRATH was written by JOHN STEINBECK.

Learn ? (question mark)

Space twice.

4 :? :? ;? ;? ?; ?; Who? What? When? Where? Why?
5 When will they arrive? Will you go? Where is he?
6 What time is it? Who called? Where is the dance?

Combine Caps Lock and ?

7 Is CSCO the ticker symbol for CISCO? What is MMM?
8 MEMORIAL DAY is in MAY; LABOR DAY is in SEPTEMBER.
9 When do the CUBS play the TWINS? Is it on SUNDAY?

10 Did Julie fly to Kansas City, MISSOURI, or KANSAS?
11 Did Dr. Rodriguez pay her DPE, PBL, and NBEA dues?
12 Did you say go TWO blocks EAST or TWO blocks WEST?

Activity 3

Cut, Copy, and Paste

| WP | • Home/Clipboard/Select Feature |

1. Read the copy at the right. Learn how to cut, copy, and paste text.
2. Open file *DF OF1 ACTVITY3*. Copy the text in this file and paste it a TS below the last line of text.
3. In the second set of steps, use Cut and Paste to arrange the steps in order.

Save as: OF1 ACTIVITY3

After you have selected text, you can use the Cut, Copy, and Paste features. The **Cut** feature removes selected text from the current location; the **Paste** feature places it at another location.

The **Copy** feature copies the selected text so it can be placed in another location (pasted), leaving the original text unchanged.

Step 1. Select text to be cut (moved).

Step 2. Click **Cut** to remove text from the current location.

Step 3. Move the insertion point to the desired location.

Step 4. Click **Paste** to place the cut text at the new location.

Activity 4

Undo and Redo

1. Read the copy at the right.
2. Learn how to use the Undo and Redo features.
3. Key the sentence at the right.
4. Delete *San Francisco* and *Tchaikovsky's*.
5. Use the Undo feature to reverse both changes.
6. Use the Redo feature to reverse the last Undo action.

Save as: OF1 ACTIVITY4

Use the **Undo** feature to reverse the last change you made in text. Undo restores text to its original location, even if you have moved the insertion point to another position. Use the **Redo** feature to reverse the last Undo action.

The **San Francisco** Symphony Orchestra performed **Tchaikovsky's** 1812 Overture Op. 49 Waltz for their final number.

Activity 5

Zoom and Print Preview

| WP | • View/Zoom/Select Feature |

| WP | • Office Buttom/Print/Print Preview |

1. Read the copy at the right.
2. Learn how to use the Zoom and Print Preview features of your software.
3. Open the *OF1 ACTIVITY1* file. Complete the steps at the right.
4. Close the file.

Use the **Zoom** feature to increase or decrease the amount of the page appearing on the screen. As you decrease the amount of the page appearing on the screen, the print will be larger. Larger print makes it easier to read and edit. As you increase the amount of the page appearing on the screen, the print becomes smaller. Other options of the Zoom feature include viewing one page, two pages, or multiple pages on the screen.

Quite often you will want to see the whole page on the screen to check the appearance (margins, spacing, graphics, tables, etc.) of the document prior to printing. You can display an entire page by using the Zoom feature or the **Print Preview** feature.

Step 1: View the document as a whole page using the Zoom feature.

Step 2: View the document at 75 percent.

Step 3: View the document at 200 percent.

Step 4: View the document as a whole page using Print Preview.

18C

New-Key Mastery

Key each line twice SS; DS between 2-line groups.

> ### Technique cue
> - Keep fingers curved and upright.
> - Key at a steady pace.

q/z
1 zoom hazy quit prize dozen freeze quizzed equalize
2 Zoe was quite amazed by the quaint city of La Paz.

p/x
3 pox expect example explore perplex explain complex
4 Tex picked six apples for a pie for Rex and Pedro.

v/m
5 move vase mean veal make vice mark very comb above
6 Mavis came to visit Mark, Vivian, Val, and Marvin.

easy
7 Their maid may pay for all the land by the chapel.
8 The auditor may do the work for the big city firm.

alphabet
9 Glenn saw a quick red fox jump over the lazy cubs.
10 Gavin quickly explained what Joby made for prizes.

18D

Block Paragraphs

1. Key each paragraph (¶) once SS; DS between ¶s; then key them again faster.
2. Key a 1' timing on each ¶; determine your *gwam*.

. . . .

For additional practice:
MicroType 5
Alphabetic Keyboarding
Lesson 18

. . . .

Paragraph 1   `gwam` 1'

A good team member is honest, does a fair share of   10
the work, and is eager to help another team member   20
if there is a need to do so. Quite often the best   30
team member must be a superb follower as well as a   40
good leader.   43

Paragraph 2

There are several other skills that a person ought   10
to acquire in order to become a good leader. Such   20
skills as the ability to think, listen, speak, and   30
write are essential for a good leader to possess.   40

`gwam` 1' | 1 | 2 | 3 | 4 | 5 | 6 | 7 | 8 | 9 | 10 |

18E

Enrichment

Key each line twice SS; DS between 2-line groups.

> ### Technique cue
> - Keep fingers upright.
> - Keep hands/arms steady.

x/:
1 To: Rex Cox, Tex Oxley|From: Max Saxe|A:B as C:D
2 Spelling words: extra, extract, exam, and explain

q/,
3 square square|quick quick|equip equip|squad squad;
4 Spelling words: quartz, quiet, quote, and quickly

p/z
5 Lopez Lopez|pizza pizza|zephyr zephyr|Perez Perez;
6 Spelling words: utilize, appeal, cozy, and pepper

m/v
7 velvet velvet|move move|remove remove|movie movie;
8 Spelling words: Vermont, Vermillion, and Vermeil.

Activity 6

Customize Status Bar

1. Read the copy at the right.
2. Learn how to customize the status bar.
3. Open the *OF1 ACTIVITY1* file. Complete the steps at the right.
4. Close the file.

There are many options (page number, vertical page position, line number, spelling and grammar check, etc.) that the software can perform. The **status bar** indicates whether the options are turned on or off. The status bar can be customized to meet the needs of the person using the software.

Step 1: Note the options that are available on the status bar.

Step 2: See what additional options are available on the status bar.

Step 3: Turn off one of the options that is currently available. Note the change on the status bar.

Step 4: Turn the option back on. Note the change on the status bar.

Step 5: Turn on the Line Number, Page Number, and Vertical Page Position if they are not already on.

Step 6: Move the insertion point and note how the status bar informs you of the location of the insertion point.

Activity 7

Apply What You Have Learned

1. Key lines 1–6, applying formatting as shown.
2. After keying the lines, make the following changes.

line 1
Change *Kennedy* to *Washington* and *Democrat* to *Federalist*.

line 4
Change *New York Times* to *Washington Post*.

line 6
Delete *frequently*. Insert or **bold** after *italic*.

Save as: OF1 ACTIVITY7

1. **Kennedy** was a *Democrat*; **Lincoln** was a *Republican*.

2. Is the correct choice <u>two</u>, <u>too</u>, or <u>to</u>?

3. Is *Harry Potter and the Deathly Hallows* still on the bestseller list?

4. There was an article on her in the *New York Times*.

5. Are the names to be **bolded** or <u>underlined</u> or **<u>bolded and underlined</u>**?

6. The <u>underscore</u> is being used less frequently than *italic*.

Activity 8

Apply What You Have Leaned

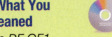

1. Open *DF OF1 ACTIVITY8*.
2. Use the select text feature to select and change the formatting of the copy as shown at the right.
3. Use the copy and paste feature to arrange the Presidents in the order they served: Roosevelt 1901–1909, Wilson 1913–1921, Truman 1945–1953, Reagan 1981–1989

Save as: OF1 ACTIVITY8

Harry S. Truman: *"The American people stand firm in the faith which has inspired this Nation from the beginning. We believe that all men have a right to equal justice under law and equal opportunity to share in the common good. We believe that all men have the right to freedom of thought and expression."*

Theodore Roosevelt: *"Much has been given us, and much will rightfully be expected from us. We have duties to others and duties to ourselves; and we can shirk neither."*

Ronald Reagan: *"We are a nation that has a government--not the other way around. And this makes us special among the nations of the Earth. Our government has no power except that granted it by the people. It is time to check and reverse the growth of government, which shows signs of having grown beyond the consent of the governed."*

Woodrow Wilson: *"We have built up, moreover, a great system of government, which has stood through a long age as in many respects a model for those who seek to set liberty upon foundations that will endure against fortuitous change, against storm and accident."*

OBJECTIVE

• To learn reach technique for **z** and : (colon).

18A

Conditioning Practice

Key each line twice SS; then key a 1' timing on line 3; determine *gwam*.

all letters learned	1	Jack quickly helped Mary Newton fix the big stove.
spacing	2	it is│if you can│by the end│when will he│to be the
easy	3	Helen may go to the city to buy the girls a shake.

| gwam | 1' | │ | 1 | │ | 2 | │ | 3 | │ | 4 | │ | 5 | │ | 6 | │ | 7 | │ | 8 | │ | 9 | │ | 10 | │ |

18B

New Keys: z and : (colon)

Key each line twice SS; DS between 2-line groups. If time permits, key lines 7–10 again.

z *Left little* finger

: *Left Shift* and tap : key

Spacing cue

Space twice after : used as punctuation.

Capitalization cue

Capitalize the first word of a complete sentence following a colon.

Learn z

1 a z a z │az az│zap zap│zip zip│raze raze│size size;
2 daze daze│maze maze│lazy lazy│hazy hazy│zest zest;
3 Utah Jazz; hazel eyes; loud buzz; zoology quizzes;

Learn : (colon)

4 ; : ; : │a:A b:B c:C d:D e:E f:F g:G h:H i:I j:J kK1L
5 M:m N:n O:o P;p Q:q R:r S:s T:t U:u V: w: X: y: Z:
6 Dear Mr. Baker: Dear Dr. Finn: Dear Mrs. Fedder:

Combine z and :

7 Liz invited the following: Hazel, Inez, and Zach.
8 Use these headings: Zip Code: Zone: Zoo: Jazz:
9 Buzz, spell these words: size, fizzle, and razor.
10 Dear Mr. Perez: Dear Ms. Ruiz: Dear Mrs. Mendez:

Lesson 17   HELP BASICS

- To gain an overview of software Help features.
- To learn to use software Help features.

17A

Overview

1. Study the information at the right.
2. Access your Help feature.

Note: The size of the Help box can be adjusted by clicking and dragging the edges of the dialog box. The Help box can also be moved to a different location on the screen (click the title bar at the top of the dialog box and drag to a new location) to allow you to see other parts of the screen.

Help Basics

Application software offers built-in Help features that you can access directly in the software as you work. Help is the equivalent of a user's manual on how to use your software. Listed below are some of the main functions that most software Help features allow you to do.

- Browse a table of contents of Help topics organized by categories.
- Search for topics in an alphabetic index.
- Point to screen items for a concise explanation of their use.
- Access technical resources, free downloads, and other options at the software manufacturer's website.

The Help features work the same way for each software application in the Office suite. For example, the Microsoft Help feature works the same in *Word* or *Excel* as it does in *PowerPoint* or *Access*.

The software's Help features can be accessed by tapping F1 or by clicking on the question mark located in the upper-right corner of the screen.

Access Help Feature

Help Menu

Use the scroll bar to see help features located at the bottom of the Help menu.

Bottom of Help Menu

Lesson 17   REVIEW

• To improve keying technique and speed.

17A

Improve Keyboarding Skill

Key each line twice SS; DS between 2-line groups.

1 Vivian may make their formal gowns for the social.
2 It may be a problem if both men work for the city.
3 The antique box is in the big field by the chapel.
4 The man paid a visit to the firm to sign the form.
5 He works with the men at the dock to fix problems.
6 The rich man may work with Jan to fix the bicycle.

17B

Speed Check

Key three 20" timings on each line. Try to go faster on each timing.

1 You will need to buy the book.
2 Jana will have to pay the late fee.
3 Scott and James left for Utah yesterday.
4 Reed has not set a date for the next meeting.
5 I will not be able to finish the book before then.
6 Enrique took the final exam before he left for Georgia.

gwam 20"	3	6	9	12	15	18	21	24	27	30	33

17C

Increase Keying Speed

Key each line twice SS; DS between 2-line groups. Key a 30" timing on each line.

1 It is a civic duty to handle the problem for them.
2 Six of the city firms may handle the fuel problem.
3 Jay may make an authentic map for the title firms.
4 Hal and Orlando work at the store by the big lake.
5 I may make a shelf for the neighbor on the island.
6 Rick and I may go to town to make the eight signs.
7 He may blame the boy for the problem with the bus.
8 Jan Burns is the chair of the big sorority social.
9 A box with the bugle is on the mantle by the bowl.

gwam 30"	2	4	6	8	10	12	14	16	18	20

For additional practice:
MicroType 5
Alphabetic Keyboarding
Lesson 17

Using Help

1. Access Microsoft Office Word Help.

2. Click *What's new;* then click *Introduction to Word 2007.* Scroll down to *What's new in Word 2007?* Change the font size to Largest.

3. Use the Back button to return to the Word Help and How-to screen.

4. Use the Forward button to return to *Introduction to Word 2007.* Scroll down to *What's where in Word?*

5. Use the Home button to return to the Home screen.

6. Click the Keep on Top button. Click outside of the Help dialog box. Click the Keep on Top button again. Click outside the Help dialog box. Notice what happens to the dialog box each time.

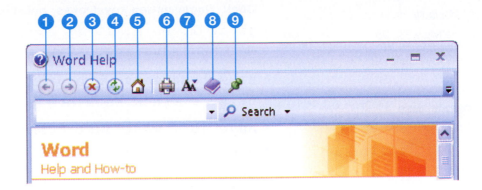

Help Buttons

1. Back
2. Forward
3. Stop
4. Refresh
5. Home

6. Print
7. Change Font Size
8. Show Table of Contents
9. Keep On Top (Not On Top)

Help Table of Contents

1. Read the information at the right.

2. Access the Table of Contents, and open a category that interests you. Open subcategories if necessary. Read the topic information. Go to related topics, if any.

3. Read two other categories that interest you. Print any information you think will be helpful in the future.

Like the table of contents in a book, the Table of Contents feature in Help lets you look for information that is organized by categories. In the Table of Contents shown below in the left-hand pane, a book icon indicates a category.

Click on the book to open it and reveal the topics available on the category.

Some categories have subcategories (see illustration below). The topics available for the subcategories can also be viewed by clicking on the book to open. Click on the desired topic, and information on the topic will be displayed in the right-hand pane.

Help Table of Contents

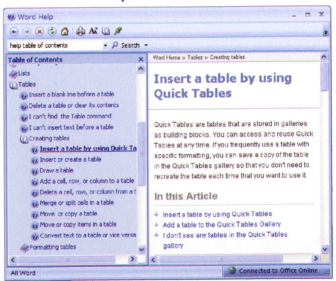

16C

New-Key Mastery

Key each line twice SS; DS between 2-line groups. If time permits, key lines 9–10 again.

Technique cues

- Reach up without moving hands away from your body.
- Use quick-snap keystrokes.

Goal: finger-action keystrokes; quiet hands and arms

reach review
1 jh fg l. o. k, I, ft sw aq de ;p fr jn jb fv jn jm
2 We can leave now. Take Nancy, Michael, and Jorge.

3rd/1st rows
3 nice bond many when oxen come vent quit very prom;
4 drive a truck|know how to|not now|when will you be

key words
5 have jail wept quit desk from goes cave yarn boxer
6 brand extra cycle event equip know fight made show

key phrases
7 when will you|may be able to|if you can|he will be
8 ask about the|need to be|where will|as you can see

all letters learned
9 The quaint old maypole was fixed by Jackie Groves.
10 Very fixed the job growth plans quickly on Monday.

16D

Technique: Spacing with Punctuation

Key each twice; DS between 2-line groups.

Spacing cue

Space once after , (comma) or ; (semicolon) used as punctuation.

1 Jay asked the question; Tim answered the question.
2 Ann, Joe, and I saw the bus; Mark and Ted did not.
3 I had ibid., op. cit., and loc. cit. in the paper.
4 The Mets, Dodgers, Cardinals, and Padres competed.

16E

Enrichment

Key each line twice SS; DS between 2-line groups.

Adjacent keys

1 ew mn vb tr op iu ty bv xc fg jh df ;l as kj qw er
2 week oily free join dash very true wash tree rash;
3 union point extra river tracks water cover weapon;

Long direct reaches

4 ny many ce rice my myself mu mute gr grand hy hype
5 lunch hatch vouch newsy bossy yearn beyond crabby;
6 gabby bridge muggy venture machine beauty luncheon

Double letters

7 book feet eggs seek cell jeer keep mall adds occur
8 class little sheep effort needle assist happy seem
9 Tennessee Minnesota Illinois Mississippi Missouri;

For additional practice:
MicroType 5
Alphabetic Keyboarding
Lesson 16

Lesson 18   SPECIAL FEATURES

OBJECTIVES

- To learn to use the pop-up description feature.
- To access additional software support on the Internet.

18A

Screen Tips

1. Read the information at the right.
2. Learn how to use the pop-up description feature of your software.
3. Take a pop-up description tour of your screen. Use the feature to learn what unfamiliar screen items do.

A valuable Help feature for new users is the pop-up description box. This feature may be called ScreenTips, Quick Tips, or something similar. It allows you to use the mouse to point to commands or other objects on the screen. After a brief period of time, a pop-up box appears, giving a concise description of the feature.

The illustration below shows what happens when you point at the Format Painter command found in the Clipboard group of the Home tab. For this particular command, the pop-up box tells you:

- The name of the command
- What it is used for
- How to use it

Sometimes the box will offer more information about the command by telling you to *Press F1 for more help.*

When you are finished reading the information, move the pointer away from the command to close the description box.

Screen Tips

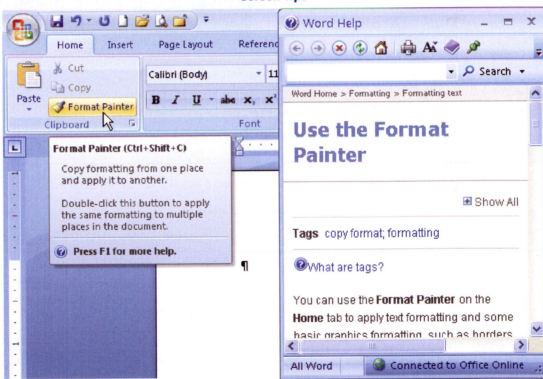

18B

Use Screen Tips

1. Use the pop-up description to learn about each of the features at the right.
2. Key a sentence or two explaining the purpose of each feature.

Thesaurus - Review Tab

Orientation – Page Layout Tab

Line Spacing – Home Tab

Lesson 16   NEW KEYS: q AND COMMA (,)

OBJECTIVE

• To learn reach technique for **q** and , (comma).

16A

Conditioning Practice

Key each line twice SS; DS between 2-line groups. If time permits, key the lines again.

all letters learned	1	dash give wind true flop comb yolk joke hunt gain;
p/v	2	prove vapor above apple voted super cover preview;
all letters learned	3	Mary forced Jack to help move six big water units.

16B

New Keys: q and , (comma)

Key each line twice SS; DS between 2-line groups.

q *Left little* finger

, (comma) *Right middle* finger

Spacing cue

Space once after , (comma) used as punctuation.

Learn q

1 a q aq | quit quit | aqua aqua | quick quick | quote quote
2 quest quest | quart quart | quite quite | liquid liquid;
3 quite quiet; quick squirrel; chi square; a quarter

Learn , (comma)

4 , k ,k ,k one, two, three, four, five, six, seven,
5 Akio, Baiko, Niou, and Joji are exchange students.
6 Juan, Rico, and Mike voted; however, Jane did not.

Combine q and , (comma)

7 Quota, square, quiche, and quite were on the exam.
8 Quin can spell Quebec, Nicaragua, Iraq, and Qatar.
9 Joaquin, Jacque, and Javier sailed for Martinique.

10 Quin, Jacqueline, and Paque quickly took the exam.
11 Rob quickly won my squad over quip by brainy quip.
12 Quit, quiet, and quaint were on the spelling exam.

Office Online

1. Read the information at the right.
2. Learn how to access the software manufacturer's website.
3. Go to the software manufacturer's website. Spend some time browsing the different options. Take advantage of two or three options. For example, print a helpful article or download clip art or a template (with your instructor's permission).

An abundance of additional help and resources is available from most software manufacturers' websites. These resources include:

- articles on software features
- downloads for templates, clip art, and "patch" files to fix problems
- online training courses

These resources can be accessed (provided you have Internet access) directly from the bottom of the Help menu by clicking on the desired link.

Microsoft Downloads Home Page

Training Home Page

Templates Home Page

Online Training

1. Access Microsoft Online Training from the Help menu.
2. Select the 2007 Office System training course.
3. Complete *Up to Speed with Word 2007*.
4. Complete the online tests.
5. Answer the questions at the right.

Training course evaluation.

1. Was the training course easy to understand?
2. What did you like best about the training course?
3. What suggestions would you give for improving the course?
4. Which of the Help options that were presented in Lessons 17–18 do you think you will use most often? Explain your answer.

15c

New-Key Mastery

Key each line twice SS; DS between 2-line groups.

Technique cues
- Reach up without moving hands away from your body.
- Reach down without moving hands toward your body.

Goal: finger-action keystrokes; quiet hands and arms

reach review
1 fv fr ft fg fb jn jm jh jy ju l. lo sx sw dc de ;p
2 free kind junk swim loan link half golf very plain

3rd/1st rows
3 oven cove oxen went been nice more home rice phone
4 not item river their newer price voice point crime

key words
5 pair pays pens vigor vivid vogue panel proxy opens
6 jam kept right shake shelf shape soap visit visual

key phrases
7 pay them|their signs|vote for|when will|if they go
8 you will be|much of the|when did they|to see their

all letters learned
9 Crew had seven of the votes; Brooks had only five.
10 They just left the park and went to see Dr. Nixon.

15d

Technique: SHIFT and ENTER Keys

1. Key each line once SS; at the end of each line, quickly tap the **ENTER** key, and immediately start the next line.
2. On lines 7 and 8, see how many words you can key in 30".

Eyes on copy as you shift and as you tap ENTER key

1 Mary was told to buy the coat.
2 Vern is to choose a high goal.

3 Jay and Livan did not like to golf.
4 Ramon Mota took the test on Monday.

5 Lexi told Scott to set his goals higher.
6 Eric and I keyed each line of the drill.

7 Roberto excels in most of the things he does.
8 Vivian can key much faster than Jack or Kate.

gwam 1' | 1 | 2 | 3 | 4 | 5 | 6 | 7 | 8 | 9 |

15e

Enrichment

Key each line twice SS; DS between 2-line groups.

Technique cues
- keep fingers upright
- keep hands/arms steady

m/p
1 plum bump push mark jump limp camp same post maple
2 Pete sampled the plums; Mark sampled the apricots.

b/x
3 box exact able except abide job expand debt extend
4 Dr. Nixon placed the six textbooks in the taxicab.

y/v
5 very verb eyes vent layer even days save yard vast
6 Darby Vance may take the gray van to Vivian today.

For additional practice:
MicroType 5
Alphabetic Keyboarding
Lesson 15

CAPITALIZATION

ACTIVITY 1

Capitalization

1. Study each of the eight rules.
   a. Key Learn line(s) beneath each rule, noting how the rule is applied.
   b. Key Apply line(s), using correct capitalization.

Capitalization

Rule 1: Capitalize the first word of a sentence, personal titles, and names of people.

Learn 1 Ask Ms. King if she and Mr. Valdez will sponsor our book club.

Apply 2 did you see mrs. watts and gloria at the school play?

Rule 2: Capitalize days of the week and months of the year.

Learn 3 He said that school starts on the first Monday in September.

Apply 4 my birthday is on the third thursday of march this year.

Rule 3: Capitalize cities, states, countries, and specific geographic features.

Learn 5 When you were recently in Nevada, did you visit Lake Tahoe?

Apply 6 when in france, we saw paris from atop the eiffel tower.

Rule 4: Capitalize names of clubs, schools, companies, and other organizations.

Learn 7 The Voices of Harmony will perform at Music Hall next week.

Apply 8 lennox corp. operates the hyde park drama club in boston.

Rule 5: Capitalize historic periods, holidays, and events.

Learn 9 The Fourth of July celebrates the signing of the Declaration of Independence.

Apply 10 henri asked if memorial day is an american holiday.

Rule 6: Capitalize streets, buildings, and other specific structures.

Learn 11 Jemel lives at Bay Shores near Golden Gate Bridge.

Apply 12 dubois tower is on fountain square at fifth and walnut.

Rule 7: Capitalize an official title when it precedes a name and elsewhere if it is a title of high distinction.

Learn 13 In what year did Juan Carlos become King of Spain?

Learn 14 Masami Chou, our class president, made the scholastic awards.

Apply 15 did the president speak to the nation from the rose garden?

Apply 16 mr. chavez, our company president, wrote two novels.

Rule 8: Capitalize initials; also, letters in abbreviations if the letters would be capitalized when the words are spelled out.

Learn 17 Does Dr. R. J. Anderson have an Ed.D. or a Ph.D.?

Learn 18 She said that UPS stands for United Parcel Service.

Apply 19 we have a letter from ms. anna m. bucks of washington, d.c.

Apply 20 m.d. means Doctor of Medicine, not medical doctor.

(continued on next page)

Lesson 15   NEW KEYS: p AND v

- To learn reach technique for **p** and **v**.

Fingers curved

Fingers upright

Hard return

15A

Conditioning Practice
Key each line twice SS; DS between 2-line groups.

one-hand words
balanced-hand words
all letters learned

1 rare gear seed hill milk lion bare moon base onion
2 town wish corn fork dish held coal owns rich their
3 Gabe Waxon may ask us to join him for lunch today.

15B

New Keys: p and v
Key each line twice SS; DS between 2-line groups. If time permits, key lines 7–9 again.

p *Right little* finger

v *Left index* finger

Learn p

1 ; p ;p ;p|put put|pin pin|pay pay|pop pop|sap sap;
2 pull pull park park open open soap soap hoop hoops
3 a purple puppet; pay plan; plain paper; poor poet;

Learn v

4 f v fv fv|van van|vain vain|very very|value value;
5 over over|vote vote|save save|move move|dove dove;
6 drive over; seven verbs; value driven; viable vote

Combine p and v

7 cave push gave pain oven pick jive keep very river
8 have revised; river view; five to seven; even vote
9 Eva and Paul have to pick papa up to vote at five.

2. Key Proofread &
Correct, using correct
capitalization.
a. Check answers.
b. Using the rule
number(s) at the left
of each line, study the
rule relating to each
error.
c. Rekey each incorrect
line, using correct
capitalization.

Save as: **CS2 ACTIVITY1**

Proofread & Correct

Rules

1,6	1	has dr. holt visited his studio at the hopewell arts center?
1,3,5	2	pam has made plans to spend thanksgiving day in fort wayne.
1,2,8	3	j. c. hauck will receive a b.a. degree from usc in june.
1,4,6	4	is tech services, inc. located at fifth street and elm?
1,2,7	5	i heard senator dole make his acceptance speech on thursday.
1,3,6	6	did mrs. alma s. banks apply for a job with butler county?
1,3	7	she knew that albany, not new york city, is the capital.
1,3	8	eldon and cindy marks now live in santa fe, new mexico.
1,6	9	are you going to the marx theater in mount adams tonight?
1,2,6	10	on friday, the first of july, we will move to Keystone Plaza.

ACTIVITY 2

Listening

Complete as directed.

Save as: **CS2 ACTIVITY2**

1. Listen carefully to the sounds around you for 3'.
2. As you listen, key a numbered list of every different sound you hear.
3. Identify with asterisks the three loudest sounds you heard.

ACTIVITY 3

Composing

1. Read the quotations.
2. Choose one and make notes of what the quotation means to you.
3. Key a ¶ or two indicating what the quotation means to you.
4. Proofread, revise, and correct.

Save as: **CS2 ACTIVITY3**

1. "A teacher affects eternity; he can never tell, where his influence stops." (Henry B. Adams)

2. "Every man I meet is in some way my superior." (Ralph Waldo Emerson)

3. "I'm a great believer in luck, and I find the harder I work the more I have of it." (Thomas Jefferson)

ACTIVITY 4

Math: Multiplying and Dividing Numbers

1. Open *DF CS2 ACTIVITY4* and print the file.
2. Solve the problems as directed in the file.
3. Submit your answers.

CAREER **Clusters**

ACTIVITY 2

You must complete Activity 1 on page 28 before completing this activity.

1. Retrieve your completed Career Clusters Interest Survey from your folder.

2. Determine your top three career clusters by adding the number of circled items in each box. Write the total number of items circled in the small box at the right of each section; then determine the boxes with the highest numbers. The box numbers correspond to the career cluster numbers on the pages you printed earlier. For example, let's say you had 15 circles in Box 6, 11 circles in Box 7, and 12 circles in Box 11. You have shown an interest in Finance (Box 6), Government & Public Administration (Box 7), and Information Technology (Box 11).

3. Return your Career folder to the storage area.

14C

New-Key Mastery

Key each line twice SS; DS between 2-line groups.

Technique Cue

- Reach up without moving hands away from your body.
- Reach down without moving hands toward your body.

Goal: finger-action keystrokes; quiet hands and arms

3rd/1st rows
1 no cut not toy but cow box men met bit cot net boy
2 torn core much oxen only time next yarn into north

space bar
3 as ox do if go oh no we of is he an to by in it at
4 jar ask you off got hit old box ice ink man was in

key words
5 mend game team card exam back hold join form enjoy
6 were time yarn oxen four dent mask when dark usual

key phrases
7 she can│go to the│if they will│make the│at the end
8 when will│we will be able│need a│take a look│I can

all keys learned
9 Fabio and Jacki said you would need the right mix.
10 Glen said that he would fix my bike for Jacob Cox.

14D

Technique: Spacing with Punctuation

Key each line twice SS; DS between 2-line groups.

Spacing Cue

Do not space after an internal period in an abbreviation, such as Ed.D.

1 Dr. Smythe and Dr. Ramos left for St. Louis today.
2 Dr. Chen taught us the meaning of f.o.b. and LIFO.
3 Keith got his Ed.D. at NYU; I got my Ed.D. at USU.
4 Sgt. J. Roarke met with Lt. Col. Christina Castro.

14E

Enrichment

Key each line twice SS; DS between 2-line groups.

Practice Cue

Keep the insertion point moving steadily across each line (no pauses).

m/x 1 Mary Fox and Maxine Cox took all six of the exams.
b/y 2 Burly Bryon Beyer barely beat Barb Byrnes in golf.
w/right shift 3 Carlos DeRosa defeated Wade Cey in the last match.
u/c 4 The clumsy ducks caused Lucy Lund to hit the curb.
./left shift 5 Keith and Mike went to St. Louis to see Mr. Owens.
n/g 6 Glen began crying as Ginny began singing the song.
o/t 7 Tom bought a total of two tons of tools yesterday.
i/r 8 Rick and Maria tried to fix the tire for the girl.
h/e 9 Helen Hale heard her tell them to see the hostess.

For additional practice:

MicroType 5
Alphabetic Keyboarding
Lesson 14

UNIT 6
Lessons 19-21
Learn/Review Symbol-Key Techniques

Lesson 19   LEARN/REVIEW /, $, %, #, &, (, AND)

OBJECTIVE

• To review control of **/**, **$**, **%**, **#**, **&**, **(**, and **)**.

19A

Conditioning Practice

Key each line twice.

alphabet	1	Quincy just put back five azure gems next to the gold watch.
fig/sym	2	Tim moved from 5142 Troy Lane to 936-123rd Street on 8/7/03.
speed	3	He lent the field auditor a hand with the work for the firm.

| gwam | 1' | 1 | 2 | 3 | 4 | 5 | 6 | 7 | 8 | 9 | 10 | 11 | 12 |

19B

Learn/Review /, $, and %

Key each line twice.

> The / is the same key as the ?.
> Key the shift of 4 for $.
> Key the shift of 5 for %.

Spacing Cue

Do not space between a figure and the / or the $ sign. Do not space between a figure and the % sign.

Learn/Review / (diagonal or slash) Reach down with the right little finger.

1 ; /|; /|;/ ;/ |;/; ;/; |2/3 4/5|and/or|We keyed 1/2 and 3/4.

2 Space between a whole number and a fraction: 5 2/3, 14 6/9.

3 Do not space before or after the / in a fraction: 2/3, 7/8.

Learn/Review $ (dollar sign) Reach up with the left index finger.

4 f R $|f R $|F$ F$|F r $ F r $|4$ 4$|f r 4 $|f r 4 $|$f$ f;

5 A period separates dollars and cents: $4.50, $6.25, $19.50.

6 I earned $33.50 on Mon., $23.80 on Tues., and $44.90 on Wed.

Learn/Review % (percent sign) Reach up with the left index finger.

7 fF 5% fF 5%|f 5 % f 5 %|f%f f%f|5f% 5f%|rF5% rF5%|T5f% T5f%.

8 Do not space between a number and %: 5%, 75%, 85%, and 95%.

9 Prices fell 10% on May 1, 15% on June 1, and 20% on July 15.

Lesson 14   NEW KEYS: m AND x

• To learn reach technique for **m** and **x**.

14A

Conditioning Practice

Key each line twice SS; DS between 2-line groups.

reach review   1   car hit bus get ice not win boy try wait knit yarn

b/y   2   body obey baby busy bury bully byway beauty subway

all letters learned   3   Jerry will take the four cans of beans to Douglas.

14B

New Keys: m and x

Key each line twice SS; DS between 2-line groups

m *Right index* finger

x *Left ring* finger

Learn m

1 j m | jm jm | jam jam | arm arm | aim aim | man man | ham hams

2 lamb some game firm come dome make warm mark must;

3 more magic; many firms; make money; many mean men;

Learn x

4 s x | sx sx | six six | axe axe | fix fix | box box | tax tax;

5 Lexi Lexi | oxen oxen | exit exit | taxi taxi | axle axle;

6 fix the axle; extra exit; exact tax; excited oxen;

Combine m and x

7 Max Max | mix mix | exam exam | axiom axiom | maxim maxim;

8 tax exams; exact amount; maximum axles; six exams;

9 Max Xiong took the extra exam on the sixth of May.

10 Mary will bike the next day on the mountain roads.

11 Martin and Max took the six boys to the next game.

12 Marty will go with me on the next six rides today.

19c

Speed Building

1. Key three 1' timings; determine *gwam*.
2. Key one 2' timing; determine *gwam*.

Respect your newspaper deliveryperson. He or she may   6

become one of the next great statesmen. One of the first jobs   12

Benjamin Franklin had was that of delivering newspapers. Later   19

in life he was recognized for his work in many diverse areas.   25

It was natural for him to become a printer and an author.   31

Benjamin Franklin is also known for his accomplishments as a   37

scientist and a philosopher. Additionally, he is quite well   43

known for his work as a diplomat and for his efforts during and   50

after the American Revolution. You combine all this and you   56

have one of the greatest statesmen of our country.   61

19d

Learn/Review #, &, (, and)

Key each line twice.

> Key the shift of the 3 for #.
> Key the shift of the 7 for &.
> Key the shift of 9 for (.
> Key the shift of 0 for).

Spacing Cue

Do not space between # and a figure; space once before and after & used to join names.

Do not space after a left parenthesis or before a right parenthesis and the copy enclosed.

For additional practice:

MicroType 5
New Key Review,
Number & Symbol
Lesson 5

Learn/Review # (number/pounds) Reach up with the left middle finger.

1 d E # d E # | D e # D e # | 3 d # 3 d # | dd #3 dd #3 | #d E3 #d E3;

2 Do not space between a number and #: 3# of #633 at $9.35/#.

3 Jerry recorded Check #38 as #39, #39 as #40, and #40 as #41.

Learn/Review & (ampersand) Reach up with the right index finger.

4 j U & j U & | J u & J u & | 7 j & 7 j & | jj &7 jj &7 | &j U7 &j U7;

5 Do not space before or after & in initials, e.g., CG&E, B&O.

6 She will interview with Johnson & Smith and Jones & Beckett.

Learn/Review ((left parenthesis) Reach up with the right ring finger.

7 l O (l O (| L o (L o (| 9 l (9 l (| ll (9 ll (9 | (l o9 (l o9.

8 As (is the shift of 9, use the l finger to key 9, (, or (9.

Learn/Review) (right parenthesis) Reach up with the right little finger.

9 ; P) ; P) | : p) : p) | 0 ;) 0 ;) | ;;)0 ;;)0 |); p0); p0.

10 As) is the shift of 0, use the ; finger to key 0,), or 0).

Combine (and)

11 Hints: (1) depress shift key; (2) tap key; (3) release both.

12 Tab steps: (1) clear tabs, (2) set stops, and (3) tabulate.

OBJECTIVES
- To improve spacing and shifting.
- To increase keying control and speed.

13A

Keyboard Mastery

Key each line twice SS; DS between 2-line groups.

Space bar (Space immediately after each word.)

1 She will be able to see the show in a week or two.
2 Jack lost the ball; Gary found it behind the door.
3 Kay and Jo went to the beach to look for starfish.

Shift keys (Shift; tap key; release both quickly.)

4 Dick and Allene went with Elaine to New York City.
5 The New York Yankees host the New York Mets today.
6 Don and Jack used the new bats that Jason brought.

13B

Speed Check

Key three 20" timings on each line. Try to go faster on each timing.

1 He can go to town for a shelf.
2 Gary can fish off the dock with us.
3 Jo thanked the girls for doing the work.
4 Becky took the girls to the show on Thursday.
5 Lance and Jared will be there until noon or later.
6 Jose and I should be able to stay for one or two hours.

| gwam 20" | 3 | 6 | 9 | 12 | 15 | 18 | 21 | 24 | 27 | 30 | 33 |

13C

Increase Keying Speed

Key each line twice SS; DS between 2-line groups. Key the word the first time at an easy speed; repeat it at a faster speed.

For additional practice:
MicroType 5
Alphabetic Keyboarding
Lesson 13

1 Juan hikes each day on the side roads near school.
2 Taki and I will take the algebra test on Thursday.
3 Fran told the four boys to take the bus to school.
4 Jordan took the dogs for a walk when he got there.
5 Sandra and I went to the store to buy new outfits.
6 Jennifer will buy the food for the January social.

Lesson 20   LEARN/REVIEW _, *, @, +, !, AND \

• To review control of _, *, @, +, !, and \.

20A

Conditioning Practice

Key each line twice.

alphabet   1   Joyce Savin fixed the big clock that may win a unique prize.

fig/sym   2   Items marked * are out of stock: #785*, #461A*, and #2093*.

speed   3   The firm paid for the rigid sign by the downtown civic hall.

gwam   1' | 1 | 2 | 3 | 4 | 5 | 6 | 7 | 8 | 9 | 10 | 11 | 12 |

20B

Learn/Review _, *, @, and +

Key each line twice.

> Key the shift of - for _.
> Key the shift of 8 for *.
> Key the shift of 2 for @.
> Key the shift of the key to the right of the hyphen for +.

Learn/Review _ (underline) Reach up with the right little finger.

1   ; _ ; _|_:_ _:_|:_:- :_;-|I shifted for the _ as I keyed _-.

2   The _ is used in some Internet locations, i.e., http2_data_2.

Learn/Review * (asterisk) Reach up with the right middle finger.

3   k I * k I *|K i * K i *|8 k * 8 k *|kk 8* ii *8|*k I8 *k I*;

4   Put an * after Gary*, Jane*, and Joyce* to show high scores.

Learn/Review @ ("at" sign) Reach up with the left ring finger.

5   s W @ s W @|S w @ S w @|2 s @ 2 s @|ss @2 dd @2|@s W2 @s W2;

6   Change my e-mail address from myers@cs.com to myers@aol.com.

Learn/Review + ("plus" sign) Reach up with the right little finger.

7   ; + ; +|;+; ;+;|+;+ +;+|7 + 7,|a + b + c < a + b + d,|12 + 3

8   If you add 3 + 4 + 5 + 6 + 7, you will get 25 for an answer.

20C   Skill Building

Guided Timings

1. Review the procedure for setting speed goals (Guided Timing Procedure, p. 22).

2. Use the procedure to key unguided and guided timings on the ¶s of 15D, p. 35.

3. Compare your gwam for the best 2' timing with your previous rate on these ¶s.

12D

New Keys: b and y

Key each line twice SS; DS between 2-line groups.

b *Left index* finger

y *Right index* finger

Learn b

1 f b | fb fb | fob fob | tub tub | bug bug | bat bat | bus bus;
2 bfb bfb | boat boat | boot boot | jobs jobs | habit habit;
3 blue bus; bit bat; brown table; a bug; big hubbub;

Learn y

4 j y | jy jy | yet yet | eye eye | dye dye | say say | day day;
5 yjy yjy | yell yell | stay stay | easy easy | style style;
6 Sunday or Friday; buy or bye; fly away; any jockey

Combine b and y

7 by by | baby baby | bury bury | lobby lobby | gabby gabby;
8 bay bridge | blue eyes | busy body | noisy boys | baby toy
9 Tabby and Barry had a baby boy with big blue eyes.

12E

New-Key Mastery

Key each line twice SS; DS between 2-line groups.

Practice Cue

- Reach up without moving hands away from your body.
- Reach down without moving hands toward your body.

reach review
1 jnj ftf ded kik hjh dcd fgf juj jyj sws lol 1.1 hg
2 how got eat was rat you ice not bat fun done only;

3rd/1st rows
3 nice hit | not now | only twice | were busy | they can be;
4 Cody told both boys before they left for the show.

key words
5 and are the can did was ask far you foil boat note
6 joke dine call ball gold feet hold wash yard flute

key phrases
7 to the | and then | if you want | when will you | you were
8 here is the | this is the | you will be able to | is the

all letters learned
9 Julio and Becky forgot to show Dick their new dog.
10 Barry found two locks by his jacket in the garage.

gwam 1' | 1 | 2 | 3 | 4 | 5 | 6 | 7 | 8 | 9 | 10 |

For additional practice:
MicroType 5
Alphabetic Keyboarding
Lesson 12

20D

Learn/Review ! and \

Key each line twice.

> Key the shift of 1 for !.
> Key the \ with the key above the ENTER key.

Spacing Cue

Space twice after an ! at the end of a sentence.

....

For additional practice:

MicroType 5
New Key Review,
Number & Symbol
Lesson 6
....

Learn/Review ! (exclamation point) Reach up with the left little finger.

1 a Q! a Q!|aq! aq!|a! a!|!a! !a!|Qa! Qa!|Felipe won the game!

2 On your mark! Get ready! Get set! Go! Go faster! I won!

3 Great! You made the team! Hurry up! I am late for school!

Learn/Review \ (backslash) Reach up with the right little finger.

4 ;\ ;\|;\; ;\; |\;\ \;\|Juan\Mary Juan\Mary|Chan\Kay Chan\Kay

5 Use the \ key to map the drive to access \\sps25\deptdir556.

6 Map the drive to \\global128\coxjg$, not \\global217\coxjg$.

Lesson 21   LEARN/REVIEW =, [ ], AND < >

OBJECTIVE

• To review control of =, [ ], and < >.

21A

Conditioning Practice

Key each line twice.

alphabet	1 Jacques paid a very sizeable sum for the meetings next week.
fig/sym	2 The desk (#539A28) and chair (#61B34) usually sell for $700.
speed	3 Pamela did the work for us, but the neighbor may pay for it.

gwam	1'	1	2	3	4	5	6	7	8	9	10	11	12

21B

Learn/Review =, [, and]

Key each line twice.

> Key the = using the same key as the +.
> Key the [with the key to the right of p.
> Key the] with the key to the right of [.

Learn/Review = ("equals" sign) Reach up with the right little finger.

1 ; = ; =|;=; ;=;|=;= =;=|a = 5, a = 5,|4 + 6 = 10|4 + 6 = 10;

2 Solve the following: 3a = 15, 5b = 30, 3c = 9, and 2d = 16.

Learn/Review [(left bracket) Reach up with the right little finger.

3 ; [; [|[;[[;[|;[; ;[;|[a [B [c [D [e [F [g [H [i [J [k [L.

4 [m [N [o [P [q [R [s [T [u [V [w [X [y [Z [1 [2 [3 [4 [5 [6.

Learn/Review] (right bracket) Reach up with the right little finger.

5 ;] ;]|];]];]|;]; ;];|A] b] C] d] E] f] G] h] I] j] K] l.

6 M] n] O] p] Q] r] S] t] U] v] W] x] Y] z] 7] 8] 9] 10] 11]].

NEW KEYS: b AND y

OBJECTIVE

• To learn reach technique for **b** and **y**.

Fingers curved

12A

Conditioning Practice

Key each line twice SS; DS between 2-line groups.

reach review 1 sw ju ft fr ki dc lo .l jh fg ce un jn o. de gu hw

c/n 2 cent neck dance count clean niece concert neglect;

all letters learned 3 Jack and Trish counted the students on the risers.

12B

Technique: Space Bar

Key each line twice.

> **Technique Cue**
>
> Space with a down-and-in motion immediately after each word.

1 Ann has an old car she wants to sell at this sale.

2 Len is to work for us for a week at the lake dock.

3 Gwen is to sign for the auto we set aside for her.

4 Jan is in town for just one week to look for work.

5 Juan said he was in the auto when it hit the tree.

12C

Technique: ENTER Key

1. Key each line twice SS; at the end of each line, quickly tap **ENTER** key, and immediately start new line.

2. On line 4, see how many words you can key in 30 seconds (30").

A **standard word** in keyboarding is five characters or any combination of five characters and spaces, as indicated by the number scale under line 4. The number of standard words keyed in 1' is called **gross words a minute** (gwam).

1 Dot is to go at two.

2 Justin said she will be there.

3 Sarah cooked lunch for all of the girls.

4 Glenda took the left turn at the fork in the road.

| gwam | 1' | 1 | 2 | 3 | 4 | 5 | 6 | 7 | 8 | 9 | 10 |

To find 1-minute (1') gwam:

1. Note on the scale the number beneath the last word you keyed. That is your 1' gwam if you key the line partially or only once.

2. If you completed the line once and started over, add 10 to the figure determined in step 1. The result is your 1' gwam.

To find 30-second (30") gwam:

1. Find 1' gwam (total words keyed).

2. Multiply 1' gwam by 2. The resulting number is your 30" gwam.

Speed Building

1. Key three 1' timings; determine *gwam*.
2. Key two 2' timings; determine *gwam*.

A   all letters used   (MicroPace)   gwam   2'

Who lived a more colorful and interesting   4
existence than this President? He was a rancher in   9
the west. He participated as a member of the Rough   14
Riders. He was a historian. He went on an African   20
safari. He was quite involved in the development of   25
the Panama Canal. He was the youngest person ever to   30
become President of the United States; however, he was   35
not the youngest person that was ever elected to the   41
office of President. And these are just a few of his   46
accomplishments.   48

Theodore Roosevelt was an active and involved   52
man. He lived life to the fullest and tried to make   57
the world a better place for others. Today, we still   63
benefit from some of his many deeds. Some of the   68
national forests in the West came about as a result of   73
legislation enacted during the time he was President.   78
He worked with college leaders to organize the   83
National Collegiate Athletic Association.   87

gwam 2' | 1 | 2 | 3 | 4 | 5 | 6 |

Learn/Review < and >

Key each line twice.

> Key the shift of comma for <.
> Key the shift of period for >.

Learn/Review < ("less than" sign) Reach down with the right middle finger.

1 K< K<|k< k<|,k< ,k<|,i< ,i<|a<b a<b|9<12 9<12|13c<4d 13c<4d;

2 If a < b, and c < d, and e < f, and a < c and e, then a < d.

Learn/Review > ("greater than" sign) Reach down with the right ring finger.

3 L> L>|l> l>|.l> .l>|.o> .o>|d>c d>c|10>8 10>8|5c>17d 5c>17d;

4 If b > a, and d > c, and f > e, and c and e > a, then f > a.

....

For additional practice:

MicroType 5
New Key Review,
Number & Symbol
Lesson 7

....

11C

New-Key Mastery

Key each line twice SS; DS between 2-line groups.

Practice Cue

Space quickly after keying each word.

Goal: finger action reaches; quiet hands and arms

w and right shift
1 Alaska; Wisconsin; Georgia; Florida; South Dakota.
2 Dr. Wick will work the two weekends for Dr. Woods.

n/g
3 eight or nine|sing the songs again|long length of;
4 Dr. Wong arranged the song for singers in Lansing.

key words
5 wet fun ask hot jar cot got use oil add run are of
6 card nice hold gnaw join knew face stew four feat;

key phrases
7 will see|it is the|as it is|did go|when will|if it
8 I will|where is the|when can|use it|and the|of the

all keys learned
9 Nikko Rodgers was the last one to see Jack Fuller.
10 Alfonso Garcia and I took Taisuke Johns to Newark.

11D

Technique: Spacing with Punctuation

Key each line twice SS; DS between 2-line groups.

Spacing Cue

Do not space after an internal period in an abbreviation; space once after each period following initials.

No space   Space once.

1 Use i.e. for that is; cs. for case; ck. for check.
2 Dr. West said to use wt. for weight; in. for inch.
3 Jason F. Russell used rd. for road in the address.
4 Dr. Tejada got her Ed.D. degree at Colorado State.

11E

Enrichment

Key each line twice SS; DS between 2-line groups.

Technique Cue

- unused fingers curved, upright over home keys
- eyes on copy as you key

u/c
1 cute luck duck dock cure junk clue just cuff ulcer
2 Luci could see the four cute ducks on the counter.

w and right shift
3 Wade and Will; Don W. Wilson and Frank W. Watkins.
4 Dr. Wise will set the wrist of Sgt. Walsh at noon.

left shift and .
5 Julio N. Ortega|Julia T. Santiago|Carlos L. Sillas
6 Lt. Lou Jordan and Lt. Jan Lee left for St. Louis.

n/g
7 gain gown ring long range green grind groan angle;
8 Last night Angie Nagai was walking along the road.

o/t
9 foot other tough total tooth outlet outfit notice;
10 Todd took the two toddlers towards the other road.

i/r
11 ik rf or ore fir fir sir sir ire ire ice ice irons
12 Risa fired the fir log to heat rice for the girls.

h/e
13 hj ed he the the hen hen when when then then their
14 He was with her when she chose her new snow shoes.

For additional practice:
MicroType 5
Alphabetic Keyboarding
Lesson 11

UNIT 7
Lessons 22-23

Build Keyboarding Skill

Lesson 22 — SKILL BUILDING

OBJECTIVES
- To improve technique on individual letters.
- To improve keying speed on 1' and 2' writings.

22A

Conditioning Practice

Key each line twice.

alphabet 1 Jack liked reviewing the problems on the tax quiz on Friday.
figures 2 Check #365 for $98.47, dated May 31, 2001, was not endorsed.
easy 3 The auditor may work with vigor to form the bus audit panel.

gwam 1' | 1 | 2 | 3 | 4 | 5 | 6 | 7 | 8 | 9 | 10 | 11 | 12 |

22B — Skill Building

Technique Mastery: Individual Letters

Key each line twice.

Technique Goals
- curved, upright fingers
- quick keystrokes

Emphasize continuity and rhythm with curved, upright fingers.

A 1 After Nariaki ate the pancake, he had an apple and a banana.
B 2 Ben Buhl became a better batter by batting big rubber balls.
C 3 Chi Chang from Creek Circle caught a raccoon for Cara Locke.
D 4 Did David and Dick Adams decide to delay the departure date?
E 5 Ed and Eileen were selected to chaperone the evening events.

F 6 Jeff Flores officially failed four of five finals on Friday.
G 7 Garth and Gregg glanced at the gaggle of geese on the grass.
H 8 His haphazard shots helped through half of the hockey match.
I 9 Ida insisted on living in Illinois, Indiana, or Mississippi.
J 10 Jackie objected to taking Jay's jeans and jersey on the jet.

K 11 Ken kept Kay's snack in a knapsack in the back of the kayak.
L 12 Lillian and Layne will fill the two small holes in the lane.
M 13 The minimum amount may make the mission impossible for many.

gwam 1' | 1 | 2 | 3 | 4 | 5 | 6 | 7 | 8 | 9 | 10 | 11 | 12 |

For additional practice:
MicroType 5
New Key Review,
Number & Symbol
Lesson 8

Lesson 11   NEW KEYS: w AND right shift

• To learn reach technique for **w** and **right shift**.

11A

Conditioning Practice

Key each line twice SS; DS between 2-line groups.

reach review   1 jn de ju fg ki ft lo dc fr l. jtn ft. cde hjg uet.

u/c   2 cut cue duck luck cute success accuse juice secure

all letters learned   3 Jake and Lincoln sold us eight large ears of corn.

11B

New Keys: w and Right Shift

Key each line twice SS ; DS between 2-line groups.

w *Left ring* finger

Right Shift *Right little* finger

Shifting cue

1. Hold down the right shift key with the little finger on the right hand.
2. Tap the letter with the finger on the left hand.
3. Return finger(s) to home key.

Learn w

1 s w sw sw|we we|saw saw|who who|wet wet|show show;

2 will will|wash wash|work work|down down|gown gown;

3 white gown; when will we; wash what; walk with us;

Learn right shift key

4 ;A ;A; |A1; A1; |Dan; Dan; |Gina; Gina; |Frank; Frank;

5 Don saw Seth Green and Alfonso Garcia last August.

6 Trish Fuentes and Carlos Delgado left for Atlanta.

Combine w and right shift

7 Will Wenner went to show the Wilsons the two cars.

8 Wes and Wade want to know who will work this week.

9 Willard West will take Akiko Tanaka to Washington.

10 Rafael and Donna asked to go to the store with us.

11 Walt left us at Winter Green Lake with Will Segui.

12 Ted or Walt will get us tickets for the two shows.

22C

Speed Check: Sentences

1. Key a 30" writing on each line. Your rate in *gwam* is shown word-for-word below the lines.
2. Key another 30" writing on each line. Try to increase your keying speed.

1 Dr. Cox is running late today.
2 Ichiro baked Sandy a birthday cake.
3 Kellee will meet us here after the game.
4 Gordon will be leaving for college on Friday.
5 Juan and Jay finished the project late last night.
6 This is the first time that I have been to Los Angeles.

gwam	30"	2	4	6	8	10	12	14	16	18	20	22

22D   Skill Building

Speed Building: Guided Writing

1. Key one 1' unguided and two 1' guided timings on each ¶; determine *gwam*.
2. Key two 2' unguided timings on ¶s 1–2 combined; determine *gwam*.
3. Key one 3' unguided timing on ¶s 1–2 combined; determine *gwam*.

Quarter-Minute Checkpoints				
gwam	1/4'	1/2'	3/4'	Time
16	4	8	12	16
20	5	10	15	20
24	6	12	18	24
28	7	14	21	28
32	8	16	24	32
36	9	18	27	36
40	10	20	30	40

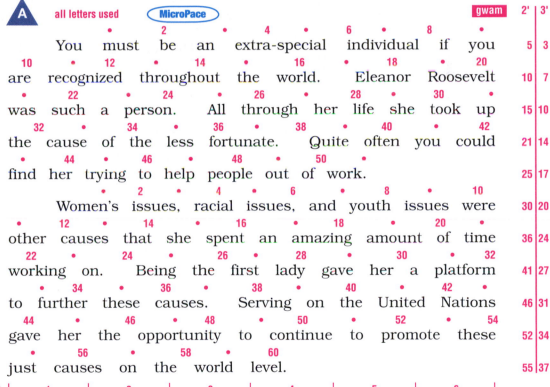

A   all letters used   MicroPace

	gwam	2'	3'

You must be an extra-special individual if you are recognized throughout the world. Eleanor Roosevelt was such a person. All through her life she took up the cause of the less fortunate. Quite often you could find her trying to help people out of work.

Women's issues, racial issues, and youth issues were other causes that she spent an amazing amount of time working on. Being the first lady gave her a platform to further these causes. Serving on the United Nations gave her the opportunity to continue to promote these just causes on the world level.

gwam	2'	1	2	3	4	5	6
	3'	1		2		3	4

10C

New-Key Mastery

Key each line twice SS; DS between 2-line groups.

Technique Cue

- Reach up without moving hands away from your body.
- Reach down without moving hands toward your body.

3rd/1st rows	1 run car nut nice cute noon touch other clean truck
	2 Lincoln coin; strike three; cut the cards; four or
left shift and .	3 Jack and Nicholas are going to Otter Lake in Ohio.
	4 Lucille took a truck to Ohio. Janet sold her car.
key words	5 call fund kind race neck golf half just toil lunch
	6 cause guide hotel feast alike joins; laugh; judge;
key phrases	7 if she can|he can do the|it is the|and then|all of
	8 till the end|tie the knot|faster than|a little red
all keys learned	9 Either Jack or Lance said the four girls are here.
	10 Hugh likes to run on the lakefront; Jack does not.

10D

Technique: Space Bar and Left Shift

Key the lines once SS; DS between 3-line groups.

For additional practice:
MicroType 5
Alphabetic Keyboarding
Lesson 10

space bar	1 Lucas asked the girls to get the dogs at the lake.
	2 Lance said he can go to Oregon to get the old car.
	3 Janice and her three dogs ran along the shoreline.
left shift	4 Jack and Joe Kern just left to go to Lake Ontario.
	5 Jo thinks it takes less than an hour to get there.
	6 Kanosh and Joliet are cities in Utah and Illinois.

10E

Enrichment

Key each line once SS; DS between 2-line groups.

Practice Cue

Try to reduce hand movement and the tendency of unused fingers to fly out or follow reaching finger.

u/c	1 cut luck such cuff lunch crush touch torch justice
	2 Okichi Kinura had juice. Lucius caught the judge.
n/g	3 gone ring fang long eggnog length; sing sang song;
	4 Glen thinks Glenda Leung can sing the eight songs.
all keys learned	5 Julian and Hector left a note for Leticia Herrera.
	6 Juan and Luisa took Jorge and Leonor to the dance.
all keys learned	7 Jack Lefstad said to take the road through Oregon.
	8 Janet and Linda caught eight fish in Lake Ontario.

Lesson 23   SKILL BUILDING

OBJECTIVES
- To improve technique on individual letters.
- To improve keying speed on 1' and 2' writings.

23A

Conditioning Practice

Key each line twice.

alphabet	1	Wayne gave Zelda exact requirements for taking the pulp job.
fig/sym	2	Add tax of 5.5% to Sales Slip #86-03 for a total of $142.79.
easy	3	Rick may bicycle to the ancient city chapel by the big lake.

gwam 1' | 1 | 2 | 3 | 4 | 5 | 6 | 7 | 8 | 9 | 10 | 11 | 12 |

23B

Technique Mastery: Individual Letters

Key each line twice.

> **Technique Cue**
> - Limit keystroking movement to fingers; keep hands and arms motionless.

Emphasize continuity and rhythm with curved, upright fingers.

N	1	A new nanny can tend Hanna's nephew on Monday and Wednesday.
O	2	Two of the seven women opposed showing more shows on Monday.
P	3	Phil's playful puppy pulled the paper wrapping off the pear.
Q	4	Quincy quickly questioned the adequacy of the quirky quotes.
R	5	Our receiver tried to recover after arm surgery on Thursday.
S	6	Russ said it seems senseless to suggest this to his sisters.
T	7	Ty took title to two cottages the last time he went to town.
U	8	Uko usually rushes uptown to see us unload the sugar trucks.
V	9	Vivian voted to review the vivid videos when she visits Val.
W	10	Will waved wildly when a swimmer went wading into the water.
X	11	Six tax experts explained that Mary was exempt from the tax.
Y	12	Your younger boy yearns to see the Yankees play in New York.
Z	13	Zelda quizzed Zack on the zoology quiz in the sizzling heat.

gwam 1' | 1 | 2 | 3 | 4 | 5 | 6 | 7 | 8 | 9 | 10 | 11 | 12 |

23C

Skill Building

Key each line twice.

Space Bar

1 day son new map cop let kite just the quit year bay vote not
2 She may see me next week to talk about a party for the team.

Word response

3 me dye may bit pen pan cow sir doe form lamb lake busy their
4 The doorman kept the big bushel of corn for the eight girls.

Double letters

5 Neillsville berry dollar trees wheels sheep tomorrow village
6 All three of the village cottonwood trees had green ribbons.

gwam 1' | 1 | 2 | 3 | 4 | 5 | 6 | 7 | 8 | 9 | 10 | 11 | 12 |

For additional practice:

MicroType 5
New Key Review,
Number & Symbol
Lesson 9

Lesson 10　　NEW KEYS: u AND c

• To learn reach technique for **u** and **c**.

10A

Conditioning Practice

Key each line twice SS; DS between 2-line groups.

reach review　1　hjh tft njn gfg iki .l. ede olo rfr it go no or hi

space bar　2　so ask let jet his got ink are and the kid off did

left shift　3　Jason and I looked for Janet and Kate at the lake.

10B

New Keys: u and c

Key each line twice SS; DS between 2-line groups.

u *Right index* finger

c *Left middle* finger

Learn u

1　j u|juj juj|uju uju|us us|due due|jug jug|sun sun;

2　suit suit|dusk dusk|four four|fund fund|huge huge;

3　just for fun; under the rug; unusual urt; found us

Learn c

4　d c|dcd dcd|act act|cash cash|card card|ache ache;

5　Jack Jack|sack sack|lock lock|calf calf|rock rock;

6　acted sick; tic toc goes the clock; catch the cat;

Combine u and c

7　duck duck|accuse accuse|cruel cruel|actual actual;

8　crucial account; cute cousin; chunk of ice; juice;

9　such success; rustic church; no luck; count trucks

10　June and Chuck told us to take four cans of juice.

11　Jack asked us for a list of all the codes he used.

12　Louise has gone to cut the cake on the green cart.

23D

Speed Check: Sentences

1. Key a 30" writing on each line.
2. If time allows, key an additional 30" on selected lines.

1 Tomas left just before supper.
2 When will you be able to return it?
3 He has two more final exams to complete.
4 Their next concert will be held in September.
5 Jacob and Sarah left for San Francisco on Tuesday.
6 Orlando wanted to see the last home game of the season.

gwam 30" | 2 | 4 | 6 | 8 | 10 | 12 | 14 | 16 | 18 | 20 | 22 |

23E   Skill Building

Speed Building

1. Key one 1' unguided and two 1' guided timings on each ¶.
2. Key two 2' unguided timings on ¶s 1–2 combined; determine *gwam*.

Quarter-Minute Checkpoints			
gwam	1/4'	1/2'	3/4'	Time
16	4	8	12	16
20	5	10	15	20
24	6	12	18	24
28	7	14	21	28
32	8	16	24	32
36	9	18	27	36
40	10	20	30	40

 A   all letters used   MicroPace   gwam 2'

•   2   •   4   •   6   •   8   •   10
Whether you are an intense lover of music or simply   5
•   12   •   14   •   16   •   18   •   20   •   22
enjoy hearing good music, you are more than likely aware of   11
•   24   •   26   •   28   •   30   •   32   •   34
the work completed by Beethoven, the German composer. He is   17
•   36   •   38   •   40   •   42   •   44   •   46   •
generally recognized as one of the greatest composers to ever   24
48   •   50   •   52   •   54   •   56   •   58
live.   Much of his early work was influenced by those who   29
•   60   •   62   •   64   •   66
wrote music in Austria, Haydn and Mozart.   33

•   2   •   4   •   6   •   8   •   10
It can be argued whether Beethoven was a classical or   39
•   12   •   14   •   16   •   18   •   20   •   22   •
romantic composer. This depends upon which period of time in   45
24   •   26   •   28   •   30   •   32   •   34   •
his life the music was written. His exquisite music has ele-   51
36   •   38   •   40   •   42   •   44   •   46   •
ments of both. It has been said that his early works brought   57
48   •   50   •   52   •   54   •   56   •   58   •
to a conclusion the classical age. It has also been stated   63
60   •   62   •   64   •   66   •   68   •   70   •   72
that Beethoven's later work started the romantic age of music.   69

gwam 2' | 1 | 2 | 3 | 4 | 5 | 6 |

OBJECTIVES

- To increase keying speed.
- To improve **Space Bar**, **left shift**, and **ENTER** technique.

9A

Keyboard Mastery

Key each line twice SS; DS between 2-line groups.

Technique Cue

- curved, upright fingers
- eyes on copy
- wrists not touching keyboard

o/t

1 too took foot told hot toes lot dot toil toga torn
2 Otto has lost the list he took to that food store.

n/g

3 gin song sing sign long ring gone green gnat angle
4 Link N. Nagle is going to sing nine songs at noon.

Left shift/.

5 Lake Ontario; Hans N. Linder; Lake Larson; J. Hill
6 Jake left for Indiana; Kathleen left for Illinois.

9B

Improve ENTER Key Technique

Key each line twice SS; DS between 2-line groups. Keep up your pace at the end of the line, tap **ENTER** quickly, and begin the new line immediately.

1 I like the dog.
2 Jan has a red dress.
3 Hal said he left it here.
4 Kate has gone to the ski hill.
5 Lane said he left the dog in Idaho.
6 Kristi and Jennifer are hiking the hill.

9C

Increase Keying Speed

Key each line twice SS; DS between 2-line groups. Key the word the first time at an easy speed; repeat it at a faster speed.

For additional practice:
MicroType 5
Alphabetic Keyboarding
Lesson 9

1 add add|ask ask|hot hot|ring ring|eat eat|off off;
2 jar jar|ago ago|feet feet|hotel hotel|other other;
3 sand sand|join join|lake lake|half half|dear dear;
4 Janet said she left three letters on his old desk.
5 Hal and Jan added three things to her latest list.
6 Jen is to go to Illinois to get the old gold ring.

Office Features 2

For each activity, read and learn the feature described, then follow instructions at the left.

Activity 1

Margins

WP • Page Layout/Page Setup/Margins

1. Key the ¶s using the default margins.
2. Change the margins to the Wide margin option.
3. Change the left and right margins to 2.5" and the top margin to 2.0" using the Custom Margins option.

Save as: OF2 ACTIVITY1

Use the **Margins** feature to change the amount of blank space at the top, bottom, right, and left edges of the paper.

The default margin settings are not the same for all software.

Margins are the white space left between the edge of the paper and the print. When the right and left margins are increased, the length of the line of text will be decreased. When the top and bottom margins are increased, the number of lines of text that can be placed on a page will be decreased.

Of course, increasing or decreasing the size of the font also changes the amount of text that can appear on a page. Changing the font will also impact the amount of text that is placed on one page. You will understand this concept better when you complete the font activity below.

Activity 2

Line Spacing

WP • Home/Paragraph/Line Spacing

Change the line spacing to DS and key the four lines (include the numbers).

Save as: OF2 ACTIVITY2

Use the **Line Spacing** feature to change the amount of white space left between lines of text. Single spacing, one-and-a-half spacing, and double spacing are common to most software.

The default setting for *Word 2007* is 1.15. This allows a little more white space between lines of type than the previous version's default setting of 1.0. The new 1.15 default is treated as single spacing. Also note that there is a default of 10 points after each paragraph. This can be removed.

1. Click the I-beam where you want the line spacing changed.
2. Access the Line Spacing feature.
3. Specify the line spacing.
4. Begin or continue keying.

> When keying the numbers, key *<number> <period> <space> <space> <text>*.

Activity 3

Font

WP • Home/Font

Read each sentence then key it in the font, font size, and font color shown.

Save as: OF2 ACTIVITY3

The **Font** is the type, or letters, in which a document is printed. The size of the printed letters can be changed by changing the **Font Size** (measured in points). The font size can also be changed by using **Grow Font** to increase the font size or **Shrink Font** to decrease the font size. The default color of the font is black. Use the **Font Color** feature to change the color.

This is 11-point font size in Calibri font.

This is 11-point font size in Times New Roman font.

This is 14-point font in Lucida Handwriting.

This is 15-point font size in Comic Sans MS font.

This is 16-point font size in Calibri font.

New-Key Mastery

Key each line twice SS; DS between 2-line groups.

- eyes on copy except when you lose your place
- out-and-down shifting

abbrev./initials

1 J. Hart and K. Jakes hired Lila J. Norton to sing.
2 Lt. Karen J. Lane took Lt. Jon O. Hall to the jet.

3rd row emphasis

3 I told her to take a look at the three large jets.
4 Iris had three of her oldest friends on the train.

key words

5 if for the and old oak jet for oil has egg jar oar
6 told lake jade gold here noon tear soil goes fade;

key phrases

7 and the|ask for|go to the|not so fast|if he|to see
8 if there is|to go to the|for the last|none of the;

all letters learned

9 Jodi and Kendra Jaeger are in the National finals.
10 Jason Lake did not take Jon Hoag for a train ride.

8d

Technique: Space Bar and ENTER Key

Key each line twice SS; DS between 2-line groups.

Spacing Cue

Immediately tap Space Bar after the last letter in each word.

1 Linda had fish.
2 Jan is on the train.
3 Nat took her to the lake.
4 He is here to see his friends.
5 Kathleen sold the large egg to her.
6 Kate and Jason hired her to do the roof.
7 Lane took all eight of the girls to the lake.

> Tap ENTER quickly and start each new line immediately.

8e

Enrichment

Key each line twice SS; DS between 2-line groups.

Spacing/shifting

1 Kellee and I did see Jed and Jonathan at the lake.
2 Jane and Hal are going to London to see Joe Hanks.
3 Lee left for the lake at noon; Kenneth left later.
4 Jo and Kate Hanson are going to take the test soon.

Keying easy sentences

5 Jessie is going to talk to the girls for the kids.
6 Harold Lett took his friends to the train station.
7 Lon and Jen are going to see friends at the lodge.
8 Natasha and Hansel are taking the train to London.

For additional practice:

MicroType 5
Alphabetic Keyboarding
Lesson 8

Activity 4

Hyphenation

WP • Page Layout/Page Setup/Hyphenation

1. Key the ¶ in Courier New 12 pt. with hyphenation off.
2. Turn on the Automatic Hyphenation feature.
3. Change the margin setting to Wide.
4. Change the right and left margins to 2.5".

Save as: OF2 ACTIVITY4

The **Hyphenation** feature automatically divides (hyphenates) words that would normally wrap to the next line. This evens the right margin, making the text more attractive.

Use the **Hyphenation** feature to give text a professional appearance. When the **Hyphenation** feature is activated, the software divides long words between syllables at the end of lines. Using hyphenation makes the right margin less ragged. This feature is particularly helpful when keying in narrow columns.

Activity 5

Spelling and Grammar Check

WP • Review/Proofing/Spelling & Grammar

1. Key the ¶ *exactly* as shown. Some errors are automatically corrected.
2. Use the Spelling and Grammar check to identify errors. Correct all errors.
3. Proofread to find errors not caught.

Save as: OF2 ACTIVITY5

Use the **Spelling and Grammar Check** to check for misspellings and grammar errors. The Spelling Check feature compares each word in the document to words in its dictionary (or dictionaries). If a word in a document is not identical to one in its dictionary, the word is flagged by a wavy red underline. Usually the Spelling Check lists words it *thinks* are likely corrections (replacements).

The Grammar Check feature flags potential grammar errors with a wavy green underline. The Grammar Check also lists words it thinks will correct the grammar error.

Note: The Grammar Check may or may not catch incorrect word usage (*too* for *to* or *two*). Even when using these features, it is important to proofread your documents.

Dr. Smith met with the students on Friday to reviiw for for there test. He told the students that their would be three sections to the test. The first secction would be multiplee choice, the second sction would be true/fals, and the last section would be shoot answer. He also said, "If you have spelling errors on you paper, you will have pionts deducted.

Activity 6

Print

WP • Office Button/Print

1. Open *OF2 ACTIVITY4* and preview the document using Print Preview.
2. Close Print Preview and open the Print dialog box to see the options.
3. Cancel the Print dialog box and use Quick Print to print the document. Close the document.

The **Print** feature under the Microsoft Office Button offers three options:

• The **Print** option opens the Print dialog box, where you select the printer, indicate which page(s) and the number of copies to be printed, etc.

• The **Quick Print** option sends the document directly to the default printer.

• The **Print Preview** option allows you to preview the document and make changes before printing it.

Lesson 8 — NEW KEYS: left shift AND period (.)

OBJECTIVE

• To learn reach technique for **left shift** and . (period).

8A

Conditioning Practice

Key each line twice SS; DS between 2-line groups.

reach review 1 ft jn fr jh de ki gf lo tf nj rf hj ed ik fg ol ng

space bar 2 so it if at or on is go do ask the and jar art lid

all letters learned 3 join the; like those; ask her to sing; define the;

8B

New Keys: Left shift and . (period)

Key each line twice SS; DS between 2-line groups. If time permits, key lines 7–9.

Down-and-in spacing

Quick out-and-tap ENTER

Left Shift *Left little* finger

. (period) *Right ring* finger

Spacing cue

• Do not space after . within abbreviations.
• Space once after . following abbreviations and initials.
• Space twice after . at end of a sentence except at the end of a line. There, return without spacing.

Shifting Cue

(1) Hold down the left shift key with the little finger on the left hand, (2) tap the letter to be keyed with the finger on the right hand, and (3) return finger(s) to home keys in a quick 1-2-3 count.

Learn left shift key

1 a J|a J|Ja Ja|Jan Jan|a K a K|Kate Kate|Hank Hank;

2 Idaho; Kansas; Ohio: Oregon: Indiana; Illinois; IL

3 Lane and I; Ida and Jane; Hal and Kate; John and I

Learn . (period)

4 l . l .|l. l.|a.l. a.l.|d.l. d.l.|j.l j.l|k.l. k.l

5 hr. hr.|ft. ft.|in. in.|rd. rd.|ea. ea.|ltd. ltd.;

6 fl. fl.|fed. fed.|alt. alt.|ins. ins.|asst. asst.;

Combine left shift and . (period)

7 I took Linda to Lake Harriet. Lt. Kerns is there.

8 I did it. Lana took it. Jett Hill left for Ohio.

9 Karl and Jake got Ida and Janet to go to the fair.

Activities 7 & 8

Horizontal Alignment: Left, Center, Right, Justify

 WP
- Home/Paragraph/Select alignment type

1. Key the lines at the right. Right-align the page number, center-align the title, and left-align the last two lines.

Save as: OF2 ACTIVITY7

2. Open *OF2 ACTIVITY4* and justify the text.

Save as: OF2 ACTIVITY8

Horizontal alignment refers to the position of a line of text on the page. Use **left** alignment to start text at the left margin. Use **right** alignment to start text at the right margin.

Use **center** alignment to center lines of text between the left and right margins. Use **justify** alignment to align text to both the right and left margin.

Page 13

THE FINAL ACT

Just before dawn the policeman arrived at the home of Ms. Kennington.

All the lights were shining brightly . . .

Activity 9

Tabs

 WP
- View Ruler

1. Set a left tab at 1", a right tab at 3", and a decimal tab at 4.5".
2. Key the first four lines using these tab settings. TS after keying the fourth line.
3. Reset tabs: left tab at 1.5", right tab at 4.0", decimal tab at 5.5"; key the last four lines.

Save as: OF2 ACTIVITY9

 Left tab

 Right tab

 Decimal tab

Most software has left tabs already set at half-inch (0.5") intervals from the left margin. However, tabs can be set at intervals you determine.

When you set a tab, the preset tabs are automatically cleared up to the point where you set the tab. Most software lets you set **left tabs, right tabs,** and **decimal tabs**.

Left tabs
Left tabs align all text evenly at the left by placing the text you key to the right of the tab setting. Left tabs are commonly used to align words.

Right tabs
Right tabs align all text evenly at the right by placing the text you key to the left of the tab setting. Right tabs are commonly used to align whole numbers.

Decimal tabs
Decimal tabs align all text at the decimal point or other character that you specify. If you key numbers in a column at a decimal tab, the decimal points will line up, regardless of the number of places before or after the decimal point.

Left tab at 1" ↓	Right tab at 3" ↓	Decimal tab at 4.5" ↓
(TAB) James Hill (TAB)	6,750 (TAB)	88.395 (ENTER)
(TAB) Mark Johnson (TAB)	863 (TAB)	1.38 (ENTER)
Sue Chen	30	115.31
Seth Ramirez	1,397	24.6580

Left tab at 1.5" ↓	Right tab at 4.0" ↓	Decimal tab at 5.5" ↓
Juan Ortiz	142,250	0.25
Marsha Black	3,219	13.6
Kay Kent	56,873	297.312
Kay Ichiro	571,490	32.68

New-Key Mastery

Key each line twice SS; DS between 2-line groups.

Technique Cue

- curved, and upright fingers
- wrists low, but not resting
- down-and-in spacing
- eyes on copy as you key

reach review
1 rf ik hj tf ol ed nj gf; lo fr ft jn de ki jh fgf;
2 it it|oil oil|the the|ink ink|here here|song song;

n/g
3 sing gone night seeing doing going ringing longest
4 sing one song; going along; long night; good angle

space bar
5 if he no as to it is so do at in so of did elk jet
6 It ask and the are let oil oar ill son odd fan sat

all keys learned
7 desk soil lark joke that done find join gold lake;
8 tank logs hand jade free toil seek said like tear;

all keys learned
9 oil free; did join; has half; go get; near the end
10 tell jokes; right here; ask her; fine desk; is it;

Enrichment

Key each line twice; DS between 2-line groups.

Technique Cue

- space immediately after each word; down-and-in motion of thumb
- maintain pace to end of line; tap **ENTER** key quickly and start new line immediately

Reach review

1 jh jh|jn jn|fg fg|fr fr|ft ft|de de|ki ki|lo lo|jh
2 no no|hot hot|oil oil|the the|gold gold|rest rest;
3 hold nest gone that nails there going alert radio;

Space Bar

4 is at if so no do as he of go it to an or is on in
5 of hen got ink and the ask jar let hit jet den far
6 no ink|on the go|hit it|ask her to|did not see the
7 he is to join her at the lake; she is not the one;

ENTER key

8 he is there;
9 ask if it is far;
10 the sign for the lake;
11 she still has three of the;
12 did he join her at the lake the;

Short words and phrases

13 on on|do do|in in|it it|go go|or or|as as|are are;
14 see see|the the|and and|are are|for for|hire hire;
15 jet jet|kid kid|fit fit|ask ask|ton ton|risk risk;
16 he is go to the ski lodge; he lost the three jars;

For additional practice:
MicroType 5
Alphabetic Keyboarding
Lesson 7

Activity 10

Text Wrapping Break

1. Key the text in the first box, tapping ENTER at the end of each line.
2. QS and key the text in the second box, holding down the Shift key and tapping ENTER as instructed.
3. Compare the difference.

Save as: OF2 ACTIVITY10

The default settings leave space after a paragraph each time the ENTER key is tapped.

The space can be removed by using the Text Wrapping Break feature (hold down the Shift key and tap the ENTER key).

Mr. Ricardo Seanez (Tap ENTER)

1538 Village Square (Tap ENTER)

Altoona, WI 54720 (Tap ENTER)

Dear Ricardo (Tap ENTER)

I will be arriving in Altoona on July 15 for the next meeting.

Mr. Ricardo Seanez (Hold Shift; Tap ENTER)

1538 Village Square (Hold Shift; Tap ENTER)

Altoona, WI 54720 (Tap ENTER)

Dear Ricardo (Tap ENTER)

I will be arriving in Altoona on July 15 for the next meeting.

Activity 11

Envelope

WP • Mailings/Create/Envelopes

Use the Envelopes feature to format a small envelope (No. 6 3/4) for Envelope 1 and a large envelope (No. 10) for Envelope 2.

Save as: OF2 ACTIVITY11-1 and OF2 ACTIVITY11-2

Use the **Envelopes** feature to format envelopes for the documents you create. This feature allows you to select the size of the envelope, enter the **return address** and the **delivery address**, and print the envelope.

The delivery address can be keyed, inserted automatically from the letter file, or inserted from your Address Book.

Electronic postage software can be used with this feature.

Return address:

Envelope 1
Carson Sanchez
270 Rancho Bauer Drive
Houston, TX 77079-3703

Envelope 2
Victoria Westmont
499 Tulpehocken Avenue
Philadelphia, PA 19117-6741

Delivery address:

Ms. Susan Keane
872 Mayflower Drive
Terre Haute, IN 47803-1199

Mr. Jacob Saunders
396 Hickory Hill Lane
Kalamazoo, MI 49009-0012

Activity 12

Apply What You Have Learned

1. Set top margin at 2.5"; side margins at 2.7".
2. Change the ¶ font to 12 pt. Arial Narrow, black. Change the line spacing to 1.0; remove the space after paragraph.
3. Justify the paragraph alignment. Leave one blank line before and after the list of books.
4. Use Print Preview, then print the document.

Save as: OF2 ACTIVITY12

Center the heading; use Lucida Handwriting, 14 pt., blue, for the font.

Leave one blank line between the heading and the text.

Put the titles of the books in italic and bold, using the colors shown. Center-align each book entry. Use 1.5 line spacing for the book listings.

CHILDREN'S BOOKS

There are several older books that have been added to this year's children's book list. With all the new books being written, we often forget about these older books. The books added include:

Little Women by Louisa May Alcott

A Christmas Carol by Charles Dickens

The Jungle Book by Rudyard Kipling

The Adventures of Tom Sawyer by Mark Twain

The Last of the Mohicans by James F. Cooper

Please be sure to present these new additions to our book list at the in-service meeting scheduled for August 29.

Lesson 7   NEW KEYS: n AND g

• To learn reach technique for **n** and **g**.

7A

Conditioning Practice

Key each line twice SS; DS between 2-line groups.

e/r | 1 rare doer fear feet tire hire read ride rest after
o/t | 2 toad told took other hotel total tools tooth torte
i/h | 3 hits idle hail hiked their fifth faith heist hairs

7B

New Keys: n and g

Key each line twice SS; DS between 2-line groups. If time permits, key lines 7–9 again.

n *Right index* finger

g *Left index* finger

Follow the *Standard Plan for Learning New Keys* outlined on p. 511.

Learn n

1 j n jn jn|njn njn|an an|on on|no no|in in|and and;
2 kind kind|none none|loan loan|find find|land land;
3 not till noon; not a need; not in; a national need

Learn g

4 f g fg fg|gfg gfg|go go|dog dog|gas gas|goes goes;
5 age age|logs logs|glad glad|eggs eggs|legal legal;
6 great grin; large frog; gold dog; eight large eggs

Combine n and g

7 gone gone|sing sing|king king|gnat gnat|ring rings
8 sing along; a grand song; green signs; long grass;
9 eight rings; a grand king; long gone; sing a song;

7C

Technique: ENTER Key

Key each line twice SS; DS between 2-line groups.

Practice Cue

Keep up your pace to end of line, tap **ENTER** key quickly, and start new line without pausing.

1 large gold jar;
2 take the last train;
3 did he take the last egg;
4 she has to sing the last song;
5 join her for a hike at the lake at;

Reach out and tap ENTER

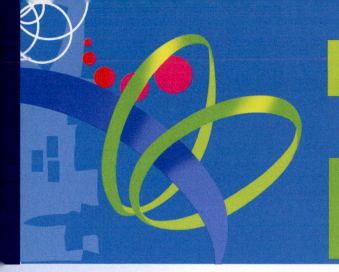

Format Guides: Interoffice Memo

Memos (interoffice memorandums) are written messages used by employees within an organization to communicate with one another. A standard format (arrangement) for memos is presented below and illustrated on p. 61.

Memo heading. The memo heading includes who the memo is being sent to (**TO**), who the memo is from (**FROM:**), the date the memo is being sent (**DATE**), and what the memo is about (**SUBJECT**). Use ALL CAPS for the headings beginning at the left margin, and space as shown below. Use initial caps for subject line.

Note: It is also acceptable to use ALL CAPS for the subject line.

TO: Tab twice to key name. SS
FROM: Tab twice to key name. SS
DATE: Tab twice to key date.   SS
SUBJECT: Tab once to key subject. SS

Memo body. The paragraphs of the memo all begin at the left margin and are SS with a SS between paragraphs.

Reference initials. If someone other than the originator of the memo keys it, his/her initials are keyed in lowercase letters at the left margin, a SS below the body.

Attachment/Enclosure notations. If another document is attached to a memo, the word *Attachment* is keyed at the left margin a SS below the reference initials (or below the last line of the body if reference initials are not used). If a document accompanies the memo but is not attached to it, key the word *Enclosure*.

Memo and Letter Margins	
Top margin (TM)	2"
Side margins (SM)	1" or default
Bottom Margin (BM)	At least 1"

Personal-Business Letter, Block Style

A letter written by an individual to deal with business of a personal nature is called a personal-business letter. Block format (see p. 66) is commonly used for formatting personal-business letters. All parts of a letter arranged in block format begin at the left margin. The paragraphs are not indented. The basic parts of the personal-business letter are described below in order of placement.

Return address. The return address (start at 2" from top edge) consists of a line for the street address and one for the city, state, and ZIP Code.

Date. Key the month, day, and year on the line below the city, state, and ZIP Code.

Letter mailing address. Key the first line of the letter mailing (delivery) address a DS below the date. A personal title (Miss, Mr., Mrs., Ms.) or a professional title (Dr., Lt., Senator) is keyed before the receiver's name.

Salutation. Key the salutation a SS below the mailing address.

Body. Begin the letter body (message) a SS below the salutation. SS and block the paragraphs with a SS between them.

Complimentary close. Key the complimentary close a SS below the last line of the body.

Name of the writer. Key the name of the writer a DS below the complimentary close. The name may be preceded by a personal title (Miss, Mrs., Ms.) to indicate how a female prefers to be addressed in a response. If a male has a name that does not clearly indicate his gender (Kim, Leslie, Pat), the title Mr. may precede his name.

Attachment/Enclosure notation. If another document is attached to a letter, the word *Attachment* is keyed at the left margin, a SS below the writer's name. If the additional document is not attached, the word *Enclosure* is used.

Note: The above instructions are based on *Word 2007* default settings. For instructions for the traditional style based on *Word 2003* default settings, see the model document on p. 67.

6C

New-Key Mastery
Key each line twice SS; DS between 2-line groups.

Technique Cue

- curved, upright fingers
- down-and-in spacing
- wrists low, but not resting
- eyes on copy as you key

Practice Cue

In lines of repeated words (lines 3, 5, and 7), speed up the second keying of each word.

reach review

1 ki lo de ft jh fr ei or th olo ere hjh iki edr iro
2 here is; the fort; their old trail; first look at;

h/e

3 the the|hear hear|here here|heat heat|sheet sheet;
4 the sheets; hear her heart; their health; heat the

i/t

5 sit sit|fit fit|silt silt|kites kites|tried tried;
6 a little tire; he tried to tilt it; he tied a tie;

o/r

7 tort tort|tore tore|fort fort|road road|roof roof;
8 a road|a door|a rose|or a rod|a roar|for her offer

space bar

9 to do it he as are hit dot eat air the ask jar let
10 if he|do it|to see|had it|is the|for her|all of it

all keys learned

11 ask jet art oil old fit hit the sad did soil risk;
12 oil the; the jail; oak door; he said; their forts;

6D

Enrichment
Key each line twice; DS between 2-line groups.

Keying Cue

Keep up your pace to the end of each line, tap the **ENTER** key quickly, and start the new line without a pause.

For additional practice:
MicroType 5
Alphabetic Keyboarding
Lesson 6

1 it is

2 the jet is

3 he had the rose

4 ask to hear the joke

5 she took the old shirt to

6 she told her to take the tests

7 at the fort; the lake road; did she

8 take the test; it is the last; he did it

9 the last jar; the old fort; he took the offer

10 take a jet; solid oak door; a red rose; ask her to

Lesson 24 FORMAT INTEROFFICE MEMOS

- To learn to format interoffice memos.
- To process memos from arranged and semi-arranged copy.

24A

Conditioning Practice

Key each line twice.

alphabet	1	Zack Gappow saved the job requirement list for the six boys.
figures	2	Jay Par's address is 3856 Ash Place, Houston, TX 77007-2491.
easy	3	I may visit the big chapel in the dismal town on the island.

gwam 1' | 1 | 2 | 3 | 4 | 5 | 6 | 7 | 8 | 9 | 10 | 11 | 12 |

At 2" (3 returns down)

TO: Maria Gutierrez, Secretary ↓1

FROM: Jackson Phipps, President ↓1

DATE: *Current Date* ↓1

SUBJECT: Next FBLA Meeting ↓1

Our next Future Business Leaders of America meeting is scheduled for this Friday at 6:30 p.m. in SSS 400F. Please put up the posters to remind members. ↓1

Default or 1" SM

Based on the attendance at the last meeting, you should have 45 copies of the attached agenda and the minutes to distribute. We will be going over five more competitive event descriptions at the meeting. You can make copies of the descriptions from the FBLA-PBL National Site (www.fbla.org). The events that we will be covering at this meeting are: ↓1

Future Business Leaders
Entrepreneurship
Electronic Career Portfolio
Word Processing 1
Business Communication ↓1

Hold down the Shift key when you return after the first four items in this list to avoid extra space between lines.

Thank you again for all the time and effort you devote to our organization. You set a great example for other FBLA members at Jefferson High School to follow. ↓1

xx ↓1

Attachment

Shown in 11-point Calibri with 2" top margin and 1" side margins, this memo appears smaller than actual size.

Interoffice Memo

Lesson 6   NEW KEYS: o AND t

OBJECTIVE

• To learn reach technique for **o** and **t**.

6A

Conditioning Practice

Key each line twice SS; DS between 2-line groups.

Fingers curved

Fingers upright

h/e 1 her head; has had a; see here; feed her; hire her;

i/r 2 hire a; fire her; his risk; fresh air; a red hair;

all keys learned 3 a lake; ask a lad; a risk; here she is; a red jar;

6B

New Keys: o and t

Key each line twice SS; DS between 2-line groups. If time permits, key lines 7–9 again.

> Follow the *Standard Plan for Learning New Keys* on p. 511.

o *Right ring* finger

t *Left index* finger

Learn o

1 l o lo lo|olo olo|fold fold|sold sold|holds holds;

2 of of|do do|oak oak|soil soil|does does|roof roof;

3 load of soil; order food; old oil; solid oak door;

Learn t

4 f t ft ft|tf tf|the the|tea tea|eat eat|talk talk;

5 at at|fit fit|set set|hit hit|talk talk|test tests

6 flat feet; the treats; the first test; take a hike

Combine o and t

7 total total|tooth tooth|toast toast|otters otters;

8 the total look; other tooth; took a toll; too old;

9 those hooks; the oath; old tree fort; took a tool;

Memos

Study the format guides on p. 60 and the memo format illustration on p. 61. Note the vertical and horizontal placement of memo parts and the spacing between them.

Memo 1

1. Key the model memo on p. 61.
2. Proofread your copy; correct all keying and formatting errors.

Save as: 24B MEM01

Memo 2

1. Format and key the information at the right as a memo.
2. The memo goes to the Foreign Language Department Students and is from Travel Abroad Coordinator Mary Seville. Date the memo November 2, 20--; supply an appropriate subject line.
3. Use the Speller; proofread and correct all errors.

Save as: 24B MEMO2

Note: Each time the year is indicated with *20--*, replace it with the current year.

Memo 3

1. Format and key the text at the right in memo format. Use your initials as the keyboard operator (reference initials).
2. Proofread your copy; correct all errors.

Save as: 24B MEMO3

Are you ready for a summer you will never forget? Then you will want to sign up for this year's Travel Abroad Program. You will travel to the country that famous writers like Virgil, Horace, and Dante called home. The music of Vivaldi, Verdi, and Puccini will come to life. You will visit art museums exhibiting the art of native sons such as Michelangelo Buonarotti and Giovanni Bellini.

*By now you have probably guessed that we will be taking a trip to Italy this summer. Touring **Rome, Florence, Venice,** and **Naples** gives you the opportunity to experience firsthand the people, the culture, the history, and the cuisine of Italy.*

If you are interested in learning more about traveling to Italy this summer, attend our open house on <u>November 15</u> at <u>3:30</u> in Room 314.

TO: Foreign Language Teachers

FROM: Mary Seville, Travel Abroad Coordinator

DATE: November 2, 20--

SUBJECT: OPEN HOUSE

I've enclosed copies of a memo announcing the open house for the Travel Abroad Program. Please distribute the copies to students in your classes.

Last year we had 25 students participate in the trip to England. If you have had the opportunity to talk with them about this experience, you know that the trip was very worthwhile and gave them memories that will last a lifetime. I am confident that the trip to Italy will be just as rewarding to those who participate. As you know, the experiences students gain from traveling abroad cannot be replicated in the classroom.

I appreciate your support of the program and your help in promoting it with your students.

xx

Enclosure

OBJECTIVES

- To increase keying speed.
- To improve **Space Bar** and **ENTER** technique.

5A

Improve Space-Bar Technique

Key each line twice SS; DS between 2-line groups. Space quickly after keying a letter or a word; begin keying the next letter or word immediately.

1 a s d f; a s d f; j k l; j k l; as; ask; he; held;
    DS
2 ask her; ask her; last sale; last sale; if he asks
    DS
3 a red jar; a red jar; she said half; she said half
    DS
4 hear a lark; hear a lark; a fire sale; a fire sale
    DS
5 he fired her; he fired her; a dark red; a dark red
    DS
6 ask her kids; ask her kids; he has had; he has had
    TS

5B

Improve ENTER Key Technique

Key each line twice SS; DS between 2-line groups. Keep up your pace at the end of the line, enter quickly, and begin the new line immediately.

1 she said;
2 a red jar is;
3 ask her if she is;
4 he said her ad is here;
5 he asked her if she had it;
6 here is; his last lead; she is;

5C

Increase Keying Speed

Key each line twice SS; DS between 2-line groups. Key the word the first time at an easy speed; repeat it at a faster speed.

1 had had|sad sad|her her|lake lake|dad dad|has has;
2 is is|lad lad|red red|jade jade|lake lake|far far;
3 sad; sad;|ask ask|desk desk|fall fall|hired hired;
4 sir sir|jar jar|like like|ash ash|far far|are are;
5 fair fair|fall fall|read read|risk risk|here here;

For additional practice:

MicroType 5
Alphabetic Keyboarding
Lesson 5

- To check knowledge of e-mail and memo formats.
- To check the level of memo processing skills.

25A

Conditioning Practice

Key each line twice.

alphabet	1	Bobby Klun awarded Jayme sixth place for her very high quiz.
figures	2	I had 50 percent of the responses (3,923 of 7,846) by May 1.
easy	3	The haughty man was kept busy with a problem with the docks.

| gwam | 1' | 1 | 2 | 3 | 4 | 5 | 6 | 7 | 8 | 9 | 10 | 11 | 12 |

25B   Formatting

Memo Processing

Memo 1

1. Format and key the memo at the right. Use your initials as the keyboard operator.
2. Use the Speller; proofread and correct all errors.

Save as: 25B MEMO1

Note: Use italic instead of underline for the play titles.

TO: Drama Students

FROM: Ms. Fairbanks

DATE: November 1, 20--

SUBJECT: Selection of Spring Play

There are three plays that I would like you to consider for next semester's performance. They include:

The Importance of Being Earnest, a comedy written by Oscar Wilde. In the play, Jack Worthing has a complicated courtship with Lady Bracknell's daughter, Gwendolen. His ward, Cecily, has fallen in love with his friend Algernon.

A Delicate Balance, a comedy written by Edward Albee. The play is a funny look at love, compassion, and the bonds of friendship and family.

A Comedy of Errors, a comedy written by William Shakespeare. The play is about mistaken identities of twins.

I have placed copies of the plays on reserve in the library. Please look them over by November 25 so that we can discuss them in class that day. We will need to make a decision before December 1 so that I can order the playbooks.

4D

New Keys: i and r

Key each line twice SS; DS between 2-line groups. If time permits, key lines 7–9 again.

Follow the *Standard Plan for Learning New Keys* on p. 511.

Follow the *Standard Plan for Learning New Keys* on p. 511.

Technique cue
- curved, upright fingers
- eyes on copy

i *Right middle* finger

r *Left index* finger

Learn i

1 k i|ki ki|ik; ik;|is; is;|lid lid|kid kid|aid aid;

2 ill; ill;|said said|like like|jail jail|file file;

3 he likes; file a lease; a slide; if he is; his kid

Learn r

4 f r|fr fr|far far|red red|are are|ark ark|jar jar;

5 dark dark|real real|rake rake|hear hear|rear rear;

6 a red jar; hear her; dark red; a real rake; read a

Combine i and r

7 ride ride|fire fire|hair hari|hire hire|liar liar;

8 air air|risk risk|fair fair|dire dire|rifle rifle;

9 fire risk; hire a; her side; like air; a fire; sir

4E

New-Key Mastery

Key each line twice SS; DS between 2-line groups.

Technique cue
- wrists low, but not resting on desk
- fingers curved
- eyes on copy

For additional practice:
MicroType 5
Alphabetic Keyboarding
Lesson 4

reach review

1 de ki jh fr ed ik rf ik ki rf jh ed ik fr jh de ki

2 are are|hair hair|hear hear|risk risk|shear shear;

h/e

3 she she|her her|seeks seeks|shed sheds|shelf shelf

4 her shelf; he had; he held a jar; he heard; he has

i/r

5 ir ir|air air|hair hair|hired hired|riddle riddle;

6 hire a kid; ride like; her hair; like her; a fire;

all keys learned

7 jar jar|half half|fire fire|liked liked|lake lake;

8 fire fire|jail jail|hire hire|sake sake|deal deal;

all keys learned

9 if she is; he did ask; he led her; he is her aide;

10 she has had a jak sale; she said he had a red fir;

Memo 2

1. Format and key the memo at the right.
2. Use the Speller; proofread and correct all errors.

Save as: 25B MEMO2

TO: Office Staff

FROM: Jennifer Green, General Manager

DATE: March 15, 20--

SUBJECT: New Box Office Coordinator

Rebecca Dunwoody has been hired to replace DeWayne Hughes as our box office coordinator. DeWayne has decided to return to school to start work on a Master of Business Administration degree. As you are aware, DeWayne has been a valuable asset to our organization for the past five years.

It was not easy finding a person with similar qualifications to replace DeWayne. His enthusiasm and love of music, combined with a degree in music as well as a minor in business administration, made filling the job particularly difficult. However, we believe we were successful when we were able to hire Ms. Dunwoody. She is a recent graduate of NYC's music program. While completing her degree, she worked as an assistant for the business manager of one of our competitors.

Please extend your appreciation and best wishes to DeWayne before he leaves on March 30 and welcome Rebecca when she arrives on March 25.

Memo 3

1. Format and key the text at the right in memo format. Use your initials as the keyboard operator.
2. Proofread your copy; correct all errors.

Save as: 25B MEMO3

TO: Foreign Language Faculty

FROM: Karla A. Washburn

DATE: December 1, 20--

SUBJECT: Travel Abroad Coordinator

As you may have heard by now, Mary Seville announced her plans to retire at the end of next summer. In addition to hiring a new French teacher, we will need to replace Mary as our Travel Abroad Coordinator. This will be a very difficult task; Mary has done an excellent job.

If you are interested in this position, please let me know before you leave for the winter break. I would like to fill the position early next semester. This will allow the new coordinator to work with Mary as she plans this year's trip. The new coordinator would be expected to travel with Mary and the students to Italy this summer.

We also need to start thinking about a retirement party for Mary. If you are interested in being on a retirement party committee, please let me know.

Lesson 4   NEW KEYS: i AND r

• To learn reach technique for **i** and **r**.

4A

Get Ready to Key

Follow the steps in the *Standard Plan for Getting Ready to Key* on p. 511.

4B

Conditioning Practice

Key each line twice SS; DS between 2-line groups.

Practice cue

• Key the line at a slow, steady pace, tapping and releasing each key quickly.

• Key the line again at a faster pace; move from key to key quickly.

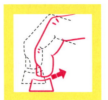

home keys 1 ll aa ff jj ss kk dd ;; jd f; ls ak sj ;a df kl ak

Tap ENTER twice to DS.

h/e 2 he he|she she|held held|heed heed|shed shed|ahead;

DS

all keys learned 3 she had a sale; a jade desk; she ask a as he fled;

Tap ENTER 3 times to TS between lesson parts.

4C

Speed Building

Key each line twice SS; DS between 2-line groups.

Keying cue

Keep up your pace to the end of each line, tap the **ENTER** key quickly, and start the new line without a pause.

1 had a deal

2 see if she did;

3 ask if she has read;

4 her dad did ask her if he

5 a sled ride; half a jar; he is

6 ask dad if she has had a real sale;

7 her aide asked if he has real dark hair;

8 she has a shed; half a flask; she has a desk;

- To learn to format personal-business letters in block format.
- To improve word choice skills.

26A

Conditioning Practice

Key each line twice.

alphabet	1	Jackie will budget for the most expensive zoology equipment.
figures	2	The rate on May 14 was 12.57 percent; it was 8.96 on May 30.
easy	3	The official paid the men for the work they did on the dock.

gwam   1' | 1 | 2 | 3 | 4 | 5 | 6 | 7 | 8 | 9 | 10 | 11 | 12 |

26B   Formatting

Personal-Business Letters in Block Format

Letter 1

Study the format guides on p. 60 and the model personal-business letter on p. 66. Note the placement of letter parts and spacing between them.

Format/key the model on p. 66.

Proofread and correct errors.

Save as: 26B LETTER1

Letter 2

Format/key Letter 2 shown at the right. Refer to the model on p. 66 as needed. Proofread and correct errors.

Save as: 26B LETTER2

Letter 3 (Optional Activity)

Format/key the model letter on p. 67 in the traditional letter style using the *Office Word 2003* Look Installed Template.

Save as: 26B LETTER3

2674 Edworthy Road
Dallas, TX 77429-6675
April 15, 20--

Ms. Addilynn Morgan
671 Meadowbank Avenue
Boston, MA 02126-6720

Dear Ms. Morgan

This year's Business Leadership Conference will be held in Dallas on December 8-9. With ethical behavior becoming more and more of an issue in today's society, the main focus of the conference will be on the importance of developing ethical business leaders.

When I was in Boston for another conference earlier this spring, I heard you speak on this topic. I believe you would be the perfect keynote speaker for our conference. Specifically, we would like you to focus your remarks on dealing with others in a fair and honest manner at all times and under all circumstances—not just when it is a matter of convenience. The title of your session would be ***Enhancing Your Company Image through Strong Ethical Leaders.***

We are offering an honorarium of $1,000 and will cover your travel expenses. Please let us know of your availability on the 8th of December. You can reach me at 972-372-8811 if you have questions about this speaking engagement.

We are looking forward to having you share your expertise with our conference participants.

Sincerely

Bella K. Jarvis
Conference Chair

New Keys: h and e

1. Use the *Standard Plan for Learning New Keys* (p. 511) for each key to be learned. Study the plan now.

2. Relate each step of the plan to the illustrations below and copy at the right. Then key each line twice SS; leave a DS between 2-line groups.

h *Right index* finger

e *Left middle* finger

Do not key the line numbers, the vertical lines separating word groups, or the labels.

Learn h

1 j h jh jh|hj hj|ha ha|has has|dash dash|hall hall;

2 jh jh|had had|ash ash|has has|half half|lash lash;

3 ha ha; a half; a dash; has had; a flash; had half;

Tap ENTER twice to DS after you complete the set of lines.

Learn e

4 d e de de|ed ed|elk elk|elf elf|see see|leak leak;

5 fake fake|deal deal|leaf leaf|fade fade|lake lake;

6 jade desk; see a lake; feel safe; see a safe deal;

Combine h and e

7 he he|she she|shelf shelf|shake shake|shade shade;

8 he has; half ashes; he fed; held a shelf; she has;

9 held a sale; he has a shed; he has a desk; she has

Tap ENTER 3 times to TS between lesson parts.

New-Key Mastery

Key each line twice SS; DS between 2-line groups.

Spacing cue

Space once after ; used as punctuation.

Fingers curved

Fingers upright

home row
1 add add|dad dad|jak jak|ask ask|lad lad|fall falls
2 all fall; as a jak; a sad lad falls; all salad ads

h/e
3 he he|had had|see see|she she|held held|shed shed;
4 half a shelf; a jade sale; she has a jak; he deals

all keys learned
5 jell jell|half half|sale sale|lake lake|held held;
6 a lake; she has half; he held a flask; a jade sale

all keys learned
7 she held a deed; a flash; a jade keel; has a shed;
8 a jak; half a flask; he has a desk; he held a sale

For additional practice:

MicroType 5
Alphabetic Keyboarding
Lesson 3

Return address 230 Glendale Court
Brooklyn, NY 11234-3721
February 15, 20— ↓ 2

Letter mailing address Ms. Julie Hutchinson
1825 Melbourne Avenue
Flushing, NY 11367-2351 ↓ 1

Salutation Dear Julie ↓ 1

Body It seems like years since we were in Ms. Gerhig's keyboarding class. Now I wish I had paid more attention. As I indicated on the phone, I am applying for a position as box office coordinator for one of the theatres on Broadway. Of course, I know the importance o having my letter of application and resume formatted correctly, but I'm not sure that I remember how to do it. ↓ 1

Default or 1" SM

Default or 1" SM

Since you just completed your business education degree, I knew where to get the help I needed. Thanks for agreeing to look over my application documents; they are enclosed. Also, if you have any suggestions for changes to the content, please share those with me too. This job is so important to me; it's the one I really want. ↓ 1

Thanks again for agreeing to help. If I get the job, I'll take you out to one of New York's finest restaurants. ↓ 1

Complimentary close Sincerely ↓ 2

Writer Rebecca Dunworthy ↓ 1

Enclosure notation Enclosure

Personal-Business Letter in Block Format—Word 2007 defaults

Lesson 3

NEW KEYS: h AND e

OBJECTIVE

• To learn reach technique for **h** and **e**.

3A

Get Ready to Key

Before starting each lesson, follow the *Standard Plan for Getting Ready to Key* at the right.

Standard Plan for Getting Ready to Key

1. Arrange work area as shown on page 506.
2. Start your word processing software.
3. Align the front of the keyboard with the front edge of the desk.
4. Position the monitor and the textbook for easy reading.

3B

Plan for Learning New Keys

All keys except the home keys (**fdsa jkl;**) require the fingers to reach in order to tap them. Follow the *Standard Plan for Learning New Keys* at the right to learn the proper reach for each new key.

Standard Plan for Learning New Keys

1. Find the new key on the keyboard chart shown on the page where the new key is introduced.
2. Look at your keyboard and find the new key on it.
3. Study the reach-technique picture near the practice lines for the new key. Read the statement below the illustration.
4. Identify the finger to be used to tap the new key.
5. Curve your fingers; place them in home-key position (over asdf jkl;).
6. Watch your finger as you reach to the new key and back to home position a few times (keep it curved).
7. Refer to the set of drill lines near the reach-technique illustration. Key each line twice SS—once slowly to learn the new reach and then again at a faster rate. DS between 2-line groups.

3C

Home-Key Review

Key each line twice SS; DS between 2-line groups.

All keystrokes learned

1 ss jj ff ;; dd ll aa kk jj ff kk ss dd ll ;; aa kk

2 fk ja ld s; aj d; fl sk ka jf ls d; jd kf sl ;a dj

3 a sad lass; all ads; ask a lad; all fall; a flask;

4 a lad ask; a salad; a fall ad; ask a dad; all fall

Tap ENTER 3 times to TS between lesson parts.

Return address 2832 Primrose Street
Eugene, OR 97402-1716
November 20, 20-- ↓4

Letter mailing address Mr. Andrew Chaney
324 Brookside Avenue NW
Salem, OR 97304-9008 ↓2

Salutation Dear Mr. Chaney ↓2

Body Thank you for taking time out of your busy schedule to speak to our **A**spiring **M**usicians **C**lub. It was great learning more about the "Masters" from you. ↓2

I particularly enjoyed learning more about the German composers. It is amazing that so many of the great musicians (Johann Sebastian Bach, Ludwig van Beethoven, Robert Schumann, Felix Mendelssohn, and Richard Wagner) are all from Germany. It is my goal to continue my study of music at the **Staatliche Hochschule fur Musik Rheinland** in Germany once I graduate from college. ↓2

Default or 1" SM

Default or 1" SM

Your insights into what it takes to make it as a professional musician were also enlightening for our members. Those of us who want to become professional musicians know we have to rededicate ourselves to that goal if we are going to be successful. ↓2

Thank you again for sharing your expertise with our club. ↓2

Complimentary close Sincerely ↓4

Writer Stephen R. Knowles
Writer's Title AMC Member

Shown in 12-point Times New Roman with 2" top margin and 1" side margins, this letter appears smaller than actual size.

Personal-Business Letter in Block Format—Word 2003 defaults

Lesson 2   REVIEW HOME KEYS (fdsa   jkl;)

- To review control of home keys (**fdsa jkl;**).
- To review control of the **Space Bar** and **ENTER**.

2A

Practice Home Keys

Key each line twice SS; DS between 2-line groups. Do not key the numbers.

1 s s ss l l ll d d dd k k kk f f ff j j jj a; a; ;a
                                                          DS
2 f f ff j j jj d d s sl fl lf al la ja aj sk ks jj;
                                                          DS
3 sa as ld dl af fa ls sl fl lf al la ja aj sk ks jj
                                                          DS
4 fj dk sl a; jf kd ls ;a ds kl df kj sd lk sa ;l jj
                                                          DS
5 fa ds jk ;f jf kd ls ;a f; dl sk aj sj ak d; fl ad
                                                          TS

2B

Improve ENTER Key Technique

Key each line twice SS; DS between 2-line groups.

- fingers curved and upright
- wrists low, but not touching keyboard
- body erect, sitting back in chair
- eyes on copy

1 alj; ksf; dak;
2 sff; ldd; ajj; lkk;
3 jaj; sls; kdk; fjf; sks;
4 ljd; fss; jdj; skj; asj; fdl;
5 afsd klj; fsda lj;k flaj s;dk fj;k
6 akdj ls;f daj; kfls jlja fsdl ;skd ajsa

2C

Improve ENTER Key Technique

Key each line twice SS; DS between 2-line groups.

For additional practice:
MicroType 5
Alphabetic Keyboarding
Lesson 2

1 a fall; a fall; a jak; a jak; asks dad; asks dad;;
2 all ads; all ads; a fad; a fad; as a lad; as a lad
3 a sad lad; a sad lad; a fall; a fall; ask a ask a;
4 a fad a fad; ask a lass; ask a lass; a dad; a dad;
5 all fall ads; all fall ads; a sad fall; a sad fall
6 a lad asks a lass; a lad asks a lass; a lad; a lad

Language Skills: Word Choice

1. Study the spelling and definitions of the words.
2. Key all *Learn* and *Apply* lines, choosing the correct word in the *Apply* lines.

Save as: 26C CHOICE

hole (n) an opening in or through something **whole** (adj/n) having all its proper parts; a complete amount or sum	**peak** (n) pointed end; top of a mountain; highest level **peek** (vb) to glance or look at for a brief time

Learn 1 The **whole** group helped dig a **hole** to bury the time capsule.

Apply 2 They ate the (hole, whole) cake before going to the water (hole, whole).

Apply 3 He told us, "The (hole, whole) is greater than the sum of its parts."

Learn 1 If you **peek** out the window, you will see the **peak** of the iceberg.

Apply 2 The (peak, peek) of the mountain came into view as they drove around the curve.

Apply 3 Students were told not to (peak, peek) at the keyboard in order to reach (peak, peek) skill.

Lesson 27   PERSONAL-BUSINESS LETTERS

OBJECTIVES
- To review format of personal-business letters in block format.
- To learn to format/key envelopes.

27A

Conditioning Practice
Key each line twice.

alphabet 1 Even Jack will be taking part of a history quiz next Monday.

fig/sym 2 Out-of-stock items (#7850*, #461A*, and #2093*) are in blue.

speed 3 Jake may sign the big form by the antique door of city hall.

gwam 1' | 1 | 2 | 3 | 4 | 5 | 6 | 7 | 8 | 9 | 10 | 11 | 12 |

27B   Formatting

Personal-Business Letters in Block Format

Letter 1

Format/key the letter at the right. Refer to the model on p. 66 as needed. Proofread and correct errors.

Save as: 27B LETTER1

Note: Line endings for opening and closing lines are indicated by color verticals. Insert a hard return at these points.

	words
610 Grand Avenue │ Laramie, WY 82070-1423 │ October 10, 20-- │	12
Elegant Treasures │ 388 Stonegate Drive │ Longview, TX 75601-	25
0132 │ Dear Armani Dealer	29

Last week when I was in Longview visiting relatives, I noticed that you had Giuseppe Armani figurines displayed in your window. You had already closed for the day, so I was not able to see if you had other figurines. — 43 56 70 73

I am interested in three sculptures that Armani had created to celebrate the new millennium. They are called **Stardust, Silver Moon,** and **Comet.** I want to buy all three sculptures. Do you have them in stock, or could you order them? If not, could you refer me to a nearby dealer? — 85 99 113 127 129

I am looking forward to adding these exquisite pieces of art to my collection. — 143 145

Sincerely │ Cynthia A. Maustin — 151

1H

Home-Key Mastery

Key each line twice (without the numbers).

Technique cue

Keep fingers curved and upright over home keys, right thumb just barely touching the Space Bar.

Spacing cue

Space once after ; (semicolon) used as punctuation.

Correct finger alignment

```
1 j j jk jk l l l; l; a a as as d d df df af kl dsj;    DS

2 jj kjk kjk ll ;l; ;l; ja ja dk dk ls ls ;f ;f kjd;    DS

3 sad sad|lad lad|all all|ask ask|jak jak|fall fall;    DS

4 a sad lass; ask all dads; a lad ask; a salad; as a    DS

5 as a dad; add a fall; ask all lads; as a fall fad;    TS
```

1I

End-of-Lesson Routine

Follow the routine shown at the right at the end of each practice session.

1. Save the document if you have not already done so. Use the word Lesson and the lesson number (Lesson 1) for the filename unless directed to use another filename.
2. Exit the software.
3. Remove disk from disk drive.

4. Turn off equipment if directed to do so.
5. Store materials as instructor directs.
6. Clean up your work area and push in your chair before you leave.

1J

Enrichment

Key each line twice SS; DS between 2-line groups.

```
1 ja js jd jf f; fl fk fj ka ks kd kf d; dl dk dj a;    DS

2 la ls ld lf s; sl sk sj ;a ;s ;d ;f a; al ak aj fj    DS

3 jj aa kk ss ll dd ;; ff fj dk sl a; jf kd ls ;a a;    DS

4 as as ask ask ad ad lad lad all all fall fall lass    DS

5 as a fad; as a dad; ask a lad; as a lass; all lads    DS

6 a sad dad; all lads fall; ask a lass; a jak salad;    DS

7 add a jak; a fall ad; all fall ads; ask a sad lass    TS
```

For additional practice:

MicroType 5
Alphabetic Keyboarding
Lesson 1

Letter 2

Format and key the text at the right as a personal-business letter in block format.

Save as: 27B LETTER2

	words
117 Whitman Avenue	Hartford, CT 06107-4518	July 2, 20--	Ms.	13
Geneva Everett	880 Honeysuckle Drive	Athens, GA 30606-9231		25
Dear Geneva	28

Last week at the Educational Theatre Association National Convention, you mentioned that your teaching assignment for next year included an Introduction to Shakespeare class. I find the Internet to be a very useful supplement for creating interest in many of the classes I teach. Here are four websites dealing with Shakespeare that you may find helpful for your new class.

http://www.shakespeares-globe.org/Default.htm
http://www.shakespeare-online.com/
http://www.shakespeare.mit.edu/
http://www.albemarle-london.com/map-globe.html

Another resource that I use is a booklet published by Cengage Learning: *Introducing Shakespeare.* A copy of the title page is attached. The booklet contains scenes from some of Shakespeare's best-known works. Scenes from my favorites (*Romeo and Juliet, A Midsummer Night's Dream,* and *Julius Caesar*) are included.

As I come across other resources, I will forward them to you. Enjoy the rest of the summer; another school year will be upon us before we know it.

Sincerely | Marshall W. Cline | Attachment

(words column: 42, 55, 69, 84, 99, 105, 114, 122, 130, 140, 152, 165, 178, 191, 203, 217, 231, 232, 241)

27C   Formatting

Envelopes

Format a small (No. 6 3/4) envelope for Letter 1 of 27B and a large (No. 10) envelope for Letter 2 of 27B.

Save as: 27C ENVELOPE1 and 27C ENVELOPE2

117 Whitman Avenue
Hartford, CT 06107-4518
July 2, 20--

Ms. Geneva Everett
880 Honeysuckle Drive
Athens, GA 30606-9231

Dear Geneva

Last week at the Educational T teaching assignment for next be a very useful supplement fe dealing with Shakespeare that

http://www.shakespeares-glo
http://www.wfu.edu/~tedfor
http://www.jetlink.net/~mass
http://www.albemarle-londo

Another resource that I use is a copy of the title page is attach works. Scenes from my favorit included.

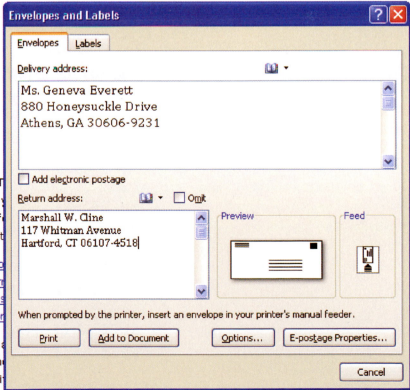

1F

Home-Key, Space-Bar, and ENTER-Key Practice

1. Place your hands in home-key position (left-hand fingers on **f d s a** and right-hand fingers on **j k l ;**).

2. Key each line once single-spaced (SS); double-space (DS) between 2-line groups. Do not key line numbers.

Fingers curved and upright

Down-and-in spacing motion

```
1 a aa s ss d dd f ff
2 a aa s ss d dd f ff
                              DS
3 j jj k kk l ll ; ;;
4 j jj k kk l ll ; ;;
                              DS
5 aj lf d; ks ja fl ;d aja
6 aj lf d; ks ja fl ;d aja
                              DS
7 djd kak s;s flf jal d;k;
8 djd kak s;s flf jal d;k;
```
Tap the ENTER key 3 times to triple-space (TS)

1G

Technique: ENTER-Key Practice

Key the lines once SS; DS between 2-line groups. Do not key the numbers.

Spacing cue

When lines are SS, tap **ENTER** twice to insert a DS between 2-line groups.

Reach out with little finger; tap the ENTER key quickly; return finger to home key.

```
 1 jj ss ll
 2 jj ss ll
                  DS
 3 aa kk dd ;; ff
 4 aa kk dd ;; ff
                  DS
 5 ll ff jj dd kk ss ;;
 6 ll ff jj dd kk ss ;;
                          DS
 7 aa aa fd l; kj j; lk af ds
 8 aa aa fd l; kj j; lk af ds
                              DS
 9 ;f; ;f; ala ala djd djd ksk ksk;
10 ;f; ;f; ala ala djd djd ksk ksk;
                                    DS
11 kkff kkff jjss jjss aall aall dd;s dd;
12 kkff kkff jjss jjss aall aall dd;s dd;
                                          TS
```

Lesson 28   PERSONAL-BUSINESS LETTERS

• To format personal-business letters in block format.

28A

Conditioning Practice

Key each line twice.

alphabet 1 Peter was amazed at just how quickly you fixed the big vans.

fig/sym 2 Of 34,198 citizens, 25,648 (75%) voted in the 2004 election.

speed 3 Orlando may make a big map to hang by the door of city hall.

gwam 1' | 1 | 2 | 3 | 4 | 5 | 6 | 7 | 8 | 9 | 10 | 11 | 12 |

28B   Formatting

Personal-Business Letters in Block Format

Letter 1

Format and key the letter at the right in block format; check spelling, proofread, and correct the letter before you save it.

Save as: 28B LETTER1

	words
1245 Park Avenue	3
New York, NY 10128-2231	8
October 28, 20--	11

Mrs. Tara Cruz — 14
4221 Beekman Street — 18
New York, NY 10038-8326 — 22

Dear Mrs. Cruz — 25

Mrs. Kenningston's fifth-grade class will be attending a production of — 40
the Broadway musical *The Lion King* on March 25 to conclude their — 53
study of the theatre. As you are probably aware, the play is based on — 67
the 1994 Disney film about a young lion's coming-of-age struggles. — 80

Attending the play will give the fifth-graders a real sense of New York — 95
theatre. The production will be at the New Amsterdam Theatre, built — 109
in 1903 and for years considered the most majestic on 42nd Street. — 122
With its recent renovation, it has been restored almost to its original — 136
grandeur. The theatre is best known as the home of the Ziegfeld — 149
Follies (1913 through 1927) and George M. Cohan's *Forty-Five Minutes* — 163
from Broadway. — 166

This will be a great experience for the fifth-graders. Mrs. Kenningston — 181
would like four parents to help chaperone on the day of the — 193
production. Are you interested and willing to assist? I will call you — 207
next week to determine your availability and discuss details. — 220

Sincerely — 222

Marsha Rhodes — 224
Parent Volunteer — 228

1C

Home-Key Position

1. Find the home keys on the keyboard illustration: **f d s a** for left hand and **j k l ;** for right hand.

2. Locate the home keys on your keyboard, and place your fingers, well curved and upright (not slanting), on them.

3. Remove your fingers from the keyboard; then place them in home-key position again, curving and holding them lightly on the keys.

Left Fingers **Right Fingers**

1D

Technique: Keystroking and Space Bar

1. Read the hints and study the illustrations at the right.

2. Place your fingers in home-key position as directed in 1C above.

3. Key the line beneath the illustration. Tap the Space Bar once at the point of each arrow.

4. Review proper position at the keyboard (1B); key the line again.

Technique Hints

Keystroking: Tap each key with the tip of the finger. Keep your fingers curved as shown.

Spacing: Tap the Space Bar with the right thumb; use a quick down-and-in motion (toward the palm). Avoid pauses before or after spacing.

Space once

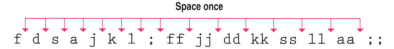

f d s a j k l ; ff jj dd kk ss ll aa ;;

1E

Technique: Hard Return at Line Endings

Read the information and study the illustration at the right.

Hard Return
To return the insertion point to the left margin and move it down to the next line, tap **ENTER**.
This is called a hard return. Use a hard return at the end of all drill lines. Use two hard returns when directed to double-space.

Hard Return Technique
Reach the little finger of the right hand to the **ENTER** key, tap the key, and return the finger quickly to home-key position.
Practice the **ENTER** key reach several times.

Letter 2

Format and key the letter at the right in block format; check spelling, proofread, and correct the letter.

Save as: 28B LETTER2

	words
1245 Park Avenue	New York, NY 10128-2231	January 5, 20--		11
Ticket Manager	New Amsterdam Theatre	214 West 42nd Street		23
New York, NY 10036	Dear Ticket Manager	31

Mrs. Kenningston's fifth-grade class from Washington Elementary 44
School will be studying theatre during the month of March. To 56
conclude their study, Mrs. Kenningston would like for them to attend 70
a Broadway production of *The Lion King* on March 25. 81

Approximately twenty children would attend the performance along 94
with five chaperones. Does your theatre offer educational discounts 108
for the matinee performance? 114

One of our students needs wheelchair accessibility. What facilities do 128
you have to accommodate this student? 136

The students are very excited about the possibility of attending a live 150
Broadway production. Please provide me with the requested information 164
as soon as possible so that the necessary arrangements can be made. 178

Sincerely | Marsha Rhodes | Parent Volunteer 186

Letter 3

Format and key the letter at the right in block format; check spelling, proofread, and correct the letter.

Save as: 28B LETTER3

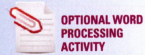

OPTIONAL WORD PROCESSING ACTIVITY

Prepare letters for the other three parents who helped chaperone the field trip. Their addresses are:

Mr. Charles Chan
389 Wadsworth Avenue
New York, NY 10040-0025

Ms. Alesha Ramirez
175 Morningside Avenue
New York, NY 10027-8735

Ms. Gwendolyn Maas
1615 Henry Hudson Parkway
New York, NY 10034-6721

Save as: 28B LETTER-3CHAN, 28B LETTER-3RAMIREZ, and 28B LETTER3MAAS

	words
*1245 Park Avenue	New York, NY 10128-2231	April 1, 20--	Mrs.*	13
*Tara Cruz	4221 Beekman Street	New York, NY 10038-8326	Dear*	26
Mrs. Cruz	28

Thank you for helping chaperone the fifth-grade class on their 41
field trip to Broadway. When I visited Mrs. Kenningston's classroom 54
yesterday, the children were still excited about having attended the play. 70
Their thank-you note is enclosed. 76

Because of parents like you, educational experiences outside the 89
classroom are possible. These experiences bring to life what the students 101
learn in school. I'm glad our children have this enrichment. 117

Thank you again for accepting the challenge of watching over 129
the fifth-graders on their exciting trip to Broadway. I know the task 143
wasn't easy, but I felt it was well worth our time. 154

Sincerely | Marsha Rhodes | Parent Volunteer | Enclosure 165

Lessons 1-16

New Key Learning

Lesson 1   HOME KEYS (fdsa   jkl;)

OBJECTIVES

• To review control of home keys (**fdsa jkl;**).
• To learn control of the **Space Bar** and **ENTER**.

1A

Work Area Arrangement

Properly arranged work area includes:

• alphanumeric keyboard directly in front of chair
• front edge of keyboard even with edge of desk
• monitor placed for easy viewing
• book at right of keyboard

© CENGAGE LEARNING

Properly arranged work area

1B

Keying Position

Proper position includes:

• fingers curved and upright (not slanted) over home keys
• wrists low, but not touching keyboard
• forearms parallel to slant of keyboard
• body erect, sitting back in chair
• feet on floor for balance
• eyes on copy

© franksiteman.com 2007

Proper position at computer

Keyboard Review

Key each line twice.

A/Z	1	Zack had a pizza at the plaza by the zoo on a hazy day.
B/Y	2	Bobby may be too busy to buy me a bag for my boat trip.
C/X	3	Ricky caught six cod to fix for the six excited scouts.
D/W	4	Wilda would like to own the doe she found in the woods.
E/V	5	Evan will give us the van to move the five heavy boxes.
F/U	6	All four of us bought coats with fur collars and cuffs.
G/T	7	Eight men tugged the boat into deep water to get going.
H/S	8	Marsha wishes to show how to make charts on a computer.
I/R	9	Ira can rise above his ire to rid the firm of a crisis.
J/Q	10	Josh quietly quit the squad after a major joint injury.
K/P	11	Kip packed a backpack and put it on a box on the porch.
L/O	12	Lola is to wear the royal blue skirt and a gold blouse.
M/N	13	Many of the men met in the hall to see the new manager.
figures	14	I worked 8:30 to 5 at 1964 Lake Blvd. from May 7 to 26.
fig/sym	15	I said, "ISBN #0-651-24879-3 was not assigned to them."

Timed Writings

1. Key two 1' timings on each ¶; determine *gwam*.
2. Key two 2' timings on ¶s 1–2 combined; determine *gwam*.
3. If time permits, key 1' guided timings on each ¶. To set a goal, add 2 to the *gwam* achieved in step 1.

LA all letters used **MicroPace**   gwam 2'

One of the best-known inaugural addresses was given   5
by President John F. Kennedy. The exact words of this   11
President are permanently imprinted into the minds of   16
numerous Americans. If you were to say, "Ask not what   21
your country can do for you but what you can do for your   27
country," quite a few Americans would know the individual   33
you were quoting.   34

These words alone make an impression. However, the   40
way John F. Kennedy delivered them with such zealousness   45
made them have an even greater impact. What do you think   51
he meant by these words? Do you think it is more or less   57
important for Americans to try and live by these words   62
today than when Kennedy delivered them in his inaugural   67
address?   68

Quarter-Minute Checkpoints

gwam	1/4'	1/2'	3/4'	1'
24	6	12	18	24
28	7	14	21	28
32	8	16	24	32
36	9	18	27	36
40	10	20	30	40
44	11	22	33	44
48	12	24	36	48
52	13	26	39	52
56	14	28	42	56

gwam 2' | 1 | 2 | 3 | 4 | 5 | 6 |

New Key Learning

Alphabetic Keying

Numeric Keypad

You will find keyboarding skills very useful in your life. To get started, this unit will help you learn to use the keyboard and the numeric keypad by "touch." You can learn or review basic keying skills in these 21 lessons. Fluent manipulation of letter, figure/symbol, and basic service keys is your goal. In the five Numeric Keypad lessons, you will learn to key numbers with speed and ease using the touch method.

Communication & Math
SKILLS 3

ACTIVITY 1

Number Expression

1. Study each of the eight rules shown at the right.
   a. Key the *Learn* line(s) beneath each rule, noting how the rule is applied.
   b. Key the *Apply* line(s), expressing numbers correctly.

Number expression

Rule 1: Spell a number that begins a sentence even when other numbers in the sentence are shown in figures.

Learn 1   Twelve of the new shrubs have died; 48 are doing quite well.

Apply 2   14 musicians have paid their dues, but 89 have not done so.

Rule 2: Use figures for numbers above ten, and for numbers from one to ten when they are used with numbers above ten.

Learn 3   She ordered 8 word processors, 14 computers, and 4 printers.

Apply 4   Did he say they need ten or 14 sets of Z18 and Z19 diskettes?

Rule 3: Use figures to express date and time (unless followed by o'clock).

Learn 5   He will arrive on Paygo Flight 418 at 9:48 a.m. on March 14.

Apply 6   Exhibitors must be in Ivy Hall at eight forty a.m. on May one.

Rule 4: Use figures for house numbers except house number One.

Learn 7   My home is at 8 Vernon Drive; my office, at One Weber Plaza.

Apply 8   The Nelsons moved from 4059 Pyle Avenue to 1 Maple Circle.

Rule 5: Use figures to express measures and weights.

Learn 9   Glenda Redford is 5 ft. 4 in. tall and weighs 118 lbs. 9 oz.

Apply 10   This carton measures one ft. by nine in. and weighs five lbs.

Rule 6: Use figures for numbers following nouns.

Learn 11   Review Rules 1 to 18 in Chapter 5, pages 149 and 150, today.

Apply 12   Case 1849 is reviewed in Volume five, pages nine and ten.

Rule 7: Spell (and capitalize) names of small-numbered streets (ten and under).

Learn 13   I walked several blocks along Third Avenue to 54th Street.

Apply 14   At 7th Street she took a taxi to the theater on 43rd Avenue.

Rule 8: Spell indefinite numbers.

Learn 15   Joe owns one acre of Parcel A; that is almost fifty percent.

Learn 16   Nearly seventy members voted; that is nearly a fourth.

Apply 17   Over 20 percent of the students auditioned for the play.

Apply 18   Just under 1/2 of the voters cast ballots for the best musician.

(continued on next page)

Communicating
YOUR PERSPECTIVE | 6

At the beginning of the 21st century, there are many differences in the world. For example, life expectancy, literacy rate, and purchasing power vary greatly among the countries of the world. The table below provides information on the three most and three least livable countries as reported in Infoplease "1999 National Events Wrap-Up." Infoplease. © 2000–2006 Pearson Education, publishing as InfoPlease. 19 Jul. 2008 http://www.infoplease.com/ipa/A0762380.html and *The CIA 2008 World Factbook*. https://www.cia.gov/library/publications/the-world-factbook/.

Country	Life Expectancy (Yrs)		Literacy Rate	Purchasing Power Parity
	Male	Female		
DIFFERENCES WITHIN OUR WORLD				
Three "Most Livable" Countries				
Iceland	78.4	82.7	99%	$ 39,400
Norway	77.1	82.6	100%	$ 55,600
Australia	77.8	83.7	99%	$ 37,500
Three "Least Livable" Countries				
Sierra Leone	38.6	43.2	35%	$ 800
Burkina Faso	50.6	54.4	22%	$ 1,200
Guinea-Bissau	45.7	49.3	42%	$ 600

When anthropologists set out to learn about a culture, one of their most important clues is food. From the cookbooks, utensils, kitchens, and garbage piles of New World settlements, anthropologists can trace the British colonists' attempts to preserve an English way of life. The colonists initially applied British cooking methods to the food that was available. Then some of the young women learned how Native American women cooked food. The colonists learned, for instance, to roast corn in the fields just after picking, to eat it on the cob, and to mix it with beans and meat in dishes like hominy and succotash.

Recipes for Boston brown bread and Virginia ham are indicators that the colonies were evolving into regions with distinct identities. Foods from different cultures reflect the waves of immigrants that introduced them. The fact that you can buy the same cereal, with the same taste, in Sacramento or St. Louis is one small example of how much of our food is now national in appeal.

Here are some questions we might ask about the food of a country or culture:

- Why are certain foods popular? Can they be grown locally? Are they inexpensive? Do they have cultural meaning?
- Examine the typical diet. Could it be improved to be more nutritional? If so, how?
- Does their diet put people at risk for or protect them from certain diseases? Which diseases are they likely to get, and why?
- Does growing any of these foods affect the environment? If so, how?

Global Awareness

ACTIVITIES

1. Read the material at the left and key the table. Does the information surprise you?

2. Conduct research to determine where the United States ranks on each of these variables. Add your findings to the table.

3. With one or two classmates, research one of the countries listed to find other factors that affected the ranking. Collaborate to write a one-page group report that combines the findings.

Cultural Diversity

ACTIVITIES

1. Read the material at the left.

2. What could someone infer about our society from the fact that we eat "fast foods"? Compose a paragraph at the keyboard to answer this question.

3. Form a group with other students. Choose a foreign country or culture. Research it, answering the bulleted questions at the left.

4. Create and key a restaurant menu for the country or culture that you chose in step 3. Format the menu attractively.

2. Key Proofread & Correct, expressing numbers correctly. Then follow the steps below.
   a. Check answers.
   b. Using the rule number at the left of each line, study the rule relating to each error you made.
   c. Rekey each incorrect line, expressing numbers correctly.

Save as: CS3 ACTIVITY1

ACTIVITY 2

Reading

1. Open *DF CS3 ACTIVITY2*.
2. Read the document; close the file.
3. Key answers to the questions at the right.

Save as: CS3 ACTIVITY2

ACTIVITY 3

Composing

1. Read the quotations.
2. Choose one and make notes of what the quotation means to you.
3. Key a ¶ or two indicating what the quotation means to you.
4. Proofread, revise, and correct.

Save as: CS3 ACTIVITY3

ACTIVITY 4

Math: Working with Decimals, Fractions, and Percents

Proofread & Correct

Rules

1	1	20 members have already voted, but 15 have yet to do so.
2	2	Only twelve of the dancers are here; six have not returned.
3	3	Do you know if the eight fifteen Klondike flight is on time?
3, 4	4	We should be at 1 Brooks Road no later than eleven thirty a.m.
5	5	This oriental mural measures eight ft. by 10 ft.
5	6	The box of books is two ft. square and weighs six lbs. eight oz.
6	7	Have you read pages 45 to 62 of Chapter two that he assigned?
7	8	She usually rides the bus from 6th Street to 1st Avenue.
8	9	Nearly 1/2 of the cast is here; that is about 15.
8	10	A late fee of over 15 percent is charged after the 30th day.

1. Will at least one member of the cast not return for the next season?
2. Has a studio been contracted to produce the show for next season?
3. Does each cast member earn the same amount per episode?
4. Is the television show a news magazine or comedy?
5. How many seasons has the show been aired, not counting next season?
6. Do all cast members' contracts expire at the same time?
7. What did the cast do three years ago to get raises?

1. "Man does not live by words alone, despite the fact that sometimes he has to eat them." (Adlai Stevenson)
2. "No man is rich enough to buy back his past." (Oscar Wilde)
3. "It is not fair to ask of others what you are unwilling to do yourself." (Eleanor Roosevelt)

1. Open *DF CS3 ACTIVITY4* and print the file.
2. Solve the problems as directed in the file.
3. Submit your answers.

From the desk of:
Julia Kingsley

Mr. McLemore would like the spreadsheet (DF Hoops SS) for the June 15-16 tournament completed with the attached information.

JK

June 15 Refs:
Stella Tarantino (All June 15 games on Court A-1)
Michael Ginobli (All June 15 games on Court A-2)
Trenton Chen (All June 15 games on Court B-1)
Travis Martinez (All June 15 games on Court B-2)

June 16 Refs:
Tamika Jackson (All June 16 games on Court A-1 plus the 3rd place game on Court A, 1st place game on Court A, and the Championship game on Court A)

Samaal Carlisle (All June 16 games on Court A-2 plus 3rd place game on Court B and the 1st place game on Court B)

Farrel Goldfarb (All June 16 games on Court B-1)
Jan Szczerbiak (All June 16 games on Court B-2)

Please add a Ref Fees column to the spreadsheet. Format the cells in the column as currency cells. Refs are paid $15 for each game on June 15 and $20 for each game on June 16. The refs are paid $25 for 1st and 3rd place games. The ref fee for the championship game is $35. Input the fees and calculate the total fees for referees.

Make these formatting changes to the spreadsheet.
- Center the text in the Court column.
- Indent all left-aligned columns 1 space.
- Center information on page horizontally.
Add a note to your tasks list to pay referees for June 15-16 games on June 18.

ACTIVITY 3

You must complete Career Exploration Activities 1 and 2 before completing this activity.

1. Retrieve your completed Career Clusters Interest Survey from your folder.

2. Review the Career Cluster Plans of Study for your top three career clusters. Do this by returning to http://www.careerclusters.org and clicking the **Free Career Cluster — Plans of Study** link. This will take you to a screen where you can establish a login address and password (be sure to record your login information in a safe place for future use). Select your top three career clusters. Click your first choice and open and print the file. Click the Back button to return to the career clusters and open and print the second career cluster. Repeat the procedure for the third career cluster.

3. Place your printed files in your folder and file it in the storage area.

Communicating
YOUR PERSPECTIVE | 1

Ethics is a set of moral principles and values. Ethical issues confront us every day. They occur in our community, nation, and world. They also arise in our personal and professional lives.

- A banker makes concealed loans to a company, helping that company inflate its profits by $1.5 billion during a four-year period. The company ends up in bankruptcy; the company stock is worthless.
- An executive of a charitable organization uses funds to remodel the executive suite rather than to support the needy.
- A teenager takes a DVD from a store without paying for it.

Deciding what to do in ethical situations isn't always easy. What is a good way to think them through? What is a good way to make an ethical decision?

1. **Get the facts.** Learn as much as possible about the situation before jumping to a conclusion. Make an intelligent decision rather than an emotional one.

2. **Don't let assumptions get in the way of the facts.** As the actor and comedian Will Rogers said, "It isn't what we don't know that gives us trouble[;] it's what we know that ain't so." You don't like it when people make assumptions about you. Make sure your judgment isn't colored by preconceptions or stereotypes.

3. **Consider the consequences for everyone.** Try to see the situation from the point of view of each party involved. What is each person or group likely to lose or gain as a result of your decision?

4. **Consider your personal values.** Apply your own beliefs and standards to the problem.

5. **Make your decision.**

Situation: In a grocery store, you see your best friend putting items under her coat.

Ethics: The Right Thing to Do

ACTIVITIES

1. Read the material at the left.

2. Think about the situation described at the bottom of the page.

3. Key a ¶ telling how you would use the five-step process at the left to make a decision on how to handle the situation.

4. Form a group with some other students. Discuss an ethical issue in your community. Make sure everyone contributes. Did everyone in the group agree?

5. In an e-mail to your teacher, briefly explain the issue chosen in step 4 and state your point of view. Include your reasons. Always present your viewpoint in a professional and respectful manner.

From the desk of:
Julia Kingsley

Mr. Zimmerscheid sent the business cards for more refs. Mr. McLemore would like them added to our Referees folder in the Contacts file.

Add to your Tasks list that we need to request referees' Business Telephone Numbers, Fax Numbers, and E-mail Addresses when we contact them.

After you have keyed the information for each of the referees, please print two copies of the Referees folder, one in Card style and one in Phone Directory style.

JK

Knight, Boyd

Mr. Boyd Knight

970-381-7834 Home

8311 Yellowstone Road
Longmont, CO 80503

Martinez, Travis

Mr. Travis Martinez

970-381-4621 Home

4173 Huntington Court
Longmont, CO 80503

Prior, Scott

Mr. Scott Prior

970-344-9011 Home

991 Gaylord Drive
Loveland, CO 80537

Chatzky, Derek

Mr. Derek Chatzky

(970) 753-2095 Work
970-348-8855 Home
chatzkydd@networld.com

185 Kenosha Court
Fort Collins, CO 80525

Ginobli, Michael

Mr. Michael Ginobli

970-344-6602 Home

29 Yorkshire Street
Fort Collins, CO 80526

Grisham, Mitchell

Mr. Mitchell Grisham

970-381-1838 Home

311 Glacier View Road
Longmont, CO 80503

Jackson, Takika

Ms. Takika Jackson

(970) 389-1128 Work
970-546-1932 Home
jackson289@yahoo.com

801 - 10th Street
Fort Collins, CO 80524

Layton, Clark

Mr. Clark Layton

970-546-2890 Home

888 Greenway Drive
Fort Collins, CO 80525

Parker, Dyan

Ms. Dyan Parker

(970) 753-5610 Work
970-490-1208 Home
parker10@comcast.net

56 Village Park Court
Fort Collins, Co 80526

Carlisle, Jamaal

Mr. Jamaal Carlisle

970-348-2209 Home

3480 Ottawa Court
Fort Collins, CO 80526

Chen, Trenton

Mr. Trenton Chen

(970) 389-8301 Work
970-344-0739 Home
trentocc@charter.ne

736 Montana Place
Loveland, CO 80538

Goldfarb, Farrel

Mr. Farrel Goldfarb

(970) 753-1080 Work
970-546-0357 Home
fgoldfa@yahoo.com

77 Broadview
Fort Collins, CO 80521

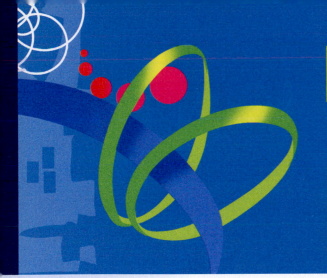

UNIT 9
Lessons 29-30

Learn to Format E-mails and Use Personal Information Management Features

Format Guides: E-mail

E-mail (electronic mail) is used in most business organizations. Because of the ease of creating and the speed of sending, e-mail messages have partially replaced the memo and the letter. Generally, delivery of an e-mail message takes place within minutes, whether the receiver is in the same building or in a location anywhere in the world. An e-mail message is illustrated below.

E-mail heading. The format used for the e-mail heading may vary slightly, depending on the program used for creating e-mail. The heading generally includes who the e-mail is being sent to (**To**), what the e-mail is about (**Subject**), and who copies of the e-mail are being sent to (**Cc**). The name of the person sending the e-mail and the date the e-mail is sent are automatically included by the software. If you don't want the person receiving the e-mail to know that you are sending a copy of the e-mail to another person, the **Bcc** feature can be used.

E-mail body. The paragraphs of an e-mail message all begin at the left margin and are SS with a DS between paragraphs.

E-mail attachments. Attachments can be included with your e-mail by using the Attachment feature of the software. Common types of attachments include word processing, database, and spreadsheet files.

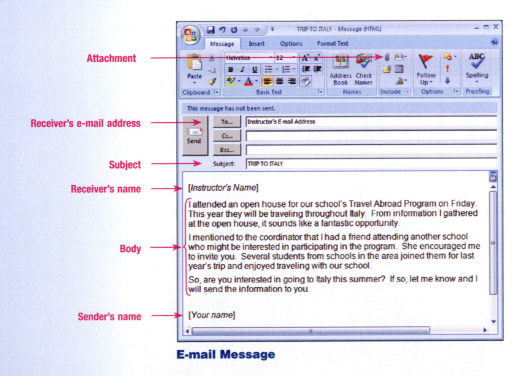

E-mail Message

Current "Hoops" Tournaments

- 3—on—3 tournaments
- Males and females
  - 11-12 years old
  - 13-14 years old
  - 15-16 years old
  - 17-18 years old
- Eight tournaments in Fort Collins

Future "Hoops" Tournaments

- 3—on—3 tournaments
- 5—on—5 tournaments
- Same age brackets for males and females
- Sponsor tournaments in:
  - Fort Collins, CO
  - Omaha, NE
  - Casper, WY
  - Ogden, UT

What Is Personal Information Management Software?

We live in a fast-paced world. Our schedules are filled with school, work, family, and extracurricular activities. We are constantly communicating with others. The latest technological advances allow us to exchange more information faster than ever before. We are inundated with information. We schedule appointments and exchange addresses, telephone numbers, cell phone numbers, fax numbers, e-mail addresses, etc.

It is critical to be organized if we are to survive in this fast-paced world. Today's personal information manager software (PIMS) provides the solution for individuals to manage this abundance of information and to be personally and professionally organized. Most PIMS have:

- an *E-mail* feature to send, receive, and manage e-mails
- a *Calendar* feature to keep track of schedules
- a *Contacts* feature to maintain information needed to contact others
- a *Tasks* feature to record items that need to be done
- a *Notes* feature to provide reminders

E-mail Inbox—Searches and Sorts

The e-mail inbox receives all incoming e-mail messages. Two features that are used to manage e-mail messages are Search and Sort. The Search feature finds specific messages based on a word, phrase, or other text.

For example, you may want to see only the messages that are from a specific person. The Inbox (Search Results) screen below shows all the messages that were received from *Parker* or that had the name *Parker* in the e-mail. Notice that the search results shown below included messages from Carter. These messages were also included in the search results because they had the word *Parker* in them.

The results of a search are normally shown by date. However, the Sort feature can be used to organize e-mail messages in a variety of ways. The more common sorts arrange e-mail messages by date, by subject, or by name of the person sending the message. The sort shown below organizes them by sender (from), thus placing all the messages from Parker together and all messages from Carter together.

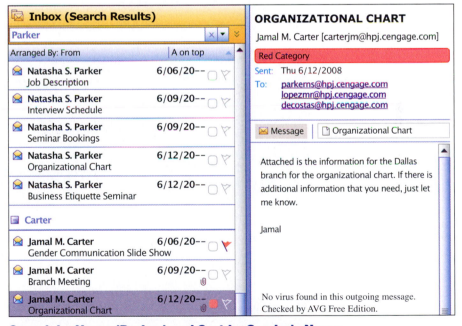

Search by Name (Parker) and Sort by Sender's Name

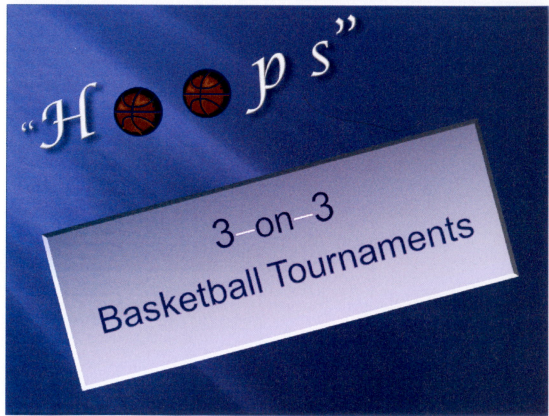

Calendar

The Calendar feature is used to record and display appointments electronically. The calendar can be displayed and printed in a variety of ways (daily, weekly, or monthly), depending on how it will be used. The daily display is illustrated at the right.

Appointments can be scheduled by using the Appointment dialog box (**CTRL + N** for *Outlook* users) or by selecting the day and then clicking in the location where you want to key the information. Recurring appointments (those that occur repeatedly) can also be scheduled. For example, if you had a music lesson every Monday at 4 p.m, you could use the Recurrence feature to automatically place the music lesson on the calendar each Monday at 4 p.m.

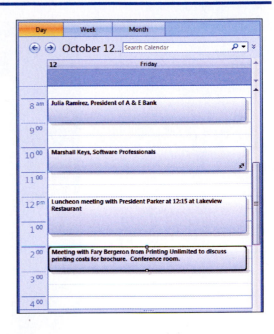

Contacts

The Contacts feature is used to store information about your associates. Generally, the person's name, business address, phone number, and e-mail address are recorded. Some software allows for recording more detailed information.

Once information has been recorded in Contacts, it can be viewed electronically or a hard copy can be printed. Hard copies can be printed in a variety of formats (card style, booklet style, phone directory style, etc.).

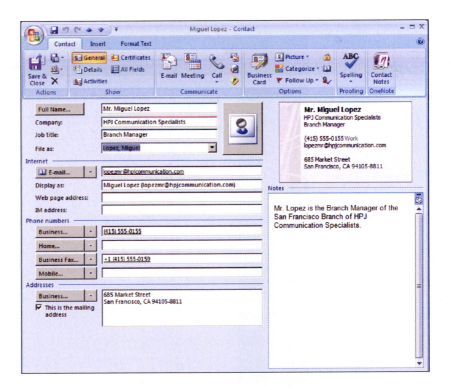

Prepare monthly calendars for June, July, and August. Use the Help feature for your software if you don't know how to prepare a calendar. Refer to the list of tournament dates I gave you (p. 486) to get the dates for August. You can choose the colors for August. Use landscape orientation and center the calendars on the page.

JK

June 20~~

"Hoops" Tournaments

Mon	Tue	Wed	Thu	Fri	Sat	Sun
					1	2
3	4	5	6	7	8	9
10	11	12	13	14	15	16
					Tournament 1	
17	18	19	20	21	22	23
					Tournament 2	
24	25	26	27	28	29	30
					Tournament 3	

July 20~~

"Hoops" Tournaments

Mon	Tue	Wed	Thu	Fri	Sat	Sun
1	2	3	4	5	6	7
					Tournament 4	
8	9	10	11	12	13	14
					Tournament 5	
15	16	17	18	19	20	21
					Tournament 6	
22	23	24	25	26	27	28
					Tournament 7	
29	30	31				

Tasks

The Tasks feature allows you to record tasks that you are responsible for completing. When a task is recorded, it is less likely to be forgotten. Completion dates and reminders can be set for each task. If no completion date is recorded, the task will appear on the TaskPad below the calendar (see below illustration). Once the task has been completed, it can be checked off as shown below.

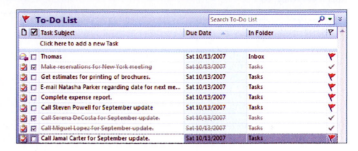

Notes

The Notes feature allows you to write yourself a reminder. The note may remain on the screen as an immediate reminder, or it may be stored for later use. Once the note is no longer needed, it can be deleted. Notes can be used for anything that a paper note could be used for.

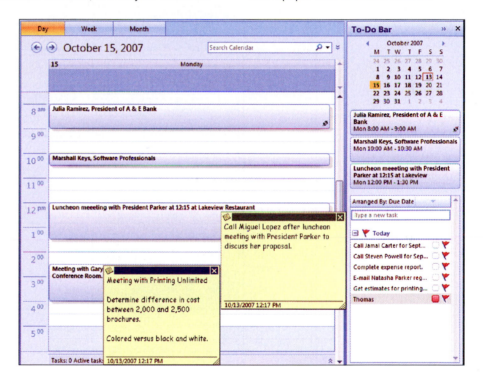

Lesson 29   FORMAT E-MAIL MESSAGES

OBJECTIVE

• To learn to format e-mail messages.

29A

Conditioning Practice

Key each line twice.

alphabet	1	Jordan placed first by solving the complex quiz in one week.
figures	2	The 389 members met on June 21, 2004, from 6:15 to 7:30 p.m.
speed	3	Jan paid the big man for the field work he did for the firm.

gwam	1'	1	2	3	4	5	6	7	8	9	10	11	12

MALES 15–16 YEARS OLD
Blue & Gold Brackets
June 15–16

	Blue Bracket Middle School Gym—Court C		Date and Time	Gold Bracket Middle School Gym—Court D	
Score	Teams			Teams	Score
	Frontiersmen Railroaders		June 15 3:00 p.m.	Cavaliers Miners	
	Rainmakers Cowboys			Ghost Shooters Pikers	
	Wolves Shooters		June 15 3:45 p.m.	Tetons Platters	
	3-Pointers Free Stylers			Pioneers Mustangs	
	Frontiersmen Rainmakers		June 15 6:00 p.m.	Cavaliers Ghost Shooters	
	Railroaders Cowboys			Miners Pikers	
	Wolves 3-Pointers		June 15 6:45 p.m.	Tetons Pioneers	
	Shooters Free Stylers			Platters Mustangs	
	Frontiersmen Cowboys		June 16 10:00 a.m.	Cavaliers Pikers	
	Railroaders Rainmakers			Miners Ghost Shooters	
	Wolves Free Stylers		June 16 10:45 a.m.	Tetons Mustangs	
	Shooters 3-Pointers			Platters Pioneers	
	3rd and 4th place games		June 16 2:00 p.m.	3rd and 4th place games	
	1st and 2nd place games		June 16 2:45 p.m.	1st and 2nd place games	
	Championship game		June 16 5:00 p.m.	Championship game	

E-mail Messages

Study the model that illustrates e-mail on p. 75.

E-mail Message 1

1. Key the model e-mail on p. 76.
2. Proofread your copy; correct all errors.

Save as: 29B EMAIL1*

*E-mail can be saved automatically in e-mail software. Use this filename only if your instructor directs you to save the message on disk.

E-mail Messages 2 and 3

1. Format and key the e-mail messages at the right; send to your instructor's e-mail address.
2. Proofread your copy; correct all errors.

Save as: 29B EMAIL2 and 29B EMAIL3

INTERNET ACTIVITY

Using an Internet search engine, gather information about a play, symphony, or concert you would like to attend. Send an e-mail inviting a friend to go with you. Include all the necessary details.

E-mail Message 2

Subject: HELP!!!

Hopefully, my sister told you that I would be e-mailing you. I'm writing a report on Mark Twain for my English class. Last weekend when Katherine was home, we were talking about this assignment. She mentioned that you were an English major and seemed to think that you had completed a course that focused on Mark Twain. She suggested that I contact you to see if you would be able to suggest some sources that I might use for this assignment.

As part of the report project, we have to read two of his books. I've already started reading *Life on the Mississippi*. Could you offer a suggestion as to what other book I should read for this assignment?

Katherine said that you are planning on coming home with her during spring break. I'll look forward to meeting you.

E-mail Message 3

Subject: WEB PAGE CREATION

As we develop our Web page, we may want to review some of those developed by other symphonies. I have already looked at several on the Web. San Francisco's was one that I felt we could model ours after.

Theirs is clear, concise, and easy to navigate. In addition to the normal sections, they have a section called "More about the San Francisco Symphony." Here they include such things as:

1. A brief history
2. The mission statement
3. Community programs
4. News items about the Symphony

To view their Web page, go to http://www.sfsymphony.org. I'll look forward to working with you at our next committee meeting.

Lesson 30   CALENDARING, CONTACTS, TASKS, AND NOTES

OBJECTIVE

• To learn to use the Calendaring, Contacts, Tasks, and Notes features.

Conditioning Practice

Key each line twice.

alphabet	1	Jack next placed my winning bid for the prized antique vase.
fig/sym	2	I deposited Lund & Lutz's $937.46 check (#2408) on April 15.
speed	3	Jan is to go to the city hall to sign the land forms for us.
gwam	1'	1 2 3 4 5 6 7 8 9 10 11 12

From the desk of:
Julia Kingsley

I attached another "Hoops" Tournament application. Ms. De Los Santos registered the Rockies for the June 15-16, June 29-30, July 13-14, and July 27-28 tournaments. Please input the information on the form in the database tables for coaches and players.

Check to see if I've updated the spreadsheet already with this information.

After you have completed entering the information in the database tables, send a letter to Ms. De Los Santos confirming receipt of her registration fees and the tournaments that the Rockies are registered for. See Job 10.
JK

"Hoops" Tournament Application

Division:	Tournament Date:	Age Level of Players:
☐ Males ■ Females	June 15-16	☐ 11–12 year age bracket ☐ 13–14 year age bracket ■ 15–16 year age bracket ☐ 17–18 year age bracket

Name of Your Team: Rockies

Coach or Contact Person (Must be 21 years of age or older):

Last Name	First	Middle Initial	E-mail Address
De Los Santos	Loretta	L.	- - - -
Street Address	City	State	ZIP	Phone
2115 Gaylord Drive	Loveland	CO	80537	303-776-1375

Player 1:

Last Name	First	Middle Initial	Age as of First Day of Tournament
De Los Santos	Maria	A.	15
2115 Gaylord Drive	Loveland	CO	80537	303-776-1375

Player 2:

Erstad	Janet	K.	16
3157 Sierra Vista Drive	Loveland	CO	80537	303-776-2909

Player 3:

Radke	Tabetha	J.	16
80 Mulberry Drive	Loveland	CO	80538	303-629-4439

Player 4:

Edmonds	Cynthia	S.	16
8880 Snowberry Place	Loveland	CO	80537	303-776-1529

Player 5:

Poquette	Paula	B.	15
672 Mustang Drive	Loveland	CO	80537	303-629-6110

Verification by Coach: To the best of my knowledge the information presented on this form is correct. Please sign below.

Signature: Loretta L. De Los Santos   Date: May 5, 20--

30B

Calendar

Using the Calendar feature, record the appointments shown at the right.

Save as: 30B CALENDAR

1. Jamison Russell, Vice President of Riley Manufacturing Company, on June 5 from 10:30 to 11:30 a.m.
2. Vivian Bloomfield, Manager of Garnett Enterprises, on June 9 from 3:30 to 4:30 p.m.
3. Department meeting from 9 to 11:30 a.m. on June 9.
4. Chamber of Commerce meeting on June 5 from 3:30 to 5 p.m.

30C

Contacts

In your contacts create a new file folder called 30C Contacts. Record the information at the right in the folder. Print a copy of the file in Business Cards view.

Save as: 30C CONTACTS

30D

Tasks

Record the tasks shown at the right using the Tasks feature.

Save as: 30D TASKS

1. Schedule an appointment with Jack Mason to discuss photo shoot.
2. Schedule a meeting with Marketing to discuss new products.
3. Turn in May expense report.
4. Meet with Erin Hollingsworth to discuss layout of annual report.

30E

Notes

Use the Notes feature to create notes for the items shown at the right.

Save as: 30E NOTES

1. Get the sales figures ready for the 3 p.m. department meeting.
2. Call Brookstone Travel Agency to change reservations.
3. Check with Paul to see if he is ready for the meeting on Friday.

Job 13—May 8

From the desk of:
Julia Kingsley

I found several copies of the blank tournament table we used last year. I've filled in a blank tournament form for the females in the 15–16-year-old bracket and attached it. Since I can't find the file, you will have to create the table shell again and input the information.

Put the heading in Cambria 26 pt.; put the subheading in Cambria 14 pt.

Save the table shell, as we will be doing similar tables for all age brackets.

JK

FEMALES 15–16 YEARS OLD
Yellow & Green Brackets
June 15–16

Yellow Bracket Middle School Gym—Court A		Date and Time	Green Bracket Middle School Gym—Court B	
Score	Teams		Teams	Score
	Columbines / Rockies	June 15 3:00 p.m.	Mavericks / Gold Nuggets	
	PikesPeakers / Bronkettes		River Rafters / Rebounders	
	Cowgirls / Larks	June 15 3:45 p.m.	Flyers / Snow Shooters	
	Jazzettes / Aggies		Vailers / Huskers	
	Columbines / PikesPeakers	June 15 6:00 p.m.	Mavericks / River Rafters	
	Rockies / Bronkettes		Gold Nuggets / Rebounders	
	Cowgirls / Jazzettes	June 15 6:45 p.m.	Flyers / Vailers	
	Larks / Aggies		Snow Shooters / Huskers	
	Columbines / Bronkettes	June 16 10:00 a.m.	Mavericks / Rebounders	
	Rockies / PikesPeakers		Gold Nuggets / River Rafters	
	Cowgirls / Aggies	June 16 10:45 a.m.	Flyers / Huskers	
	Larks / Jazzettes		Snow Shooters / Vailers	
	3rd and 4th place games	June 16 2:00 p.m.	3rd and 4th place games	
	1st and 2nd place games	June 16 2:45 p.m.	1st and 2nd place games	
	Championship game	June 16 5:00 p.m.	Championship game	

Office Features 3

For each activity, read and learn the feature described, then follow instructions at the left.

Activity 1

Format Painter

WP
- Home/Clipboard/Format Painter

Open *DF OF3 ACTIVITY1*. Use Format Painter to copy the formatting for University of Wisconsin—Eau Claire from line 1 and apply the formatting to lines 2–4.

Save as: OF3 ACTIVITY1

Use the **Format Painter** feature to copy formatting from one place and apply it in another. Click the paintbrush once to apply the formatting to one place in a document; double-click to apply it to multiple places.

1. The **University of Wisconsin—Eau Claire** was founded in 1916.
2. The **University of Wisconsin—Eau Claire** has over 10,000 students.
3. The **University of Wisconsin—Eau Claire** was rated as a "Best Midwestern College" for 2008 in *The Princeton Review*.
4. The **University of Wisconsin—Eau Claire** was rated No. 5 among the top regional public universities in the Midwest in the 2008 edition of *America's Best Colleges* (*U.S. News & World Report magazine*).

Activity 2

Sort

WP
- Home/Paragraph/Sort

Open *DF OF3 ACTIVITY2*. Use the Sort feature to alphabetize the names in ascending order and the numbers in descending order.

Save as: OF3 ACTIVITY2

Use the **Sort** feature to arrange text in alphabetical order and numbers in numerical order. Ascending order is from A to Z and 0 to 9; descending order is Z to A and 9 to 0.

Entire lists can be sorted, or parts of a list can be selected and sorted.

Ascending Order

Barrett, James
Benavides, Eduardo
Buza, Margaret
Clemens, Nancy
Flannigan, Marsha
George, Theodore

Activity 3

Center Page

WP
- Page Layout/Page Setup Dialog Box/Layout

1. Key the copy DS; center the copy horizontally and vertically.
2. Use Print Preview to see how the copy looks on the page.

Save as: OF3 ACTIVITY3

Use the **Center Page** feature to center lines of text between the top and bottom margins of the page. This feature leaves an equal (or nearly equal) amount of white space above and below the text. Inserting one hard return below the last keyed line gives the document a more centered look.

Pot of Gold

by Dianna Vermillion

Together we chased after the rainbow

To find the pot of gold; but in each other,

We found our own treasure to unfold.

[Insert one hard return]

Job 10—May 3

From the desk of:
Julia Kingsley

When a "Hoops" Tournament application is returned, send the attached e-mail message to the coach confirming that we have received it. If the coach didn't list an e-mail address, you will need to send a letter instead.

Two coaches already returned their applications. Matthew Trussoni registered for Tournaments 1, 2, and 3. Brett Perkins registered for the June 15-16 tournament.

JK

Your "Hoops" Tournament application for the June 15-16, June 22-23, and June 29-30 tournaments has been received. We are looking forward to having the Frontiersmen participate in these tournaments.

As soon as your bracket has been filled and the schedule completed, we will mail the schedule to you. If you have any questions before then, please e-mail me or call the office. Our office hours are 10:30 a.m. to 3:30 p.m. Monday through Friday.

Note: Please adjust the message to fit the situation. If someone registers for only one tournament, you will have to modify the message slightly.

Job 11—May 3

From the desk of:
Julia Kingsley

Mr. McLemore received the attached e-mail. He would like you to start a New Folder in the Contacts file; label the folder **Referees**. Enter the information for the two refs. There will be more to enter later.

JK

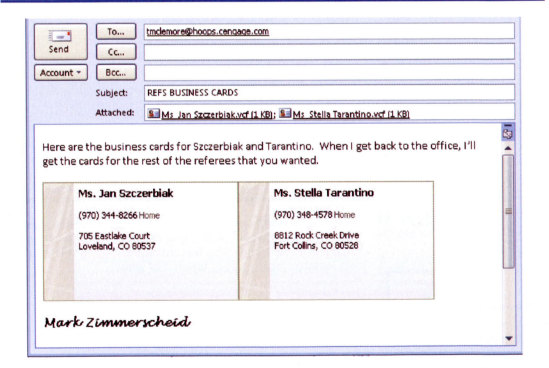

> To... tmclemore@hoops.cengage.com
> Cc...
> Bcc...
> Subject: REFS BUSINESS CARDS
> Attached: Ms_Jan Szczerbiak.vcf (1 KB); Ms_Stella Tarantino.vcf (1 KB)
>
> Here are the business cards for Szczerbiak and Tarantino. When I get back to the office, I'll get the cards for the rest of the referees that you wanted.
>
> **Ms. Jan Szczerbiak**
> (970) 344-8266 Home
> 705 Eastlake Court
> Loveland, CO 80537
>
> **Ms. Stella Tarantino**
> (970) 348-4578 Home
> 8812 Rock Creek Drive
> Fort Collins, CO 80528
>
> *Mark Zimmerscheid*

Job 12—May 3

From the desk of:
Julia Kingsley

Robert Van Bleek (Park Place Plaza) returned the advertiser form without including a check. Send a letter to him similar to the one sent for Job 6. Get the address for Park Place Plaza from the *D4 HOOPS ADVERTISERS* database file. Mr. Van Bleek wants a full-page ad.

JK

Activity 4

Thesaurus

WP
• Review/Proofing/ Thesaurus

Key the ¶ at the right DS. After keying the ¶, use the Thesaurus to replace each word in blue with one suggested in the Thesaurus.

Save as: OF3 ACTIVITY4

Use the **Thesaurus** to find words that have a similar meaning to a word in your document.

If you are writing and can't think of the right word to use or are not quite content with the word you presently have down, you can use the Thesaurus to find words that have a comparable meaning (synonym). This can be a very important tool if you do a lot of writing for your occupation.

Activity 5

Hard Page Break

WP
• Insert/Pages/Page Break

1. Key the roster signup sheet for the Red Sox shown at the right. Leave a 2" top margin on each page. Use 14-pt. Comic Sans for the font; 1.15" spacing below the title and between the numbers; 12 players will be signing up for the team.
2. Insert a hard page break at the end of the Red Sox Roster page. Create sign-up sheets for the Mets, the Dodgers, and the Cubs.

Save as: OF3 ACTIVITY5

Word processing software has two types of page breaks: **soft** and **hard**. Both kinds signal the end of a page and the beginning of a new page. The software inserts a soft page break automatically when the current page is full. You insert hard page breaks manually when you want a new page to begin before the current one is full. When a hard page break is inserted, the wp software adjusts any following soft page breaks so that those pages will be full before a new one is started. Hard page breaks do not move unless you move them. To move a hard page break, you can (1) delete it and let the software insert soft page breaks, or (2) insert a new hard page break where you want it.

RED SOX ROSTER

1.

2.

11.

12.

Activity 6

Widow/Orphan

WP
• Page Layout/Paragraph Dialog Box/Line and Page Breaks

1. Open *DF OF3 ACTIVITY6*. An orphan line appears at the top of p. 4.
2. Turn on the Widow/ Orphan feature at the beginning of that line. The line is automatically reformatted to prevent an orphan line.

Save as: OF3 ACTIVITY6

The **Widow/Orphan** feature ensures that the first line of a paragraph does not appear by itself at the bottom of a page (**orphan line**) or the last line of a paragraph does not appear by itself at the top of a page (**widow line**).

2

well organized, and easy to read.

Finally, support your report with a list of references from which you paraphrased or directly quoted. Quoting or paraphras-

Example of widow line

From the desk of:
Julia Kingsley

I have roughed out what I would like the spreadsheet for the tournament registration revenues to look like. Several other tournament registrations have come in since I did the rough. Prepare a spreadsheet that contains the information shown at the right plus the information shown below.

Team: **Cowgirls**
Amount Paid: **$400**
For Tournaments: **1, 2, 3, 4**
Coach: **Steve Chi**

Team: **Aggies**
Amount Paid: **$300**
For Tournaments: **1, 3, 8**
Coach: **Tanya Hanrath**

Team: **3-Pointers**
Amount Paid: **$100**
For Tournaments: **1**
Coach: **Marge Jenkins**

JK

From the desk of:
Julia Kingsley

Mr. McLemore is out of the office today. In order for him to stay apprised of the Fort Collins tournament revenues, he would like you to e-mail him a copy of the registration revenues spreadsheets. Compose a message to accompany the spreadsheet. His e-mail address is tmclemore@ hoops.cengage.com.

JK

Registraton Reve

Team Name	Coach	Tournament 1 June 15-16	Tournament 2 June 22-23	Tournament 3 June 29-30
Frontiersmen	Trussoni M.	$100	$100	$100
Boulder "Dashers"	Perkins B.	100		
Rockies	De Los Santos L.	100		100
Jazzettes	Woodward D.	100	100	100
Gold Nuggets	McKinney K.	100		
Cavaliers	Quaid M.	100	100	100
Mustangs	Brady S.	100		
Huskers	Reed S.	100		100
	Totals	**$800**	**$300**	**$500**

Revenues

	Tournament 4 July 6-7	Tournament 5 July 13-14	Tournament 6 July 20-21	Tournament 7 July 27-28	Tournament 8 August 3-4
0					
00					
00		100		100	
0	100	100	100	100	100
00					
		100		100	
0	100				
	$300	**$200**	**$100**	**$300**	**$100**

Activity 7

Page Numbers

 WP • Insert/Header & Footer/ Page Number

1. Open *OF3 ACTIVITY6*.
2. Number all five pages with the page number at the bottom center of the page. Hide the number on p. 1.
3. Use Print Preview to verify that the page numbers have been added (pp. 2–5) or hidden (p. 1).

Save as: OF3 ACTIVITY7

Use the **Page Number** feature to place page numbers in specific locations on the printed page. Most software allows you to select the style of number (Arabic numerals—1, 2, 3; lowercase Roman numerals—i, ii, iii; uppercase Roman numerals—I, II, III).

You can place numbers at the top or bottom of the page, aligned at the left margin, center, or right margin. Use the Different First Page feature to keep the page number from appearing on the first page.

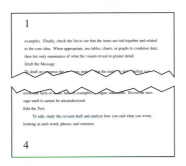
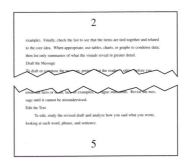
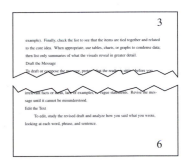

Page numbering positions

Activity 8

Indentations

 WP • Home/Paragraph Dialog Box/Indents and Spacing

1. Set margins at Wide. Use Century Gothic, 14-pt. font.
2. Key the three ¶s, indenting them as indicated.

Save as: OF3 ACTIVITY8

Use the **Indent** feature to move text away from the margin. A **left indent (paragraph indent)** moves the text one tab stop to the right, away from the left margin. A **hanging indent** moves all but the first line of a paragraph one tab stop to the right.

No indent — This example shows text that is not indented from the left margin. All lines begin at the left margin. *DS*

Left (paragraph) indent 0.5" — This example shows text that is indented from the left margin. Notice that each line begins at the indentation point. *DS*

Hanging indent 0.5" — This example shows hanging indent. Notice that the first line begins at the left margin, but the remaining lines begin at the indentation point.

Activity 9

Styles

WP • Home/Styles/select style

1. Open *DF OF3 ACTIVITY9*.
2. Select the text for the first line (Title).
3. Click on the Title style feature.
4. Select the next line of text and click on the corresponding style (Subtitle).

Repeat for each of the remaining lines of text.

Save as: OF3 ACTIVITY9

The **Styles** feature provides a collection of preset formats for titles, subtitles, headings, etc. It is easy to format text using the Styles feature. Simply select the text to be formatted and click on the style with the desired formatting.

Before Style Applied	After Style Applied
Title	Title
Subtitle	*Subtitle*
Heading 1	**Heading 1**
Heading 2	**Heading 2**
Intense Quote	*Intense Quote*
Intense Reference	INTENSE REFERENCE

"Hoops" Tournament Application

Division:	Tournament Date:	Age Level of Players:		
☐ Males ☑ Females	June 15–16	☐ 11–12 year age bracket ☑ 13–14 year age bracket ☐ 15–16 year age bracket ☐ 17–18 year age bracket		
Name of Your Team: Boulder "Dashers"				

Coach or Contact Person (Must be 21 years of age or older):

Last Name	First	Middle Initial	E-mail Address	
Perkins	Brett	P.	bpperkins@cs.com	

Street Address	City	State	ZIP	Phone
837 Roundtree Court	Boulder	CO	80302	303-347-3728

Player 1:

Last Name	First	Middle Initial	Age as of First Day of Tournament
Baxter	Barbara	A.	14

Street Address	City	State	ZIP	Phone
830 Dennison Lane	Boulder	CO	80303	303-368-2839

Player 2:

Last Name	First	Middle Initial	Age as of First Day of Tournament
Washington	Natasha	K.	13

Street Address	City	State	ZIP	Phone
892 Hazelwood Court	Boulder	CO	80302	303-368-1427

Player 3:

Last Name	First	Middle Initial	Age as of First Day of Tournament
Thurston	Jane	M.	14

Street Address	City	State	ZIP	Phone
890 Driftwood Place	Boulder	CO	80301	303-347-2225

Player 4:

Last Name	First	Middle Initial	Age as of First Day of Tournament
Santiago	Maria	A.	13

Street Address	City	State	ZIP	Phone
834 Dennison Lane	Boulder	CO	80303	303-368-7877

Player 5:

Last Name	First	Middle Initial	Age as of First Day of Tournament
Kelley	Rebecca	C.	14

Street Address	City	State	ZIP	Phone
1711 Rockmont Circle	Boulder	CO	80303	303-368-5678

Verification by Coach: To the best of my knowledge the information presented on this form is correct. Please sign below.

Signature:	Brett P. Perkins	Date:	April 16, 20--

Activity 10

Apply What You Have Learned

1. Set spacing for DS—no space before or after ¶; set top margin for 2".
2. Key headings in Title style; key text in 12 pt. font.
3. SS the second ¶; indent the ¶ 0.5" from the left.
4. Place the References on a separate page. Use the Hanging Indent feature to key the reference lines SS.
5. Use the Spelling and Grammar checker; then proofread.

Save as: **OF3 ACTIVITY10**

Famous Speeches

Many famous speeches have been delivered over the years. The content of these speeches continues to be used to inspire, motivate, and unify us today. Winston Churchill and Abraham Lincoln delivered two great examples of such speeches.

Winston Churchill served his country as soldier, statesman, historian, and journalist. His military career and work as a reporter took him to India, Cuba, and the Sudan. He was elected to Parliament in 1900, again from 1906–1908, and from 1924–1945. He held dozens of other key posts, including that of Prime Minister. (LaRocco and Johnson, 1997, 49)

Reference

LaRocco, Christine B., and Elaine B. Johnson. *British & World Literature for Life and Work.* Cincinnati: South-Western, Cengage Learning, 1997.

Activity 11

Apply What You Have Learned

1. Open file *DF OF3 ACTIVITY11.*
2. **Bold** the names of the states and change the font size to 14pt. *Italicize* the names of the state flowers.
3. At the end of each line, key (bold and italicize) the state nickname in blue.
4. Sort the lines alphabetically in ascending order by state.
5. Center the text vertically and horizontally on the page.

Save as: **OF3 ACTIVITY11**

Michigan, Lansing - *Apple Blossom* - **The Great Lakes State**

Florida, Tallahassee - *Orange Blossom* - **The Sunshine State**

Massachusetts, Boston - *Mayflower* - **Bay State**

North Carolina, Raleigh - *Dogwood* - **The Tar Heel State**

California, Sacramento - *Golden Poppy* - **The Golden State**

Washington, Olympia - *Rhododendron* - **Evergreen State**

New York, Albany - *Rose* - **Empire State**

New Jersey, Trenton - *Purple Violet* - **Garden State**

Texas, Austin - *Bluebonnet* - **Lone Star State**

Illinois, Springfield - *Violet* - **Prairie State**

Hint: After making the formatting changes to Michigan, place the insertion point on Michigan, double-click the Format Painter, and then click on each state.

Activity 12

Apply What You Have Learned

1. Set the left and right margins at 1.7"; set the top margin at 2".
2. Key each quote on a separate page using the Title style for the name and date and the Subtitle style for the quote.
3. Place page numbers at bottom center of each page.

Save as: **OF3 ACTIVITY12**

Albert Einstein (1879–1955)

"Every day I remind myself that my inner and outer life are based on the labors of other men, living and dead, and that I must exert myself in order to give in the same measure as I have received and am still receiving."

Abraham Lincoln (1809–1865)

"Nearly all men can stand adversity, but if you want to test a man's character, give him power."

Helen Keller (1880–1968)

"Character cannot be developed in ease and quiet. Only through experience of trial and suffering can the soul be strengthened, ambition inspired, and success achieved."

Winston Churchill (1874–1965)

"All great things are simple, and many can be expressed in single words: freedom, justice, honor, duty, mercy, hope."

"Hoops" Tournament Application

Division:	Tournament Date:	Age Level of Players:
■ Males ☐ Females	June 15–16	☐ 11–12 year age bracket ☐ 13–14 year age bracket ■ 15–16 year age bracket ☐ 17–18 year age bracket

Name of Your Team:	
Frontiersmen	

Coach or Contact Person (Must be 21 years of age or older):

Last Name	First	Middle Initial	E-mail Address
Trussoni	Matthew	P.	mtrussoni@home.com

Street Address	City	State	ZIP	Phone
732 Bozeman Trail	Cheyenne	WY	82009	307-376-8756

Player 1:

Last Name	First	Middle Initial	Age as of First Day of Tournament
Sinclair	Mark	A.	16

Street Address	City	State	ZIP	Phone
615 Clark Street	Cheyenne	WY	82009	307-376-7652

Player 2:

Last Name	First	Middle Initial	Age as of First Day of Tournament
Finch	Jeff	R.	15

Street Address	City	State	ZIP	Phone
879 Columbus Drive	Cheyenne	WY	82007	307-345-7733

Player 3:

Last Name	First	Middle Initial	Age as of First Day of Tournament
Remmington	Jay	M.	16

Street Address	City	State	ZIP	Phone
33 Sagebrush Avenue	Cheyenne	WY	82009	307-376-1090

Player 4:

Last Name	First	Middle Initial	Age as of First Day of Tournament
Martinez	Felipe	J.	16

Street Address	City	State	ZIP	Phone
458 Yellowstone Road	Cheyenne	WY	82009	307-345-5648

Player 5:

Last Name	First	Middle Initial	Age as of First Day of Tournament
Roberts	Reece	R.	16

Street Address	City	State	ZIP	Phone
730 Piute Drive	Cheyenne	WY	82001	307-376-9023

Verification by Coach: To the best of my knowledge the information presented on this form is correct. Please sign below.

Signature:	Matthew P. Trussoni	Date:	April 15, 20--

Format Guides: Unbound Reports

Short reports are often prepared without covers or binders. If they consist of more than one page, the pages are usually fastened together in the upper-left corner by a staple or paper clip. Such reports are called unbound reports.

Standard Margins

The standard margins for unbound reports are presented below.

	First Page	Second page and subsequent pages
Side Margins (SM)	1"	1"
Top Margin (TM)	2"	1"
Bottom Margin (BM)	Approximately 1"	Approximately 1"
Page number	Optional; bottom at center if used	Top; right-aligned

Internal Spacing of Reports

All parts of the report are SS using the 1.15 default line spacing.

Page Numbers

The first page of an unbound report may or may not include a page number. *The reports keyed for this unit will not include a page number on the first page.* On the second and subsequent pages, the page number should be right-aligned at the top of the page. The Page Number feature of your software can be used to automatically place the page number in the location you specify.

Titles and Headings

The title of the report is formatted using the Title style. The default Title style is 26-point Cambria font (Dark Blue, Text 2) with a bottom border. The default Title style will be used in this unit.

Side headings are keyed at the left margin and formatted using Heading 1 style. The default Heading 1 style is 14-pt. Cambria font (Blue, Accent 1). Capitalize the first letters of all words except prepositions in titles and side headings.

Textual (Within Text) Citations

References used to give credit for paraphrased or quoted material—called textual citations—are keyed in parentheses in the body of the report. *The textual citation method of documentation will be used for this unit.* Textual citations include the names(s) of the author(s), year of publication, and page number(s) of the material cited. *Note*: For electronic (Internet) references, textual citations include the name(s) of the author(s) and the year of publication. When there are two articles by the same author, the title of the article will also be included, as shown on p. 89.

Quotations of up to three keyed lines are enclosed in quotation marks. Long quotations (four lines or more) are indented 0.5" from the left margin. Paraphrased material is not enclosed in quotation marks, nor is it indented.

An ellipsis (. . .) is used to indicate material omitted from a quotation. An ellipsis is three periods, each preceded and followed by a space. If the omitted material occurs at the end of a sentence, include the period or other punctuation before the ellipsis.

> In ancient Greece, plays were performed only a few times a year. . . . The festivals were held to honor Dionysius in the hope that he would bless the Greeks. . . . (Prince and Jackson, 1997, 35)

Reference Lists

All references used in a report are listed alphabetically by author's last name at the end of the report on a separate page under the title References (or Bibliography or Works Cited). The References section is formatted with the same margins as the first page of the report.

The page number for the References page is placed at the top right of the page. *References* is keyed 2" from the top margin using the Title style. Begin the first line of each reference at the left margin; indent other lines 0.5" (hanging indent format).

Job 6—April 24

From the desk of:
Julia Kingsley

Ms. Radeski, manager of the Sub Shoppe, returned the advertisement form to place a half-page ad in the tournament program. She did not include payment for the advertisement. Format and key the letter I've drafted on the attached sheet.

Make a note to contact Ms. Radeski by phone if you haven't heard from her by May 15.

JK

April 24, 20--

Ms. Karin Radeski
The Sub Shoppe
88 Manchester Circle
Fort Collins, CO 80526-1118

Dear Ms. Radeski:

Thank you for returning your form for placing an advertisement in the "Hoops" Tournament Program. In order for your advertisement to appear in the program, we will need to receive your check for $400 for the half-page advertisement before we have the programs printed. Our deadline for submitting the program to the printer is May 28.

If you have any questions or would like to preview your advertisement, you can call or stop by the office between 10:30 a.m. and 3:30 p.m. Monday through Friday.

Sincerely,

Todd McLemore
Tournament Director

xx

Job 7—April 30

From the desk of:
Julia Kingsley

The first "Hoops" Tournament applications for the June 15–16 tournament arrived. Please create a database for the tournament. Set the database up so there will be two separate tables—one for Coaches and one for Players. I've listed the fields to be included in each table on the attached sheet. After you create the database, enter the information from the two applications that appear on the next two pages. Print a copy of the Players table in landscape orientation.

JK

Table for Coaches
- ✓ Division
- ✓ Age Level
- ✓ Team
- ✓ Last Name
- ✓ First Name
- ✓ Initial
- ✓ E-mail
- ✓ Street Address
- ✓ City
- ✓ State
- ✓ ZIP
- ✓ Phone

Table for Players
- ✓ Division
- ✓ Age Level
- ✓ Team
- ✓ Last Name
- ✓ First Name
- ✓ Initial
- ✓ Age
- ✓ Street Address
- ✓ City
- ✓ State
- ✓ ZIP
- ✓ Phone

Title

Effective Communicators (Title style)

1" SM

Communication is the thread that binds our society together. Effective communicators are able to use the thread (communication skills) to shape the future. To be an effective communicator, one must know how to put words together that communicate thoughts, ideas, and feelings. These thoughts, ideas, and feelings are then expressed in writing or delivered orally. Some individuals are immortalized because of their ability to put words together. A few examples of those who have been immortalized are Patrick Henry, Nathan Hale, Abraham Lincoln, and Susan B. Anthony.

Side heading

Patrick Henry (Heading 1 style)

Words move people to action. Patrick Henry's words ("I know not what course others may take; but as for me, give me liberty or give me death!") helped bring about the Revolutionary War in 1775.

Side heading

Nathan Hale (Heading 1 style)

Words show an individual's commitment. Who can question Nathan Hale's commitment when he said, "I only regret that I have but one life to lose for my country."

Side heading

Abraham Lincoln (Heading 1 style)

Words can inspire. The Gettysburg Address, delivered in 1863 by Abraham Lincoln, inspired the Union to carry on its cause. Today many Americans, still inspired by Lincoln's words, have committed to memory at least part of his address. "Four score and seven years ago, our fathers brought forth on this continent a new nation, conceived in liberty, and dedicated to the proposition that all men are created equal. Now we are engaged in a great civil war . . ."

Side heading

Susan B. Anthony (Heading 1 style)

Words bring about change. "The only question left to be settled now is: Are women persons? And I hardly believe any of our opponents will have the hardihood to say they are not. Being persons, then, women are citizens; and no state has a right to make any law, or to enforce any old law, that shall abridge their privileges or immunities."

at least 1"

Unbound Report – Word 2007

From the desk of:
Julia Kingsley

Create a Hotel Information sheet with the information shown on the attached sheet. Center the information on the page. Mark your calendar for April 26 at 2 p.m. to go over the final copy with me.

JK

Hotel Information

Hotel and Address	Price Range	Features
Country Inn 2208 Main Street Fort Collins, CO 80524-1733 Phone: 970-555-6553 E-mail: countryinn@fortcollins.com	$45-93	Nonsmoking rooms, onsite restaurant, free full breakfast, kitchenettes, whirlpool, indoor pool, fitness center
Cozy Cottage Inn 689 Center Avenue Fort Collins, CO 80526-2210 Phone: 970-555-7752	$30-$55	Cable, pets allowed, nonsmoking rooms, complimentary coffee
Four Season Suites 4817 Main Street Fort Collins, CO 80524-2056 Phone: 970-555-9805	$59-79	Suites, nonsmoking rooms, onsite restaurant, free continental breakfast, cable, in-room Jacuzzi, indoor pool, courtesy van, free local calls
The Inn 310 Main Street Fort Collins, CO 80524-1403 Phone: 970-348-7382	$49-$119	Suites, nonsmoking rooms, onsite restaurant, free continental breakfast, kitchenettes, indoor pool, fitness center
Red Cedar Inn 453 Cedar Street Fort Collins, CO 80524-1237 Phone: 970-555-5610	$30-$45	Budget motel, nonsmoking rooms, waterbeds, kitchenettes, cable, pets allowed

Insert a row in the table before the Red Cedar Inn for the information given below.

Park Place Plaza
320 Park Place Court
Fort Collins, CO 80525-1621
Phone: 970-348-1239
E-mail: mail@parkplaceplaza.com

$60-$140

Nonsmoking rooms, free continental breakfast, kitchenettes, cable, in-room whirlpools, indoor and outdoor pool, sauna, fitness center, Internet connections in rooms

Lesson 31 — UNBOUND REPORT MODEL

OBJECTIVES
- To learn format features of unbound reports.
- To process a one-page unbound report in proper format.

31A

Conditioning Practice

Key each line twice.

alphabet	1	Jack will help Mary fix the quaint old stove at the big zoo.
figures	2	Check Numbers 197, 267, 304, and 315 were cashed on June 28.
easy	3	Jan and Sydney may wish to make gowns for the civic socials.

gwam 1' | 1 | 2 | 3 | 4 | 5 | 6 | 7 | 8 | 9 | 10 | 11 | 12 |

31B

Report Formatting/Editing

Open *15C TITLES*. For each of the five stories, reformat the title, author, and first sentence in report format as shown at the right. Each entry should appear on a separate page.

Save as: 31B REPORT

2" TM

(Title) **Farmer Boy** Title style

(Author) *by Laura Ingalls Wilder* Subtitle style ↓ 2

(First sentence) It was January in northern New York State, sixty-seven years ago. Snow lay deep everywhere.

Page number centered at the bottom of the page.

1

31C — Formatting

Unbound Report

Save as: 31C REPORT

1. Read the format guides on p. 86; study the model report on p. 87.

2. Key the model report; proofread and correct errors.

Lesson 32 — UNBOUND REPORT MODEL

OBJECTIVES
- To process a two-page unbound report in proper format.
- To format textual citations in a report.
- To process references.

32A

Conditioning Practice

Key each line twice.

alphabet	1	Jessica moved quickly to her left to win the next big prize.
figures	2	Kevin used a comma in 3,209 and 4,146 but not in 769 or 805.
easy	3	The key is to name the right six goals and to work for them.

gwam 1' | 1 | 2 | 3 | 4 | 5 | 6 | 7 | 8 | 9 | 10 | 11 | 12 |

From the desk of: Julia Kingsley

A tournament packet will be sent to last year's participants and to new inquiries. We will include "Hoops" Tournament Rules (copy shown at right) and a flyer ("Hoops" Tournament Schedule Flyer) in the packet. Use your creativity and decision-making skills to create these two documents.

Format and key the copy at the right with the changes shown on the copy. Center the document on the page; DS before and after each of the main bullets.

The tournament flyer should contain relevant tournament information along with the tournament dates (given on p. 486) and appropriate graphics. The Internet has some great basketball graphics that could be imported.

Include an entry on your Task list to have tournament packets ready to mail by May 1.

JK

From the desk of: Julia Kingsley

One of the businesses that advertised in last year's program was missing from the letters I signed yesterday. Send a letter to:
Ms. Glenna McCormack
21st Century Sports
749 Center Avenue
Fort Collins, CO 80526-1394

Update the database to include 21st Century Sports. Also make the change noted on the attached letter to the database and print a copy of the letter.

JK

"Hoops" Tournament Rules

- Each team may consist of up to five players; three players will play at one time. *There will be a male division and a female division.*

- Teams will be grouped by age level. ∧Copies of participants' birth certificates must accompany registration materials. Participants may be required to verify their age at the tournament if another team requests verification. ∧

- The age-level groupings are as follows: *Age is based on first day of tournament.*

  - 11–12 years old
  - 13–14 years old
  - 15–16 years old
  - 17–18 years old
  - ~~19 and over~~ ℓ

  Players can play up one age level. For example, an 11-year-old can play on a team of 13- and 14-year-olds. However, players cannot play down; a 17-year-old player cannot play on a team of 15- and 16-year-olds.

- A team is guaranteed at least three games each tournament and may have as many as five games if they advance to the championship game. Each grade level will have a maximum of 16 teams competing. The 16 teams will be divided into two brackets. The first-place winners in each bracket will play each other for the championship of the age level.

- Games will be played on half court and will have a 25-minute time limit.

- Game scoring is as follows:

  - One point for baskets under 20 feet
  - Two points for baskets over 20 feet

Todd McLemore, Tournament Director
"Hoops" Tournaments
618 Center Street
Fort Collins, CO 80526-1392

April 17, 20--

~~Mr. Jason Dixon~~
Pizza Palace
608 Main Street
Fort Collins, CO 80524-1444

Dear Mr. ~~Dixon~~:

Mr. Justin Kummerfeld bought the Pizza Palace. Redo the letter, addressing it to Mr. Kummerfeld. Update the database.

"Hoops" will again be sponsoring 3-on-3 basketball tournaments each weekend from June 15-August 4. Over 600 basketball players plus their families and relatives will travel to Fort

Title # Samuel Clemens ("Mark Twain")

Report body

Samuel Clemens was one of America's most renowned authors. The colorful life he led was the basis for his writing. Although his formal education ended when he was 12 years old with the death of his father, his varied career interests provided an informal education, not unlike many others of his generation. Clemens brings these rich experiences to life in his writing.

Textual citation

Sam Clemens was recognized for his fiction as well as for his humor. It has been said that " . . . next to sunshine and fresh air Mark Twain's humor has done more for the welfare of mankind than any other agency" (Railton, "Your Mark Twain," 2003). By cleverly weaving fiction and humor, he developed many literary masterpieces. Some say his greatest masterpiece was "Mark Twain," a pen name (pseudonym) Clemens first used in the Nevada Territory in 1863. This fictitious name became a kind of mythic hero to

Textual citation

the American public (Railton, "Sam Clemens as Mark Twain," 2003).

Mark Twain was brought to national prominence when his first book, *The Celebrated Jumping Frog of Calaveras County and other Sketches*, was published in 1867. The book was comprised of 27 sketches, some of which had previously been published in newspapers. Some of his masterpieces that are among

1" SM

his most widely read books are *The Adventures of Tom Sawyer, Adventures of Huckleberry Finn,* and *The Prince and the Pauper*.

Side heading

The Adventures of Tom Sawyer

The Adventures of Tom Sawyer was first published in 1876. Such characters as Tom Sawyer, Aunt Polly, Becky Thatcher, and Huck Finn have captured the attention of readers for generations. Boys and girls, young and old, enjoy Tom Sawyer's mischievousness. Who can forget how Tom shared the privilege of whitewashing Aunt Polly's fence? What child isn't fascinated by the episode of Tom and Becky lost in the cave?

Side heading

Adventures of Huckleberry Finn

Adventures of Huckleberry Finn, the story about a boy who runs away from home and lives in the wild, has appealed to young and old alike since it was first published in 1885. Many of the characters included in *The Adventures of Tom Sawyer* surface again in *Huckleberry Finn*. The widow Douglas and the widow's sister, Miss Watson, provide formidable foes for Huckleberry despite their good intentions.

Children are able to live vicariously through Huck. What child hasn't dreamed of sneaking out of the house at night and running away to live a lifestyle of their own making?

About 1" BM

Unbound Report with Textual Citations, page 1 – Word 2007

(continued on next page)

From the desk of:
Julia Kingsley

Please format and key the attached as a form letter to last year's advertisers. The Advertisers' database file, DF Hoops Advertisers, can be found on your network or Web source. Print a copy of the form letter to Mona Lisa's Cuisine and Park Place Plaza.

When our letterhead design is final, you should begin using it. Make a reminder note to check with the graphic artist on Thursday to see if the letterhead is ready.

JK

April 17, 20--

\<Courtesy Title> \<First Name> \<Last Name>
\<Business>
\<Address>
\<City>, \<State> \<ZIP>

Dear \<Courtesy Title> \<Last Name>:

"Hoops" will again be sponsoring 3-on-3 basketball tournaments each weekend from June 15-August 4. Over 600 basketball players plus their families and relatives will travel to Fort Collins for each of the nine weekends. This will have a huge impact on the economy of the Fort Collins area.

We are starting to work on the program that will be distributed at the tournaments to players, coaches, and spectators. Last year you purchased advertising space in the program for \<Business>. The advertisement appeared in each of the five tournament programs. This year we have increased the number of tournaments from five to eight.

As you know, we have three different sizes of advertisements. The costs for the different advertisement sizes are as follows:

Quarter-page advertisement	$200
Half-page advertisement	$400
Full-page advertisement	$750

If you are interested in placing an advertisement in this year's tournament programs, please complete the enclosed form and return it by May 15.

Sincerely,

Todd McLemore
Tournament Director

xx

Enclosure

Textual
citation

Perhaps the greatest testimony to this book was given by Ernest Hemingway when he said, "All modern American literature comes from one book by Mark Twain called Huckleberry Finn . . . . There was nothing before. There had been nothing as good since" (Waisman, "About Mark Twain," 2003).

Unbound Report with Textual Citations, page 2 – Word 2007

3

Title

References

List of
references

Railton, Stephen. "Your Mark Twain." http://etext.lib.virginia.edu/railton/sc_as_mt/yourmt13.html (accessed October 23, 2007).

Railton, Stephen. "Sam Clemens as Mark Twain." http://etext.virginia.edu/railton/sc_as_mt/cathompg.html (accessed October 14, 2007).

Waisman, Michael. "About Mark Twain." http://www.geocities.com/swaisman/huckfinn.htm (accessed October 18, 2007).

References Page – Word 2007

"Hoops" Tournament Application

Division:	Tournament Date:	Age Level of Players:
☐ Males		☐ 11-12 year age bracket
☐ Females		☐ 13-14 year age bracket

Name of Your Team:	☐ 15-16 year age bracket
	☐ 17-18 year age bracket
	~~☐ 19 and over age bracket~~

Coach or Contact Person (Must be 21 years of age or older):

Last Name	First	Middle Initial	E-mail Address

Street Address	City	State	ZIP	Phone

Player: 1

Last Name	First	Middle Initial	~~Birth Date (Month, Day, Year)~~ Age

Street Address	City	State	ZIP	Phone

Player: 2

Last Name	First	Middle Initial	~~Birth Date (Month, Day, Year)~~ Age

Street Address	City	State	ZIP	Phone

Player: 3

Last Name	First	Middle Initial	~~Birth Date (Month, Day, Year)~~ Age

Street Address	City	State	ZIP	Phone

Player: 4

Last Name	First	Middle Initial	~~Birth Date (Month, Day, Year)~~ Age

Street Address	City	State	ZIP	Phone

Player: 5

Last Name	First	Middle Initial	~~Birth Date (Month, Day, Year)~~ Age

Street Address	City	State	ZIP	Phone

Verification by Coach: To the best of my knowledge the information presented on this form is correct. Please sign below.

Signature: Date:

shade in gold   *shade in gold*

32B

Unbound Report

Save as: 32B REPORT

1. Review the format guides on p. 86; study the model report on pp. 89–90.
2. Key the model report. Proofread and correct errors.

Optional Internet Activity

Search the Internet for more information about Samuel Clemens and his literary works. Be prepared to present orally what you found.

32C · Language Skills

Language Skills: Word Choice

1. Study the spelling and definitions of the words.
2. Key all *Learn* and *Apply* lines, choosing the correct words in the *Apply* lines.

Save as: 32C CHOICE

know (vb) to be aware of the truth of; to have understanding of	**your** (adj) of or relating to you or yourself as possessor
no (adv/adj/n) in no respect or degree; not so; indicates denial or refusal	**you're** (contr) you are

Learn 1 Did she **know** that there are **no** exceptions to the rule?

Apply 2 I just (know, no) that this is going to be a great year.

Apply 3 (Know, no), she didn't (know, no) that she was late.

Learn 1 When **you're** on campus, be sure to pick up **your** schedule.

Apply 2 (Your, You're) mother left (your, you're) keys on the table.

Apply 3 When (your, you're) out of the office, notify (your, you're) supervisor.

Lesson 33   UNBOUND REPORT MODEL

OBJECTIVES
- To process a poem.
- To process a two-page unbound report and references page in proper format.

33A

Conditioning Practice

Key each line twice.

alphabet 1 Jacob Lutz made the very quick trip to France six weeks ago.

figures 2 Only 1,359 of the 6,487 members were at the 2004 convention.

easy 3 They may turn down the lane by the shanty to their big lake.

gwam	1'	1	2	3	4	5	6	7	8	9	10	11	12

33B

WP Enrichment Activity

Format the poem shown at the right. Leave a 2" TM; center-align the body. Key the title in 14 pt. (bold), the subtitle in 12 pt. (bold blue, Accent 1), and italicize the body.

Save as: 33B POEM

Note: This poem will be used in Unit 12.

Source: *Encyclopedia Americana*, Vol. 25 (Danbury, CT: Grolier Incorporated, 2001), p. 637.

THE NEW COLOSSUS

By Emma Lazarus

Not like the brazen giant of Greek fame,
With conquering limbs astride from land to land;
Here at our sea-washed, sunset gates shall stand
A mighty woman with a torch, whose flame
Is the imprisoned lightning, and her name
Mother of Exiles. From her beacon-hand
Glows world-wide welcome; her mild eyes command
The air-bridged harbor that twin cities frame.
"Keep ancient lands, your storied pomp!" cries she
With silent lips. "Give me your tired, your poor,
Your huddled masses yearning to breathe free,
The wretched refuse of your teeming shore.
Send these, the homeless, tempest-tost to me,
I lift my lamp beside the golden door!"

"Hoops" Simulation

Read the copy at the right to familiarize yourself with the workplace simulation you are about to begin. Be prepared to produce standard business documents for a manager and company whose specialty is recreational basketball tournaments.

McLemore, Todd

Todd McLemore
"Hoops" Tournaments
Tournament Director

(970) 555-1100 Work
tmclemore@hoops.cengage.com

618 Center Street
Fort Collins, CO 80526-1392

Work Assignment

You have been hired to work part-time (two to three afternoons a week) for "Hoops." "Hoops" plans, organizes, and manages 3-on-3 basketball tournaments in Fort Collins, Colorado, throughout the summer. The owner of "Hoops" is Todd McLemore; his administrative assistant is Julia Kingsley.

The position requires the following skills:

- Word processing
- Database
- Spreadsheet
- Electronic Presentations
- Interpersonal
- Telephone
- Calendaring
- Contacts

You will be assisting Ms. Kingsley in processing all information dealing with the tournaments. The work includes:

- Processing letters and e-mail messages to advertisers, coaches, and players.
- Creating a database for advertisers, coaches, and players.
- Updating a database as registrations and advertising fees are received.
- Formatting tournament forms.
- Preparing tournament information.
- Creating a spreadsheet to keep track of tournament registrations.
- Updating spreadsheets for registration fees and refs' schedules.
- Formatting and keying tournament brackets.
- Preparing a slide show for electronic presentation.
- Preparing tournament calendars.

Ms. Kingsley will attach general processing instructions to each task you are given. If a date is not provided on the document, use the date included on the instructions. If the instructions given with the document are not sufficiently detailed, use your decision-making skills to process the document. Since "Hoops" has based its office manual on the *Century 21* textbook, you can also use the text as a reference.

Documents should be attractively formatted. You are expected to produce error-free documents, so proofread and correct your work carefully before presenting it for approval.

Mr. McLemore likes his letters formatted in block format with mixed punctuation. Use the following for the closing lines of his letters:

> Sincerely,
>
>
> Todd McLemore
> Tournament Director

Tournament Dates

"Hoops" Tournament Schedule

June 15 – August 4

For additional information contact:

Todd McLemore, Tournament Director
"Hoops" Tournaments
618 Center Street
Fort Collins, CO 80526-1392

Tournament Dates:

June 15-16	July 13-14
June 22-23	July 20-21
June 29-30	July 27-28
July 6-7	August 3-4

Unbound Reports

Report 1

Open *DF 33C REPORT* and finish keying the report from the text at the right. Refer to the guidelines on p. 86 as needed.

After you are done keying, use the format painter to copy the formatting for the *Statue of Liberty* heading and apply it to *Central Park* and *Yankee Stadium* headings. Copy the formatting for the *New York City Today* heading and apply it to *Summary* heading.

Prepare a References page from the information below.

Fodor's New York City, 2nd Edition. New York: Fodor's Travel Publications, 2006.

"History of New York City," http://en.wikipedia.org/wiki/History_of_New_York_City (accessed 24 October 2007).

Save as: 33C REPORT

Note: This report will be used in Unit 12.

Statue of Liberty. The Statue of Liberty, located in New York Harbor, is a symbol of political freedom. The statue was given to the United States by the people of France in 1886. The statue was often what the immigrants first saw as they came to the United States from Europe.

Central Park. Central Park provides an opportunity to get away from the hectic pace of New York City and relax. A terrific view of the skyscrapers is always available as a backdrop to the park. The park is perfect for biking, jogging, and rollerblading. Statues throughout the park memorialize famous individuals such as Beethoven and Shakespeare.

Yankee Stadium. New York has many sports teams. The Yankees, however, with their rich tradition, is the team that brings so much attention to New York City. Yankee Stadium, "The House That Ruth Built," is a landmark in the city. When you think of baseball, you think of the Yankees, winners of 26 World Series.

Summary

New York City is like no other city in the United States. It is a hub of activity, offering something for everyone—shopping, entertainment, dining. The city is well known for its extraordinary cultural activities, numerous landmarks, and variety of sporting activities. New York has it all!

Lesson 34   UNBOUND REPORT MODEL

OBJECTIVES

- To process a two-page unbound report in *Word 2003* format (traditional style).
- To process a references page.

Conditioning Practice

Key each line twice.

alphabet	1	Opal Weber made five or six quick flights to Zurich in July.
figures	2	The firm had 15 accountants in 1987 and 134 in 2006 or 2007.
easy	3	Orlando made the panel suspend the pay of the six officials.

gwam	1'	1	2	3	4	5	6	7	8	9	10	11	12

From the desk of Audry Bates

Use the information at the right and in DF 161 JOB17 to prepare a draft of a program. Format the program on two pages, using 8.5" x 11" paper in landscape orientation. These two pages will be folded into a four-page program with each page measuring 5½" x 8½".

AB

Save as: 161 JOB17A and 161 JOB17B

Outside Back Cover

- *List names of the Class Officers*
  - Audry Chomas Bates, President
  - Blaine Check, Vice President
  - Gaynell Eastwood, Secretary
  - Paul Thompson, Treasurer
  - Janice Bondi Aberle, Historian
- *List names of Reunion Committee Members in alpha order*
  - Janice Bondi Aberle
  - Audry Chomas Bates
  - Fred Brydebell
  - Blaine Check
  - Gaynell Eastwood
  - Tom Stark
  - Helen Linton Ward
  - Barbara Staffen Wills

Outside Front Cover

- 25-Year Reunion
- Salk High School
- Class of 19--
- Saturday, August 15, 20--
- Highlands Country Club, Elizabeth, PA

Job 18

From the desk of Audry Bates

Create a report from the database that includes all the fields. Sort the records by state, then by last name in ascending order. Use stepped layout and landscape orientation. Use Concourse style. Use Address by State for the heading.

AB

Address by State

State	Last Name	Title	First Name	Maiden	Address Line 1	City
CA						
	Aiken	Mr.	Eugene		17735 Owens Street	Fontana
	Pascoe	Ms.	Linda		636 Highland Avenue	Half Moon Bay
CT						
	Sutton	Mr.	Kurt		10 Sherry Drive	East Hampton
FL						
	Juno	Mrs.	Janice	Horn	State Route 3, Box 280	DeLand
	Sutes	Mr.	Roy		12360 SW 109th Street	Miami
IL						
	Dyer	Mr.	Thomas		631 Mildred Avenue	Glen Ellyn
	Gilbert	Mrs.	Carol	Uveges	1420 Concord Drive	Downers Grove
	Thompson	Mr.	Paul		813 sunnydale Drive	Streamwood
IN						
	Sorg, III	Mr.	William		1821 Lincoln Street	Portage
KY						
	Achtzehn	Mr.	William		713 Issac Shelby Circle	Frankfort
MD						
	Nundini	Mr.	Larry			
MI						
	Malady	Mrs.				

IMMIGRATION TO AMERICA ↓2

America has often been called the "melting pot." The name is derived from America's rich tradition of opening its doors to immigrants from all over the world. These immigrants came to the United States looking for something better. Most of them did not possess wealth or power in their home countries. Most were not highly educated. Other than these few commonalities of what they didn't possess, their backgrounds were vastly different. The thread, however, that bound these immigrants together was their vision of improving their current situation.

Emma Lazarus, in a poem entitled "The New Colossus," which is inscribed on the pedestal of the Statue of Liberty, tells of the invitation extended to those wanting to make America their home. " . . . 'Give me your tired, your poor, your huddled masses yearning to breathe free,' . . ." (*Encyclopedia Americana*, 2001, Vol. 25, 637).

Immigration Before 1780

Many have accepted the invitation to make America their home. Most of the immigrants before 1780 were from Europe.

The "melting pot" concept can be better understood by the following quote. "I could point out to you a family whose grandfather was an Englishman, whose wife was Dutch, whose son married a French woman, and whose four sons have wives of different nations" (Luedtke, 1992, 3).

Recent Immigration

Recent immigration patterns have changed; the reasons have not. Individuals and families still come to the United States with a vision of improving their lives. The backgrounds of

Job 13

From the desk of Audry Bates

Design a document to record reservations, and then enter the ones at the right. Make it attractive by using font sizes, colors, borders, and shading. Add an appropriate title as a header. Insert a footer that contains a page number and the current date. Sort the data alphabetically by last name.

AB

Save as: 161 JOB13

First	Maiden	Last	Spouse	Guest	Check Number	Amount Paid
Tom		Stange			3275	$35
Janice	Bondi	Aberle	David		2371	$70
Audry	Chomas	Bates	Tom		3571	$70
Blaine		Check	Karen		564	$70
Gaynell		Eastwood		Jerry	116	$70
Louise		Moore			783	$35
Ruth	Young	Todd			2430	$35
Helen	Linton	Ward	Bill		457	$70
Bill		Achtzhen		Mary	587	$70
Guy		Dolata	Jill		7889	$70
Jackie		Thomas		Gary	543	$70

Job 14

From the desk of Audry Bates

There's a worksheet in DF 161 JOB14-WS. Use it to create a pie chart. Include a chart title and legend. Paste the chart at the end of the memo (DF 161 JOB14). Size and center the chart to make it attractive; add your reference initials to the memo.

AB

Save as: 161 JOB14

Job 15

From the desk of Audry Bates

I keyed the start of the May newsletter on DF 161 JOB15. I'd like to have the title span the width of the page and equal-width columns separated by vertical lines. You decide all other formatting features. Insert the three paragraphs at the right as text boxes at appropriate places within the newsletter. I'll review it when you get this portion done.

AB

Save as: 161 JOB15

Want to serve on a committee? Call Janice Bondi Aberle at 412-555-0189 or e-mail her at aberle@starnet.com.

Check out http://www.salkalumni.org to see who is coming to the reunion and how to get good deals at local hotels.

Check out http://www.salkalumni.org to find out how you can sign up for the August 14 golf outing, 5K walk, or tennis matches.

Job 16

From the desk of Audry Bates

Open either the worksheet named 161 JOB3 or DF 161 JOB16 and insert the following note below the worksheet using word processing software.

AB

Save as: 161 JOB16

Blaine, Gaynell, and Janice:

Here's a copy of the budget that we approved at our meeting on February 23. Please review it and see if you believe it needs to be revised. We can discuss your thoughts at our next meeting. Thanks.

Audry

today's immigrants expand beyond the European borders. Today they come from all over the world. At a 1984 oath-taking ceremony in Los Angeles, there were nearly a thousand individuals from the Philippines, 890 from Mexico, 704 from Vietnam, 110 from Lebanon, 126 from the United Kingdom, and 62 from Israel. Although not as large a number, there were also individuals from Lithuania, Zimbabwe, and Tanzania (Luedtke, 1992, 3).

Unbound Report with Textual Citations, page 2 – Word 2003

Word 2003. The REFERENCES title is bolded, centered, and keyed in ALL CAPS in 14 pt. 2" from TM.

REFERENCES

Encyclopedia Americana, Vol. 25. "Statue of Liberty." Danbury, CT: Grolier Incorporated, 2001.

Luedtke, Luther S., ed. *Making America*. Chapel Hill: University of North Carolina Press, 1992.

References Page – Word 2003

34B Formatting

Unbound Report

Save as: 34B REPORT

Note: This report will be used in Unit 12.

1. Review the notes on the top of p. 93. Study the model report on pp. 93–94.
2. Key the model report using the *Office Word 2003* Look template. Access the template by opening a new document, clicking on Installed Templates, and clicking on Office Word 2003.
3. Correct errors as you key

Note: Poem shown in its entirety on p. 91.

Internet Activity
Search the Web for additional information about immigration.

Be prepared to make a few comments to your classmates about what you found.

From the desk of
Audry Bates

Create a query of the database to get the classmates who live in Elizabeth or McKeesport. Do not include their maiden names in the query.
(Save as: Elizabeth or McKeesport.) Key the letter (Save as: 161 JOB11-MAIN1) and merge it with the query you just created. Exclude Auberle, Check, Eastwood, and me from the merge. Print the first letter for me to review.

AB

Save merged letters as:
161 JOB11-LETTERS

From the desk of
Audry Bates

Print mailing labels for the letters. Use label Vendors: Avery US Letter, Product No.: 5160.

AB

Save as: 161 JOB11
LABELS

Job 12

From the desk of
Audry Bates

Mrs. Aberle has found a DJ for the reunion, and I need to send a confirmation letter on our letterhead and a $100 deposit. Address the letter to:
Attention Business Manager
Music Selections
2539 Rose Garden Road
Pittsburgh, PA 15220-1880
Add **CLASS OF 19--**
REUNION COMMITTEE *as a company name in the closing lines.*

AB

Save as: 161 JOB12

March 5, 20--

<<AddressBlock>>
<<GreetingLine>>:

As you may have learned, the Salk High School Class of 19-- is having its 25-year reunion on August 15, 20--, at the Highlands Country Club.

Presently, the Class Officers who still live in the area are organizing the event, but your help is needed. Will you serve on a committee? Help is needed with registration, gathering door prizes from neighborhood businesses, and table decorations.

<<First Name>>, please give Janice Bondi Aberle (412.555.0189), Blaine Check (412.555.0102), Gaynell Eastwood (412.555.0172), or me (412.555.0113) a call to let us know the committee to which you want to be assigned.

Since this is such a major milestone in our lives, we expect a large turnout for the reunion. I hope we can count on you.

Sincerely,

Audry Chomas Bates, Chair
Reunion Committee

xx

April 5, 20--

Ladies and Gentlemen

CONTRACT FOR SERVICES

This letter confirms that Salk High School's Class of 19-- will employ one of your disc jockeys to play music at our 25th reunion on August 15, 20--.

The reunion will be held at Highlands Country Club, 619 Walker Road, Elizabeth, PA. You are to provide music from 8:30 p.m. until 1 a.m. for $350. The enclosed $100 check is the deposit required to reserve your services. The $250 balance will be paid at the end of the evening's activities.

If you have any questions or need additional information, call me at 412-555-0113. Thank you.

Sincerely
Audry Chomas Bates, Chair

xx
Enclosure

Office Features 4

For each activity, read and learn the feature described, then follow instructions at the left.

Activity 1

Insert Table

WP • Insert/Tables/Table

1. Create and key the table shown at the right.
2. Key the main heading in ALL CAPS, bold, and centered above the table.

Main Heading: AMERICAN LEAGUE MOST VALUABLE PLAYERS

Save as: **OF4 ACTIVITY1**

Use the **Insert Table** command to create a grid for arranging information into rows and columns. Tables consist of vertical columns and horizontal rows. **Columns** are labeled alphabetically from left to right; **rows** are labeled numerically from top to bottom. The crossing of columns and rows makes **cells**.

When text is keyed in a cell, it wraps around in that cell—instead of wrapping around to the next row. A line space is added to the cell each time the text wraps around.

To fill in cells, use the TAB key or right arrow key to move from cell to cell in a row and from row to row. (Tapping ENTER will simply insert a blank line space in the cell.) To move around in a filled-in table, use the arrow keys, TAB, or the mouse (click the desired cell).

Year	Player	Team
2003	Alex Rodriguez	Rangers
2002	Miguel Tejada	Athletics
2001	Ichiro Suzuki	Mariners
2000	Jason Giambi	Athletics
1999	Ivan Rodriguez	Rangers
1998	Juan Gonzalez	Rangers
1997	Ken Griffey, Jr.	Mariners

Activity 2

Insert and Delete Rows and Columns

WP • Table Tools/Layout/Rows & Columns/Insert or Delete

1. Open the table you created for Activity 1 (*OF4 ACTIVITY1*).
2. Insert the information for 2004–2006.
3. Delete the 1997–1999 award winners.
4. Delete the column showing the team the award winner played for.
5. Undo the last change made to restore the deleted column.

Save as: **OF4 ACTIVITY2**

The **Table Tools Layout** tab can be used to edit or modify existing tables. The commands found in the **Rows & Columns** group are used to insert and delete rows in an existing table.

A cell, row, column, or entire table can be deleted using the Delete command. Use the Insert commands to place rows above or below existing rows and columns to the right or left of existing columns.

AMERICAN LEAGUE MOST VALUABLE PLAYERS

Year	Player	Team
2006	Justin Morneau	Twins
2005	Alex Rodriguez	Yankees
2004	Vladimir Guerrero	Angels
2003	Alex Rodriguez	Rangers
2002	Miguel Tejada	Athletics
2001	Ichiro Suzuki	Mariners
2000	Jason Giambi	Athletics

Job 8

From the desk of
Audry Bates

Gaynell prepared this information that will become a web page we will post later. Arrange it attractively on one page and save it as a web page.

AB

Save as: 161 JOB8

25th Reunion for Salk High School Class of 19--

August 15, 20--

Highlands Country Club

6:30 p.m. reception

7:30 p.m. dinner

8:30 p.m. to 1 a.m. dancing and conversation

To save your spot, e-mail your name (First, Last, and Maiden, if applicable), address, telephone number, and name of spouse/guest to:

Blaine Check (checkb@hostnet.com)

Payment of $35 per person is due by July 15. Make check payable to 19-- Class Reunion and mail it to:

Blaine Check, 922 Grant Street, Elizabeth, PA 15037

Classmates Attending	"Lost… Classmates	Highlands Country Club

---

Job 9

From the desk of
Audry Bates

Design a letterhead for our reunion, using this information.

AB

Save it as a building block called 161 JOB9.

Salk High School Class of 19-- 25th Reunion

3393 Long Hollow Road   Elizabeth, PA 15037-9823   412-555-0113

Job 10

From the desk of
Audry Bates

Key this letter on our letter-head; date it March 1; and address it to **Mr Ronald Pimilo, 780 Peairs Road, Elizabeth, PA 15037-5779.** Use **Audry Chomas Bates, Chair, Reunion Committee,** in the closing.

AB

Save as: 161 JOB10

The Salk High School Class of 19-- is holding its 25th reunion on August 15, 20--, at 6:30 p.m. at the Highlands Country Club, and the Reunion Committee wants you and your wife, Carole, to be our guests for the evening.

We expect to have a great turnout of classmates for this major milestone in our lives. As our class sponsor for four years, you have had the opportunity to know us very well as we worked on our various fundraisers and activities like the Junior Prom and Senior Day.

I will telephone you within a few days to see if you will be able to attend and to give you more details.

(Postscript) Gene Aiken and Fred Brydebell have said that if you don't come, they're not coming! I'm sure others feel the same way!

Activity 3

Table Styles and Heading Styles

WP • Table Tools/Design/Table Styles/Select Style

WP • Home/Styles/Select Style

1. Open the table you created for Activity 2 (*OF4 ACTIVITY2*).
2. Format the table in the table style Light Shading — Accent 1.
3. Use Heading 2 style for the main heading for the table.
4. Center the main heading above the table.

Save as: OF4 ACTIVITY3

After a table has been created, the commands found on the **Table Tools Design** tab can be used to change the table style.

Before or after text has been keyed, the **Styles** group on the **Home** tab can be used to enhance the appearance of the title or other text within the table.

AMERICAN LEAGUE MOST VALUABLE PLAYERS

Year	Player	Team
2006	Justin Morneau	Twins
2005	Alex Rodriguez	Yankees
2004	Vladimir Guerrero	Angels
2003	Alex Rodriguez	Rangers
2002	Miguel Tejada	Athletics
2001	Ichiro Suzuki	Mariners
2000	Jason Giambi	Athletics

Activity 4

Merging Cells and Changing Column Width

WP • Table Tools/Layout/Merge/Merge Cells

1. Open the file *DF OF4 ACTIVITY4*.
2. Merge the cells of row 1.
3. Adjust the column widths so that the name of the sales representative fits on one line. Adjust the width of other columns as needed.

Save as: OF4 ACTIVITY4

Use the **Merge Cells** command to join two or more cells into one cell. This feature is useful when information in the table spans more than one column or row. The main title, for example, spans all columns.

In a newly created table, all columns are the same width. You can change the width of one or more columns to accommodate entries of unequal widths.

SALES REPORT					
Sales Rep.	Territory	Jan.	Feb.	March
Juan Ramirez	Washington	12,325	13,870	12,005
Shawn Hewitt	Oregon	15,680	17,305	7,950
Maria Hernandez	Idaho	9,480	16,780	14,600
Cheryl Updike	Washington	10,054	8,500	17,085
Tanya Goodman	Washington	19,230	11,230	15,780
Jason Graham	Oregon	15,900	16,730	9,290
Carolyn Plummer	Idaho	20,370	13,558	12,654
Scott Bowe	Idaho	15,750	14,560	16,218
Brandon Olson	Oregon	14,371	11,073	19,301
Laura Chen	Washington	17,320	9,108	18,730

From the desk of
Audry Bates

Key these minutes that
Gaynell Eastwood wrote at
the 2/23 meeting.
AB

Save as: 161 JOB6

From the desk of
Audry Bates

I drafted a news release for
the reunion, but I didn't have
a chance to proofread it.
Please open DF 161 Job7 and
use track changes to make
any necessary corrections or
revisions to the content.
AB

Save as: 161 JOB7

CLASS OF 19-- REUNION COMMITTEE MEETING

February 23, 20--

Participants: Audry Bates, Chair; Janice Aberle; Blaine Check; Gaynell Eastwood

1. The reunion was set for Saturday, August 15, 20--, from 6:30 p.m. to 1 a.m. at the Highlands Country Club.

2. These dates and major activities were established:
   - On February 25, Audry will place a $100 deposit at Highlands Country Club to reserve the facilities.
   - Audry and Blaine will prepare and send first mailing by March 31.
   - Janice will select a DJ by April 30.
   - Gaynell will print tickets and order decoration material and supplies by June 30.
   - Audry and Blaine will prepare and make second mailing by June 30.

3. The budget was approved. It projects revenues of $3,500 from 100 people, each paying $35. (Refreshments at the reception are not included in the $35.) Expenses are projected to be $3,410. If there is an excess of revenue over expenses, the amount will be donated to the Salk High School Alumni Association.

4. The members submitted their updated address lists; and after a lengthy discussion, it was decided that the revised data source table would be used for the first mailing.

5. Mr. Ronald Pimilo, sponsor for the Class of 19--, and his wife will be invited to attend the reunion as our guests.

6. Gaynell will draft information to be posted on the Salk High School Alumni Association's Web page. It should suggest those planning on attending to e-mail information to Blaine and indicate that payment is expected by July 15.

7. The next meeting is set for March 28 at 9 a.m. at Mike's Restaurant. Each member is to make an oral progress report.

Activity 5

Make Table Formatting Changes

1. Open the file *OF4 ACTIVITY4* created in Activity 4.
2. Make the formatting changes given below.
   a. Bold and center the main heading and column headings.
   b. Center-align column B.
   c. Right-align columns C, D, and E.
   d. Bold and italicize the highest sales figure for each month.
   e. Apply an appropriate Table Style design.

Save as: OF4 ACTIVITY5

The formatting changes (bold, italicize, different alignment, etc.) that you have learned to make to text can also be made to the text within a table. You can do this prior to keying the text into the table, or it can be done after the text has been keyed. After the table is complete, make changes by selecting the cell (or row or column) to be changed and then selecting the software command to make the change.

SALES REPORT				
Sales Rep.	**Territory**	**Jan.**	**Feb.**	**March**
Juan Ramirez	Washington	12,325	13,870	12,005
Shawn Hewitt	Oregon	15,680	*17,305*	7,950
Maria Hernandez	Idaho	9,480	16,780	14,600
Cheryl Updike	Washington	10,054	8,500	17,085
Tanya Goodman	Washington	19,230	11,230	15,780
Jason Graham	Oregon	15,900	16,730	9,290
Carolyn Plummer	Idaho	*20,370*	13,558	12,654
Scott Bowe	Idaho	15,750	14,560	16,218
Brandon Olson	Oregon	14,371	11,073	*19,301*
Laura Chen	Washington	17,320	9,108	18,730

Activity 6

Centering Tables

1. Open *OF4 ACTIVITY5*.
2. Center the table vertically and horizontally.

Save as: OF4 ACTIVITY6

Use the **Center alignment** command to center a table horizontally on the page. This will make the side margins (right and left margins) equal. See illustration on p. 99.

Use the **Page Vertical alignment** or **Center Page** feature to center a table vertically on the page. This will make the top and bottom margins equal. See illustration on p. 99.

Activity 7

Change Cell Size & Alignment

WP
• Layout/Cell Size/Specify Cell Size

WP
• Layout/Alignment/Specify Alignment Type

1. Open *OF4 ACTIVITY6*. Change row height as follows: title row, 0.6"; column headings, 0.5"; other rows, 0.4".
2. Change vertical alignment as follows: main heading and column headings, center; other rows, bottom alignment.

Save as: OF4 ACTIVITY7

Use the **Layout Cell Size** commands to change the height of the rows in a table. The height of all the rows of the table can be changed to the same height, or each row can be a different height.

Use the **Layout Alignment** commands to change the alignment of the text in cells. The text within a cell can be top-aligned, center-aligned, or bottom-aligned.

Cell Alignment and Row Height

Top Left – .3"	Top Center – .3"	Top Right – .3"
Center Left – .4"	Center – .4"	Center Right – .4"
Bottom Left – .5"	Bottom Center – .5"	Bottom Right – .5"

From the desk of Audry Bates

Here's a budget that I need for the 2/23 meeting. Use spreadsheet software to calculate the row and column totals. The cash on hand is computed by adding the cash on hand at the end of the last month to the month's revenues and then subtracting the month's expenses. Make the budget easy to read and colorful.

AB

Save as: 161 JOB3

CLASS OF 19-- REUNION BUDGET	February	March	April	May	June	July	August	Total
Revenue								
$35/person	$350	$350	$350	$700	$875	$525	$350	
Expenses								
Food	$100						$2,250	
DJ			$100				$250	
Tickets					$25			
Decorations					$25	$25	$100	
Door Prizes						$200		
Flyers		$40			$40			
Paper	$10				$25			
Labels	$30							
Name Badges							$30	
Postage		$45			$45			
Sponsor							$70	-
Total Expenses								
Cash on Hand								-

CLASS OF 19-- REUNION COMMITTEE MEETING
February 23, 20--, 9 a.m.
Third Street Diner

1. Call meeting to order.
2. Confirm reunion date, time, and place.
3. Establish time line for activities.
4. Review and approve budget.
5. Finalise database.
6. Establish next meeting date and ajourn.

From the desk of Audry Bates

Here are the missing addresses plus a couple of address changes that need to be made in our database. Use the search feature to quickly find each person.

AB

Save as: 161 JOB5-DATA

Last Name	Address 1	City	State	Postal Code
Amos	1374 Foxwood Drive	Monroeville	PA	15146-4522
Brydebell	6229 Smithfield Street	Boston	PA	15135-8873
Dale	602 Elizabeth Avenue	Elizabeth	PA	15037-1956
Dyer	631 Mildred Avenue	Glen Ellyn	IL	60137-2061
Malady	4265 Quick Road	Holly	MI	48442-4016
Nundini	4513 Orangewood Lane	Bowie	MD	20715-1160
Pascoe	636 Highland Avenue	Half Moon Bay	CA	94019-6339
Stange	258 Hope Lane	Monongahela	PA	15063-2593
Tepe	332 Bailey Road	Lordstown	OH	44481-0635
Todd	734 Holly Hills Drive	Biloxi	MS	39532-7337
Zezeck	5835 Garden Oak Circle	Memphis	TN	38210-1920

Activity 8

Table Sort

WP
- Table Tools/Layout/ Data/Sort

1. Open *OF4 ACTIVITY7*.
2. Sort the table by Territory in descending order as shown.
3. Sort the table again by March sales in ascending order.

Save as: OF4 ACTIVITY8

Activity 9

Converting Tables to Text

WP
- Table Tools/Layout/Data/ Convert to Text/Tabs

1. Open *OF4 ACTIVITY8*.
2. Convert the table to text, separating text with tabs.

Save as: OF4 ACTIVITY9

The **Sort** feature arranges text in a table in a specific order. The feature will sort alphabetic or numeric text in ascending (A to Z, 0 to 9) or descending (Z to A, 9 to 0) order.

The **Convert to Text** feature converts a table to regular text.

SALES REPORT				
Sales Rep.	Territory	Jan.	Feb.	March
Juan Ramirez	Washington	12,325	13,870	12,005
Cheryl Updike	Washington	10,054	8,500	17,085
Tanya Goodman	Washington	19,230	11,230	15,780
Laura Chen	Washington	17,320	9,108	18,730
Shawn Hewitt	Oregon	15,680	*17,305*	7,950
Jason Graham	Oregon	15,900	16,730	9,290
Brandon Olson	Oregon	14,371	11,073	*19,301*
Maria Hernandez	Idaho	9,480	16,780	14,600
Carolyn Plummer	Idaho	*20,370*	13,558	12,654
Scott Bowe	Idaho	15,750	14,560	16,218

*Table shown sorted by **Territory** in descending order.

Activity 10

Apply What You Have Learned

1. Open the file *DF OF4 ACTIVITY10*.
2. Insert a column for the dates; center and key the heading and dates.
3. Merge cells in row 1.
4. Bold and center main heading and column headings.
5. Adjust column widths to fit the information in each cell on one line.
6. Sort the Date column in ascending order.
7. Select a table style to enhance the table.
8. Adjust vertical alignment in cells: main heading and column headings, center; other rows, bottom alignment.
9. Center table on the page.

Save as: OF4 ACTIVITY10

INVENTIONS		
Date	Invention	Inventor
1877	Phonograph	Thomas Edison
1805	Railroad locomotive	Richard Trevithick
1846	Sewing machine	Elias Howe
1867	Revolver	Samuel Colt
1820	Calculating machine	Charles Babbage
1867	Typewriter	Christopher Sholes

OBJECTIVES

- To demonstrate your ability to integrate your knowledge and skills.
- To demonstrate your ability to solve problems and make correct decisions.

161–165A

Conditioning Practice

Key each line twice daily.

alphabet 1 Mary Jane quickly realized that the beautiful gown was expensive.

fig/sym 2 After a 45-minute delay, Tour 8374 left from Gate 26 at 1:09 p.m.

speed 3 When I visit the man in a wheelchair, we may go to the town mall.

gwam 1' | 1 | 2 | 3 | 4 | 5 | 6 | 7 | 8 | 9 | 10 | 11 | 12 | 13 |

161–165B

Work Assignments

Job 1

From the desk of
Audry Bates

I started a Salk Alumni Association database with the mailing information for our 25-year class reunion. Please add these classmates to it. Before you start, create a form. That will make data easier to enter and verify once entered. After you have entered this information to the db, sort the file in alpha order by last name, then first name.

AB

Save as: 161 JOB1-DATA

Mr James Wythe 1401 Second Avenue Beaver PA 15009-7667	Ms Mary O'Donnell Box 142 Bunola PA 15020-3210	Ms Louise Moore 6220 Smithfield Street Boston PA 15135-1098
Mrs Sue Dainty Lewis 298 Mohawk Drive McKeesport PA 15135-8429	Mrs Janice Horn Juno State Route 3, Box 280 DeLand FL 32720-2863	Ms Kimberly White 535 Lewis Run Road Clairton PA 15025-1262
Mrs Jane Resh O'Hare 6320 Holsing Street Boston PA 15135-4321	Mr Paul Thompson 813 Sunnydale Drive Streamwood IL 60107-2468	Ms Jackie Thomas 3305 Oakland Avenue McKeesport PA 15132-7913
Mrs Tina Smith Gray 810 Golfview Drive McKeesport PA 15135-0641	Mrs Ann Toth Booth 4114 Faith Court Arlington VA 22311-0934	Mr Harry Zadmik 1930 N Evans Street McMinnville OR 97128-4800
Mr Martin Megela 1388 Fayette Street Donora PA 15033-3974	Mr Tim Justin 111 Sandro Street Indiana PA 15701-4085	Mrs Sandy Lutes May 2540 W Second Street Brooklyn NY 11223-2863
Mr Paul Tagliari 600 Amberson Ave Pittsburgh PA 15232-9135	Mrs Ruth Young Todd 115 Ground Oaks Lane Chicora PA 16025-8024	Mrs Freda Rippel Ruby 37 Colonial Drive McKeesport PA 15135-5432

Job 2

From the desk of
Audry Bates

Key this memo from me to the Reunion committee Members. Include 161 JOB1-DATA as an enclosure.

AB

Save as: 161 JOB2

TO: *Janice Aberle, Blaine Check, and Gaynell Eastwood*

FROM: *Audry Bates*

DATE: *Current date*

SUBJECT: FEBRUARY 23, 20-- MEETING

Please plan to attend the Saturday, February 23, 20--, meeting at the Third Street Diner at 9 a.m. Among other things, we need to complete the database so we can send our first mailing soon. I suggest we each do an Internet search to verify that the information is current. Will each of you take about 20 names from the enclosed list (Janice--A through C; Blaine--D through L; and Gaynell--M through S). I'll do the rest. If you cannot confirm that the address we have is current, please contact a friend or family member of the classmate to get one that is current.

Format Guides: Tables

Although you will use a word processing feature to create tables, you will need these guidelines for making your tables easy to read and attractive.

Parts of a Table

A table is an arrangement of data (words and/or numbers) in rows and columns. Columns are labeled alphabetically from left to right; rows are labeled numerically from top to bottom. Tables range in complexity from those with only two columns and a title to those with several columns and special features. The tables in this unit are limited to those with the following parts:

- Main heading (bold, ALL CAPS, centered in first row or placed above the gridlines of the table).
- Secondary heading (bold, capital and lowercase letters, centered in second row or placed a DS below the main title above the gridlines).
- Column headings (bold, centered over the column).
- Body (data entries).
- Source note (bottom left in last row or may be placed beneath the gridlines of the table. If placed beneath the gridlines, use the Add Space Before Paragraph feature to place space between the gridlines and the source note. (Home/Paragraph/Line Spacing/Add Space Before Paragraph) and set a tab to place the source note at the table's left edge.
- Gridlines (may be hidden).

Table Format Features

The following features (illustrated on p. 100) can be used to make your tables attractive and easy to read.

Vertical placement. A table may be centered vertically (equal top and bottom margins), or it may begin 2" from the top edge of the page.

Horizontal placement. Tables are most attractive when centered horizontally (side to side) on the page.

Column width. Generally, each column should be only slightly wider than the longest data entry in the column. Table columns should be identical widths or markedly different widths. Columns that are only slightly different widths should be avoided.

Row height. All rows, including title rows, may be the same height. To enhance appearance, the main title row height may be slightly more than the secondary title row height, which may be more than the column heading row height. The column heading row height may be more than the data entry rows.

Vertical alignment. Within rows, data entries can be aligned at the top, center, or bottom. Most often you will use center vertical alignment for the headings and bottom vertical alignment for data rows beneath the headings. If a source note is included, it should also be bottom-aligned.

Horizontal alignment. Within columns, words may be left-aligned or center-aligned. Whole numbers may be center-aligned or right-aligned. If a column total is shown, numbers should be right-aligned. Decimal numbers are decimal-aligned.

Table Styles design. The Table Styles feature of the software provides a quick way to enhance the appearance of a table. Table styles can be selected and applied at any time after a table has been inserted into a document. Once the table style has been applied, changes to the format for the selected style can be made such as bolding or removing preset bolding, changing font size, changing alignment, etc., to further enhance the appearance of the table.

Work Assignment

This unit is designed to give you experiences you likely would have working in an administrative specialist position.

Assume you are a student at Jonas E. Salk High School who is completing a service-learning requirement. You have been assigned to the Salk High School Alumni Association to help a committee organize a 25-year class reunion. You work directly for Mrs. Audry Bates, class president, who is chairing the reunion committee. Three other class officers who still reside in the area also serve on the committee. They are Mr. Blaine Check, Ms. Gaynell Eastwood, and Mrs. Janice Aberle.

As an administrative specialist, your main duty is to process the documents Mrs. Bates and the other committee members need for the reunion.

For the purposes of this simulation, assume that the class having the reunion was graduated 25 years before the current year, and use that year to identify the graduating class. For example, if the current year is 2009, the reunion is for the class of 1984.

You have completed an orientation program that focused on committee activities and goals, the kinds of documents you will prepare, and the hours you will work through the remainder of the school year. To help you further, Mrs. Bates has established these guidelines for you.

General

1. You are to follow all directions that are given.

2. If a formatting guide or direction is not given, use what you have learned in this class to prepare the documents.

3. Always be alert to and correct errors in punctuation, capitalization, spelling, and word usage.

Correspondence

Prepare all letters in modified block format with mixed punctuation and ¶ indentations. Supply an appropriate salutation and complimentary close, and use your reference initials.

Tables, Worksheets, and Charts

Use spreadsheet, word processing, or database software to prepare tables or worksheets, whichever you decide is better. Prepare charts using spreadsheet software. Be sure to format and identify the various parts of these documents so the reader can easily read or interpret the data you present.

Data Source File

You will help create a data source file of classmates' names and addresses to use for the mailings. Mrs. Bates will determine the fields that are to be included, and you may use word processing or database software to process the data source file.

Mailing Labels

Use a standard mailing label that is 1" × 2.63", such as Avery 5160.

Filenames

Since Mrs. Bates and others may need to access the files, she will provide filenames for you to use.

Main heading

Secondary
heading

Column headings

Body

BROADWAY GROSSES		
Week Ending 7/22/2007		
Production	Gross This Week	Gross Last Week
Wicked	$1,472,649	$1,468,400
The Lion King	1,283,279	1,291,898
Mary Poppins	1,226,944	1,191,101
Jersey Boys	1,197,014	1,211,053
Beauty and the Beast	1,139,499	1,095,124
Legally Blonde	946,840	939,285
Mamma Mia!	935,608	940,187
The Color Purple	926,764	974,904
Hairspray	865,744	809,462
Curtains	837,138	821,457
Totals	$10,831,479	$10,742,871

Source

Source: http://www.broadwayworld.com/grosses.cfm (24 July 2007).

Three-Column Table Centered Horizontally and Vertically

Activity 13

Timed Writing

Two 5' writings on the three ¶s; determine *gwam;* count errors.

A   all letters used   (MicroPace)

	gwam	3'	5'

Attempts to maximize the standard of living for humans — 4 | 2
through the control of nature and the development of new products — 8 | 5
have also resulted in the pollution of the environment. In some — 13 | 8
parts of the world, the water, air, and soil are so polluted that — 17 | 10
it is unsafe for people to live there because of the heightened — 21 | 13
risk from disease. — 23 | 14

Pollution of the air, land, and water has existed since — 27 | 16
people began to live in cities. People living in these early — 31 | 19
cities took their garbage to dumps outside the main part of — 35 | 21
the city or just put it into the streets or canals. Both of these — 40 | 24
disposal methods helped create the pollution process. — 44 | 26

Pollution is one of the most serious problems facing — 47 | 28
people today. Clean air, water, and land are needed by all living — 52 | 31
things. Bad air, water, and soil cause illness and even death — 56 | 34
to people and other living things. Bad water quickly kills fish — 61 | 36
and ruins drinking water; bad soil reduces the amount of land — 65 | 39
that is available for growing food. — 67 | 40

gwam   3' | 1 | 2 | 3 | 4
       5' | 1 | 2 | 3

- To learn placement/arrangement of basic table parts.
- To format tables using the Table Format feature.

35A

Conditioning Practice

Key each line twice SS.

alphabet	1	Meg saw an extra big jet zip quickly over the frozen desert.
fig/sym	2	My income tax for 2003 was $4,178.69--up 5% over 2002's tax.
speed	3	Rick may make a bid on the ivory gowns they got in the city.

gwam	1'	1	2	3	4	5	6	7	8	9	10	11	12

35B   Formatting

Format Table

1. Study the format guides for tables on p. 98 and the model table on p. 99.
2. Using the following information, key Tables 1–3 shown at right and on p. 102.
   - Center, bold, and key the main heading in all CAPS.
   - SS after keying the main heading, change the alignment to left, and turn bold off.
   - Create the table and key the data.
   - Center and bold the column headings.
   - Center the table vertically.

Table 1

Save as: **35B TABLE1**

Table 2

Save as: **35B TABLE2**

POEMS TO IMPROVE OUR LIVES

Poem	Written By
Great Men	Ralph Waldo Emerson
Success	Henry Wadsworth Longfellow
If	Rudyard Kipling
The Road Not Taken	Robert Frost
Will	Ella Wheeler Wilcox
The Sin of Omission	Margaret E. Sangster
Good and Bad Children	Robert Louis Stevenson
Lady Clare	Alfred Tennyson

THE PHANTOM OF THE OPERA

Character	Cast Member
Christine Daae	Susan Medford
Phantom of the Opera	Ramon DeRosa
Raoul	Martin Selbach
Monsieur Andre	Justin Wyman
Meg Giry	Sarah Henrich
Carlotta Guidicelli	Rebecca Haynes
Madame Giry	Sandra Keller
Ubaldo Piangi	Richard Kummerfeld
Monsieur Firmin	Clark Gerhig
Don Attilio	Anthony Blass

Activity 10

Update Linked Word Processing and Worksheet Files

Complete steps 1–3 to revise a worksheet and to update a wp document that is linked to it.

1. Open the worksheet file *CA4 ACTIVITY9-WS* and insert the amounts for Week 3:

   D3: 45   D4: 36   D5: 35   D6: 37

2. Save as **CA4 ACTIVITY9-WS** and close the file.

3. Open *CA4 ACTIVITY9-WP.* Update the worksheet and revise the last ¶ to reflect the most recent sales data.

   Save as: **CA4 ACTIVITY9-WP**

Activity 11

Database

Open the database table from *DF CA4 ACTIVITY11*, and do the following:

1. Enter the *Graduation Term* for the students shown at the right.
2. Run a query that includes:
   - ✓ Last Name
   - ✓ First Name
   - ✓ Resident GPA
   - ✓ 1st Semester
   - ✓ Graduation Term (Use the Criteria feature to select only those students who have graduated.)

Save the query as Graduates.

Last Name	First Name	Graduation Term
Pichler	Javier	Fall 2008
Brancatelli	Kristin	Spring 2009
Frank	Justin	Spring 2008
Lynch	Lance	Spring 2009
Shue	Sara	Spring 2008

Activity 12

Database

Create a report from the query with the information shown at the right. Group the information by 1st Semester. Sort the information by Resident GPA in descending order. Use stepped layout and landscape orientation. Use Office style. Adjust column widths to fit the information, and attractively arrange the copy on the page.

Graduates

1st Semester	Resident GPA	Last Name	First Name	Graduation Term
Fall 1999				
	3.14	Eisenhuth	Dee	Spring 2004
	2.94	Graham	Seth	Fall 2006
Fall 2000				
	3.61	McHale	Laura	Spring 2003
	3.50	Hanson	Kristen	Spring 2003
	2.83	Hudson	Brett	Fall 2002
	2.70	Tilkens	Gordon	Spring 2003
	2.52	Chiu	Kent	Fall 2006
Fall 2001				
	3.76	Traczek	Helen	
	3.65	Holmes		

Table 3

Save as: **35B TABLE3**

FAMOUS PAINTINGS

Artist	Painting
Claude Monet	The Boat Studio
Paul Cezanne	Riverbanks
Rembrandt	The Mill
Michelangelo	The Holy Family
Leonardo da Vinci	The Mona Lisa
Vincent van Gogh	The Starry Night
Raphael	The School of Athens
Berthe Morisot	Little Girl Reading
Pierre-Auguste Renoir	Girls at the Piano
Jan Vermeer	The Milkmaid

Lesson 36   TABLE LAYOUT AND DESIGN

OBJECTIVES

- To use table layout and design features.
- To format two-column tables with main, secondary, and column titles.

36A

Conditioning Practice

Key each line twice SS.

alphabet 1 Jay was amazed at how quickly a proud man fixed the big van.

fig/sym 2 Review reaches: $70, $64, 95%, #20, 5-point, 1/8, B&O 38's.

speed 3 Lane is to fix the big sign by the chapel for the neighbors.

gwam 1' | 1 | 2 | 3 | 4 | 5 | 6 | 7 | 8 | 9 | 10 | 11 | 12 |

36B   Formatting

Format Tables

Table 1

1. Open file
   DF 36B TABLE1.
2. Make the format changes given at the right.

Save as: **36B TABLE1**

1. Change the width of column A to 3.5"; column B to 2".
2. Merge the cells of row 1; center the main heading.
3. Merge the cells of row 2; center the secondary heading.
4. Center column headings.
5. Apply Light Shading – Accent 3 Table Style design to the table.
6. Bold Column B heading.
7. Change the row height of the main heading to 0.5"; the secondary heading to 0.4"; the column headings to 0.35"; the data rows to 0.3".
8. Change the alignment for the first three rows to Center; column A data rows to Bottom Left; column B data rows to Bottom Center.
9. Center the table horizontally and vertically.

Table 2

1. Open file
   DF 36B TABLE2.
2. Make the format changes given at the right.

Save as: **36B TABLE2**

1. Change the row height for all rows to 0.4".
2. Apply Medium Grid 3 – Accent 4 Table Style design to the table.
3. Change alignment for the column headings to Center; the data rows to Bottom Center.
4. Change the width of column A to 2.5"; column B to 2.3".
5. Change the font size for the main heading and column headings to 14 pt.
6. Center the table horizontally and vertically.
7. Insert two new rows at the end of the table and include the following:

Diego Velazquez — Juan de Pareja

Jean-Auguste-Dominique Ingres — Princess de Broglie

Activity 8

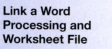

Worksheet

1. Open *DF CA4 ACTIVITY8*.
2. Complete steps 1–10 at the right.

1. Indent the text in cells A4, A10, and A13 one additional position.
2. Write formulas to perform these calculations:
   - In cell B4, subtract cell B3 from cell B2.
   - In cell B8, add cells B6 and B7.
   - In cell B10, subtract cell B9 from cell B8.
   - In cell B11, subtract cell B10 from cell B4.
   - In cell B13, subtract cell B12 from cell B11.
3. Insert a double accounting underline beneath the number in cell B13.
4. In cell C1, key **% of Net Revenues** and wrap the text.
5. You need to determine what percent each number in cells B2:B13 is of the number in cell B4 and display the result in cells C2:C13. Therefore, enter a formula in cell C2 that will calculate the percent that B2 is of B4 and that can be copied to cells C3:C13. Copy the formula to cells C3:C13.
6. Insert a row at the top of the worksheet and merge cells A1:C1. Key **Borders Construction, Inc. Income Statement** in the merged cells, using left alignment.
7. Change the name of Sheet 1 worksheet tab to **Net Profit** and color the tab red. Delete Sheet 2 and Sheet 3 tabs.
8. Set the gridlines and row and column headings to print.
9. You decide other formatting features.
10. Print the worksheet.

Save as: **CA4 ACTIVITY8**

Activity 9

Link a Word Processing and Worksheet File

1. Open wp file *DF CA4 ACTIVITY9-WP*, and save it as **CA4 ACTIVITY9-WP**.
2. Create a worksheet from the data given. Calculate the total and percents. Format it appropriately. Save it as **CA4 ACTIVITY9-WS**.
3. Paste a linked copy of *CA4 ACTIVITY9-WS* into *CA4 ACTIVITY9-WP* below the ¶.
4. Key the text at the right below the worksheet.
5. Save and close both files without changing the filenames.

FBLA Calendar Sales					
Team	**Week 1**	**Week 2**	**Week 3**	**Week 4**	**Total**
Team 1	34	36			70
Team 2	43	32			75
Team 3	39	42			81
Team 4	29	39			68
Totals	145	149	0	0	294

As you can see, sales increased slightly from Week 1 to 2. Team 2 sold the most calendars in Week 1; Team 3 sold the most calendars in Week 2. Team 3 has sold the most calendars to date.

Tables 3–4

Use the information below to format and key Tables 3 and 4. Complete the steps in this order:

1. Create table.
2. Change the width of column A to 2.4" and column B to 2.1".
3. Change the row height to 0.4" for all rows.
4. Merge the cells in row 1 and in row 2.
5. Key the information—ignore bolding and centering until after applying table style.
6. Use Medium Shading 2 – Accent 1 for the Table Style design for Table 3; use Medium Shading 2 – Accent 2 for Table 4.
7. Change the main heading to 16-pt. font, secondary heading to 12-pt. font, and the column headings to 14-pt. font.
8. Use Center alignment for all heading rows.
9. Use Bottom Left alignment for column A data rows; use Bottom Center alignment for column B data rows.
10. Bold the main heading and the column headings; do not bold the secondary headings.
11. Center the table on the page.

Table 3

Save as: 36B TABLE3

Table 4

Save as: 36B TABLE4

CHILDREN'S STORIES	
By Laura Ingalls Wilder	
Book	**Year Published**
Little House in the Big Woods	1932
Little House on the Prairie	1935
On the Banks of Plum Creek	1937
By the Shores of Silver Lake	1939
The Long Winter	1940
Little Town on the Prairie	1941
These Happy Golden Years	1943

LONGEST BROADWAY RUNS	
As of May 25, 2006	
Broadway Show	**No. of Performances**
The Phantom of the Opera	7,637
Cats	7,485
Les Miserables	6,680
A Chorus Line	6,137
Oh! Calcutta (revival)	5,959
Beauty and the Beast	4,964
Rent	4,185
Miss Saigon	4,092
Chicago (revival)	3,963
The Lion King	3,555

Source: *Time Almanac 2007*.

OPTIONAL INTERNET ACTIVITY

Update Table 4 to reflect the most current data available. Use the Internet to search for the *longest running Broadway plays*.

Activity 6

Newsletter

1. Open *DF CA4 ACTIVITY5*.
2. Complete steps 1–9 at the right and on the next page.

1. Key the following information at the top of the newsletter:

Recycling Works!

Marion Township Recycling Guidelines   January 20--

2. Format as a three-column newsletter, but have the information you inserted span the width of both columns.
3. Use WordArt to display the newsletter name.
4. Use 1.0 line spacing, 10-pt. spacing after ¶s, justification, and hyphenation for the report body.
5. Format the side headings in Heading 1 style.
6. Insert a vertical line between the columns.
7. Insert the text below in a shaded text box between the first and second paragraphs in the first article on page 1.

Where do we get our Waste?

About 32% of all waste comes from household packaging.

8. Insert the text below in a shaded text box between the second and third articles on page 1.

Recover your containers promptly after collection.

9. You decide all other formatting.

Save as: CA4 ACTIVITY6

Activity 7

Worksheet

1. Open *DF CA4 ACTIVITY7*.
2. Complete steps 1–13 at the right.

1. Insert **FBLA Region 14 Job Interview Results** as a centered header and your name as a left-aligned footer.
2. Separate the names in column A so the first names remain in A and the last names appear in column B.
3. In each row in column G, sum the scores for each student.
4. Insert two rows at the top of the worksheet.
   - Merge cells E1:G1; key **Scores** in the merged cells.
   - Merge cells A1 and B1; key **Name** in the merged cells.
   - Key **First** in cell A2, **Last** in B2, **School** in C2, **Class** in D2, **Application** in E2, **Interview** in F2, **Combined** in G2.
   - Center align and bold all entries in cells A1:G2.
5. AutoFit the column widths.
6. Sort the list by Combined Score (Largest to Smallest).
7. In column E, apply conditional formatting to shade the cells that are above average.
8. Apply the same conditional formatting to the cells in column F.
9. In column H, write an IF statement that prints *Advance* next to each cell in column G that is above 189.
10. You decide other formatting features for the worksheet.
11. Save as **CA4 ACTIVITY7-WS**; print and keep it open.
12. Save the worksheet as a Web page. Use **Job Interview Results** for the page title and **CA4 ACTIVITY7-WEB** for the filename.
13. Open *CA4 ACTIVITY7-WEB* in your browser; view and print it from your browser.

OBJECTIVES

- To format tables with main, secondary, and column titles.
- To improve language skills (word choice).

37A

Conditioning Practice

Key each line twice SS.

alphabet   1   Eight extra pizzas will be quickly baked for the jovial men.

fig/sym   2   Kaye said, "Can't you touch-key 45, 935, $608, and 17 1/2%?"

speed   3   Orlando and the girls may do the work for the big city firm.

gwam   1' | 1 | 2 | 3 | 4 | 5 | 6 | 7 | 8 | 9 | 10 | 11 | 12 |

37B   Language Skills

**Language Skills:
Word Choice**

1. Study the spelling and definitions of the words.
2. Key all *Learn* and *Apply* lines, choosing the correct words in the *Apply* lines.

Save as: 37B CHOICE

cite (vb) to quote; use as support; to commend; to summon

sight (n/vb) ability to see; something seen; a device to improve aim; to observe or focus

site (n) the place something is, was, or will be located

their (pron) belonging to them

there (adv/pron) in or at that place; word used to introduce a sentence or clause

they're (contr) a contracted form of *they are*

Learn   1   He will **cite** the article from the web**site** about improving your **sight**.

Apply   2   You need to (cite, sight, site) five sources in the report due on Friday.

Apply   3   The (cite, sight, site) he chose for the party was a (cite, sight, site) to be seen.

Learn   1   **There** is the car **they're** going to use in **their** next play production.

Apply   2   (Their, there, they're) making (their, there, they're) school lunches.

Apply   3   (Their, there, they're) is the box of (their, there, they're) tools.

37C   Formatting

Format Tables

Table 1 Format and key the table at the right as directed below.

Main title: 16-pt. font
Secondary title: 12-pt. font
Table Style design: Medium Shading 1 – Accent 3 (do not bold column headings or column A text)
Column headings: row height 0.4"; Center alignment; 14-pt. font
Data rows: row height 0.3"; 12-pt. font
Column A row width 2.3"; Bottom Left alignment
Column B row width 1.0"; Bottom Center alignment
Column C row width 1.2"; Bottom Right alignment
Center table on page

Save as: 37C TABLE1

ALL-TIME TOP MOVIE BOX OFFICE GROSSES
As of May 29, 2006

Movie	Year	Revenue
Titanic	1997	$600,788,188
Star Wars	1977	460,998,007
Shrek 2	2004	436,471,036
E.T. The Extra-Terrestrial	1982	434,949,459
Star Wars: Episode I-The Phantom Menace	1999	431,088,295
Spider-Man	2002	403,706,375

Source: *Time Almanac 2007.*

Last Name	Title	Company
Adams	Mrs.	Adams Medical Association
Aitken, Albert	Mr.	Compilers Plus
Aitken, Barbara	Mrs.	Database & More
Gioia	Mr.	Four Springs Golf Course
Harris	Mr.	Brite House Electricians
McClintock	Mr.	Banquets Unlimited
Springer	Mrs.	County Motors

Activity 3

Mail Merge: Letters

1. Create a main document in modified block letter format with mixed punctuation and indented ¶s to merge with *CA4 DATA2*. Save the main document file as **CA4 MAIN1**.

2. Perform the mail merge and print the last two letters.

Saved merged letters as: CA4 ACTIVITY3

Activity 4

Mail Merge: Address Labels

1. Prepare a standard address label for each record in the data source *CA4 DATA2*. Include the company name in the address. Save the main document file as **CA4 MAIN2**.

2. Print the address labels.

Saved merged letters as: CA4 ACTIVITY4

February 15, 20--

<<AddressBlock>>

<<GreetingLine>>

This letter is to inform you that your company has been selected to participate in an experimental recycling program for various businesses in Ohio. The program will begin March 1 and is scheduled to end August 31.

<<Title>><<Last Name>>, this recycling program requires you to separate paper products into four categories for recycling purposes. The categories are white paper, newspapers, cardboard boxes, and mixed paper. The enclosed pamphlet describes in detail the kinds of paper that are to go into each of these categories.

Early in September, we will send you a survey to complete. The survey results will provide us with much of the information we need to determine if the paper recycling program will be continued and expanded to other business in the state.

Your cooperation and compliance throughout this six-month period is expected and appreciated. If you have any questions that are not answered by the information in the pamphlet, give me a call at 214-555-0119.

Sincerely, | OHIO RECYCLING AUTHORITY | Jeremy Morales | Executive Director | xx | Enclosure |

Activity 5

Report

1. Open *DF CA4 ACTIVITY5* and format as a report.

2. Key **Recycling Works** as the first line of the report. Format it in Title style.

3. Format the side headings in Heading 1 style.

4. Insert a page number at the bottom center of the pages, but hide it on p. 1.

5. Insert a table of contents prior to p. 1. It should contain page numbers, dot leaders, and hyperlinks.

6. Key **Page** above the first page number.

7. Key **Table of Contents** in Title Style as the first line on the page.

8. Change the Style Set to Formal.

9. Key **Return to Top** below the last line of the report.

10. Bookmark the title of the report.

11. Hyperlink the text *Return to Top* to the bookmark.

Save as: CA4 ACTIVITY5

Table 2

Create the table at the right using the information given below.

Main title: 16-pt. font

Table Style design: Colorful List – Accent 3

Column headings: row height 0.5"; Center alignment; 14-pt. font

Data rows: row height 0.3"

Column A and C: 2.0" wide; Bottom Left alignment

Column B: 1.4" wide; Bottom Center alignment

Center: table on page

Save as: 37C TABLE2

Table 3

Arrange the information at the right as a table. Use **MOST FREQUENTLY PRODUCED OPERAS** for the main title; **1996–2006** for the secondary title; and **Operas**, **Composer**, and **No. of Productions** for the three column headings. Source: *Time Almanac 2007*.

Save as: 37C TABLE3

Table 4

Open Table 2 (*37C TABLE2*). Insert the information at the right. Delete the year each author died; change column heading to **Year Born**. Sort the information by Year Born in ascending order.

Save as: 37C TABLE4

SELECTED WORKS BY AMERICAN AUTHORS

Author	Life	Work
Robert Lee Frost	1874-1963	West-Running Brook
Henry W. Longfellow	1807-1882	Ballads
Carl Sandburg	1878-1967	Smoke and Steel
Louisa May Alcott	1832-1888	Little Women
William Faulkner	1897-1962	The Sound and the Fury
Samuel L. Clemens	1835-1910	Adventures of Tom Sawyer
F. Scott Fitzgerald	1896-1940	All the Sad Young Men

La boheme	Puccini	300
La traviata	Verdi	281
Madama Butterfly	Puccini	272
Carmen	Bizet	250
Tosca	Puccini	204
Don Giovanni	Mozart	201
Rigoletto	Verdi	171

Arthur Miller	1915	Death of a Salesman
Oliver W. Holmes	1809	Old Ironsides

Lesson 38 TABLE LAYOUT AND DESIGN

OBJECTIVES

- To format tables with main, secondary, and column titles.
- To make independent decisions regarding table format features.

38A

Conditioning Practice

Key each line twice SS.

alphabet	1	David will buy the six unique jackets from Grady for prizes.
fig/sym	2	Glen's 2001 tax was $4,875, almost 7% ($396) less than 2000.
speed	3	Glen works with vigor to dismantle the downtown city chapel.

gwam 1' | 1 | 2 | 3 | 4 | 5 | 6 | 7 | 8 | 9 | 10 | 11 | 12 |

CYCLE 4
Assessment

• To assess Cycle 4 document processing, computer application, and straight-copy skills.

Conditioning Practice

Key each line twice.

alphabet	1	Zemjaw caught seven very quiet lions before they exited the park.
fig/sym	2	Order 97-431 for Series 608 storm windows was shipped on June 25.
speed	3	The eight busy men may do the work for the city if she pays them.

gwam 1' | 1 | 2 | 3 | 4 | 5 | 6 | 7 | 8 | 9 | 10 | 11 | 12 | 13 |

Activity 1

Data Source

1. Create a data source file for the eight records.
2. Sort in ascending order by postal code and then alphabetically by last name and then first name.

Save as: CA4 DATA1

Doris Adams 2405 Grandview Avenue Cincinnati, OH 45206-2220	Roger Harris 4381 Antioch Drive Enon, OH 45323-6492
Albert Aitken 440 Long Pointe Drive Avon Lake, OH 44012-2463	Larry McClintock 6821 Burgundy Drive Canton, OH 44720-4592
Barbara Aitken 440 Long Pointe Drive Avon Lake, OH 44012-2463	Mary Springer 81 Mayflower Drive Youngstown, OH 44512-6204
Bruce Gioia Route 3, Box 416 Marietta, OH 45750-9057	William Eiber 387 Cranberry Run Youngstown, OH 44512-2504

Activity 2

Edit Data Source

1. Open *CA4 DATA1*.
2. Add a Title field, add the four records, and delete the Eiber record.
3. Add the titles and company names for the other records as given.
4. Sort by postal code in descending order and then alphabetically by last name and then first name.

Save as: CA4 DATA2

Mr. Gerald Bruni Bruni Auto Parts 11184 Greenhaven Drive Navarre, OH 44662-9650	Mrs. Mary Phillip Union Cleaning Co. 123 Marrett Farms Union, OH 45322-3412
Ms. Ruth O'Hara Warren Florists 426 Forest Street Warren, OH 44483-3825	Mr. Henry Lewis Lewis Printing 3140 Beaumont Street Massilon, OH 44647-3140

(continued on next page)

Format Tables

Table 1

Format the information at the right as a table. Use **FAMOUS COMPOSERS** for the main title and **1756–1899** for the secondary title. Apply the Medium Grid 3 – Accent 2 Table Style design. Adjust column width and height to attractively arrange the information on the page. Use the Sort feature to arrange the composers in alphabetical order.

Save as: 38B TABLE1

Table 2

Format the table at the right, arranging the data attractively.

Use **TOP TEN DAILY NEWSPAPERS** for the main title and **United States** for the secondary title. Source: *Time Almanac 2007*.

Apply the Colorful List – Accent 4 Table Style design.

Save as: 38B TABLE2

Table 3

Use **TOP BASEBALL MOVIES** for the main title; **July 27, 2007** for the secondary title; **Rank**, **Movie**, **Year**, and **Percent of Votes** for the column headings.

The tenth movie is **Pride of the Yankees** made in **1942**, **1.9** percent of votes. Include a source note: **Source: ESPN – Page 2 Mailbag.** http://espn.go.com/page2/s/users/baseball/films.html (27 July 2007).

Use the Sort feature to arrange the movies in order by rank; apply an appropriate table style.

Save as: 38B TABLE3

Composer	Nationality	Life	Music
Mozart	Austrian	1756-1791	Don Giovanni
Beethoven	German	1770-1827	Ninth Symphony
Berlioz	French	1803-1869	Romeo and Juliet
Mendelssohn	German	1809-1847	Reformation
Chopin	Franco-Polish	1810-1849	Sonata in B Minor
Schumann	German	1810-1856	Rhenish Symphony
Wagner	German	1813-1883	Rienzi
Strauss	Austrian	1825-1899	Blue Danube

Rank	Newspaper	Location	Circulation
1	USA Today	Arlington, VA	2,528,437
2	Wall Street Journal	New York, NY	2,058,342
3	Times	New York, NY	1,683,855
4	Times	Los Angeles, CA	1,231,318
5	Post	Washington, D.C.	960,684
6	Tribune	Chicago, IL	957,212
7	Daily News	New York, NY	795,153
8	Inquirer	Philadelphia, PA	705,965
9	Post/Rocky Mountain News	Denver, CO	704,806
10	Chronicle	Houston, TX	692,557

4	Bull Durham	1988	13.4
9	A League of Their Own	1992	3.1
8	Bad News Bears	1976	3.3
2	Major League	1989	19.2
3	The Natural	1984	15.9
6	For the Love of the Game	1999	4.4
1	Field of Dreams	1989	23.5%
5	The Sandlot	1993	10.8
7	Eight men Out	1988	4.0

Note: Because of rounding, the amounts do not add up to 100 percent.

Activity 12

Database

Create a report from the query created in Activity 11 similar to the one shown at the right. Group the information by Type of Service. Sort the information by ZIP Code in Ascending order. Use stepped layout and portrait orientation. Use Technic style. Adjust column widths to fit the information attractively on the page.

Type of Service Customer List

Type of Service ZIP Code		Last Name	First Name	Address
Daily				
	11215	Gomez	Brandon	1204 8th Avenue
	11215	Bostock	Lance	1105 8th Avenue
	11215	Etheridge	Grant	1107 8th Avenue
	11215	Vanderbilt	Kyle	1240 8th Avenue
	11217	Vine	Javier	230 Berkeley Place
	11217	Farrell	Marsha	203 St. Johns Place
	11217	Franco	Elizabeth	315 Flatbush Avenue
	11217	DiMarco	Leah	224 Lincoln Place
	11217	Bostock	Siera	207 Berkeley Pl...
	11217	Marquis	Trave	
	11217	Foxworthy		

Activity 13

Timed Writings

Two 5' writings on the three ¶s; determine *gwam*; count errors.

A — all letters used — MicroPace

	gwam	3'	5'

Sleep is a very important element of staying healthy. Many | 4 | 3

people who do not get the proper amount of sleep quickly become | 9 | 5

edgy, fatigued, and tired. In addition, people who do not get | 13 | 8

enough sleep are more likely to be attacked by various diseases. | 17 | 10

It is, therefore, important that you get the amount of sleep that | 22 | 13

your body needs. | 23 | 14

Science knows very little about sleep. There is evidence | 27 | 16

that the amount of sleep each individual needs to maintain good | 31 | 19

health varies. Some believe that the amount of sleep people need | 36 | 21

lessens with age. For example, children below four years of age | 40 | 24

frequently need to sleep about half of each day while teenagers | 44 | 26

need just eight to ten hours each day to perform adequately. | 47 | 29

Most people realize that a good mattress, one that is neither | 53 | 32

too hard nor too soft; a quiet room; and darkness are conditions | 57 | 34

that help them get enough sleep to restore body power. Also help- | 61 | 37

ful are covers and electric blankets that are warm but not too | 66 | 39

heavy. It is also helpful to avoid excitement and heavy eating | 70 | 42

before going to sleep. | 71 | 43

gwam	3'	1		2		3		4	
	5'		1		2		3		

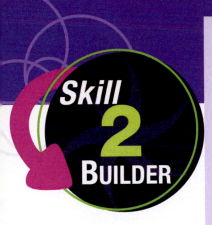

Speed Building

1. Key each line twice with no pauses between letters or words.
2. Key a 1' timing on lines 2, 4, 6, 8, and 10; determine *gwam* on each timing.

space	1	and the she big city disk held half firm land paid them make
bar	2	Jane and the man may handle the problems with the city firm.
shift	3	Moorcroft, WY; Eau Claire, WI; New York City, NY; Newark, DE
keys	4	M. L. Ramirez left for San Francisco on Tuesday, January 23.
adjacent	5	wire open tire sure ruin said trim quit fire spot lids walks
keys	6	Katrina opened a shop by the stadium to sell sporting goods.
long direct	7	many vice brag stun myth much cents under check juice center
reaches	8	I brought a recorder to the music hall to record my recital.
word	9	their visit signs aisle chapel dials handy shake shelf usual
response	10	Their dog slept by the oak chair in the aisle of the chapel.

gwam 1' | 1 | 2 | 3 | 4 | 5 | 6 | 7 | 8 | 9 | 10 | 11 | 12 |

Timed Writings

1. Key a 1' timing on each ¶; determine *gwam*.
2. Key a 2' timing on ¶s 1–2 combined; determine *gwam*.
3. Key a 3' timing on ¶s 1–2 combined; determine *gwam* and number of errors.

Quarter-Minute Checkpoints

gwam	1/4'	1/2'	3/4'	1'
24	6	12	18	24
28	7	14	21	28
32	8	16	24	32
36	9	18	27	36
40	10	20	30	40
44	11	22	33	44
48	12	24	36	48
52	13	26	39	52
56	14	28	42	56
60	15	30	45	60

A all letters used MicroPace

gwam 2' | 3'

"I left my heart in San Francisco." This expression 5 | 4
becomes much easier to understand after an individual has 11 | 7
visited the city near the bay. San Francisco is one of 17 | 11
the most interesting areas to visit throughout the entire 23 | 15
world. The history of this city is unique. Even though 28 | 19
people inhabited the area prior to the gold rush, it was 34 | 23
the prospect of getting rich that brought about the fast 40 | 26
growth of the city. 42 | 28

It is difficult to write about just one thing that this 47 | 31
exquisite city is known for. Spectacular views, cable cars, 53 | 35
the Golden Gate Bridge, and Fisherman's Wharf are only a 59 | 39
few of the many things that are associated with this amazing 65 | 43
city. The city is also known for the diversity of its people. 71 | 48
In fact, there are three separate cities within the city, 77 | 51
Chinatown being the best known. 80 | 54

gwam 2' | 1 | 2 | 3 | 4 | 5 | 6 |
3' | 1 | 2 | 3 | 4 |

Activity 9

Link a Word Processing and Worksheet File

1. Open wp file *DF CR4 ACTIVITY9-WP* and save it as **CR4 ACTIVITY9-WP**.

2. Create a worksheet from the data given. Calculate the total and percents. Format it appropriately. Save it as **CR4 ACTIVITY9-WS**.

3. Paste a linked copy of *CR4-ACTIVITY9-WS* into *CR4 ACTIVITY9-WP* between ¶s1 and 2. Save and close both files without changing the filenames.

CURRENT INVESTMENT PORTFOLIO		
Type of Fund	**Dollars**	**Percent of Total**
Growth Funds	$ 45,982.00	
Growth-and-Income Funds	$ 76,135.00	
Equity-Income Funds	$ 30,971.00	
Bond Funds	$ 82,068.00	
Money Market Funds	$ 23,504.00	
Total Portfolio		

Activity 10

Update Linked Word Processing and Worksheet Files

Complete steps 1–3 to revise a worksheet and to update a wp document that is linked to it.

1. Open the worksheet file *CR4 ACTIVITY9-WS*, and key the new numbers in the cells:

   B3: $43,789   B4: $73,778   B5: $28,765   B6: $85,089   B7: $27,854

2. Save as **CR4 ACTIVITY9-WS** and close the file.
3. Open *CR4 ACTIVITY9-WP*, update the worksheet, and save as **CR4 ACTIVITY9-WP**.

Activity 11

Database

Open the database table from *DF CR4 ACTIVITY11* and do the following:

1. Add the two new subscriptions shown at the right to the *Route 153 Customer List* table.

2. Run a query that includes:
   ✓ Last Name
   ✓ First Name
   ✓ Address
   ✓ ZIP Code
   ✓ Type of Service

Save the query as: **Type of Service Customer List.**

NY-Today
Subscriptions

Last Name: Chan
First Name: Marsha   Courtesy Title: Ms.
Address: 347 St. Johns Place
City: Brooklyn
State: NY   ZIP Code: 11238
Type of Service: Weekend Only

NY-Today
Subscriptions

Last Name: LaFranz
First Name: Sterling   Courtesy Title: Mr.
Address: 238 Park Place
City: Brooklyn
State: NY   ZIP Code: 11238
Type of Service: Weekend Only

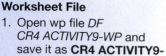

PRONOUN AGREEMENT

Pronoun Agreement

1. Study each of the four rules.
   a. Key the Learn lines beneath each rule, noting how the rule is applied.
   b. Key the Apply lines, choosing correct pronouns.

Pronoun Agreement

Rule 1: A personal pronoun (*I, we, you, he, she, it, their*, etc.) agrees in **person** (first, second, or third) with the noun or other pronoun it represents.

Learn 1 We can win the game if we all give each play our best effort. (1st person)

Learn 2 You may practice dancing only after you finish all your homework. (2nd person)

Learn 3 Andrea said that she will drive her car to the antique mall. (3rd person)

Apply 4 Those who saw the exhibit said that (he, she, they) were impressed.

Apply 5 After you run for a few days, (my, your) muscles are less sore.

Apply 6 Before I take the test, I want to review (your, my) class notes.

Rule 2: A personal pronoun agrees in **gender** (feminine, masculine, or neuter) with the noun or other pronoun it represents.

Learn 7 Miss Kimoto will give her talk after the art exhibit. (feminine)

Learn 8 The small boat lost its way in the dense fog. (neuter)

Apply 9 Each winner will get a corsage as she receives (her, its) award.

Apply 10 The ball circled the rim before (he, it) dropped through the hoop.

Rule 3: A personal pronoun agrees in **number** (singular or plural) with the noun or other pronoun it represents.

Learn 11 Celine drove her new car to Del Rio, Texas, last week. (singular)

Learn 12 The club officers made careful plans for their next meeting. (plural)

Apply 13 All workers must submit (his, their) vacation requests.

Apply 14 The sloop lost (its, their) headsail in the windstorm.

Rule 4: A personal pronoun that represents a collective noun (*team, committee, family*, etc.) may be singular or plural, depending on the meaning of the collective noun.

Learn 15 Our men's soccer team played its fifth game today. (acting as a unit)

Learn 16 The drill team took their positions on the field. (acting individually)

Apply 17 The jury will render (its, their) verdict at 1:30 today.

Apply 18 The Social Committee had presented (its, their) written reports.

(continued on next page)

4. Use 1.0 line spacing, 10-pt. spacing after paragraphs, justification, and hyphenation for the report body.
5. Format the side headings in Heading 1 style.
6. Insert a vertical line between the columns.
7. Insert the text below in a shaded text box between the first and second articles on p. 1.

Tip of the Week

Skiers may injure their thumbs when falling if they're using ski poles with molded plastic grips, which are not flexible. The American Physical Therapy Association recommends using ski poles with soft webbing or leather straps.

8. You decide all other formatting.

Save as: **CR4 ACTIVITY6**

Activity 7

Worksheet

1. Open *DF CR4 ACTIVITY7*.
2. Complete steps 1–10 at the right to complete the worksheet.

1. AutoFit the column widths.
2. Insert **Tri-County Fabulous 15 Offensive Football Players** as a left-aligned header and your name as a right-aligned footer.
3. Separate the names in column A so the first names remain in A and the last names appear in column B. Change the column headings to **First Name** and **Last Name**, wrapping text if needed. Autofit columns A and B to fit the widths.
4. Sort the list by last name (A-Z).
5. Apply a Data Bar conditional format to values in column F.
6. In column C, apply conditional formatting to highlight the cell if the player is a senior.
7. You decide other formatting features for the worksheet.
8. Save as **CR4 ACTIVITY7-WS**; print and keep it open.
9. Save the worksheet as a Web page. Use **Fab 15** for the page title and **CR4 ACTIVITY7-WEB** for the filename.
10. Open *CR4 ACTIVITY7-WEB* in your browser; view and print it from your browser.

Activity 8

Worksheet

1. Open *DF CR4 ACTIVITY8*.
2. Complete steps 1–7 at the right to complete the worksheet.

1. Insert a row at the top of the worksheet. Key **Budget Category** in cell A1, **Estimates** in cell B1, and **% of Income** in cell C1. Rotate and bold the text in cells A1:C1 on a 45-degree angle.
2. Indent the text in cells A4:A11.
3. In cell B12, sum the numbers in cells B4:B11.
4. You need to determine what percent each number in cells B2:B12 is of the number in cell B2 and display the result in cells C2:C12. Therefore, enter a formula in cell C2 that will calculate the percent that B2 is of B2 and that can be copied to cells C4:C12. Copy the formula to cells C4:C12. Format all percent columns to one decimal place.
5. Change the name of Sheet 1 worksheet tab to **Budget** and color the tab blue. Delete Sheet 2 and Sheet 3 tabs.
6. Set the gridlines and row and columns headings to print.
7. Print the worksheet.

Save as: **CR4 ACTIVITY8**

2. Key Proofread & Correct, using correct pronouns.
   a. Check answers.
   b. Using the rule number at the left of each line, study the rule relating to each error you made.
   c. Rekey each incorrect line, using correct pronouns.

Save as: CS4 ACTIVITY1

Proofread & Correct

Rules

2	1	Suzy knew that (he, she, they) should read more novels.
3	2	People who entered the contest say (he, she, they) are confident.
3	3	As soon as art class is over, I like to transcribe (our, my) notes.
2, 3	4	Mrs. Kelso gave (her, his, their) lecture in Royce Hall.
2	5	The yacht moved slowly around (her, his, its) anchor.
1	6	As you practice the lines, (his, your) confidence increases.
1	7	I played my new clarinet in (my, their, your) last recital.
3	8	The editors planned quickly for (its, their) next newsletter.
4	9	The women's volleyball team won (its, their) tenth game today.
4	10	Our family will take (its, their) annual trip in August.

ACTIVITY 2

Listening

1. Open *DF CS4 ACTIVITY2*.
2. Listen to the weather forecast and take notes. Then close the file.
3. Key answers to the questions.

Save as: CS4 ACTIVITY2

1. What were the high and low temperatures for today?
2. What are the predicted high and low temperatures for Tuesday?
3. Is it likely to rain tomorrow?
4. How many days are likely to have rain in the five-day forecast?
5. What is the highest temperature predicted in the five-day forecast?
6. What is the lowest temperature predicted in the five-day forecast?

ACTIVITY 3

Write to Learn
Save as: CS4 ACTIVITY3

1. Using word processing or voice recognition software, write a paragraph explaining how to insert a 3 × 4 table.
2. Write a second paragraph explaining how to change the row height to 0.3".

ACTIVITY 4

Math: Finding the Part of a Whole

1. Open *DF CS4 ACTIVITY4* and print the file.
2. Solve the problems as directed in the file.
3. Submit your answers.

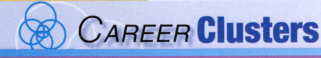

CAREER **Clusters**

ACTIVITY 4

You must complete Career Exploration Activities 1–3 before completing this activity.

1. Retrieve your Career folder and find the printed Career Cluster Plan of Study for the career cluster that is your first choice.

2. Review the plan and write a paragraph or two about why you would or would not consider a career in this cluster. Print your file, then save it as Career4, and keep it open.

3. Exchange papers with a classmate. Have the classmate offer suggestions for improving the content and correcting any errors he or she finds in your paragraph(s). Make the changes that you agree with and print a copy to turn in to your instructor. Save it as Career4 and close the file.

4. Return your folder to the storage area. When your instructor returns your paper, file it in your Career folder.

Activity 3

Mail Merge: Letters

1. Create a main document in modified block letter format with mixed punctuation and indented ¶s to merge with *CR4 DATA2*. Save the main document file as *CR4 MAIN1*.
2. Perform the mail merge and print the last two letters.

Save merged letters as: CR4 ACTIVITY3

Activity 4

Mail Merge: Address Labels

1. Prepare a standard address label for each record in the data source *CR4 DATA2*. Save the main document file as *CR4 MAIN2*.
2. Print the address labels.

Save merged file as: CR4 ACTIVITY4

September 15, 20-- |

<<AddressBlock>>

<<GreetingLine>>

Thank you for attending the adult educational series that focused on disease management issues. It appears that the series was a success from the many positive comments we have received.

<<FirstName>>, since you have been a strong supporter of the Beakin County United Way for several years, we want to be certain that you know about our upcoming events:

❏ The Pediatric Educational Program with breakout sessions for teenagers and parents on three Monday evenings beginning October 11 at Beakin County Community College.

❏ The "Evening with Da Vinci" Annual Gala on October 27 at the Beakin Club.

❏ The Pace Setter 5K-Run/Walk for the Cure of Disease on November 5 at Valley View Park.

❏ Funder's Golf Classic on November 8 at Harris Heights Golf Club.

If you want more information about any of these events, please e-mail me at jenko@united-way.org or call me at 713-555-0144. I have enclosed a form that you can complete and return to register.

Sincerely, | Janice Jenko | Executive Director | xx | Enclosures |

<<FirstName>>, Jerry Helco is arranging foursomes for the golf outing and he wants you to be a part of one of them. He'll call you in a few days to see if you have any preferences for partners.

Activity 5

Report

1. Open *DF CR4 ACTIVITY5* and format it as a report.
2. Key **Jones Memorial Hospital Update** as the first line of the report. Format it in Title style.
3. Format the side headings in Heading 1 style.
4. Insert a page number at the bottom center of the pages, but hide it on page 1.
5. Insert a table of contents prior to p. 1. It should contain page numbers, dot leaders, and hyperlinks.
6. Key **Page** above the first page number.
7. Key **Table of Contents** in Title Style as the first line on the page.
8. Change the Style Set to Formal.
9. Key **Return to Top** below the last line of the report.
10. Bookmark the title of the report.
11. Hyperlink the text *Return to Top* to the bookmark.

Save as: CR4 ACTIVITY5

Activity 6

Newsletter

1. Open *DF CR4 ACTIVITY5*.
2. Complete steps 1–9 at the right and on the next page.

1. Key the following information at the top of the newsletter:

Healthscape

Published by Jones Memorial Hospital   February 20--

2. Format as a two-column newsletter, but have the information you inserted span the width of both columns.
3. Use WordArt to display the newsletter name (*Healthscape*).

UNIT 12
Lessons 39-45

Learn Electronic Presentation Basics

What Is an Electronic Presentation?

Electronic presentations are computer-generated visual aids (usually slide shows) that can be used to help communicate information. Electronic presentations can combine text, graphics, audio, video, and animation to deliver and support key points. With the powerful features of presentation software such as *Microsoft PowerPoint*, attractive and engaging presentations can be created with ease.

Presentations are an important part of communication in business. Presentations are given to inform, to persuade, and/or to entertain. Visual aids generally make a speaker more effective in delivering his/her message. That is because the speaker is using two senses (hearing and sight)

rather than just one. The probability of a person understanding and retaining something seen as well as heard is much greater than if it is just heard. For example, if you had never heard of a giraffe before, you would have a better idea of what a giraffe was if the speaker talked about a giraffe and showed pictures of one than if the speaker only talked about what a giraffe was.

With presentation software, visuals (slides) can be created that can be projected on a large screen for a larger audience to view, or viewed directly on a computer by a smaller audience. Web pages, color or black-and-white overheads, audience handouts, and speaker notes can be created using electronic presentation software.

What Are the Key Features of Electronic Presentation Software?

Learning how to use **PowerPoint** is quite easy for individuals who have had experience with **Word**. *PowerPoint* has many of the same features as *Word* and is set up the same way, using ribbons, groups, and tabs. However, you will learn new features unique to *PowerPoint*.

In this unit you will learn how to:
- Create text slides
- Insert illustrations on a slide
- Create diagrams and tables
- Create charts and graphs
- Create and deliver a presentation

What Is a Design Theme?

PowerPoint comes with files containing design themes (see examples on next page). A theme has everything set up. All the person creating the presentation has to do is select the slide layout and key in their information. The font and font size, places for keying information, background design, and

color schemes are preset for each design theme. Even though these themes are preset, they can be changed to better fit the needs of the user. Using design themes gives your presentations a professional appearance.

CYCLE 4
Review

- To prepare for assessment of Cycle 4 document processing, computer application, and straight-copy skills.

Conditioning Practice

Key each line twice.

alphabet	1	Zelda will judge quickly and pay them for excellent book reviews.
fig/sym	2	A loan (#397-4) was made on 5/1/2005 for $68,000 at a rate of 6%.
speed	3	The official paid the men for the handiwork they did on the dock.

gwam 1' | 1 | 2 | 3 | 4 | 5 | 6 | 7 | 8 | 9 | 10 | 11 | 12 | 13 |

Activity 1

Data Source

1. Create a data source file for the eight records.
2. Sort alphabetically by last name and then first name.

Save as: CR4 DATA1

Jodi Duerr Box 1099 Twain Harte, CA 95383-1099	Miguel Rugeirio 18803 S. Alfred Street Cerritos, CA 90701-0230
Scott Letwin 3209 Synder Avenue Modesto, CA 95356-0140	Gina Mysliwiec 28881 Aloma Avenue Laguna Niguel, CA 92677-1406
Denise Ehrhardt 23633 Real Court Valencia, CA 91355-2125	William Joyce 6022 Poplar Street Weldon, CA 93283-6022
Beverly Erickson 38-381 Desert Green Drive Palm Desert, CA 92260-1009	Lori Rugeirio 18803 S. Alfred Street Cerritos, CA 90701-0230

Activity 2

Edit Data Source

1. Open *CR4 DATA1*.
2. Add a title field, add the four records, and delete the Joyce record.
3. Add the titles for the other records as given.
4. Sort alphabetically by last name and then first name.

Save as: CR4 DATA2

Mrs. Patricia Medich 1640 Fountain Springs Circle Danville, CA 94526-5635	Mr. Mitchell Lacey 284 Turf Paradise Rancho Mirage, CA 92270-2847
Mrs. Ruth Flynn 6214 Rosalind Avenue El Cerrito, CA 94530-2682	Mr. Charles Oates 9922 Cedar Avenue Bloomington, CA 92316-1850

Duerr	Mrs.	Mysliwiec	Mrs.
Ehrhardt	Ms.	Rugeirio, Lori	Mrs.
Erickson	Ms.	Rugeirio, Miguel	Mr.
Letwin	Mr.		

What Is Slide Layout?

Layout refers to the way text and graphics are arranged on the slide. Presentation software allows the user to select a slide layout for each slide that is created. Some of the more common layouts (see examples below) include:

- Title Slide layout
- Title and Content layout
- Section header layout
- Two Content layout
- Comparison layout
- Title Only layout
- Blank layout
- Content with Caption
- Picture with Caption layout

Illustrations of Design Themes with Common Slide Layouts

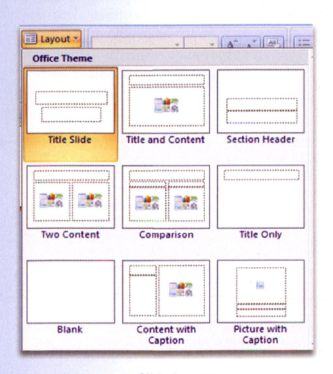

Slide Layout

Title Slide Layout

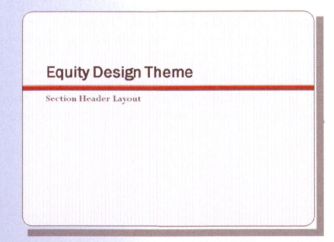

Section Header Layout

Title and Content Layout

Activity 2

Web Page Construction

1. Create a new folder called **U36-WPC-XXX** (*XXX* represents your initials).
2. Create the Web pages, including the hyperlinks, for the website you designed in Activity 1.
3. Name the files and save them in your U36-WPC-XXX folder.
4. Submit your website to your instructor as required.

Activity 3

Web Page Design Tips

1. Form groups.
2. Review the Web Page Design Tips above.
3. Search the Internet for additional tips on designing Web pages or sites.
4. Summarize the tips you find and present them in a wp document along with the Web address where the tips were located.

   Save as: 158 ACT3

5. Discuss the tips that each member found, and choose the ones that you want to include with those given at the right.
6. Each group should design a Web page that integrates your group's tips with those at the right. Include the Web addresses for the tips you add.

   Save as Web page: U36-158-TIPS

Activity 4

Web Page Critique

1. Using what you have learned about Web page design in Activity 3, have your group members critique each other's Web pages that were created in Activity 2.
2. Using the suggestions of the group, revise the Web pages you constructed in Activity 2.
3. Submit your revised Web pages to your instructor as required.
4. If permitted, post your website to your school's intranet or the Internet.

158–160c

Language Skills: Word Choice

1. Study the spelling and definitions of the words.
2. Key the *Learn* and *Apply* lines, choosing the correct word(s) in the *Apply* lines.

Save as: 160C CHOICE

> **pole** (n) a long, slender, rounded piece of wood or other material
>
> **poll** (n) a survey of people to analyze public opinion
>
> **plain** (adj/n) with little decoration; a large flat area of land
>
> **plane** (n) an airplane or hydroplane

Learn 1 He posted the results of his **poll** on the **pole** outside his office.
Apply 2 Judy will hang the banner on each (pole/poll) near the school.
Apply 3 John conducted a (pole/poll) to see what the students preferred.

Learn 1 Greg was a served a **plain** bagel on the **plane** this morning.
Apply 2 John was told to hurry as the (plain/plane) was departing soon.
Apply 3 I plan to wear a (plain/plane) brown skirt on the (plain/plane).

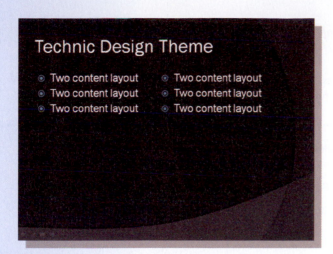

Two Content Layout   **Two Content Layout**

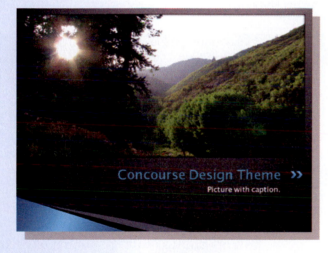

**Picture with Caption
Shown with Three Design Themes**

What View Options Are Available to View Slides?

As you create a presentation, there are different view options available. Each view serves a distinct purpose for creating, editing, and viewing slides.

View Options:
- Normal View
- Slide Sorter View
- Slide Show View

These views are explained and illustrated on the next page.

- To apply skills you have learned to design Web pages.
- To create and then improve a functional interactive website.

158–160B

Activity 1

Web Page Design

1. Read the directions at the right.
2. Select a purpose for your website.
3. Obtain approval of your website purpose from your instructor.
4. Read the Web Page Design Tips in the chart on the next page.
5. Using wp software, outline the structure and content of each Web page within your site.

Save as: 158 ACT1

You are to design Web pages for a website that you choose. The website must have these elements:

- At least three Web pages that have hyperlinks to each other.
- One or more graphics from the Internet or clip art.
- One or more pictures with descriptive text from the Internet or from files.
- One or more hyperlinks to another website.
- Two or more hyperlinks to different locations within the same Web page. "Return to the Top" can be used as one of the hyperlinks.
- One or more hyperlinks to e-mail addresses—may be fictional.
- Tables within each page.
- A background with texture, color, picture, or image.
- Font color that is compatible with the background.

Web Page Design Tips	
Use a background and font color combination that is attractive but easy to read.	Do not use big blocks of text. Users tend to scan text and not read long blocks of text carefully or thoroughly.
Keep pictures and graphics small to avoid long download times.	Use hyperlinks in long Web pages to reduce the need for users to scroll long distances.
Use hyperlinks that enable the user to move from one website to another, one Web page to another, and within a Web page easily.	Use descriptive titles in the title bar and headings at the beginning of each Web page so the user always knows where he/she is.

Illustrations of View Options

Normal View (Outline) – The Normal View with outline is used for creating and editing individual slides, outlining, and creating notes.

Normal View (Slides) – The Normal View with slides is used for creating and editing individual slides, viewing miniatures of slides that have already been created, and creating notes.

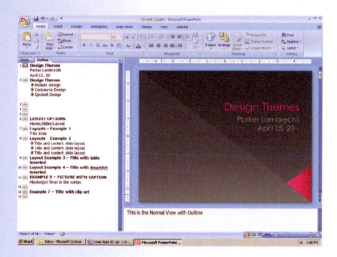

Normal View - Outline

Normal View - Slides

Slide Sorter View – The Slide Sorter View shows all the slides in miniature. This is helpful for rearranging slides and for applying features to several slides at a time.

Slide Show View – The Slide Show View is used to see how the slides will look on the screen. This view is helpful for rehearsing and presenting your slide show.

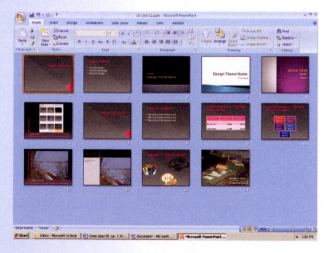

Slide Sorter View

Slide Show View

Activity 5

Hyperlinks to Other Web Pages Within the Same Website

1. Read the text.
2. Learn to create a hyperlink to a different file within the same website.
3. Complete steps 1–2.

You can hyperlink to other Web pages (files) within a website by selecting the text or graphic that the user will click to access the other file. As with other hyperlinks, the hypertext link usually appears in a different font color and underlined. Once the path has been followed, the hypertext link usually changes to another color to indicate that the hyperlink has been used.

In the illustration, the first hyperlink (in blue) has not been followed; the second hyperlink (in purple) has been followed.

In this activity, hyperlinks using text will lead to other files within the BPSAF website.

> This text represents a portion of a Web page done using a red font. This <u>first hyperlink</u> is in blue and is underlined. In this example, blue is used as the color for a hyperlink that has not been followed. This <u>second hyperlink</u> uses purple to indicate that this link has been followed.

1. Open *index* and insert the following five hyperlinks in the 3 × 2 table:
   - *index* to *U36 BPSAF* by making *About BPSAF* the hyperlinked text.
   - *Index* to *U36 BDMBRS(2)* by making *Board Members* the hyperlinked text.
   - *Index* to *U36 FINANCES* by making *Finances* the hyperlinked text.
   - *index* to *U36 DONORS* by making *Donors* the hyperlinked text.
   - *Index* to *U36 EVENTS* by making *Events* the hyperlinked text.

2. Open each of the following Web pages in the appropriate *Office* program, and link the *Home* at the bottom of the Web page to the home page (*index* file). Verify that each hyperlink works properly. Save each file as a Web page with the same filename.

Word files: *U36 BDMBRS(2), U36 DONORS,* and *U36 EVENTS*

Excel file: *U36 FINANCES*

PowerPoint file: *U36 BPSAF (Home* is on the last slide*)*

Activity 6

Bookmarks and Hyperlinks in a Web Page

1. Read the text.
2. Review how to create bookmarks and hyperlinks.
3. Complete steps 1–7.

In Unit 30, you learned to insert bookmarks and hyperlinks into a long document so the reader could move from one part of the document to another quickly, without needing to scroll through several pages of text.

Bookmarks and hyperlinks are also frequently used in a Web page that is longer than a window and contains multiple sections. Bookmarks are inserted into the Web page

text to mark the different locations you want the user to be able to move to quickly. Also, hyperlinks are frequently inserted at strategic points in a Web page to allow the user to return to the top of the Web page quickly, if desired.

In this activity, you are going to link to specific places (bookmarks) within the Web page titled *U36 EVENTS*:

1. Open *U36 EVENTS* and preview this activity by scrolling through the Web page looking for these items:
   a. Locate *Recent Events* and *Upcoming Events* in the top table. You will use these headings as your hyperlinks.
   b. Locate the heading *Recent Events* in the Web page. You will bookmark this text so your hyperlink will move the user to it.
   c. Locate the heading *Upcoming Events* in the Web page. You will bookmark this text so your hyperlink will move the user to it.
   d. Locate the *Return to the Top* phrase in the Web page. You will hyperlink this phrase to the top of the document.

2. Select the *Recent Events* heading in the Web page, and insert a bookmark at this point.
3. Select the *Upcoming Events* heading in the Web page, and insert a bookmark at this point.
4. Link *Recent Events* in the top table to the *Recent Events* bookmark.
5. Link *Upcoming Events* in the top table to the *Upcoming Events* bookmark.
6. Link *Return to the Top* to the top of the Web page.
7. Preview the Web page in your browser and verify that the hyperlinks move the user to the various places within the Web page.

Save as Web page: U36 EVENTS

OBJECTIVES

- To navigate through an existing electronic presentation.
- To create a title slide.
- To create a bulleted list slide.

39A–45A

Conditioning Practice

Key each line twice SS.

alphabet	1	Jake Lopez may give a few more racquetball exhibitions in Dallas.
figures	2	Ray quickly found the total of 8.16, 9.43, and 10.25 to be 27.84.
speed	3	Bob's neighbor may dismantle the ancient shanty in the big field.

gwam 1' | 1 | 2 | 3 | 4 | 5 | 6 | 7 | 8 | 9 | 10 | 11 | 12 |

39B

View Presentation

1. Open *DF 39B PP*. The file will open in Normal View (Slides).
2. Click the Slide Show View button at the bottom of the screen and view the slide show, noting the design themes and layout options. Click the mouse button to advance to the next slide.
3. When you are done viewing the slide show, click Slide Sorter View.
4. Click Normal View; read the notes beneath each slide, then use the down arrow key to go to the next slide.
5. Close without saving.

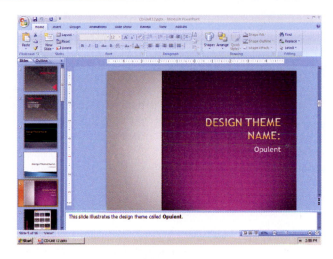

Normal View   Slide Sorter View   Slide Show View

39C

Create Title Slide

P • Design/Themes/Module

P • Home/Slides/Layout/ Title Slide

1. Start a new presentation.
2. Select the Module design theme (or another if Module is not available).
3. Select Title Slide layout.
4. Create the title slide as shown.
5. Increase the font size for the name of the presenter and the company name to 24 pt.

Save as: **39C PP**

Title slide. A presentation should begin with a title slide. Include the presentation title, presenter name, and other relevant information.

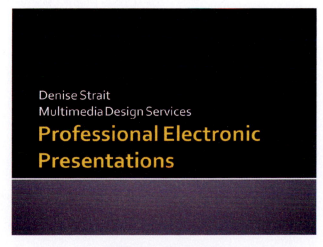

Slide 1 – Title Slide

1. Open *index* and select *Webmaster* (the last word in the last line of text) to create a hyperlink to this e-mail address: kvarati@cengage.com. Use **Kimberly Varati** as the screen tip.

Save as Web page: index

2. Open *U36 BDMBRS*. Insert a column at the right; key **E-mail** for the column heading; merge cells as needed. Key each e-mail address in the last column so that the entire e-mail address is the hyperlink. Use the default screen tip, and key each person's e-mail address in lowercase letters. The e-mail address for each person is the **first initial** of his or her name plus the **last name**, followed by **@cengage.com** —for example, ahess@cengage.com and hmalone@cengage.com.

Save as Web page: U36 BDMBRS(2)

3. Open *U36 EVENTS* and create an e-mail hyperlink to *Alex Rendulic* (arendulic@cengage.com) by inserting the mailbox graphic file (*MAILBOX* in U36-BP-XXX folder) between *mailbox* and *to* in the *Golf Outing* section. Use **Alex Rendulic** as the screen tip. Key **REQUEST FOR BPSAF GOLF OUTING INFO** as the subject in the subject line in the Insert Hyperlink dialog box.

Save as Web page: U36 EVENTS

Activity 4

Hyperlinks to a Different Website

1. Read the text.
2. Learn to create a hyperlink to a different website using a graphic and text.
3. Complete steps 1 and 2.

As with e-mail, hyperlinks to other websites can be inserted by using a graphic, selecting text, or using the site's URL. When the site's URL is used as the hyperlink, the software will usually create the hyperlink.

The three methods are illustrated at the right.

Using a graphic	
Using selected text	Bristol Point High School
Using the URL as the text	http://www.bphs.cengage.com

1. Open *index*.
   - Create a hyperlink to *Bristol Point School District* using the lion mascot. The URL is http://www.bpsd.cengage.com. Use **BPSD** as the screen tip.
   - Create a hyperlink to Bristol Point High School using the text in the lower right cell of the 3 × 2 table. The URL is http://www.bphs.cengage.com.

Save as Web page: index

2. Open *U36 EVENTS*.
   - Create a hyperlink to the text *Joplin's Public Golf Course* (in the *Upcoming Events* section). The URL is http://www.joplins.cengage.com. Use the default screen tip.
   - Create a hyperlink to *Bristol Point School District* using the lion mascot. The URL is http://www.bpsd.cengage.com. Use **BPSD** as the screen tip.

Save as Web page: U36 EVENTS

Create Title and Content Slide

P • Home/Slides/Layout/ Title and Content

1. Read the information at the right.
2. Open *39C PP* and insert two new slides with the Title and Content (bulleted list) layout after the slide you created in 39C.
3. Create the slides as shown below.

Save as: 39D PP

Title and Content (bulleted list). Use the Title and Content layout for lists to guide discussion and help the audience follow a speaker's ideas. If too much information is placed on a single slide, the text becomes difficult to read. Keep the information on the slide brief—do not write complete sentences. Be concise.

When creating lists, be sure to:
• focus on one main idea.
• add several supporting items.
• limit the number of lines on one slide to six.
• limit long wraparound lines of text.

Presentation Planning

▪ Consider the audience.
▪ Consider the subject.
▪ Consider the equipment.
▪ Consider the facilities.

Slide 2 - Bulleted List 1

Message Development

▪ Introduction
▪ Body
▪ Summary and/or Conclusion

Slide 3 - Bulleted List 2

Change Template Design

P • Design/Themes/Aspect (Concourse, Solstice, Opulent)

Open *39D PP*; change the template design to two other designs, and see how the appearance of the different layouts changes with each template. Close the file without saving.

Professional Electronic Presentations
Denise Strait
Multimedia Design Services

Aspect Design Theme

Professional Electronic Presentations
Denise Strait
Multimedia Design Services

Concourse Design Theme

Presentation Planning
• Consider the audience.
• Consider the subject.
• Consider the equipment.
• Consider the facilities.

Solstice Design Theme

PRESENTATION PLANNING
⊛ Consider the audience.
⊛ Consider the subject.
⊛ Consider the equipment.
⊛ Consider the facilities.

Opulent Design Theme

• To learn to insert various kinds of hyperlinks in Web pages.

157B

Activity 1

Table

1. Open *U36 BKGRD*, delete the text; save it as a Web page named *U36 DONORS*.

2. Format the tables as a Web page consistent with others in Lesson 156.

3. Key **BPSAF** as the Web page title.

Save as Web Page: U36 **DONORS**

BPSAF DONORS	
Amount	**Last Year's Donors**
$500 or more	Paul Adamek, Bob Rothey, Kristine Wood
$250–$499	Toni Bauer, Cyd Booth, Jon Burd, Ira Mays, Dee Spahr
$100–$249	Harry Held, Eugene Lytle, Dennis Marks, Wallace Rapp, Jen Sinclair, Bob Turner, Laura Weigel
Up to $100	Connie Cain, Debbie Cole, Sue Cranston, Jeremy Davis, Janet Krise, Stanley Lang, Victor Ophar, Walter Suchy, Michael Wray

Home

Activity 2

Hyperlinks

1. Read the text.

2. Consider how hyperlinks can streamline moving between documents.

Web pages can be enriched through the use of **hyperlinks.** Graphic or text hyperlinks usually appear in a different font color and underlined. When hyperlinks are inserted into a Web page, the user can click them to go to a different location.

The location can be a different website, a different Web page within the same website, another location within the same Web page, or an e-mail address.

In the next four activities, you will insert each of the four kinds of hyperlinks into the Web pages for the Bristol Point High School.

Activity 3

Hyperlinks to an E-mail Address

1. Read the text and Learning Cue.

Learning Cue

When the user moves the pointer over a hyperlink (graphic or text), a screen tip generally appears in a rectangle above the pointing hand. You can use the default screen tip, or you can insert other text for the screen tip. When the hyperlink is to an e-mail address, the default is generally *mailto:* followed by the e-mail address.

2. Learn to create a hyperlink to an e-mail address.

3. Complete steps 1–3.

When a user clicks a hyperlink to an e-mail address, a new e-mail message box is created with the linked e-mail address appearing in the To line. The user then keys the subject line and e-mail message and clicks **send**.

The illustrations show three methods of creating hyperlinks to an e-mail address. The first is to an address that is represented by the mailbox graphic. When the user clicks the mailbox, the e-mail message box will open.

The second is an e-mail address that is used as a hyperlink. It appears in a different font color and is underlined. Most often, the software will recognize the format of an e-mail address and automatically create a hyperlink as soon as the Space Bar is tapped after the last character of the e-mail address is keyed.

The third box also uses text to hyperlink to an e-mail address, but in this example, the text is the person's name rather than the person's e-mail address.

For additional information, contact:

 Jerry Hernandez

 Rosalind Porter

For additional information, contact:

Jerry Hernandez,
hernanj@webgate.com

Rosalind Porter,
porter@webgate.com

For additional information, contact:

Jerry Hernandez

Rosalind Porter

Lesson 40 INSERTING ART AND DRAWING OBJECTS

OBJECTIVES

- To understand how to use appropriate graphic images, lines, and shapes.
- To insert, position, and size graphic images, photos, lines, and shapes.
- To create slides with graphic enhancements.

40B

Insert Clip Art

P • Insert/Illustrations/Clip Art

1. Read the information at the right.
2. Learn how to insert clip art in a slide and how to size and position graphics.
3. Open *39D PP*. Insert an appropriate piece of clip art from your software or from Clip Art on Office Online on slides 2 and 3. If clip art isn't available, use the clip art from *DF 40B&40F PP*. Size and position the clip art attractively. See slide 2 illustration below.

Save as: **40B PP**

Art, or graphics, can enhance a message and help convey ideas. Graphic images might include clip art from your software collection or other sources such as the Internet. Graphic images could also include photo images or even original artwork scanned and converted to a digitized image.

Use graphics only when they are relevant to your topic and contribute to your presentation. Choose graphics that will not distract the audience. Clip art can often be used to add humor. Be creative, but use images in good taste. An image isn't necessary on every slide in a presentation.

40C

Insert Photo

P • Home/Copy
• Home/Paste

1. Learn how to insert photos in a slide and how to size and position the picture.
2. Open *39D PP*.
3. Open *DF 40C PP*. Copy photo 1 shown at the right and insert on slide 2 as shown below. Copy photo 2 and insert on slide 3. Size and position the picture attractively.

Save as: **40C PP**

Photo 1

Photo 2

Presentation Planning

- Consider the audience.
- Consider the subject.
- Consider the equipment.
- Consider the facilities.

Slide 2 - Bulleted List with Clip Art

Presentation Planning

- Consider the audience.
- Consider the subject.
- Consider the equipment.
- Consider the facilities.

Slide 3 - Bulleted List with Photo

a. Open *index*. Copy the mascot (lion) graphic. Close the file. Paste the lion centered below the second table in *U36 EVENTS*.

b. Make the new pictures 3" wide but keep them in proportion and center-align them, if possible.

4. View *U36 EVENTS* as a Web page and make any needed changes.

5. Key **BPSAF Events** as the Web page title.

Save as Web Page:
U36 EVENTS in your
U36-BP-XXX folder.

➢ BPSAF's **2d Annual 5K Run and Walk** was held at the Holt Trail in June. Over 125 residents participated in this fundraising event.

Insert TRAIL (a JPEG file) here.

➢ When the school district decided to renovate the stadium entrance, six members of the BPSAF Board agreed to donate their time and expertise to support this endeavor.

Insert STADIUM (a JPEG file) here.

Return to the Top

Upcoming Events

Additional information on each of these events can be obtained from the Webmaster.

➢ The **5th Annual Alumni Golf Outing** will be held at Joplin's Public Golf Course on Saturday, July 15, at 9:30 a.m. Use this mailbox to get more information on how you can support this fundraising event.

Insert GOLF (a JPEG file) here.

➢ Recipients of loans for the coming year will be decided early in July. All residents seeking loans must submit their applications by June 30.

Home

Activity 7

Excel and PowerPoint Web Pages

1. Using *Excel*, open 155 ACT5E.

2. Format the worksheet using fill and font colors consistent with those used in this website.

3. Add a home box in cell B28. Format it appropriately.

4. Save as a Web page named *U36 FINANCES* in the U36-BP-XXX folder. Key **BPSAF Financial Statements** as the title of this Web page.

5. Using *PowerPoint*, open *155 POWERPOINT*.

6. Apply a slide design that is consistent with the colors used in this website.

7. Save as a Web page named *U36 BPSAF* in the U36-BP-XXX folder. Key **About BPSAF** as the title of this Web page.

Insert Shapes

P • Insert/Illustrations/Shapes

1. Read the information at the right.
2. Learn how to use the Shapes features of your software.
3. Open *40C PP*. Create a simple logo for Multimedia Design Services. Use a circle, box, or other shape and add a fill to it. Put clip art or text on or around the shape. Place your logo attractively on the title slide.

Save as: 40D PP

Ready-made shapes can be inserted into your PowerPoint presentation. These shapes include:

- Lines
- Basic shapes
- Block arrows
- Equation shapes
- Flowchart
- Stars and banners
- Callouts

- Shapes like arrows can focus an audience's attention on important points.
- Lines can be used to separate sections of a visual, to emphasize key words, or to connect elements.
- Boxes, too, can separate elements and provide a distinctive background for text.
- Decorative borders can call attention to the contents of a box.

Lines

Equation Shapes

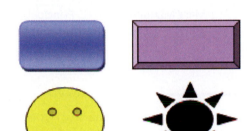

Basic Shapes

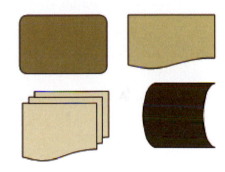

Flowchart Shapes

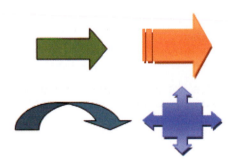

Block Arrows

Stars, Banners, and Callouts

Create a Slide with Shapes

1. Open *40D PP*. Insert a fourth slide with a Title Only layout.
2. Use the Draw Shapes feature to create the slide at the right. Use the Arial font (24-pt. bold and 18-pt. bold) for the text boxes.

Save as: 40E PP

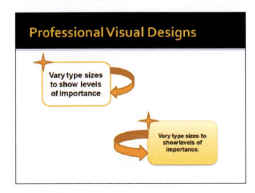

Slide 4

Activity 4

Application

1. Open *U36 BKGRD*, delete the text, and save it as a Web page named *U36 BDMBRS* in the U36-BP-XXX folder. Key **BPSAF Board Members** as the Web page title.

2. Format the tables so they are attractive, easy to read, and consistent with other Web pages of this website.

Save as Web Page: **U36 BDMBRS**

BPSAF Board Members		
Name	**Office**	**Years Served**
Adrian Hess	President	12
Harry Malone	Vice President	8
William Evans	Secretary	20
Amanda Egan	Treasurer	7
Barbara Narick	Legal Counsel	2
Alex Rendulic		5
Gladys Young		9
Paul Lyman		1
Susan Rhymond		8
Kimberly Varati		3
Ex-Officio Members		
Name	**Affiliation**	
Charles Shaw	Superintendent, BPSD	
Mary McHolme	BPHS Principal	
Margaret Julio	BPHS Guidance Counselor	

Home

Activity 5

Insert Clip Art in a Web Page

1. Read the text.
2. Complete steps 1–3.

Clip art can be inserted into Web pages in the same manner as it is inserted into other *Office* documents. Once inserted, it can be moved, edited, and used as a hyperlink, if desired.

(Hyperlinks are presented in Lesson 157.) **Note:** If you use clip art from an Internet Web page, first check the copyright policy. If necessary, give proper credit to that website.

1. Open *index*.
2. Using clip art, find a lion to represent Bristol Point School District's mascot.
3. Insert the graphic in the horizontal center after the first heading. Size the image so it is about 1.5" wide. Format it appropriately.

Save as Web page: **index**

Activity 6

Insert a Picture in a Web Page

1. Read the text.
2. Open *U36 BKGRD* and save it as a Web page named *U36 EVENTS* in the U36-BP-XXX folder.
3. Delete the existing text and key the information at the right using a background, font, and color that are consistent with the other Web pages in the website.

(continued on next page)

Picture and graphic files, like clip art, can be inserted into Web pages just as they are inserted into wp documents. Once inserted, a picture can be moved, edited, and used as a hyperlink. **Note:** If you use pictures from another website, you must give proper credit to that website.

BPSAF Events

Recent Events	Upcoming Events

Insert copy of lion in index file here.

Recent Events

➢ William Evans was recognized at the Board's meeting for his 20 years of service to BPSAF. He received a plaque noting his service to the community and BPSAF.

(continued on next page)

Create Slides with Clip Art

1. Open *40E PP*.
2. Insert two slides with Two Content layout after slide 4.
3. Create the slides as shown at the right. Insert an appropriate piece of clip art from your software, or use the Clip Art from Office Online or from *DF 40B&40F PP*.

Save as: **40F PP**

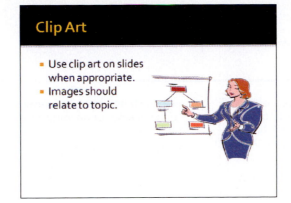

Clip Art

- Use clip art on slides when appropriate.
- Images should relate to topic.

Slide 5

Presenter Tips

- Dress professionally
- Speak clearly
- Maintain eye contact
- Use natural gestures
- Smile

Slide 6

Lesson 41-42   CREATING DIAGRAMS AND TABLES

OBJECTIVES
- To learn how diagrams and tables can portray processes and ideas.
- To create diagrams using the choice, stair steps, cluster, and flowchart designs.
- To create tables to enhance a presentation.

Create a Choice Diagram

P • Design/Background/ Background Styles/ Format Background

1. Start a new presentation using the Solstice design theme.
2. Choose the Title and Content layout.
3. Learn how to change the background of the slide. Change the slide background to Texture fill —Stationery.
4. Move the box in which you will key the bulleted text to the bottom of the slide.
5. Use the Shapes feature to create the choice diagram in the space above the bulleted list.
6. Key the bulleted list.

Save as: **41-42B PP**

A diagram is a drawing that explains a process or idea. Diagrams can help an audience understand relationships or a sequence of events. Text can be arranged in boxes that are connected with lines or arrows to help the audience visualize the individual steps in a process or the parts of an idea.

The diagram below indicates that a choice must be made between two options. The arrows pointing in opposite directions indicate an either/or situation. This same technique can be used to represent conflict.

Presentation software allows you to use different backgrounds for the entire slide or parts of the slide. The backgrounds fill effects include:

- Solid Fill
- Gradient Fill
- Picture or Texture Fill

Notice the difference in the background of the strip down the side of the slides below.

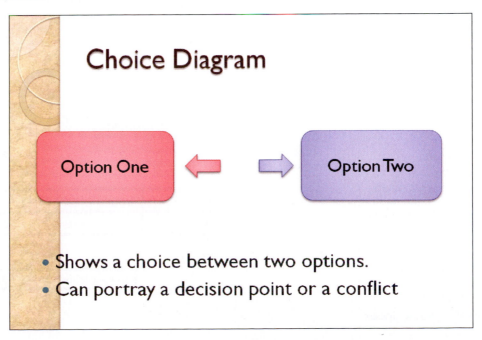

Choice Diagram

Option One ← → Option Two

- Shows a choice between two options.
- Can portray a decision point or a conflict

Slide 1

OBJECTIVE

• To create Web pages with tables, graphics, and pictures.

156B

Activity 1

Website for Bristol Point Student Aid Fund

In this and the next lesson, you will complete the first few pages of a website for the Bristol Point Student Aid Fund.

1. Find the folder named DF U36-BP-XXX and change its name by deleting **DF** and replacing the *XXX* with your initials.

   Note: All files relating to the Bristol Point Student Aid Fund website must be filed in the U36-BP-XXX folder so hyperlinks to your files can be easily inserted in later activities. The

website then can be uploaded to the Internet or an intranet, if applicable.

2. Open a new *Word* document and apply a Page Color that uses red and blue, Bristol Point School District's school colors.

3. Key your name in a font and font color that are

attractive and easy to read. Select a font from Arial, Calibri, Comic Sans, or Verdana.

4. Save the background and font selections as a Web page file named *U36 BKGRD* in the U36-BP-XXX folder. This file will be used for the three BPSAF Web pages in Lessons 156–157.

Activity 2

Review

1. Open *U36 BKGRD*, delete the text, and save it as a Web page named **index** in the U36-BP-XXX folder. The filename for the home page for the BPAA website is *index*.

2. Key the text at right as the home page of the website, keying the first line in 36-pt. font; the next two lines in 24-pt. font; the first ¶ in 12-pt. font; and the last ¶ in italic 10-pt. font.

3. View it as a Web page. Save the Web page as **index** in the U36-BP-XXX folder.

Bristol Point Student Aid Fund

Supporting Residents of Bristol Point School District Since 1976

Mission Statement

BPAA's mission is to provide loans to needy and deserving residents of Bristol Point School District who are enrolled in undergraduate programs of study at an accredited higher education institution. By supporting such students, BPSAF fosters pride in academic attainment.

This site is maintained by Bristol Point High School students and the BPAA Webmaster. Please e-mail your feedback to the Webmaster.

Activity 3

Tables

1. Read the text.
2. Open *index*.
3. Insert the tables below the mission statement. Center them horizontally; use a 12-pt. bold font; and use colored borders around the cells.
4. Key **Bristol Point Student Aid Fund** as the Web page title.

Save as Web Page: index

Many Web pages use tables to organize information in an attractive manner. The Table feature of your word processor can be used to create tables for your Web pages.

You can use features you learned in previous units to format the tables so they are attractive, easy to read, and consistent with your background and font colors.

About BPSAF	Board Members	Finances
Donors	Events	Bristol Point High School

Voice Mailbox	*535-555-0193*

Create a Stair Steps Diagram

1. Read the information at the right.
2. Open *41-42B PP* and insert a slide for slide 2. Create slide 2 using the Title and Content layout.
3. Use the Shapes features to create the stair steps diagram for slides 3–6.

Hint: Use the following steps to create the boxes:

1. Create the bottom box.
2. After creating the first box, copy and paste it to make the remaining boxes (steps).
3. Edit the text and color of the pasted boxes.

Save as: **41-42C PP**

The diagram below shows a series of ideas. The stair steps diagram begins with a box at the bottom containing the text for the first idea being explained. Additional boxes with text are positioned to look like stairs going up. For a slide show, you could prepare four separate slides so that the stair steps appear one at a time as the discussion progresses. After completing the first slide, copy and paste it. Make the changes for the second slide; then copy and paste it to make the third slide, etc.

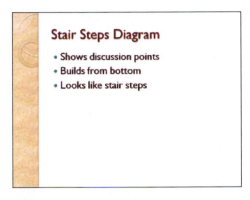

Slide 2

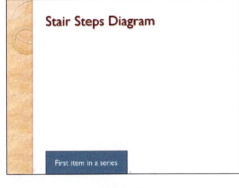

Slide 3

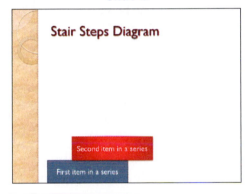

Slide 4

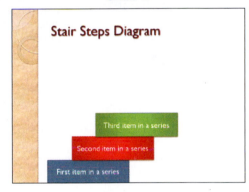

Slide 5

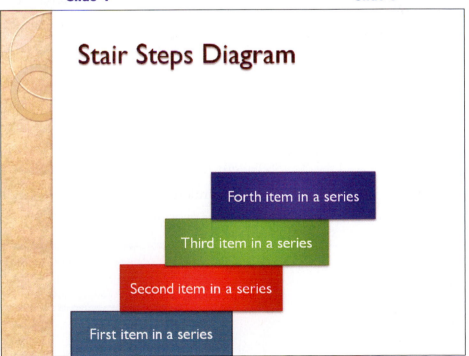

Slide 6

Office Tip for *Excel*: A picture background can be added to an Excel Web page **(Page Layout/Page Setup/ Background)**.

Office Tip for *PowerPoint*: The background in the design theme used for the slides will be the background that appears when displayed in a browser **(Design/Themes)**.

a. Create backgrounds using solid colors of your choice.
b. Create backgrounds using textures of your choice.
c. Create backgrounds using patterns of your choice.
d. Create a background using the picture with the filename *PICTURE* (find *PICTURE* in the U36 GRAPHICS folder).
e. Choose a background and font color that you believe to be very easy to read and attractive. Show your instructor what you have chosen.
f. Save the file in Web Page format named *155 ACT4*, preview it, and print it. (The background won't print.)

Activity 5

Set Page Title

1. Read the text.
2. Learn to create a page title on a Web page.
3. Open *155 WORD*.
4. Key **Ms. Dilligan's Home Page** as the Web page title.

Save in Web Page format as *155 ACT5W*.

Each Web page has a title displayed in the browser title bar at the top of the window. If you do not specify a title for a Web page, the software will create one for you. Since you want the title to accurately describe the content of the Web page, you should specify a title to be displayed. In *Word*, go to the Save as Web Page dialog box and specify a Web page title. Click the Change Title button, click in the Set Page Title dialog box, and key the desired title.

The illustration shows the Save as Web Page dialog box that is accessed from the Change Title button that appears in the Save as dialog box after the Web Page format is selected in the Save as type list.

5. Open *155 EXCEL* and key **Bristol Student Aid Fund** as the Web page title.
Save in Web page format as *155 ACT5E*.

6. Preview each document in the browser, noting the title that is displayed in the browser's tabs.

Activity 6

Application

1. Open a new *Word* document.
2. Key the text at the right, using the directions given in the text.
3. Key **Lesson 155: Activity 6** as the title of the Web page.
4. Preview the document in your browser.
5. Compare the Web page text with the text you keyed and directions you followed. Does your browser support all of the wp features used in this activity?

Save in Web Page format as *155 ACT6*.

Center-align this text using 36-pt. Verdana font

Left-align this text using 18-pt. Verdana font

Right-align this text using 18-pt. Verdana font

Using left alignment, 12-pt. Verdana font, and a bullet style you select, list the following lines:

- Bullet 1
- Bullet 2
- Bullet 3

Using 16-pt. Comic Sans MS font, indent the following lines as directed:

    Indent this line 0.5" from left margin

        Indent this line 1" from left margin

            Indent this line 1.5" from left margin

> Center a shaded text box with a border.
> Use 14-pt. Comic Sans MS font for the text. Select a font color.

Create a Flowchart

P • Insert/Illustrations/Shapes/Flowchart symbol

1. Read the information at the right.
2. Start a **new** presentation using the **Median** design theme.
3. Create a title slide using **Flowchart** for the title. Use your name for the subtitle. Use **Stationery** for the slide background.
4. For slides 2–5, use Title Only layout; change the **slide** background to **Stationery**. Create four additional slides using the Shapes feature. The last of the slides is shown at the right. The first slide would only include *Start*. The next slide would include *Start* and *Step*. The third slide would include *Start*, *Step*, and *Input*.

Note: This is a horizontal flowchart. Flowcharts may also be shown vertically.

Save as: **41-42D PP**

The flowchart below shows steps in a process, connected by arrows. Flowcharts can use pictures or shapes. In a flowchart with shapes, each shape has a certain meaning. An oval shows the beginning or end of a process. A parallelogram shows input or output. A diamond shows a decision to be made, worded as a question. Two arrows, one marked *Yes* and one marked *No*, extend from the diamond to the flowchart step that results from the decision. A rectangle shows a step that does not require a decision.

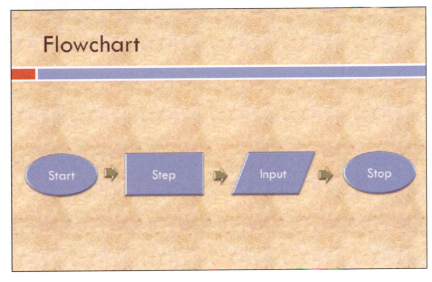

Slide 5

Create a Table

P • Home/Slides/New Slide/Layout/Title and Content/Insert Table

1. Read the information at the right.
2. Create a new presentation using the Technic design theme.
3. Using the Title and Content layout, insert a table to include the information shown at the right.
4. Create the slide.

Save as: **41-42E PP**

Tables can be used to organize information that can be displayed in presentations to compare and contrast facts or figures and to list data.

Tables can be created in *PowerPoint*, or they can be created in *Word* or *Excel* and inserted into *PowerPoint*.

FBLA Membership by Year

Year	Members	+/- from Previous Year
2005	20	-
2006	28	8
2007	39	11
2008	56	17
2009	75	19

Activity 2

Open a Web Page

1. Read the text.
2. Learn to open a Web page in *Word, Excel,* and *PowerPoint.*
3. Complete steps a–f:
   a. Open *DF 155 WORD*.
   b. Save in Web Page format named *155 WORD*.

After saving an *Office* document as a Web page, you can open the Web page in the *Office* program in which it was created. For example, if you save an *Excel* workbook in Web Page format and then reopen the Web page file in *Excel*, the workbook will look the same as the original worksheet you created in *Excel*. *Excel,*

   c. Open *DF 155 EXCEL*.
   d. Save in Web Page format named *155 EXCEL*.

like *Word* and *PowerPoint,* preserves the original formatting of the document. This allows you to easily switch from the file in HTML format (Web Page) to the standard *Office* program format and back again as needed when you are creating or editing Web pages.

   e. Open *DF 155 POWERPOINT*.
   f. Save in Web Page format named *155 POWERPOINT*.

Activity 3

Preview Web Page in Browser

1. Read the text.
2. Learn to preview Web pages in *Office* documents.
3. Complete steps a–i:
   a. Open *155 WORD*.
   b. Preview as a Web page.
   c. Save in Web Page format using same filename.
   d. Open *155 EXCEL*.
   e. Preview as a Web page.
   f. Save in Web Page format using same filename.
   g. Open *155 POWER-POINT*.
   h. Preview as a Web page.
   i. Save in Web Page format using same filename.

You can see how any *Office* document will look after it is posted on the Internet or intranet by previewing the Web page. This enables you to see if there are any errors that need to be corrected or formatting features that need to be added, changed, or deleted. Previewing the Web page is similar to using the Print Preview feature before you print a document.

To preview your Web page, click the Web Page Preview button on the Quick Access Toolbar. This command opens a browser and displays the document as a Web page in it. If the Web Page Preview button is not on your toolbar, follow the steps at the right to add it.

Web Preview Button

Placing the Web Preview Button on the Quick Access Toolbar

1. Display the Customize Quick Access Toolbar options by clicking the list arrow to the right of the Quick Access Toolbar.
2. Select *More Commands*.
3. Under *Choose commands from*, select *All Commands*.
4. Scroll down the All Commands list to *Web Page Preview*, select it, and then click *Add* to insert it into the existing list of commands on the Quick Access Toolbar.
5. Click OK.

Learning Cue

When using *Word*, a document can be viewed as a Web page by using Web Layout View on the status bar.

Activity 4

Word: Page Color

1. Read the text.
2. Open *155 WORD*.
3. Complete steps a–f on the next page to create different backgrounds for *155 WORD*.

Page Color (background) can be used to create attractive Web pages in *Word*. With Page Color, you can apply various colors and fill effects: a solid color, a color in a variety of textures or patterns, different gradients that use one or two colors, or a picture.

A good practice is to select the background and the color of the font together so the combination is easy to read and attractive.

The illustration shows the Theme Colors, No Color, More Colors, and Fill Effects options for backgrounds. Use Fill Effects to select gradients, textures, patterns, and pictures as backgrounds.

Lesson 43 — CREATING GRAPHS AND CHARTS

OBJECTIVES

- To learn which graph or chart to use for particular situations.
- To learn to create graphs.
- To learn various graph elements.

43B

Learn Graph Elements

1. Read the information at the right.
2. Locate the various graph elements in bar chart below.
3. Learn how to create charts and graphs in your software.

Numeric information can be easier to understand when shown as **a graph** or **chart** rather than in text or a table. The relationship between data sets or trends can be compared with bar graphs, line graphs, area graphs, or pie charts. Each type of graph or chart is best suited for a particular situation.

- **Bar graph**—comparison of item quantities
- **Line and area graphs**—quantity changes over time or distance
- **Pie chart**—parts of a whole

Elements common to most graphs are identified on the bar graph shown below. They include:

- **X-axis**—the horizontal axis; usually for categories
- **Y-axis**—the vertical axis; usually for values

- **Scale**—numbers on the Y- or X-axis representing quantities
- **Tick marks**—coordinate marks on the graph to help guide the reader
- **Grids**—lines that extend from tick marks to make it easier to see data values
- **Labels**—names used to identity parts of the graph
- **Legend**—the key that identifies the shading, coloring, or patterns used for the information shown in the graph

To change the design of the graph, click on the graph. This activates the Chart Tools. The Chart Styles under the Design tab allow you to select from a variety of preset designs. Notice the difference between the appearance of the two graphs shown below.

43C

Create Bar Graph

P • Home/Slides/New Slide/Layout/Title andContent/Insert Chart/Column

1. Read the information at the right.
2. Open *41-42E PP* and create the bar graph as shown below for slide 2. Use the data from 41-42E in the previous lesson.
3. Change the Chart Style design to Style 34 (Design/Chart Style/Style 34).

Save as: **43C PP**

Bar graphs compare one or more sets of data that are plotted on the horizontal X-axis and the vertical Y-axis. The X-axis usually contains category information (such as years or months); the Y-axis usually contains measured quantity values (numbers).

Vertical bars (columns) are easy to interpret; the baseline on the Y-axis should begin at zero for consistent comparisons when several graphs are used. Special effects can be added, but a simple graph is effective for showing relationships.

Graph Elements

OBJECTIVES

- To learn to open, title, save, and preview Office documents as Web pages.
- To learn to apply a background to *Word* Web pages.

155A–160A

Conditioning Practice

Key each line twice.

alphabet	1	Danny bought major equipment to vitalize work after the tax cuts.
figures	2	Call 712-9648 in 30–35 days to get the orders Sean has requested.
speed	3	The busy maid bid for the ivory soap dish and antique ivory bowl.

gwam 1' | 1 | 2 | 3 | 4 | 5 | 6 | 7 | 8 | 9 | 10 | 11 | 12 | 13 |

155B

Activity 1

Create and Save Office Documents as Web Pages

1. Read the text.
2. Learn to save *Word, Excel,* and *PowerPoint* documents in Web Page format.
3. Open a new *Word* document and key your name, the date, and your school's name on three lines in the upper-left corner of the document.
4. Save in Web Page format named *155 ACT1WD.*
5. Open a new *Excel* document and key your name, the date, and your school's name in cells A1, A2, and A3.
6. Save in Web Page format named *155 ACT1EX.*
7. Open a new *PowerPoint* document and key your name, the date, and your school's name on the title slide.
8. Save in Web Page format named *155 ACT1PP.*

An Office document can be saved as a Web Page in three formats. The desired format is selected from the "Save as type" list in the Save As dialog box. The formats available in *Word* are:

- Web Page
- Single File Web Page
- Web Page, Filtered

Excel and *PowerPoint* do not offer the Web Page, Filtered format.

The illustration below shows the Save As dialog box in *Word* with the three formats in Save As showing in the Save as type list. The Web Page format is selected, and the other formats are listed above and below it in the illustration.

All three formats automatically insert HTML code into the document. Without the HTML code, browsers are unable to display the document on the Internet or intranet.

The **Web Page** format saves the document in one file and creates a folder to hold the graphics used in the Web page.

The **Single File Web Page** format saves the document and supporting graphics in one file. This format may be used when the Web page is to be viewed in an *Internet Explorer* browser, Version 4.0.1 or later.

The **Web Page, Filtered** format is similar to the Web Page format except some of the HTML code is removed, making the file smaller than it is when saved in Web Page format. This option should only be used when you are finished editing the document as a *Word, Excel,* or *PowerPoint* file, since it may lose some of its HTML coding that is needed to display the document in its original format. Because of this, it is wise to save a version of the file in its original format when using the Web Page, Filtered option.

All Web pages in this unit will be saved in the Web Page format to increase the likelihood they will be supported by most browsers. In addition, we may want to open the document in its original format to edit further.

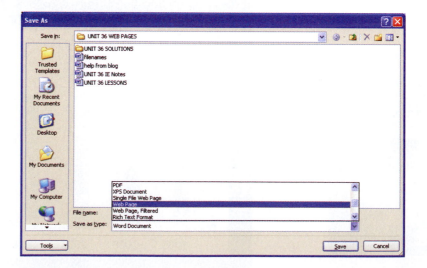

Create Line Graph

P • Home/New Slide/Layout/ Title and Content/Insert Chart/Column

1. Start a new presentation using the Paper design theme with Title and Content layout. Create a line graph showing the number of employees using the following data:
   - 1980 30
   - 1985 38
   - 1990 45
   - 1995 42
   - 2000 40
   - 2005 47
   - 2010 60
2. Display the data labels above the line.

Save as: 43D PP

Same slide with different chart style

Line graphs display changes in quantities over time or distance. Usually the X-axis shows a particular period of time or distance. The Y-axis shows measurements of quantity at different times or distances. The baseline of the Y-axis should be zero to provide a consistent reference point when several graphs are used in a presentation.

When the numbers for the X-axis are entered, lines appear connecting the values on the graph to reflect the changes in amounts. A grid with vertical lines helps the viewer interpret quantities.

Several sets of data can be displayed by using lines in different colors. Various options are available for placing titles, legends, and labels on line graphs.

Line Graph

Create an Area Graph

P • Design/Type/Change Chart Type/Area

1. Open *43D PP*.
2. Change the Chart Type from line graph to area graph.
3. Do not display the data values.

Save as: 43E PP

Same slide with different chart style

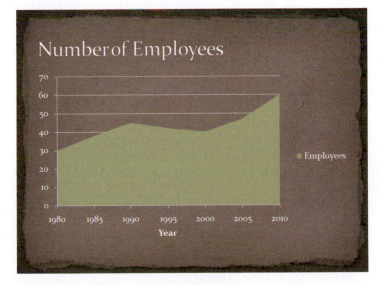

Area Graph

Creating Web Pages

There are many different ways to create Web pages. Often, large companies employ expert programmers who write time-consuming code to create and maintain complicated websites. Other businesses may contract with Web page design companies or consultants to create their Web pages. Some businesses create and maintain their websites by using Web page design software that does not require knowledge of **HTML (HyperText Markup Language)**—a computer language that specifies the codes that browsers use to format and display the document.

Many smaller companies, and individuals creating personal websites, use word processing, spreadsheet, or electronic presentation software to create Web pages. Pages created with these general application packages can be very effective. They are likely, however, to lack some of the "bells and whistles" that specialized software and expert programmers can provide.

Microsoft Office and Web Pages

The *Microsoft Office* programs (*Word, Excel, PowerPoint,* etc.) provide tools you need to create and save your documents as a Web page in HTML format without needing to learn HTML. Once saved in HTML format, a document can be previewed in the *Office* program or in a browser such as Internet Explorer. When the Web page is previewed in a browser, you are able to see the *Office* document as if it were already on the Web.

When you preview your Web page, your Web page format may look a little different than it does when viewed within the *Office* program, since browsers do not support all *Office* software features. For example:

- Character formatting such as shadow, emboss, and engrave is not supported by all browsers.
- Tab settings may not appear when the browser is used.
- Spacing after the punctuation ending a sentence may change from two spaces to one space.
- The alignment of pictures and graphs and the placement of wrapped text may change.
- Headers and footers and page numbers may not appear.
- Row height in tables may change.

Web Page Activities

Word, Excel, and *PowerPoint* software will be used to create Web pages in this unit. *Internet Explorer* will be the browser used to preview the Web pages, unless you have another browser set as your default browser.

In Lessons 155–157, you will create Web pages for a high school alumni association. The pages include a background and text in various font sizes, styles, and colors.

Hyperlinks connect to places within the same Web page, to other Web pages within the same website, to different websites, and to e-mail addresses. Pictures, graphics, and tables are used.

In Lessons 158–160, you have an opportunity to create a website of your choice. It can be Web pages for yourself, your family, your school, a business, an organization, etc. You should, therefore, think about the purpose of your website and identify the Web pages you will include in your site as you complete the activities in Lessons 155–157.

Create Pie Charts

P • Home/ New Slide/Layout/ Title and Content/Insert Chart/Pie

Pie Chart 1

1. Read the information at the right.
2. Open *43C PP*.
3. Create the pie chart shown at right as slide 3.

Chart data:

2005	20
2006	28
2007	39
2008	56
2009	75

Save as: 43F PP

Pie charts are best used to display parts of a whole. They show clearly the proportional relationship of only one set of values. Without any numbers displayed, the chart shows only general relationships. In the examples shown below, the different colors used for the pie slices are identified in a legend. Colors used on the pie chart should provide adequate contrast between the slices. Consider also the color scheme of your entire presentation so that the pie chart will coordinate with other visuals.

Pie Chart, Legend at Right, Outside Labels

Pie Chart 2

P • Insert/Type/Change Chart Type/Pie/Explode

P • Layout/Labels/Legend/ None

P • Layout/Labels/Data labels/ More Label Options/Cat. Name, Percent

1. Change Pie Chart 1 to give it a 3D appearance and to emphasize the pie slices by exploding them.
2. Remove the legend.
3. Display Category Name labels and percentages with each slice.

Save as: 43F-2 PP

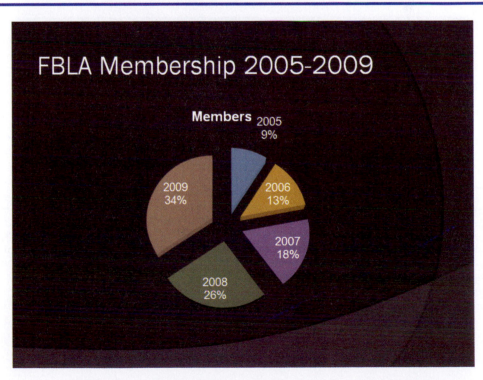

3D Pie Chart, Inside Category Name, Legend, and Labels

154D

What If

1. If needed, open *154C WORKSHEET* and answer this question: What is the total payroll if the hourly rate is increased to $10.75?

2. Clear the conditional formatting in column J, and then reapply to highlight those who would earn more than $430.

   Save as: **154D WORKSHEET**

154E

Letter with Linked Worksheet

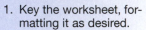

1. Key the worksheet, formatting it as desired.

   Save as:
   154E WORKSHEET

2. Copy the worksheet, with a link, into *DF 154E WP* between the first two ¶s.

   Save as: **154E WP**

FRAMES BY yourframes.com				
Size	Quantity			
	1-6	7-12	13-24	24+
4" X 6"	$ 17.98	$ 16.18	$ 14.56	$ 13.11
5" X 7"	$ 19.98	$ 17.98	$ 16.18	$ 14.57
8" X10"	$ 21.98	$ 19.78	$ 17.80	$ 16.02

154F

Update Letter with Link

1. Open *154E WORKSHEET* and increase each amount by $2.00.

2. Open wp file *154E WP*, which will update the letter with the new amounts. Use today's date and address it to:

   Dr. Patricia Kurtz
   1246 Warren Drive
   Denver, CO 80221-7463

   Save as: **154F WP**

154G

Multiple Worksheets and 3-D References

1. Open *DF 154G WORKSHEET* and make Sheet 1 active, if needed.

2. Write an If function in cell H4 to calculate the number of hours in excess of 40 during each week.

3. Copy this formula to cells H4 in each of the worksheets 2, 3, 4, and 5 and then to H5:H14 in each of the five worksheets.

4. Calculate the total overtime hours in cell H15 in worksheet 1, and then copy it to H15 in the other four worksheets.

5. Rename each of the worksheets using the last name of the employee and then arrange them in alphabetical order starting at the left.

6. Insert a new worksheet. Position it to so it is the first worksheet.

7. Rename the new worksheet **OVT RPT** and key the information as shown in the worksheet at the right.

	A	B
1	Employee	Overtime Hours
2	Carney	
3	Connors	
4	Greene	
5	Tillitson	
6	Zanetti	

8. In cell B2 of the *OVT RPT* worksheet, insert a 3-D reference to cell H15 in the *Carney* worksheet.

9. In a similar manner, enter a 3-D cell reference in cells B3, B4, B5, and B6 in the OVT RPT worksheet to cell H15 in each of the employee's worksheets.

10. Embed the following text as a *Word* file using 9-pt. font below row 6 in *OVT RPT*:

This worksheet shows the total overtime hours worked by each employee.

11. Print the *OVT RPT* worksheet.

Save as: **154G WORKSHEET**

• To create an electronic presentation

44B

Create an Electronic Presentation

Open *DF 44B PP* and review the pictures of New York City. Read the poem and reports you keyed for 33B, 33C, and 34B on the city. Use the Internet to learn more about it.

Using these pictures and the information from the reports and the Internet, prepare an electronic presentation to give to your classmates on the sights of New York City.

Shown at the right are a few examples of what can be done with the pictures. Use your creativity to make the presentation interesting as well as informative.

Save as: 44B PP

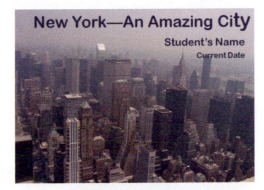

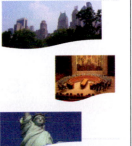

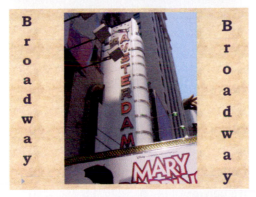

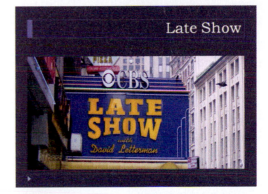

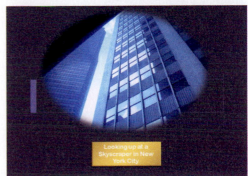

Application

1. Open *DF 153F WORKSHEET*.
2. Use data bars to apply conditional formatting to cells B6:I6.
3. Create a column chart with a title and legend using information in cells A2:I5.
4. Move the chart to a chart sheet.
5. Embed the text at the right below the worksheet.
6. You decide all other formatting features for the worksheet, chart, and embedded file.

Save as: 153F WORKSHEET

This activity required me to apply what I have learned in this lesson. I applied specialized conditional formatting, created a chart and chart sheet, and embedded a new Word file in a worksheet.

Lesson 154   SPREADSHEET APPLICATIONS

OBJECTIVE

• To apply what you have learned in this and the previous spreadsheet units.

Integrate Word and Excel and Charting

1. Key the wp table at the right.

Save as: 154B WP

2. Copy the table into a blank worksheet; make formatting adjustments as desired.
3. Create a column chart with title, legend, and other features you choose.
4. Move the chart to a chart sheet.

Save as:
154B WORKSHEET

CORRESPONDENCE REPORT					
TYPE	MON	TUE	WED	THU	FRI
U.S. Postal Service	10	12	11	10	9
Interoffice	14	12	10	8	11
E-mail	24	18	15	14	12
Facsimile	8	7	10	11	6
Private carrier	9	11	10	13	8

Worksheet with Calculations and Conditional Formatting

1. Open *DF 154C WORKSHEET*.
2. Calculate the hours worked by each employee in column G.
3. Write an IF function for calculations in column H so that all hours worked

up to and including 40 are paid at the hourly rate in cell D17.

4. Write an IF function for column I to calculate overtime pay that is paid at 1.5 the hourly rate in D17 for all hours worked over 40.
5. In column J, calculate each employee's gross pay and apply conditional formatting to high-light those who earned more than $425.

6. Calculate totals for cells G15-J15.
7. Calculate the average pay in cell D18, the minimum pay in D19, and the maximum pay in D20.
8. Use two decimal places for currency.
9. Use data bars in column I (cell I4:I14) to show different levels of overtime pay.

Save as: 154C WORKSHEET

OBJECTIVE

- To give a presentation using electronic slides.

45B

Practice Presenting

1. Read the information about delivering a presentation.

2. Practice giving the presentation that you created in 44B.

Presenting Delivery

Planning and preparing a presentation is only half the task of giving a good presentation. The other half is the delivery. Positive thinking is a must for a good presenter. Prepare and practice before the presentation. This will help you be confident that you can do a good job. Don't worry that the presentation will not be perfect. Set a goal of being a better speaker each time you give a speech, not of being a perfect speaker each time. Practice these tips to improve your presentation skills.

- **Know your message.** Knowing the message well allows you to talk with the audience rather than read to them.
- **Look at the audience.** Make eye contact with one person briefly (for two to three seconds). Then move on to another person.
- **Look confident.** Stand erect and show that you want to communicate with the audience.
- **Let your personality come through.** Be natural; let the audience know who you are. Show your enthusiasm for the topic you are presenting.
- **Vary the volume and rate at which you speak.** Slow down to emphasize points. Speed up on points that you are sure your audience is familiar with.
- **Use gestures and facial expressions.** A smile, frown, or puzzled look, when appropriate, can help communicate your message. Make sure your gestures are natural.
- **Know how to use the visuals.** Practice using the visual aids you have chosen for the presentation. Glance at each visual as you display it. Then focus on the audience.

45C

Give a Presentation

1. Review the evaluation at the right.
2. Break up into groups of three. Each student in your group will give the presentation that was developed in Lesson 44. While one student is giving the presentation, the other two will evaluate it using the form shown at the right.

The evaluation form is available in the data files: *DF 45C Eval Form.*

	Excellent	Good	Need(s) Improvement	Comments
The introduction to the topic is				
The body of the presentation is				
The visual aids are				
The speaker's ability to use the visual aids is				
The speaker's enthusiasm is				
The speaker's eye contact is				
The speaker's gestures are				
The speaker's confidence is				
The speaker's vocal variation is				
The speaker's facial expressions are				
The closing is				

153C

Embed a File

SS • Insert/Text/Object

1. Read the text.
2. Learn to embed a *Word* file in an *Excel* file.
3. Open *DF 153C WORK-SHEET* and save it as *153C WORKSHEET-S*.
4. Click in cell A30. Choose to embed a new *Word* file.
5. Size the *Word* writing window so it spans cells A30 to J32.
6. Key the text at the right in the *Word* writing window, using Arial 10-pt. red font.

Save as:
153C WORKSHEET

Embedding inserts a copy of a file created in one program (source file) into a file created in another program (destination file). Once inserted, the embedded file can be edited with the commands and toolbar buttons used to create the source file. Any changes you make in the embedded file appear only in the destination file and not the source file since they are not linked. The source file can be an existing file or a new file created in the destination file.

In Unit 30, you embedded a worksheet in a word processing document when you used *Excel* Spreadsheet in the Insert Table feature. In this activity, you will create a *Word* file (source file) in an *Excel* file (destination file).

Directions: Record a score for each member of your group, excluding yourself. Be sure to take into consideration each group member's contribution to the planning and preparation as well as the visual and oral presentations.

153D

Review Charting

Complete steps 1–3.

1. Open *DF 153D WORK-SHEET1* and create a bar chart with chart and axis titles and gridlines. Enlarge the chart as needed to make it easy to read.

   Save as:
   153D WORKSHEET1

2. Open *DF 153D WORK-SHEET2* and create a column chart with chart and axis titles, gridlines, and legend. Enlarge the chart as needed to make it easy to read.

   Save as:
   153D WORKSHEET2

3. Open *DF 153D WORK-SHEET3* and create a pie chart with chart title, legend, and data labels showing %. Enlarge the chart as needed to make it easy to read.

   Save as:
   153D WORKSHEET3

153E

Create Chart Sheet

SS • Chart Tools/Design/ Location/ Move Chart

1. Study the text.
2. Learn to display a chart as a chart sheet.
3. Open *153D WORK-SHEET1* and move the chart to a new chart sheet.

Save as:
153E WORKSHEET1

4. Repeat step 3 for *153D WORKSHEET2* and *153D WORKSHEET3*.

Save as:
153E WORKSHEET2 and 153E WORKSHEET3

Charts can be created and displayed two ways—as an embedded object or as a new chart sheet. Charts created previously have been created and displayed as embedded objects. That is, the chart is placed within the worksheet so the chart and data can be viewed at the same time.

In this activity, charts will be created and placed in a new chart sheet. The chart sheet is a separate sheet in the workbook. You can access the chart sheet by clicking the chart tab to the left of the worksheet tab near the bottom of the worksheet. Chart sheets are saved when the worksheet is saved. You can

use the default name(s) assigned or give each chart sheet a specific name. Several charts can be prepared from a worksheet if chart sheets are used.

CYCLE 1
Review

• To review Cycle 1 formatting skills, *Office Suite* features, and straight-copy skills.

Conditioning Practice

Key each line twice SS.

alphabet	1	Quincy just put back five azure gems next to the gold watch.
fig/sym	2	Tim moved from 5142 Troy Lane to 936--123rd Street on 8/7/03.
speed	3	He lent the field auditor a hand with the work for the firm.

gwam 1' | 1 | 2 | 3 | 4 | 5 | 6 | 7 | 8 | 9 | 10 | 11 | 12 |

Activity 1

Memo

Format and key the text at the right as a memo. Proofread your copy; correct all keying and format errors.

Save as: CR1 ACTIVITY1

TO: Marguerite Mercedes, Director

FROM: Justin Mathews, Administrative Assistant

DATE: March 5, 20--

SUBJECT: BALLET COMPANY ADDRESSES

Attached is the address list for the ballet companies that you requested. I was unable to secure an address for the Bolshoi Ballet in Moscow.

I have seen the Royal Swedish Ballet, the American Ballet Theatre, and the Paris Opera Ballet perform. They were all excellent. The patrons of our Artist Series would be extremely pleased with any of the three performances.

Even though I have not personally seen performances by any of the other groups on the list, I have heard excellent comments by others who have been fortunate enough to see them perform. I don't think we can go wrong by inviting any of those on the list to be a part of next year's Artist Series.

xx

Attachment

152D

Copy a Worksheet Chart to a Word Processing Document

1. Open *DF 152D WORKSHEET* and save it as *152D WORKSHEET-S*.
2. Open *DF 152D WP* and save it as *152D WP*.
3. Copy and paste the chart in *152D WORKSHEET-S* into *152D WP* as a *Microsoft Office Excel* Chart Object with a link.
4. Save and close *152D WP*.
5. If needed, open *152D WORKSHEET-S*.

Like worksheets, worksheet charts can be copied into a wp document by using Copy and Paste (or Paste Special) commands to avoid recreating the chart. The chart can be pasted in a variety of ways: With or without a link to the source document, with source file or destination file formatting, or as a chart that can be edited in Word or Excel, etc. In this activity, paste the chart so it is linked to the worksheet, can be edited as an Excel document, and retains the formatting of the source document.

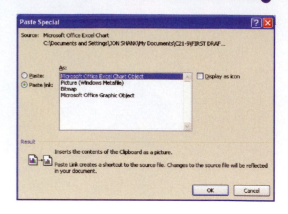

6. Change the contents of cell B2 to **158**, C2 to **162**, B3 to **164**, and cell C3 to **166**.

Save as: 152D WORKSHEET-S

7. Open *152D WP* and update the data in the table.

Save as: 152D WORKSHEET

152E

Application

1. Open *DF 152E WORKSHEET* and save it as *152E WORKSHEET-S*.
2. Open *DF 152E WP* and save it as *152E WP*.

3. Copy and paste the chart in *152E WORKSHEET-S* into *152E WP* as a *Microsoft Office Excel* Chart Object with a link.
4. Save and close *152E WP*.
5. If needed, open *152E WORKSHEET-S*.

6. Change the contents of cell B2 to **1450**, C2 to **360**, B3 to **1600**, cell C3 to **425**, B4 to **1250**, and C4 to **275**.

Save as: 152E WORKSHEET-S

7. Open *152E WP* and update the data in the table.

Save as: 152E WORKSHEET

Lesson 153   FORMATTING, EMBEDDING, AND CHARTING WORKSHEETS

OBJECTIVE

• To apply specialized conditional formats, to embed a *Word* file in an *Excel* file, to create a chart sheet.

153B

Apply Specialized Conditional Formatting

SS • Home/Styles/Conditional Formatting

1. Open *DF 153B WORKSHEET*.
2. Apply a Data Bar conditional format to values in column B.
3. Apply a Color Scale conditional format to values in column C.
4. Apply an Icon Set conditional format to values in column D.

Save as:
153B WORKSHEET

You can use data bars, color scales, and icon sets as specialized conditional formats. A **data bar** shows the value of a cell relative to other cells—larger values have a longer data bar. A **color scale** uses a two- or three- color gradient to show how values vary—the shade of the color represents the value in the cell. An **icon set** can classify data into three to five categories—each icon represents a value in the cell. The settings for each of these specialized conditional formats can be changed by selecting the More Rules options in each list.

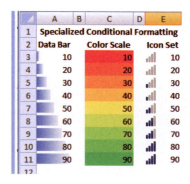

Activity 2

Letter

Format and key the text at the right as a personal-business letter. Proofread your copy; correct all keying and format errors.

Save as: CR1 ACTIVITY2

810 Lake Grove Court | San Diego, CA 92131-8112 | March 30, 20-- | Ms. Barbara Knight | 2010 Rosewood Place | Riverside, CA 92506-6528 | Dear Barbara

Can you believe that we will be in London in less than three months? London is one of my favorite places to visit.

I've done some checking on London's theatres. Do any of the three plays I've listed below interest you? If so, let me know, and I'll make the arrangements.

Les Miserables: Story revolves around nineteenth-century French Revolution with its struggles, passion, and love.

Amadeus: Story about the life of Mozart in eighteenth-century Vienna and his rivalry with composer Sallieri.

Starlight Express: Musical by Andrew Lloyd Weber with lyrics by Richard Stilgoe.

Les Miserables is being performed at the Palace Theatre, *Amadeus* at The Old Vic, and *Starlight Express* at the Apollo Victoria. The Palace Theatre and The Old Vic were both built in the 1800s.

I've confirmed our reservations at the Copthorne Tara. If there is anything else that you would like me to check, let me know.

Sincerely | Jessica C. Holloway

xx

Activity 3

E-mail

Key the e-mail message at the right to your instructor. If you do not have access to e-mail, format and key the text as an interoffice memo using the following information:

TO: Jessica Holloway
FROM: Barbara Knight
DATE: March 15, 20—
SUBJECT: LONDON EXCURSION

Proofread your message; correct all errors.

Save as: CR1 ACTIVITY3

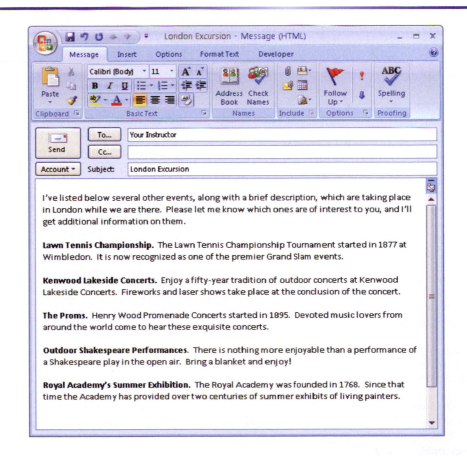

I've listed below several other events, along with a brief description, which are taking place in London while we are there. Please let me know which ones are of interest to you, and I'll get additional information on them.

Lawn Tennis Championship. The Lawn Tennis Championship Tournament started in 1877 at Wimbledon. It is now recognized as one of the premier Grand Slam events.

Kenwood Lakeside Concerts. Enjoy a fifty-year tradition of outdoor concerts at Kenwood Lakeside Concerts. Fireworks and laser shows take place at the conclusion of the concert.

The Proms. Henry Wood Promenade Concerts started in 1895. Devoted music lovers from around the world come to hear these exquisite concerts.

Outdoor Shakespeare Performances. There is nothing more enjoyable than a performance of a Shakespeare play in the open air. Bring a blanket and enjoy!

Royal Academy's Summer Exhibition. The Royal Academy was founded in 1768. Since that time the Academy has provided over two centuries of summer exhibits of living painters.

Application

Complete steps 1–5 to create and revise a worksheet and to update a wp document that is linked to it.

1. Open the wp file *DF 151F WP* and save it as *151F WP*.
2. Open the worksheet *DF 151F WORKSHEET* and save it as *151F WORKSHEET*.
3. Delete values in the worksheet file *151F WORKSHEET-S* for Last Year; move the values for This Year to Last Year; and move the values for Next Year to This Year.
4. Key these new numbers for Next Year from left to right, formatting as necessary:

   6 $68,217   104 $47,248   15 $49,017
5. Save *151F WORKSHEET* changes. Open, update, and save *151F WP* changes.

Lesson 152   INTEGRATE WORKSHEETS AND WORD PROCESSING DOCUMENTS

OBJECTIVE

- To convert a word processing table to a worksheet, copy a worksheet chart to a word processing document, and embed a word processing document in a worksheet.

152B

Convert a Word Processing Table to a Worksheet

1. Study the text.
2. Learn to convert a wp document to a worksheet.
3. Complete steps 1–4.

Save as:
152B WORKSHEET

Data from a wp table can be converted to a worksheet, and then calculations can be performed on the data. If the wp document is a table or data separated by tabs, it will be copied to separate cells in the worksheet; otherwise, the information will be copied into the highlighted cell of the worksheet.

1. Open the wp document *DF 152B WP* and copy it into a blank worksheet.
2. Add a column at the right with **Total Hits** as the heading; add a row at the bottom with **Totals** as an indented row heading.
3. Perform the calculations in the added column and row.
4. Adjust font size, row height, and column width as needed to improve the appearance.

152C

Application

1. Key the WP table and save it as *152C WP*. Copy the table into a blank worksheet.
2. Add **Bonus** and **Total** columns at the right of the worksheet.
3. Calculate bonuses: Bonuses are 25% of the salary if the sales are more than $1,900. If not, no bonus is earned.
4. Total each salesperson's pay for April.
5. Add an indented **Totals** row at the bottom, and calculate a total for each column.
6. Format the worksheet to make it attractive.

Save as:
152C WORKSHEET

APRIL PAY SCHEDULE			
Salesperson	**Sales**	**Commission**	**Salary**
Frederick Adams	$1,856	$464	$600
Janice Brown	$2,235	$558	$625
Carlos Cruz	$1,975	$493	$600
Enrico Duarte	$1,857	$464	$575
Lisa Ford	$1,785	$446	$600
Marian Mosley	$2,145	$536	$650
Jerry Roberts	$2,098	$524	$600
Leona Williams	$1,674	$418	$575

Activity 4

Timed Writings

1. Key a 1' timing on each ¶; determine *gwam*.
2. Key a 2' timing on ¶s 1–2 combined; determine *gwam*.
3. Key a 3' timing on ¶s 1–2 combined; determine *gwam* and number of errors.

A all letters used MicroPace

	gwam	2'	3'

In deciding upon a career, learn as much as possible about — 5 | 4

what individuals in that career do. For each job class, there are — 11 | 7

job requirements and qualifications that must be met. Analyze — 17 | 11

these tasks very critically in terms of your personality and what — 23 | 15

you like to do. — 28 | 19

A high percentage of jobs in major careers demand education or — 34 | 23

training after high school. The training may be very specialized, — 40 | 26

requiring intensive study or interning for two or more years. You — 42 | 28

must decide if you are willing to expend so much time and effort. — 47 | 31

After you have decided upon a career to pursue, discuss the — 53 | 35

choice with parents, teachers, and others. Such people can help — 59 | 39

you design a plan to guide you along the series of steps required — 65 | 43

in pursuing your goal. Keep the plan flexible and change it when- — 71 | 48

ever necessary. — 77 | 51

gwam 2' | 1 | 2 | 3 | 4 | 5 | 6
3' | 1 | 2 | 3 | 4

Quarter-Minute Checkpoints				
gwam	1/4'	1/2'	3/4'	1'
24	6	12	18	24
28	7	14	21	28
32	8	16	24	32
36	9	18	27	36
40	10	20	30	40
44	11	22	33	44
48	12	24	36	48
52	13	26	39	52
56	14	28	42	56

Activity 5

Unbound Report

Format and key the text at the right as an unbound report. Use **Theatre** for the title of the report. Proofread and correct all keying and format errors.

Save as: CR1 ACTIVITY5

Tonight the house lights will dim, and another performance will begin on Broadway. Perhaps it will be another performance of *The Phantom of the Opera*, the longest-running show in the history of Broadway with 8,251 performances as of November 25, 2007 (Hernandez). Or perhaps it will be the play that replaces *The Phantom of the Opera*.

Somewhere, sometime today, another enactment of one of Shakespeare's plays will take place. It may be in a high school auditorium, or it may be at a professional Shakespearean playhouse.

Theatre has enriched the lives of people for many years. No one really knows when the first play production was performed. However, historians say, "Theatre is as old as mankind. There have been primitive forms of it since man's beginnings" (Berthold, 1991, 1). The more commonly recognized form of theatre, the play, dates back to what is referred to as "Greek Theatre" and "Roman Theatre."

151D

Update a Worksheet and Linked Word Processing Document

1. Study the text.
2. Learn to update a link.
3. Complete steps 1–3.

After you make the following changes to the source file (151C WORKSHEET-S), the destination file (*151C WP*) can be updated when you open it.

1. Open *151C WORKSHEET-S* and change the numbers to those given below:

Increase in net assets	
Operations	
Net investment income	$ 415,676
Net realized gain	$ 3,297,811
Change in net unrealized appreciation (depreciation)	$ 2,877,590
Net increase in net assets resulting from operations	$ 6,591,077
Distributions to shareholders	
From net investment income	$ (399,456)
From net realized gain	$ (2,195,315)
Total distributions	$ (2,594,771)
Share transactions	
Net proceeds from sales of shares	$ 897,120
Reinvestment of distributions	$ 2,987,407
Cost of shares redeemed	$ 10,976,866
Net increase in net assets resulting from share transactions	$ 897,120
Total increase in net assets	$ 10,082,968
Net assets	
Beginning of period	$ 48,595,195
End of period	$ 58,678,163

2. Save the changes to *151C WORKSHEET-S*.
3. Open *151C WP*, click Yes, and note that the numbers in the financial report have been updated automatically.

Save as: 151D WP

151E

Application

1. Open wp file *DF 151E WP* and save it as *151E WP*.
2. Create the worksheet (*151E WORKSHEET-S*) from the data given, and copy it into *151E WP* between the ¶s.

Save as: 151E WP

Business	Address	Points	Amount
Avenue Deli	309 Franklin Avenue	92	$15,000
Ford's Newsstand	302 Franklin Avenue	88	$15,000
Hannon Shoes	415 Shefield Avenue	86	$10,000
Unger Appliances	525 Station Street	83	$10,000
Best Food Market	311 Franklin Avenue	76	$ 5,000
Avenue Restaurant	376 Franklin Avenue	76	$ 5,000

Activity 6

References List

Use the information below to create a references list on a separate page. Proofread and correct all keying and format errors.

References

Berthold, Margot. *The History of World Theatre*. New York: The Continuum Publishing Company, 1991.

Hernandez, Ernio. "Playbill News: Long Runs on Broadway." http://www.playbill.com/celebritybuzz/article/ 75222.html (accessed November 25, 2007).

Prince, Nancy, and Jeanie Jackson. *Exploring Theatre*. Minneapolis/St. Paul: West Publishing Company, 1997.

Save as: **CR1 ACTIVITY6**

Greek Theatre

Greek Theatre started around 500 B.C. Sophocles and Aristophanes are two of the well-known Greek playwrights whose works are still being performed today.

Religious festivals that honored the Greek god of wine and fertility (Dionysus) were part of the culture of Greece around this time. The Greeks felt that if they honored Dionysus, he would in turn bless them with many children, rich land, and abundant crops. Plays were performed as part of these festivals.

To accommodate the large number of people who attended the plays (as many as 14,000 to 17,000 people, according to historians), theatres were built into a hillside. The plays were staged in the morning and lasted until sunset, since there was no electricity for lighting (Prince and Jackson, 1997, 35).

Roman Theatre

Roman Theatre was the next widely recognized form of the theatre. The first Roman theatrical performance, historians believe, was performed around 365 B.C. Seneca, Plautus, and Terence are the best known of the early Roman playwrights. Seneca was known for his tragedies, while the other two were known for their comedies.

The Roman plays were similar to those of the Greeks. Unlike the Greeks, however, the Romans did not limit the number of actors in each play. Another major difference between the Greek and Roman theatres was the theatre buildings. *The Romans were great engineers and architects. They built theatres that were unified, free-standing structures several stories in height (Prince and Jackson, 1997, 44).*

Activity 7

Table 1

Create the table at the right.
- Table Styles – Medium Shading 1 – Accent 4
- Center the table horizontally and vertically.
- **Main title:** row height 0.5"; align center; 14-pt. font
- **Column headings:** row height 0.4"; align center
- **Data rows:** row height 0.3"; bottom vertical alignment
- Adjust column widths to arrange material attractively on the page.

Save as: **CR1 ACTIVITY7**

American Literature – 1900s	
Literature	Author
A Rose for Emily (1930)	William Faulkner
The Grapes of Wrath (1939)	John Steinbeck
The Scotty Who Knew Too Much (1940)	James Thurber
House Made of Dawn (1968)	N. Scott Momaday
Everyday Use (1973)	Alice Walker
I Ask My Mother to Sing (1986)	Li-Young Lee
The Phone Booth at the Corner (1989)	Juan Delgado

Application

1. Open *DF 150G WORKSHEET*.
2. Apply conditional formatting to format the following. You choose the format and clear the rules as needed.

a. Highlight all boys and girls whose club is Seneca.

Save as: 150G WORKSHEET1

b. Highlight the scores of all boys who earned between 350 and 400 points.

Save as: 150G WORKSHEET2

c. Highlight the times of the girls whose time was below 101.

Save as: 150G WORKSHEET3

d. Format the points of the boys who earned more than the average points.

Save as: 150G WORKSHEET4

Lesson 151 INTEGRATE WORKSHEETS AND WORD PROCESSING DOCUMENTS

OBJECTIVE

• To learn to copy and link a worksheet to a word processing document.

151B

Copy a Worksheet into a Word Processing Document

1. Study the text.
2. Open a wp document and learn how to copy/paste a worksheet into it.
3. Complete steps 1–4.

Save as: 151B WP

Note: A file that is to become a source copy for an activity will be saved with a filename that ends in "S." For example, the source file for this activity is named *151B WORKSHEET-S*.

Frequently, worksheets are copied into a wp document by using Copy and Paste (or Paste Special) commands to avoid rekeying the information. The worksheet can be pasted in a variety of ways: with or without a link to the source document; with source file or destination file formatting; as a table, text, hyperlink, etc. In this activity, paste the worksheet as a *Word* table that can be formatted using *Word* table formatting features but is not linked to the source file.

	A	B	C	D	E	F
1	FOURTH ANNUAL TRI-HIGH GOLF MATCH					
2	First Name	Last Name	Gender	Class	School	Best Round
3	Suari	Al-Shah	Male	12	White Bank	74
4	Robert	Banks	Male	12	Johnson	75
5	Torborn	Bergston	Male	12	Johnson	72
6	Diane	Blust	Female	10	White Bank	75

1. Open the wp document *DF 151B WP*.
2. Open the worksheet *DF 151B WORKSHEET* and save it as *151B WORKSHEET-S*.
3. Copy the worksheet into the document, placing it about a DS below the last line of the memo body. Leave about one blank line after the table, and then key your initials.
4. Center the table between the left and right margins with gridlines. Format the table in Calibri 10 pt. to keep the memo to one page. You decide other formatting features.

151C

Link a Worksheet to a Word Processing Document

1. Study the text.
2. Learn how to link data between a worksheet and a word processing document.
3. Complete steps 1–5.

Save as: 151C WP

Oftentimes, data in a worksheet that has been copied into a wp document is routinely updated. To eliminate the need to rekey the wp document and copy the worksheet each time the data is updated, a link between the wp document and the worksheet can be created.

With linking, data changed on the source file (worksheet) is automatically updated in the destination file (wp document). The **Paste Special** command is used to establish this link.

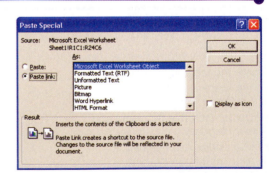

1. Open the wp document *DF 151C WP*.
2. Open the worksheet *DF 151C WORKSHEET* and save it as *151C WORKSHEET-S*.
3. Use Paste Special to paste the worksheet into the document and to link the worksheet and wp document.
4. Place the table a DS below the last line of the memo body. Leave about one blank line after the table, and then key your initials.
5. Center between the left and right margins with gridlines. You decide other formatting features.

Activity 8

Table 2

Create the table shown at the right using the information given for Activity 7, Table 1.

Use Medium Shading 2 – Accent 1 for the Table Style.

Save as: **CR1 ACTIVITY8**

WILLIAM SHAKESPEARE

Play	Year Written	Category
The Comedy of Errors	1590	Comedy
Richard II	1595	History
Romeo and Juliet	1595	Tragedy
Much Ado About Nothing	1599	Comedy
Julius Caesar	1599	Tragedy
Hamlet	1601	Tragedy
King Lear	1605	Tragedy
The Tempest	1611	Comedy

Activity 9

Electronic Presentations

Create the slides as shown at the right. Choose appropriate clip art if the art shown at the right isn't available with your software.

Slide 1: Title slide

Slide 2: Section Header

Slide 3-6: Title and Content slides

Save as: **CR1 ACTIVITY9**

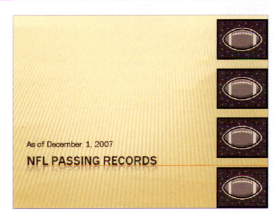

Slide 1

Slide 2

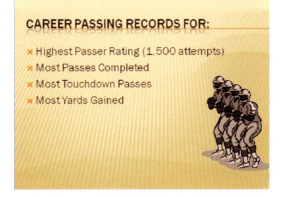

Slide 3

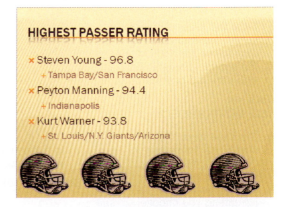

Slide 4

(continued on next page)

Application

1. Key the worksheet.
2. In column F, calculate average score to nearest whole number.
3. In column G, key an IF function that compares the scores in column F to a score of 75. If the score is less than 75, print **TUTORING** in column G. If it is 75 or more, print nothing.
4. You decide all formatting features.

Save as:
150E WORKSHEET

	A	B	C	D	E	F	G
1	GRADE BOOK						
2	NAME	TEST 1	TEST 2	TEST 3	TEST 4	AVG	NEEDS TUTORING
3	ABEL	78	85	72	78		
4	BOGGS	64	66	71	73		
5	CARR	78	82	86	75		
6	FRYZ	90	93	88	86		
7	GOOD	95	82	86	92		
8	MILLS	71	75	73	76		
9	POPE	62	71	73	66		
10	SIA	75	76	81	71		
11	TODD	66	65	50	61		
12	WILLS	75	64	75	70		
13	ZEON	81	74	65	60		

Apply Conditional Formatting

SS • Home/Styles/Conditional Formatting

1. Study the text.
2. Learn to apply conditional formatting.
3. Open *DF 150F WORK-SHEET*.
4. Apply conditional formatting so that all test scores above 93 are highlighted with green fill and dark green text.

Save as:
150F WORKSHEET1

5. Clear the rules. Apply conditional formatting to display the Top 10% of the scores in column G with dark red outline.

Save as:
150F WORKSHEET2

6. Clear the rules. Apply conditional formatting to display scores in column G that are below the average score with formatting you choose.

Save as:
150F WORKSHEET3

Conditional formatting enables you to quickly apply formatting features in a cell when the data in the cell meet specified conditions. For example, your teacher can apply conditional formatting to change the font color and cell fill color to quickly identify students who have (1) scores above, below, or equal to a specific value; (2) the top and bottom score(s); and (3) scores above or below the average score on a test.

Conditional formats remain until they are cleared. Also, revisions that cause cell data to meet the specified condition will display the conditional formats, and revisions that cause cell data to not meet the specified condition will not display the conditional formats.

In this activity, you will use conditional formatting within the Highlight Cells Rules options and the Top/Bottom Rules.

7. Clear the rules. Apply conditional formatting to highlight all scores of 100 with formatting you choose.

Save as: 150F WORKSHEET4

8. Clear the rules. Apply conditional formatting to highlight all duplicate test scores in column D with formatting you choose.

Save as: 150F WORKSHEET5

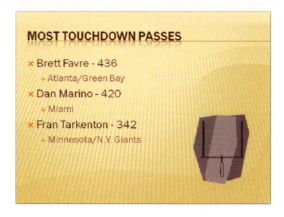

MOST TOUCHDOWN PASSES

× Brett Favre - 436
   + Atlanta/Green Bay
× Dan Marino - 420
   + Miami
× Fran Tarkenton - 342
   + Minnesota/N.Y. Giants

Slide 5

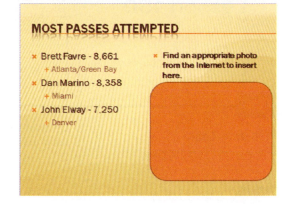

MOST PASSES ATTEMPTED

× Brett Favre - 8,661
   + Atlanta/Green Bay
× Dan Marino - 8,358
   + Miami
× John Elway - 7,250
   + Denver

× Find an appropriate photo from the Internet to insert here.

Slide 6

Activity 10

Timed Writings

1. Key a 1' timing on each ¶; determine *gwam*.
2. Key a 2' timing on ¶s 1–2 combined; determine *gwam*.
3. Key a 3' timing on ¶s 1–2 combined; determine *gwam* and number of errors.

 A   all letters used   (MicroPace)   gwam   2' | 3'

	gwam 2'	3'
Atlanta, the capital of Georgia, is a gem of the South.	6	4
It is the largest city in the state and exists because of	12	8
railroads. The original site was selected as the end of the	18	12
line for the railroad to be built northward. Eight years	23	16
later, the area became known as Atlanta. Because of the	29	19
railroad, Atlanta was the key supply center for the Confederacy	36	24
and was virtually destroyed during the Civil War.	40	27
One of the more famous Atlanta citizens was Margaret	46	30
Mitchell. The book she wrote exquisitely portrays the area	52	34
during the Civil War period. During the war, much of the city	58	39
was destroyed. However, a few of the elegant southern homes	64	43
of this time period have been restored and are open for the	70	47
public to see. Today, Atlanta is recognized as a modern city	76	51
that gives those who visit as well as the residents of the city	83	55
a variety of cultural and sporting events for their enjoyment.	89	59

gwam 2' | 1 | 2 | 3 | 4 | 5 | 6 |
3' | 1 | 2 | 3 | 4 |

Lesson 150

ANSWER "WHAT IF" QUESTIONS AND USE THE IF FUNCTION AND CONDITIONAL FORMATTING

• To answer "what if" questions and use the IF function and conditional formatting.

150B

Prepare to Learn

1. Open *DF 150B WORK-SHEET*

2. Calculate Next Year's Quota by multiplying column B values by cell A2.

3. You decide all formatting features.

Save as: 150B WORKSHEET

150C

Answer "What If" Questions

1. Study the text.

2. Using *150B WORK-SHEET*, answer the three "what if" questions.

3. Print the worksheet after each question, unless directed to do otherwise.

Save the final worksheet as: 150C WORKSHEET

An advantage of ss software is its ability to show the effects on all cells of a change in one cell. For example, in the worksheet in Activity 150B, you determined next year's quota for each salesperson if the company were to make the new quotas 1.05 (105%) of this year's quota. By changing the 1.05 in cell A2 to other numbers representing other possible changes, the effect of the change on the quotas for all salespersons can be computed at once.

1. What if the goal is decreased to 95% of this year's quota?

2. What if the goal is increased to 105.5% of this year's quota?

3. What if the goal is increased to 110% of this year's quota?

150D

Use the IF Function

SS • Formulas/Function Library/Logical

1. Study the text.

2. Learn to write IF functions using logical operators:

Logical Operators

= (value of two cells are *equal*)

< (value of one cell is *less than* the other)

> (value of one cell is *greater than* the other)

<= (value of one cell is *less than* or *equal* to the other)

>= (value of one cell is *greater than* or *equal* to the other)

<> (values are *unequal*)

3. Complete steps 1–4.

4. Print the worksheet with gridlines and row and column headings.

Save as: 150D WORKSHEET

The IF function compares the contents of two cells. Conditions that contain logical operators (listed at the left) provide the basis for the comparison. For example, an instructor could use the following IF function (see formula bar below) to determine whether a student passed or failed a course:

	A	B	C	D	E	F
				fx	=IF(D2>60, "Pass","Fail")	
1	Name	Quiz 1	Quiz 2	Average	Pass/Fail	
2	Joe	89	84	86.5	Pass	
3	Maria	55	62	58.5	Fail	
4	Chu	94	98	96	Pass	
5	Abdul	78	74	76	Pass	

This IF function involves three arguments. The first is the comparison of the scores in column B to the criteria (a score that is greater than [>] 60 in the example). The second argument is the text or value ("Pass" in the example) that is to be displayed if the comparison is true. The third is the text or value ("Fail") that is to be displayed if the comparison is false.

As illustrated, the arguments of the IF function are keyed inside parentheses and are separated from each other with commas. If text is to be displayed for argument 2 or 3, the text should be keyed inside quotation marks. Quotes are not keyed if values are to be displayed.

1. Key **25** in cell A1 and **35** in cell B1. In cell C1, key an IF function that prints EQUAL if A1=B1 or UNEQUAL if A1 and B1 are unequal.

2. In cell D1, key an IF function that prints HELP if the sum of A1+B1 is less than 75 and NO HELP if the sum is 75 or greater.

3. In cell A3, key **679805**; in cell B3, **354098**; in cell C3, **350507**. In cell D3, key an IF function that prints EQUAL if A3-B3=C3 and UNEQUAL if A3-B3 does not equal C3.

4. In cell A5, key **11**; **22** in cell B5; **33** in cell C5; **44** in cell D5. In cell E5, key an IF function that prints 1-149 if the sum of A5:D5 is less than 150 and 150+ if the sum of A5:D5 is greater than 150.

OBJECTIVE

• To assess Cycle 1 document processing, computer application, and straight-copy skills.

Conditioning Practice

Key each line twice SS.

alphabet 1 John was quite amazed by his blocking of seven extra points.

fig/sym 2 In 1994, we had only 345 computers; as of 2004 we owned 876.

speed 3 Rick and Jan may pay for the antique box for their neighbor.

gwam	1'	1	2	3	4	5	6	7	8	9	10	11	12

Activity 1

Memo

Format and key the text at the right as a memo to **Suzanne Hamlin** from **Elizabeth A. Ross**. Date the memo **May 6, 20--**; use **Summer Trip** for the subject line. Correct all errors.

Save as: CA1 ACTIVITY1

Here are some of the costs that our group will incur on our trip to The Breakers.

The admission fee for The Breakers is $10. I'll check on group rates this week. Round-trip airfare from Portland to T. F. Green Airport is $235. Of course, you know that rates vary considerably during the summer months. My travel agent will inform me of any summer specials.

I'm still waiting for rates for the hotel accommodations. I've narrowed the list to Castle Hill Inn and Resort, Vanderbilt Hall, and Hotel Viking. Any of the three would provide excellent accommodations. As soon as they send the rates, I'll forward them to you.

Activity 2

E-mail

Format and key the text at the right as an e-mail message to your instructor. Use **MACBETH QUOTE** for the subject line.

Correct all spelling, keying, and formatting errors.

Save as: CA1 ACTIVITY2

I enjoyed our visit last week at the class reunion. How quickly time passes; it seems like only yesterday that we graduated. Of course, a class reunion is a quick reminder that it *wasn't* yesterday.

I was able to find the quote that we discussed with the group on Friday. Your memory definitely serves you better than mine; it was a quote from George Bernard Shaw. However, he was referring to Shakespeare's *Macbeth*. Here is the exact quote by Shaw: "Life is not a 'brief candle.' It is a splendid torch that I want to make burn as brightly as possible before handing it on to future generations."

I was glad to see that so many of our classmates are living lives as "splendid torches" rather than as "brief candles."

149D

Use 3-D Cell References

1. Study the text.
2. Learn to enter 3-D cell references.
3. Open *DF 149D WORKSHEET*.
4. Enter a 3-D cell reference so cell B3 in Sheet 2 references the value in cell C6 in Sheet 1.
5. Enter a 3-D cell reference so cell B4 in Sheet 2 references the value in cell D6 in Sheet 1.

Save as:
149D WORKSHEET

A 3-D cell reference refers to a cell or range of cells on another worksheet. A 3-D cell reference contains the cell or range name preceded by the worksheet name and the exclamation (!) mark. As shown at the right, a 3-D reference in cell D1 in Sheet 2 to cell A3 in Sheet 1 would appear as =Sheet1!A3 in the formula bar when cell D1 in Sheet 2 is selected.

Clipboard		Font		Alig
D1		f_x	=Sheet1!A3	

	A	B	C	D	E
1				345	
2					

To insert a 3-D reference:

1. Click the cell that is to contain the reference.
2. Key an = sign.
3. Click the tab for the worksheet that has the cell or range of cells you want to reference.
4. Select the cell or range of cells to be referenced. Tap ENTER.

To confirm the 3-D cell reference:

1. Activate the worksheet and then the cell where the reference was entered.
2. Read the information in the formula bar to verify it has been referenced correctly.

149E

Application

1. Key the worksheet.
2. Calculate the % of Net Revenues for each item (use two decimal places).
3. Format the worksheet as desired.
4. Print centered on the page.

Save as:
149E WORKSHEET

Learning Tip: % of Net Revenue = Value in column B/C2.

Jones Electric

	12/31/20--	% of Net Revenues
Revenues	$2,257,650	
Returns and Allowances	$ 1,568	
Net Revenues	$2,256,082	
Cost of Goods Sold		
Beginning Inventory	$ 125,612	
Purchases	$ 834,972	
Cost of Goods Available for Sale	$ 960,584	
Ending Inventory	$ 126,829	
Cost of Goods Sold	$ 833,755	
Gross Profit	$1,422,327	
Expenses	$1,165,750	
Net Profit	$ 256,577	

149F

Application

1. Open *DF 149F WORKSHEET*.

2. In the Loans worksheet, enter a 3-D reference in cell C3 that refers to the value in cell G3 in the Bates worksheet.

3. Insert the same 3-D reference in cells C4, C5, and C6 for Evans, Martinez, and Pope, respectively.

Save as: 149F WORKSHEET

Activity 3

Letter

Format and key the text at the right as a personal-business letter from **Elizabeth A. Ross.**

Supply an appropriate salutation and complimentary close. Be sure to include your reference initials and an attachment notation. Correct all errors.

Return Address and Date:

183 Lennox Street
Portland, ME 04103-5282
May 3, 20--

Letter Address:

Ms. Suzanne Hamlin, President
Portland Historical Society
1821 Island View Road
Portland, ME 04107-3712

Save as: CA1 ACTIVITY3

After doing research on possible historical destinations for our Annual Portland Historical Society trip, I narrowed our choices to the Hildene House in Manchester, Vermont, and The Breakers in Newport, Rhode Island. The Hildene House was built in 1902 for Robert Todd Lincoln, the son of Abraham Lincoln; The Breakers was built for Cornelius Vanderbilt II in 1895.

I met with our planning committee yesterday to share the information I was able to obtain. After discussing the merits of both places, our recommendation is The Breakers for this year's trip. Even though we liked both places, the committee felt that many of our members would have already visited the Hildene House since it is so close to Portland.

I've attached some information on The Breakers. As soon as I receive the additional information I requested about expenses, I will send it to you. You should have it in plenty of time for the June meeting.

Activity 4

Timed Writings

1. Key a 1' timing on each ¶; determine *gwam*.
2. Key two 3' timings on ¶s 1–2 combined; determine *gwam* and number of errors.

 all letters used MicroPace

	gwam	1'	3'

New York City, a city of many large buildings, is the — 11 | 4
largest city in the United States. The city is recognized all — 23 | 8
over the world for its theater, finance, fashion, advertising, — 36 | 12
and exquisite stores. New York City is said to be a city of — 48 | 16
extremes. It is a city with a diverse population, a melting — 60 | 20
pot of people from various backgrounds. No individual group — 72 | 24
forms a majority. In addition to its wealthy citizens, New — 85 | 28
York also has a large number of people living on the street. — 97 | 32

Not only is New York the largest city in the United — 10 | 36
States, it is also one of the largest cities in the entire — 22 | 40
world. Because of its size, the city has many cultural and — 34 | 44
sporting activities for an individual to attend. Baseball, — 46 | 48
football, and basketball are just a few of those available. — 58 | 52
Carnegie Hall, the Lincoln Center, and the New York State — 70 | 56
Theater are several of the places where the performing arts — 82 | 60
can be taken in throughout the year. The harbor, parks, art — 94 | 64
galleries, and museums provide other interesting attractions — 106 | 68
for those who live within New York City as well as for those — 119 | 72
who go there to visit. — 123 | 73

gwam	1'	1	2	3	4	5	6	7	8	9	10	11	12
	3'		1			2			3			4	

1. Key this worksheet.

	A	B	C	D	E	F	G
1				**Cell Referencing**			
2	**Numbers**			**Relative**	**Absolute**	**Mixed**	**Mixed**
3	1	2	3				
4	4	5	6				
5	7	8	9				
6	10	11	12				
7	13	14	15				

2. In cell D3, key **=A3+B3+C3** and then copy to cells D4:D7. Notice that the formula added the numbers in columns A–C across each row since relative cell referencing was used.

3. In cell E3, key **=$A$3+$B$3+$C$3** and then copy to cells E4:E7. Notice that the formula added the numbers in columns A, B, and C across the same row (row 3) since absolute cell referencing was used for the row.

4. In cell F3, key **=A$3+B$3+C3** and then copy to cells F4:F7. Notice that the formula always added the numbers in columns A and B, row 3, to each value in column C as the formula was copied to each row.

5. Copy cell F3 to cell G3 and then copy cell G3 to cells G4:G7. In cells G3:G7, notice that the A changed to B and B changed to C in each cell reference in column G since the A and B are relative references. The $3 remained the same in each row in column G since it is an absolute reference. Since C3 is a relative reference, it changed to D3 when copied to cell G3, and then the number changed each time it was copied to a new row in column G.

149c

Application

1. Key the worksheet as shown, supplying the totals (*TOT*) in column I and row 15.

2. Specify column A width at 6, B–I at 5, and J at 9.

3. Make all rows 0.25" high.

4. Calculate the total revenue (*$ REV*) in column J by multiplying column I values by cell A17. Format column J as Currency with two decimal places.

5. Add a nine-character column at the right with the heading **% of REV.**

6. Calculate each room's percent of the total revenue (cell J15) and display it in the *% of REV* column. Format it as Percentage with two decimal places.

Save as:
149C WORKSHEET

	A	B	C	D	E	F	G	H	I	J
1	**CANDY BAR SALES BY HOMEROOM**									
2	ROOM	MON	TUE	WED	THU	FRI	SAT	SUN	TOT	$ REV
3	101	23	45	32	66	66	72	23		
4	103	45	65	82	45	45	56	33		
5	105	45	23	10	75	75	63	77		
6	107	34	23	15	34	56	45	23		
7	109	23	35	46	53	53	49	66		
8	111	22	33	55	88	88	46	23		
9	113	24	57	80	76	76	62	54		
10	115	23	56	80	55	55	65	29		
11	117	78	67	56	46	61	33	60		
12	119	35	65	73	59	92	47	59		
13	121	44	56	71	48	98	32	45		
14	123	35	58	56	59	84	15	38		
15	TOT									
16	CANDY BAR PRICE									
17	$1.25									

Activity 5

Unbound Report

Format and key the text at the right as an unbound report. Correct all spelling, keying, and formatting errors.

Save as: CA1 ACTIVITY5

The castles listed on A&E's *America's Castles* belonged to the rich and famous. By looking at the history of some of the families that owned these castles, it is easy to see why people say that America is the land of opportunity.

Cornelius Vanderbilt was a man who took advantage of the opportunities America had to offer. He was born on May 27, 1794, to a family of modest means. Cornelius ended his formal schooling by the age of 11 (*Encyclopedia Americana*, 2001, Vol. 27, 891). He achieved success because he was industrious. He knew how to work, and he knew the value of the money that came from hard work. Other qualities that made him successful were perseverance, enterprise, courage, and trustworthiness. Being trustworthy meant he could command better prices than others doing the same job (Smith, 528, 1886). Because of these qualities, Cornelius Vanderbilt was able to amass one of the largest fortunes ever made in America from his shipping and railroad enterprises.

Three of America's castles were built by descendents of the man who came out of humble beginnings to amass such a large fortune. The Biltmore House, The Breakers, and Marble House were all built by Cornelius Vanderbilt's descendents.

Biltmore House

The Biltmore House, the largest private residence in America, is located on the Biltmore Estate of 8,000 acres near Asheville, North Carolina. The house and grounds are the most visited historic tourist destination in the nation. The mansion, built for George W. Vanderbilt by Richard Morris Hunt (the late nineteenth century's most renowned architect), was styled after a French Renaissance Chateau (*Visitor's Guide to the Biltmore Estate*, 2007).

The Breakers

The Breakers is located in Newport, Rhode Island. It was built for Cornelius Vanderbilt II. The 70-room castle (Italian Renaissance) was started in 1895. Upon its completion, the castle was filled with antiques from France and Italy (A&E, *America's Castles*, "The Breakers," 2000).

Marble House

Marble House is also located in Newport, Rhode Island. During the 1890s, Newport became the summer colony of New England's wealthiest families. Marble House was built by William K. Vanderbilt, a grandson of Cornelius Vanderbilt, for his wife's birthday. The castle cost $11 million; the 500,000 cubic feet of white marble that it took to build it cost $7 million alone (*Architecture*, "Vanderbilt Marble House," 2003).

UNIT 35
Lessons 149-154
Enhance Spreadsheet Skills

Lesson 149   CELL REFERENCES

• To use relative, absolute, mixed, and 3-D cell references.

149A-154A

Conditioning Practice

Key each line twice.

alphabet	1	Pam will acquire two dozen red vinyl jackets for the big exhibit.
figures	2	The library has 95,684 books, 1,205 periodicals, and 3,457 tapes.
speed	3	They may sign the usual proxy if they make an audit of the firms.

gwam 1' | 1 | 2 | 3 | 4 | 5 | 6 | 7 | 8 | 9 | 10 | 11 | 12 | 13 |

149B

Learn Relative, Absolute, and Mixed Cell References

1. Study the text.
2. Learn to enter relative, absolute, and mixed cell references.
3. Complete steps 1–5 on the next page.

Save as:
149B WORKSHEET

You have learned that ss software copies a formula across a row or up or down a column. It also adjusts the formula copied into the new cells to reflect its new address and the address of other cells used in the formula.

When formulas are copied in this manner, the software is using **relative cell referencing**. That is, the copy of the cell is related to its new address. For example, if cell D1 contains the formula =B1+C1, when this formula is copied to E2, it changes automatically to =C2+D2. Since E2 is down one row and one column over, the cells in the formula are also down one row and one column over from the cells in the original formula.

Sometimes you will not want to change a formula to reflect its new address when copying across a row or up or down a column.

In these instances, you will use **absolute cell referencing**. Absolute cell referencing is used by keying a $ sign before the column and row reference in the cell address that is not to change. For example, if you want to divide all the numbers in column B by a number that is in A1, you would make A1 an absolute cell address by keying a $ before the A and a $ before the 1 ($A$1).

A **mixed cell reference** is one that maintains a reference to a specific row or column but not to both. For example, D$1 is a mixed cell reference. The reference to column D is relative and the reference to row 1 is absolute. When copied to another cell, the reference to column D will change, but the reference to row 1 will remain the same.

Cell Reference	Example	Explanation
Relative	A1	Column A and row 1 *will change* when copied to a new cell.
Absolute	$A$1	Column A and row 1 *will not change* when copied to a new cell.
Mixed	$A1	Column A *will not change* when copied to a new cell (absolute), but row 1 *will change* when copied (relative)
Mixed	A$1	Column A *will change* when copied to a new cell (relative), but 1 will not change when copied (relative)

Activity 6

References List

Use the information at the right to create a references list on a separate page. Proofread and correct all spelling, keying, and format errors.

Save as: CA1 ACTIVITY6

REFERENCES

A&E, *America's Castles*, "The Breakers." http://www.aetv.com/tv/shows/castles/breakers.html (26 January 2000).

Architecture, "Vanderbilt Marble House." http://www.architecture.about.com/library/blmarblehouse.htm (17 November 2003).

Encyclopedia Americana Vol. 27, "Cornelius Vanderbilt." Danbury, CT: Grolier Incorporated, 2001.

Smith, Helen Ainslie. *One Hundred Famous Americans*. Reprint of 1886 ed. Freeport, NY: Books for Libraries Press, 1972.

"Visitor's Guide to the Biltmore Estate." http://www.willowwinds.com/biltmore-estate-guide.htm (4 December 2007).

Activity 7

Assessment: Keying Skills

1. Key a 1' timing on each ¶ of Activity 4, p. 133; determine *gwam*.

2. Key two 3' timings on ¶s 1–2 combined (Activity 4, p. 133); determine *gwam* and number of errors.

Activity 8

Create the table at the right using the Dark List – Accent 3 table style. Center the table on the page.

Main heading: row height 0.7"; align center; 14-pt. font for 1st line.

Column headings: row height 0.4" align center; 12 pt. font.

Data rows: row height 0.3"; align column 1 bottom left, align column 2 bottom center.

Column widths: Adjust column widths to arrange material attractively on the page.

Save as: CA1 ACTIVITY8

VAN NOY ART GALLERY	
June—August Exhibits	
Exhibit	**Opening/Closing Dates**
Emerging Artists	June 1–June 10
19th-Century European Paintings	June 11–June 20
Colonial American Art	June 21–June 30
Old Masters' Paintings	July 1–July 15
American Oil Paintings	July 16–July 31
19th-Century French Prints	August 1–August 15
American Impressionists	August 16–August 30

1. Open *CS14 ACTIVITY4* and print the file.
2. Solve the problems as directed in the file.
3. Submit your answers.

CAREER Clusters

ACTIVITY 14

You must complete Career Exploration Activities 1–3 before completing this activity.

1. Retrieve your Career folder and the information in it that relates to the three career clusters you have chosen.

2. Identify the career cluster that is now your second choice.

3. Use the Internet to search for schools that you could attend after you are graduated from high school to pursue an occupation in this cluster. Then write a paragraph or two describing what kind of school it is, where it is, the cost to enroll, whether it has resident students and/or commuter students, and other information that interests you. Print your file, save it as Career14, and keep it open.

4. Exchange papers with a classmate and have the classmate offer suggestions for improving the content and correcting any errors he or she finds in your paragraph(s). Make the changes you agree with and print a copy to turn in to your instructor. Save your file as Career14 and close it.

5. Return your folder to the storage area. When your instructor returns your paper, file it in your Career folder.

PHOTODISC/GETTY IMAGES

Activity 9

Create the table shown at the right using Colorful Grid – Accent 1. Center the table and adjust column widths to arrange material attractively on page.

Include the following source note: A&E, *America's Castles*, http://www.aetv.com/tv/shows/castles/index2.html (26 January 2000).

Save as: CA1 ACTIVITY9

AMERICA'S CASTLES

Eastern Region

Castle	Location
The Breakers	Newport, Rhode Island
Chesterwood	Stockbridge, Massachusetts
Drumthwacket	Princeton, New Jersey
George Eastman House	Rochester, New York
Hildene	Manchester, Vermont
Longwood	Kennett Square, Pennsylvania
Lyndhurst Mansion	Tarrytown, New York
Marble House	Newport, Rhode Island
Sunnyside	Tarrytown, New York

Activity 10

Create the table shown at the right using Colorful List – Accent 6. Use the table formatting features that you learned to attractively arrange the information at the right as a table.

Save as: CA1 ACTIVITY10

THEATER VOCABULARY WORDS

April 7–25

Week of April 7	Week of April 14	Week of April 21
Blackout	Callbacks	Choreography
Conflict	Critique	Cues
Dialogue	Ensemble	Feedback
Floor plan	Illusion	Imagination
Improvisation	Intermission	Literary merit
Melodrama	Narrator	Playwright
Run-throughs	Screenplay	Soliloquy
Theme	Tragedy	Visualization

Activity 11

Electronic Presentations

Create the slides shown at the right. Choose appropriate clip art if the art shown at the right isn't available with your software.

Slide 1: Title slide
Slides 2 & 5: Section Headers slides
Slides 3: Comparison
Slides 4, 6, 7: Title and Content slides

Note: Text on some slides has been enlarged for readability.

Save as: CA1 ACTIVITY11

Slide 1

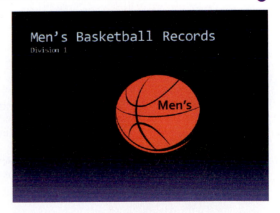

Slide 2

Communication & Math
SKILLS 14

ACTIVITY 1

Application: Commas

Key lines 1–10, inserting commas correctly.

Save as: CS14 ACTIVITY1

1 When you get to State Street make a right turn at the light.

2 She will ask Ken you and me to serve on the planning committee.

3 They moved to Las Cruces New Mexico on September 15 2004.

4 Elden be sure to turn off all equipment before you leave.

5 Ms. Rogers said "Keep the insertion point moving steadily."

6 Winona who is our class treasurer couldn't attend the meeting.

7 By the middle of 2006 we had 273 employees; in 2009 318.

8 The probability is that only 1 in 280000 have the same DNA.

9 Dr. Woodburn has a strong pleasant personality.

10 The choir director Elena Spitz is planning a special program.

ACTIVITY 2

Application: Punctuation

Key lines 1–10, punctuating each sentence correctly.

Save as: CS14 ACTIVITY2

1 Vanessa Williams sang the quite beautiful Colors of the Wind

2 After you see the film *Pocahontas*, she said, write a review.

3 Miss Tallchief signed a two year contract as ballet director.

4 Dr. Cho said that 30 second and 1 minute spurts build speed.

5 The dance competition is scheduled for 9 15 a.m. on October 15.

6 My goal is to develop 1 self-confidence and 2 self-esteem.

7 "A textual citation follows the quote" Sanchez, 2005, 273.

8 Who, she asked, is your all time favorite country singer?

9 Ms. Ott said: Read Frost's poem The Housekeeper by Monday.

10 *Home Improvement* was a very popular TV show in the late 1990s.

ACTIVITY 3

Listening

Complete as directed.

Save as: CS14 ACTIVITY3

1. Open sound file *DF CS14 ACTIVITY3* that contains three mental math problems.
2. Each problem starts with a number, followed by several addition, subtraction, multiplication, and division steps. Key or handwrite the new answer after each step, but compute the answer mentally.
3. Record the last answer for each problem.
4. After the third problem, close the sound file.

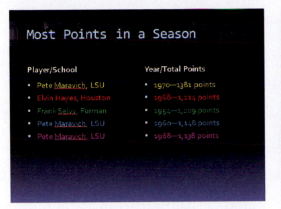

Slide 3

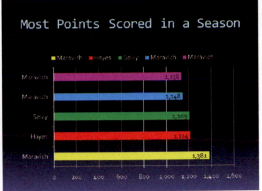

Slide 4

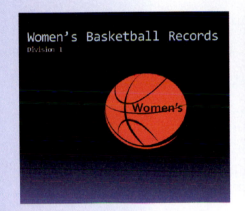

Slide 5

Slide 6

Slide 7

Activity 12

Timed Writings

1. Key a 1' timing on each ¶; determine *gwam*.
2. Key two 3' timings on ¶s 1–2 combined; determine *gwam*; count errors.

A   **all letters used**   **MicroPace**

	gwam	1'	3'

The Arlington House is a place filled with the very interesting history of our country. The exquisite house built for the grandson of Martha Washington, George Custis, in time became the home of General Lee. The house was built in an amazing location which today looks out over the capital city of our nation.

gwam	1'	3'
	11	4
	23	8
	33	11
	44	15
	55	18
	63	21

The home and land are also linked to other famous people of United States history. Soon after the Civil War started, the home became the headquarters of the Union army with much of the land to ultimately be used for what is today known as Arlington National Cemetery. President Kennedy and President Taft are just a few of the notables buried on the former estate of General Lee.

	1'	3'
	11	25
	23	29
	34	32
	45	36
	57	40
	69	44
	77	47

gwam	1'	1	2	3	4	5	6	7	8	9	10	11	12
	3'		1		2			3			4		

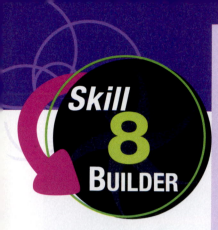

Skill 8 Builder

Timed Writing

1. Key three 1' writings on each ¶; determine *gwam*. Count errors. If errors are two or fewer on any writing, goal is to increase speed by one or two words on next writing. If errors on any writing are more than two, goal is control on next writing.

2. Key two 3' writings on ¶s 1–3 combined; determine *gwam* and count errors.

3. Key a 5' writing on ¶s 1–3 combined; determine *gwam* and count errors.

A all letters used MicroPace

	gwam	3'	5'

You are nearing the end of your keyboarding classes. The skill level you have attained is much better than that with which you started when you were given keyboarding instruction for the very first time. During the early phase of your training, you were taught to key the letters of the alphabet and the figures by touch. During the initial period of learning, the primary emphasis was placed on your keying technique.

After learning to key the alphabet and figures, your next job was to learn to format documents. The various types of documents formatted included letters, tables, and manuscripts. During this time of training, an emphasis also was placed on increasing the rate at which you were able to key. Parts of the lessons keyed at this time also were used to help you recognize the value of and to improve language skills.

The final phase of your training dealt with increasing your skill at producing documents of high quality at a rapid rate. Directions were provided for keying special documents; drills were given to build skill; and problems were provided to assess your progress. You were also given a number of simulations to allow you to apply what you had learned. Now you have a skill that you will be able to use throughout your life.

gwam	3'	5'
	4	2	53
	8	5	55
	13	8	58
	17	10	61
	22	13	64
	26	16	66
	28	17	67
	32	19	70
	36	22	72
	40	24	75
	44	27	77
	49	29	80
	53	32	82
	56	34	84
	60	36	86
	64	38	89
	68	41	91
	72	43	94
	77	46	96
	81	49	99
	84	51	101

gwam 3' 1 2 3 4
5' 1 2 3

Communicating
YOUR PERSPECTIVE | 2

A growing number of "fair trade" organizations provide artists, artisans, and farmers, often from developing countries, with a means of marketing their goods globally at a fair price. One such organization, PEOPLink, works with a network of Trading Partners (more than 1,400 organizations in 44 countries, representing over 200,000 artisans).* PEOPLink gives its Trading Partners digital cameras to photograph products and markets those products in its online catalog. The organization also provides online information about the work and lives of the artisans, teaches them to build and maintain their own Web catalogs, gives them online training, and helps them develop their products. The table below shows a few of the partners.

FAIR TRADE ARTS AND CRAFTS

Country	Product
Cameroon	Wood Carving
Guatemala	Ceramics
Nepal	Artwork
Panama	Molas
Uzbekistan	Chess Sets
Uganda	Baskets

*Source: PEOPLink. "Linking People Around the Globe via E-commerce." (15 May 2008) http://www.PEOPLink.org/EN/history.html.

Global Awareness

1. Key and format the table at the left. Use the table formatting features that you have learned to arrange the information attractively on the page.

2. Form a group with some other students. Develop a plan for a school fair in which you could showcase the work of artists from your school and community. Include details such as the date of the fair, where it would be held, how you would invite participants, how many you could invite, and where and how you would advertise the event.

Music has a rich cultural history. From ancient times, different cultures have developed their own styles of music and have invented different instruments with which to express them.

In music, the influence of one culture on another can be clearly seen and can produce exciting results. Take the American composer Aaron Copland, for example. Some of Copland's best-known compositions were based on American folk music, such as the ballets *Billy the Kid* (1938), *Rodeo* (1942), and *Appalachian Spring* (1944). His *El salon Mexico* was inspired by Mexican folk music.

Radio, television, the Internet, and high-quality sound and video recording have made music from many different cultures accessible to listeners worldwide. They have also helped to make music even more multicultural. For example, South Indian *cine*, or motion-picture music, uses both Indian and Western musical instruments and mixes classical Indian music with Western rock and jazz.*

*Source: David Butler, B.SC., M.A., Ph.D. "Music." Microsoft® Encarta® Online Encyclopedia 2008 http://encarta.msn.com (16 July 2008).

Cultural Diversity

1. Pair up with a student who likes a musician that you also like. Talk about this musician. Address the following questions, taking notes on the answers.

   - Does this musician's work show the influence of other musicians or other kinds of music? If so, in what way?
   - Do you think people in another country might form perceptions of this musician's country based on his or her music? If so, what might they be?
   - Think of the music you like to listen to and the music your parents like. How important is culture to being able to appreciate a particular kind of music?

2. Develop your notes and key them into a one-page unbound report.

Activity 6
Report

Create a report called **August Sales** similar to the one shown at the right for *Rockwell Technologies – District 14*. Include the sales rep's Last Name, First Name, Territory, and August Sales. Group the reps by Territory and sort by August Sales in ascending order. Select an appropriate layout and style.

Rockwell - District 14

Territory	August Sales	Last Name	First Name
California			
	$34,780.00	Weiss	Daniel
	$39,716.00	Miller	Michelle
	$47,343.00	Keller	Loretta
	$49,655.00	Ryan	Terri
	$49,763.00	Phillips	Lori
	$50,845.00	Taylor	Dean
	$54,900.00	McGraw	Katherine
	$55,428.00	Montessa	Carlos
	$57,381.00	Gonzalez	Renae
	$58,332.00	Zimmer	Albert
	$58,675.00	Winfield	Kevin
	$59,659.00	Chi	Xi
	$59,752.00	Wilkins	
	$60,230.00	Pizar	
	$62,385.00		

Activity 7
Mailing Labels

Prepare a set of mailing labels similar to the ones shown at the right for *District 14* sales reps. Use Avery 5160 labels. Print the labels.

Save as: **147B Activity 7 Labels**

Mr. Justin Hughes
313 Glenwood Drive
Vancouver, WA 98662-1148

Ms. Rose Winters
1472 Prescott Street
Portland, OR 97217-8755

Mr. Chad Chambers
2317 Silver Dollar Avenue
Las Vegas, NV 89102-9964

Mrs. Harriet Hanson
1890 Rancho Verde Drive
Reno, NV 89511-2221

Mrs. Mai Yang
2187 Klamath Street
Salem, OR 97306-9031

Mr. Albert Zimmer
330 Van Ness Avenue
Los Angeles, CA 90020-3341

Activity 8
Query and Mail

Prepare a mail merge letter from the information below and at the right for *Rockwell Technologies – District 14* sales reps with August sales greater than $70,000.

- Date the letter **September 16, 20--**
- Provide an appropriate complimentary close
- The letter is from **Leslie R. Fenwick, President**

Save as: **147B Activity 8 Merge Letters**

<<Title>> <<First_Name>> <<Last_Name>>
<<Address>>
<<City>>, <<State>> <<ZIP>>

Dear <<Title>> <<Last_Name>>

Congratulations! The sales report I received from your district manager lists your name as one of the three sales representatives in District 14 with sales over $70,000 for the month of August.

August was a very good month for District 14 sales representatives. They averaged over $56,104 of sales during August. This was an increase of approximately 4.3 percent over July and an increase of 7.8 percent over last August. This increase is due in large part to your efforts during the month.

We appreciate your hard work to make this the best year ever at Rockwell Technologies.

CYCLE 2

No matter what career you choose or what jobs you have along the way, a computer—and a computer keyboard—almost certainly will be at the center of your work. You will use new technology to build on existing keying skills.

In Cycle 2 you will refine keying techniques, increase communication skills, and learn advanced word processing features. You will work on your electronic presentation skills. You will process e-mail with attachments, reports with footnotes, and tables with borders and shading, to name a few. And that's not all.

You will go to work in the home office of a growing organization with branches in five cities. Your work for the President/CEO often takes you to the company's Web page.

Let's get started!

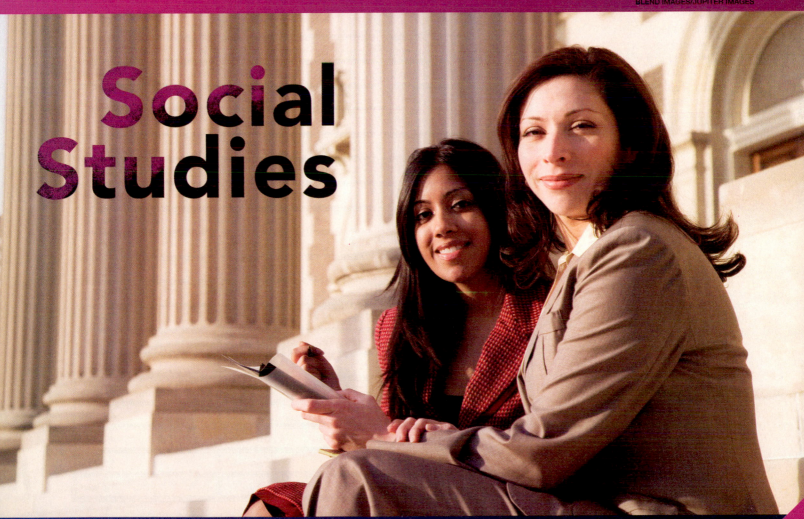

Social Studies

Activity 3
Add Fields to an Existing Database Table

1. Add the fields shown below to the *Rockwell Technologies – District 14* table.

   July Sales
   August Sales

2. Enter into the table the information shown at the right.

Activity 4
Query

1. Run a query called *Total Sales* on the table. Include First Name, Last Name, Territory, and July and August Sales.

2. Add a new column for **Total Sales**. Use the Expression Builder to compute the total sales.

3. Sort the query by *Total Sales* in descending order. Print a copy of the query.

Activity 5
Computed Fields

1. Create a form called **Total Sales** using the query created in Activity 4 of all the sales reps that shows Last Name, First Name, July Sales, August Sales, and Total Sales. Use Tabular layout with Equity style.

2. Sort the query by last name in ascending order. Adjust the columns to fit the longest entry in each column.

3. Print the form in landscape orientation.

SALES REPRESENTATIVES		
Last Name	*July Sales*	*August Sales*
Hughes	$55,671	$63,339
Winters	65,882	73,563
Chambers	43,812	54,650
Hanson	50,092	39,751
Yang	27,389	48,762
Zimmer	63,982	58,332
Aguilera	60,010	69,756
Winfield	44,396	58,675
Gonzalez	39,792	57,381
Keller	74,981	47,343
Wilkins	49,201	59,752
Bushlack	70,500	75,306
Lopez	65,730	62,385
Weiss	54,750	34,780
Culver	47,980	58,656
Miller	29,760	39,716
Sherman	80,754	54,354
Bailey	49,753	50,330
Stockton	75,880	82,791
Pizarro	54,900	60,230
Davis I.	39,763	48,655
Rice	65,830	66,385
Gilmore	40,340	37,381
Chi	52,379	59,659
Phillips	38,751	49,763
Taylor	57,925	50,845
Ryan	42,700	49,655
Backwith	68,524	62,566
Davis B.	57,247	62,318
Bolling	42,700	47,930
Montessa	59,650	55,428
McGraw	49,831	54,900

UNIT 13
Lessons 46-48

Build Keyboarding Skill

Lesson 46 KEYING TECHNIQUE

OBJECTIVES

- To improve keying techniques.
- To improve keying speed and control.

46A-48A

Conditioning Practice

Key each line twice.

alphabet	1	Extensive painting of the gazebo was quickly completed by Jerome.
figures	2	At least 456 of the 3,987 jobs were cut before November 18, 2005.
speed	3	Keith and I may go to the island to dismantle the bicycle shanty.

gwam 1' | 1 | 2 | 3 | 4 | 5 | 6 | 7 | 8 | 9 | 10 | 11 | 12 | 13 |

46B Skill Building

Technique: Letter Keys

Key each line twice.

Technique Cue

Limit keystroking action to the fingers; keep hands and arms motionless.

Emphasize continuity and rhythm with curved, upright fingers.

A 1 Katrina baked Marsha a loaf of bread to take to the Alameda fair.
B 2 Barbara and Bob Babbitt both saw the two blackbirds in the lobby.
C 3 Carl, the eccentric character with a classic crew cut, may catch.
D 4 David and Eddie dodged the duck as it waddled down the dark road.
E 5 Ellen needed Steven to help her complete the spreadsheet on time.
F 6 Before I left, Faye found forty to fifty feet of flowered fabric.
G 7 George and Greg thought the good-looking neighbor was gregarious.
H 8 John, Hank, and Sarah helped her haul the huge bush to the trash.

gwam 1' | 1 | 2 | 3 | 4 | 5 | 6 | 7 | 8 | 9 | 10 | 11 | 12 | 13 |

46C Skill Building

Technique: Number Keys/Tab

Key each line twice (key number, tap TAB, key next number).

Concentrate on figure location; quick tab spacing; eyes on copy.

95	107	403	496	572	824	590	576	871
82	458	314	307	891	103	721	980	645
73	669	225	218	600	206	843	109	312

147–148B

Activity 1
Enter Information into Forms

Open the *Rockwell Technologies – District 14* database. Enter the information shown at the right into the form.

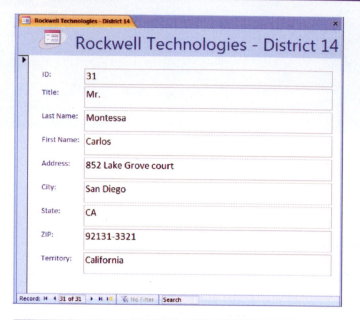

Activity 2
Editing Records

Make the changes shown at the right to the records in the *Rockwell Technologies – District 14* table.

1. Change *Winters'* address to **1472 Prescott Street.**
2. Change the ZIP Code for *Culver* to **97301-8824.**
3. Change *Phillips'* address to **387 Ferguson Avenue, Modesto, 95354-3210.**

Speed Forcing Drill

Key each line once at top speed; then try to complete each sentence on the 15", 12", or 10" call as directed by your instructor. Force speed to higher levels as you move from sentence to sentence.

Emphasis: high-frequency balanced-hand words

	gwam	15"	12"	10"
Hal paid the men for the work they did on the rig.		40	50	60
Orlando and I did the work for the eight busy men.		40	50	60
Helen and Rodney may do the handiwork for the neighbor.		44	55	66
When I visit the neighbor, Jan may go down to the dock.		44	55	66
Alan and I laid six of the eight signs by the antique chair.		48	60	72
Pamela and Vivian may sign the proxy if they audit the firm.		48	60	72
Chris may go with the widow to visit the city and see the chapel.		52	65	78
The maid may go with them when they go to the city for the gowns.		52	65	78

Skill Check

1. Key a 1' timing on ¶ 1; determine *gwam*.
2. Add 2–4 *gwam* to the rate attained in step 1; determine quarter-minute checkpoints from the chart below.
3. Key two 1' guided timings on ¶ 1 to increase speed.
4. Practice ¶ 2 in the same way.
5. Key two 3' timings on ¶s 1 and 2 combined; determine *gwam* and the number of errors.

Quarter-Minute Checkpoints

gwam	1/4'	1/2'	3/4'	Time
16	4	8	12	16
20	5	10	15	20
24	6	12	18	24
28	7	14	21	28
32	8	16	24	32
36	9	18	27	36
40	10	20	30	40

A   all letters used   MicroPace

	gwam	1'	3'
Which of the states has the least number of people?		10	3
Few people realize that this state ranks first in coal,		21	7
fifth in natural gas, and seventh in oil production. Quite		33	11
a significant number of deer, antelope, and buffalo dwell		44	15
within the boundaries of this exquisite state. A major		55	18
portion of Yellowstone National Park is located in the		66	22
state. If you still don't know which state is being		77	26
described, it is Wyoming.		82	27
Wyoming is located in the western portion of the		92	31
United States. The state is bordered by six different		103	34
states. Plains, mountain ranges, and national parks make		114	38
up a vast portion of the landscape of the state. Several		126	42
million people come to the state each year to view the		137	46
beautiful landscape of this unique state. Visitors and		148	49
the extraction of natural resources make up a major portion		159	53
of the economy of the state.		165	55

gwam	1'	1	2	3	4	5	6	7	8	9	10	11	12
	3'		1		2			3			4		

Lesson 146   PREPARING MAILING LABELS AND ENVELOPES

146B

Mailing Labels and Envelopes

Activity 1
Mailing Labels

1. Create mailing labels (illustrated at the right) for the merge letters generated for *Rockwell Technologies* in Lessons 144–145 using the Mail Merge Wizard.

2. Label specifications:
   Label vendor: Avery US Letters
   Product No.: 5160

Save as: Rockwell Labels

Activity 2
Mailing Labels

1. Create mailing labels for the merge letters generated for *Eastwick School of Dance* in Lessons 144–145.

2. Use Avery Product No. 5160 labels.

Save as: Eastwick Labels

Activity 3
Envelopes

1. Create and print envelopes as illustrated at the right for the merge letters generated for *Franklin High School FBLA* in Lessons 144–145.

2. Use Standard Size 10 envelopes and only print envelopes for Lockwood and Van Buren.

The return address is:

Future Busines Leaders of America
Franklin High School
300 California Street
San Francisco, CA 94104

Save as: FBLA Envelopes

Mailing labels and envelopes can be created by using the mailing labels and envelopes features of Mail Merge in conjunction with your database file.

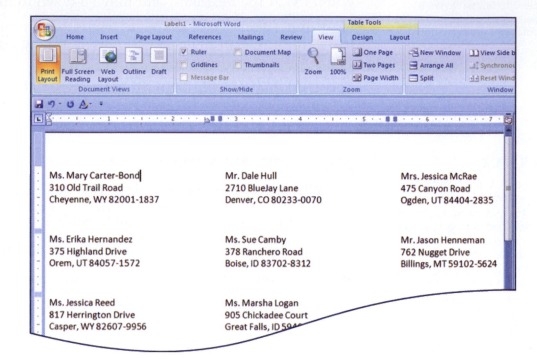

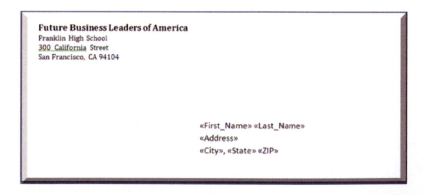

Lesson 47

KEYING TECHNIQUE

OBJECTIVES
- To improve keying techniques.
- To improve keying speed and control.

47B   Skill Building

Technique: Letter Keys

Key each line twice.

Technique Cue

Keep fingers curved and upright.

Emphasize continuity and rhythm with curved, upright fingers.

I 1 Michigan, Illinois, Indiana, and Missouri are all in the Midwest.

J 2 Jeff juggled jobs to join Jane for juice with the judge and jury.

K 3 Katie knocked the knickknacks off the kiosk with her knobby knee.

L 4 Please allow me to be a little late with all legal illustrations.

M 5 Mary is immensely immature; her mannerisms make me extremely mad.

N 6 Nancy knew she would win the nomination at their next convention.

O 7 Roberto opposed opening the store on Monday mornings before noon.

P 8 Pam wrapped the peppermints in purple paper for the photographer.

Q 9 Qwin quietly queried Quincy on the quantity and quality of quail.

gwam 1' | 1 | 2 | 3 | 4 | 5 | 6 | 7 | 8 | 9 | 10 | 11 | 12 | 13 |

47C   Skill Building

Technique: Number Keys/TAB

1. Set tabs at 2" and 4".
2. Key the copy at the right.

Technique Cue

Eyes on copy.

Concentrate on figure location; quick tab spacing; eyes on copy.

703 Sandburg Trl.	65 Yates Ave.	656 Winter Dr.
5214 Chopin St.	423 Clement St.	187 Ocean Ave.
3769 Orchard Rd.	641 Boone Ct.	410 Choctaw St.
158 Hartford St.	901 Cassia Dr.	792 Fairview Dr.

47D

Speed Building

1. Key a 1' timing on ¶ 1; key four more 1' timings on ¶ 1, trying to go faster each time.
2. Repeat the procedure for ¶ 2.

 all letters used (MicroPace)

gwam 1'

Government is the structure by which public laws are   11
made for a group of people.   It can take many forms.   For   22
example, in one type of structure, the populace has the right   34
to elect citizens to govern for them and make the laws and   46
policies.   This way of making the laws is called a represen-   58
tative government.   62

Democracy or republic form of government are two names   12
that are quite often used to refer to this type of governance   24
by the people.   This type of a structure is in direct contrast   37
to a dictatorship, in which all the decisions are made by just   49
one person.   52

gwam 1' | 1 | 2 | 3 | 4 | 5 | 6 | 7 | 8 | 9 | 10 | 11 | 12 |

1. Send the letter at the right to the following chapter members of Franklin High School FBLA:
   Julia Radclif
   Jason McWilliams
   Alison Massena
   Greg Lockwood
   Dianna Van Buren

Hint: In the Mail Merge recipient's list, click the √ to the right of the Data Source. Then click in the box under the √ next to the names of the individuals to receive the letter.

2. Print the letters to Radclif and Lockwood.

Save as: FBLA Form

Save as: FBLA Merge

Activity 3
Merging Sources

1. Create the form letter shown at the right to send to the parents of students who have not paid their September dance fees.

2. Update the address file to include a field for the person's *Title*. Supply an appropriate courtesy title of **Mr.** or **Mrs.** for each person.

3. Create a query from the *Address* file and the *Fee* file that includes all of the fields shown at the right needed to complete the mail merge plus September fees. Set the criteria for September fees = to 0 to determine who should receive a letter.

4. Merge and print the letters to Finley and Dye.

Save as: Eastwick Form

Save as: Eastwick Merge

January 15, 20--

<<First_Name>> <<Last_Name>>
<<Street_Address>>
<<City>>, <<State>> <<ZIP>>

Dear <<First_Name>>,

At last week's meeting, you indicated an interest in participating in one of the events at the FBLA Regional Leadership Conference, which will be held March 5-6 in Sacramento. Event signup will take place at our February 2 meeting.

I have enclosed a pamphlet that lists all the events along with a brief description of the events. If you have questions about any of the events, please stop in and see our advisor, Ms. King.

We are looking forward to having you take part in this year's leadership conference; I know that you will have a great time.

Sincerely,

Judy S. Loganberry
Leadership Conference Coordinator

October 15, 20--

<<Title>> <<First_Name_Guardian>> <<Last_Name_Guardian>>
<<Address>>
<<City>>, <<State>> <<ZIP>>

Dear <<Title>> <<Last_Name_Guardian>>:

Please check your records to see if you have paid for <<First_Name>>'s September dance fees. Our records show that we have not received the fees in the amount of $<<Monthly_Fees>>. Let us know if our records are incorrect or send the fees with <<First_Name>> to her next dance class.

I have enjoyed working with <<First_Name>> this fall. Observing the students' progress from one skill level to the next is always very satisfying to me. The students are looking forward to performing for you at the December recital.

Sincerely,

Ashley Eastwick
Dance Instructor

Skill Building

Speed Forcing Drill

Key each line once at top speed; then try to complete each sentence on the 15", 12", or 10" call as directed by your instructor. Force speed to higher levels as you move from sentence to sentence.

Emphasis: high-frequency balanced-hand words

	gwam	15"	12"	10"
Glen and I may key the forms for the city auditor.		40	50	60
He may make a sign to hang by the door of the bus.		40	50	60
They may make a profit if they do all of the busy work.		44	55	66
Six of the men may bid for good land on the big island.		44	55	66
If he pays for the bus to the social, the girls may also go.		48	60	72
The neighbor paid the maid for the work she did on the dock.		48	60	72
It is their civic duty to handle their problems with proficiency.		52	65	78
Helen is to pay the firm for all the work they do on the autobus.		52	65	78

Lesson 48   KEYING TECHNIQUE

OBJECTIVES

- To improve keying techniques.
- To improve keying speed and control.

48B   Skill Building

Technique: Letter Keys

Key each line twice.

Technique Cue

Limit keystroking action to the fingers; keep hands and arms motionless.

Emphasize continuity and rhythm with curved, upright fingers.

R 1 Raindrops bore down upon three robbers during the February storm.
S 2 The Mets, Astros, Reds, Twins, Jays, and Cubs sold season passes.
T 3 Trent bought the teal teakettle on the stove in downtown Seattle.
U 4 Ursula usually rushes to the music museum on Tuesday, not Sunday.
V 5 Vivacious Eve viewed seven vivid violets in the vases in the van.
W 6 We swore we would work with the two wonderful kids for two weeks.
X 7 Rex Baxter explained the extra excise tax to excited expatriates.
Y 8 Yes, Ky is very busy trying to justify buying the yellow bicycle.
Z 9 Dazed, Zelda zigzagged to a plaza by the zoo to see a lazy zebra.

gwam	1'	1	2	3	4	5	6	7	8	9	10	11	12	13

48C   Skill Building

Technique: Number Keys/TAB

1. Set tabs at 2" and 4".
2. Key the copy at the right.

Concentrate on finger location; quick tab spacing; eyes on copy.

331 Summit St.	589 Gabriel Ave.	364 Topaz Ave.
2490 Tucker Ave.	981 Toweridge Rd.	72 Viking Rd.
587 Telemark Ct.	207 Maplewood Trl.	481 Osceola Ave.
6021 Mission Hills	365 Westover St.	2963 Hunt St.
467 Sycamore Dr.	440 Radcliff Blvd.	50 Saratoga Ln.
809 Danbury Ave.	13 Plum Way	83 Ravine Dr.
9987 Park Pl.	224 Norton Way	745 Sinclair Ct.

Mail Merge Illustration

The illustration at the right shows how the data file was merged with the wp file to produce the letter at the bottom of the illustration.

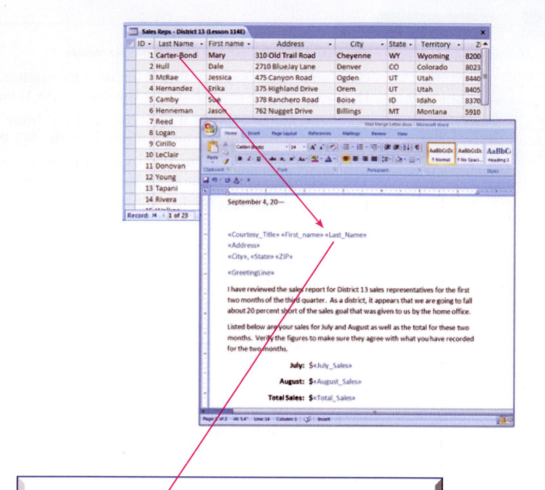

Speed Forcing Drill

Key each line once at top speed; then try to complete each sentence on the 15", 12", or 10" call as directed by your instructor. Force speed to higher levels as you move from sentence to sentence.

Emphasis: high-frequency balanced-hand words

	gwam	15"	12"	10"
Janel may go to the dock to visit the eight girls.		40	50	60
She is to go with them to the city to see the dog.		40	50	60
The sorority girls paid for the auto to go to the city.		44	55	66
She is to go to the city with us to sign the six forms.		44	55	66
Dick may go to the big island to fix the auto for the widow.		48	60	72
Hank and the big dog slept by the antique chair on the dock.		48	60	72
Rick is to make a turn to the right at the big sign for downtown.		52	65	78
Vivian may go with us to the city to do the work for the auditor.		52	65	78

Skill Check

1. Key a 1' timing on ¶ 1; determine *gwam*.
2. Add 2–4 *gwam* to the rate attained in step 1; determine quarter-minute checkpoints from the chart below.
3. Key two 1' guided timings on ¶ 1 to increase speed.
4. Practice ¶ 2 in the same way.
5. Key two 3' timings on ¶s 1 and 2 combined; determine *gwam* and the number of errors.

Quarter-Minute Checkpoints

gwam	1/4'	1/2'	3/4'	Time
16	4	8	12	16
20	5	10	15	20
24	6	12	18	24
28	7	14	21	28
32	8	16	24	32
36	9	18	27	36
40	10	20	30	40

A **all letters used** (MicroPace)

	gwam	3'
Extraordinary would be an appropriate word to use to de-	4	71
scribe Michelangelo. It would be a good word to express how	8	75
an individual may feel about the statue of David. It would	12	79
also be an excellent choice of words for describing the exqui-	16	84
site works of art on the ceiling of the Sistine Chapel. It	20	88
would be just as fine a word to use to describe the dome of	24	92
St. Peter's Basilica. Each of these outstanding works of art	28	96
was completed by Michelangelo, quite an extraordinary person.	32	100
The paintings, sculptures, and architecture of this man	36	104
are recognized throughout the world. Michelangelo was born in	40	108
Caprese, Italy, but spent much of his early life in the city	44	112
of Florence. Here he spent a great deal of time in the work-	48	116
shops of artists. His father did not approve of his doing so,	52	120
because artists were considered to be manual laborers. His	56	124
father considered this to be beneath the dignity of his family	61	128
members. This did not stop the young artist, who would even-	65	132
tually become one of the greatest of all times.	68	135

144–145B

Using Mail Merge

Read the text at the right and study the illustration on the next page to learn how information from two sources is combined into one document.

Activity 1
Merging Sources

1. Use the Mail Merge Wizard to create the form letter shown at the right to send to the sales reps in the *Rockwell Technologies – District 13* database.

Save as: **144B Rockwell Form**

2. Merge and print the letters to Hernandez, Tapani, and Butler.

Save as: **144B Rockwell Form**

Note: Fields to be inserted are shown in color. To get the address spaced correctly, use More items to insert each field for the address rather than using Address block. Be sure to include your reference initials.

The Merge feature is used to combine information from two sources into one document. It is often used for mail merge, which merges a word processing file (form letter) with a database file.

The database file contains a record for each recipient. Each record contains field(s) of information about the person such as first name, last name, address, city, state, ZIP, etc.

The wp file contains the text of the document (constant information) plus the field codes and field names (variable information). The field codes and names are positioned in the document where the variable information from the database is to appear. A personalized letter to each recipient is the result of merging the two files.

September 4, 20--

<<Courtesy_Title>> <<First_name>> <<Last_Name>>
<<Address>>
<<City>>, <<State>> <<ZIP>>

<<GreetingLine>>

I have reviewed the sales report for District 13 sales representatives for the first two months of the third quarter. As a district, it appears that we are going to fall about 20 percent short of the sales goal that was given to us by the home office.

Listed below are your sales for July and August as well as the total for these two months. Verify the figures to make sure they agree with what you have recorded for the two months.

        July: $<<July_Sales>>

      August: $<<August_Sales>>

    Total Sales: $<<Total_Sales>>

Please make every effort possible during September to reach the goal that was set for your territory last May. It is my understanding that most of the other districts are going to meet or exceed the goals that were given to them.

If I can provide additional assistance to you to help you meet your goal, please contact me.

Sincerely,

Paul M. Vermillion
District Sales Manager

Communication & Math
SKILLS 5

SUBJECT/VERB AGREEMENT

Subject/Verb Agreement

1. Study each of the six rules.
   a. Key the *Learn* line(s) beneath each rule, noting how the rule is applied.
   b. Key the *Apply* line(s), choosing correct verbs.

Subect/Verb Agreement

Rule 1: Use a singular verb with a singular subject (noun or pronoun); use a plural verb with a plural subject and with a compound subject (two nouns or pronouns joined by *and*).

Learn	1	The speaker was delayed at the airport for over thirty minutes.
Learn	2	The musicians are all here, and they are getting restless.
Learn	3	You and your assistant are to join us for lunch.
Apply	4	The member of the chorus (is, are) to introduce the speaker.
Apply	5	Dr. Cho (was, were) to give the lecture, but he (is, are) ill.
Apply	6	Mrs. Samoa and her son (is, are) to be at the craft show.

Rule 2: Use the plural verb *do not* or *don't* with pronoun subjects *I, we, you,* and *they* as well as with plural nouns; use the singular verb *does not* or *doesn't* with pronouns *he, she,* and *it* as well as with singular nouns.

Learn	7	I do not find this report believable; you don't either.
Learn	8	If she doesn't accept our offer, we don't have to raise it.
Apply	9	They (doesn't, don't) discount, so I (doesn't, don't) shop there.
Apply	10	Jo and he (doesn't, don't) ski; they (doesn't, don't) plan to go.

Rule 3: Use singular verbs with indefinite pronouns (*each, every, any, either, neither, one,* etc.) and with *all* and *some* used as subjects if their modifiers are singular (but use plural verbs with *all* and *some* if their modifiers are plural).

Learn	11	Each of these girls has an important role in the class play.
Learn	12	Some of the new paint is already cracking and peeling.
Learn	13	All of the dancers are to be paid for the special performance.
Apply	14	Neither of them (is, are) well enough to sing today.
Apply	15	Some of the juice (is, are) sweet; some (is, are) quite tart.
Apply	16	Every girl and boy (is, are) sure to benefit from this lecture.

Rule 4: Use a singular verb with a singular subject that is separated from the verb by the phrase *as well as* or *in addition to*; use a plural verb with a plural subject so separated.

Learn	17	The letter, in addition to the report, has to be revised.
Learn	18	The shirts, as well as the dress, have to be pressed again.
Apply	19	The vocalist, as well as the pianist, (was, were) applauded.
Apply	20	Two managers, in addition to the president, (is, are) to attend.

Rule 5: Use a singular verb if *number* is used as the subject and is preceded by *the*; use a plural verb if *number* is the subject and is preceded by *a*.

| Learn | 21 | A number of them have already voted, but the number is small. |
| Apply | 22 | The number of jobs (is, are) low; a number of us (has, have) applied. |

Rule 6: Use a singular verb with singular subjects linked by *or* or *nor*, but if one subject is singular and the other is plural, the verb agrees with the nearer subject.

Learn	23	Neither Ms. Moss nor Mr. Katz was invited to speak.
Learn	24	Either the manager or his assistants are to participate.
Apply	25	If neither he nor they (go, goes), either you or she (has, have) to.

Activities 1 and 2
Creating Reports

1. Open *Software Professionals*.
2. Create the reports with the information requested at the right.

Save as: Software Price List and Software Sales

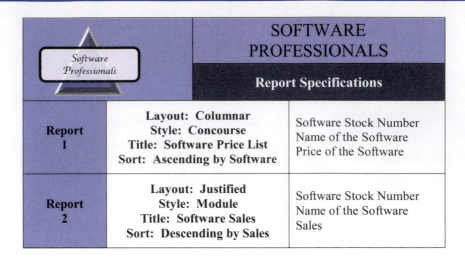

	SOFTWARE PROFESSIONALS	
	Report Specifications	
Report 1	Layout: Columnar Style: Concourse Title: Software Price List Sort: Ascending by Software	Software Stock Number Name of the Software Price of the Software
Report 2	Layout: Justified Style: Module Title: Software Sales Sort: Descending by Sales	Software Stock Number Name of the Software Sales

Activities 3 and 4
Creating Reports

1. Open *Eastwick School of Dance*.
2. Create reports with the information requested at the right.

Save as: Student Address List and Student Telephone List

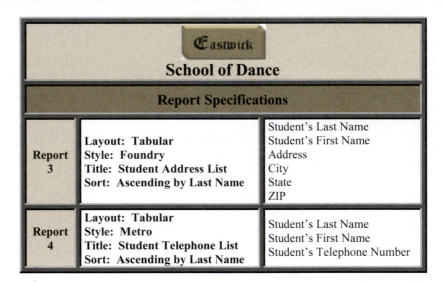

	School of Dance	
	Report Specifications	
Report 3	Layout: Tabular Style: Foundry Title: Student Address List Sort: Ascending by Last Name	Student's Last Name Student's First Name Address City State ZIP
Report 4	Layout: Tabular Style: Metro Title: Student Telephone List Sort: Ascending by Last Name	Student's Last Name Student's First Name Student's Telephone Number

Activities 5 and 6
Creating Reports

1. Open *Rockwell Technologies*.
2. Create reports with the information requested at the right.

Save as: July/August Sales and July/August Sales by Territory

Hint: Using the query you created for 141C Activity 1, go into Design View and add **Territory** as one of the fields. After running the report, you will need to adjust the column width to accommodate the Total Sales column.

	ROCKWELL TECHNOLOGIES	
	Report Specifications	
Report 5	Layout: Tabular Style: Office Title: July/August Sales Sort: Descending by Total Sales	Sales Rep's Last Name Sales Rep's Territory Sales Rep's July Sales Sales Rep's August Sales Sales Rep's Total Sales
Report 6	Prepare a sales report with the same information used in Report 5. Group the sales by territory. Use **July/August Sales by Territory** for the report title.	

2. Key Proofread & Correct, using correct verbs.
   a. Check answers.
   b. Using the rule number at the left of each line, study the rule relating to each error you made.
   c. Rekey each incorrect line, using correct verbs.

Save as: CS5 ACTIVITY1

ACTIVITY 2

Reading

1. Open *DF CS5 ACTIVITY2*
2. Read the document; close the file.
3. Key answers to the questions using complete sentences.

Save as: CS5 ACTIVITY2

ACTIVITY 3

Composing

1. Study the quotations.
2. Compose a ¶ to show your understanding of honesty and truth.
3. Compose a 2nd ¶ to describe an incident in which honesty and truth *should* prevail but don't.
4. Proofread and correct.

Save as: CS5 ACTIVITY3

ACTIVITY 4

Math: Finding What Percent One Number Is of Another

Proofread & Correct

Rules

1	1	Sandra and Rich (is, are) running for band secretary.
1	2	They (has, have) to score high on the SAT to enter that college.
2	3	You (doesn't, don't) think keyboarding is important.
2	4	Why (doesn't, don't) she take the test for advanced placement?
3	5	Neither of the candidates (meet, meets) the performance criteria.
3	6	One of your art students (is, are) likely to win the prize.
5	7	The number of people against the proposal (is, are) quite small.
4	8	The manager, as well as his assistant, (is, are) to attend.
6	9	Neither the teacher nor her students (is, are) here.
3	10	All the meat (is, are) spoiled, but some items (is, are) okay.

1. What kinds of positions are being filled?
2. What is the minimum number of hours each employee must work each week?
3. Is weekend work available?
4. What kind of service is being offered to those who have to care for elderly people?
5. Is the pay based solely on performance?
6. When are the openings available?
7. Does everyone work during the day?
8. How can you submit a resume?

Honesty's the best policy.
—Cervantes

Piety requires us to honor truth above our friends.
—Aristotle

To be honest . . . here is a task for all that a man has of fortitude.
—Robert Louis Stevenson

The dignity of truth is lost with protesting.
—Ben Jonson

1. Open *DF CS5 ACTIVITY4* and print the file.
2. Solve the problems as directed in the file.
3. Submit your answers.

CAREER Clusters

ACTIVITY 5

You must complete Career Activities 1–3 before this activity.

1. Retrieve the printed Career Cluster Plan of Study for the career cluster that is your second choice.
2. Review the plan and write a paragraph or two about why you would or would not consider a career in this cluster. Print your file, save it as Career5, and keep it open.
3. Exchange papers with a classmate. Have the classmate offer suggestions for improving the content and correcting any errors he or she finds in your paragraph(s). Make the changes that you agree with and print a copy to turn in to your instructor. Save it as Career5 and close the file.
4. Return your folder to the storage area. When your instructor returns your paper, file it in your Career folder.

Report Illustration 2

The report at the right was created using the Report Wizard feature. The report is in Portrait orientation with Justified layout in Foundry style. The report is sorted in Descending order by Ending Inventory. Only the first three entries of the report are shown.

Ending Inventory

Ending Inventory	
	4127
Stock Number	
B658	
Software	
Telephone Directory	
Ending Inventory	
	4020
Stock Number	
B952	
Software	
Tax Assistant	
Ending Inventory	
	2247
Stock Number	
E758	

Report Illustration 3

The report at the right is in Portrait orientation with Columnar layout in Concourse style. The report is sorted in Ascending order by Ending Inventory. Only the first four entries of the report are shown.

Ending Inventory

Ending Inventory	60
Stock Number	B821
Software	Data Controller
Ending Inventory	325
Stock Number	B833
Software	Office Layout
Ending Inventory	350
Stock Number	E561
Software	Creative Letters
Ending Inventory	463
Stock Number	B586
Software	Graphic Designer

Office Features 5

For each activity, read and learn the feature described, then follow instructions at the left.

Activity 1

Review Features

Key sentences 1–5; <u>underline</u>, *italicize*, and **bold** text as you key. Use the Hanging Indent feature to align the second line of text under the first line.

Save as: **OF5 ACTIVITY1**

1. **Benjamin Britten's** *Four Sea Interludes* include ***Dawn, Sunday Morning, Moonlight,*** and ***Storm***.
2. <u>**Brad Pitt,**</u> <u>**Cate Blanchett,**</u> <u>**Kimberly Scott,**</u> **and** <u>**Jason Flemyng**</u> star in ***The Curious Case of Benjamin Button***.
3. The titles of **books** and **movies** should be <u>underlined</u> or *italicized*.
4. <u>The Bourne Ultimatum</u> is an **adventure/action** movie; <u>Fred Clause</u> is a **comedy**; and <u>The Assassination of Jesse James</u> is a **western**.
5. *Success* was written by <u>Henry Wadsworth</u> **Longfellow**; <u>Samuel</u> **Longfellow** wrote *Go Forth to Life*.

Activity 2

Review Features

1. Open DF *OF5 ACTIVITY2*.
2. <u>Underline</u>, *italicize*, and **bold** text as shown at the right.

Save as: **OF5 ACTIVITY2**

6. During the first week of February, *The Testament* by **John Grisham** was No. 1 on the <u>Best Sellers</u> list.
7. <u>Time</u> and <u>Newsweek</u> featured articles on **Princess Diana** a decade after her tragic death.
8. <u>Cut</u>, <u>Copy</u>, and <u>Paste</u> were presented in **OF1**; <u>margins</u> were presented in **OF2**.
9. Do you know the difference between **their** and **there**?
10. *The Village Blacksmith* (**Longfellow**) and *The Road Not Taken* (**Frost**) were discussed in class on Friday.

Activity 3

Review Features

1. Open *DF OF5 ACTIVITY3*.
2. Use the Format Painter feature to copy formatting from line 1 and apply it to lines 2–6.

Save as: **OF5 ACTIVITY3**

1. The state capital of **Alabama** is **Montgomery**.
2. The state capital of **Arizona** is **Phoenix**.
3. The state capital of **Georgia** is **Atlanta**.
4. The state capital of **Indiana** is **Indianapolis**.
5. The state capital of **New Jersey** is **Trenton**.
6. The state capital of **Ohio** is **Columbus**.

143B

Preparing Reports

Read the text at the right to learn about Report features.

The Report features of the database are used for summarizing, formatting, and printing selected data from the database.

Summarizing: Generally, only a portion of the data contained in a database is needed for a particular application. The Summarizing feature allows selection of specific data for inclusion in the report.

Formatting: Formatting can be accomplished automatically using the Wizard feature of the software. The form can be modified by using the Design View feature.

Printing: Once the data has been specified and formatted, professional-looking hard copies can be printed and distributed for information and decision-making purposes. Today, electronic distribution of reports is also quite common.

Report Illustration 1

The report shown below was created using the Report Wizard feature. The report was sorted in Ascending order by Ending Inventory. The report was formatted in Tabular layout with Portrait orientation using Module style.

Ending Inventory

Ending Inventory	Stock Number	Software
60	B821	Data Controller
325	B833	Office Layout
350	E561	Creative Letters
463	B586	Graphic Designer
600	E320	English Enhancement
826	E786	Computerized Reading
827	B839	Art Gallery
1241	B615	Language Skills
1513	B689	Financial Advisors
1622	B929	Basic Spreadsheets
1700	E641	Spelling Mastery
1961	E910	Math Tutor
2050	E246	Computer Geography
2121	B794	
2122	B731	
2247		

Activity 4

Review Features
Envelope

Use the Envelopes feature to format a small envelope (No. 6 ¾) for Envelope 1 and a large envelope (No. 10) for Envelope 2.

Save as: **OF5 ACTIVITY4-1**

Save as: **OF5 ACTIVITY4-2**

Return address:

Envelope 1

Felix S. Vidro
720 Dorado Beach NE
Albuquerque, NM 87111-3827

Envelope 2

Jesus Rios
310 Joe Louis Avenue
Raleigh, NC 27610-3386

Delivery address:

Ms. Erin Cooper
840 Torinita Avenue
Trenton, NJ 08610-3728

Ms. Kendra Eastwick
748 Gertrude Lane
Lafayette, IN 47905-3882

Activity 5

Review Features
Tabs

1. Set a left tab at .5", a right tab at 3", and a decimal tab at 5".
2. Starting at 2" from the top of the page, key the text (DS) at the right.

Save as: **OF5 ACTIVITY5**

Left tab at .5"	Right tab at 3"	Decimal tab at 5"
↓	↓	↓
One-eighth	1/8	.125
One-sixth	1/6	.1667
One-fourth	1/4	.25
One-third	1/3	.3333
One-half	1/2	.5
Two-thirds	2/3	.6667
Three-fourths	3/4	.75
One	1/1	1.0

Activity 6

Copy Text to Another File

1. Read the copy at the right.
2. Open *Microsoft Word*.
3. Open *DF OF5 ACTIVITY 6-1*; copy sentences 6–10.
4. Open *DF OF5 ACTIVITY 6-2*; place the copied text a DS below sentence 5.

Save as: **OF5 ACTIVITY6**

Use the **Copy** and **Paste** features to copy text from one file to another.

Use the **Cut** and **Paste** features to move text from one file to another.

Steps to Copy, Cut, and Paste:

1. Select the text.
2. Copy (or cut) the selected text.
3. Open the document in which you want to place the copied (or cut) text.
4. Place the insertion point where you want to place the text.
5. Paste the text at the insertion point.

Activity 7

Reinforce Copying Text to Another File

Open the files:
DF OF5 ACTIVITY7-1
DF OF5 ACTIVITY7-2
DF OF5 ACTIVITY7-3

Create a copy of the Gettysburg Address as directed at the right.

Save as: **OF5 ACTIVITY7**

The initial words of each of the three ¶s of the Gettysburg Address are shown at the right. The names of the files where these ¶s can be found are shown in parentheses.

Copy the ¶s from *OF5 ACTIVITY7-2* and *OF5 ACTIVITY7-3* and place them in the correct order in *OF5 ACTIVITY7-1*. Leave a DS between ¶s.

Paragraph 1: Four score and seven years ago, our fathers brought forth on this continent . . . (*OF5 ACTIVITY7-1*)

Paragraph 2: Now we are engaged in a great civil war, testing . . . (*OF5 ACTIVITY7-2*)

Paragraph 3: But in a large sense we cannot dedicate, we cannot consecrate, we cannot hallow this ground. The brave . . . (*OF5 ACTIVITY7-3*)

Activity 2
Creating Forms

1. Open *Franklin High School FBLA*.
2. Create a form in the database with the information requested at the right.

Save as: **Membership List**

Activity 3
Creating Forms

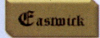

1. Open *Eastwick School of Dance*.
2. Create a form in the database with the information requested at the right

Save as: **Eastwick Student Enrollment**

Activities 4 and 5
Creating Forms

1. Open *Rockwell Technologies*.
2. Create forms in the database with the information requested at the right.

Save Activity 4 as:
Rockwell Sales for July and August

Save Activity 5 as: **Sales Reps' Territory**

Hint: To expand column width, click View/Layout view. Click in the column where you want to change the width. Then click and drag the right side of the box to the desired width.

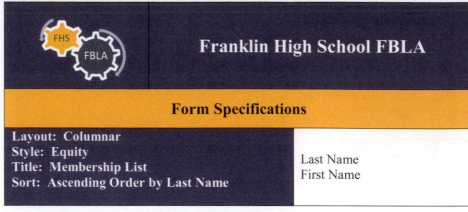

Franklin High School FBLA

Form Specifications

Layout: Columnar	Last Name
Style: Equity	First Name
Title: Membership List	
Sort: Ascending Order by Last Name	

Eastwick

School of Dance

Form Specifications

Layout: Tabular	Last Name
Style: Median	First Name
Title: Eastwick Student Enrollment	Dance Class 1
Sort: Ascending Order by Last Name	Dance Class 2

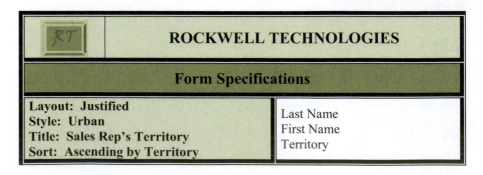

ROCKWELL TECHNOLOGIES

Form Specifications

Layout: Tabular	Last Name
Style: Northwind	First Name
Title: Rockwell Sales for July and August	July Sales
Sort: Ascending by Last Name	August Sales

ROCKWELL TECHNOLOGIES

Form Specifications

Layout: Justified	Last Name
Style: Urban	First Name
Title: Sales Rep's Territory	Territory
Sort: Ascending by Territory	

Navigate a Document

1. Read the copy at the right. Learn to move the insertion point using HOME, END, PgUp/PgDn, and CTRL + arrow keys.
2. Key sentence 1; edit as instructed in sentences 2, 3, and 4, using only the insertion point to navigate.

Save as: OF5 ACTIVITY8

The **HOME**, **END**, **PgUp**, and **PgDn** keys can be used to *navigate* (move the insertion point quickly from one location to another) in a document.

The **CTRL** key in combination with the arrow keys can be used to move the insertion point to various locations.

1. Key the following sentence.

   The basketball game is on Friday.

2. Make the following changes, using the insertion point move keys.

   The basketball game is on Friday, ~~next~~ February 20.

3. Make these additional changes, using the insertion point move keys.

   The next basketball game is on Friday, February 20, varsity *at 7 p.m.*

4. Make these changes.

   The next varsity basketball game is on ~~Friday,~~ February 20, at 7 p.m. Saturday against Sundance.

Inserting the Date

1. Read the copy at the right; learn to use the features described.
2. Key the information at the right using the Insert Date and AutoComplete features as indicated. If AutoComplete is not available with your software, use the Insert Date feature.

Save as: OF5 ACTIVITY9

Use the **Insert Date** feature to enter the date into a document automatically. Some software has an Update Automatically option along with Insert Date. When the update option is used, the date is inserted as a date field. Each time the document is opened or printed, the current date replaces the previous date. The date on your computer must be current to insert the correct date in a document.

Some software provides an **Automatic Completion (AutoComplete)** feature, which also inserts the date automatically. When you start keying the month, AutoComplete recognizes the word and shows it in a tip box above the insertion point. By tapping the **ENTER** key, you enter the remainder of the month automatically, without keying it. When you tap the Space Bar, the tip box shows the complete date. Tapping the **ENTER** key enters the complete date.

Part I
<Insert Date>

Mr. Gavin Garfield
5104 Hyde Park Blvd., S
Chicago, IL 60615-3291

<Insert hard page break>

Part II
<Insert Date Field, Update Automatically>

Ms. Tabitha Cicero
3678 Regal Street
Charleston, SC 29405-1348

<Insert hard page break>

Part III
1. Today is <AutoComplete>.
2. Your balance as of <Insert Date Field, Update Automatically> is $42.83.
3. I received your check today, <Insert Date>.
4. You will need to make sure that today's date, <Insert Date Field, Update Automatically>, is included on the form.

142B

Using a Wizard to Create Forms

Create/Forms/More Forms/Form Wizard

Read the text at the right to learn about creating forms.

Form Illustration

The forms at the right were created using the Form Wizard feature. The first form includes the fields in the *Software Professionals* database. The second form includes only the *Stock Number, Software,* and *Ending Inventory* fields. Both forms are in Columnar layout. The third form shows the same fields as the second, but in Tabular layout, which allows you to view multiple records on the screen at the same time. The first two forms let you view one record at a time on the screen.

You can use forms to enter or view the information in a database. When using the Forms feature, you have the option of viewing only one record or multiple records at a time. When doing the former, it is easy to enter and view data in the clearly labeled fields.

Using the Wizard makes it easy to create well-designed forms. The Wizard feature allows you to have all the fields in a database included in the form or only selected fields.

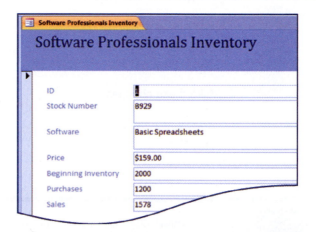

Activity 1
Creating Forms

1. Open *Software Professionals*.
2. Create the three forms shown at the right using the Form Wizard.
3. Use Columnar layout and Office style for the first two forms. Title the first form **Software Professionals Inventory** and the second form **Ending Inventory**.
4. Use Tabular layout and Office style for the third form, and title it **Ending Inventory 1**.

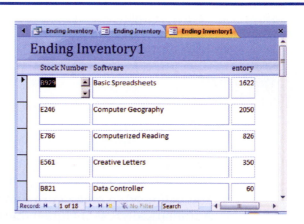

Format Guides

In Unit 8, you learned to format memos and personal-business letters. In this unit, you will learn to format business letters and memos with special features.

Since business letters have the return address printed as part of the letterhead, the return address does not need to be keyed.

Special Features for Memos and Letters

In addition to the basic parts presented in Unit 8, memos and letters may include the special features described below and illustrated on pp. 151 and 156.

Reference initials. If the memo or letter is keyed by someone other than its originator, the initials of the keyboard operator should be placed in lowercase letters at the left margin one line below the body (memos) or the originator's name and title (letters).

Attachment/Enclosure notation. If another document is attached to a memo or letter, the word *Attachment* is keyed at the left margin one line below the reference initials. If a document is included but not attached, the word *Enclosure* is used instead. If reference initials are not used, the notation is keyed one line below the body (memos) or the writer's name and title (letters).

Copy notation. A copy notation indicates that a copy of a memo or letter is being sent to someone other than the addressee. Use *c* followed by a space and then the name(s) of the person(s) to receive a copy. Place a copy notation one line below the last line of the enclosure notation or the reference initials if there is no enclosure. If there is more than one name, list names vertically.

c   Hector Ramirez
    Ursula O'Donohue

Blind copy notation. When a copy of a memo or letter is to be sent to someone without disclosing to the person receiving the

memo or letter, a blind copy (*bc*) notation is used. When used, *bc* and the name of the person receiving the blind copy are keyed at the left margin one line below the last memo or letter part on all copies of the memo *except* the original.

bc   Arlyn Hunter
     Miguel Rodriguez

Memo distribution list. When a memo is sent to several individuals, a distribution list is used. Format the memo distribution list as shown below:

To: Tim Burroughs
     Charla Dunwoody
     Alexandra Williams
     Ramon Garcia

Attention line for letters. An attention line should only be used when the writer does not know the name of the person who should receive the letter. For example, if a writer wants a letter to go to the director of special collections of a library but doesn't know the name of that person, *Attention Special Collections Director* or *Attention Director of Special Collections* could be used. When an attention line is used in a letter addressed to a company, key it as the first line of the letter and envelope address. Within the letter, the correct salutation is *Ladies and Gentlemen*.

Subject line for letters. The subject line specifies the topic discussed in the letter. Key the subject line in ALL CAPS, a SS below the salutation.

Tables. Tables may be inserted in memos and letters. Single-space before and after the table. To leave extra space following the table, click the Line spacing drop-down list arrow, and click Add Space Before Paragraph. This will make the spacing before and after the table equal. If space allows, indent the table at least .5" from the right and left margins.

Activity 1
Creating Computed Fields

1. Review the example on the previous page.
2. Create a query with the four fields shown at the right.

Save as: 141C Activity 1

3. Use the Expression Builder to create a formula to calculate the Total Sales in the column next to August Sales.
4. Print the query.

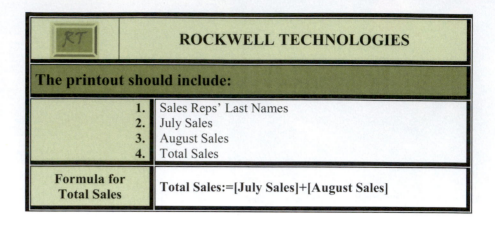

		ROCKWELL TECHNOLOGIES
		The printout should include:
	1. 2. 3. 4.	Sales Reps' Last Names July Sales August Sales Total Sales
Formula for Total Sales		**Total Sales:=[July Sales]+[August Sales]**

Activity 2
Creating Computed Fields

1. Create a query with the five fields shown at the right.

Save as: 141C Activity 2

2. Use the Expression Builder to create a formula to calculate the Total Fees Paid.
3. You will need to insert $0.00 in the cells where the fee has not been received.
4. Print the query.

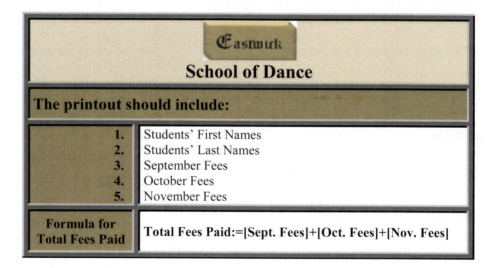

		School of Dance
		The printout should include:
	1. 2. 3. 4. 5.	Students' First Names Students' Last Names September Fees October Fees November Fees
Formula for Total Fees Paid		**Total Fees Paid:=[Sept. Fees]+[Oct. Fees]+[Nov. Fees]**

Activity 3
Creating Computed Fields

1. Create a query with the five fields shown at the right.

Save as: 141C Activity 3

2. Use the Expression Builder to create a formula to calculate the Ending Inventory.
3. Print the query.

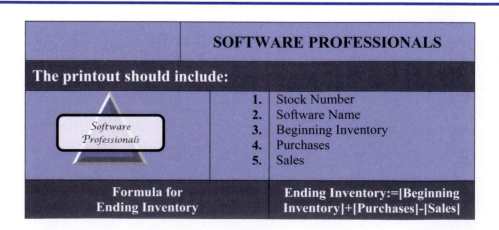

		SOFTWARE PROFESSIONALS
		The printout should include:
	1. 2. 3. 4. 5.	Stock Number Software Name Beginning Inventory Purchases Sales
Formula for Ending Inventory		**Ending Inventory:=[Beginning Inventory]+[Purchases]-[Sales]**

Memo Distribution List TO: American History I
American History II ↓1

FROM: Ms. Schultz ↓1

DATE: February 1, 20-- ↓1

SUBJECT: FINAL PROJECT ↓1

Body The table below lists the topics that you can choose from for your final project in American History. After you select a topic, sign up for it on Desire2Learn. Remember that only two students can select the same topic. The sooner you sign up, the more likely you are to get your first choice. ↓1

Default or 1" Left Margin

American History Topics for Final Project		
American Revolutionary War	Cuban Missile Crisis	Reconstruction
California Gold Rush	Great Depression	September 11, 2001
Civil Rights Act of 1964	Industrialization	Vietnam War
Civil War	Korean War	Wall Street Crash of 1929
Cold War	Louisiana Purchase	War of 1812
Colonial America	Persian Gulf War	Watergate
Constitutional Convention	Prohibition	World War I
Continental Army	Reaganomics	World War II

Default or 1" Right Margin

↓1

The guidelines for the final project are attached. Look them over before class on Monday, and I'll answer any questions you have at that time. Remember that each of you will be assigned to a faculty member of the English department to work with on the written part of this project. ↓1

Reference Initials xx ↓1

Attachment Notation Attachment ↓1

Copy Notation c Ms. Conway
Mr. Brockton
Mr. Dickson
Ms. McGee

Shown in 11-point Calibri with 2" top margin and 1" side margins, this memo appears smaller than actual size. Table heading is keyed in 13-point.

Memo with Special Features

Creating Computed Fields

Calculations can be done on existing fields by using the Expression Builder in the Query feature.

In the illustration at the right, Total Sales were calculated for each Rockwell Technologies sales representative:

STEPS:

1. Create a query on your Rockwell Technologies database table to include the following fields
   - **Last Name**
   - **First Name**
   - **July Sales**
   - **August Sales**

2. Save query as **Total Sales**.

3. Place the cursor in the column to the right of August Sales, and click *Builder* in the Query Setup group.

4. With the cursor in the Expression Builder, key **Total Sales:**

5. Click =, which is located beneath the Expression Builder input box.

6. Double-click *July Sales*, in the middle column beneath the Expression Builder input box.

7. Click + beneath the Expression Builder input box.

8. Double-click *August Sales*. Your expression should look like this:

   Total Sales: = [July Sales] + [August Sales]

9. Click OK.

10. Save the query.

11. Run the query to view the results.

Expression Builder

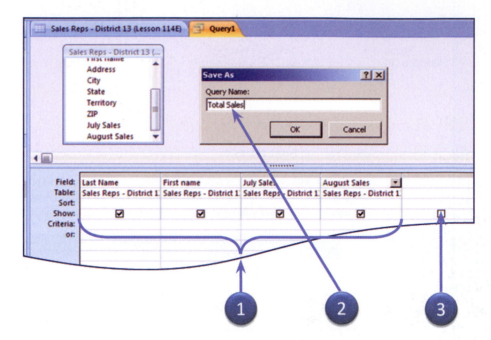

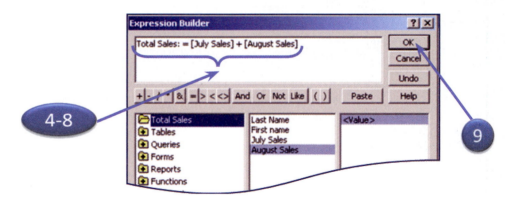

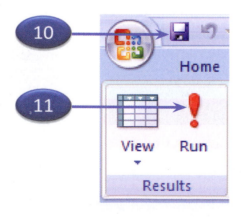

Lesson 49

IMPROVE MEMO FORMATTING SKILLS

- To increase proficiency at formatting memos.
- To format memo distribution lists.

49A–54A

Conditioning Practice

Key each line twice.

alphabet	1	Gavin Zahn will buy the exquisite green jacket from the old shop.
figures	2	Check No. 183 was used to pay Invoices 397 and 406 on October 25.
speed	3	Glen may pay the haughty neighbor if the turn signals work right.

gwam 1' | 1 | 2 | 3 | 4 | 5 | 6 | 7 | 8 | 9 | 10 | 11 | 12 | 13 |

49B Formatting

Memos

Memo 1

After reviewing the formatting guides on p. 150, key the model memo on p. 151. Use Light List – Accent 1. Do not bold the entries in Column 1.

Save as: 49B MEMO1

Memo 2

Format and key the text at the right as a memo. Include a blind copy notation to **Kevin Hefner**.

Save as: 49B MEMO2

TO: Marsha Hanson, Director | FROM: Jack Vermillion | DATE: Current Date | SUBJECT: ANTHONY AND STANTON DISCUSSION

Even though the Virginia Women's Museum is primarily for recognizing those women who contributed greatly to Virginia's history, I think it appropriate to recognize some early leaders of the women's movement on a national level.

Susan B. Anthony and Elizabeth Cady Stanton are two women who led the struggle for women's suffrage at the national level. They organized the National Woman Suffrage Association. Shouldn't they be recognized for their gallant efforts in our museum as well?

Please include a discussion of this issue on the next agenda. | xx

---

Memo 3

Format and key the text at the right as a memorandum. Send copies of the memo to **Timothy Gerrard** and **Maria Valdez**.

Save as: 49B MEMO3

TO: Andrew Nelson, Manager; Amy McDonald, Assistant Manager; Judith Smythe, Assistant Manager | FROM: Malcolm McKinley, Travel Agent | DATE: May 3, 20-- | SUBJECT: CIVIL WAR BUS TOUR

Yes, I think there would be an interest in a bus tour of some of the battle campaigns of the Civil War. My recommendation would be to start with a six-day tour that includes some of the most famous battlefields.

Of course, the one that comes to mind right away is Gettysburg, where over 158,000 Union (George G. Meade) and Confederate (Robert E. Lee) soldiers fought courageously for their causes. This battle (July 1-3, 1863) resulted in an estimated 51,000 lives being lost. Being able to visit the place where President Lincoln delivered the Gettysburg Address would also be of real interest to those considering the trip. I've looked at several websites, and evidently something of interest is always going on in or near Gettysburg.

The other battlefields that I recommend including on the tour are Manassas (Virginia) and Antietam (Maryland). Both of these battlefields were key encounters of the Civil War.

Within the next week, I will provide you with more details on a tour such as the one I've briefly presented. | xx

Activity 1
Execute a Query

1. Open the *Software Professionals* database.
2. Use the Queries feature to answer the questions at the right.
3. Print the results of query No. 4.

SOFTWARE PROFESSIONALS

No.	Query	Fields to Include	Criteria
1	What are the names of the software that was designated as "Educational" (Stock No. starting with E)?	Stock Number Software	Like "E*"
2	What software sells for more than $150?	Stock Number Software Price	>150
3	What software sold more than 1,500 units?	Stock Number Software Sales	>1500
4	What software sold less than 500 units?	Stock Number Software Sales	<500

Activity 2
Execute a Query

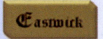

1. Open the *Eastwick School of Dance* database.
2. Use the Queries feature to answer the questions at the right.
3. Print the results of query No. 3.

School of Dance

No.	Query	Fields to Include	Criteria
1	What are the names and addresses of the students living in Minneapolis/St. Paul?	First Name Last Name Address State City ZIP	"Minneapolis" Or "St. Paul"
2	What are the names and addresses of the students living in Wisconsin?		"WI"
3	Which students have not paid their September fees?	Last Name First Name September Fees	Is Null

Activity 3
Execute a Query

1. Open the *Rockwell Technologies* database.
2. Use the Queries feature to answer the questions at the right.
3. Print the results of query No. 2.

ROCKWELL TECHNOLOGIES

No.	Query	Fields to Include	Criteria
1	What are the names and addresses of our Arizona sales reps?	First Name Last Name Address City	"Arizona"
2	What are the names and addresses of our Montana and Wyoming sales reps?	State ZIP Territory	"Montana" or "Wyoming"
3	Which sales reps had sales of more than $55,000 during July?	First Name Last Name July Sales	>55000

IMPROVE MEMO FORMATTING SKILLS

OBJECTIVE

- To increase proficiency in formatting and keying memos.

50B Formatting

Memos

Memo 1

Format and key a memo to **John Ewing** from **Duncan Sedgwick** using the current date. Include your reference initials and a blind copy notation to **Sally Enders**.

Save as: 50B MEMO1

SUBJECT: FIELD TRIP PROPOSAL | In our American History class, my students are studying the American Revolution. To bring this unit to life, I would like to take the class on a field trip to the Valley Forge Historical Society Museum.

According to their website, the museum

. . . offers visitors to Valley Forge the opportunity to understand the value of the sacrifice made by the 12,000 men who camped here during the winter of 1777-78. The spirit of Valley Forge is chronicled through galleries and displays that present the letters, weapons, and personal effects of the great and everyday Continental soldier.

I believe this would be an excellent educational experience for our students. When would you be available to meet with me to discuss a field trip of this nature?

Memo 2

Format the text at the right as a memo to **Kara Hundley, Chair**. The memo is from **Richard Ashmore**. Use the **current date** and a subject line of **RECOMMENDATION FOR CORPORATE GIVING FUNDS**.

Save as: 50B MEMO2

Remember the Alamo!!! As part of our annual corporate giving program, I am recommending that we make a contribution to the Alamo, managed by the Daughters of the Republic of Texas. They depend entirely on donations and proceeds from the gift shop for covering operating costs.

I believe it is important for us to honor those who played integral roles in the history of our state. Our children need to be reminded of the lives of James Bowie, David Crockett, and William Barret Travis, who made the ultimate sacrifice for freedom. And who can forget the role Sam Houston played as the commander in chief of the Texan army in the revolution against Mexico? Memories of Texan legends are preserved at the Alamo.

Please list the Alamo as a potential recipient in our corporate giving program next year. Of course, we will discuss it when we meet. | xx

Memo 3

Compose a memo using the information shown at the right.

Save as: 50B MEMO3

50C

Drill: Memos

Key two 2' timings on Memo 2. Try to key at least four additional words on the second 2' timing.

Jason Lopez, the FBLA president, would like you to send a memo to four of your teachers asking them to announce the first FBLA meeting of the year in their classes. The purpose of the meeting is to recruit new members; Mr. Chen will be the guest speaker, talking about the importance of co-curricular activities. The meeting will be held on September 8 at 3:30 in Ms. Jackson's room (308). Compose and format an appropriate memo; send a copy of the memo to Jason Lopez.

Creating Queries (cont.)

The Queries feature is used to extract and display specific information from a table. The Criteria line of the Query Design box is where instructions are given to the software that tell it which information to display. The basic criteria expressions are:

equal to (=)

greater than (>)

less than (<)

In the illustration at the right, *=CO* was used to extract only those sales reps from Colorado. If the criteria had been *=CO or AZ*, the sales reps from both Colorado and Arizona would have been displayed.

Follow these steps to design a query.

1. Open *Rockwell Technologies* database.

2. Activate Query Design feature.

3. Highlight table to draw Query from; click Add; click Close.

4. Select the field(s) you want to include in the query by double-clicking the field name.

5. Enter the desired search criteria (=CO).

6. To save query, click Save and enter name for query; click OK.

or

To view query, click ! (Run).

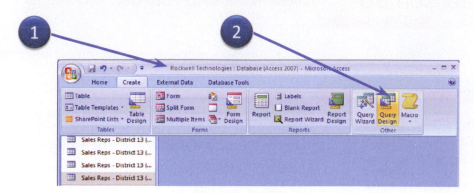

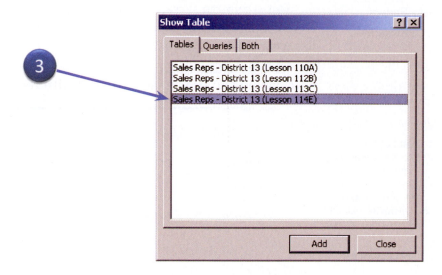

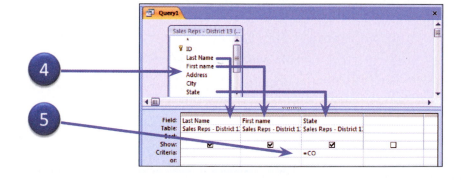

- To review personal-business letter formatting.
- To improve language skills.
- To increase proficiency in keying opening and closing lines of letters.

51B **Formatting**

Personal-Business Letters

Letter 1

Review the model personal-business letter on p. 66. Key in block format the letter shown at the right.

Save as: **51B LETTER1**

672 Saratoga Place | Boston, MA 02120-3857 | July 15, 20--

Ms. Annette Banks | 91 Kenwood Street | Brookline, MA 02446-2412 | Dear Ms. Banks |

At our meeting this summer, we decided to dedicate one unit of instruction to John F. Kennedy. As you will recall, I was assigned the responsibility for proposing a curriculum for this particular unit of instruction.

The possibilities of what to include in this unit were unlimited. It was very difficult squeezing everything into a one-week unit (see enclosure). However, I enjoyed the challenge of trying to do so. JFK is one of my favorite Presidents; many of my childhood memories are centered around the few short years that he was President.

What do you think of taking our classes on a tour of his birthplace? The home he was born in at 83 Beals Street is now a National Historic Site. Wouldn't this be a great way to conclude our unit and impress upon our students that the 35th President of the United States lived in a modest home only a few blocks away from our school?

If this is of interest to you, I will start making arrangements for both of our classes. I'm already getting excited about returning to school in the fall.

Sincerely | Blake Finley | xx | Enclosure

Letter 2

Format and key in block format the letter shown at the right.

Save as: **51B LETTER2**

325 Manhattan Avenue | New York, NY 10025-3827 | May 7, 20--

Ms. Suzanne E. Salmon | 1116 Tiffany Street | Bronx, NY 10459-2276 | Dear Ms. Salmon

I would be more than happy to meet with you to discuss my experiences during my assignment in the Persian Gulf region. It was one of the most, if not the most, exciting assignments I've worked on. The night the attack on Baghdad began will be with me for the rest of my life.

I will share with you the events in Kuwait that precipitated the war. I believe we should also discuss how these events led up to the next conflict, *Iraqi Freedom*.

Please call me at 212-183-8211 so we can arrange a time and location to meet. I'm looking forward to meeting you.

Sincerely | Mitchell Clevenger | Reporter | xx | bc Enrique Jaden

Lesson 141 — CREATING QUERIES AND COMPUTED FIELDS

141A-148A

Conditioning Practice

Key each line twice daily.

alphabet	1	Jeff Pizarro saw very quickly how Jason had won the boxing match.
figures	2	Our team average went from .458 on April 17 to .296 on August 30.
speed	3	Nancy may go to the big social at the giant chapel on the island.

gwam 1' | 1 | 2 | 3 | 4 | 5 | 6 | 7 | 8 | 9 | 10 | 11 | 12 | 13 |

141B

Creating Queries

Read the text at the right. Study the information below and the illustration to understand how queries can be used to extract information from a database table.

The answers to many questions can be found in a well-organized database. The *Sales Reps – District 13* table of the *Rockwell Technologies* database can be used to answer:

• Who are the sales reps from Colorado?
• Who are the sales reps with ZIP Codes starting with 5?
• Which sales reps had July sales of more than $50,000?

To generate answers to these questions, a query to the database must be made. A **query** is a question structured in a way that the software (database) can understand.

I •	Last Name ▾	First name ▾	Address ▾	City ▾	State ▾	Territory ▾	ZIP ▾	July Sales ▾	August ▾
1	Carter-Bond	Mary	310 Old Trail Road	Cheyenne	WY	Wyoming	82001-1837	$45,351.00	$37,951.00
2	Hull	Dale	2710 BlueJay Lane	Denver	CO	Colorado	80233-0070	$53,739.00	$49,762.00
3	McRae	Jessica	475 Canyon Road	Ogden	UT	Utah	84404-2835	$33,371.00	$38,978.00
4	Hernandez	Erika	375 Highland Drive	Orem	UT	Utah	84057-1572	$39,371.00	$40,790.00
5	Camby	Sue	378 Ranchero Road	Boise	ID	Idaho	83702-8312	$42,173.00	$65,386.00
6	Henneman	Jason	762 Nugget Drive	Billings	MT	Montana	59102-5624	$17,219.00	$29,737.00
7	Reed	Jessica	817 Herrington Drive	Casper	WY	Wyoming	82607-9956	$53,791.00	$59,349.00
8	Logan	Marsha	905 Chickadee Court	Great Falls	ID	Montana	59404-3883	$49,712.00	$21,790.00
9	Cirillo	Mathew	1208 Whitaker Road	Pocatello	ID	Idaho	83202-7523	$29,731.00	$37,956.00
10	LeClair	Justin	830 Whitehead Drive	Grand Junction	CO	Colorado	81503-2270	$63,212.00	$40,321.00
11	Donovan	Kellee	765 Coal Mine Avenue	Littleton	CO	Colorado	80123-0091	$37,198.00	$45,865.00
12	Young	Marsha	7563 Ferncrest Circle	Salt Lake City	UT	Utah	84118		
13	Tapani	Devlin	543 Lookout Mountain	Rapid City	SD				
14	Rivera	Jose	756 Royal Crest Drive						

Sales Reps – District 13 Table

Query 1 was designed to include *Last Name, First Name, State*.

The criteria for the state field was set to *=CO* to extract those reps from the state of Colorado.

Last Name ▾	First name ▾	State ▾
Hull	Dale	CO
LeClair	Justin	CO
Donovan	Kellee	CO
Rivera	Jose	CO
Bell	Scott	CO

Record: I◀ 1 of 5 ▶ ▶I ▶⊕ No Filter Search

Query 1

Query 2 was designed to include *Last Name, First Name, ZIP*.

The criteria for the ZIP field was set to *<6* to extract only those reps with ZIP codes starting with 5.

Last Name ▾	First name ▾	ZIP ▾
Henneman	Jason	59102-5624
Logan	Marsha	59404-3883
Tapani	Devlin	57702-9932
Wetteland	Cynthia	59803-8388
Doolittle	Lisa	57106-7621

Record: I◀ 1 of 5 ▶ ▶I ▶⊕ No Filter Search

Query 2

Query 3 was designed to include *Last Name, First Name, July Sales*.

The criteria for the July Sales field was set to *>50000* to extract only those sales reps with sales of more than $50,000.

Last Name ▾	First name ▾	July Sales ▾
Hull	Dale	$53,739.00
Reed	Jessica	$53,791.00
LeClair	Justin	$63,212.00
Rivera	Jose	$55,400.00
Reese	Jay	$67,890.00
Doolittle	Lisa	$64,890.00

Record: I◀ 1 of 7 ▶ ▶I ▶⊕ No Filter Search

Query 3

Illustrations on the next page show the steps required to run a query.

Language Skills: Word Choice

1. Study the spelling and definitions of the words.
2. Key all *Learn* and *Apply* lines, choosing the correct word in the *Apply* lines.

Save as: 51C CHOICE

to (prep/adj) used to indicate action, relation, distance, direction	**cents** (n) specified portion of a dollar
too (adv) besides; also; to excessive degree	**sense** (n/vb) meaning intended or conveyed; perceive by sense organs; ability to judge
two (pron/adj) one plus one in number	**since** (adv/conj) after a definite time in the past; in view of the fact; because

Learn   1   I plan on going **to** at least **two** of the games if you go **too**.

Apply   2   (To, Too, Two) of the history students are going (to, too, two) take the exam early.

Apply   3   You will need (to, too, two) bring (to, too, two) boxes (to, too, two).

Learn   1   **Since** I changed the dollars and **cents** columns, the figures make **sense**.

Apply   2   (Cents, Sense, Since) you gave me a dollar, you will get 77 (cents, sense, since) back.

Apply   3   (Cents, Sense, Since) he doesn't have common (cents, sense, since), be careful.

Drill: Personal-Business Letter

1. Take a 3' timing on the letter to determine *gwam*.
2. Key two 1' timings on opening lines through first ¶ of letter. If you finish the lines before time is called, QS and start over. Try to key four more words on the second timing.
3. Key two 1' writings on ¶ 3 through closing lines. If you finish before time is called, QS and start ¶ 3 again. Try to key four more words on the second timing.
4. Key another 3' timing on the letter. Try to increase your *gwam* by 4–8 words over your rate in step 1.

	words
622 Main Street	Moorcroft, WY 82721-2342	January 5, 20--	13
Ms. Dorothy Shepard	P.O. Box 275	Moorcroft, WY 82721-2342	25
Dear Ms. Shepard	29

Are you interested in serving on a planning committee for a women's   43
historical museum in Wyoming? The state's nickname (Equality State)   56
stems from the fact that Wyoming women were the first women in the   70
U.S. to achieve voting rights (1869).   78

Since then, many women have played an important part in shaping   90
the history of Wyoming. Are you aware that the first woman governor   104
in the U.S. came from Wyoming? Nellie Tayloe Ross became governor   118
of Wyoming in 1925.   122

Let's build a museum to recognize these women--a place for people to   136
reflect on events of the past and contemplate the future. I will call you   151
next week to see if you are willing to serve on the committee.   164

Sincerely | William P. Shea | xx   170

Lesson 140   COLUMN DOCUMENTS

• To apply what you have learned to prepare column documents.

140B

Newsletter 1

1. Using the copy at right, prepare a newsletter with two columns of equal width, separated by a vertical line. The newsletter title and publication information should span both columns.

2. Open *DF 140B NEWS1* and add the articles in the file to the end of the newsletter article at the left.

3. You decide all formatting features for the newsletter and make it fit on two pages using portrait or landscape orientation. Position the Health Tip text box wherever you prefer.

Save as: **140B NEWS**

ENVIRONMENTAL ALERT!

Volume 12, No. 9   November 20--

Where to Get Help
Have you ever wondered where to turn for answers to environmental problems? One good place to start is the United States Environmental Protection Agency's (EPA) website. The home page contains numerous links to general and specific information that will be of help. You can link to sections for concerned citizens, small businesses, industry, and even get EPA telephone numbers and addresses.

Protection of the environment is a big job. Federal, state, and local agencies across the nation are all involved, employing thousands of citizens who care about their health and natural resources. Every city, county, and state networks with federal groups to share and provide information. If the first person you contact can't answer a question, he or she will know who can.

No longer can we say, "I'm too busy to be concerned with the environment-- someone else can take care of it."

140C

Announcement

1. Open *DF 140C ANN*.
2. Format the text into two columns of equal width.

3. Insert appropriate clip art near the top of the page.
4. Use the Drop Cap feature as desired, and place a Draft watermark behind the text.
5. You decide all other formatting features to make the document attractive and easy to read.

Save as: **140C ANN**

140D

Word Choice

1. Study the spelling and definitions of the words.
2. Key the *Learn and Apply* lines, choosing the correct word(s) in the *Apply* lines.

Save as: **140D CHOICE**

Choose the right word

passed (vb) past tense of "pass"; already occurred; moved by; gave an item to someone	**waist** (n) narrowed part of the body between chest and hips; middle of something
past (adv/adj/prep/n) gone or elapsed; time gone by	**waste** (n/vb/adj) useless things; rubbish; spend or use carelessly; nonproductive

Learn 1 I think he **passed** his goal in the **past** month.

Apply 2 Judy worked every Monday during the (passed/past) year.

Apply 3 Alberto (passed/past) the runner on the left.

Learn 1 Greg did not **waste** any time putting the belt around his **waist**.

Apply 2 John was told not to (waist/waste) time during study hall.

Apply 3 I need to measure his (waist/waste) for his new uniform.

140E

Internet Activity
Energy-Saving Tips

1. Access the U.S. Department of Energy's website via http://school.cengage.com/keyboarding/c21key.
2. Explore the website to find energy-saving tips you can use.
3. Key a list of at least five energy saving tips you can use.

Save as: **140E INTERNET**

2" TM

Date February 15, 20-- ↓2

Letter mailing address Ms. Ariel McKenzie, Principal
4608 Delaware Avenue
Baltimore, MD 21215-8794 ↓1

Salutation Dear Ms. McKenzie ↓1

Subject Line NEW TEXTBOOKS

Body Thank you for meeting with the history department instructors to discuss our priority list for the next school year. The proposed curriculum revisions are not going to happen without incurring significant costs in terms of textbooks, technology resources, and faculty development. As we agreed, we will start with textbooks. The table below shows the books that are essential for next year. ↓1

Default or 1" Right Margin

Textbook	Author	Copyright
The Glorious Cause: The American Revolution, 1763-1789	Robert Middlekauff	2007
The American Revolution: A History	Gordon S. Wood	2002
The Women of the American Revolution	Elizabeth Ellet	2004

↓1

Default or 1" Left Margin

At our last meeting, the history instructors agreed to develop a tentative budget for the technology resources and faculty development costs. The budget is attached.

I've scheduled the library conference room for our next meeting on February 23. ↓1

Complimentary close Sincerely ↓2

Writer Barbara Segee ↓1
Writer's Title Curriculum Coordinator

Reference Initials xx

Attachment Notation Attachment

Copy Notation c Rebecca Schultz
Marshall Woodward
Gavin Sanchez

Shown in 11-point Calibri with 2" top margin and 1" side margins, this letter appears smaller than actual size. Change the default bottom margin to .5" to fit copy on the page.

Business Letter with Special Features

OBJECTIVE

• To prepare a four-page program booklet.

139B

Program Booklet

1. Prepare a program booklet for the High School Honor Society Induction Ceremony.

2. The brochure will be formatted on *two pages*, using 8.5" x 11" paper in landscape orientation (see illustration at right):

    Page 1 will have the text for the outside back and front covers.

    Page 2 will have the text for the inside left page and the inside right page.

3. Set top, bottom, and side margins on both pages at 0.5".

4. Select landscape orientation and two pages per sheet. (**Page Layout/ Page Setup dialog box/ Margins tab/Orientation: Landscape and Pages:** 2 pages per sheet)

5. Set columns as follows:

    a. **Outside Back Cover:** two columns, each 2" wide, with 0.5" between them.

    b. **Outside Front Cover:** one 4.5" column.

    c. **Inside Left Page:** one 4.5" column.

    d. **Inside Right Page:** two columns, each 2" wide with 0.5" between them.

6. Key the information that is given for the covers and pages at the right. You decide all other formatting features and graphics that will be inserted.

Save p. 1 as *139B PRO1* and p. 2 as *139B PRO2*.

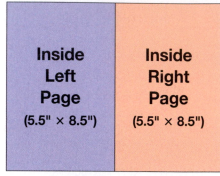

Page 1

| Outside Back Cover (5.5" × 8.5") | Outside Front Cover (5.5" × 8.5") |

One 8.5" × 11" paper in landscape orientation

Page 2

| Inside Left Page (5.5" × 8.5") | Inside Right Page (5.5" × 8.5") |

One 8.5" × 11" paper in landscape orientation

Outside Back Cover:

1. Key **SENIOR MEMBERS** as a title that spans both columns.

2. Insert the senior members' names from the file *DF 139B NAMES*. Balance the names in two columns. If needed, change to 1.15 line spacing with 0 pts. spacing before and after.

Outside Front Cover:

1. Arrange the following information attractively: **High School Honor Society**, **Induction Ceremony**, **Laurel High School**, **December 15, 20--**, **6:30 p.m.**

2. Insert the following text in a shaded text box or shape:

> **The High School Honor Society inducts students who have achieved academic excellence, displayed good character, demonstrated leadership qualities, and served the school and community.**

Inside Left Page:

After keying the title **PROGRAM**, insert this information, including dot leaders:

Welcome . . . . Rob Jansante, President
Opening Remarks . . . . Dr. Paul Henry, Principal
Speaker . . . . Dr. Helen Rapp, Laurel Community College
Induction Ceremony
    Scholarship . . . . Matt Roman, Vice President
    Character . . . . Jessica Roman, Treasurer
    Leadership . . . . Stephanie Davis, Secretary
    Service . . . . Meghan Johnson, Historian
Pledge . . . . Rob Jansante
Presentation of Certificates . . . Rob Jansante and Dr. Paul Henry
Closing . . . . Rob Jansante

All members and guests are invited to a reception in the Library immediately following the Induction Ceremony.

Inside Right Page:

1. Key **INDUCTEES** as a title that spans both columns.

2. Insert the names of the inductees from the file *DF 139B NAMES*. Balance the names in two columns. If needed, change to 1.15 line spacing with 0 pts. spacing before and after.

FORMAT BUSINESS LETTERS

OBJECTIVE

• To learn to format business letters.

Formatting

Letters

Letter 1
Key the model business letter on p. 154.

Save as: 52B LETTER1

Letter 2
Format and key the text at the right as a business letter in block format.

Save as: 52B LETTER2

February 20, 20-- | Mr. and Mrs. Eric Russell | P.O. Box 215 | Moorcroft, WY 82721-2152 | Dear Mr. and Mrs. Russell

Wyoming women were the first women in the United States to have the right to vote (1869). Ester Morris of South Pass City became the first woman judge in 1870. Wyoming was the first state to elect a woman to state office when Estelle Reel was elected State Superintendent of Public Instruction in 1894. Nellie Tayloe Ross became the first female governor in the United States when she was elected governor of Wyoming in 1925.

It is time to honor women such as these for the role they played in shaping Wyoming and U.S. history. A Wyoming Women's Historical Museum is being planned. With your help, the museum can become a reality.

Our community would benefit from the increased tourist activity. Thousands of tourists visit the nation's first national monument, Devil's Tower, each year. Since Moorcroft is only 30 miles from Devil's Tower, a museum would draw many of them to our city as they travel to and from the Tower.

National and state funds for the project are being solicited; however, additional funding from the private sector will be required. Please look over the enclosed brochure and join the Wyoming Women's Historical Museum Foundation by making a contribution.

Sincerely | William P. Shea | xx | Enclosure

Letter 3
Format and key the text at the right as a business letter in block format.

Save as: 52B LETTER3

August 10, 20-- | Ms. Dorothy Shepard | P.O. Box 275 | Moorcroft, WY 82721-2342

Dear Ms. Shepard

GROUNDBREAKING CEREMONY

¶The planning committee is thrilled to announce the groundbreaking ceremony for the **Wyoming Women's Historical Museum** will take place on Saturday, August 25.

¶As one who played an important role in reaching this milestone, you are invited to a luncheon before the ceremony. The luncheon will be held at the Mead House at 11:30. The groundbreaking will begin at 1:30.

¶The museum will be a source of great pride for Wyoming residents and will give them a sense of their history. Visitors will be reminded of the part Wyoming women played in the history of the state and nation.

Sincerely | William P. Shea | Committee Chair | xx

1. Format the two articles below as a newsletter with three columns of equal width and nearly equal length.

2. The title and publication information should span the columns and be formatted appropriately. Use WordArt to format the title.

3. Correct all errors.
4. Use a 2-line drop cap for the first word in each ¶.
5. Insert vertical lines between columns.

6. You decide other formatting features.
7. Hyphenate and justify the columns.

Save as: **137B NEWS3**

STRATEGIES FOR SUCCESS

Vol. 6, No. 3 Spring, 20--

Reputation and Choice

Reputation is the image people have of your standards of conduct--your ethical and moral principals. Most people think that a good reputation is needed to succeed in any job; and it is, therefore, one of the most important personal assetts you can acquire in your life.

> A bad reputation can result from one misdeed.

A good reputation is a valued asset that requires time, effort, and discipline to develop and project. A bad reputation can be a longterm liability established in a short time. It can be a result from just one misdeed and can be a heavy burden to carry throughout life.

It is very important to realize, therefore, that most of you have an opportunity to develope and protect the reputation you want. You have many choices to make that will destroy or enhance the image you want to extned. The choices are hard; and honestly, loyalty, and dedicatoin are most often involved.

> Choices you make destroy or enhance your reputation.

Learnig About People

Many aspects of a job present challenges to those who strive to do their best in all they do. The most critical challenge all workers face is being able to relate will to the many individuals with whom they have to work. It is common for workers to have dailty dealings with bosses, peers,

and subordinates. Also, most workers will interact with telephone callers and visitors from outside and inside the company daily.

> Relating well to others is a critical challenge.

While it is critical to learn all you can about your job and company, it is often just as cirtical to learn about the people with whom you will work and interact. Frequently, you can rely upon experienced workers for information that will help you analyze the formal and informal structures of the organization. What you learn may help you determine what an employer expects and likes, or dislikes, and will help you make a good adjustment to your workplace.

> Learn from experienced workers.

- To format business letters.
- To increase straight-copy keying skill.

53B   **Formatting**

Business Letters

Key in block format the business letters shown at the right.

Letter 1

Date: **May 23, 20--**

Letter address:

Mr. Jamison Cooper
882 Elderberry Drive
Fayetteville, NC 28311-0065

Letter 1 is from **Susanne J. Warrens** who is the **Program Chair**. Supply an appropriate salutation, complimentary closing, and reference initials. Send a copy of the letter to **Marsha Edinburgh, President**.

Save as: 53B LETTER1

Letters 2 & 3

Date (Letter 2): **June 4, 20--**
Date (Letter 3): **June 10, 20--**

Letter Address:

Ms. Susanne J. Warrens
Program Chair
8367 Brookstone Court
Raleigh, NC 27615-1661

The letters are from **Jamison R. Cooper**, who is a **Program Committee Member**. Supply an appropriate salutation and complimentary closing. Be sure to include an Enclosure notation and reference initials on each letter.

Save as: 53B LETTER2 and 53B LETTER3

Last week at our meeting, you mentioned several individuals you thought would be excellent presenters for the opening and closing sessions of next year's convention. I accept your offer to contact them. When you contact them, please share with them the theme of our convention and determine what they would propose as an opening or closing session for our convention. Of course, we need to be concerned with the budget; please determine the fee they would charge.

The information will be needed before June 15 for our meeting. Your willingness to serve on this committee is greatly appreciated. I'll look forward to seeing you in a couple of weeks.

Here is the information you requested. The presenter's name, the title of the presentation, a brief description of the presentation, and the fees charged are included. I've heard Kai Westmoreland and Steve Harmon present; they were excellent.

Kai Westmoreland--*The Great Depression.* Dr. Westmoreland explores the Great Depression in terms of the stock market crash, the economy, income distribution, and international and federal factors. The suffering that millions of American families endured during the depression is brought to life by Dr. Westmoreland's captivating style of presenting. ($500 plus expenses)

Steve Harmon--*World War II.* What better person to have speak about World War II than one of the 156,000 Allied soldiers who crossed the English Channel in the D-Day invasion of France in June of 1944? Harmon's presentation depicts the grim realities of a world war through the eyes of a young soldier. ($350 plus expenses)

Members who attended this year's convention recommended two other presenters--Tayt McCauley and Judith Earnhardt. McCauley's presentations deal with the Kennedy years; Earnhardt is well known for her presentations on women's suffrage. I have contacted them, but I've not yet heard from them. As soon as I do, I will get the information to you.

Here is the information on Judith Earnhardt and Tayt McCauley that I said I would send to you. Only a brief sketch on each person is given below; their complete resumes (enclosed) arevery impressive. Evidently these two as well as the two I previously sent would all be excellent choices for our convention. It's just a matter of deciding which two we want to go with and then contacting them to make surethey are available. We will want to do that as quickly as possible, as I'm sure all four are in high demand.

Judith Earnhardt--*Women's Suffrage.* Dr. Earnhardt explores the women's movement and the impact of such organizations as the American Woman Suffrage Association and the National Woman Suffrage Association. The presentation brings to life the early advocates of women's rights--Elizabeth Cady Stanton, Susan B. Anthony, Lucy Stone, and Julia Ward Howe. ($500 plus expenses)

Tayt McCauley--*The Kennedy Years.* Dr. McCauley recounts the events that touched the nation during the years of John F. Kennedy's administration. Included in the presentation are the Bay of Pigs, the Cuban Missile Crisis, the Moon Landing, Civil Rights, and the Kennedy Assassination. ($450 plus expenses)

If you think we need to identify additional presenters, I will be happy to do so. Please let me know if you want me to take care of anything else before our next meeting.

What's Up! with our Colleagues

Michelle Glatzko, Central Service, presented "Isolation Carts and Universal Precautions as Related to Central Service Technicians" at the fall conference of the Tri-County Central Service Association and was elected secretary.

Maurice Tarli, volunteer coordinator, was elected secretary of the board, Society of Directors of Volunteer Services, Western chapter.

Two staff members, Larry Szerbin, RN, and Ann Tokar, RN, received degrees. Larry completed a bachelor of science in business administration degree with a major in nursing management from Lynn College. Ann earned a master of science degree in long-term health care from Upton University.

Investment Performance

If you participate in the Upton Retirement Program or Supplemental Retirement Annuity plans, daily balances of your accounts can be obtained via the Internet. All you need to do is visit http://www.hiaa.com and establish a PIN. With your social security number and your PIN, you can obtain end-of-day balances at any time. You no longer need to wait for the quarterly reports to see how your money is growing.

Farewell, Rudy

A retirement tea will be held for Rudy Beissel, Environmental Support Services, on Thursday, June 24, from 1:30 p.m. to 3 p.m. in the Jones Conference Center. Rudy is retiring after 35 years with Upton.

Career Track

Lorretta Slobodnick recently was named as an administrative assistant, Medical Records. She reports to Erika Cooper, head, Medical Records. Lorretta earned her associate degree from Upton County Community College and specialized in medical technology. Please welcome her at Extension 1505 or slobodni@upton.com.

Patient Praises

To Susan Getty, nurse: "Thank you for the compassionate and knowledgeable care ."--a stroke patient

"Thanks to all who helped nurse me back to health!"--a Unit 15D patient

To Jill Holt, nurse: "Thanks, thanks, thanks! Your skill is appreciated."--a new mom

---

FORMAT LETTERS WITH SPECIAL PARTS

OBJECTIVE

• To increase skill at formatting business letters with special features.

54B   Formatting

Business Letters

Key in block format the business letters shown at the right.

Letter 1

Date: **March 14, 20--**
Letter Address:

Ms. Gwen English, President
3801 Wedgewood Road
Wilmington, DE 19805-9921

Letter 1 is from **Marsha J. Johnson, Display Coordinator**. Supply all missing letter parts.

Save as: 54B LETTER1

Letter 2

Revise Letter 1; address it to the Florida State President:

Ms. Sandra Ortiz, President
723 Majestic Pines Court
Orlando, FL 32819-3487

Change the letter to reflect this Florida information:

Capital: Tallahassee
Nickname: The Sunshine State
Admitted to the Union: No. 27 on March 3, 1845

Save as: 54B LETTER2

Letter 3

Use the Insert Date feature to insert the current date.

Letter address:

Attention Special Collections Director
University of Virginia Library
Alderman, 2 East
Charlottesville,
VA 22903-0011

Supply a salutation, complimentary closing, and reference initials. The letter is from **Gregg G. Elway, Doctoral Candidate**.

Save as: 54B LETTER3

At last year's national convention, our displays highlighted the U.S. Presidents. This year's exhibits will spotlight the states. Each delegation will have a table to display items relating to their state. Exhibits will be in the order the states were admitted to the Union. State presidents are being asked to coordinate the display for their state.

Each display area will include a backdrop, a table, and two chairs for representatives from your state. The table (2' x 6') will be covered with a white cloth. Your state flag will be displayed in front of the backdrop on the far right. The 10-foot-wide backdrop will have a cutout of your state, along with the following information.

Delaware
Capital: Dover
State Nickname: The Diamond State
Admitted to the Union: No. 1 on December 7, 1787

Each delegation can decide what they want to exhibit on the table. We hope that you will include something to give to the people attending the convention. You know how attendees like freebies. We anticipate about eight hundred people at the convention.

We are excited about the state exhibits and hope that you and your officers will make **Delaware's** display the best one at the convention.

I'm doing my dissertation on the Civil War generals and their families. Of course, it is easy to gather the needed information on U. S. Grant and Robert E. Lee. So much has been written about these icons of the Civil War that the problem is deciding what to include.

However, I'm not having as much luck with some of the other generals. I'm particularly interested in Galusha Pennypacker, who was claimed to be the youngest general of the Civil War, and in John E. Wool, who was claimed to be the oldest Civil War general. I believe Pennypacker was from Pennsylvania and Wool from New York. From the little I've been able to gather, I believe Pennypacker didn't reach voting age until after the war and Wool was on active duty at the age of 77 when the war began.

I'm going to be in Washington, D.C., next month. Would it be worth my time to drive to Charlottesville to have access to the archives at the University of Virginia? Since I have very limited time on this trip, I want to use it in the best way possible. If you don't feel that your library would be the best place to visit, could you suggest where my time might be better spent?

1. Key the text at the right using default settings for line spacing and font. Indent first line of ¶s in articles .25" and use light blue shading on headings.

2. Format *What's Up!* In Title style and then italicize it. Format the volume, number, and date in Intense Emphasis style.

3. Format the shaded article titles in Subtitle style.

4. Format the text below the volume, number, and date line in two balanced columns.

5. Justify and hyphenate the text. Adjust for any spacing inconsistencies.

6. Size the text box to fit within the column margin. Format the title within the text box in Intense Emphasis style.

7. Place a **DRAFT** watermark behind the columns.

8. Balance the columns as needed.

9. If desired, apply an appropriate style, color combination, and/or font combination.

Save as: 137B NEWS2

What's Up!

Volume 6, Number 6   June, 20--

Satisfaction Survey Established

Upton General Hospital has established patient satisfaction as a major organizational goal and is committed to establishing a hospital-wide patient satisfaction survey. Patient satisfaction is recognized as a critical business issue and is a mechanism to demonstrate high-quality care and service to employers, insurers, and the community. "Patient satisfaction surveying is an important tool to help us learn more about our patients' expectations," said Freda Banks, RN, DNS, vice president, Nursing. "By understanding their needs better, we can deliver care in ways that are more satisfying to them."

The first phase of the patient satisfaction survey process will be implemented in July. Patients in the burn center, in-patient surgery, emergency, and same-day surgery will be surveyed. Preliminary results will be reported to the board of directors and corporate officers at the August board meeting, and then distributed to department heads.

Upton Says Thanks

Upton says thanks to all the steering committee members for their hard work in preparing for and hosting the on-site review by the Joint Review Committee on Accreditation of Healthcare Providers (JRCAHP). All steering committee and subcommittee members are asked to stop by the Arcadia Dining Room between 11 a.m. and 2 p.m. on Friday, June 25, to enjoy soup and salad and discuss the team's oral exit report. Night-shift staff can enjoy bagels and coffee and a similar discussion in the Main Dining Room from 2 a.m. to 3 a.m. on Saturday, June 26. Watch *What's Up!* for the JRCAHP findings.

New Requirements for Ordering CT Scans

Due to recent changes in third-party payer requirements, referring physicians are advised to request all necessary imaging studies when placing orders with the Radiology Department. Radiologists cannot extend the examination coverage or add additional studies.

The abdominal computed tomography (CT) scan is a common order affected by the recent changes. In the past, inclusion of the pelvic region in an abdominal CT scan was common. However, now it is necessary to specifically order an abdomen and pelvis examination if an image of the pelvic region is deemed necessary.

For more information about the new requirements, contact Stephen Antoncic, MD, director, Radiology Department, at Extension 3512 or antoncic@upton.com.

(continued on next page)

Letter Editing

Open the file *53B LETTER1* and make the changes shown at the right. Include a subject line: **KEYNOTE SPEAKERS**. Leave the rest of the letter as it is.

Save as: 54C LETTER

...When you contact them, please ~~share with~~ *tell* them the theme of our convention and determine what they ~~would~~ propose as an opening or closing session ~~for our convention.~~

~~Of course, we need to be concerned with the budget; please determine what they would charge.~~ *As I am sure you are aware, we have a very limited budget. The budget often determines whom we invite. As you discuss fees with them, make sure they are aware that we are an educational institution. Oftentimes, professional presenters are willing to give "educational discounts."*

The information will be needed before June 15 for our *speaker* meeting. ...

Enrichment Activities
Editing Business Letters

Open *54B LETTER1*; revise and send it to the Massachusetts and Arizona state presidents with the information shown at the right. Make sure you change the state at the very end of the letter.

Save as: 54B LETTER1-R and 54B LETTER1-R2

Letter Address:
Ms. Judith Austin, President
711 Colonial Way
New Bedford, MA 02747-0071

Massachusetts
Capital: Boston
State Nickname: The Bay State
Admitted to the Union: No. 6 on
February 6, 1788

Letter Address:
Mr. Scott Mathews, President
55 Rio Cancion, N.
Tucson, AZ 85718-3399

Arizona
Capital: Phoenix
State Nickname: The Grand
Canyon State
Admitted to the Union: No. 48 on
February 14, 1912

Timed Writings

1. Key a 1' timing on each ¶; determine *gwam*.
2. Key two 2'timings on ¶s 1–2 combined; determine *gwam*.

LA   **all letters used**   MicroPace   gwam 2'

	gwam 2'
The Bill of Rights includes the changes to the	4
constitution that deal with human rights of all people.	10
The changes or amendments were to improve and correct the	16
original document. They were made to assure the quality of	22
life and to protect the rights of all citizens.	27
One of the changes provides for the right to religious	32
choice, free speech, and free press. Another addresses the	38
right to keep and bear firearms. Another deals with the	44
rights of the people with regard to unreasonable search and	50
seizure of person or property. Two others deal with the	55
right to an immediate and public trial by a jury and the	61
prevention of excessive bail and fines.	65

gwam 2' | 1 | 2 | 3 | 4 | 5 | 6 |

UNIT 33
Lessons 137-140

Enhance Desktop Publishing Skills

OBJECTIVE

- To prepare newsletters using balanced columns, vertical lines, shaded text, drop caps, text boxes, WordArt, shapes, and watermarks.

137A-140A

Conditioning Practice
Key each line twice daily.

alphabet	1	Waj and Zogy are quick at solving complex problems with formulas.
figures	2	William's 169 stores in 48 states served over 320,750 last month.
speed	3	The men may focus on their work if they are apt to make a profit.

gwam 1' | 1 | 2 | 3 | 4 | 5 | 6 | 7 | 8 | 9 | 10 | 11 | 12 | 13 |

137-138B

Newsletters

Newsletter 1

1. Format the two articles using three equal-width columns that are balanced.
2. Format titles in Subtitle style.
3. Shade the second ¶ in the first article in light blue.
4. Insert the tip below in a text box between the articles. Use 1.0 line spacing and 9-pt. font for the text. Format the title using Emphasis style. Fill the text box with the same color used to shade ¶ 2. Format with a border.

This Issue's Tip
If you've asked for a doggie bag to take home from a restaurant, you should refrigerate it within two hours. Reheat leftovers to 165 degrees Fahrenheit until warmed throughout.

5. Select the Paper colors combination.
6. Justify and hyphenate.

Save as: 137B NEWS1

Basic Life Support Renewal Courses

The School of Nursing at North Hills Hospital will hold its annual basic life support (BLS) renewal courses in March. The courses are open to all staff.

Staff members whose jobs require them to hold a valid BLS completion card must attend a renewal course every two years, according to American Heart Association guidelines. Heart Saver Plus (adult) and Health Care Provider (adult, infant, and child) BLS renewal courses will be offered.

Renewal courses will be held Monday through Friday, March 15 through March 19, and March 22 through March 26, from 7 a.m. to 8 p.m. Renewal courses also will be held Saturday, March 20, from 7 a.m. to 2 p.m. All courses will be held in Wilkins Hall, Room 135.

Staff should allow 60 to 90 minutes to complete the renewal course. To receive a BLS renewal, staff will be required to complete a written test and demonstrate their BLS skills. The renewal course is open to anyone who is due to take a renewal course, even if it is not required for his or her job.

Science Judges Sought

An additional 25 judges with expertise in science and an interest in children are needed for the 61st annual North Hills Science and Engineering Fair. The competition will be held from 8 a.m. to 1 p.m. March 31 at the North Hills Science Center.

Jeffrey Sidora, science fair coordinator, said 60 judges are needed to examine exhibits created by 150 students from 6 area schools. The judges should have technical backgrounds, such as master's degrees in biology, chemistry, physics, computer science, mathematics, engineering, robotics, medicine, microbiology, earth science, or environment.

The judges have to be willing to make a time commitment from 8 a.m. to 1 p.m. Lunch will be provided. At the fair, students in grades 6 through 12 compete for the best science and engineering projects in their age brackets.

Special E-mail Features

E-mail Address List. Names and e-mail addresses of persons (contacts) you correspond with often may be kept in an address list. An address can be entered on the TO line by selecting it from the list.

E-mail Copies. Copies of e-mail can be sent to additional addresses at the same time you send the original message. The **Cc:** (courtesy copy) and **Bcc:** (blind courtesy copy) features of e-mail software are used to send copies.

Reply and Forward. The Reply feature automatically puts the e-mail address of the person you are replying to in the TO area of the e-mail heading. The Forward feature allows you to send a copy of an e-mail message you received to other individuals.

Request Delivery Receipt. Request Delivery Receipt notifies you when an e-mail has been delivered successfully.

Request a Read Receipt. Request a Read Receipt notifies you when an e-mail has been read.

Signature. Signatures are a way of personalizing your e-mail messages and making them appear more professional. For business, a signature usually includes your name, your professional title, the company name, the company address, and the company phone number.

Delay Delivery. The Delay Delivery features allows you to specify a date and time for an e-mail message to be sent. This allows a message to be created early but not sent until the specified date and time. For example, your teacher may give you an assignment that is due in two weeks and may automatically remind you two days before the assignment is due by creating a reminder message today with a delayed delivery date.

E-mail Distribution List. When e-mail is regularly sent to the same group of contacts, use a distribution list. A distribution list is a collection of contacts. For example, if you are part of a team in your American History class, you can create a distribution list called *American History Project* that includes the names of all team members. When you want to e-mail them, you can use the distribution list rather than listing each individual separately. This feature is very helpful when you send e-mails frequently to the same people, especially when there is a large number.

When a distribution list is selected and it appears in the TO area of the e-mail heading, a + appears in front of the name of the distribution list. By clicking the +, all of the names and address of the individuals who are part of the distribution list appear in the TO area. If you do not want an individual included, highlight the name and tap DELETE.

Activity 5

Balanced Column Lengths

WP • Page Layout/Page Setup/ Breaks/Column

Complete steps 1–3, making certain to leave no widow/orphan lines.

Oftentimes, columns need to be balanced (equal or nearly equal in length). The desired balance can be achieved by inserting column breaks as needed.

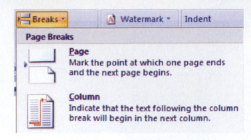

1. Open *DF OF13 ACTIVITY5* and balance the columns.

Save as: OF13 ACTIVITY5A

2. Reformat *OF13 ACTIVITY5A* into two balanced columns using the Right Preset format.

Save as: OF13 ACTIVITY5B

3. Reformat *OF13 ACTIVITY5B* into a three-column document with balanced lengths.

Save as: OF13 ACTIVITY5C

Activity 6

Vertical Lines Between Columns

WP • Page Layout/Page Setup/ Columns/More Columns/ Line Between

Complete steps 1–2.

If desired, vertical lines can be placed between columns to enhance the appearance of the document. The lines can be inserted before or after keying the document.

1. Open *OF13 ACTIVITY4B* and add vertical lines between the columns.

Save as: OF13 ACTIVITY6A

2. Reformat *OF13 ACTIVITY4B* into two columns of unequal width by using the Left Preset. If needed, insert a vertical line between the columns.

Save as: OF13 ACTIVITY6B

Activity 7

Watermarks

WP • Page Layout/Page Background/Watermark

Open *OF13 ACTIVITY6A* and add the word CONFIDENTIAL as a diagonal watermark.

Save as: OF13 ACTIVITY7

A watermark is any text or graphic that, when printed, appears behind the document's text. For example, your school's mascot may appear as a watermark on the school newspaper or stationery. A watermark stating *draft* or *confidential* is often added to letters or memos.

If a picture is used, you can lighten it, or wash it out, so it doesn't interfere with the document text.

Watermarks are visible only in Print Layout and Full Screen Reading and on the printed page. Watermarks can be changed, removed, or made to appear only on selected pages of a document.

CAREER FAIR

The Annual Career Fair will be held May 15 from 9 a.m. to 12:30 p.m. in Gymnasium A. A list of the 20 employers who will attend will be published next week. The employers represent many different areas that hire scientists, technicians, and engineers within the environmental field. Therefore, there will be a variety of career opportunities for our students to explore.

All junior and senior students are urged to attend and speak to as many of the employers as possible. To ensure that students speak to many employers, they will need to obtain signatures of the employers they visit and give the signatures to the Career Fair Coordinator when they leave the gymnasium.

It is important that students dress and act appropriately during the Career Fair. Standard or casual business dress is suggested. Students should have up-to-date resumes to distribute. Also, students should use correct grammar and speak clearly without using slang to improve their chances of making a favorable first impression.

Distribution List Illustrations

A distribution list is created with the e-mail addresses of those you want included from the contacts list.

A distribution list is used to send the same e-mail to all those on the list (see below).

To see who is on the list and to delete any one you don't want to receive the e-mail, click on the + (see below).

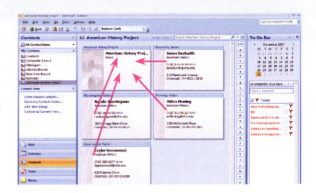

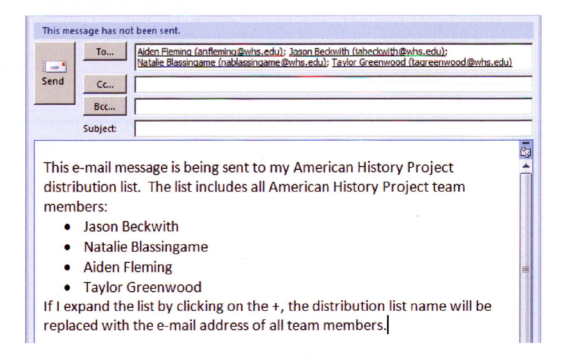

Attachments/Inserts

Various items may be sent with your e-mails including files, previously sent or received e-mails, business cards, calendars, etc. An example of a calendar being attached to an e-mail is shown on the next page. You can choose to show availability only, limited details as shown below, or full details of your calendar in the e-mail.

Activity 3

Columns

WP • Page Layout/Page Setup/Columns

Key the text using a 3.5" top margin, 4" bottom margin, and three columns of equal width.

Save as: OF13 ACTIVITY3

Except for tables and labels, the documents you have created in *Word* have had a single column of text that extended from the left margin to the right margin.

Multiple-column documents, such as pamphlets, brochures, and newsletters, use the Columns feature to divide a document into two or more vertical columns that are placed side by side on a page. The columns may be of equal or unequal width.

As you key, text fills the length of a column before moving to the next column to the right.

CAREER FAIR

The Annual Career Fair will be held May 15 from 9 a.m. to 12:30 p.m. in Gymnasium A. A list of the 20 employers who will attend will be published next week. The employers represent many different areas that hire scientists, technicians, and engineers within the environmental field. Therefore, there will be a variety of career opportunities for our students to explore.

All junior and senior students are urged to attend and speak to as many of the employers as possible. To ensure that students speak to many employers, they will need to obtain signatures of the employers they visit and give the signatures to the Career Fair Coordinator when they leave the gymnasium.

It is important that students dress and act appropriately during the Career Fair. Standard or casual business dress is suggested. Students should have up-to-date resumes to distribute. Also, students should use correct grammar and speak clearly without using slang to improve their chances of making a favorable first impression.

Activity 4

Changing the Number and Width of Columns

 WP • Page Layout/Page Setup/ Columns or Columns Dialog Box

Complete steps 1–2.

The number and width of columns can be changed using the Columns feature. The changes can be made before or after keying the text, and both the number and width of columns can vary on a page. Typically, you can select from several preset formats, or you can design a specific format you need.

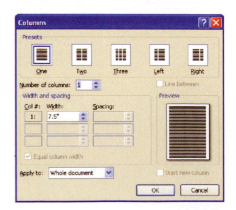

1. Open *OF13 ACTIVITY3* and reformat the text into two columns of equal width.

Save as: OF13 ACTIVITY4A

2. Open *OF13 ACTIVITY4A* if necessary and reformat, changing the top margin to 3.0"; formatting the title, *Career Fair*, in a single column in Title style. Center the title. Format the text into three columns of nearly equal width below the title.

Save as: OF13 ACTIVITY4B

Attach a Calendar to an E-mail Illustration

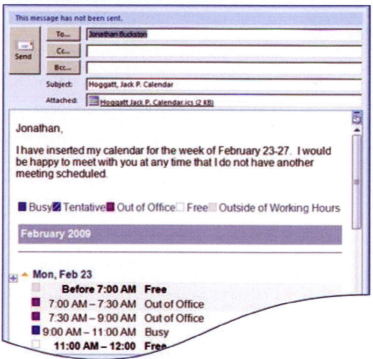

Out of Office Assistant

The Out of Office Assistant automatically sends your out-of-the-office message to those who send you an e-mail message. Use this feature when you are not going to be checking your e-mail messages for an extended period of time to let individuals know when they can expect to hear from you or who to contact in your absence. An example is shown on the next page.

Office Features 13

Activity 1

Shaded Paragraphs

WP
- Home/Paragraph/ Shading

Complete steps 1–2.

Save as: OF13 ACTIVITY1

Paragraphs can be shaded in various colors to focus the reader's attention to their contents. The illustration below shows a shaded paragraph.

> This is an example of a paragraph that has been shaded. Readers are more apt to pay attention to its contents. Various colors can be selected for the shading.

1. Open *DF OF13 ACTIVITY1*.
2. Using light colors, shade each ¶ differently.

Activity 2

Drop Cap

WP
- Insert/Text/Drop Cap

Complete steps 1–4.

Save as: OF13 ACTIVITY2

You can format paragraphs to begin with a large initial capital letter that takes up one or more vertical lines of regular text. Drop caps are objects that can be formatted and sized. Two drop cap formats are usually available. One capitalizes the first letter of the first word in the paragraph with a large dropped capital letter and then wraps the text around the drop cap. The second creates a dropped capital letter, but places it in the margin beginning at the first line.

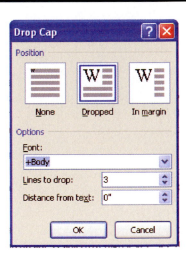

1. Open *DF OF13 ACTIVITY2*.
2. Format ¶ 1 with a drop cap with text wrapped around it.
3. Format ¶ 2 with a drop cap that is placed in the left margin.
4. Format ¶ 3 the same as ¶ 1, but drop the cap only two lines and change it to Times New Roman font.

Out of Office Assistant
Message Illustration

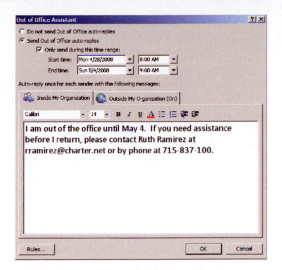

IMPROVE E-MAIL FORMATTING SKILLS

Lesson 55

OBJECTIVES

- To create a distribution list.
- To process e-mail messages with attachments and copy notations.

55A-57A

Conditioning Practice

Key each line twice.

alphabet	1	Tom saw Jo leave quickly for her job after my dog won six prizes.
fig/sym	2	Check No. 203 ($1,486.17) and Check No. 219 ($57.98) are missing.
speed	3	Did their auditor sign the key element of the forms for the firm?

| gwam | 1' | 1 | 2 | 3 | 4 | 5 | 6 | 7 | 8 | 9 | 10 | 11 | 12 | 13 | |

55B

Create a Distribution List

Create a distribution list following the instructions at the right.

1. Create a folder for your contacts for your American history project. (Your instructor will assign four students to be part of your group.) See the illustrations on p. 160 and below.

2. Create a contact card for each student assigned to your group. For this project, you only need to include their names and e-mail addresses.

3. Create a distribution list that includes the students in your group.

Communicating
YOUR PERSPECTIVE | 5

I should have . . . I shouldn't have . . . Sometimes we find ourselves thinking, after we have taken an action, that we were wrong. Making good ethical decisions doesn't end with the choice itself. You need to take the time to look at your decision again later, especially if you think it was wrong.

Often, a bad choice is the result of something beyond our control. Something happened that we couldn't have expected. There was something important that we couldn't have known. But other times, the problem is that we were not careful enough in the way we made our decision. An article in *Issues in Ethics*, the online journal of the Markkula Center for Applied Ethics at Santa Clara University, identifies three things that can cause people to unintentionally take unethical actions at work.

The first factor is something psychologists call scripts. Scripts are tasks we have performed so many times that they have become automatic—we do them without thinking. An example might be braking at a stop sign. Scripts can be a problem when they cause you not to pay attention to a situation that demands it. Suppose a security guard is responsible for checking employee ID cards. She is so used to doing this that she barely glances at the forged ID of a potential thief and lets the thief into the building.

The second factor is distractions. Distractions take our focus from one thing to another. If you are studying hard for a very important test, a loud radio or television can be a distraction. If an employee is focusing all his attention on a project that is due, he might barely glance at a memo that points out safety flaws in a product because he sees the memo as a distraction.

The third factor is moral exclusion. Moral exclusion means not showing some individuals or groups the same consideration that you give everyone else. You may have come across a store clerk who is courteous and respectful to all customers except teenagers. The clerk may think that teenagers don't have much money to spend. What do you think will happen when a high school student tries to warn this clerk of a theft in progress?

When we recognize the three factors, we can find solutions. A Japanese drug company came up with a good solution to a moral exclusion problem. The company decided its employees needed a better understanding of the people who used its products. After a week of training, the company sent 100 managers to work with sick people. The program grew to include more than 1,000 employees. The company produced many new drugs as a result.

Source: Dennis J. Moberg. "When Good People Do Bad Things at Work." *Issues in Ethics* vol. 10, no. 2. http://www.scu.edu/ethics/publications/iie/v10n2/peopleatwork.html (19 July 2008).

Ethics: The Right Thing to Do

ACTIVITIES

1. Read the material at the left.

2. Key a list of scripts that you or others use.

3. To be sure that you understand the three factors, have a group or class discussion in which you give new examples of scripts, distractions, and moral exclusion.

4. Suppose you are planning a presentation about effective workplace decisions. You are to inform others about the three factors discussed on this page. How would you present the information? Develop and key an outline of the points you will address.

Send/Receive E-mail and Attachments

Document 1 (Attachment)

1. Format and key the text at the right. Leave a 2" top margin; SS paragraphs. Use the Title style for the heading and Heading 1 style for your name and the date.
2. Use 12-pt. Calibri for the text beneath the heading. Bold all names.
3. Correct all spelling, keying, and formatting errors.

Save as: 55C
ATTACHMENT1

INTERNET ACTIVITY

Search the Web to learn more about one of the individuals whose names appear at the right or one of those listed in Document 3 (p. 164). Compose a ¶ or two about the individual.

Document 2 (E-mail)

Key the text at the right as an e-mail and send to your American history project distribution list; copy your instructor. Use **American History Project** for the subject line and attach Document 1 (*55C ATTACHMENT1*).

When you receive the message from one of your classmates, reply indicating that you will be there.

Save as: 55C EMAIL1

American History

Your Name

March 18, 20--

Albert Einstein: American physicist whose theory of relativity led to the harnessing of nuclear energy.

Benjamin Franklin: A leading American statesman, inventor, philanthropist, publisher, author, revolutionary, and thinker.

Abraham Lincoln: The sixteenth President of the United States; helped keep the Union together during the Civil War, which led to the abolishment of slavery; recognized for his honesty and compassion.

Franklin Roosevelt: Thirty-second President of the United States; led the country during two critical periods in United States history (the Great Depression and World War II).

George Washington: Commander in Chief of the Continental Army during the American Revolution; first President of the United States.

Attached is the list of the five Americans who I feel had the greatest impact on our history. A few notes about the individuals are provided after each name. Narrowing the list to five was very difficult. ¶ I've reserved a room in the library for us to meet on Thursday, March 25, at 3 p.m. By then we should have received and reviewed each other's lists. Be prepared to decide on the final ten individuals to include in the report for Ms. Graham. ¶ I look forward to receiving each of your lists.

ACTIVITY 5

Math: Applying Math Skills by Using Mental Math

1. Open *DF CS13 ACTIVITY5* and print the file.
2. Solve the problems as directed in the file.
3. Submit your answers.

CAREER Clusters

ACTIVITY 13

You must complete Career Exploration Activities 1–3 before completing this activity.

1. Retrieve your Career folder and the information in it that relates to the three career clusters that you have chosen.

2. If your interests have changed as a result of completing the first 12 Career Exploration activities, identify the career cluster that is now your first choice, second choice, and third choice.

3. Using the career cluster that is now your first choice and the Internet, search for schools that you could attend after you are graduated from high school to pursue an occupation in this cluster. Write a paragraph or two describing what kind of school it is, where it is, the cost to enroll, whether it has resident students and/or commuter students, and other information that interests you. Print your file, save it as Career13, and keep it open.

4. Exchange papers with a classmate and have the classmate offer suggestions for improving the content and correcting any errors he or she finds in your paragraph(s). Make the changes that you agree with and print a copy to turn in to your instructor. Save your file as Career13 and close it.

5. Return your folder to the storage area. When your instructor returns your paper, file it in your Career folder.

BLEND IMAGES/JUPITER IMAGES

Document 3 (Attachment)

Key the list centered horizontally on the page. Leave a 1.5" TM.

Title: **Suggestions for American History Report**

Use the Title style for the heading. Key the names in Calibri 14 pt.

Save as: **55C**

ATTACHMENT2

Susan B. Anthony
Neil Armstrong
Alexander Graham Bell
Thomas Alva Edison
Albert Einstein
Benjamin Franklin
Ulysses S. Grant
Patrick Henry
Thomas Jefferson
Martin Luther King, Jr.

Abraham Lincoln
Douglas MacArthur
Thomas Paine
Sir Walter Raleigh
Eleanor Roosevelt
Franklin Roosevelt
Harriet Beecher Stowe
Henry David Thoreau
George Washington

Lesson 56 IMPROVE E-MAIL FORMATTING SKILLS

OBJECTIVES

- To increase proficiency at formatting e-mails.
- To use the Attachment feature to attach calendars and business cards to e-mails.

56B

Calendars

Using the Calendar feature, record the class and lab hours shown at the right for January 23.

January 23

1. English 110 (8 to 8:50 a.m.)
2. Biology 101 (10 to 10:50 a.m.)
3. Math 246 (1 to 1:50 p.m.)
4. Biology Lab (3 to 5:00 p.m.)

56C

Contacts

Record the information on the business card at the right in your *Outlook* contacts file.

HPJ COMMUNICATION

HPJ Communications

Troy McNeil
Communication Specialist

142 Colebrooke Lane
Louisville, KY 40219-1221
Phone: 502.555.0105
Fax: 502.555.0102
TMCNEIL@hpj.com

Communication & Math
SKILLS 13

SUBJECT/PREDICATE AGREEMENT, CAPITALIZATION, AND NUMBER EXPRESSION

ACTIVITY 1

Application: Subject/ Predicate Agreement

Key lines 1–10, selecting the proper verb.

Save as: CS13 ACTIVITY1

1 (Wasn't, Weren't) you aware that the matinee began at 2:30 p.m.?

2 Our senior debate team (has, have) won the city championship.

3 A number of our workers (are, is) to receive proficiency awards.

4 Either the coach or an assistant (are, is) to speak at the assembly.

5 Maria (doesn't, don't) know whether she can attend the beach party.

6 Ms. Yamamoto and her mother (are, is) now American citizens.

7 (Was, Were) the director as well as his assistants at the meeting?

8 The number of applicants for admission (are, is) greater this year.

9 The logic behind their main arguments (elude, eludes) me.

10 It (doesn't, don't) matter to me which of the two is elected.

ACTIVITY 2

Application: Capitalization and Number Expression

Key lines 1–10, capitalizing and expressing numbers correctly.

Save as: CS13 ACTIVITY2

1 "the jury," said the judge, "must reach a unanimous decision."

2 for what percentage of total sales is mrs. rhodes responsible?

3 i need a copy of the *dictionary of composers and their music*.

4 miss valdez told us to go to room eight of corbett hall.

5 the institute of art is at fifth avenue and irving place.

6 "don't you agree," he asked, "that honesty is the best policy?"

7 is the "tony award show" to be shown on tv on april seventeen?

8 dr. robin j. sousa is to address fbla members in orlando.

9 see page 473 of volume one of *encyclopedia americana*.

10 here is pbc's check #2749 for $83 (less ten percent discount).

ACTIVITY 3

Write to Learn

Complete as directed.

Save as: CS13 ACTIVITY3

Using word processing or voice recognition software, write a ¶ explaining the steps you would take to scan a document into your computer.

ACTIVITY 4

Preparing to Speak

Complete as directed.

Save as: CS13 OUTLINE and CS13 SOUND

You will attend a meeting of a club you joined recently. The members likely will ask you to introduce yourself briefly (about 1' to 2').

1. Prepare an outline of the points you want to include. Suggestions follow:

- State your name and year in school, and mention your hobbies.

- Describe your aspirations after graduation.

- Tell the audience about other things you do or like.

2. If time and resources permit, record your speech in a sound file.

E-mails

E-mail 1

Send the text at the right as an e-mail to the American history distribution list created in 55B. Attach Document 3 (*55C ATTACHMENT2*).

When you receive this e-mail message from one of your class-mates, forward one message to your instructor.

Save as: 56D EMAIL1

E-mail 2

Format and key the text at the right as an e-mail message for Professor Perry (use your instructor's e-mail address).

Save as: 56D EMAIL2

E-mail 3

Format and key the text at the right as an e-mail message to Professor Perry (use your instructor's e-mail address). Attach the calendar you created for 56B.

Save as: 56D EMAIL3

Subject: Meeting Reminder

Don't forget our meeting tomorrow. Since the librarian wouldn't give me a specific room ahead of time, let's plan on meeting at the front desk at 3:00 p.m. ¶ I went ahead and created a combined list of all the names you sent me via e-mail. A total of 19 individuals were named at least once. The alphabetical list is attached. ¶ See you tomorrow at 3 p.m.

Subject: Next Exam

Here is the information about next week's exam. The exam will cover Chapter 22, pages 702–727, and Chapter 23, pages 740–769.

The main emphasis of Chapter 22 is the New Deal. You will be expected to explain what the New Deal was, why some people criticized it while others praised it, and the impact of the New Deal on the U.S. economy.

Between 1933 and 1937, many pieces of legislation associated with the New Deal were passed. Make sure you know the purpose of each of the following acts.

* Emergency Banking Act
* Agricultural Adjustment Act
* Federal Emergency Relief Act
* Home Owners Refinancing Act
* National Industrial Recovery Act
* Emergency Relief Appropriation Act
* National Labor Relations Act
* Social Security Act

Chapter 23 covers World War II. We thoroughly discussed this chapter in class. Make sure you review your notes carefully.

If you are knowledgeable about these topics, you should do well on the exam.

Professor Perry,

Thank you for sending the information on next week's exam. I have several questions on Chapter 22 that I would like to discuss with you.

Would you be available to meet with me on January 23? I have attached my schedule for that day. I would be available any time that is shown as "Free" on my calendar. Let me know if any of the times will work with your schedule.

Skill Check

1. Key three 1' writings on each ¶ for speed; determine *gwam*.
2. Key two 3' writings on all ¶s combined for control; circle errors.
3. Key two 5' writings on all ¶s combined. Record and retain your better 5' *gwam* and error count and compare it to the score received in 135D.

 A   **all letters used**   **MicroPace**   **gwam**   3'   5'

	3'	5'
Speaking before a group of people can cause a great deal of	4	2	60
anxiety for an individual. This anxiety is so extensive that it	8	5	63
was ranked as the greatest fear among adults in a recent survey.	13	8	66
Such fear suggests that many people would rather perish than go	17	10	68
before the public to give a talk. Much of this fear actually	21	13	71
comes from a lack of experience and training in giving public	25	15	73
speeches. People who excel in the area of public speaking have	30	18	76
developed this unique skill through hard work.	33	20	78

	3'	5'
Planning is a key part to giving a good talk. The speech	36	22	80
should be organized into three basic parts. These parts are the	41	24	83
introduction, the body, and the conclusion. The introduction is	45	27	85
used to get the attention of the audience, to present the topic of	50	30	88
the talk, and to establish the credibility of the speaker. The	54	32	90
body of the speech is an organized presentation of the material	58	35	93
the speaker is conveying. The conclusion is used to summarize	62	37	95
the main points of the talk.	64	39	97

	3'	5'
Several things can be done to lower the level of anxiety	68	41	99
during a talk. Learning as much as possible about the audience	72	43	101
prior to the talk can reduce uncertainty. Advance planning and	77	46	104
preparing are essential; the lack of either is a major cause of	81	49	107
anxiety. Having the main points written on note cards to refer	85	51	109
to when needed is also helpful. Using visual aids can also lessen	90	54	112
the exposure a person feels. These are but a few ideas that may	94	56	114
be used to develop better speaking skills.	97	58	116

gwam   3' | 1   2   3   4
      5' | 1   2   3

E-mail 4

Format and key the text at the right as an e-mail message to Professor Perry (use your instructor's e-mail address). Attach the business card for Troy McNeil (created in 56C above) to your e-mail.

Save as: 56D EMAIL4

Professor Perry,

I've talked with Mr. McNeil, a communication specialist from HPJ Communications, about the possibility of his presenting to our class. He would like you to contact him to discuss the specifics of what you would like him to present. He is interested in discussing the communication styles of our most successful Presidents.

I've attached his business contact information. If there is anything else you would like me to do, please let me know.

Lesson 57   SPECIAL E-MAIL FEATURES

OBJECTIVES

- To increase proficiency in formatting and keying e-mails.
- To learn special e-mail features.
- To improve language skills.

57B

E-mail Special Features

Request a Read Receipt

Format and key the text at the right as an e-mail message to the distribution list created in 55B. Request a Read Receipt.

Save as: 57B EMAIL1

Out of Office Assistant

Use the Out of Office Assistant to have the message shown at the right sent to incoming e-mail messages for the next two days.

Send a message to yourself to see if it works (you should get the message you send plus the Out of Office Message). Forward the message to your instructor.

Cancel the Out of Office Message.

Delay Delivery

Send yourself two e-mails with the messages shown at the right using the Delay Delivery feature. The first one should be delivered tomorrow at 3:30 p.m.; the second should be delivered tomorrow at 11:30 p.m.

I know this is very short notice, but I think that we should meet one more time before we turn in the report on Friday. I've combined each of our parts into one report. However, we need to work on the transitions between the parts and proofread the report one more time to make sure there are no additional keying, formatting, spelling, or grammar errors.

We could meet in the library this evening. Does 6:30 work for you?

I will not be reading my e-mails until next Tuesday, (include the date). If you would like to contact me before then, please call me at (include your telephone number).

Remember:
- English paper due tomorrow.
- Algebra quiz tomorrow.

Remember:
- Piano lesson at 4:30 p.m.
- Play practice on Saturday – 3:30 to 5:30.

KEYING TECHNIQUES

OBJECTIVES

- To improve language skills.
- To improve keyboarding techniques and straight-copy speed and control.

136B

Word Choice

1. Study the spelling and definitions of the words.
2. Key the *Learn* and *Apply* lines, choosing the correct word(s) in the *Apply* lines.

Save as: **136B CHOICE**

Choose the right word

It's (contr) it is; it has	**wear** (vb/n) to bear or have on one's person; diminish by use
its (pron) possessive form of *it*	**where** (adv/conj/n) at, in, or to what degree; hat place, source, or cause

Learn   1 **It's** been a long time since the dog ate all of **its** food.

Apply   2 The auto lost (**it's/its**) shine from the dust.

Apply   3 (**It's/its**) good to get e-mail; (**it's/its**) been a long time.

Learn   1 Jim knows **where** he will **wear** his new suit.

Apply   2 (**Wear/where**) did the runner go when he left the stadium?

Apply   3 Do you think the rain will (**wear/where**) the stone's finish?

136C

Technique: Response Patterns

1. Key each line twice with a continuous pace.
2. Take a 1' writing on each line group.

Home row

1 ha has kid lad led last wash lash gaff jade fads half sash haggle   13
2 ask dad add jug leg gas lads hall lass fast deal fall leaf dashes   26
3 at had sad jigs lash adds gall legs fish gash lakes halls haggles   39

Consecutive direct reaches

4 many much loan sold vice side cent code thus fund told wide price   13
5 golf slow gift grow cloth delay fifty chance checks manual demand   26
6 fold music brown hence forums enemy bright signed editor specific   39

Adjacent finger

7 this time find help give plan mail into sent item high file might   13
8 five vote else dues which plans claim giving during thanks always   26
9 fine inform plant blank civil light wishes single quality furnish   39

gwam 1' | 1 | 2 | 3 | 4 | 5 | 6 | 7 | 8 | 9 | 10 | 11 | 12 | 13 |

Signature

Using the E-mail Signature feature, create a signature block that will go out with all your e-mails. Include the information shown at the right. Choose a quote that reflects your personality. If you don't have a favorite quote, use an Internet search engine to search for famous quotes and select one from those you find.

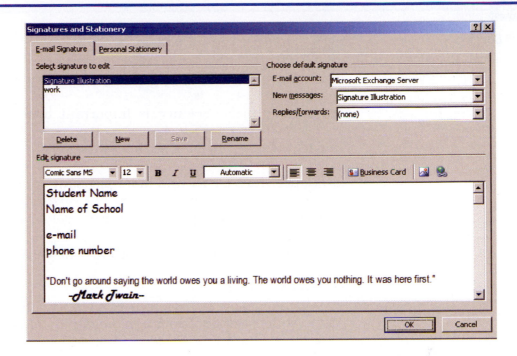

57C | **Language Skills**

Language Skills: Word Choice

1. Study the spelling and definitions of the words.
2. Key all *Learn* and *Apply* lines, choosing the correct word in the *Apply* lines.

Save as: **57C CHOICE**

hole (n) an opening in or through something **whole** (adj/n) having all its proper parts; a complete amount or sum	**peak** (n) pointed end; top of a mountain; highest level **peek** (vb) to glance or look at for a brief time

Learn 1 The **whole** team is responsible for the **hole** in the wall.

Apply 2 The (hole, whole) team dug a (hole, whole) in which to put the doughnut (holes, wholes).

Apply 3 The (hole, whole) project is just getting to be too much to handle.

Learn 1 If you **peek** out the door, you can see the **peak** of the new building.

Apply 2 The clouds covered the (peak, peek) of the mountain.

Apply 3 Did you get a chance to take a (peak, peek) at your exam after it was graded?

57D

E-Mail

Choose the three e-mail features that you think you will use most often from those listed at the right. Send an e-mail to your teacher explaining why you chose the three features.

Send a copy of the e-mail to the student in front of you. Request a Read Receipt and delay delivery for 2 hours.

- E-mail copies
- Attachments/Inserts
- Request Delivery Receipt/Read Receipt
- Delay Delivery
- E-mail Distribution List
- Out of Office Assistant
- Signature

135D

Skill Check

1. Take three 1' writings on each ¶; find *gwam* and errors.
2. Take two 3' writings on all ¶s combined; find *gwam* and errors.
3. Take one 5' writing on all ¶s combined; find *gwam* and errors.

A **all letters used** (MicroPace) `gwam` 3' | 5'

	3'	5'
Have you ever stopped to ponder how important science is in	4	2
your daily life? Science is important to everyone. It has played	8	5
a part in many amazing advances that make our homes, schools, and	13	8
work activities easier and more pleasant. Science has improved how	17	10
we produce goods, provide services, get from one place to another,	21	13
and speak to each other. Science has even made it possible for	26	15
us to live longer.	27	16
Your science education began in elementary school in the	31	19
early grades where you learned to describe, to measure, and to	35	21
draw conclusions. You got simple explanations of what makes it	40	24
rain, what keeps airplanes in the sky, and how sound moves so	44	26
quickly from one place in the world to another through or without	48	29
wires. From these general ideas about the world, you began to	52	31
build an understanding of science.	55	33
In subsequent grades, science learning was more formal when	59	35
it became a separate subject. In high school you are likely to	63	38
take a science course each year so that you can learn more about	67	40
the specific fields of science. In addition, you are apt to take	72	43
other courses and complete projects that enable you to apply the	76	46
science concepts learned in your specific science courses.	80	48

`gwam` 3' | 1 | 2 | 3 | 4
5' | 1 | 2 | 3

Office Features 6

For each activity, read and learn the feature described, then follow instructions at the left.

Activity 1

Review Office Features

1. Format and key the copy at the right, using a 1.5" left margin and a 1" right margin. DS ¶ 1; SS ¶ 2.
2. Use the Left (Paragraph) Indent feature to indent the long quote (¶ 2) 0.5" from the left margin.

Save as: OF6 ACTIVITY1

Another speech of significant magnitude was delivered by Winston Churchill (1940, 572). His words not only lifted the spirits of the British but also were motivational to those committed to the Allied cause.

> We shall go on to the end, we shall fight in France, we shall fight on the seas and oceans, we shall fight with growing confidence and growing strength in the air, we shall defend our island, whatever the cost may be, we shall fight on the beaches, we shall fight on the landing grounds, we . . . .

Activity 2

Review Office Features

1. Set a 1.5" left margin and a 1" right margin. Use the Page Number feature to place the page number (6) in the upper-right corner.
2. Key **References** 2" from the top of the page, using Title style. Use the Hanging Indent feature to format and key the references at the right.
3. SS references; DS between references.

Save as: OF6 ACTIVITY2

6

REFERENCES

Churchill, Winston. "We Shall Fight in the Fields and in the Streets." London, June 4, 1940. Quoted by William J. Bennett, *The Book of Virtues.* New York: Simon & Schuster, 1993.

Henry, Patrick. "Liberty or Death." Richmond, VA, March 23, 1775. Quoted in *North American Biographies*, Vol. 6. Danbury, CT: Grolier Education Corporation, 1994.

Lincoln, Abraham. "The Gettysburg Address." *Wikipedia,* "Gettysburg Address," http://en.wikipedia.org/wiki/Gettysburg_Address (accessed September 3, 2007).

Activity 3

Review Office Features

The text shown at the right completes the quote by Winston Churchill in Activity 1.

1. Open *Microsoft Word*.
2. Open file *DF OF6 ACTIVITY3A* and copy the text.
3. Open *DF OF6 ACTIVITY3B*.
4. Paste the copied text at the ellipsis; then delete the ellipsis.

Save as: OF6 ACTIVITY3

shall fight in the fields and in the streets, we shall fight in the hills; we shall never surrender, and even if, which I do not for a moment believe, this island or a large part of it were subjugated and starving, then our Empire beyond the seas, armed and guarded by the British fleet, would carry on the struggle, until in God's good time, the New World, with all its power and might, steps forth to the rescue and the liberation of the old.

UNIT 32
Lessons 135-136

Build Basic Skills

Lesson 135   KEYING TECHNIQUE

OBJECTIVES

• To improve keyboarding techniques.
• To improve straight-copy speed and control.

135A–136A

Conditioning Practice

Key each line twice.

alphabet	1	Zev and Che saw pilots quickly taxi many big jets from the gates.
figures	2	She sold 105 shirts, 28 belts, 94 skirts, 36 suits, and 47 coats.
speed	3	Jen sat by the right aisle for the sorority ritual at the chapel.

gwam 1' | 1 | 2 | 3 | 4 | 5 | 6 | 7 | 8 | 9 | 10 | 11 | 12 | 13 |

135B

Word Choice

1. Study the spelling and definitions of the words.
2. Key the *Learn* and *Apply* lines, choosing the correct word(s) in the *Apply* lines.

Save as: 135B CHOICE

Choose the right word

accept (vb) to receive; to give approval; to take	**threw** (vb) past tense of throw; to toss
except (prep) with the exclusion or exception of	**through** (prep/adj) beginning to end of; finished

Learn   1   I think they will **accept** all my revisions **except** for Unit 8.
Apply   2   Juliana works every day (accept/except) Saturday and Sunday.
Apply   3   Adolpho will attend the banquet to (accept/except) the award.

Learn   1   Greg **threw** the football perfectly **through** two quarters.
Apply   2   When they were (threw/through), I (threw/through) a party.
Apply   3   The cheer was (threw/through), so I (threw/through) the ball.

135C

Technique: Response Patterns

1. Key each line twice with a continuous pace.
2. Take a 1' writing on each line group.

gwam by line group

Third row

1	or up it us we you pop top rut yip wit pea tea pit wet were quiet	13
2	pew toe tie rep per hope pour rope quip your pout tore ripe quirk	26
3	tip out tar war per tour keep roar fret puppy youth pretty yuppie	39

Bottom row

4	ax can bam zag sax cab mad fax vans buzz knack caves waxen banana	13
5	ax ban man zinc clan band calm lamb vain back amaze bronze buzzer	26
6	box nab and bag van name vane clam oxen main none climb mezzanine	39

gwam 1' | 1 | 2 | 3 | 4 | 5 | 6 | 7 | 8 | 9 | 10 | 11 | 12 | 13 |

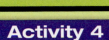

Activity 4

Cover Page

• Insert/Pages/Cover Page

1. Key a cover page using the Tiles style with the following information.
   Title: Plains Indians
   Author: Your Name
   Date: Current Date
2. *Note*: For placeholders not used, click on the placeholder and tap the Space Bar to remove the placeholder from the page.
3. Apply a different style to the cover page you created.
4. Change the style back to Tiles Style.

Save as: OF6 ACTIVITY4

The Cover Page feature inserts a fully-formatted cover page. Placeholders are provided for keying the title, author, and date information.

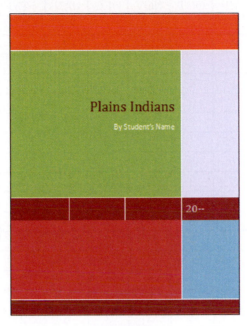

Tiles Style

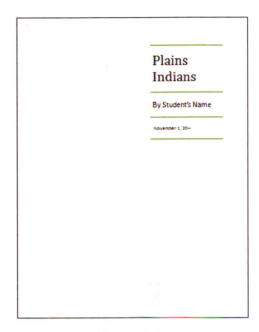

Stacks Style

Activity 5

Footnote and Endnote

1. Open file *DF OF6 ACTIVITY5*. Insert the three footnotes shown at the right where indicated in the file. Insert a blank line between footnotes.
2. Delete (*Insert footnote No.* x) from the copy.

Save as: OF6 ACTIVITY5

Use the **Footnote and Endnote** feature to identify sources quoted in your text. Footnotes are automatically positioned at the bottom of the same page as the reference. Endnotes are automatically placed on a separate page at the end of the report. As you edit, add, or delete footnotes and endnotes, changes in numbering and formatting are automatically made.

[1]David J. Rachman and Michael H. Mescon, *Business Today* (New York: Random House, 1987), p. 529.

[2]Greg Anrig, Jr., "Making the Most of 1988's Low Tax Rate," *Money*, February 1988, pp. 56–57.

[3]Andrew Chamberlain, "Twenty Years Later: The Tax Reform Act of 1986," http://www.taxfoundation.org/blog/show/1951.html (accessed September 7, 2007).

Activity 6

Superscript

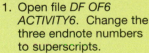

1. Open file *DF OF6 ACTIVITY6*. Change the three endnote numbers to superscripts.
2. Delete (*Apply superscript . . .*) from the copy.
3. Format endnotes 2 and 3 (at the right) on p. 4 of the file, below endnote 1.

Save as: OF6 ACTIVITY6

Text may be placed slightly higher than other text on a line by using the Superscript feature. The superscript is commonly used for footnotes and endnotes *not* inserted with the Footnote and Endnote feature, and for mathematical formulas and equations.

[1]Edmund Morgan, *American Slavery, American Freedom* (London: W. W. Norton & Company, 2003), p. 368.

[2]Steven Mintz and Susan Kellogg, *Domestic Revolutions: A Social History of American Family Life* (New York: The Free Press, 1988), p. 4.

[3]Gordon S. Wood, *The Americanization of Benjamin Franklin* (New York: Penguin, 2004), pp. 23–24.

Community Service Record

1. Create a worksheet, indenting and merging cells as shown at the right.
2. Calculate all totals using the most efficient method.
3. Within each team, sort by each person's total (descending), and then by name (ascending).
4. Rotate the months and the Totals heading in row 3.
5. You decide all other formatting features.
6. Center horizontally and vertically in portrait orientation and print the worksheet.

Save as:

134C WORKSHEET

COMMUNITY SERVICE										
TEAM	HOURS SERVED									
	SEP	OCT	NOV	DEC	JAN	FEB	MAR	APR	MAY	TOTALS
Givers										
Young	3	6	2	4	2	4	1	3	5	?
Yarry	2	4	4	3	6	3	5	4	1	?
Estrada	4	4	3	6	2	4	2	4	2	?
Johnson	1	3	5	4	4	3	6	2	2	?
Totals	?	?	?	?	?	?	?	?	?	?
Servers										
Chin	2	4	4	3	6	3	2	5	1	?
Poole	3	3	4	3	6	2	4	2	4	?
Everett	2	3	5	1	2	4	4	3	6	?
Morris	3	6	6	2	5	1	1	2	4	?
Totals	?	?	?	?	?	?	?	?	?	?
V'Teers										
Quinnones	3	3	4	4	4	3	6	1	4	?
Nester	1	2	5	2	3	5	5	2	4	?
Veres	2	4	4	3	5	2	2	4	4	?
Cox	5	2	3	5	5	2	4	3	3	?
Totals	?	?	?	?	?	?	?	?	?	?
Grand Totals	?	?	?	?	?	?	?	?	?	?

Activity 7

Bullets and Numbering

1. Key Activity A at the right using the ✓ Bullet style; TS after keying.
2. Key Activity B using the Numbering feature.

Save as: OF6 ACTIVITY7

Bullets (special characters) are used to enhance the appearance of text. Bullets are often used to add visual interest or emphasis. Examples of bullets: ❖ ➢ ✓ •

Numbering is used to show the proper order of a series of steps. Use numbers instead of bullets whenever the order of items is important.

Activity A

Please be sure to bring the following:

- ✓ Paper
- ✓ Pencil
- ✓ CD-R
- ✓ Keyboarding book

Activity B

The standings in the American League East as of September 8, 2007, are:

1. Red Sox
2. Yankees
3. Blue Jays
4. Orioles
5. Devil Rays

Activity 8

Leader

WP • Home/Paragraph dialogue box/Tabs/Select Leader Style

Format and key the copy at the right, leaving a 2" TM and setting a right dot leader tab at the right margin. Leave a space before and after inserting the dot leader tab to enhance the appearance of the text. Use the Title style for the heading.

Save as: OF6 ACTIVITY8

The Leader feature automatically places leaders (. . . . .) between columns of text. The leaders lead the eyes from the text in the first column to the text in the second column. A *right* leader tab inserts the text to the left of the tab setting; a *left* leader tab inserts the text to the right of the tab setting.

In the illustration below, a right tab was set at the right margin using the Leader feature. Several type of leaders are available, such as periods, broken lines, and solid lines.

To leave a space before and after the leader, space once before tapping TAB and once after tapping TAB.

TELEPHONE EXTENSIONS

Javier Pizzaro	9458
Mark Cortez	6351
Helen Etheridge	4187
Rachel LaBonte	3067

Activity 9

Text from File

WP • Insert/Text/Object/Text from file/file name

1. Leaving a 2" TM, key the copy at the right (except words printed in red). Use the Title style for the heading.
2. Insert the files where indicated at the right.

Save as: OF6 ACTIVITY9

To insert text from an existing file into a file that you are currently working on, use the Text from File feature.

TABLE EXAMS

Here is a list of the software features you will need to know for the first exam on tables.

Insert *DF OF6 ACTIVITY9A* file.

For the second exam on tables, you will need to know the following table formatting software features.

Insert *DF OF6 ACTIVITY9B* file.

Application

1. Open *DF 133G WORKSHEET*.
2. Complete steps 1–4.

1. Key this data into the worksheet:
   Morris Towers, 5-story office building, $4.53, $4.86
2. Hide column C and sort by present value (Smallest to Largest). Save as *133G WORKSHEET1* and print the worksheet.
3. Unhide column C, hide column D, and sort by Property Cost (Largest to Smallest) and then by Property Name (A–Z). Save as *133G WORKSHEET2* and print the worksheet.
4. Unhide column D, hide column B, and sort by Property Name (A–Z). Save as *133G WORKSHEET3* and print the worksheet.

Application

Open *130F WORKSHEET* and complete steps 1–4.

Save as:

133H WORKSHEET

1. Sort the information in cells A4:D9 by Percent Change in Largest to Smallest order.
2. Sort the information in cells E4:H9 by Percent Change in Largest to Smallest order.
3. Confirm that your name is a right-aligned header and today's date is a left-aligned footer.
4. Center and print the worksheet in landscape orientation.

Lesson 134   SPREADSHEET APPLICATIONS

OBJECTIVE

- To apply previously learned formatting and formula skills.

Golf Match Information Sheet

1. Open *DF 134B WORK-SHEET*.
2. Complete steps 1–18.

Save as:

134B WORKSHEET

1. In cell I1, key **Round Score** (use Wrap Text) as a column heading, and then calculate the total score for each golfer in column I.
2. Specify column widths as follows: columns B and F at 12; C, D, G, H, and I at 8; and E at 16.
3. Format column B as social security number and column E as phone number.
4. Insert a row at the top, and key **FOURTH ANNUAL TRI-HIGH GOLF MATCH** centered across all columns.
5. Center-align all columns except A.
6. Make all row heights 24 pts. except row 2.
7. Rotate the text in row 2 to 75°, and adjust row height to 65. Horizontally center-align all row 2 text.
8. Separate the names in column A so the first names remain in A and the last names appear in column B. Change the column headings to First Name and Last Name. Adjust width of columns A and B to fit the contents.
9. Sort by Gender (A–Z); then by Round Score (Smallest to Largest); then by Last Name (A–Z).
10. Insert a page break so the females print on p. 1 and males print on p. 2.
11. Set up the pages so they will print horizontally and vertically centered in landscape orientation with gridlines showing. Column headings in rows 1 and 2 (cell range A1:J2) are to be repeated on p. 2.
12. Change font size as desired.
13. Add shading and color as desired.
14. Make other formatting changes as desired.
15. Insert your name as a centered header in 14-pt. font and today's date as a right-aligned footer in 14-pt. font.
16. Hide the Gender column.
17. Rename Sheet 1 tab **4th Annual**.
18. Print the worksheet.

In Unit 10, you learned to format short, **unbound** reports using the textual citation method of documentation. In this unit, you will learn to format longer, **bound** reports. The endnote and footnote methods of documentation are used in this unit.

Bound Reports

Longer reports are generally bound at the left margin. The binding takes about one-half inch (0.5") of space. To accommodate the binding, the left margin is increased to 1.5" on all pages.

Standard Margins

The standard margins for bound reports are presented below.

	First Page	Second page and subsequent pages
Left Margin (LM)	1.5"	1.5"
Right Margin (RM)	1"	1"
Top Margin (TM)	2"	1"
Bottom Margin (BM)	Approximately 1"	Approximately 1"
Page number	Optional, bottom at center if used	Top; right-aligned

Because an exact 1" bottom margin is not always possible, the bottom margin may be adjusted to prevent a side heading or first line of a paragraph from printing as the last line on a page (orphan); or to prevent the last line of a paragraph from occurring at the top of a new page (widow). The Widow/Orphan software feature (p. 83) also may be used to prevent these problems.

Page Numbering

The first page of a report is usually not numbered. However, if a page number is used on the first page, position it at the bottom of the page using center alignment. On the second and subsequent pages, position the page number at the top of the page using right alignment.

Internal Spacing

All parts of the report are SS using the 1.15 default line spacing.

Long quotes. Quoted material of four or more lines should be indented 0.5" from the left margin.

Enumerated items. To format numbers and bullets, the default 0.25" indentation should be used.

Titles and Headings

Title. The title of the report is formatted using the Title style (26-pt. Cambria, Dark Blue, Text 2 font).

Side headings. Side headings are keyed at the left margin and formatted using Heading 1 style (14-pt. Cambria, Blue, Accent 1 font). Capitalize the first letters of all words except prepositions in titles and side headings.

Paragraph headings. Paragraph headings are keyed at the left margin in 11-pt. Cambria and are bolded and italicized. Capitalize only the first letter of the first word and any proper nouns. Place a period after the heading.

Cover/Title Page

A cover or title page is prepared for most bound reports. To format a title page, center and bold the title (14-pt.) in ALL CAPS 2" from the top. Change to 11-pt. type and center the writer's name in capital and lowercase letters 5" from the top. The school name is centered a DS below the writer's name. The date should be centered 9" from the top. Margin settings are the same as the report body. The Cover Page feature of the software can also be used to format professional-looking cover pages.

133D

Print Row and Column Titles on each Page

SS • Page Layout/Page Setup/ Print Titles/Sheet Tab

1. Study the text and illustration.
2. Learn to repeat rows and columns.
3. Complete steps 1–2.

Save as:

133D WORKSHEET

As worksheets expand to two or more pages, it is very helpful to repeat the row and/or column headings on each page to make the second page and subsequent pages easier to read.

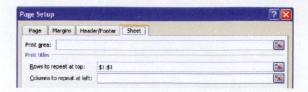

1. Open *DF 133D WORKSHEET*.
2. Print the worksheet, repeating the column headings in row 1 on each page.

133E

Sort

SS • Data/Sort & Filter/Sort

1. Study the text and illustration.
2. Learn to sort.
3. Open *DF 133E WORK-SHEET* and save it as 133E WORKSHEET.
4. Complete steps 1–4, printing gridlines and column and row headings when directed to print.

Information in a worksheet can be sorted. Sorting reorganizes data to place it in an order that is more meaningful. You can sort in different orders (A–Z, Z–A, Largest to Smallest, Oldest to Newest, etc.) You can sort on information in one column or multiple columns.

It is always best to rename and save the worksheet before doing the sort to retain the information in its original order.

1. Open *133E WORKSHEET* and sort by Date Received (Oldest to Newest). Print the first 12 rows that include data for 9/10.

   Save as: **133E WORKSHEET1**

2. Open *133E WORKSHEET* and sort the information by Last Name and then First Name, both in A–Z order. Freeze row 1 and hide columns E and G. Print rows 35–54.

   Save as: **133E WORKSHEET2**

3. Open *133E WORKSHEET* and sort the list by Meal Choice (Z–A), then Last Name (A–Z), and then First Name (A–Z). Hide column G. Print the last five C and first five B meals.

   Save as: **133E WORKSHEET3**

4. Open *133E WORKSHEET* and sort the information by Ticket No. (Largest to Smallest) and then Last and First Names (A–Z). Hide columns F and G. Print p. 1 of the worksheet.

   Save as: **133E WORKSHEET4**

133F

Application

1. Open *DF 130B WORKSHEET*.
2. Complete steps 1–4.

Save as:

133F WORKSHEET

1. Hide columns B–G.
2. Sort by Gross Pay in Smallest to Largest order.
3. Use your name as a right-aligned header and today's date as a right-aligned footer.
4. Print the worksheet with gridlines and row and column headings, scaled to fit on one page with 2" side margins and centered vertically.

Table of Contents

A table of contents lists the headings of a report and the page numbers where those headings can be found in the report. The side and top margins for the table of contents are the same as those used for the first page of the report. Include Table of Contents (using the Title style, 2" from top). Then list side and paragraph headings (if included). Side headings are started at left margin; paragraph headings are indented 0.5". Page numbers for each entry are keyed at the right margin; use a right dot leader tab to insert page numbers. Space once before inserting the dot leader and once after inserting the dot leader to leave a space after the heading and before the page number.

Documentation

Documentation is used to give credit for published material (electronic as well as printed) that is quoted or closely paraphrased (slightly changed). Three types of documentation will be used in this unit: textual citation, footnotes, and endnotes.

Textual citation. The textual citation method of documentation was used in Unit 10. This method includes the name(s) of the author(s), the date of the referenced publication, and the page number(s) of the material cited as part of the actual text:

`(McWilliams, 2009, 138)`

When the author's name is used in the text introducing the quotation, only the year of publication and the page number(s) appear in parentheses:

`McWilliams (2009, 138) said that . . .`

For electronic references, include the author's name and the year.

Footnotes. The footnotes method of documentation identifies the reference cited by a superscript number . . . .[1]

The complete documentation for the reference is placed at the bottom of the same page and is identified with the same superscript number (see model on p. 178).

`[1]Richard G. Harris, "Globalization, Trade, and Income," Canadian Journal of Economics, November 1993, p. 755.`

Each footnote is SS, with a DS between footnotes. Footnotes should be numbered consecutively throughout the report.

Endnotes. The endnotes method of documentation identifies the reference cited by a superscript Roman numeral . . . .[1]

The complete documentation for the reference is placed at the end of the report. The references listed in the endnotes section appear in the same order they appear in the report. A corresponding superscript number identifies the reference in the text.

`[1]W. J. Wood, Battles of the Revolutionary War (Cambridge, MA: Da Capo Press, 2003), pp. 63-64.`

Each endnote is SS with a DS between endnotes.

References Page. Each of these three types of documentation (textual citation, footnotes, and endnotes) requires a reference page. All references cited in the report are listed alphabetically by author surnames at the end of a report under the heading References (Title style). The References page can also be called Works Cited or Bibliography.

Use the same margins as for the first page of the report, and include a page number. SS each reference; DS between references. Begin the first line of each reference at the left margin; indent other lines 0.5" (hanging indent).

**Bound Report with
Long Quotation, Footnotes**

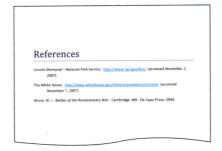

References Page

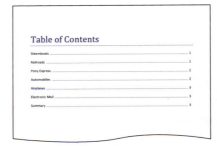

Table of Contents

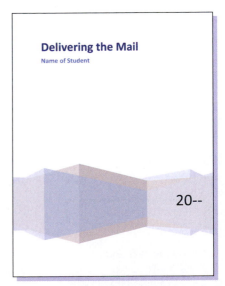

**Bound Report Title Page
using Cubicles Style**

Application

Complete steps 1–10 to create an answer sheet.

1. Specify height of rows 1–27 at 0.25" (18 pts.) and row 28 at 54 pts.
2. Specify the following widths:

   column A and C at 4
   column B and D at 10
   column E at 2
   column F at 50

3. Merge cells A1 to F1 and key **ANSWER SHEET**, centered in 16-pt. bold font.
4. Key **Item** in cells A2 and C2 and **Answer** in cells B2 and D2. Center the headings.
5. In cell F2, key **SHORT ANSWER RESPONSES**, centered.
6. Merge the following cells: F3 to F10; F11 to F18; F19 to F27; and E2 to E28.
7. Merge cells A28 to D28 and key **Student Name**, centered horizontally and top-aligned. Key **Subject and Period** in cell F28 with the same alignment.

8. Use Fill to enter numbers **1–25** in column A cells A3 to A27 and **26–50** in column C cells C3 to C27.
9. Center horizontally and top-align **ANSWER 1**, **ANSWER 2**, and **ANSWER 3** in the three large merged cell areas in column F, with ANSWER 1 being in the first merged cell.
10. Center the worksheet on the page, and print with gridlines.

Save as: 132G WORKSHEET

Lesson 133 · FREEZE, HIDE, REPEAT, AND SORT

OBJECTIVES

• To freeze and hide column and rows.
• To sort worksheet information alphabetically and numerically.

Freeze/Unfreeze Columns and Rows

SS • View/Window/Freeze Panes

1. Study the text and illustration.
2. Learn to freeze and unfreeze columns and rows.
3. Complete steps 1 and 2.

Often an entire worksheet cannot be seen on the screen because as you scroll through the worksheet, the information in the column and row headings disappears from the screen. You can freeze the column and row headings so they remain visible as you scroll to other parts of the worksheet. In the illustration, row 1 was frozen and rows 2–49 disappeared from the screen as the user scrolled to row 50.

Rows and columns can be unfrozen when that feature is no longer needed.

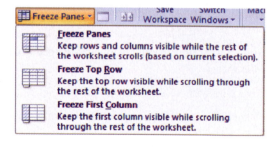

1. Open *DF 133B WORKSHEET*, freeze row 1, and then scroll through the worksheet. Notice that the column headings remain visible.
2. Unfreeze row 1 and close.

Hide Columns and Rows

SS • Home/Cells/Format

1. Study the text and illustration.
2. Learn to hide and unhide columns and rows.
3. Complete steps 1–4.

Save as:
133C WORKSHEET

Rows and columns can be temporarily hidden to enable you to view only those parts of a worksheet that you want to see or print.

Rows and columns can be unhidden when you need to see or print them.

1. Open *DF 133C WORKSHEET*. Hide columns B, C, D, E, and G and rows 8, 9, 10, and 11.
2. Unhide columns B, C, D, and E.
3. Hide columns C, D, and E.
4. Print page 1 of the worksheet.

58A–63A

OBJECTIVES
- To format a bound report with textual citations and references.
- To improve word choice skills.

Conditioning Practice

Key each line twice.

alphabet	1	Zack and our equipment manager will exchange jobs for seven days.
figures	2	If you call after 12:30 on Friday, you can reach him at 297-6854.
speed	3	The eight men in the shanty paid for a big bus to go to the city.

| gwam | 1' | 1 | 2 | 3 | 4 | 5 | 6 | 7 | 8 | 9 | 10 | 11 | 12 | 13 |

58B — Formatting

Bound Report

Document 1 (Report Body)

1. Review the format guides on pp. 173–174.
2. Format the text at the right and on pp. 176–177 as a bound report with textual citations. Insert text files as noted.
3. Proofread your copy and correct any errors.

Save as: 58B REPORT1

PLAINS INDIANS

The Plains Indians [American] are among the most [best] known of all Native Americans. These Indians played a significant role in shaping the history of the West. Some of the more noteworthy Plains Indians were big Foot, Black Kettle, Crazy Horse, Red Cloud, Sitting Bull, and Spotted Tail.

Big Foot

Big Foot (?1825-1890) was also known as Spotted Elk. Born in the northern Great Plains, he eventually became a Minneconjou Teton Sioux chief. He was part of a tribal delegation that traveled to Washington, D.C., and worked to establish schools throughout the Sioux territory. He was one of those massacred at Wounded Knee in December 1890 (Bowman, 1995, 63).

Black Kettle

Black Kettle (?1803-1868) was born near the Black Hills in present-day South Dakota. He was recognized as a Southern Cheyenne peace chief for his efforts to bring peace to the region. However, his attempts at accommodation were not successful and his band was massacred at sand creek in 1864. Even though he continued to seek peace, he was killed with the remainder of his tribe in the Washita Valley of Oklahoma in 1868 (Bowman, 1995, 67).

(continued on next page)

132D

Format Worksheet Tabs

SS • Right Click Sheet Tab/Select Option

1. Study the text and illustrations.
2. Learn how to rename, reposition, and format worksheet tabs.
3. Open a new worksheet and complete steps 1–4.

Save as:

132D WORKSHEET

Sheet tabs (at the bottom of the worksheet) are for each worksheet in a workbook. By default, workbooks usually contain three sheet tabs (Sheet 1, Sheet 2, and Sheet 3)—one for each of the worksheets. Sheet tabs can be renamed, added or deleted, repositioned (that is, moved from first to third, third to second, etc.), or colored.

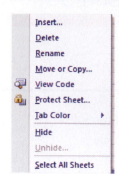

1. Rename Sheet 1 **Section A**, Sheet 2 **Section D**, and Sheet 3 **Section C**.
2. Insert a new sheet tab between Section A and Section D sheet tabs. Rename the sheet tab **Section B**.
3. Reposition sheet tabs so they are in alpha order with Section A being the first sheet tab.
4. Apply a different color to each sheet tab.

132E

Convert Text to Columns

SS • Data/Data Tools/ Text to Columns

1. Study the text and illustrations.
2. Learn how to convert text to columns.
3. Open *DF 132E WORK-SHEET* and complete steps 1–3.

Save as:

132E WORKSHEET

The Convert Text to Columns feature helps you separate information entered in cells in one column into cells in multiple columns. For example, if the cells in a column contain the first and last names, you can separate them so the first name appears in one column and the last name appears in a second column without rekeying the names. The Convert to Columns Wizard is used to make this change. The Wizard uses commas, tabs, spaces, etc. to separate the information.

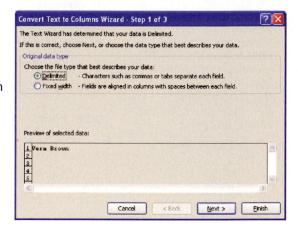

1. Insert a new column between column A and B.
2. Convert the text in cells A1:A10 to two columns (A and B) by using the space between the names as the delimiter.
3. Convert the text in cells C1:C10 to two columns (C and D) by using the comma between the city and state as the delimiter.

132F

Application

1. Open *DF 132F WORKSHEET*.
2. Complete steps 1–11.

Save as:

132F WORKSHEET

1. In column B, use Fill to complete assigning consecutive payroll numbers (127–134).
2. Rotate text in column headings at least 70°.
3. Make rows 2 through 9 0.5" high.
4. Format column C numbers as social security numbers.
5. Display column D numbers as dates in the March 14, 2001 format.
6. Display column E numbers as telephone numbers.
7. Apply a thick red border around all cells in the range A2:G9.
8. Add a new column between columns A and B. Separate the text in column A into two columns (first name in column A; last name in column B).
9. Cut and paste *Employee* from cell A1 to cell B1. Adjust width of columns to fit contents.
10. Rename Sheet 1 **Employee Data** and Sheet 2 **Payroll**. Color each tab.
11. Delete the Sheet 3 tab.

Crazy Horse

Crazy Horse (?1842–1877) was also born near the Black Hills. His father was a medicine man; his mother was the sister of Spotted Tail. He was recognized as a skilled hunter and fighter. Crazy Horse believed he was immune from battle injury and took part in all the major Sioux battles to protect the Black Hills against white intrusion. He was named supreme war and peace chief of the Oglalas in 1876 and led the Sioux and Cheyenne to victory at the battle of Rosebud in January that year. Perhaps he is remembered most for leading the Sioux and Cheyenne in the battle of the Little Bighorn, where his warriors defeated Custer's forces. Crazy Horse is regarded as the greatest leader of the Sioux and a symbol of their heroic resistance (Bowman, 1995, 160–161).

WP Activity

Insert *DF 58B RED CLOUD* text file. Make the corrections shown at the right.

Red Cloud

Red Cloud (1822–1909) was born near the Platte River in present-day Nebraska. Because of his intelligence, strength, and bravery, he became the the chief of the Oglala Sioux. "Red Cloud's War" took place between 1865 and 1868. These battles forced the closing of the Bozeman trail and the signing of the Fort Laramie Treaty in 1868. In exchange for peace, the U.S. government accepted the territorial claims of the sioux (Bowman, 1995, 601).

Sitting Bull

Sitting Bull (?1831–1890), a leader of the Sioux, was born in the region of the Grand River in South Dakota (Encarta, 2004). He was known among the Sioux as a warrior even during his youth. He was bitterly opposed to white encroachment, but made peace in 1868 when the U.S. government guaranteed him a large reservation free of white settlers. When gold was discovered in the Black Hills, he joined the Arapaho and Cheyenne to fight the invaders (Bowman, 1995, 673). According to fellow tribesmen, the name Sitting Bull suggested an animal possessed of great endurance that planted immovably on its haunches to fight on to the death (Utley, 1993, 15).

(continued on next page)

OBJECTIVES

- To use Fill, change text orientation, and convert text to columns.
- To rename, format, and reposition worksheet tabs.

132B

Use Fill

1. Read the text.
2. Learn to use Fill.
3. Complete steps 1–9.

Save as:

132B WORKSHEET

Information can be quickly copied to adjacent cells by using the Fill feature. This feature can be used to enter a series of days (Monday, Tuesday, Wednesday,...), months (Jan, Feb, Mar,...), years (2002, 2003, 2004,...) consecutive numbers (100, 101, 102,...), or numbers in intervals (2, 4, 6, 8,... or 2, 4, 8, 16,...) in adjacent cells.

1. Key **FILL** in cell A1 and then use Fill to copy it to cells A2:A15.
2. Use Fill Right to copy cell A5 to B5:J5.
3. Key **Monday** in C7 and use Fill to enter the days in cells C8:C18.
4. Key **1850** in cell B1 and use Fill to enter the years through **1858** in the cells to the right of B1.
5. Key **Jan** in E7 and use Fill to enter the months through **Dec** below E7.
6. Key **1** in F7 and use Fill to enter numbers 2-12 below F7.
7. Key **100** in H7 and use Fill to enter numbers in intervals of 5 to 150 below H7.
8. Use Fill to enter each power of 2 from 2 to 1024 beginning in A19 and moving right.
9. Print worksheet with gridlines and column and row headings on one page, using a left margin of 1.25" and top margin of 3".

132C

Change Text Orientation

SS
- Home/Alignment/Orientation

1. Study the copy and illustration.
2. Learn to rotate text.
3. Key the worksheets. Use Angle Counterclockwise to rotate the text in the column headings in the first worksheet. Use Rotate Text Up to rotate the text in the column heading in the second.

Save as:

132C WORKSHEET1 and 132C WORKSHEET2

When column headings are considerably longer than the information in the columns, the column headings can be rotated to save space.

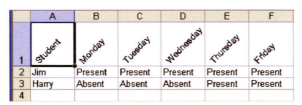

Orientation button

Student	Monday	Tuesday	Wednesday	Thursday	Friday
Jim	Present	Present	Present	Present	Present
Harry	Absent	Absent	Absent	Present	Present

Month	Albert	Mary Ann	Roberto	Yin Chi	Zeb
Sep	1	0	0	0	1
Oct	0	0	0	0	0
Nov	1	1	0	2	0
Dec	1	0	0	1	3
Jan	1	0	0	0	0
Feb	0	0	0	0	1

Insert *DF 58B SPOTTED TAIL* text file. Make the corrections shown at the right.

Document 2 (Reference Page)

Prepare a separate reference page from the information at the right. Proofread; correct errors.

Save as: 58B REPORT2

INTERNET ACTIVITY

Use the Internet to learn more about a person named in the report. Compose a ¶ about the person.

Save as: 58B INTERNET

Spotted Tail

Spotted Tail (?1833-1881) was born along the White River, *either* in present-day South Dakota or near present-day Laramie, Wyoming. He be came the leader of the Brulé Sioux and was one of the signers of the Fort Laramie Treaty of 1868. Eventually, he became the government-appointed chief of the agency Sioux and made frequent trips to Washington, D.C. in that capacity (Bowman, 1995, 688). Starting in 1870 spotted Tail became the statesman that made him the greatest chief the Brulés ever new (Fielder, 1975, p. 29).

Bowman, John S. (ed). *The Cambridge Dictionary of American Biography*. Cambridge: Cambridge University Press, 1995.

Encarta, http://encarta.msn.com/encyclopedia_761578750/sittingbull.html (5 February 2004).

Fielder, Mildred. *Sioux Indian Leaders*. Seattle: Superior Publishing Company, 1975.

Utley, Robert M. *The Lance and the Shield: The Life and Times of Sitting Bull*. New York: Henry Holt and Company, 1993. (accessed February 5, 2004)

58C Language Skills

Language Skills: Word Choice

1. Study the spelling and definitions of the words.
2. Key all *Learn* and *Apply* lines, choosing the correct word in the apply lines.

Save as: 58C CHOICE

some (n/adv) unknown or unspecified unit or thing; to a degree or extent	**hour** (n) the 24th part of a day; a particular time
sum (n/vb) the whole amount; the total; to find a total; summary of points	**our** (adj) of or relating to ourselves as possessors

Learn 1 The total **sum** awarded did not satisfy **some** of the people.

Apply 2 The first grader said, "The (some, sum) of five and two is seven."

Apply 3 (Some, sum) of the students were able to find the correct (some, sum) for the problem.

Learn 1 The first **hour** of **our** class will be used for going over the next assignment.

Apply 2 What (hour, our) of the day would you like to have (hour, our) group perform?

Apply 3 Minutes turned into (hours, ours) as we waited for (hour, our) turn to perform.

Lesson 59 REPORT WITH FOOTNOTES

OBJECTIVES

- To format a bound report with footnotes.
- To format a reference page.

59B Skill Building

Timed Writing

1. Your instructor will provide a timed writing. Key a 3' timing on ¶s 1–3 combined; determine *gwam* and number of errors.

2. Key two 1' timings on each ¶, trying to better the rate achieved in step 1 by three words or more. Don't worry about errors.

3. Key another 3' timing on ¶s 1–3 combined, trying to increase your *gwam* over the 3' timing of step 1.

131E

Review Checking Spelling

1. Study the text.
2. Learn to check spelling.
3. Open *DF 131E WORK-SHEET* and use the spell checker to help proofread and correct errors in the worksheet.

Save as:

131E WORKSHEET

Spreadsheet software checks spelling in much the same way as wp software does. Words are checked for correct spelling against the words in the dictionary but not always for context. Numbers are not checked at all. It is therefore important that *you proofread* all words and numbers for accuracy and context after the checker has been used. Proper names should be checked carefully, since the dictionary may not contain many proper names.

131F

Application

Complete steps 1–8 to create a two-day daily planner.

Save as:

131F WORKSHEET

1. Specify column A width at 7; column B width at 50.
2. Merge cells A1 and B1 and key **Daily Planner For** _____ (left-aligned) in the merged cell.
3. In column A, key the time in one-hour intervals in every fourth cell. Start with **8 a.m.** in cell A2 and end **7 p.m.** in cell A46.
4. In column B, merge every four rows together. The first four cells to be merged are B2:B5 and the last are B46:49.
5. Make a copy of this planner by copying the cells in the range A1:B49 to a new area beginning with cell A50.
6. Key and left-align your name as a header and the page number as a footer.
7. Insert a page break so each copy of the daily planner will print on a separate page.
8. Center the worksheet on the page and then print the second page with gridlines.

131G

Application

1. Key the worksheet (wrap and indent text as shown).
2. Calculate the correct number to be inserted at each set of question marks. The Ending Cash Balance becomes the Opening Cash Balance for the next quarter.
3. Key **ROARING SPRINGS GOLF CLUB** as a centered heading in 18-pt. bold font and your name and date as a left-aligned footer.
4. You decide all other formatting features.
5. Check spelling and preview before printing.

Save as:

131G WORKSHEET

PROJECTED CASH FLOW FOR 20--

	January to March	April to June	July to September	October to December
Cash Receipts				
Gross Cash Receipts	9500	11000	19000	6550
Returns	445	555	935	305
Net Cash Receipts	???	???	???	???
Cash Disbursements				
Expenses				
Operating Expenses	2335	2357	2390	2240
Other Expenses	150	400	500	300
Cash Disbursements	???	???	???	???
Net Cash Flow				
Opening Cash Balance	9606	???	???	???
Net Cash Receipts	???	???	???	???
Cash Disbursements	???	???	???	???
Ending Cash Balance	???	???	???	???

Title # Globalization

We live in a time of worldwide change. What happens in one part of the world impacts people on the other side of the world. People around the world are influenced by common developments.[1]

Footnote Superscript

The term "globalization" is used to describe this phenomenon. According to Harris, the term is being used in a variety of contexts.[2] However, in the broadest context globalization can be defined as:

Long Quote

> . . . a process of interaction and integration among the people, companies, and governments of different nations, a process driven by international trade and investment and aided by information technology. This process has effects on the environment, on culture, on political systems, on economic development and prosperity, and on human physical well-being in societies around the world.[3]

1.5" LM

The business world uses this term in a narrower context to refer to the production, distribution, and marketing of goods and services at an international level. Everyone is impacted by the continued increase of globalization in a variety of ways. The types of food we eat, the kinds of clothes we wear, the variety of technologies we utilize, the modes of transportation available to us, and the types of jobs we pursue are directly linked to globalization. Globalization is changing the world we live in.

1.0" RM

Side Heading ## Causes of Globalization

Harris indicates that there are three main factors contributing to globalization. These factors include:

Footnotes

---

[1] Robert K. Schaeffer, *Understanding Globalization* (Lanham, MD: Rowman & Littlefield Publishers, Inc., 1977), p. 1.

[2] Richard G. Harris, "Globalization, Trade, and Income," *Canadian Journal of Economics*, November 1993, p. 755.

[3] "Globalization 101.org," http://www.globalization101.org/What_is_Globalization.html (accessed November 1, 2007).

Bound Report with Footnotes

OBJECTIVE

• To select print area, set page breaks, select paper size, and check spelling.

131B

Set Print Area

SS • Office Button/Print/ Print Range or Print What options

1. Study the text and illustration.
2. Learn to set the print area.
3. Open *DF 131B WORK-SHEET* and complete steps 1–2.

By default, most ss software prints all the information in a worksheet. If you need to print only a portion (one or more pages, one cell, or a range of cells), you can set the print area by using the Print dialog box shown at the right. The print area selected is the section of the worksheet that prints.

The print area can also be set, cleared, and added to by using the Print Area options in the Page Setup group on the Page Layout tab.

1. Select cells in the range A1:E12, and then print just those cells.
2. Specify and then print only the second page of the worksheet.

131C

Set Page Breaks

SS • Page Layout/Page Setup/Breaks

1. Study the text and illustration.
2. Learn to adjust page breaks.
3. Open *DF 131B WORK-SHEET* and complete steps 1–3.

Save as:
131C WORKSHEET

When you are working with multiple-page worksheets, the spreadsheet software will insert automatic page breaks the same as wp software inserts breaks in multiple-page documents. You can see the automatic page breaks (represented by dotted lines within the worksheet) in the Page Break Preview view. You can use the Breaks feature in the Page Setup group on the Page Layout tab to insert and delete page breaks.

Alternatively, you can move page breaks to the different locations by dragging them to the desired location while using the Page Break Preview View.

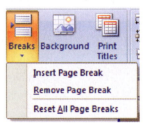

1. Verify that *DF 131B WORKSHEET* contains three seating charts.
2. Adjust the page breaks so that one chart is printed per page.
3. Print only the first seating chart. Show gridlines, use portrait orientation, and center horizontally and vertically on the page.

131D

Select Paper Size

SS • Page Layout/Page Setup/Size

1. Study the text and illustration.
2. Learn to select paper size.
3. Open *DF 130D WORK-SHEET* and complete steps 1–2.

Save as:
131D WORKSHEET

You can specify the size of paper on which the worksheet is to be printed. If you do not make a selection, it will print on 8.5" by 11" paper.

1. Open *DF 130D WORKSHEET* and set print area as cells A1:G12.
2. Print on Executive size paper (7.25" by 10.5") centered horizontally and vertically using portrait orientation.

Bound Report

1. Review the report format guides on pp. 173–174; study the model report on p. 178. Note the format of the footnotes.
2. Key the first page of the "Globalization" report from the model on p. 178; continue keying the report from the rough-draft copy shown at the right. The information for footnotes 4–6 is given below.
3. Proofread your copy and correct errors.

Footnotes 4–6

[4]Harris, p. 763.

[5]*Encyclopedia Americana*, Vol. 26, "Trade Policy" (Danbury, CT: Grolier Incorporated, 2001), p. 915.

[6]Louis S. Richman, "Dangerous Times for Trade Treaties," *Fortune*, September 20, 1993, p. 14.

Save as: 59C REPORT

Note: You will finish keying the report in Lesson 60.

- The reduction in trade and investment barriers in the post-world war II period.

- The rapid growth and increase in the size of developing countries' economies.

- Changes in technologies.[4]

Trade Agreements

Originally, each nation established its own rules governing foreign trade. Regulations and tariffs were often the outcome, leading to the tariff wars of the 1930s. However, [*Not a long quote, don't Indent*]

"During the 1950's a concerted effort was made to reduce these artificial barriers to trade, and as a result the quotas and other controls limiting foreign trade were gradually dismantled."[5]

Many trade agreements exist in the world today. Three of those agreements (General Agreement on Tariffs and Trade [GATT], the European Community, and the North American Free Trade Agreement [NAFTA]) have had or will have a significant impact on the United States.

GATT. The first trade agreement of major significance was the General Agreement on Tariffs and Trade. The purpose of GATT was aimed at lowering tariff barriers among its members. The success of the organization is evidenced by its membership. Originally signed by 23 countries in 1947, the number of participating countries continues to grow.

The Uruguay Round of GATT is the most ambitious trade agreement ever attempted. Some 108 nations would lower tariff and other barriers on textiles and agriculture goods; protect one another's intellectual property; and open their borders to banks, insurance companies, and purveyors of other services.[6]

The European Community. The European Community is another example of how trade agreements impact the production, distribution, and marketing of goods and services. The 12 member nations of the European Community have dismantled the internal borders of its members to enhance trade relations.

Dismantling the borders was only the first step toward an even greater purpose--the peaceful union of European countries.

130E

Insert Headers and Footers

1. Study the text and illustration.
2. Learn to insert headers and footers.
3. Open *DF 130D WORKSHEET* and complete steps 1 and 2.

Save as:

130E WORKSHEET

Tip: The header/footer font does not change automatically when font changes are made in the worksheet.

Worksheets can contain headers and footers in much the same way as wp documents can. You can select predefined headers/footers from the ss software, or you can create custom headers/footers. Special codes can be entered in the header/footer to print the date, time, page number, filename, etc. The font, font style, and font size can also be specified. In addition, the header/footer may be left-, center-, or right-aligned and can be set so it does not appear on the first page of a worksheet.

Header/Footer Tools—Right side of Design tab features

Header/Footer Tools—Left side of Design tab features

1. Using Arial 14-pt. bold font, insert the filename as a right-aligned header and your name and date as a centered custom footer.
2. Set left and right margins at 1.25". Preview the worksheet. Print the worksheet in landscape orientation without gridlines or column/row headings when it is arranged attractively on one page.

130F

Application

1. Key the worksheet, making the changes in steps 1–4.
2. Calculate totals and percent of change (use Percent to one decimal place).
3. Format the worksheet attractively.
4. Print in landscape orientation, centered on page with your name as a right-aligned header and today's date as a left-aligned footer, both in 18-pt. font.

Save as:

130F WORKSHEET

JENNCO MONTHLY SALES REPORT

| | Northern Division | | | Southern Division | |
| | | Same | | | Same |
Office	This Month	Month Last Year	Office	This Month	Month Last Year
Boston	1540000	1444975	Atlanta	1653450	1582625
Baltimore	1562675	1375755	Dallas	1345870	1467050
Cleveland	2143750	2307450	Mobile	1873525	1852840
Chicago	1957500	2010730	Memphis	2769200	2652810
Boise	780560	755050	Omaha	2459550	2234800
Seattle	2289570	2185525	San Diego	3000540	2750750
Totals			Totals		

1. Specify all column widths at 12.
2. Format numbers as Currency with no cents.
3. Insert an 8-character column between C and D and a similar column at the right of the last column.
4. Use **Percent Change** for the new column headings (wrap the text).

- To format a bound report with footnotes.
- To format a references page and a title page.

60B   Formatting

Bound Report

Document 1

Finish the Globalization report started in Lesson 59. Insert the file *DF 60B GLOBAL* after the last sentence in *59C REPORT*. Make the changes shown at the right.

Footnotes 7–9

[7]**"Fact Sheet: European Community,"** Vol. 4, No. 7, Washington, D.C.: *U.S. Department of State Dispatch*, February 15, 1994, p. 89.

[8]Mario Bognanno and Kathryn J. Ready, eds., *North American Free Trade Agreement* (Westport, CT: Quorum Books, 1993), p. xiii.

[9]Rahul Jacob, "The Big Rise," *Fortune,* May 30, 1994, pp. 74–75.

The first step was ~~done~~ *accomplished* by the Paris and Rome treaties, which established the european community and consequently removed the economic barriers. The treaties called for members to establish a *common* market; a *common* customs tariff; and *common* economic, agricultural, transport, and nuclear policies.[7]

NAFTA. A trade agreement that will have an *significant* impact on the way business is conducted in the United States is the North American *Free* Trade Agreement. This trade agreement involves Canada, the United States, and Mexico. Proponents of NAFTA claim that the accord will not only increase trade throughout the Americas, but it will also moderate product prices and create jobs in all *three of* the countries.[8]

Over the years a number of trade agreements have been enacted that promote trade. The result of these agreements has been a better quality of life because of the increased *enhanced* access to goods and services produced in other countries.

Growth in Developing Countries' Economies

The growth in developing countries' economies is another major reason for globalizaiton. According to Jacob, the *global* surge means more consumers who need goods and services.[9] These needs appear because of the increase in per capita incomes of the developing countries.

According to the U.S. Department of Commerce, the world's ten biggest emerging markets include:

- Argentina
- Brazil
- China
- India
- Indonesia
- Mexico
- Poland
- South Africa
- South Korea
- Turkey

Adjust Page Margins and Center and Scale Worksheets

SS
- Page Layout/Page Setup/Margins

1. Study the text and illustration.
2. Learn to set margins and center and scale worksheets.
3. Complete steps 1–3.

To arrange worksheets attractively on a page, you can change margin settings, center the worksheet horizontally and/or vertically, and/or scale the worksheet to fit specific page widths and lengths.

To change the top, bottom, and side margins, use one of the preset options (Normal, Wide, or Narrow) or **Page Layout/ Page Setup/Margins/Custom Margins/ Margins tab** to set other margins sizes.

Use **Page Layout/Page Setup/ Margins/ Custom Margins/Margins tab** to center the worksheet horizontally and/or vertically on the paper.

Use **Page Layout/Page Setup/ Margins/ Custom Margins/Page tab** to set the scaling settings to fit on the number of pages desired.

1. Open *DF 130C WORKSHEET*; change the side margins to Narrow. Print the worksheet in landscape orientation without gridlines or headings.

   Save as: 130C WORKSHEET1

2. Open *DF 130C WORKSHEET*; center the worksheet vertically and horizontally. Print in landscape orientation with gridlines and headings.

   Save as: 130C WORKSHEET2

3. Open *DF 130C WORKSHEET*, scale the worksheet to fit on one page in portrait orientation, center it vertically and horizontally, and print it without gridlines or headings.

   Save as: 130C WORKSHEET3

Use Print Preview

SS
- Office Button/Print/ Print Preview

1. Study the text and illustration.
2. Learn to use Print Preview.
3. Open *DF 130D WORKSHEET* and complete steps 1–3.

Save as:

130D WORKSHEET

Note: Print Preview can also be accessed by launching the Page Setup dialog box in the Page Setup group on the Page Layout tab.

A worksheet should be previewed before it is printed to make sure it is arranged on the page as desired. If it is not, adjustments can be made to the worksheet before it is printed. These adjustments include changing margins, centering the worksheet, or scaling the worksheet to the desired size. As shown in the illustration, Print Preview can be accessed by clicking Print on the Office button list.

1. Review the worksheet to see the numbers of columns it has, paying particular attention to the names of the columns near the right.

2. Select Print Preview. If the worksheet doesn't fit on one page in landscape orientation, scale it to one page and then center it horizontally and vertically.

3. Use Print Preview as many times as needed to ensure the entire worksheet is arranged correctly, and then print it with gridlines and column and row headings.

Document 1 cont.
Complete the Globalization report. Format and key the text at the right following the data file *DF 60B GLOBAL* that you inserted.

Footnotes 10–11

[10]"India's Income Per Capita Way Behind China," http:// in.news.yahoo.com /021204/43/1ysk5.html (accessed February 9, 2004).

[11]Pete Engardio, "Third World Leapfrog," *Business Week,* May 18, 1994, p. 47.

Save as: 60B REPORT1

Document 2 (Cover Page)

Review the Cover Page section of the format guides, p. 173. Prepare a cover page for the Globalization report.

Save as: 60B REPORT2

Use the Cover Page feature (Puzzle format) to prepare a cover page. Compare the two cover pages.

Save as: 60B REPORT2A

Document 3 (References Page)

Review the format guides for preparing a references page, p. 174. Use the information from the footnotes and the information shown at the right to prepare a references page for the report. Refer to p. R18 for format of references.

Save as: 60B REPORT3

Of these emerging markets, the most dramatic increase is in the East Asian countries. India, for example, has been able to achieve higher growth in incomes, longer life expectancy, and better schooling through increased integration into the world economy.[10]

Recent technological developments have also contributed to globalization. Because of these developments, the world is a smaller place; communication is almost instant to many parts of the world. The extent of the technological developments can be sensed in Engardio's comments:[11]

> Places that until recently were incommunicado are rapidly acquiring state-of-the-art telecommunications that will let them foster both internal and foreign investment. It may take a decade for many countries in Asia, Latin America, and Eastern Europe to unclog bottlenecks in transportation and power supplies. But by installing optical fiber, digital switches, and the latest wireless transmission systems, urban centers and industrial zones from Beijing to Budapest are stepping into the Information Age. Videoconferencing, electronic data interchange, and digital mobile-phone services already are reaching most of Asia and parts of Eastern Europe.

> All of these developing regions see advanced communications as a way to leapfrog stages of economic development.

Summary

The world continues to become more globalized. The trend will continue because of three main factors: new and improved trade agreements, rapid growth rates of developing countries' economies, and technological advances. All of these factors foster globalization.

Engardio article pp. 47–49	Jacob article pp. 74–90
"Fact Sheet" article pp. 87–93	Richman article p. 14
Harris article pp. 755–776	

Lesson 61   REPORT WITH ENDNOTES

OBJECTIVES
- To format a bound report with endnotes.
- To format a references page.

61B   Skill Building

Timed Writings

1. Your instructor will provide a timed writing. Key a 3' timing on ¶s 1–3 combined; determine *gwam* and number of errors.
2. Key two 1' timings on each ¶, trying to better the rate achieved in step 1 by three words or more. Don't worry about errors.
3. Key another 3' timing on ¶s 1–3 combined, trying to increase your *gwam* over the 3' timing of step 1.

Application

1. Key **States** in cell A1 and **Capitals** in cell B1.
2. In cells A2:A11, list the ten states that have two words in their name.
3. In cells B2:B11, list the capital of each state named in column A.
4. Shrink to fit the contents of each cell.

Save as: **129F WORKSHEET**

Application

1. Key the worksheet as shown.
2. Calculate the sum in cells D8, D13, D17, and D18.
3. Format numbers in column B as percents with two decimal places, column C with a thousands separator, and column D as currency with no cents.
4. Using the Present Value for each industry and the Total Portfolio Value as the base, calculate the percent in cells B8, B13, and B17.
5. Right-align all numbers and apply shading to make the worksheet attractive and easy to read.

Save as:
129G WORKSHEET

MXP COMMON STOCK FUND
December 31, 20--

Industry and Company	Percent of Portfolio	Shares	Present Value
Aerospace			
Fleet Company		4627	205601
Textran		748	37607
Kite Technologies		1312	69459
Total Aerospace			
Energy			
HPNGCO Electric		1701	103855
Gertin Corp		7362	395719
SH Oil		6333	348722
Total Energy			
Real Estate			
The Troyer Company		2151	45324
Suburban Malls, Inc		6446	164791
Total Real Estate			
Total Portfolio Value			

Lesson 130   PAGE SETUP AND PRINT

OBJECTIVES

- To use Print Preview and print in landscape orientation.
- To change margins, center and scale worksheets, and insert headers and footers.

Landscape Orientation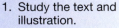

1. Study the text and illustration.
2. Learn to use landscape orientation.
3. Open *DF 130B WORKSHEET* and print the worksheet in landscape orientation.

Save as:
130B WORKSHEET

Most documents, including letters, memos, reports, tables, and forms, are printed in portrait orientation, or across the width of the paper (the 8.5" side of paper that is 8.5" by 11"). Many worksheets are wider than 8.5"; these can be printed in landscape orientation, which prints across the length of the paper (the 11" side of 8.5" by 11" paper).

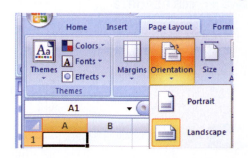

Bound Report

Document 1 (Report Body)

1. Format the copy shown at the right as a bound report with endnotes.
2. Information for the endnotes is shown below.

Save as: 61C REPORT1

Information for Endnotes

¹W. J. Wood, *Battles of the Revolutionary War* (Cambridge, MA: Da Capo Press, 2003), pp. 63-64.

²Lincoln Memorial-- National Park Service, http://www.nps.gov/linc/ (2 November 2007).

³The White House, http://www.whitehouse.gov/history/presidents/tj3.html (accessed November 7, 2007).

Document 2 (Reference Page)

Use the endnotes information to prepare a references page. See p. R18 for format.

Save as: 61C REPORT2

WASHINGTON D.C.

Our nation's capital, Washington D.C., is a magnificent city to visit. It is known for the monuments, memorials, and cemetery that honor those who have given their lives in the cause of freedom and democracy. Some of the more widely recognized tributes to those who have fought for freedom and democracy include:

- Washington Monument
- Lincoln Memorial
- Jefferson Memorial
- Arlington Cemetery

Washington Monument

Few men have impacted the history of this country as much as George Washington. The birth of this nation can in large part be attributed to the Continental Army under the leadership of George Washington. His leadership is easily imagined when reading Wood's book on the Revolutionary War. "He stands on the bank of the stream, wrapped in his cloak, superintending the landing of his troops. He is calm and collected, but very determined. The storm is [again] changing to sleet and cuts like a knife."[i]

Recognized for his leadership abilities, Washington was elected by the American people as the first President following the conclusion of the Revolutionary War. Naming the nation's capital after him and erecting a 555-foot monument in his honor ensure that George Washington's contributions to his country will always be remembered.

Lincoln Memorial

The Lincoln Memorial, another symbol of freedom, is a tribute to the sixteenth President of the United States. While Washington is recognized for fighting for the birth of this nation in the Revolutionary War, Lincoln is recognized for trying to preserve the nation during the Civil war.

The Lincoln Memorial was built to resemble a Greek temple. The 36 columns of the memorial represent the 36 states at the time of Lincoln's death. A sculpture of a seated Lincoln done by Daniel Chester French is the focal point of the memorial. Inscribed above the seated Lincoln are these words, "In this temple, as in the hearts of the people for whom he saved the Union, the memory of Abraham Lincoln is enshrined forever."[ii]

Prominently displayed on the walls of the memorial are the Gettysburg Address (often referred to as Lincoln's most famous speech) and Lincoln's second inaugural address. The words "Four score and seven years ago . . ." and "With malice toward none; with charity for all . . ." need no formal introduction.

Jefferson Memorial

The man recognized as the primary drafter of the Declaration of Independence is memorialized in the Jefferson Memorial. A powerful advocate of liberty and an eloquent correspondent, Jefferson drafted the Declaration of Independence for the Continental Congress in 1776 at the age of 33.[iii] He became the third president in 1801.

Declaration of Independence

We hold these truths to be self-evident, that all men are created equal, that they are endowed by their Creator with certain unalienable Rights, that among these are Life, Liberty and the pursuit of Happiness. — That to secure these rights, Governments are instituted among Men, deriving their just powers from the consent of the governed, —

Arlington Cemetery

The most widely known cemetery in the United States is Arlington Cemetery. Arlington Cemetery is the final resting place of many veterans--every war that the U.S. has been involved in is represented. Perhaps the best known of the memorials at Arlington is the "Tomb of the Unknown Soldier." Other well-known memorials include:

(continued on next page)

129C

Wrap Text in Cells

SS
- Home/Alignment/Wrap Text

1. Study the text and illustration.
2. Learn to wrap text in cells.
3. Open a new worksheet and complete steps 1–4.
4. Print the worksheet with gridlines and row and column headings.

Save as:
129C WORKSHEET

Text that is too long for a cell will extend into the adjacent cell if the cell to the right is empty. If the cell to the right is not empty, the text that does not fit will not display. You can choose to have the text wrap within the cell's width in the same way sentences are wrapped in a wp document. The row height will adjust as shown in the illustration at the right.

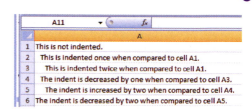

1. Center-align **UNION HIGH SCHOOL ENROLLMENT REPORT** in cells A1:G1 (merge cells).
2. Center-align **Females** in cells B2:D2 and **Males** in cells E2:G2.
3. Center-align and vertically center **Grade** in A2:A3.
4. Using wrap, center-align **Fall 2004 Semester** in cell B3 and again in cell E3; **Fall 2005 Semester** in cell C3 and again in F3; and **Percent Change** in cells D3 and G3.

129D

Shrink Text to Fit

1. Study the text and illustration.
2. Learn to shrink text to fit.
3. Open a new worksheet and complete steps 1–3.
4. Print the worksheet with gridlines and row and column headings.

Save as:
129D WORKSHEET

SS
- Home/Alignment Dialog Box launcher/Alignment tab/Shrink to Fit

Cell contents can be shrunk to fit within the available space so the column width and height do not need to be changed to achieve an attractive appearance.

1. Center-align **GREENE COUNTY RECYCLING MATERIALS** in cells A1:D1.
2. Using the default cell width and height, key **Newspaper** in cell A2; **Clear Glass** in B2; **Aluminum** in C2; and **Electronics** in D2.
3. Shrink to fit the contents of cells A2, B2, C2, and D2.

129E

Increase/Decrease Cell Indents

SS
- Home/Alignment/Increase Indent or Decrease Indent

1. Study the text and illustration.
2. Learn to use increase/decrease indent features.
3. Key and format the worksheet as directed in steps 1–6.
4. Print the worksheet with gridlines and row and column headings.

Save as:
129E WORKSHEET

Use the Increase Indent and Decrease Indent features to help distinguish categories or set text apart within cells. The amount of the indent can be increased or decreased by clicking the proper Indent button in the Paragraph group on the Home tab or changing the indent setting in the Format Cells dialog box.

Distributions to shareholders	Amount
From net investment income	
Class A	$ 43,523
Class B	$ 10,325
In excess of net investment income	
Class A	$ 2,354
Class B	$ 574
From return on capital	
Class A	$ 2,765
Class B	$ 750
Total distributions	$ 60,291

1. Indent column A rows 2, 5, and 8 once.
2. Indent column A rows 3, 4, 6, 7, 9, and 10 twice.
3. Indent column A row 11 three times.
4. Format numbers as Accounting with dollar signs and no cents.
5. Bold as shown.
6. Use AutoFit to set column widths to widest entry.

- President John F. Kennedy
- Audie Murphy--one of the most decorated WWII soldiers
- Tomb of Unknown Civil War Dead--remains of Union soldiers
- Confederate Monument--remains of many Confederate soldiers
- Iwo Jima--U.S. Marine Corps Memorial
- Anita Newcomb McGee--organizer of Army Nurse Corps

Lesson 62   REPORT WITH ENDNOTES

OBJECTIVES
- To format a bound report.
- To format endnotes.

62B   Formatting

Bound Report

Document 1 (Report Body)

1. Review the format guides on reports on pp. 173–174 as needed.
2. Format the copy at the right as a bound report with endnotes. The endnotes are shown below and on p. 184.
3. When you finish, use the Speller feature and proofread.

Save as: 62B REPORT

Document 1 (Endnotes)

[1]Wayne E. Fuller, *The American Mail* (Chicago: University of Chicago Press, 1972), p. ix.

[2]William M. Leary, *Aerial Pioneers* (Washington, D.C.: Smithsonian Institution Press, 1985), p. 238.

[3]Richard Wormser, *The Iron Horse: How Railroads Changed America* (New York: Walker Publishing Company, Inc., 1993), p. 26.

[4]Leary, p. 238.

DELIVERING THE MAIL

For years, people have used written communication as one of their primary means of exchanging information. Those using this form of communicating have depended on the U.S. mail to transport their messages from one place to another.

> For much of American history, the mail was our main form of organized communication. Americans wanting to know the state of the world, the health of a friend, or the fate of their business anxiously awaited the mail. To advise a distant relative, to order goods, to pay a bill, to express views to their congressman or love to their fiancée, they used the mail. No American institution has been more intimately involved in daily hopes and fears.[1]

The history of the U.S. mail is not only interesting but also reflective of the changes in American society, specifically transportation. A variety of modes of transporting mail have been used over the years. Speed, of course, was the driving force behind most of the changes.

Steamboats

Congress used inventions to move the mail from place to place. In 1813, five years after Robert Fulton's first experiments on the Hudson River, Congress authorized the Post Office to transport mail by steamboat.[2] Transporting mail to river cities worked very well. However, the efficiency of using steamboats to transport mail between New York and San Francisco was questionable. "The distance was 19,000 miles and the trip could take as long as six to seven months."[3]

Railroads

Although mail was carried by railroads as early as 1834, it was not until 1838 that Congress declared railroads to be post roads.[4] Trains eventually revolutionized mail delivery. The cost of sending a letter decreased substantially, making it more affordable to the public.

> No aspect of American life was untouched by the revolution that the trains brought in bringing mail service almost to the level of a free good. (For many years--ironically enough, until the Depression called for an increase in the cost of a first-class letter to three cents--an ordinary first-class letter went for two cents.)[5]

Pony Express

The Pony Express was one of the most colorful means of transporting mail. This method of delivery was used to take mail from St. Joseph, Missouri, westward.

(continued on next page)

UNIT 31
Lessons 129-134

Extend Spreadsheet Skills

Lesson 129   **FORMAT CELLS AND COLUMNS**

OBJECTIVE

• To merge cells, wrap and indent text in cells, and specify column widths.

129A-134A

Conditioning Practice

Key each line twice daily.

alphabet	1	Jim avoids fizzling fireworks because they often explode quickly.
fig/sym	2	Runner #3019-A was first (49' 35"); runner #687-D was last (62').
speed	3	Nancy works in the big cornfield down by the lake with the docks.

gwam 1' | 1 | 2 | 3 | 4 | 5 | 6 | 7 | 8 | 9 | 10 | 11 | 12 | 13 |

129B

Merge Cells

SS • Home/Alignment/Merge & Center

1. Study the text and illustration.
2. Learn to merge cells.
3. Open a new worksheet and complete steps 1–4.
4. Print the worksheet with gridlines and row and column headings.

Save as:

129B WORKSHEET

As with cells in a word processing table, cells within a worksheet can be merged with adjacent cells. The text within the merged cells can be center-, left-, or right-aligned horizontally and top-, bottom-, or center-aligned vertically. This is useful for centering worksheet titles and entering column and row entries that span more than one column or row.

The illustration shows a title centered within cells A1:G1. It also shows column and

row headings and entries that span multiple columns or rows.

Merge Cell button

1. Center-align **PROPERTY TAX CALCULATIONS** in cells A1:G1 (merge cells).
2. Center-align **Value (in 000s)** in cells B2:C2 and **Taxes** in D2:F2.
3. Left-align and vertically center **Lot** in cells A2:A3. Right-align and vertically center **Total Tax** in G2:G3.
4. Center-align **Market** in B3; **Assessed** in C3; **School** in D3; **City** in E3; and **County** in F3.

Endnotes (cont.)

[5]Albro Martin, *Railroads Triumphant* (New York: Oxford University Press, 1992), p. 94.

[6]Fred Reinfeld, *Pony Express* (Lincoln: University of Nebraska Press, 1973), p. 55.

[7]Carl H. Scheele, *A Short History of the Mail Service* (Washington, D.C.: Smithsonian Institution Press, 1970), p. 117.

[8]Fuller, p. 9.

[9]"Zen and the Art of the Internet," http://www.cs.indiana.edu/docproject/zen/zen-1.0_4.html (accessed February 8, 2004).

Note: You will finish keying the report "Delivering the Mail" in Lesson 63.

April 3, 1860, remains a memorable day in the history of the frontier, for that was the day on which the Pony Express began its operations—westward from St. Joseph and eastward from San Francisco. Even in those days San Francisco had already become the most important city in California.[6]

With the East Coast being connected to the West Coast by railroad in 1869, the Pony Express had a relatively short life span.

Automobiles

The invention of the automobile in the late 1800s brought a new means of delivering mail in the United States.

An automobile was used experimentally for rural delivery as early as 1902 at Adrian, Michigan, and in 1906 the Department gave permission for rural carriers to use their automobiles. The change from horse and wagon to the motor car paralleled improvements in highways and the development of more reliable automotive equipment . . . .[7]

Airplanes

The next major mode of transporting used by the Postal Service was airplanes. Speed was the driving force behind using airplanes. ". . . so closely has speed been associated with the mails that much of the world's postal history can be written around the attempts to send mail faster each day than it went the day before."[8]

Electronic Mail

"People have always wanted to correspond with each other in the fastest way possible . . ."[9] A new way of communicating via the written word became available with the creation of the Internet. The creation of the Internet provides a way of transporting the written word almost instantaneously. Electronic Mail (e-mail) messages generally arrive at their destination within seconds of when they were sent. More and more written messages are being delivered via e-mail.

Lesson 63 — COVER PAGE AND TABLE OF CONTENTS

OBJECTIVES
- To complete formatting a bound report.
- To format reference page, title page, and table of contents.

63B   Formatting

Bound Report

Document 1 (Report Summary)

Complete the report "Delivering the Mail" that you started in Lesson 62. Insert the file *DF 63B REPORT* at the end of the report and make the corrections shown at the right.

Save as: 63B REPORT1

Summary

(now the U.S. Postal Service)

    The Post Office has been the primary means for transporting
written messages for many years. As the information age continues
to emerge, technologies will play a significant roll in getting written messages from the sender to the reciever. Again this change is
directly attributable to speed. Instead of talking in terms of months
required for delivering a message from the east coast to the west
coast, we now talk in terms of seconds. Today, e-mail and faxes are just as
important to a successful business operation as the Post Office.

1. Open *DF CS12 ACTIVITY5* and print the file.
2. Solve the problems as directed in the file.
3. Submit your answers.

CAREER **Clusters**

ACTIVITY 12

You must complete Career Exploration Activities 1–3 before completing this activity.

1. Retrieve your Career folder and the information in it that relates to the career cluster that is your third choice.

2. Use the Internet to search for the education that is recommended for occupations in this career cluster and then compose a paragraph or two explaining what you have learned. Print your file and then save it as Career12 and keep it open.

3. Exchange papers with a classmate and have the classmate offer suggestions for improving the content and correcting any errors he or she finds in your paragraph(s). Make the changes that you agree with and print a copy to turn in to your instructor. Save your file as Career12 and close the file.

4. Return your folder to the storage area. When your instructor returns your paper, file it in your Career folder.

©LISA F. YOUNG 2008/USED UNDER LICENSE FROM SHUTTERSTOCK.COM

Document 2 (Cover Page)

Use the Cover Page feature to create a cover page using the Cubicles format. Format and key a title page for "Delivering the Mail" as shown below.

Save as: 63B REPORT2

Document 3 (Table of Contents)

Review the guidelines for formatting a table of contents on p. 173. Format and key a table of contents for "Delivering the Mail." Verify the page numbers with your report page numbers.

Save as: 63B REPORT3

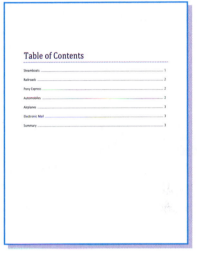

63C · Formatting

Bound Report

Table of Contents

In previous lessons, you keyed a report titled "Globalization." The headings in that report are shown at the right. Format and key a table of contents for the report.

Open the file (*60B REPORT1*); verify that the page number for each heading is the same as in your report. Change the table of contents as needed.

Save as: 63C REPORT

Table of Contents

63D · Skill Building

Timed Writings

1. Your instructor will provide a timed writing. Key a 3' timing on ¶s 1–3 combined; determine *gwam* and number of errors.

2. Key two 1' timings on each ¶, trying to better the rate achieved in step 1 by three words or more. Don't worry about errors.

3. Key another 3' timing on ¶s 1–3 combined, trying to increase your *gwam* over the 3' timing of step 1.

Proofread & Correct

2. Key Proofread & Correct, using parentheses and dashes correctly.
   a. Check answers.
   b. Using the rule number(s) at the left of each line, study the rule relating to each error you made.
   c. Rekey each incorrect line, using parentheses and dashes correctly.

Save as: CS12 ACTIVITY1

Rules

Rules		
1	1	The appendices Exhibits A and B utilize computer graphics.
2	2	The three areas are 1 ethical, 2 moral, and 3 legal.
2	3	Emphasize: 1 writing, 2 speaking, and 3 listening.
3	4	You cited the "Liberty or Death" speech Henry, 1775 twice.
4	5	The payment terms 2/10, n/30 are clearly shown on the invoice.
4	6	The article and I know you're interested is in *Newsweek*.
5	7	"The finger that turns the dial rules the air." Will Durant
1	8	The contract reads: "For the sum of $600 Six Hundred Dollars."
4	9	Albert Camus, as you know a Frenchman was an existentialist.
2	10	Her talk addressed two issues: A family values and B welfare.

ACTIVITY 2

Listening

Complete as directed.

Save as: CS12 ACTIVITY2

1. You have answered a telephone call from Maria MacDonald, who serves as an officer in the alumni association of which your mother is president.

   She asks you to take a message.

2. Open *DF CS12 ACTIVITY2* and listen to the message, taking notes as needed.

3. Close the file.
4. Using your notes, key a message in sentence form for your mother.

ACTIVITY 3

Write to Learn

Complete as directed.

Save as: CS12 ACTIVITY3

Using word processing or voice recognition software, write a ¶ explaining the voice recognition commands you can use to move around in a document.

ACTIVITY 4

Preparing to Speak

You have been nominated for treasurer of your regional Future Business Leaders of America (FBLA). Now you must make a 1' to 2' speech to the voting delegates from each school in your region. Follow the steps at the right.

Save as: CS12 OUTLINE and CS12 SOUND

1. Key an outline of the major points you want to make about yourself and your qualifications for being treasurer. Include experiences that show you to be capable, reliable, responsible, and trustworthy. Examples follow:

   - Math, accounting, and other applicable courses you have completed or are taking
   - Leadership positions you hold/held in other organizations
   - Jobs you hold/held

   - Experiences handling money (writing checks, making deposits, following a budget, investing, etc.)

2. If time and resources permit, record your speech in a sound file.

Communication & Math
SKILLS 6

TERMINAL PUNCTUATION

ACTIVITY 1

Terminal Punctuation: Period, Question Mark, Exclamation Point

1. Study each of the five rules.
   a. Key the Learn line(s) beneath each rule, noting how the rule is applied.
   b. Key the *Apply* line(s), using correct terminal punctuation
2. Key Proofread & Correct, using correct terminal punctuation.
   a. Check answers.
   b. Using the rule number(s) at the left of each line, study the rule relating to each error you made.
   c. Rekey each incorrect line, using correct terminal punctuation.

Save as: CS6 ACTIVITY1

Terminal Punctuation: Period

Rule 1: Use a period at the end of a declarative sentence (a sentence that is not regarded as a question or exclamation).

Learn 1 I wonder why *Phantom of the Opera* has always been so popular.

Apply 2 Fran and I saw *Cats* in London We also saw *Sunset Boulevard*

Rule 2: Use a period at the end of a polite request stated in the form of a question but not intended as one.

Learn 3 Matt, will you please collect the papers at the end of each row.

Apply 4 Will you please call me at 555-0140 to set up an appointment

Terminal Punctuation: Question Mark

Rule 3: Use a question mark at the end of a sentence intended as a question.

Learn 5 Did you go to the annual flower show in Ault Park this year?

Apply 6 How many medals did the U.S.A. win in the 1996 Summer Games

Rule 4: For emphasis, a question mark may be used after each item in a series of interrogative expressions.

Learn 7 Can we count on wins in gymnastics? in diving? in soccer?

Apply 8 What grade did you get for history for sociology for civics

Terminal Punctuation: Exclamation Point

Rule 5: Use an exclamation point after emphatic (forceful) exclamations and after phrases and sentences that are clearly exclamatory.

Learn 9 The lady screamed, "Stop that man!"

Learn 10 "Bravo!" many yelled at the end of the Honor America program.

Apply 11 "Yes" her gym coach exclaimed when Kerri stuck the landing.

Apply 12 The burglar stopped when he saw the sign, "Beware, vicious dog"

Proofread & Correct

Rules

5 "Jump" the fireman shouted to the young boy frozen with

1 fear on the window ledge of the burning building "Will you

3 catch me" the young boy cried to the men and women holding a

1, 5, 1 safety net forty feet below "Into the net" they yelled

Mustering his courage, the boy jumped safely into the net and

1 then into his mother's outstretched arms

INTERNAL PUNCTUATION

Internal Punctuation: Parentheses and Dash

1. Study each of the five rules.
   a. Key the *Learn* line(s) beneath each rule, noting how the rule is applied.
   b. Key the *Apply* line(s), using parentheses and dashes correctly.

Internal Punctuation: Parentheses

Rule 1: Use parentheses to enclose parenthetical or explanatory matter and added information. (Commas or dashes may be used instead.)

Learn 1 Vice President Gore (a Democrat) ran for the presidency in 2000.

Learn 2 The contracts (Exhibits C and D) need important revisions.

Apply 3 Sean Duncan the person with highest sales is being honored.

Apply 4 The Sixth Edition 2009 copyright date has been delivered.

Rule 2: Use parentheses to enclose identifying letters or figures of lists within a sentence.

Learn 5 Check for these errors: (1) keying, (2) spelling, and (3) grammar.

Apply 6 The focus group leaders are 1 Ramos, 2 Zahn, and 3 Pyle.

Apply 7 The order of emphasis is 1 technique and 2 speed of motions.

Rule 3: Use parentheses to enclose a name and date used as a reference.

Learn 8 Thousands of us heard the "I Have a Dream" speech (King, 1963).

Apply 9 He cited "The Gettysburg Address" Lincoln, 1863 in his report.

Apply 10 We read *The Old Curiosity Shop* Dickens, 1841 in class.

Internal Punctuation: Dash

Rule 4: Use a dash (two hyphens with no space before or after) to set off clarifying or added information, especially when it interrupts the flow of the sentence.

Learn 11 The skater--in clown's disguise--dazzled with fancy footwork.

Apply 12 Our trade discounts 10%, 15%, and 20% are the best available.

Apply 13 The gown a copy of an Italian original sells for only $150.

Rule 5: Use a dash before the author's name after a poem or quotation.

Learn 14 "All the world's a stage. . . ." --William Shakespeare

Apply 15 "I have taken all knowledge to be my province." Francis Bacon

(continued on next page)

ACTIVITY 2

Listening

Complete as directed.

Save as: CS6 ACTIVITY2

1. Open sound file *DF CS6 ACTIVITY2*, which is a set of driving directions.
2. Take notes as you listen to the directions to the Mansfield Soccer Field.
3. Close the sound file.
4. Using your notes, key the directions in sentence form.

ACTIVITY 3

Write to Learn

Complete as directed.

Save as: CS6 ACTIVITY3

1. Using word processing or voice recognition software, write a paragraph explaining how you would split a window so you can display a document in two panes.
2. Write a second ¶ explaining what a style is and how you can use the Style feature.

ACTIVITY 4

Composing

1. Read the ¶.
2. Compose a ¶ indicating what you think the results of your poll would be and what your response would be.
3. Proofread, revise, and correct.

Save as: CS6 ACTIVITY4

   If you were to take a poll of your classmates, what percent of them would believe that current TV and movie fare glamorizes violence and sex without portraying the negative consequences of immoral behavior? What percent would have the opposite belief?

ACTIVITY 5

Finding the Whole of a Number

1. Open *DF CS6 ACTIVITY5* and print the file.
2. Solve the problems as directed in the file.
3. Submit your answers.

CAREER Clusters

ACTIVITY 6

You must complete Career Exploration Activities 1–3 before completing this activity.

1. Retrieve your Career folder and find the printed Career Cluster Plan of Study for the career cluster that is your third choice.

2. Review the plan and write a paragraph or two about why you would or would not consider a career in this cluster. Print your file, save it as Career6, and keep it open.

3. After composing a paragraph or two, print a copy of your response and exchange papers with a classmate. Have the classmate offer suggestions for improving the content and correcting any errors he or she finds in your paragraph(s). Make the changes that you agree with and print a copy to turn in to your instructor. Save your file as Career6 and close it.

4. Return your folder to the storage area. When your instructor returns your paper, file it in your Career folder.

1. Open *123 BUSPLAN*. Spell-check and proofread the entire document.

2. Hyphenate the document.

3. If needed, make adjustments so the footnote appears on the correct page, ¶s and bullets are divided correctly, headings are kept with text correctly, and tables are not split between pages.

4. Insert a Table of Contents before the first page of the report. Display the headings formatted as Heading 1, Heading 2, and Heading 3. Include page numbers for each page, dot leaders to the left of the page numbers, and hyperlink the headings to the respective heading in the body or appendices.

5. Use Quick Parts to select a cover page named Cubicles. Key **Casa Di Italia** as the title of the report, **Business Plan** as the subtitle, **Michelle Calvini and Rachel Costanzo** as the authors, and the **current year** as the year.

6. Key **Casa Di Italia Business Plan** as a header on all pages except the cover page, first page of the Table of Contents, and first page of the report body.

7. Insert a page number as a footer on all pages except the cover page, first page of the Table of Contents, and first page of the report body.

8. Print the complete report, unless directed otherwise.

Integrity is having strong moral values and living by those values no matter what the circumstances may be. A person of high integrity has strong ethical standards. He/she always tries to do the right thing.

What Will You Do?

Situation 1: You just cashed your payroll check. As usual, you step away from the bank teller window to let the next person in line be waited on and start counting the money to make sure that you have the right amount. You find that two new fifty dollar bills were stuck together and that you receive fifty dollars more than you should have. What will you do?

Situation 2: You are on the Student Council Election Committee. Your best friend is running for president. She is a very honest person who works very hard at everything she does; she would make an excellent president. She is running against a person you don't like. The person copied your paper last year and then told the teacher you were the one who had copied her paper. You ended up having to write another paper and only getting half credit for it. The person was vice president this year and was very undependable.

You and another member of the Election Committee, Sandra, are counting the votes when she is called to the office. When Sandra leaves for the office, each person has the same number of votes. While she is gone you look at the remaining nine ballots and determine that the other person is going to win the election by one vote. It would be very easy to take two of the ballots and ensure that your friend wins. What will you do?

Situation 3: Steve, a good friend of yours, has always wanted to go to a very prestigious college that has high entrance requirements. He has met all the requirements except the ACT test score requirement. He didn't achieve a high enough score on the math part of the exam and is having to retake the exam. You are retaking the exam because you didn't do very well on the science part, but you did very well on the math part. During the exam you see Steve copying your math answers. Afterwards you confront him about it. He responds: "It was only a few answers. Those few answers could make the difference between my getting accepted and not getting accepted. What's the big deal?" What will you do?

Ethics: The Right Thing to Do

1. Read each situation at the left.

2. Key a brief ¶ explaining how you would handle each situation.

3. Form a group with three other students. Have each one explain how he or she would handle each of the situations.

4. Discuss the responses and see if your group can agree on one answer to each situation.

Activity 8

1. Open *123 BUSPLAN*.
2. Insert the table after the word *assumptions:* in the *Financials* section. Center the table between the side margins.
3. Print the page on which the table appears.

Save as: **123 BUSPLAN**

Activity 9

1. Open *123 BUSPLAN*.
2. On the new page after Appendix A, key **Appendix B** in Heading 1 style 2" from the top.
3. Insert the *Excel* spreadsheet at the right.
4. Key the following headings in column F:
   cell F1: **YEAR 1**
   cell F2: **9/15-9/14**
5. Calculate the yearly totals in cells F3: F15. Format dollar amounts in Accounting format and underline using Single or Double Accounting as shown.
6. Increase the vertical size and decrease the horizontal size so only rows/columns appear in *Word*.
7. Bookmark *Appendix B* and name it **APP_B**.
8. Search for *Appendix B* in the report body. Select and hyperlink it to the bookmark named *APP_B*.
9. Bookmark *Financials* (side heading before the hyperlink); name it **FINANCIALS**.
10. Use the Appendix B hyperlink to go to Appendix B. Below Appendix B, key **Return to Financials Section** in 8-pt. italic font. Hyperlink the text to the *FINANCIALS* bookmark.
11. Print the page on which the worksheet appears.

Save as: **123 BUSPLAN**

---

restaurants take reservations, one has call ahead seating, and one does not take reservations in any form. The 6 nearby Italian restaurants and their distance from Casa Di Italia are given below.

The Italian Warehouse--2.5 miles to the east

The Pepper Garden--1.3 miles to the northeast

Mike's Pasta House--1.6 miles to the west

Carbonara Ristorante--5 miles to the north

Calabro's--3.6 miles to the southwest

Sestilli's Restaurant--4.3 miles to the northwest

Quarter	Customers Each Day	Revenues Per Customer	Total Revenues
September 15 to December 14	140	$20	$252,000
December 15 to March 14	150	$20	$270,000
March 15 to June 14	155	$20	$279,000
June 15 to September 14	130	$20	$234,000

	QTR 1 9/15-12/14	QTR 2 12/15-3/14	QTR 3 3/15-6/14	QTR 4 6/15-9/14
Revenue	$252,000	$270,000	$279,000	$234,000
Cost of sales	$ 93,240	$ 99,900	$103,230	$ 86,580
Gross profit	$158,760	$170,100	$175,770	$147,420
Expenses				
Salaries and wages	$ 68,040	$ 68,040	$ 68,040	$ 68,040
Employee benefits	$ 13,860	$ 13,860	$ 13,860	$ 13,860
Direct operating expenses	$ 12,600	$ 13,500	$ 13,950	$ 11,700
Marketing	$ 6,300	$ 6,750	$ 6,975	$ 5,850
Energy and utility service	$ 10,080	$ 10,800	$ 11,160	$ 9,360
Administrative and general	$ 9,576	$ 10,260	$ 10,602	$ 8,892
Repairs and maintenance	$ 5,040	$ 5,400	$ 5,580	$ 4,680
Building costs	$ 15,624	$ 15,624	$ 15,624	$ 15,624
Total expenses	$141,120	$144,234	$145,791	$138,006
Net income	$ 17,640	$ 25,866	$ 29,979	$ 9,414

UNIT 17
Lessons 64-65
Build Keyboarding Skill

Lesson 64   KEYING TECHNIQUE

OBJECTIVES
- To improve keying techniques.
- To improve keying speed and control.

64A-65A

Conditioning Practice
Key each line twice.

alphabet	1	Jack Lopez will attend the quality frog exhibits over the summer.
figures	2	Tim's score was 79 percent; he missed Numbers 18, 26, 30, and 45.
speed	3	Helena may blame the men for the problem with the neighbor's dog.

gwam 1' | 1 | 2 | 3 | 4 | 5 | 6 | 7 | 8 | 9 | 10 | 11 | 12 | 13 |

64B   Skill Building

Keying Skill: Speed
Key each line twice.

Balanced-hand words of 2-5 letters

1 if me go he so us to am or by an of is to row she box air pay the

2 dig got due map jam own she box ant busy when city fish half rush

3 goal down dial firm keys pens rock odor sick soap tubs wish title

4 to do|to us|by the|if they|held a|the pen|their dog|is it|to make

5 a big fox|do the work|the gown is|when is it|he may go|a rich man

6 by the chair|he may make|did he spend|for the girls|for the firms

7 The maid may make the usual visit to the dock to work on the map.

8 Dick and Jay paid the busy man to go to the lake to fix the dock.

9 The girls may visit them when they go to the city to pay the man.

gwam 1' | 1 | 2 | 3 | 4 | 5 | 6 | 7 | 8 | 9 | 10 | 11 | 12 | 13 |

64C   Skill Building

Technique: Number Keys/Tab

Key each line twice (key number, tap TAB, and key next number).

Concentrate on figure location; quick tab spacing; eyes on copy.

264	189	357	509	768	142	642	135	9,607
258	147	630	911	828	376	475	390	1,425
763	905	481	208	913	475	609	173	2,458

gwam 1' | 1 | 2 | 3 | 4 | 5 | 6 | 7 |

Activity 6

1. Open *123 BUSPLAN*.
2. Insert a page break at the end of the business plan.
3. On the new page, key *Appendix A 2"* from the top of the page in Heading 1 style.
4. Key the comment card at the right. You decide the layout and format of the card.
5. Bookmark *Appendix A* and name it **APP_A**.
6. Search for *Appendix A* in the report body. Select and hyperlink it to the Bookmark named *APP_A*.
7. Bookmark *Quality Control* (side heading before the hyperlink); name it **QUAL_CONTROL**.
8. Use the Appendix A hyperlink to go to Appendix A. Below Appendix A, key **Return to Quality Control** section in 8-pt. italic font. Hyperlink the text to the *QUAL_CONTROL* bookmark.
9. Print Appendix A.

Save as: 123 BUSPLAN

Activity 7

1. Open *123 BUSPLAN*.
2. Key the text after the *Target Market* section.
3. Format *Direct Competition* in Heading 2 style.

Proofreading Alert

The rough-draft copy contains embedded errors. Proofread your work carefully, checking to make sure all errors have been corrected.

4. Print the page(s) on which this text appears.

Save as: 123 BUSPLAN

Dear Customer:

Your opinions are very important to the owners and employees of Casa Di Italia. Will you, therefore, take a moment to complete this card? Thank you.

Michelle Calvini and Rachel Costanzo, Owners

Rate the quality of the food:

Superior		Adequate		Poor
5	4	3	2	1

Rate the quality of the service:

Superior		Adequate		Poor
5	4	3	2	1

Please tell us what we did that pleased or did not please you: _____

_____

_____

Direct Competition

Casa Di Italia will face strong competition from area restaurants, especially Italian restaurants, and specialty food stores. There is won store specializing in Italian foods within 2 miles of our location. Only on-street parking is available to its customers. There are 6 Italian restaurants within a 5-mile radius of Casa Di Italia. Four of these are well established and two have opened within the past 2 years. Spot checks during peak dining hours reveal that all but one is attracting customers in adequate or large numbers. Four of the restaurants offer free parking in a restaurant lot, one offers valet parking only, and one has only on street parking available. One restaurants serves high priced meals, four serve moderately priced meals, and one offers low priced meals. None of these restaurants has a specialty food store housed within the restaurant. Four

(continued on next page)

Speed Forcing Drill

Key each line once at top speed. If you finish all lines before time is called, key them again, trying to go faster.

Emphasis: high-frequency balanced-hand words

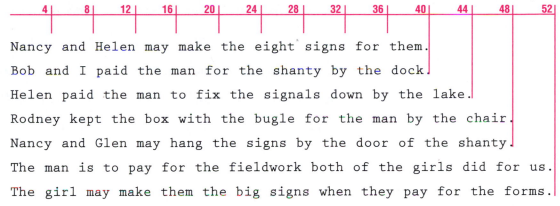

	4	8	12	16	20	24	28	32	36	40	44	48	52

Nancy and Helen may make the eight signs for them.

Bob and I paid the man for the shanty by the dock.

Helen paid the man to fix the signals down by the lake.

Rodney kept the box with the bugle for the man by the chair.

Nancy and Glen may hang the signs by the door of the shanty.

The man is to pay for the fieldwork both of the girls did for us.

The girl may make them the big signs when they pay for the forms.

gwam 15" | 4 | 8 | 12 | 16 | 20 | 24 | 28 | 32 | 36 | 40 | 44 | 48 | 52 |

Skill Check

1. Key a 1' timing on ¶ 1; determine *gwam*.
2. Add 2–4 *gwam* to the rate attained in step 1, and note quarter-minute checkpoints from the chart below.
3. Key two 1' guided timings on ¶ 1 to increase speed.
4. Practice ¶ 2 in the same way.
5. Key two 3' timings on ¶s 1 and 2 combined; count *gwam* and determine errors.

Quarter-Minute Checkpoints

gwam	1/4'	1/2'	3/4'	1'
24	6	12	18	24
28	7	14	21	28
32	8	16	24	32
36	9	18	27	36
40	10	20	30	40
44	11	22	33	44
48	12	24	36	48
52	13	26	39	52
56	14	28	42	56
60	15	30	45	60

A   all letters used   MicroPace   gwam   1' | 3'

	1'	3'
When you talk about famous Americans, it doesn't take	4	2
long to come up with a long list. However, some individuals would	8	5
appear on nearly everyone's list. George Washington would be one	13	8
of those on most people's list. He is often referred to as the	17	10
Father of our Country because of the role he played in the Ameri-	21	13
can Revolution and being our first president.	24	15
Abraham Lincoln would also be included on most lists. He is	29	17
often referred to as Honest Abe. He always gave the extra ef-	33	20
fort. Because of this, he was successful. Whether the job was	37	22
splitting logs, being a lawyer, or being president, Lincoln gave	42	25
it his best. Dealing with the Civil War required a president who	46	28
gave his best.	47	28
Harriet Tubman is recognized as another prominent individ-	51	31
ual. She risked her own life for the freedom of others. After	55	33
becoming a free woman in the North, she returned to the South to	60	36
assist several hundred slaves escape. She also took part in the	64	38
Civil War, serving the country as a Union spy and scout.	68	41

gwam 1' | 1 | 2 | 3 | 4 | 5 | 6 | 7 | 8 | 9 | 10 | 11 | 12 | 13 |
gwam 3' | 1 | | 2 | | 3 | | 4 |

Activity 4

1. Open *123 BUSPLAN* and insert the text after ¶ 2 of the *Baldwin Hills Growth* section.
2. Insert *Market Share* and apply Heading 1 style to it. Apply Heading 2 style *Target Market*.
3. Select a character for bulleted items. Apply it to the bullets in this insert and to other bulleted items in the business plan.

Proofreading Alert

The rough-draft copy contains one embedded error. Proofread your work carefully, checking to make sure all errors have been corrected.

4. Print the page(s) on which this inserted text appears.

Save as: 123 BUSPLAN

Activity 5

1. Open *123 BUSPLAN*.
2. Move the *Management Structure* section to make it the last section in *Management and Organization*.
3. Print the page(s) on which the *Management Structure* section appears.

Save as: 123 BUSPLAN

Casa Di Italia will develop a strong presence in the Baldwin Hills area by serving high-quality, healthy Italian entrees at moderate prices and providing superior service. The competitive advantage will be strengthened by the award-winning chef that/who has agreed to work at Casa Di Italia, ~~and the specialty retail area that will provide quality products.~~

Target Market

Casa Di Italia target's a variety of people, but for the most part they have these characteristics:

(change to bulleted list)

1. Located in the Baldwin Hills area
2. Make buying decisions based on quality, service, and convenience
3. Part of the middle to upper socioeconomic group
4. Between the ages of 25 and 70
5. Married or dating couples

The census data for ~~the~~ Young County shows the following characteristics for the population in the restaurant's primary service area:

- ❑ 57% of the population is between the ages 25 and 69
- ❑ 75% or more households have an annual income of $45,000 or higher *(3)*
- ❑ 49% of the population is married
- ❑ Italian heritage is the third-highest ethnic group in Young County
- ❑ 17% of the families are working married couples with children at home
- ❑ 13% of the families are working married couples with no children at home
- ❑ 20% of the households are singles ~~and~~ living ~~at home~~ alone

OBJECTIVES
- To improve keying techniques.
- To improve keying speed and control.

65B   Skill Building

Technique: Letter Keys

Key each line twice.

One-hand words of 2–5 letters

1 be no up we at in ax my as on add bag car dad war tax sat saw see

2 dad oil egg lip cab joy fee pop art you age him sad mom seat look

3 save milk race pull star pink grade onion grass polio serve pupil

4 as my│at a rate│we are│no war│get set│at my best│you were│a great

5 as few│you set a date│my card│water tax│act on a│tax date│in case

6 my only date│water rate│my tax case│tax fact│my best date│my card

7 No, you are free only after I act on a rate on a state water tax.

8 Get him my extra database only after you set up exact test dates.

9 You set my area tax rate after a great state case on a water tax.

gwam 1' │ 1 │ 2 │ 3 │ 4 │ 5 │ 6 │ 7 │ 8 │ 9 │ 10 │ 11 │ 12 │ 13 │

65C   Skill Building

Speed Forcing Drill

Key each line once at top speed. If you finish all lines before time is called, key them again, trying to go faster.

Emphasis: high-frequency balanced-hand words

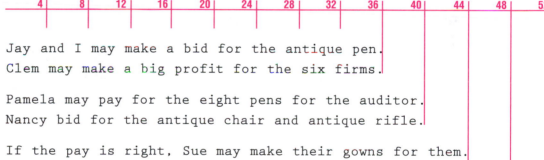

```
            4    8    12   16   20   24   28   32   36   40   44   48   52

Jay and I may make a bid for the antique pen.
Clem may make a big profit for the six firms.

Pamela may pay for the eight pens for the auditor.
Nancy bid for the antique chair and antique rifle.

If the pay is right, Sue may make their gowns for them.
When did the auditor sign the audit forms for the city?

Laurie kept the men busy with the work down by the big lake.
Diana may go with us to the city to pay them for their work.

Did the firm bid for the right to the land downtown by city hall?
Jay may suspend the men as a penalty for their work on the docks.
```

gwam 15" │ 4 │ 8 │ 12 │ 16 │ 20 │ 24 │ 28 │ 32 │ 36 │ 40 │ 44 │ 48 │ 52 │

Activity 3

1. Open *123 BUSPLAN* and insert the text before the side heading *Baldwin Hills Growth*.
2. Apply appropriate styles to headings.
3. Insert a reference for footnote #1 at the end of the first ¶, and key the following footnote using the same font and size as the text in the business plan:

[1]National data used in the business plan are from the National Restaurant Association obtained at http://www.restaurant.org/research in November 2007.

Note: Do not be concerned if the footnote "splits" between two pages. You will make adjustments as necessary in Activity 10.

Proofreading Alert

The rough-draft copy contains two embedded errors. Proofread your work carefully, checking to make sure all errors have been corrected.

4. Print the page(s) on which *Industry Analysis* and *National Growth* sections appear.

Save as: 123 BUSPLAN

Industry Analysis

Casa Di Italia will be *is* part of an industry that has established itself as an integral part of an American lifestyle. More than 45% of today's food dollar is spent away from home and almost 1/2 *half* of all adults are restaurant patrons on a typical day. Children, *teenagers,* and young adults are more familiar with restaurants and knew cuisines than ever before and are increasing their restaurant visits *spending*. The same is true for the baby boomers and members of the older generations who have been empowered by strong *economic* growth and gains in income.

National Data

The restaurant industry has enjoyed a 66.5% increase in sales from 1997 to 2007, from $322.5 billion to an estimated $536.9 billion. Eating places accounted for an estimated $363 billion (67.6%) of the estimated 2007 sales. This *These* demand for restaurant service is expected to remain strong in the near future since for out of five (80%) of consumers agree that going out to a restaurant is a better way to use their leisure time than cooking and cleaning up. In 2005, the average houshold *household* expenditure for food away from home was $2,634, or $1,054 per person.

Technique: Number Keys/TAB

1. Set tabs at 2" and 4".
2. Key the copy at the right.

Concentrate on figure location; quick tab spacing; eyes on copy.

910 Ponderosa Drive	301 Princeton Way	608 Peachwood Drive
283 Kincaid Court	201 Neilson Terrace	99 Laura Lee Lane
476 Rio Grande Court	342 Remington Ridge	658 Santiago Road
5132 Grey Stone Court	256 Windsor Gardens	790 Blue Ridge Lane
4765 Cherokee Way	756 Woodward Court	231 Meeker Street
908 Glenridge Lane	809 Greenbriar Drive	106 Hanaford Court
576 Red Rock Avenue	142 Timberline Drive	235 Eagles Nest Road
489 Parkview Avenue	357 Gardenia Drive	498 Hancock Court

Skill Check

1. Key a 1' timing on ¶ 1; determine *gwam*.
2. Add 2–4 *gwam* to the rate attained in step 1, and note quarter-minute checkpoints from the chart below.
3. Key two 1' guided timings on ¶ 1 to increase speed.
4. Practice ¶ 2 in the same way.
5. Take two 3' timings on ¶s 1 and 2 combined; determine *gwam* and number of errors.

Quarter-Minute Checkpoints

gwam	1/4'	1/2'	3/4'	1'
24	6	12	18	24
28	7	14	21	28
32	8	16	24	32
36	9	18	27	36
40	10	20	30	40
44	11	22	33	44
48	12	24	36	48
52	13	26	39	52
56	14	28	42	56
60	15	30	45	60

A — all letters used — **MicroPace**

	gwam	3'	5'

One of the great statesmen of our nation was Benjamin | 4 | 2
Franklin. Among other things, the man is quite well known for his | 8 | 5
work as an author, as a philosopher, as a scientist, and as a | 12 | 7
diplomat and representative of our country. Recognized as one of | 16 | 10
the excellent leaders of the Revolution, he is considered a founding | 21 | 13
father of the United States. His name can be seen on the | 25 | 15
Declaration of Independence as well as the United States | 29 | 17
Constitution. | 29 | 18

Some of the things that Franklin is given the credit for | 33 | 20
include the Franklin stove, the lightning rod, bifocals, and many, | 38 | 23
many witty quotes in his almanac. Franklin once said, "If you | 42 | 25
would not be forgotten as soon as you are dead, either write | 46 | 27
something worth reading or do things worth the writing." Because | 50 | 30
of his many personal accomplishments and the written documents | 54 | 33
that his signature appears on, Mr. Franklin will not likely be | 58 | 35
forgotten very soon! He is a role model that all Americans should | 63 | 38
try to model their life after. | 65 | 39

gwam | 3' | 1 | 2 | 3 | 4
| 5' | 1 | 2 | 3

OBJECTIVES

- To prepare a long report with a title page, table of contents, and appendices.
- To demonstrate your ability to integrate your knowledge and skills.

123–128A

Conditioning Practice

Key each line twice.

alphabet	1	Zeke opened jam jars quickly but avoided ruining the waxed floor.
fig/sym	2	I wrote checks 398-430 and 432-457 in July and 458-461 in August.
speed	3	Jane may work with the girls to make the ritual for the sorority.

| gwam | 1' | 1 | 2 | 3 | 4 | 5 | 6 | 7 | 8 | 9 | 10 | 11 | 12 |

123–128B

Business Plan

Activity 1

1. Complete steps 1–5.
2. Print pp. 1 and 9 of the business plan.

Save as: 123 BUSPLAN

1. Open *DF 123 BUSPLAN* and preview the business plan quickly to familiarize yourself with its content, organization, and length.
2. Check for inconsistencies in spacing and ¶ indentations, and for spelling errors. Key a list of the errors you find.

Save as: 123 ACTIVITY1

3. Correct the errors you found.
4. Use the format guides on p. 380 to verify margin settings, line spacing, etc.
5. Apply title and heading styles as follows:
   - Use Title style for the title on page 1 that is centered and keyed in bold font.
   - Use Heading 1 style for headings that are centered in regular font.
   - Use Heading 2 style for all side headings except these: *Public Areas, Employee Areas, The Head Chef*, and *The Assistant Chef*. These four side headings should be formatted in Heading 3 style.

Activity 2

1. Open *123 BUSPLAN* and key the text at the right after the first ¶ of the business plan.
2. Apply Heading 2 style to the side headings.

Proofreading Alert

The rough-draft copy contains one embedded error; correct it as you process the copy.

3. Print p. 1.

Save as: 123 BUSPLAN

Mission Statement

The mission of Casa Di Italia is to serve and sell hi-quality Italian foods at moderate prices in a friendly, ~~family type~~ healthy atmosphere that offers ~~good~~ superior service to customers.

Vision Statement

Within 5 years, Casa Di Italia ~~hopes to~~ will be recognized as one of the top 5 moderately priced Italian restaurants in the Brenthall area.

Office Features 7

For each activity, read and learn the feature described, then follow instructions at the left.

Activity 1

Review Table Formatting Features

Open the file *DF OF7 ACTIVITY1* and change the table format to make it appear as shown at the right. Center the table on the page.

Save as: **OF7 ACTIVITY1**

MAJOR LEAGUE BASEBALL					
National League			American League		
East	West	Central	East	West	Central
Atlanta Florida Montreal New York Philadelphia	Arizona Colorado Los Angeles San Diego San Francisco	Chicago Cincinnati Houston Milwaukee Pittsburgh St. Louis	Baltimore Boston New York Tampa Bay Toronto	Anaheim Oakland Seattle Texas	Chicago Cleveland Detroit Kansas City Minnesota

Activity 2

Portrait/Landscape Orientation

WP • Page Layout/Page Setup/Orientation

1. Open *OF7 ACTIVITY1*.
2. Change the page orientation to landscape.

Save as: **OF7 ACTIVITY2**

Portrait orientation. The way text is printed on a page determines what type of orientation is used. Portrait orientation, sometimes referred to as vertical – 8 ½" x 11", has the short edge of the paper at the top of the page.

> Portrait

Landscape orientation. Landscape orientation, sometimes referred to as horizontal – 11" x 8 ½", has the wider edge of the paper at the top of the page. When a table is too wide to fit on the page in portrait orientation, switching to the landscape orientation gives 2 ½" more inches to fit the table.

> Landscape

Activity 3

AutoFit Contents/AutoFit Window

WP • Table Tools/Layout/Cell Size/AutoFit

1. Open *OF7 ACTIVITY2*.
2. Change the page orientation to portrait.
3. Apply AutoFit Contents.
4. Change the page orientation to landscape.
5. Apply AutoFit Window.

Save as: **OF7 ACTIVITY3**

AutoFit Contents. Automatically resizes the column widths based on the text in each column. AutoFit Contents leaves less white space in the columns, but more white space in the margins.

> AutoFit Contents

AutoFit Window. Automatically resizes the column widths to give maximum white space between columns. AutoFit Window leaves more white space in the columns but less in the margins.

> AutoFit Window

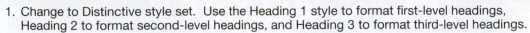

1. Change to Distinctive style set. Use the Heading 1 style to format first-level headings, Heading 2 to format second-level headings, and Heading 3 to format third-level headings.
2. Insert a page break at the beginning of the document to create a blank page 1, and move the insertion point to the first line of page 1.
3. Insert a table of contents by selecting the built-in Automatic Table 2 style.
4. Print the table of contents only, and save the document as *OF12 ACTIVITY6A*.
5. If needed, open *OF12 ACTIVITY6A*.
6. Remove the table of contents.
7. Insert a new table of contents with headings that serve as hyperlinks and page numbers. Insert dot leaders between the headings and the page numbers.
8. Key **Table of Contents** in Title style.
9. Verify that the hyperlinks work as intended.
10. Print the table of contents only, and save the document as *OF12 ACTIVITY6B*.

Activity 7

Create *Excel* Spreadsheet in a *Word* Document

WP • Insert/Tables/Excel Spreadsheet

Open *DF OF12 ACTIVITY7* and complete the steps as directed in the file

Save as: **OF12 ACTIVITY7**

You can create an *Excel* spreadsheet in an open *Word* document. When the blank (new) worksheet is opened, the *Excel* ribbons, tabs, and commands replace those used with *Word*. Create the worksheet using the *Excel* commands.

You can return to *Word* by clicking outside the worksheet area. You can return to *Excel*

by double-clicking inside the table grid. While in *Excel*, the worksheet can be sized as needed by dragging the selection handles to the desired location. This is helpful if you are trying to delete blank rows and columns. While in *Word*, the worksheet can be centered horizontally by selecting it and using the Center Align command.

Quarter	East	West	North	South	Total
1	$22,396	$29,753	$32,901	$30,502	
2	$27,098	$25,987	$31,208	$26,424	
3	$26,016	$25,736	$29,375	$30,126	
4	$28,554	$31,743	$25,380	$31,673	
Totals					

Activity 8

Apply What You Have Learned

1. Open *DF OF12 ACTIVITY8*.
2. Format the report title in Title style, the centered headings in Heading 1 style, the side headings in Heading 2, and the paragraph headings in the *Athletic Trainers* section in Heading 3.
3. Change the style set to Modern, color combinations to Civic, and font combinations to Aspect.
4. Insert a Table of Contents at the beginning of the file consisting of Headings 1, 2, and 3. Include page numbers, dot leaders, and headings that are hyperlinks.
5. Insert a section break above the report title, and key **Table of Contents** on the first line of the added page. Format it in Title style and position it about 2" from the top.
6. Insert page numbers at the bottom center on each page. The table of contents should be numbered with lowercase Roman numerals.

Save as: **OF12 ACTIVITY8**

Activity 4

Split Cells/Merge Cells

- TableTools/Layout/ Merge/Merge or Split Cells

1. Open the *DF OF7 ACTIVITY4* file.
2. Finish keying any columns that are incomplete.
3. Use the Split Cells and Merge Cells features to complete the formatting. (You will shade the table as part of Activity 5.)
4. Center the table vertically and horizontally.

Save as: OF7 ACTIVITY4

Use the Split Cells table feature to split (divide) cells horizontally or vertically.

Use the Merge Cells table feature to merge (join) cells horizontally or vertically.

ACCOUNTING MAJOR					
General Electives (40 credits)				Business Core (32 credits)	Accounting Requirements (28 credits)
Category I (9 Credits)	Category II (9 Credits)	Category III (11 Credits)	Category IV (11 Credits)	Acct 201 Acct 202 Bcom 206 Bcom 207 MIS 240 Bsad 300 Bsad 305 Fin 320 Mktg 330 Mgmt 340 Mgmt 341 Mgmt 449	Acct 301 Acct 302 Acct 314 Acct 315 Acct 317 Acct 321 Acct 450 Acct 460 Fin 326 Fin 327
CJ 202 Math 111 Math 245	Biol 102 Chem 101 Geog 104	Econ 103 Econ 104 Psyc 100 Soc 101	No specific courses required.		
Category I – Communications and Analytical Skills Category II – Natural Sciences Category III – Social Sciences Category IV – Humanities					

Activity 5

Shading

- TableTools/Design/Table Styles/Shading/Select Color

1. Open *DF OF7 ACTIVITY5*. Shade lines of the table as shown.

Save as: OF7 ACTIVITY5A

2. Open *OF7 ACTIVITY3* (Activity 3 file). Shade *National League* red. Shade *American League* blue.
3. For both the National and American Leagues; shade *East* yellow, *West* green, and *Central* purple.

Save as: OF7 ACTIVITY5B

4. Open the Activity 4 file (*OF7 ACTIVITY4*). Apply shading as shown in Activity 4, above.

Save as: OF7 ACTIVITY5C

Use the Shading feature to enhance the appearance of tables to make them easier to read. The Shading feature allows you to fill in areas of the table with varying shades of color.

Shading covers the selected area. It may be the entire table or a single cell, column, or row within a table.

SEVEN WONDERS OF THE WORLD		
Ancient	New	
	Wonder	Location
Colossus of Rhodes	Chichen Itza Pyramid	Mexico
Great Pyramid of Giza	Colosseum	Italy
Hanging Gardens of Babylon	Great Wall of China	China
Lighthouse of Alexandria	Machu Picchu	Peru
Mausoleum at Halicarnassus	Petra	Jordan
Statue of Zeus at Olympia	Statue of Christ Redeemer	Brazil
Temple of Artemis at Ephesus	Taj Mahal	India

Source: http://www.new7wonders.com

Activity 5

Bookmarks and Hyperlinks

WP
- Insert/Links/Bookmark or Hyperlink

Open *DF OF12 ACTIVITY5* and follow the directions in the file to use bookmarks and hyperlinks.

Save as: OF12 ACTIVITY5

Bookmarks assign a name to a specific point in a document. Hyperlinks create a link from a point in the document to the bookmark. For example, if (*Refer to Appendix A*) appears in the body of a report and you want to make it easy for the reader to move quickly to Appendix A at that point, you can bookmark the title *Appendix A* in the appendices and then hyperlink the text (*Refer to Appendix A*) in the body of the report. By clicking on the

hyperlink, the reader would move directly to Appendix A, the bookmarked text.

If you want the reader to be able to quickly return to the hyperlink, you can bookmark text near the hyperlinked text in the report body and add text such as *Return to Report* at the end of *Appendix A* so readers can click it to quickly return to the appropriate point in the report body they were reading before navigating to the *Appendix A* bookmark.

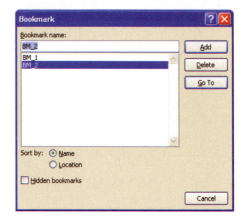

Activity 6

Table of Contents

WP
- References/Table of Contents/Table of Contents

Open *DF OF12 ACTIVITY6* and follow the directions in steps 1–10.

A table of contents (TOC) can be created automatically by choosing the heading styles of the headings within the report body that are to appear in the TOC. *Word* searches for the headings that match the styles chosen, formats and indents the TOC entry according to the heading level, and then inserts the TOC into the document at the insertion point.

Each heading in the TOC can serve as a hyperlink to the corresponding heading in

the report body. The page number on which the heading appears within the report body can be printed in the TOC, right-aligned with or without a leader tab. The TOC can contain either page numbers or hyperlinks or both.

TOCs can be updated if the headings or page numbers change, and they can be removed easily.

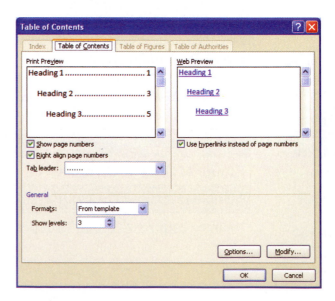

(continued on next page)

Activity 6

Borders

- TableTools/Design/Table Styles/Borders/Select Border

1. Open file *DF OF7 ACTIVITY6* from the data files. Complete the table so that it appears as shown at the right.
2. Increase the row height of the heading rows to enhance the appearance.
3. Bold team names and put a bolder border around the 5th grade Altoona games.

Save as: OF7 ACTIVITY6A

4. Open *OF7 ACTIVITY6A*. Change the orientation to landscape and apply AutoFit Window. Change margins to Narrow to fit table on page.

Save as: OF7 ACTIVITY6B

Use the Borders feature to enhance the appearance and readability of tables. The Borders feature allows a border to be added around an entire table or selected parts of it.

FIFTH & SIXTH GRADE TOURNAMENT SCHEDULE					
Altoona					
February 26					
Middle School Gym 5th Grade		Time	High School Gym 6th Grade		
Score	Teams		Teams	Score	
	Bruce Somerset	9:00	Bruce Somerset		
	St. Croix Central St. Croix Falls		St. Croix Central St. Croix Falls		
	Menomonie Rice Lake	10:10	Menomonie Rice Lake		
	Altoona Eau Claire		Altoona Eau Claire		
	St. Croix Falls Bruce	11:20	St. Croix Falls Bruce		
	St. Croix Central Somerset		St. Croix Central Somerset		
	Rice Lake Eau Claire	12:30	Rice Lake Eau Claire		
	Menomonie Altoona		Menomonie Altoona		
	St. Croix Falls Somerset	1:40	St. Croix Falls Somerset		
	St. Croix Central Bruce		ST. Croix Central Bruce		
	Rice Lake Altoona	2:50	Rice Lake Altoona		
	Menomonie Eau Claire		Menomonie Eau Claire		

Activity 7

Gridlines

- TableTools/Layout/Table/ View Gridlines

Open *OF7 ACTIVITY5A*; apply the No border setting; then hide the gridlines.

Save as: OF7 ACTIVITY7

When you remove table borders (No Border or None), light blue lines, called gridlines, replace the borders. These gridlines give you a visual guide as you work with the table; they do not print. The blue gridlines can be turned off by activating the **Hide Gridlines** option. This allows you to see what the table will look like when it is printed.

Activity 3

Show/Hide ¶

WP • Home/Paragraph/¶

1. Key the text using bullets.
2. Show formatting marks and refer to them to answer these questions below the text you keyed:
   a. How many times was ENTER tapped?
   b. How many tabs appear in the copy?
   c. How many times was the Space Bar tapped twice before keying a character?

Save as: **OF12 ACTIVITY3**

Word processing documents contain invisible formatting marks that can be displayed. Commonly used marks are:

¶ to show a new line,
→ to show a tab,
· to show a space between words.

Being able to see the formatting marks is helpful when editing a document or solving formatting problems. The formatting marks do not print.

```
¶
¶
The·¶·mark·indicates·there·are¶
two·blank·lines··above·this¶
·text·and·that·ENTER·was·tapped¶
·at·the·end·of·each·line.·¶
The·→··indicates·that·the··→··TAB¶
·key·was·tapped·after·two·occurrences¶
·of·the·word·THE·in·line·5.··The·dots¶
·indicate···the·number·of·spaces¶
·entered.··There·are·three·spaces¶
·between·INDICATE·and·THE·in¶
·line·8.¶
```

You can incorporate fitness into your daily routine by doing these three activities:
• Walk up stairs for one minute each day instead of taking the elevator. Within a year you should be a pound lighter without changing any other habits.
• Walk the dog, don't just watch the dog walk. In a nutshell–get moving!
• Perform at least 30 minutes of moderate activity each day. If necessary, do the 30 minutes in 10-minute intervals.

Activity 4

Change Styles

WP • Home/Styles/Change Styles

1. Open *DF OF12 ACTIVITY4*.
2. Change the style set to Formal, the color combinations to Foundry, and the font combinations to Foundry.
3. Complete the steps at the right.

A style is a predefined set of formatting options that have been named and saved so they can be used again to save time and add consistency to a document. In previous activities, you have used the *Office 2007* style set, the default style.

When a style set is used, many formatting commands are applied at one time. For example, when you select the Title style within the *Office 2007* style set, the title is formatted in 26-pt. Cambria font (Dark Blue, Text 2) with a bottom border; the paragraph spacing after the text is set to 15 pts.; and the horizontal alignment is set to left. All these formatting commands are applied immediately in just one step.

If you prefer, the style set can be changed from *Office 2007* style set to one of many built-in style sets, or you can create a different one. Within each built-in style set, you can choose from an array of color combinations and font combinations available in the Change Styles drop-down list.

1. Format *Career Opportunities in Sports Medicine* on p. 1 in Title style.
2. Format the two bold side headings in Heading 1 style.
3. Format the remaining side headings in Strong style.
4. Format paragraph headings in Subtle Emphasis style.

Save as: **OF12 ACTIVITY4A**

1. Open *OF12 ACTIVITY4A*.
2. Change the style, colors, and fonts to sets of your choice.

Save as: **OF12 ACTIVITY4B**

Format Guide: Tables

Tables are used to organize and present information in a concise, logical way to make it easy for the reader to understand and analyze it. The table format can make information easier or more difficult to understand.

You will be required to use the Table word processing features presented in OF 4 (pp. 95–98) and OF 7 (pp. 193–195) to format the tables in this unit. Most of the tables are already organized; you simply need to create them to look like the examples in the text. However, some of the tables will require you to use your decision-making skills to organize the information before formatting and keying them. To complete this unit, you will need to understand the format features given below.

Table Format Features

Landscape orientation. When tables contain a large number of columns and are too wide to fit on the page, the page orientation can be changed from portrait (vertical – 8½" × 11") to landscape (horizontal – 11" × 8½").

Vertical placement. Center tables vertically. The top and bottom margins will be equal.

Horizontal placement. Center tables horizontally. The left and right margins will be equal.

Column width and row height. Adjust column width and row height to put more white space around data in the rows and columns. Additional white space makes data easier to read.

Vertical alignment. Within rows, data may be aligned at the top, center, or bottom. Title rows most often use center alignment. Data rows usually are either center- or bottom-aligned.

Horizontal alignment. Within columns, words may be left-aligned or center-aligned. Whole numbers are right-aligned if a column total is shown; decimal numbers are decimal-aligned. Other figures may be center-aligned.

Delete/Insert rows and/or columns. Delete empty rows or columns wherever they occur in a table. Also, insert a row(s) as needed above or below an existing row. Insert a column(s) to the left or right of an existing column as needed.

Merge/Split cells. To make a table attractive and easy to read, merge (join) two or more cells into one cell for the main title, source note, and other data as needed. Any existing cell can be split (divided) into two or more smaller cells if necessary.

AutoFit Contents. To save space, resize the columns to the size of the longest entry in the column automatically with the AutoFit Contents feature.

AutoFit Window. To use the entire page to attractively display information, resize the columns to maximum width automatically with the AutoFit Window feature.

Shading. Use shading (colors) to enhance table appearance and to highlight selected columns, rows, or individual cells.

Borders. Borders may be applied around an entire table or around cells, rows, or columns within a table. Borders improve appearance as well as highlight the data within them.

Sort. In a table column, text can be sorted alphabetically in ascending (A to Z) or descending (Z to A) order. Also, numbers and dates can be sorted numerically (chronologically), in either ascending or descending order.

Note: When you complete a table in this unit, check your work. Correct all spelling, keying, and formatting errors before closing or printing the file.

Office Features 12

Activity 1

Split Window

Complete steps 1–4.

Save as: OF12 ACTIVITY1

Often it is helpful to be able to see two parts of a document that do not appear in the same window. The Split Window feature is used to display a document in two panes, each with its own scroll bars to help you move around in each pane. If needed, the panes can be resized.

This feature can be used when you copy or move text between parts of a long document or when you need to see text that is not visible in the window where you are keying.

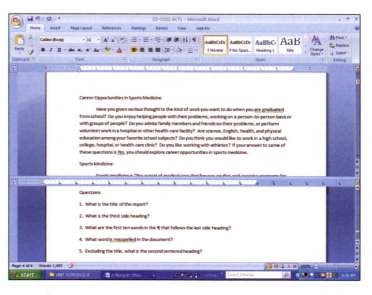

1. Open *DF OF12 ACTIVITY1* and split the window.
2. In the lower pane, find *Questions*.
3. Move through the text in the top pane to find the answers to the five questions that appear in the bottom pane, and key your answers in the space between the questions.
4. Move the questions and your answers to the top of p. 1 and print p.1.

Activity 2

Go To

WP • Home/Editing/Find or Replace/Go To

Complete steps 1–4.

Save as: OF12 ACTIVITY2

A quick way to move to a certain page or point in a long document is to use the Go To command. This command can be used to go directly to a specific page, comment, footnote, or bookmark, for example.

1. Open *DF OF12 ACTIVITY2* and split the window.
2. In the lower pane, find *Questions*.
3. Answer the questions by using Go To to move through the text in the top pane.
4. Print the page with the questions and your answers.

Lesson 66 — IMPROVE TABLE FORMATTING SKILLS

OBJECTIVES
- To improve table formatting skills.
- To improve language skills.

66A–71A

Conditioning Practice

Key each line twice.

alphabet	1	Karla justified a very low quiz score by explaining her problems.
fig/sym	2	My property tax increased by 12.7% ($486); I paid $3,590 in 2001.
speed	3	They may work with us to make a profit for the eighty auto firms.

gwam 1' | 1 | 2 | 3 | 4 | 5 | 6 | 7 | 8 | 9 | 10 | 11 | 12 | 13 |

66B — Language Skills

Language Skills: Word Choice

1. Study the spelling and definitions of the words.
2. Key all *Learn* and *Apply* lines, choosing the correct word in the apply lines.

Save as: 66B CHOICE

> **do** (vb) to bring about; to carry out
>
> **due** (adj) owed or owing as a debt; having reached the date for payment
>
> **for** (prep/conj) used to indicate purpose; on behalf of; because; because of
>
> **four** (n) the fourth in a set or series

Learn 1 **Do** you know when the three library books are **due**?
Apply 2 The next payment will be (do, due) on Tuesday, March 24.
Apply 3 I (do, due) not know when I will be available to meet again.

Learn 1 The **four** men asked **for** a salary increase **for** the next **four** years.
Apply 2 The manager left (for, four) an hour just before (for, four) o'clock.
Apply 3 The (for, four) coaches were mad after waiting (for, four) an hour.

66C — Formatting

Review Table Formatting

Key Tables 1–3 shown at right and on p. 198.

Table 1

1. Determine the number of rows and columns needed.
2. Create a table and fill in the information. Adjust column widths as needed.
3. Center and bold the main title and column headings.
4. Change the row height to 0.35" for all rows.
5. Change alignment to *Center* for the column headings and to *Bottom Left* for all other rows.
6. Center the table on the page.

Save as: 66C TABLE1

CIVIL WAR PERSONALITIES

Name	Position
Davis, Jefferson	Confederate Commander in Chief
Grant, Ulysses S.	Union Army Commanding General
Jackson, Stonewall	Confederate Army General
Johnston, Joseph E.	Confederate Army General
Lee, Robert E.	Confederate Army Commanding General
Lincoln, Abraham	Union Commander in Chief
Longstreet, James	Confederate Army General
Mead, George	Union Army General
Sheridan, Philip H.	Union Army General
Sherman, William T.	Union Army General
Stuart, J. E. B. (Jeb)	Confederate Army General
Thomas, George H.	Union Army General

Source: *Encyclopedia Americana*, Vol. 6 (Danbury, CT: Grolier Incorporated, 2001), pp. 789–790.

Business Plan

A business plan is a blueprint for a company. Developing a business plan helps entrepreneurs take an objective, critical look at a business. A well-written plan communicates the company's ideas and message to lenders, investors, and employees. A written business plan also is a management tool that helps measure the performance of the business.

The key elements of a business plan are:

1. A **market analysis** that defines the market and specifies the strategies to be used to achieve the revenues.

2. An **action plan** to guide the implementation of the strategies.

3. **Financial projections** that show the expected results.

Print and Electronic Reports

Business plans may be distributed in printed or electronic form. When distributed as printed copies, the document is frequently bound at the left to accommodate a binder and formatted without much color to avoid higher printing costs.

The business plan in this unit will be prepared for electronic distribution. It will, therefore, be formatted as an unbound report using color, fonts and font sizes, and paragraph spacing to make it attractive and easy to read on the computer monitor. Hyperlinks to bookmarks and headings will be inserted to make it easy for the reader to navigate from one part of the document to another.

Margins and Line Spacing. The business plan is to be prepared using default top (except page 1, which has a 2" top margin), bottom, and side margins and 1.15 line spacing.

Header, Footer, and Page Numbering. A header with the company name followed by the words *Business Plan* blocked at the LM, and a footer containing a centered page number with *Page* preceding the number are keyed on all pages of the report body and appendices except the first page of the report body, the first page of the table of contents, and the cover (title) page. Use lowercase Roman numeral(s) for the TOC page(s).

Text. Paragraphs and single-line bulleted lists should have at least two lines (or bullets) at the bottom of the page and carry over at least two lines to the next page. Headings and at least two lines of text should be kept together. Footnotes should be the same typeface and font size as the text. Tables and worksheets should not be split between pages. The report body should be left-aligned and hyphenated.

Style Set

The Formal Style Set, Aspect Colors, and Office Fonts are to be used to format all parts of the report in the report body, appendices, table of contents, and cover (title) page.

Table of Contents. Prepare a table of contents (TOC) that contains hyperlinks from the TOC headings to the corresponding headings in the report and page numbers with dot leaders. Level 1, Level 2, and Level 3 headings are to be included in the TOC. Key *TABLE OF CONTENTS* in Title style at the top of the TOC page.

Create Tables 2 and 3 using the information given below.

Table 2

Main Title: Row height 0.9"; Center alignment; bold text.

Column headings: Row height 0.4"; Center alignment; bold text.

Data Rows: Row height 0.3"; column A Bottom Left align; column B Bottom Center align.

Table placement: Center the table on the page.

Save as: 66C TABLE2

MAJOR LAND BATTLES of the CIVIL WAR

Battle	Dates
Fort Sumter	*April 12–14, 1861*
First Bull Run (Manassas)	*July 21, 1861*
Harpers Ferry	*September 12–15, 1862*
Second Bull Run (Manassas)	*August 28–30, 1862*
Antietam	*September 17, 1862*
Fredericksburg	*December 11–15, 1862*
Chancellorsville	*April 30–May 6, 1863*
Gettysburg	*July 1–3, 1863*
Wilderness	*May 5–7, 1864*
Spotsylvania	*May 8–21, 1864*
Siege & Battles around Petersburg	*June 8, 1864–April 2, 1865*
Appomattox	*April 2–9, 1865*
Battles for Atlanta	*July 20–September 1, 1864*

Source: Margaret E. Wagner, *The Library of Congress Civil War Desk Reference* (New York: Simon & Schuster, 2002), p. 241.

Table 3

Main Title: Row height 0.7"; center vertical alignment; bold text.

Column Titles: Row height 0.4"; Center align; bold text.

Data Rows: Row height 0.35"; column A Bottom Left align; columns B and C Bottom Center align.

Save as: 66C TABLE3

THE CONFEDERATE STATES OF AMERICA

State	Seceded from Union	Readmitted to Union[1]
South Carolina	December 20, 1860	July 9, 1868
Mississippi	January 9, 1861	February 23, 1870
Florida	January 10, 1861	June 25, 1868
Alabama	January 11, 1861	July 13, 1868
Georgia	January 19, 1861	July 21, 1868
Louisiana	January 26, 1861	July 9, 1868
Texas	March 2, 1861	March 30, 1870
Virginia	April 17, 1861	January 26, 1870
Arkansas	May 6, 1861	June 22, 1868
North Carolina	May 20, 1861	July 4, 1868
Tennessee	June 8, 1861	July 24, l866

[1]Date of readmission to representation in U.S. House of Representatives.

Source: *Time Almanac and Information Please 2007* (Upper Saddle River, NJ: Pearson Education, 2006), p. 104.

ACTIVITY 5

Math: Working with Probability

1. Open *DF CS11 ACTIVITY5* and print the file.
2. Solve the problems as directed in the file.
3. Submit your answers.

CAREER Clusters

ACTIVITY 11

You must complete Career Exploration Activities 1–3 before completing this activity.

1. Retrieve your Career folder and the information in it that relates to the career cluster that is your second choice.

2. Use the Internet to search for the education that is recommended for occupations in this career cluster, and then compose a paragraph or two explaining what you have learned. Print your file, save it as Career11, and keep it open.

3. Exchange papers with a classmate and have the classmate offer suggestions for improving the content and correcting any errors he or she finds in your paragraph(s). Make the changes that you agree with and print a copy to turn in to your instructor. Save it as Career11 and close the file.

4. Return your folder to the storage area. When your instructor returns your paper, file it in your Career folder.

IMAGE SOURCE BLACK/JUPITER IMAGES

Lesson 67 — APPLY SHADING TO TABLES

OBJECTIVES
- To improve table formatting skills.
- To enhance tables with shading.

67B

Table Editing

1. Open *66C TABLE1*. Include the information shown at the right at the end of the table.
2. Sort the table to arrange the new entries alphabetically with the rest of the entries.

Save as: 67B TABLE1

McClellan, George B.	Union Army General
Forrest, Nathan Bedford	Confederate Army General
Johnston, Albert Sidney	Confederate Army General
McDowell, Irvin	Union Army General

67C — Formatting

Table Formatting

Table 1

Format and key Table 1 (shown below) attractively on the page. Adjust row height, column width, alignment, placement, etc. Shade the column headings as shown. Use a 12-pt. font for headings and a 10-pt. font for body and source note of table.

Save as: 67C TABLE1

Table 2

Open *67C TABLE1*. Change orientation to landscape; apply AutoFit Window. Change main heading to 16 pt. font; secondary headings to 14 pt. font; body and source note to 12 pt. font. Alphabetize columns 1, 3, and 5 of Table 1 by last name in ascending order.

Save as: 67C TABLE2

FAMOUS AMERICANS					
Thinkers and Innovators		**Politics**		**Arts and Entertainment**	
Name	**Life**	**Name**	**Life**	**Name**	**Life**
George W. Carver	1864–1943	Frederick Douglass	1817–1895	Louis Armstrong	1901–1971
W. E. B. DuBois	1868–1963	Rosa Parks	1913–	Billie Holiday	1915–1959
Madam C. J. Walker	1867–1919	Harriet Tubman	1823–1913	Duke Ellington	1899–1974
Booker T. Washington	1856–1915	Thurgood Marshall	1908–1993	Ella Fitzgerald	1917–1996
Benjamin Banneker	1731–1806	Colin Powell	1937–	Bill Cosby	1937–
Mary McLeod Bethune	1875–1955	Shirley Chisholm	1924–	Alex Haley	1921–1992
Charles Drew	1904–1950	Martin Luther King, Jr.	1929–1968	Oprah Winfrey	1954–

Source: "Black History Innovators," *USA Today*, February 15, 2000, http://www.usatoday.com (accessed June 28, 2008).

Proofread & Correct

Rules

Rules		
1	1	The coach asked, How many of you practiced during the summer?
1	2	Didn't Browne say, "There is no road or ready way to virtue?"
2	3	Do you and your sister regularly watch National Geographic on TV?
2	4	My mom's column, Speak Up, appears in the local newspaper.
3	5	You have trouble deciding when to use accept and except.
1,4	6	I said, I must take, as Frost wrote, 'the road less traveled.
5	7	Jae boasted, "I'm almost twenty one; you're thirty two."
6	8	My older self confident cousin sells life insurance door to door.
6	9	The hard working outfitter readied our canoe faster than I expected.
6	10	Over the counter sales showed a great increase last month.

---

2. Key Proofread & Correct, using quotation marks and hyphens correctly.

a. Check answers.

b. Using the rule number(s) at the left of each line, study the rule relating to each error you made.

c. Rekey each incorrect line, using quotation marks and hyphens correctly.

Save as: CS11 ACTIVITY1

ACTIVITY 2

Preparing to Speak

Complete as directed.

Save as: CS11 OUTLINE and CS11 SOUND

You have been selected to introduce a speaker, Douglas H. Ruckert, to your class. You can find his resume in DF CS11 ACTIVITY2. The introduction is to be 30" to 1'.

The audience is your classmates.

1. Review the resume and decide which points you will include in your introduction.

2. Key an outline of these points.

3. If time and resources permit, record your speech in a sound file.

ACTIVITY 3

Write to Learn

Complete as directed.

Save as: CS11 ACTIVITY3

1. Using word processing or voice recognition software, write a ¶ explaining how to insert clip art from a file into a word processing document.

2. Write a second ¶ explaining how to add a border to a title page.

ACTIVITY 4

Reading

1. Open DF CS11 ACTIVITY4.

2. Read the document; close the file.

3. Key answers to the questions, using complete sentences.

Save as: CS11 ACTIVITY4

1. What service does WebGate provide?

2. What is the amount of the most recent acquisition?

3. Was WebGate founded more than five years ago?

4. In what states does WebGate do business?

5. In what state does the most recent acquisition do business?

6. Have all acquisitions been financed by a Charlotte bank?

7. About how many customers does WebGate serve?

Table 3

Key the table at the right and insert the following three names beside the individual's accomplishments.

Albert Einstein
Thomas Alva Edison
Andrew Carnegie

Use the table format features that you have learned to arrange the information attractively on the page.

Save as: 67C TABLE3

Table 4

Open *66C TABLE1*. Shade the cells with gray shading for the Confederate officers' names and light blue for the Union officers' names.

Save as: 67C TABLE4

INTERNET ACTIVITY

Select one of the names listed in the table at right. Use the Internet to find out more about the individual you select. Compose a ¶ or two telling about his or her contribution to American history.

Save as: 67C INTERNET

KEY PEOPLE IN AMERICAN HISTORY

Name	Accomplishment	Life
Alexander Grayam Bell	Invented the telephone in 1977.	1847–1922
John Wilkes Boothe	Actor; Assassin of President Lincoln, April 14, 1865	1838–1865
	Scotish immigrant who built a fortune by building steel mills.	1835–1919
Crazy Horse	Sioux Indian chief who resisted government demands for his tribe to leave the Black Hills.	18421877
Jefferson David	President of the confederate States of America.	1808–1889
	American physicist; Theory of Relativity led to harnessing nuclear energy.	1879–1955
Thomas Jefferson	Third president of the United States; author of the Declaration of Independence.	1743–1826
Martin Luther King	Civil rights leader; belief in nonviolence was patterned after Mohandas Gandi.	1929–1968
Eleanor Roosevelt	Franklin D. Roosevelt's wife and a major champoin for civil rights and humanitarian issues.	1884–1962
Elizabeth stanton	American social reformer; led the struggle for women's sufferage with Susan B. Anthony.	1815–1902
	American inventor of the incandescent light bulb and the phonograph.	*1847–1931*

Source: James R. Giese, *The American Century* (New York: West Educational Publishing, 1999), pp. 929–935.

Lesson 68 — PRESENT INFORMATION IN TABLES

OBJECTIVES

- To improve table formatting skills
- To use decision-making skills to organize information in a table.

Communication & Math
SKILLS 11

QUOTATION MARKS AND HYPHEN USAGE

Internal Punctuation: Quotation Marks and Hyphens

1. Study each of the 6 rules.
   a. Key the *Learn* line(s) beneath each rule, noting how the rule is applied.
   b. Key the *Apply* lines, using quotation marks and hyphens correctly.

Internal Punctuation: Quotation marks

Rule 1: Use quotation marks to enclose direct quotations. **Note:** When a question mark applies to the entire sentence, place it outside the quotation marks.

Learn 1 Professor Dye asked, "Are you spending the summer in Europe?"

Learn 2 Was it Emerson who said, "To have a friend is to be one"?

Apply 3 Marcella asked, May I borrow your class notes from yesterday?

Apply 4 Did John Donne say, No man is an island, entire of itself?

Rule 2: Use quotation marks to enclose titles of articles, poems, songs, television programs, and unpublished works, such as theses and dissertations.

Learn 5 Kari read aloud the poem "Fog" from Sandburg's <u>Selected Poems</u>.

Apply 6 The song Getting to Know You is from The King and I.

Apply 7 The title of his term paper is Computer Software for Grade 4.

Rule 3: Use quotation marks to enclose special words or phrases used for emphasis or for coined words (words not in dictionary usage).

Learn 8 My problem: I have "limited resources" and "unlimited wants."

Apply 9 His talk was filled with phrases like ah and you know.

Apply 10 She said that the words phony and braggart describe him.

Rule 4: Use a single quotation mark (the apostrophe) to indicate a quotation within a quotation (including titles and words as indicated in Rules 2 and 3, above).

Learn 11 I wrote, "We must have, as Tillich said, 'the courage to be.'"

Apply 12 I said, "As Milton wrote, he is 'sober, steadfast, and demure."

Apply 13 I say, "Don't lie, for Swift said, facts are stubborn things."

Internal Punctuation: Hyphen

Rule 5: Use a hyphen to join compound numbers from twenty-one to ninety-nine that are keyed as words.

Learn 14 Sixty-seven students met in the gym; about twenty-seven wore the uniform.

Apply 15 Thirty five guests attended Anita's twenty-first birthday party.

Apply 16 Thirty four delegates went to the national convention.

Rule 6: Use a hyphen to join compound adjectives preceding a noun they modify as a unit.

Learn 17 End-of-term grades will be posted outside the classroom.

Apply 18 The most up to date fashions are featured in the store window.

Apply 19 Their new computer programs feature state of the art graphics.

(continued on next page)

Table Editing

Open *67C TABLE3* and make the following changes.

1. Delete *John Wilkes Booth* and *Thomas Jefferson* from the table.
2. Add the three names shown at right (in alphabetical order).
3. Make any adjustments necessary to make the table fit on one page.

Save as: 68B TABLE1

Tisquantum	*Taught the Pilgrims farming techniques; helped them establish treaties with native tribes.*	*1580–1622 (approx.)*
Sir Walter Raleigh	*English adventurer who settled the region from South Carolina north to present-day New York City under a charter from Queen Elizabeth I of England.*	*1554–1618*
John D. Rockefeller	*Oil magnate and philanthropist; founded Standard Oil Company in 1870.*	*1839–1937*

Formatting

Table Formatting

Key Tables 1–4 using the information given below.

Table 1

Table Style: Medium Shading 2 - Accent 4; make adjustments to alignment of rows as shown at right; increase size of last column to fit date on one line.

Font Size: Main heading 14 pt.; column headings 12 pt.; column A 11 pt. columns B, C, D, E 10 pt.

Row Height: Column heading row 0.5"; all other rows 0.4".

Save as: 68C TABLE1

KNOW YOUR COUNTRIES

Country	Term for Citizens	Capital	Largest City	Independence
Australia	Australian(s)	Canberra	Sydney 4.2 million	January 1, 1901
China	Chinese	Beijing	Chongqing 30.5 million	February 12, 1912
Kenya	Kenyan(s)	Nairobi	Nairobi 1.3 million	December 12, 1963
Vietnam	Vietnamese	Hanoi	Ho Chi Minh City 5.6 million	September 2, 1945
Mexico	Mexican(s)	Mexico City	Mexico City *16 million	September 16, 1810
India	Indian(s)	New Delhi	Mumbai 16.4 million	August 15, 1947
Germany	German(s)	Berlin	Berlin 3.4 million	October 3, 1990 Reunification Date
France	French	Paris	Paris *11.3 million	July 14, 1789
Morocco	Moroccan(s)	Rabat	Casablanca 3.5 million	March 2, 1956
Jordan	Jordanian(s)	Amman	Amman 2 million	May 25, 1946
Colombia	Colombian(s)	Bogota	Bogota 4.3 million	July 20, 1810
South Korea	Korean(s)	Seoul	Seoul 11 million	August 15, 1945

*Denotes Greater Metropolitan Population.
Source: http://lcweb2.loc.gov/frd/cs/profiles.html, August 6, 2007.

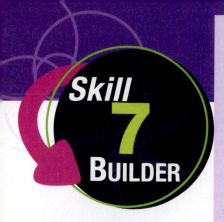

Skill 7 Builder

Technique: Keystroking Patterns

Key each line twice.

Timed Writings: Straight Copy

1. Key three 1' writings on each ¶; determine *gwam*. Count errors. If errors are two or fewer on any writing, goal is to increase speed by one or two words on next writing. If errors on any writing are more than 2, goal is control on next writing.

2. Key two 3' writings on ¶s 1–3 combined; determine *gwam* and count errors.

3. Key a 5' writing on ¶s 1–3 combined; determine *gwam* and count errors.

Adjacent key

1 ore her has sag ion oil wet new art join drop sage hope grew
2 err gas rent ever past same void week view weave short pound
3 more maker lease salsa radio prior opera trial choice import

One hand

4 as bag car dad ear fad gas him ill gave hymn kilo noon onion
5 oil pop red see tar ump vat yoyo zest ages best caves zebras
6 beef crews defer fears graft holly milky puppy excess pompom

Balanced hand

7 it ant bow cod doe elf fit got ivy jake keys naps odor prowl
8 rod sow torn vial worn yams zori auto buck clams forks giant
9 hair idle kept lapel proxy quake theory turkey naught mentor

gwam 1' | 1 | 2 | 3 | 4 | 5 | 6 | 7 | 8 | 9 | 10 | 11 | 12 |

A all letters used (MicroPace) gwam 3' | 5'

One of the many attributes that has made our country one — 4 | 2
of the greatest in the world is the willingness of so many of our — 8 | 5
citizens to assist others. Our country has many individuals who — 13 | 8
willingly give back to our communities instead of always taking — 17 | 10
from others. These caring people donate their time and skills in — 21 | 13
addition to the monetary wealth they have accumulated. — 25 | 15

It is not too early for you to begin giving back to your — 29 | 17
community. Many students your age conduct exciting service — 33 | 20
projects that make their community a better place. These projects — 37 | 22
often help students gain self-respect, believe in themselves, and — 41 | 25
gain leadership skills. Plus, others in the community gain respect — 46 | 28
for you and confidence that the future will be in good hands. — 50 | 30

There are many ways for you to start or join a group that — 54 | 32
provides community service. The group can be members of your — 58 | 35
family or friends from your school, church, or neighborhood. You — 62 | 37
can do service projects for the aquarium, the zoo, or a civic — 67 | 40
club. The projects may help you learn about pertinent issues and — 71 | 43
to solve real problems. — 73 | 44

gwam 3' | 1 | 2 | 3 | 4
     5' | 1 | 2 | 3

Table 2

Column headings: Row height 0.4"; Center alignment; bold text.

Data rows: Row height 0.4"; Bottom Left alignment.

Table placement: Center the table horizontally and vertically.

Save as: 68C TABLE2

WHAT AMERICANS REMEMBER

Top Five Events

Rank	Age Group			
	18–34	35–54	55–64	65 and Over
1	Oklahoma City Bombing	Oklahoma City Bombing	JFK Death	JFK Death
2	Challenger	JFK Death	Moon Walk	Pearl Harbor
3	Gulf War Begins	Challenger	Oklahoma City Bombing	WWII Ends
4	Reagan Shot	Moon Walk	Challenger	Moon Walk
5	Berlin Wall Falls	Gulf War Begins	MLK Death	FDR Death

Source: The Pew Research Center, "America's Collective Memory," July 28, 2007, http://people-press.org/reports/display.php3?PageID=283.

Table 3

Column headings: Row height 0.4"; Center alignment; bold text; 15% shading.

Data rows: Row height 0.4"; Bottom alignment.

Table placement: Center horizontally and vertically.

Save as: 68C TABLE3

Table 4

Note how Table 3 contains the same information as Table 2, but arranged in a different way. Use your decision-making skills to create a third table from the information, arranging it in still another way.

Save as: 68C TABLE4

WHAT AMERICANS REMEMBER

Top Five Events

Event	Age Group			
	18–34	35–54	55–64	65+
■ Berlin Wall Falls	5	*	*	*
■ Challenger	2	3	4	*
■ Franklin D. Roosevelt Death	*	*	*	5
■ Gulf War Begins	3	5	*	*
■ John F. Kennedy Death	*	2	1	1
■ Martin Luther King Death	*	*	5	*
■ Moon Walk	*	4	2	4
■ Oklahoma City Bombing	1	1	3	*
■ Pearl Harbor	*	*	*	2
■ Reagan Shot	4	*	*	*
■ World War II Ends	*	*	*	3
1 = Ranked First, 2 = Ranked Second, etc.; * = Not ranked in top five by this age group.				

Source: The Pew Research Center, "America's Collective Memory," July 28, 2007, http://people-press.org/reports/display.php3?PageID=283.

Language Skills: Word Choice

1. Study the spelling and definitions of the words.
2. Key all *Learn* and *Apply* lines, choosing the correct word(s) in the *Apply* lines.

Save as: 122D CHOICE

> **personal** (adj) private; individual
> **personnel** (n) employees
>
> **wait** (vb/n) to stay in place; to pause; to serve as a waiter; act of waiting
> **weight** (n) amount something weighs

Learn 1 The **personnel** committee took a **personal** interest in all workers.

Apply 2 Max thought the case too (personal, personnel) to discuss openly.

Apply 3 The (personal, personnel) manager will mediate the dispute.

Learn 1 Opal wants to **wait** until her **weight** loss is complete.

Apply 2 I'll gain more (wait, weight) the longer I (wait, weight).

Apply 3 He will (wait, weight) to gain (wait, weight) to wrestle heavier.

122E

INTERNET ACTIVITY

1. Read the two ¶s at the right.
2. Perform a search on an exercise topic of your choice and then compose (either at the keyboard or using speech recognition software) two or three ¶s describing what you learned.
3. Print one or two pages from an Internet site that relate to what you wrote.

Save as: 122E INTERNET

Exercise is very important to maintaining a healthy body and mind. People exercise to lose weight, get in shape and stay in shape, reduce stress, improve overall health, increase muscular strength, recover from an illness or injury, etc.

Maybe you know what you want to accomplish through exercise, but don't know where to start. This activity requires you to search the Internet to find information about a method of exercise that interests you. For example, you may want to search the broad topic *exercise* and then follow links that interest you. Or you may want to narrow your search by selecting a few exercise routines that are of particular interest to you and searching for them—e.g., aerobics, bodybuilding, climbing, cycling, martial arts, running, swimming, walking, yoga, etc.

APPLY BORDERS TO TABLES

- To improve table formatting skills.
- To format tables with enhanced borders and shading.

69B   Formatting

Table Formatting

Table 1

Key the table at the right using the Arial font and landscape orientation. Use the table format features that you have learned to arrange the information attractively on the page. Use a table border and shading similar to the illustration. Adjust column width so that each entry fits on a single line.

Save as: 69B TABLE1

Table 2

Update the table to include information about Presidents since 2009. Use the Internet site shown in the source note.

Save as: 69B TABLE2

PRESIDENTS 1953–2009			
President	**Dates in Office**	**State of Birth**	**Undergraduate Degree**
Dwight D. Eisenhower	1953–1961	Texas	West Point
John F. Kennedy	1961–1963	Massachusetts	Harvard
Lyndon B. Johnson	1963–1969	Texas	Texas State University-San Marcos
Richard M. Nixon	1969–1974	California	Whittier College
Gerald R. Ford	1974–1977	Nebraska	University of Michigan
James E. Carter, Jr.	1977–1981	Georgia	Naval Academy
Ronald W. Reagan	1981–1989	Illinois	Eureka College
George H. W. Bush	1989–1993	Massachusetts	Yale University
William J. Clinton	1993–2001	Arkansas	Georgetown University
G. W. Bush	2001–2009	Connecticut	Yale University
Blue = Republican Party Affiliation		Red = Democratic Party Affiliation	

Source: http://www.whitehouse.gov/history/presidents/, August 6, 2007.

Table 3

Create a table with the information shown at right. Use **PRESIDENT BUSH'S CABINET** for the main heading and **August 4, 2007** for the secondary heading. Use **Executive Department** and **Head of Department** for the column headings. Apply an appropriate border.

Save as: 69B TABLE3

Table 4

Using the source shown at the right, update the table with the current President's cabinet information.

Save as: 69B TABLE4

Department of Agriculture - Secretary Mike Johanns

Department of Commerce - Secretary Carlos Gutierrez

Department of Defense - Secretary Robert M. Gates

Department of Education - Secretary Margaret Spellings

Department of Energy - Secretary Samuel W. Bodman

Department of Health & Human Services - Secretary Michael O. Leavitt

Department of Homeland Security - Secretary Michael Chertoff

Department of Housing & Urban Development - Secretary Alphonso Jackson

Department of the Interior - Secretary Dirk Kempthorne

Department of Justice - Attorney General Alberto Gonzales

Department of Labor - Secretary Elaine Chao

Department of State - Secretary Condoleezza Rice

Department of Transportation - Secretary Mary E. Peters

Department of the Treasury - Secretary Henry M. Paulson, Jr.

Department of Veterans Affairs - Secretary Jim Nicholson

Source: http://www.whitehouse.gov/government/cabinet.html, August 8, 2007.

OBJECTIVE

• To use Mail Merge to prepare mailing labels, name badges, and a directory.

122B

Mail Merge Applications

1. Read the text.
2. Learn to use Mail Merge to prepare labels (address labels and name badges) and a directory.
3. Use data source *DF 122B DATA* to prepare the address labels, name badges, and directory as directed at the right.

Mail Merge can be used for many other tasks. Frequently, labels (address labels, name badges, etc.) and directories are prepared by using the Mail Merge Wizard to create the label or directory in the same manner it was used to create personalized letters.

Address Labels

1. Use all fields except EMail to prepare a standard address label for each record. Save the merged file as *122B LABELS*.

Name Badges

2. Use the First Name, Last Name, and City fields to prepare an attractive name badge for each record. Save the merged file as *122B BADGES*.

Directory

3. Using the Last Name, First Name, and EMail fields, prepare an e-mail directory for each record that has PA in the State field. List the last names in alpha order; insert a comma between the Last Name and First Name fields; align the names at the left margin. Align the e-mail addresses at the right margin using a right dot leader tab. Insert an appropriate heading for the directory. Save the merged document as *122B DIRECTORY*.

122C

Mail Merge Applications

Use data source *119C DATA2* to prepare the address labels, name badges, and directory as directed at the right.

Address Labels

Prepare a standard mailing label for each record that has *Garland* or *Mesquite* in the City field. Save the merged file as *122C LABELS*.

Name Badges

Prepare a name badge for each record that has *Plano* or *Irving* in the City field. Sort the badges in alpha order by last name. Horizontally center the First Name & Last Name fields on one line. Center the City field on the next line. Save the name badges as *122C BADGES*.

Directory

Prepare a directory listing all records in alphabetical order by City and then by Last Name within City. Left-align last and first names and set a dot leader right tab at the 6.5" position for the city. Include a heading *CITY DIRECTORY*, center-aligned before the directory entries. Save the directory as *122C DIRECTORY*.

OBJECTIVES
- To improve table formatting skills.
- To format tables with enhanced borders and shading.

70B   Formatting

Table Formatting

Table 1

Key the table at the right; insert each of the following three names next to the individual's accomplishments.

Alex Haley
Thurgood Marshall
Colin Powell

Use the table format features that you have learned to arrange the information attractively on the page. Use a border similar to the one shown.

Save as: **70B TABLE1**

FAMOUS AMERICANS

Name	Significant Accomplishments
Charles Drew	Developed a means for preserving blood plasma for transfusion.
	First black officer to hold the highest military post in the U.S., Chairman of the U.S. Joint Chiefs of Staff.
Shirley Chisholm	First black woman to be elected to the U.S. Congress.
	First black member of the U.S. Supreme Court.
Booker T. Washington	Organized a teaching and industrial school for African Americans—Tuskegee Institute.
Benjamin Banneker	First African American to receive a presidential appointment. Famous for his role as a planner for Washington, D.C.
W.E.B. DuBois	Cofounder of the organization that became the National Association for the Advancement of Colored People (NAACP).
Alice Walker	Pulitzer Prize-winning writer and poet. Novels include *The Color Purple* and *In Love and Trouble*.
	Pulitzer Prize-winning author. Wrote *Roots*, which was made into the highest-rated television miniseries of all time.
Frederick Douglass	Eminent human rights leader of the 19th century; the first black citizen to hold a high rank in the U.S. government.

Source: "Black History Innovators," *USA Today*, February 15, 2000, http://www.usatoday.com.

Mail Merge: Letters to Selected Recipients

1. Read the text.
2. Learn to select records.
3. Complete steps 1–2.

Save as: 120C PLANO

When linking the data source file to the main document, you can edit the recipient list in a variety of ways. One frequent edit is to specify those in the data source who are not to receive the merged document. When the merge is performed, a letter will not be created for the records not selected.

You can also refine your recipient list by sorting the records on one or more of the fields in the record and by filtering your list to include only the records you want to include in the merge.

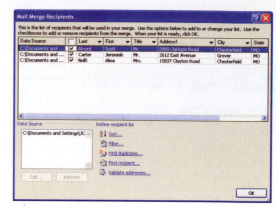

Mail Merge Recipient List

1. Using *120B MAIN2* and *119C DATA2*, create a letter for each record with *Plano* in the City field.
2. Print the letters.

Apply Mail Merge: Letters

1. Create a main document file (*120D MAIN*) using modified block letter format with mixed punctuation and merge it with *119D DATA2*.
2. Edit the recipient list so letters are sent to all except those with Inglewood in the City field. Save merged letters as *120D MERGE*.

May 25, 20--

<<AddressBlock>>

<<GreetingLine>>

We know what a burden it is for small businesses like <<Company>> to offer excellent health insurance benefits to employees. That is why First Health is holding an informational session at the Hartley Hotel on Wednesday, June 10, from 4:30 p.m. to 6 p.m.

<<Title>> <<Last Name>>, we invite you and another representative from <<Company>> to join us. You will learn about the major features of our medical, dental, and long-term disability coverage so that you can compare them to your present plan's features. We are convinced that you will be pleasantly surprised by what we can offer at affordable premiums.

Please use the enclosed card to reserve your places at the informational session. Refreshments will be served, and you will have ample time to discuss your specific needs with one of our staff members who will be attending.

Sincerely,

Robyn L. Young-Masters

Regional Marketing Manager

xx

Enclosure

<<First Name>>, Tom Durkin has told me a great deal about the success of <<Company>>, and I am looking forward to meeting you to find what you are doing to be so successful in such a competitive field.

Table 2

Key the table at the right. Use the table format features that you have learned to arrange the information attractively on the page. Use a border and shading similar to the illustration. DS between each data entry.

Include the following source note outside the table:

Source: Matthew T. Downey, et al. *United States History (New York: National Textbook Company, 1997), p. 158.

Save as: 70B TABLE2

THE CONSTITUTION		
The Executive Branch	**The Legislative Branch**	**The Judicial Branch**
• President administers and enforces federal laws • President chosen by electors who have been chosen by the states	• A bicameral or two-house legislature • Each state has equal number of representatives in the Senate • Representation in the House determined by state population • Simple majority required to enact legislation	• National court system directed by the Supreme Court • Courts to hear cases related to national laws, treaties, the Constitution; cases between states, between citizens of different states, or between a state and citizens of another state

Table 3

Key the table at the right. Use the table format features that you have learned to arrange the information attractively on the page. Use a border and shading similar to the illustration. Use landscape orientation and AutoFit Window.

Include the following source note outside the table:

Source: http://www.pollingreport.com/prioriti.htm, August 6, 2007.

Save as: 70B TABLE3

CNN/OPINION RESEARCH CORPORATION POLL
May 4-6, 2007

"How important will each of the following issues be to your vote for president next year?"					
Issue	Extremely Important %	Very Important %	Moderately Important %	Not That Important %	Unsure %
The situation in Iraq	51	37	9	2	-
Terrorism	45	35	14	6	-
Education	44	37	16	3	-
Health care	43	35	18	4	-
Gas prices	43	31	16	10	1
Corruption and ethical standards in government	41	36	17	7	-
The situation in Iran	38	39	17	5	1
Social Security and Medicare	38	37	20	4	-
The economy	33	46	16	4	-
Illegal immigration	31	32	26	10	1

4. Preview the letters and make any necessary formatting changes.

5. Complete the merge process.

6. View the letters in the merged file and print the Popelas letter. Save merged document as *120B MERGE1*.

January 15, 20--

<<AddressBlock>>

<<GreetingLine>>

It was a pleasure to meet you last week to discuss your long-term health-care needs. As you requested, I have charted the various policy features from three leading insurance providers.

The chart will show the various options each provider extends and the cost for each option. You can select those that meet your needs the best.

I will call you in a week to arrange an appointment so we can discuss this matter thoroughly.

Sincerely,

Katherine Porter

Agent

xx

Enclosure

Mail Merge 2: Letters

1. Use the information at the right and on the next page to create and save a main document (*120B MAIN2*) using block letter format with mixed punctuation and merge it with *119D DATA2*.

2. Print the Raible and White letters. Save merged letters as *120B MERGE2*.

October 5, 20--

<<AddressBlock>>

<<GreetingLine>>

¶ Thank you for attending the recent open house reception sponsored by the Dallas Area Environmental Health Association. We hope that you enjoyed meeting our expert staff of scientists, physicians, nutritionists, technicians, and others who work on your behalf to improve your quality of life.

¶ Headaches, sinusitis, fatigue, joint aches, and asthma are some of the common ailments that are often caused by our environment. The Dallas Area Environmental Health Association is dedicated to conducting the research that documents the link between the common ailments and the environment so effective treatments can be offered.

¶ <<Title>> <<Last Name>>, now that you know more about the Association, we ask you to schedule a 20-minute consultation with one of our staff members to discuss your health concerns. This consultation is free and carries no obligation to use our services. Just call me at 972-555-0119 to schedule a mutually convenient time.

Sincerely,

Margarita L. Jiminez

Director of Services

xx

- To improve table formatting skills.
- To format tables with enhanced borders and shading.

71B

Table Formatting

Table 1

Combine the information shown in the two tables at the right into one table as shown in the illustration below. Using the data from July 2005, rank the most populated states in descending order and the least populated states in ascending order.

Main Heading: MOST AND LEAST POPULATED STATES

Secondary Heading: 1990 Compared to 2005

Orientation: landscape

Source Note: *Time Almanac 2007*, p. 122.

Save as: 71B TABLE1

SELECTED STATE POPULATIONS
July 1990

Most Populated States		Least Populated States	
State	Population	State	Population
California	29,760,021	Wyoming	453,588
Texas	16,986,510	Vermont	562,758
Illinois	11,430,602	South Dakota	696,004
New York	17,990,455	North Dakota	638,800
Ohio	10,847,115	Montana	799,065
Pennsylvania	11,881,643	Delaware	666,168
Florida	12,937,926	Alaska	550,043

SELECTED STATE POPULATIONS
July 2005

Most Populated States		Least Populated States	
State	Population	State	Population
California	36,132,147	Wyoming	509,294
Texas	22,859,968	Vermont	623,050
New York	19,254,630	North Dakota	636,677
Florida	17,789,864	Alaska	663,661
Illinois	12,763,371	South Dakota	775,933
Pennsylvania	12,429,615	Delaware	843,524
Ohio	11,464,042	Montana	935,670

Most Populated States					Least Populated States				
State	1990		2005		State	1990		2005	
	Ranking	Population	Ranking	Population		Ranking	Population	Ranking	Population

1. Open *DF 119D DATA2*.
2. Add the records in the ADD RE-CORDS chart at the right to *DF 119D DATA2*.
3. Add a **Company** field and a **Plan** field to the data source table, and then key the information in the ADD FIELDS table in each record.

Save as: **119D DATA2**

ADD RECORDS			
Field Name	Record 1	Record 2	Record 3
Title	Mrs.	Dr.	Ms.
First name	LaJunta	Vijay	Rita
Last name	Greene	Awan	Martz
Address Line 1	8606 Wiley Post Avenue	1148 Hyde Park Boulevard	601 Centinela Avenue
City	Los Angeles	Inglewood	Inglewood
State	CA	CA	CA
ZIP Code	90045-8600	90302-2640	90302-5519

ADD FIELDS					
Records 1-4			Records 5-8		
Last Name	Company	Plan	Last Name	Company	Plan
Perez	P & B Auto Trim	Family	Barichal	Ace Auto Parts	Husband/Wife
Brletich	Security Auto Service	Family	Greene	Greene Auction House	Husband/Wife
Kamerer	Bank and Trust	Individual	Awan	Inglewood Orthopedics	Individual
Neumann	Lawndale Bakery	Individual	Martz	Hercules.com	Parent/Child

Lessons 120–121   CREATE MAIN DOCUMENT FILES AND USE MAIL MERGE

OBJECTIVES

- To create main document files.
- To merge main document files and data source files.

120–121B

Create a Main Document; Set Up and Perform a Mail Merge

Mail Merge 1: Letters

1. Read the text.
2. Learn to create a main document.
3. Create the main document shown on the next page, and link the data source in *119D DATA1* to your main document when setting up the merge. Save main document as *120B MAIN1*.

The main document file contains the generic text and format of the document that remain constant in each letter, plus the merge fields. After the data source has been selected, the merge fields are inserted into the main document file where the variable information from the data source is to appear.

The merge process will create the merged file, which consists of a document for each record included in the merge. Each document will contain the personalized information for each individual in the data source.

January 7, 20--

«Title» «FirstName» «LastName»
«Address1»
«City», «State» «PostalCode»

Dear «Title» «LastName»:

This is an example of a merged document with a main document file. The **data sour**

Main Document with Merge Fields in Chevrons

(continued on next page)

Table 2

Format and key one table that includes all the information shown at the right. Use **INFORMATION ABOUT SELECTED STATES** as a title. Data about each state should make up one row of the table. Alphabetize the rows by state. Include this source note:

Source: James R. Giese, et al. *The American Century*, New York: West Educational Publishing, 1999, pp. 922–925.

Place a border around each cell that has a **1** and color the cell light green. Place a border around each cell with a **50** and color the cell light purple.

Save as: 71B TABLE2

Alaska	Idaho	Montana
Rank Entering Union: 49 Rank Land Area: 1 Rank Population: 49	Rank Entering Union: 43 Rank Land Area: 13 Rank Population: 42	Rank Entering Union: 41 Rank Land Area: 4 Rank Population: 44
California Rank Entering Union: 31 Rank Land Area: 3 Rank Population: 1	**Illinois** Rank Entering Union: 21 Rank Land Area: 24 Rank Population: 6	**Nebraska** Rank Entering Union: 37 Rank Land Area: 15 Rank Population: 36
Delaware Rank Entering Union: 1 Rank Land Area: 49 Rank Population: 46	**Kansas** Rank Entering Union: 34 Rank Land Area: 14 Rank Population: 32	**Rhode Island** Rank Entering Union: 13 Rank Land Area: 50 Rank Population: 43
Hawaii Rank Entering Union: 50 Rank Land Area: 47 Rank Population: 41	**Michigan** Rank Entering Union: 26 Rank Land Area: 23 Rank Population: 8	**Wyoming** Rank Entering Union: 44 Rank Land Area: 9 Rank Population: 50

Table 3

1. Open *DF 71B TABLE3 2007*.
2. Change the page orientation to landscape. Insert the new columns and make the changes to the headings as shown at the right.
3. Open *DF 71B TABLE3 2003* to get the information for the new columns.
4. Key the data for the new columns.
5. The *Inquirer* had a circulation of **365,154** and was ranked **19** in 2003; the *Rocky Mountain News* had a circulation of **390,938** and was ranked **27** in 2003.
6. Change the source note to include both 2007 and 2003.

Save as: 71B TABLE3

CHANGES IN TOP TEN U.S. DAILY NEWSPAPERS
Comparison of 2007 to 2003

2007 Rank	2003 Rank	Newspaper	Location	2007 Circulation	2003 Circulation
1		*USA Today*	Arlington, VA	2,528,437	
2		*Wall Street Journal*	New York, NY	2,058,342	
3		*Times*	New York, NY	1,683,855	
4		*Times*	Los Angeles, CA	1,231,318	
5		*Post*	Washington, D.C.	960,684	
6		*Tribune*	Chicago, IL	957,212	
7		*Daily News*	New York, NY	795,153	
8		*Inquirer*	Philadelphia, PA	705,965	
9		*Post/Rocky Mountain News*	Denver, CO	704,806	
10		*Chronicle*	Houston, TX	692,557	

Source: *Time Almanac and Information Please 2007* (Upper Saddle River, NJ: Pearson Education, 2006).

Title	First Name	Last Name	Address Line 1	City	State	ZIP Code
Mr.	Peter	Como	701 W. State Street	Garland	TX	75040-0701
Ms.	Karen	Rolle	1026 F Avenue	Plano	TX	75074-3591
Mr.	Dale	Zeman	4412 Legacy Drive	Plano	TX	75024-4412
Mr.	Yu	Wei	12726 Audelia Road	Dallas	TX	75243-7789
Ms.	Anne	Sige	532 N. Story Road	Irving	TX	75061-0506
Mr.	David	White	3700 Chaha Road	Rowlett	TX	75088-3700

119D

Edit Data Sources

Data Source 1

1. Read the text.
2. Learn how to make changes to records and fields.
3. Open *119C DATA1* and make the changes in steps 1–4.

Save as: **119D DATA1**

You can edit both records and fields in a data source. For example, you can add records to, delete records from, revise records in, or sort records in an existing data source file.

Also, you can add, delete, or revise fields in an existing data source file.

Data source files can be word processing, spreadsheet, database, or e-mail files.

1. In Record 3, change Elizabeth's title to **Mrs.** and last name to **Popelas.**
2. Delete the record for Harold Dominicus and add these two records:

   Dr. Eugene Whitman, 531 Kiefer Road, Ballwin, MO 63025-0531
   Ms. Joyce Royal, 417 Weidman Road, Ballwin, MO 63011-0321

3. Change the orientation of the file to Landscape.
4. Add two fields (**Company** and **EMail**), and then insert the company name and e-mail address in each record as indicated below:

   Mueller—**Allmor Corporation; mueller@AC.com**
   Popelas—**Kurtz Consumer Discount; epopelas@kurtz.com**
   Whitman—**Whitman Family Practice; whitman@wfc.com**
   Royal—**Better Delivery, Inc.; jroyal2@betdel.com**

Skill 3 Builder

Reading/Keying Response Patterns

1. Key each line three times (slowly, faster, top speed).
2. Key two 1' timings on lines 7–9; determine *gwam* on each timing.

Emphasize quick finger reaches, wrists low and relaxed.

balanced-hand words
1 is by do if go he so us to me of jam row rug she bus air but city
2 both also busy held duck dial form make rush sick soap when towns
3 visit widow theme title ivory proxy quake shape amend burnt chair

Emphasize high-speed phrase responses.

balanced-hand phrases
4 He owns it | make the signs | paid the man | go to work | if they fix the
5 Go to the | they may make | to the problem | with the sign | and the maps
6 With the city | the eighth neighbor | social problem | the big ornament

Emphasize high-speed, word-level response; quick spacing.

balanced-hand sentences
7 Pamela paid the man by the city dock for the six bushels of corn.
8 Keith may keep the food for the fish by the big antique fishbowl.
9 The haughty girls paid for their own gowns for the island social.

gwam 1' | 1 | 2 | 3 | 4 | 5 | 6 | 7 | 8 | 9 | 10 | 11 | 12 | 13 |

Techniques: Figures

1. Set 0.5" side margins.
2. Clear all tabs; then set tabs 2", 4", and 6" from the left margin.
3. Key the lines, tabbing from column to column; key the lines again at a faster rate.

Keep eyes on copy.

$17.84	638-38-4911	(389) 392-8256	11/20/86
$65.67	832-17-0647	(465) 709-7294	05/25/49
$91.03	541-78-0924	(513) 330-5760	06/20/59

Timed Writings

1. Key two 1' timings on each ¶; determine *gwam*.
2. Key three 2' timings on ¶s 1–2 combined; determine *gwam*.

A **all letters used** *MicroPace*

gwam 1' | 2'

A business is in business to make a profit. They do | 11 | 5
this by employing individuals who help the organization | 22 | 11
achieve its goals. In the past, various styles of | 32 | 16
leadership were used. Today, however, one of the most | 42 | 21
common styles used is the democratic style. This is where | 54 | 27
decisions are made by a team of individuals rather than | 65 | 33
by just one person. | 69 | 34

Because more and more companies are operating as a | 79 | 40
team, it is important for you to learn to participate as | 90 | 45
part of a team. This requires an effort on your part. | 101 | 51
Good team members listen to the opinions of other individuals | 113 | 57
on the team. Good team members are considerate of others. | 125 | 62
Good team members respect the rights of others. Good team | 136 | 68
members are excellent communicators. | 144 | 72

gwam 1' | 1 | 2 | 3 | 4 | 5 | 6 | 7 | 8 | 9 | 10 | 11 | 12 |
2' | 1 | 2 | 3 | 4 | 5 | 6 |

Create Data Sources

WP • Insert/Tables/Insert or Draw Table

Data Source 1
1. Read the text.
2. Learn to create a data source.
3. Open a new wp file.
4. Use the wp table feature to create a data source with three records, each with seven fields, as shown at the right.

Save as: 119C DATA1

Data Source 2
1. Create a data source using the 15 records on this and the next page.
2. Use the column headings as field names.

Save as: 119C DATA2

The **data source** file contains unique information for each individual or item. Each individual or item is called a **record**, and each record contains **fields**. Fields are the information about the item or individual, such as her or his title, first name, last name, street address, city, state, postal code, etc. The column headings in the data source table are the names of the fields.

When you create a main document, you will insert the fields (called **placeholders** or **merge fields**) into the document at the desired locations.

Once you have created your data source and inserted the merge fields into the main document, you can perform the merge.

Title	First Name	Last Name	Address Line 1	City	State	ZIP Code
Mr.	Harold	Dominicus	14820 Conway Road	Chesterfield	MO	63025-1003
Mrs.	Noreen	Mueller	15037 Clayton Road	Chesterfield	MO	63017-8734
Ms.	Elizabeth	Theilet	1843 Ross Avenue	St. Louis	MO	63146-5577

Title	First Name	Last Name	Address Line 1	City	State	ZIP Code
Mr.	Daniel	Raible	13811 Seagoville Road	Dallas	TX	75253-1380
Ms.	Sally	Lysle	3707 S. Peachtree Road	Mesquite	TX	75180-3707
Mrs.	Luz	Ruiz	13105 Timothy Lane	Mesquite	TX	75180-1310
Mrs.	Jane	Alam	1414 Alstadt Street	Hutchins	TX	75141-3792
Ms.	Stacey	Bethel	1717 Castle Drive	Garland	TX	75040-1717
Dr.	Jash	Sharik	2021 E. Park Boulevard	Plano	TX	75074-2021
Mr.	Jack	Dunn	4007 Latham Drive	Plano	TX	75023-4000
Mrs.	Helen	Wever	1001 Cuero Drive	Garland	TX	75040-1001
Ms.	Ann	Buck	1919 Senter Road	Irving	TX	75060-1919

(continued on next page)

COMMA USAGE

ACTIVITY 1

Internal Punctuation: Comma

1. Study each of the 6 rules.
   a. Key the *Learn* line(s) beneath each rule, noting how the rule is applied.
   b. Key the *Apply* lines, inserting commas correctly.

Internal Punctuation: Comma

Rule 1: Use a comma after long (five or more words) introductory phrases, after clauses, or after words in a series.

Learn	1	When you finish keying the report, please give it to Mr. Kent.
Learn	2	We will play the Mets, Expos, and Cubs in our next home stand.
Apply	3	If you attend the play take Mary Jack and Tim with you.
Apply	4	The last exam covered memos simple tables and unbound reports.

Rule 2: Do not use a comma to separate two items treated as a single unit within a series.

Learn	5	Her favorite breakfast was bacon and eggs, muffins, and juice.
Apply	6	My choices are peaches and cream brownies or ice cream.
Apply	7	Trays of fresh fruit nuts and cheese and crackers awaited guests.

Rule 3: Use a comma before short direct quotations.

Learn	8	The man asked, "When does Flight 787 depart?"
Apply	9	Mrs. Ramirez replied "No, the report on patriotism is not finished."
Apply	10	Dr. Feit said "Please make an appointment for next week."

Rule 4: Use a comma before and after a word or words in apposition (words that come together and refer to the same person or thing).

Learn	11	Coleta, the assistant manager, will chair the next meeting.
Apply	12	Greg Mathews a pitcher for the Braves will sign autographs.
Apply	13	The personnel director Marge Wilson will be the presenter.

Rule 5: Use a comma to set off words of direct address (the name of a person spoken to).

Learn	14	I believe, Tom, that you should fly to San Francisco.
Apply	15	Finish this assignment Mary before you start on the next one.
Apply	16	Please call me Erika if I can be of further assistance.

Rule 6: Use a comma to set off nonrestrictive clauses (not necessary to the meaning of the sentence); however, do not use commas to set off restrictive clauses (necessary to the meaning of the sentence).

Learn	17	The manuscript, which I prepared, needs to be revised.
Learn	18	The manuscript that presents voting alternatives is complete.
Apply	19	The movie which won top awards dealt with human rights.
Apply	20	The student who scores highest on the exam will win the award.

(continued on next page)

- To perform a mail merge.
- To create and edit a data source file.

119B

Perform a Mail Merge

WP
- Mailings/Start Mail
- Merge/Step by Step
- Mail Merge Wizard

1. Study the text and illustration.
2. Learn how to perform a mail merge using an existing main document and data source.
3. Prepare three letters by merging the files as directed in steps 1–4.

Save as: 119B LETTERS

TIP: To save a copy of all the letters, click Edit Individual Letters in the task pane in step 6 of the Mail Merge Wizard. Choose All in the Merge New Document dialog box. Click OK and then save the letters as *119B LETTERS*. The letters may be saved before or after the one or more of the letters are printed.

The Merge feature is often used to merge a letter file (**main document**) with a name and address file (**data source**) to create a personalized letter (**merged file**) to each person in the data source file. Mail Merge can also be used to create labels for envelopes, name badges, etc.

Data sources can be word processing, spreadsheet, database, or e-mail files. In this unit, you will use data sources created in *Word*.

You can use the Mail Merge Wizard task panes to lead you through the process of setting up and performing a mail merge. Or you can use the commands on the Mailings tab. In this unit, you will use the Mail Merge Wizard to set up and perform mail merges.

Step 1 of 6 in the Mail Merge Wizard task pane

1. Open the main document file (*DF 119B MAIN*), and complete steps 1–3 to select the type of document (choose *Letters*), starting document (choose *Use the current document*), and recipients (choose *Use an existing list* and then browse for *DF 119B DATA*).
2. In step 4, the letter is written and the merge fields are inserted. Since the letter is already written and contains the needed merge fields, step 3 is completed; proceed to Step 5.
3. In step 5, preview the three letters by using the forward or backward chevrons in the task pane.
4. In step 6, select the Print option in the task pane and choose to print the Current record.

2. Key Proofread & Correct, inserting commas correctly.
   a. Check answers.
   b. Using the rule number(s) at the left of each line, study the rule relating to each error you made.
   c. Rekey each incorrect line, inserting commas correctly.

Save as: CS7 ACTIVITY1

ACTIVITY 2

Reading

1. Open *DF CS7 ACTIVITY2*.
2. Read the document; close the file.
3. Key answers to the questions, using complete sentences.

Save as: CS7 ACTIVITY2

ACTIVITY 3

Composing

1. Key the ¶, correcting word-choice errors. (Every line contains at least one error.)
2. Compose a 2nd ¶ to accomplish these goals:
   • Define what respect means to you.
   • Identify kinds of behavior that help earn your respect.
   • Identify kinds of behavior that cause you to lose respect.
3. Proofread, revise, and correct.

Save as: CS7 ACTIVITY3

Proofread & Correct

Rules

1	1	My favorite sports are college football basketball and soccer.
1	2	If you finish your history report before noon please give me a call.
1,2	3	I snacked on milk and cookies granola and some raisins.
3	4	Miss Qwan said "I was born in Taiwan."
4	5	Mr. Sheldon the historian will speak to our students today.
5	6	Why do you persist Kermit in moving your hands to the top row?
6	7	The report which Ted wrote is well organized and informative.
6	8	Only students who use their time wisely are likely to succeed.
3	9	Dr. Sachs said "Take two of these and call me in the morning."
6	10	Yolanda who is from Cuba intends to become a U.S. citizen.

1. What was the final score of yesterday's soccer match?
2. Was the winning goal scored in the first or second half?
3. Will last year's City League champion be playing in this year's championship match?
4. Will the top-ranked team in the state be playing in this year's championship match?
5. Will the top-ranked team in the city be playing in the championship match?
6. Is the championship game to be played during the day or the evening?
7. Has one or both of the teams playing in the championship match won a City League championship before?

That all individuals want others too respect them is not surprising. What is surprising is that sum people think their do respect even when there own behavior has been unacceptable or even illegal. Key two the issue is that we respect others because of certain behavior, rather then in spite of it. Its vital, than, to no that what people due and say determines the level of respect there given buy others. In that regard, than, respect has to be earned; its not hour unquestioned right to demand it. All of you hear and now should begin to chose behaviors that will led others to respect you. Its you're choice.

Letter 2

Use modified block, mixed punctuation, ¶ indentations, and Calibri, 12 pt.

Save as: 118B LETTER2

Letter 3

1. Format Letter 2 as a two-page block letter with open punctuation and Times New Roman, 14 pt. with 1.25" side margins.
2. Add the subject line: **EMPLOYEE TRIAL MEMBERSHIP**
3. Bold the name of the fitness center in the body of the letter.
4. Add the center's name as a company name in the closing lines.

Save as: 118B LETTER3

Letter 4

Use block format, mixed punctuation, and Tahoma, 12 pt.

Save as: 118B LETTER4

Letter 5

Format Letter 4 in modified block; use open punctuation, ¶ indentations, and Arial, 12 pt.

Save as: 118B LETTER5

Letter 6

1. Open *DF 118B LETTER6* and format the text as a block letter with mixed punctuation.
2. Key the ¶ at the right as the final ¶.

Proofreading Cue

Find and correct the four errors in the file.

Save as: 118B LETTER6

March 5, 20-- | Attention Human Resources Department | Central Life Assurance, Inc. | 1520 W. Ohio Street | Indianapolis, IN 46222-1578 | Ladies and Gentlemen

The Action Fitness and Exercise Center is offering an introductory membership to employees of area corporations. This membership is for 90 days and costs only $50, the regular monthly membership fee.

During this 90-day trial period, your employees can use the indoor running track, weight-lifting stations, and exercise equipment (including treadmills, stair climbers, and rowing machines).

Your employees can also enroll in any of the aerobics, weight-control, and healthy-eating classes that are offered on a regular basis.

To take advantage of this offer, distribute the enclosed cards to interested employees. These cards can be presented on the first visit.

Sincerely | Ned V. Mowry | President | xx | Enclosure | c Mary Parker, Club Membership Coordinator

May 17, 20-- | REGISTERED | Susan T. Kipin, M.D. | 404 E. Washington Street | Indianapolis, IN 46204-8201 | Dear Dr. Kipin | CHANGE IN HAZARDOUS REMOVAL CONTAINERS

The waste removal containers that we have located at your office will be removed on May 30 and replaced with new containers that provide greater safety for your patients, your employees, and you. A brochure showing the container dimensions is enclosed.

Our technician will fasten a container to the wall in each room you designate. Please be certain that your office manager knows the specific locations.

Once the new containers have been installed, TRT technicians will schedule a time when the waste can be removed daily.

Sincerely | Dorothy C. McIntyre | Service Manager | DCM:xx | Enclosure | bc Harry Williams, Technician

¶ The association's staff thanks you for supporting this important nonprofit organization. Without contributions from citizens such as you, thousands more men and women would suffer fatal heart attacks each year.

1. Open *DF CS7 ACTIVITY4* and print the file.
2. Solve the problems as directed in the file.
3. Submit your answers.

CAREER Clusters

ACTIVITY 7

You must complete Career Exploration Activities 1–3 before completing this activity.

1. Retrieve your Career folder and the information in it that relates to the career cluster that is your first choice.

2. Reflect on the skills and knowledge you have gained in the courses you have taken and the extracurricular activities in which you are involved that will be beneficial in the career you selected as your first choice. Then compose a paragraph or two describing the connection between what you have learned and/or your activities and this career. Print your file, save it as Career7, and keep it open.

3. Exchange papers with a classmate and have the classmate offer suggestions for improving the content and correcting any errors he or she finds in your paragraph(s). Make the changes that you agree with and print a copy to turn in to your instructor. Save your file as Career7 and close the file.

4. Return your folder to the storage area. When your instructor returns your paper, file it in your Career folder.

© STOCKBYTE/GETTY IMAGES

OBJECTIVES
- To review letters with special parts.
- To review format features of two-page letters.

118B

Two-Page Letters with Special Parts

Letter 1

Use block format, mixed punctuation, and Calibri 14-pt font.

Save as: **118B LETTER1**

Formatting Cue

When a company name is used in the closing lines, tap **ENTER** once after the complimentary close and key the name in ALL CAPS; then tap **ENTER** twice and key the writer's name.

April 3, 20-- | SPECIAL DELIVERY | Mrs. Carol T. Yao | Director of Human Resources | Franklin Tool & Die Company | 600 E. Lake Street | Addison, IL 60101-3492 | Dear Mrs. Yao: | YOUR REQUEST FOR ADDITIONAL INFORMATION

Thank you for agreeing to give further consideration to making Protect III available to your employees, beginning with the open enrollment period that starts in June.

Protect III has been among the leaders in the health insurance industry for the past 15 years. Our plan is now used by hundreds of thousands of people in Illinois and is accepted by almost every physician, hospital, and pharmacy in your area.

The enclosed materials will provide you with more information about Protect III that should help you prepare the proposal for your vice president. The following materials are included:

- ❑ "Top Choice Protection" brochure that explains Protect III's key features.

- ❑ A benefit summary chart that outlines specific benefits.

- ❑ A provider directory that lists all the Illinois primary care physicians and facilities participating in Protect III.

- ❑ A pharmacy directory that lists the pharmacies your employees can use as part of the Protect III prescription plan.

- ❑ A chart of monthly fees for the various levels of coverage your employees may choose.

If you have any questions about Protect III features, the provider network, or the fees that will apply to Franklin Tool & Die Company, call me at 1-800-555-0113.

Sincerely | PROTECT III, INC. | Carlos V. Santana | Corporate Account Rep | CVS:xx | Enclosures | Carol, thank you for giving Protect III the opportunity to provide your company's health care benefits. We're looking forward to serving you and your employees.

Electronic presentations can be enhanced by using the capabilities of the presentation software. Enhancements, however, should not be overdone.

Slide Animations

Rather than have a slide appear in its entirety, animations can be used to make text, graphics, and other objects appear one at a time. This allows control of how the information is presented as well as adding interest to the presentation.

A variety of animations are available to choose from. For example, text and objects on a slide can be animated to fade in, spin, float, ascend, or descend. **Animation schemes** are options that are preset. They range from very subtle to very glitzy. The scheme chosen should add interest without taking away from the message. **Custom animation** allows several different animations to be included on each slide.

Slide Transitions

Slide transition is the term used to describe how the display changes from one slide to the next. When no transition is applied, slides go from one directly to the next. Transition effects can make it appear as though the next slide dissolves in or appears through a circle, for example. There are numerous transitions to choose from.

Hyperlinks

A hyperlink is text that is colored and underlined that you click to take you from the current location in the electronic file to another location.

This means that a presenter can create hyperlinks to move from the current slide in a presentation to an Internet site that relates to what he/she is talking about.

Slide with Hyperlink

Timing

The Slide Timing feature controls the speed with which one slide replaces another. Setting times tells the software how long each slide will remain on the screen.

Pictures

In addition to clip art, pictures can be inserted in an electronic presentation from a number of different sources such as scanners, cameras, files, and the Internet. Care must be taken not to violate copyright laws. Movies can also be inserted into a presentation.

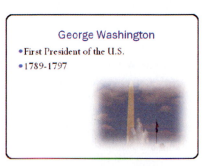
Example of Slide with Picture

SmartArt Graphics

Graphics are used to visually communicate information. SmartArt graphics include list, process, cycle, hierarchy, relationship, matrix, and pyramid.

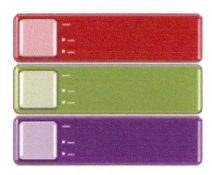
Example of SmartArt

Sound

Sound is another way to enhance a presentation. When people hear something as well as see it, they are much more likely to retain it.

Most electronic presentation software allows you to insert sound from a prerecorded clip organizer or from a sound file, play music from a CD, or record sound directly into the presentation.

The sound capability allows a presenter to bring variety and credibility to a presentation. Hearing John F. Kennedy say "Ask not what your country can do for you, ask what you can do for your country" has much more of an impact than if the presenter reads the quote. Having background music play as you show pictures has more of an impact than just showing the pictures.

Document 2 (Letter)

Use block format, open punctuation, and Arial font, 12 pt.

Save as: **117B LETTER2**

Document 3 (Letter)

1. Format Document 2 in modified block with open punctuation and ¶ indentations.
2. Use Times New Roman font, 14 pt.
3. Center the letter vertically.

Save as: **117B LETTER3**

Document 4 (Letter)

1. Use modified block format with mixed punctuation and no ¶ indentations.
2. Use Century Gothic font, 12 pt.

Save as: **117B LETTER4**

Document 5 (Letter)

1. Format Document 4 in block format with open punctuation.
2. Use Courier New font, 12 pt.

Save as: **117B LETTER5**

Document 6 (Memo)

1. Format, using this information:
   DATE: April 16, 20--
   TO: Harriett Gross
   FROM: Helen Otto
   SUBJECT: BEST DENTAL CHOICE
2. Use Times New Roman font, 18 pt.

Save as: **117B MEMO6**

(Current date) | Mr. Max R. Rice | 23 Oak Street | Schiller Park, IL 60176-6932 | Dear Mr. Rice

If the health plan you chose last year has not delivered everything you thought it would, we have some good news for you. Health Plus is now available to you during this open enrollment period.

Health Plus is the area's largest point-of-service plan that combines the managed care features of an HMO with the freedom of choice of a traditional health plan. As the enclosed directory indicates, this plan gives you access to the best doctors and medical facilities in the area.

To enroll, simply complete the enclosed application and return it to your benefits office within 30 days.

Sincerely | Ms. Peg Jerzak | Account Specialist | xx | Enclosure

---

October 2, 20-- | Ms. Paula Kenney | Sterling Medical Supplies | 4259 Rosegarden Road | Long Beach, CA 98766-4259 | Dear Ms. Kenney

Please accept this invitation to participate in East High's Fifth Annual Health Occupations Career Fair that will be held on Thursday, November 17, from 2 to 4 p.m. at East High.

Last year's career fair attracted 26 employers and associations and more than 400 students. The employers represented hospitals, long-term health-care providers, outpatient clinics, medical insurance providers, medical supply and equipment vendors, and large physician practices. In addition, several associations attended to provide students with career information related to the technical areas.

To reserve a table for your company, please fill out and return the enclosed registration form by November 1. We look forward to having you present.

Sincerely | Lawrence R. Aamont | Health Occupations | xx | Enclosure

---

A representative from Best Dental Choice will be visiting the Benefits Office on Tuesday, April 25, to explain the advantages of that dental insurance plan.

Please arrange your schedule so you can attend the 2 p.m. meeting, during which the Best Dental Choice sales rep will outline the features of the plan and compare the benefits to our present plan.

Please bring one of your assistants who works closely with the dental plan to the meeting.

OBJECTIVES
- To review how to create an electronic presentation.
- To create an electronic presentation with graphics and pictures.
- To add slides to an existing electronic presentation.

72A–75A

Conditioning Practice

Key each line twice SS.

alphabet	1	Zachary James always purchased five or six large antique baskets.
figures	2	Only 1,548 of the 1,967 expected guests had arrived by 12:30 p.m.
speed	3	The neighbor may fix the problem with the turn signal on the bus.

gwam 1' | 1 | 2 | 3 | 4 | 5 | 6 | 7 | 8 | 9 | 10 | 11 | 12 | 13 |

72B

Create a Presentation

1. Review Unit 12, pp. 110–125.
2. Learn how to copy pictures and graphics from the Internet.
3. Create the 12 slides shown at the right and on the next page. The slides will be used again in Lessons 73–75. The illustrations at the right use the Equity design theme with Office colors.

Save as: 72B PP

Source for slide 3:
http://www.whitehouse.gov/government/exec.html

Source for slides 6–7 and 72B slide 2:
http://www.whitehouse.gov/government/cabinet.html

Government of the United States of America

Student's Name
Current Date

Slide 1

Branches of U.S. Government

- Executive Branch
- Judicial Branch
- Legislative Branch

Slide 2

Executive Branch

- The power of the executive branch is vested in the President, who also serves as Commander in Chief of the Armed Forces.

Slide 3

George Washington

- First President of the U.S.
- 1789-1797

Slide 4

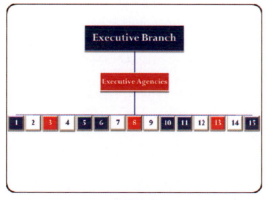

Slide 5

Slide 6

(continued on next page)

Lesson 117   **REVIEW LETTERS AND MEMOS**

OBJECTIVES
• To review block and modified block letter and memo formats.
• To review open and mixed punctuation and basic letter and memo parts.

117A-122A

Conditioning Practice

Key each line twice.

alphabet	1	Avoid fizzling fireworks because they just might explode quickly.
figures	2	He surveyed 3,657 women, 2,980 men, and 1,400 children last June.
speed	3	It may be a big problem if both of the men bid for the dock work.

gwam 1' | 1 | 2 | 3 | 4 | 5 | 6 | 7 | 8 | 9 | 10 | 11 | 12 | 13 |

117B

Business Letters and Memos

Document 1 (Memo)

1. Format, adding any memo parts that may be missing.
2. Correct the marked errors and the five embedded errors.

Save as: **117B MEMO1**

TO: Olu T. Sangoeyhi, Physical Therapy

FROM: William M. Glause, Administrative Services

DATE: May 14, 20-- *Change this and all other occurrences of "brochure" to "pamphlet."*

SUBJECT: PHYSICAL THERAPY BROCHURE

Here is the first draft of the physical theraphy brochure that
has been ~~okayed~~ *authorized* for publication in this years budget. Please *proofread* ~~check~~
the copy ~~very~~ carefully. *and make sure the pictures are correct.*

The public relations staff is in the process of getting
permission to use each persons picture in the brochure. All
permision forms should be completed within the next (10) *sp* days, If
there are ~~any~~ changes in the pictures ~~we are using~~, I will see that
you get to review ~~all the~~ changes ~~before we go to printing~~ *new pictures.*
Please ~~make the necessary~~ changes ~~in the copy~~ and retun the *mark your suggested*
brochure to me by next Monday.

Enclosure

72B (continued)

Slide 7

Source for slide 8:
http://www.whitehouse.gov/government/legi.html

Legislative Branch

- The legislative branch of the federal government consists of the Congress, which is divided into two chambers—the Senate and the House of Representatives.

Slide 8

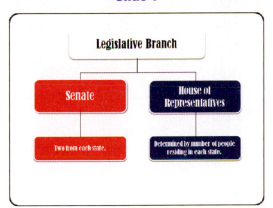

Slide 9

Source for slide 10:
http://www.whitehouse.gov/government/judg.html

Judicial Branch

- The judicial branch hears cases that challenge or require interpretation of the legislation passed by Congress and signed by the President.

Slide 10

Slide 11

U.S. Supreme Court
- The Supreme Court consists of nine justices.
- Justices are nominated by the President and confirmed by the Senate.

Slide 12

72C

Insert Slides

Learn how to insert new slides. Create the two slides shown at the right and insert them as instructed.

Create a similar one for the Legislative Branch (insert it before the Legislative Branch description) and one for the Judicial Branch (insert it before the Judicial Branch description).

Save as: 72C PP

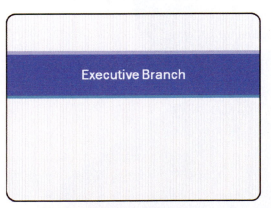

Insert between Slides 2 and 3

Insert between Slides 7 and 8

CYCLE 4

LESSONS 117-170

We all have a responsibility as citizens of the world to learn about and care for the environment. "Environment" encompasses a wide range of topics including health, population, climate, pollution, recycling, forestry, food, sports, and many more. Some of you may choose environmental careers. You could work in the wilderness or in a corporate office. You could become a teacher or join the Peace Corps.

Whatever career you choose will require some basic skills, including the ability to create effective business documents. Your keying skills, organizational abilities, and facility with computer software will give you an edge.

In this cycle, you will complete activities using business documents on health and environmental subjects.

You will improve your keying and computer skills while learning about such diverse topics as exercise, physical therapy, environmental websites, and careers in sports medicine and training. You'll learn to create a program booklet, work on a newsletter, and even prepare a business plan. You'll enhance your database and spreadsheet skills, and you'll create a Web page.

Whether you decide to go into business for yourself, choose a career in an environmental or health field, or take another direction, your keyboarding and software skills will serve you all of your life. Use the skillbuilding lessons in this unit to help you stay in the game!

Environment & Health

Lesson 73

ENHANCING PRESENTATIONS WITH GRAPHICS AND ANIMATION/TRANSITIONS

OBJECTIVES

- To copy and insert graphics from the Internet.
- To use the transition and animation features to enhance a slide show.
- To create and print slide show notes pages.

73B

Slide Show Enhancement

1. Learn how to copy and insert graphics from the Internet.

2. Review the information on transitions and animation on p. 212.

3. Learn how to add transitions and animation to your slide show.

4. Make the changes outlined at the right and insert pictures as shown. *DF 73B Washington* has a picture of the Washington Monument.

5. In Slide Sorter view, add a transition to all slides except the first. Include at least three types of transitions.

6. Animate the bulleted items so they appear one at a time for slides 2 and 16.

7. Use the Wedge animation effect for the illustration for slide 16. Use the Effects option to group graphics One by one.

8. Insert a slide following slide 9 (3rd Executive Agencies slide). Select Section Headers layout. Use **President's Cabinet** for the main heading.

9. Learn how to insert a hyperlink.

10. On the newly inserted slide, include a hyperlink to: http://www.whitehouse.gov/government/cabinet.html

Save as: **73B PP**

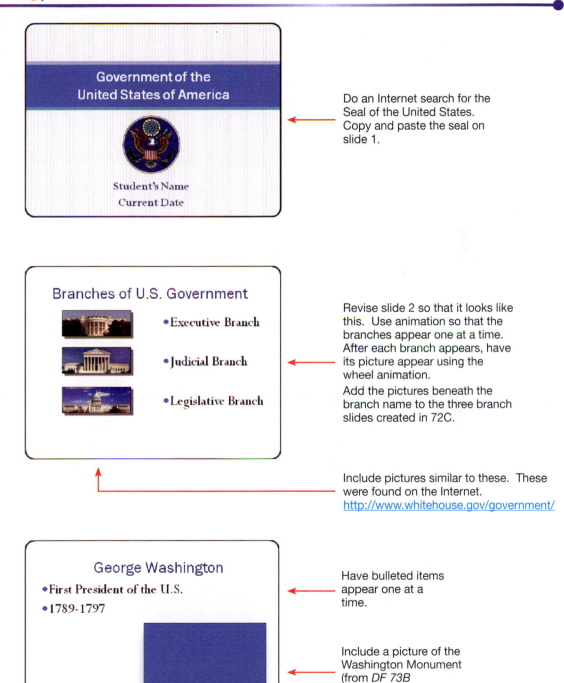

Do an Internet search for the Seal of the United States. Copy and paste the seal on slide 1.

Revise slide 2 so that it looks like this. Use animation so that the branches appear one at a time. After each branch appears, have its picture appear using the wheel animation.

Add the pictures beneath the branch name to the three branch slides created in 72C.

Include pictures similar to these. These were found on the Internet. http://www.whitehouse.gov/government/

Have bulleted items appear one at a time.

Include a picture of the Washington Monument (from *DF 73B Washington*)

Job 12

Prepare this announcement and then below it add the form that is on D4 TSEA JOB12 so it can be cut off and returned. Try to have the form begin and end with the margins for the announcement. Also, insert some appropriate clip art where you think it fits best.

YP

Job 13

I reviewed the letter you drafted and used track changes to show my suggestions. Open D4 TSEA JOB13 and accept the changes after you have reviewed them. Please use a 14-pt. font.

YP

Job 14

I need you to design an 8.5" x 11" poster that we can send out to the science departments in school districts in the Tri-County area. The information I jotted down at the right should be included. If you think something else should be added, please do it. Make it attractive, colorful, and applicable to science teachers.

YP

TSEA GOLF OUTING

Announcement and Registration Form

The TSEA 18-hole golf outing will be held on June 14 at the well-known Twin Lakes Golf Course. A shotgun start is scheduled at 11:20 a.m. Plan to be at the course no latter than 10:45 a.m. Round-trip transportation from the Russell Hotel will be provided.

The cost for the outing is $75 for green and cart fees. The cookout at 4:30 p.m. is $12. The outing will end in time for you too be at the TSEA opening general session at 7:30 p.m.

If you plan to participate complete the form below and return it by June 5 to:

Nancy Hyduk
East Lake Middle School
9600 Southern Pines Boulevard
Charlotte, NC 28273-5520

✂----------------------✂----------------------✂----------------------✂

- Name, dates, and location of the conference.
- Mention that there will be many sessions and exhibitors focusing on effective instructional resources and strategies for science educators.
- Give the cost of the conference registration, the two special workshops, banquet, and lunch.
- Mention the optional golf outing and cookout—give the name of the course and the costs associated with it.
- Let them know they can get a registration form and additional information from the TSEA website at www.cengage.com/school/keyboarding/tsea.nc.org.

I believe you can find all the information you need in the jobs you have completed. Let me know if you can't.

Add Notes

You will be giving the slide show you just created to foreign exchange students at your school. Learn how to create notes pages, and key the notes shown at the right and on the next page for each slide.

Copy the first slide and insert it at the end of your presentation as slide 18.

Print copies of your notes pages to have available for Lesson 75.

Save as: 73C PP

1. The government of the United States as we know it today has evolved over time. Its beginnings date back prior to the U.S. gaining its independence from England.

2. Today we have three branches of government. They include:

   the Executive Branch

   the Legislative Branch, and

   the Judicial Branch

3. Let's start by talking about the Executive Branch.

4. As you can see, the President of the United States is in charge of the Executive Branch. He serves as Commander in Chief of the Armed Forces, appoints cabinet members, and oversees various executive (government) agencies that we will be discussing later on in the presentation.

5. The first Commander in Chief of the Armed Forces was our first President, George Washington. Interestingly enough, he was named the army's Commander in Chief by the Second Continental Congress before he was ever elected president.

6. This slide shows a diagram of the 15 Executive Agencies.

7. The Executive Agencies include: the Department of Agriculture, the Department of Commerce, the Department of Defense, the Department of Education, the Department of Energy,

8. the Department of Health and Human Services, the Department of Homeland Security, the Department of Housing and Urban Development, the Department of the Interior, the Department of Justice,

9. the Department of Labor, the Department of State, the Department of Transportation, the Department of the Treasury, and the Department of Veterans Affairs.

10. Let's take a look at the President's Cabinet.

11. Now that we know a little about the Executive Branch, let's talk briefly about the Legislative Branch of government.

12. The Legislative Branch consists of Congress. Congress has two parts—the Senate and the House of Representatives.

13. As shown on this slide, there are two senators elected from each state. They are elected for a term of six years. The terms of the senators are staggered so that one-third of the Senate seats are up for election every two years. With each state having two senators, each state is given equal representation regardless of size or population.

Registration

The conference registration form has been designed and will be included with the next TSEA newsletter ~~that is mailed~~. Additionally, a separate ~~mailing that contains~~ *flyer announcing* conference highlights and registration procedures will be ~~sent~~ *mailed* to all science teachers in the Tri-County area ^ by May 1. The early-bird registration fee *approved at our last meeting* will ~~be~~ *apply* ~~offered~~ to all who register before June 5. Efforts are underway to recruit teachers to staff the registration tables throughout the conference.

Special Events

The *popular* conference golf outing will be held on June 14 at the Twin Lakes Golf Club, prior to the first general session at 7 p.m. Up to 72 golfers can be accommodated. The customary cookout will begin at 4:30 p.m. and all Executive Board members are encouraged to attend. The cost has increased only slightly--from $73 last year to 77 this year.

Hospitality

I will be ~~working very~~ closely with Connie Taylor ~~during the~~ next week to bring her up-to-date with what Janice Pearson ~~had~~ arranged. With that information, Connie will be able to finalize all of the gifts and information we need to ~~provide our conference~~ *give to* participants.

Conclusion

The Conference Board *that you appointed* is an excellent one. The members are very responsible, eager to work, knowledgeable, and cooperative. Their goal*s* *are* is to provide an excellent conference at a reasonable price and to generate income for TSEA. I will have ~~each committee's~~ *the Conference Board's* final budget and estimated conference revenues for you*r* to review ~~and~~ act*tion* ~~upon~~ at ~~the~~ *our* next meeting.

73C (continued)

The House of Representatives, on the other hand, is based on the population of each state. As the population changes within states, the number of representatives allocated to that state may also change.

14. The third branch of our government is called the Judicial Branch.

15. The Judicial Branch hears cases that challenge or require interpretation of the laws passed by Congress. The Judicial Branch has the responsibility of protecting the rights of all Americans that were granted by the Constitution.

16. The judicial system is three-tiered; the first tier is the U.S. District Courts. Trials take place in these courts. If a person loses in a district court, he/she can usually appeal the decision. These appeals are heard in U.S. Courts of Appeals. Finally, there is the U.S. Supreme Court.

17. The Supreme Court consists of nine justices who have been nominated by the President and confirmed by the Senate. Even though there are many cases submitted to the Supreme Court, very few cases are ever acted upon by this court.

18. This is a very brief overview of our government. You will learn much more about it during the time you spend here. And we hope to learn about your country as well. Welcome to the United States.

Lesson 74 — ENHANCING PRESENTATIONS WITH SOUND

OBJECTIVES
- To insert sound from the Clip Organizer.
- To record sound.
- To play a CD audio track during parts of the slide show.

74B

Insert Sound

1. Read the information at the right.
2. Learn how to insert sound from the Clip Organizer for your software.
3. Insert "America the Beautiful" from the sound Clip Organizer on the first and last slide of the presentation created for Lessons 72 and 73. Have the sound start automatically for slide 1 and manually for slide 18.

Save as: 74B PP

There are several different types of sounds that can be added to your presentation. These include:

- Sounds from the Clip Organizer
- Sounds from a file
- Sounds from a CD audio track
- Sounds that you record—Recorded Sounds

Sounds from Clip Organizer—Prerecorded sounds available with the software.

Sounds from a file—Sounds that you have recorded and saved as a file that can be linked to the presentation.

Sounds from a CD audio track—Music that is played directly from a CD. Particular parts of the CD can be specified for playing.

Recorded sounds—With recording capability, words (using your voice or the voice of someone else), sounds, or music can be recorded to specific slides.

change in the makeup of the board: Connie Taylor replaced Janice
Pearson who had to relinquish~~ed~~ her position as Hospitality Chair due
to illness, *in her family*.

Program

The Program Committee has designed the (entire) program for the
3-day conference and has mailed a Call for Papers to all TSEA
members. To date, 15 papers have ~~been received~~ *come in*. Reviewers are
deciding if the ~~content is~~ *papers* *are* appropriate for conference presentation**s**.
Within the next two months, the Program Committee plans to have ~~pre~~
~~senters~~ *speakers* for all concurrent and general sessions (confirmed). Two
publishing ~~houses~~ *companies* have been asked to sponsor the two general session
speakers. ~~If they agree to do this,~~ *As sponsors* they will pay ~~for~~ the speakers'
travel and lodging expenses and provide a generous honorarium. In
return for this ~~contribution~~ *support* each publisher**s** will receive promi-
nent, public recognition~~for their significant contribution.~~

Exhibitors

The Conference Board members, led by Jim Herriott, Exhibits
Chair, are making a **n** ~~concerted~~ effort to increase conference revenues
by increasing the number of exhibit spaces sold. They are doing
this in two ways:

* Increase the number of exhibitors. **to**
* Increas**ing** the number of tables exhibitors buy.

The following chart indicates how revenue may be increased *by more than $2,500* if
we attract four new exhibitors averaging two tables each, retain
all exhibitors from last year, persuade last year's exhibitor's to
purchase 7 additional spaces, and ~~there is~~ *make* no change in the exhibit
fee per table.

make rows higher

REVENUE FROM EXHIBITS					
Last Year			This Year		
Vendors	Tables	Revenue	Vendors	Tables	Revenue
7	1	$1,750	4	1	$1,000
5	2	$2,250	11	2	$4,950
2	3	$1,200	3	3	$1,800
14		$5,200	18		$7,750

(continued on next page)

Record Sound

1. Create the slides shown at the right. *DF 75 Photos* includes a picture of the Lincoln Monument.

2. Enhance the slide presentation with appropriate animation and transitions.

3. Learn how to use the Record Sound feature of your software.

4. The script for slides 2 through 9 is on p. 219. Read through the script and practice it several times. Using the script, record the narration for the slide show.

5. Learn how to play a CD audio track during a slide show presentation.

6. Select music that would be appropriate to play during the slide presentation. Specify where you want the music to start and where you want it to stop. Consider whether you will need to have the music loop.

7. Learn how to program the Slide Timing feature.

8. Set the Slide Timing feature so that the slide show will run automatically.

Save as: 74C PP

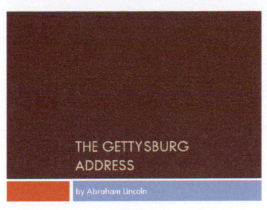

Slide 1

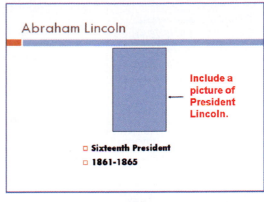

Include a picture of President Lincoln.

Slide 2

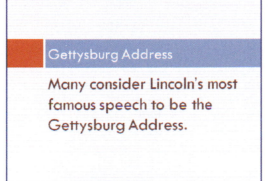

Slide 3

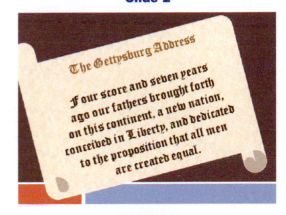

Slide 4

Slide 5

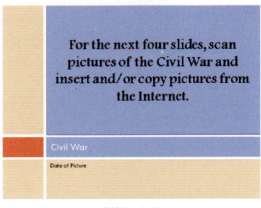

Slide 6–9

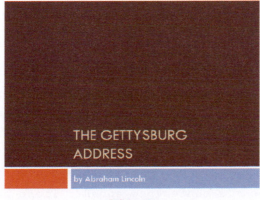

Slide 10

(continued on next page)

Job 8

I drafted a news release. Open DF TSEAJ JOB8 and prepare a final copy for me. It is for immediate release and I am the contact person.

YP

Job 9

Using your favorite Internet search engine, try to find museums in the 28202 ZIP Code area. If you find some, give me a list or a table with the names, addresses, telephone numbers, and hours. I need to give this information to Connie Taylor.

YP

Job 10

I need you to team with a classmate who is also working on this conference. Together, you need to design a worksheet that we can use to record registration information for those who are attending. The information you need to include in the worksheet is noted at the right.

YP

Job 11

Here are my corrections for the progress report I have to present to the board. Format it as a report using Word 2007 Style Set. Include a footer that shows the current date on each page. Include the title and page number on all pages, except p. 1. Correct any errors.

YP

Exhibits. J. Herriott ~~reported that he~~ is gathering data on past exhibitors and ~~is~~ identifying prospective exhibitors.

Hospitality. C. Taylor had nothing to report this time.

Special events. N. Hyduk is planning to have the golf outing at Twin Lakes Golf Course. She hopes to have confirmation in a few ~~matter of~~ days.

3. **Unfinished business:** Y. Porterfield ~~stated that she~~ set a meeting with Russell Hotel personnel and ~~that~~ she and J. Herriott will meet with them soon. Other committee chairs ~~are invited to the meeting. If they~~ need**ing** specific information about hotel facilities and services are to tell Y. Porterfield within ten days.

4. **New business:** Security for the exhibits area was discussed ~~and it was decided to request~~ funding *will be requested* to post a security guard during all hours the exhibits are *closed* ~~not open~~ to ~~the~~ conference participants.

Committee chairs are to submit ~~a~~ final request for funds ~~that they need~~ at the next meeting so that Y. Porterfield can present a final budget to the TSEA Executive Board for approval.

5. **Next meeting:** The next meeting date was not set, *but* all agreed that a Tuesday *would be* ~~was~~ best. Y. Porterfield will set the date and notify each Conference Board member.

Person's name, ZIP Code, and school name. Record the $50 registration fee they paid and the amount paid for one or both of the two special workshops that cost $30 each. Record if they paid $25 for the June 14 banquet and/or $15 for the June 15 luncheon. Also, record the total amount each registrant paid.

We need to know the number of persons paying each of the fees above. Likewise, record the total amount of money received for each of these events that require payment.

By the way, insert three or four fictitious names and fees paid so we can verify the accuracy of your calculations; format the worksheet so it is attractive and easy to read.

TSEA CONFERENCE BOARD PROGRESS REPORT

(Yvonne Porterfield, Conference Director)

Satisfactory progress is being made in all areas as the Conference Board continue**s** to make ~~all the~~ arrangements for the Sixth Annual TSEA Conference that is scheduled at the Russell Hotel (Charlotte) from June 14–16. *through June*

Conference Board *12-pt. bold*

The Conference Board has met monthly since it was appointed shortly after last year's conference ended. There has been one

(continued on next page)

74C (continued)

Script for the Gettysburg
Address by Abraham
Lincoln slide presentation

Slide 2

Abraham Lincoln is one of the best-known presidents of the United States. He was our sixteenth president and held office from 1861 until 1865, when he was assassinated.

Slide 3

The Gettysburg Address is a speech delivered by President Lincoln at the dedication of the Gettysburg National Cemetery to honor those who died in the Battle of Gettysburg during the Civil War.

Slide 4

Four score and seven years ago our fathers brought forth on this continent, a new nation, conceived in Liberty, and dedicated to the proposition that all men are created equal.

Slide 5

Now we are engaged in a great civil war, testing whether that nation, or any nation so conceived and so dedicated, can long endure. We are met on a great battlefield of that war.

Slide 6

We have come to dedicate a portion of that field, as a final resting place for those who here gave their lives that that nation might live. It is altogether fitting and proper that we should do this.

Slide 7

But, in a larger sense, we cannot dedicate—we cannot consecrate—we cannot hallow—this ground. The brave men, living and dead, who struggled here, have consecrated it, far above our poor power to add or detract.

Slide 8

The world will little note, nor long remember what we say here, but it can never forget what they did here. It is for us the living, rather, to be dedicated here to the unfinished work which they who fought here have thus far so nobly advanced.

Slide 9

It is rather for us to be here dedicated to the great task remaining before us—that from these honored dead we take increased devotion to that cause for which they gave the last full measure of devotion—that we here highly resolve that these dead shall not have died in vain—that this nation, under God, shall have a new birth of freedom—and that government of the people, by the people, for the people, shall not perish from the earth.

Job 4

Prepare this letter for my signature, please.

YP

Job 5

Open DF TSEAJ JOB5 and accept or reject the changes and note the comments.

YP

Job 6

Prepare a draft of this worksheet. It will be used to record registrations. Insert formulas to make the calculations, and then compute the amount due for these three fictitious people so we can verify the formulas are correct.

YP

Job 7

Here's a rough draft of the minutes I need to take to the conference board meeting next Tuesday. Please prepare a final draft. Insert the first Tuesday of last month as the date. Proofread carefully because I didn't.

YP

Mr. Carlos Bautista, Sales Manager, Russell Hotel, 222 E 3d Street, Charlotte, NC 28202-0222

This letter is to confirm a meeting that Mr. James Herriott and I have with you next Friday afternoon at the Russell Hotel.

The primary purpose of the meeting is to tour areas of the hotel that will be used for sessions, exhibits, dining, and registration at the TSEA Tri-County Science Education Conference that is scheduled for June 14-16, 20--.

In the session rooms, we need to see different various seating arrangements and determine what AV audiovisual and other aids speakers can use. We will need access to the Web Internet in at least two three of the rooms. Also, we need to discuss security issues relating to the exhibit area and discuss the electrical service to each exhibit space.

James and I will meat you in your office next Friday at 3:30 p.m.

GOLF OUTING AND COOKOUT REGISTRATIONS

Name	Fees	Rental	Cookout	Total Cost	Deposit	Amount Due
John Doe	75	10	12		50	
Jane Doe			12		0	
Jim Doe	75				40	

Add rows at the bottom to calculate totals and count the entries for columns B–G.

SS all A's; DS between

TSEA Conference Board

Participants: R. Acosta, M. Coughenour, J. Herriott, N. Hyduk, Y. Porterfield, C. Taylor

Recorder of minutes: J. Herriott

1. **Call to order:** Conference Director Yvonne Porterfield called the meeting to order at 4:15 p.m. at the Russell Hotel.

2. **Committee reports: Program.** R. Acosta reported that he has prepared the Call for Papers that will be mailed to all members within a week. In addition, he has contacted two publishing houses to sponsor keynote speakers for the general sessions.

   Registration. M. Coughenour has designed the registration form, and it will be included in the next newsletter as well as and the special conference mailing that will be sent. She stated she needed assistance with getting teachers to work the registration table during the conference.

(continued on next page)

OBJECTIVE

• To deliver a presentation using electronic slides.

75B

Practice Presenting

1. Read the information at the right.
2. Review the suggestions for presentation delivery on p. 124.
3. Practice giving the *Government of the United States of America* presentation that you created in Lessons 72 and 73.

Speaker notes. The notes that you created for the *Government of the United States of America* presentation should only be used as an aid when you are practicing your presentation. They should remind you of what you want to say during your practice sessions.

You will know when you have practiced the presentation enough, because you will be able to give the presentation by simply looking at the slides as they appear on the screen. The words on the slides will act as an outline to remind you of the key points you want to make.

Don't be concerned about giving the presentation word for word as it appears in the notes. If you do, it sounds memorized. Memorized speeches come across as unnatural; the speaker is not able to develop a rapport with the audience.

However, experts generally advise speakers to have the first sentence memorized. This allows the speaker to have a strong opening and come across as knowledgeable and confident. If the speaker does memorize the first sentence, he/she should practice it so that it seems natural. This can be done by pausing in appropriate places and using vocal variety—speed, volume.

Definitely don't make the mistake that is often made by beginning presenters—bringing the speaker notes to the podium and then reading to, rather than presenting to, the audience. Speakers who read to their audience are not as credible.

By being well prepared and only glancing at the screen as the next slide comes up, the speaker comes across as natural. This also allows the speaker to focus on the audience rather than on his/her notes.

75C

Give a Presentation

1. Review the evaluation sheet on p. 125.
2. Break up into groups of three. Each student in your group will give the presentation that was developed in Lessons 72–73. While one student is giving the presentation, the other two will evaluate it using the form shown on p. 125.
3. The evaluation form is available in the data files: *DF 75C EvalForm*.

SOMETHING EXTRA

Planning, Preparing, and Delivering A Presentation

APPLY WHAT YOU HAVE LEARNED

Use the report prepared for 61C (pp. 182–183) and the photos from *DF 75 Photos* as a basis for preparing a presentation that you will be giving on the sites of Washington D.C. If you need more information, use other sources. The presentation will be two to three minutes in length. Develop a slide show to aid you in delivering the presentation to your classmates. Some ideas are shown on the next page.

Plan and organize the presentation:

1. Create an outline of what you want to include.
2. Review the file photos (*DF 75 Photos*) and illustrations and Design Tips on p. 221. Plan and create the slides to be included.
3. Prepare notes and practice the presentation.
4. Give the presentation to two or three of your classmates.

Save as: **75 Sites of DC**

Mr. Herriott wants you to add these exhibitors to the database in DF TSEAJ JOB1. Create a form called Exhibitors to make data entry and verification easier. Sort the records in alpha order by company. Print 2 copies—one for the TSEA president and one for the VP.

YP

Adante Technologies, Tara Olen, 8539 Monroe Road, Charlotte 28212-7525, 704-555-0110, 1

Compulink, Anne Crevar, 5018 Sunset Road, Charlotte 28269-2749, 704-555-0156, 1

CT Science Laboratories, Bill Hughes, 5212 W. Highway 74, Monroe 28110-8458, 704-555-0131, 1

DFA Labs, Ed White, 820 Tyvola Road, Ste. 100, Charlotte 28217-3534, 704-555-0107, 1

MTI, Sidorn Huynh, 227 Franklin Avenue., Concord 28025-4908, 704-555-0145, 1

MAR WIN School Supplies, Martha Winter, 700 Hanover Drive, Concord 28027-7827, 704-555-0121, 1

Job 2

Key this memo from me. Print: 2.

YP

TO: Katherine Moorcroft, TSEA President
           Darrin Thiem, TSEA Vice President
SUBJECT: EXHIBITORS FOR TSEA

Enclosed is a list of the businesses that exhibited at the TSEA Conference last year. Will you review the list and add businesses that you would like Mr. Herriott to invite to this year's conference.

Return your additions to me within 10 days. I will add them to the list; then James Herriott, Exhibits Chair, will write letters to the new exhibitors as well as to those who exhibited last year.

Thank you.

Job 3

Add these exhibitors to the exhibitor database using the Exhibitors form created in Job 1. Since these are first-time exhibitors, key a zero in the last column. After you have entered and verified the entries, prepare a report (TSEAJ-3-Exhibitor Report). Group the data by Years Exhibited, and sort the list by company name in alpha order. Use Stepped layout and Landscape orientation. Use Verve for the style.

YP

CAI Books
Russ Alarmi
4002 Concord Highway
Monroe 28110-8233
704-555-0119

Adobe Systems
Joyce Farno
6701 Carmel Road, Ste. 203
Charlotte 28226-0200
704-555-0149

Toor Publishers
Karen Fernandez
9812 Rockwood Road,
Charlotte 28215-8555
704-555-0198

Liberty Press
Vera Green
3601 Rose Lake Drive
Charlotte 28217-2813
704-555-0159

FirstPlus Experiments
Ralph McNash
525077 Center Drive, Ste. 150
Charlotte 28226-0705
704-555-0191

Integra Biology
John Petroni
5795 Gettysburg Drive
Concord 28027-8855
704-555-0167

Design Tips

As you create the slide show, consider the following design Do's and Don't's:

- Do use bulleted lists to present concepts one at a time.
- Do use key words and phrases rather than complete sentences.
- Do use contrasting background colors that make text stand out. Use light text against a dark background or dark text against a light background.
- Do choose a font size that the audience can read—even in the back of the room.
- Do use sound and animation to make a point, but not to distract from your message.
- Don't overcrowd slides. Two slides might be better than one.
- Don't overuse clip art. Photos have more impact.

Sites of Washington D. C.

- Washington Monument
- Lincoln Memorial
- Jefferson Memorial
- The White House
- The Treasury Building
- U.S. Capitol Building
- Eleanor Roosevelt Memorial
- Arlington National Cemetery
- World War II Memorial

Washington Monument
Tribute to the 1st President of the
United States of America

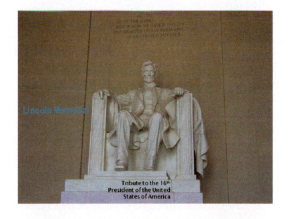

Our Nation's Capitol

Lincoln Memorial

Tribute to the 16th President of the United States of America

Washington Monument
Tribute to the 1st President of the
United States of America

Tomb of the Unknown Soldier

One of the most popular sites to visit at Arlington is the Tomb of the Unknown Soldier

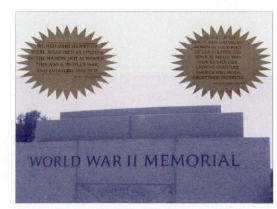

WORLD WAR II MEMORIAL

UNIT 28
Lessons 112-116

Integrated Workplace Simulation, TSEA: A Science Conference

Work assignment. Assume that you are participating in a school-based work program for Ms. Yvonne Porterfield, a high school biology teacher. Ms. Porterfield is serving as conference director for the Tri-County Science Education Association's Conference that will be held at the Russell Hotel in Charlotte, NC, in June.

Another teacher, Mr. James Herriott, is serving as Exhibits Chair for the conference. You will work for him as well, but Ms. Porterfield will give his work to you.

As an administrative specialist, your main duty is to process documents needed for the conference.

You completed a job orientation that focused on policies, procedures, and routines Ms. Porterfield wants you to follow. To help you further, she wrote these guidelines for you:

Correspondence. Center all letters vertically in modified block format with mixed punctuation and paragraph indentations. I do not use *Ms.* before my name in the closing lines of letters. Use *Conference Director* as my title.

Supply an appropriate salutation and complimentary close; use your reference initials; and include enclosure and copy notations as needed.

Tables and worksheets. Print gridlines and change and adjust column widths and row heights to appropriate sizes. Choose all other formatting features to make tables and worksheets easy to read and attractive.

Reports. Format reports as unbound and number all pages except the first. Begin and end tables and worksheets at the margins. Do not use templates to format meeting minutes and news releases.

Other.

- Be alert to and correct errors in capitalization, punctuation, spelling, and word usage.
- If a formatting guide or direction is not given, use your knowledge and judgment to complete the task.
- Unless otherwise directed, use the current date and print one copy of each job.
- Name all files you create with *TSEAJ*, followed by the job number (*TSEAJ JOB1*, *TSEAJ JOB2*, etc.). If a job involves more than one document, add *A*, *B*, *C*, etc., to the filename. Data files have *DF* as a prefix.

Lessons 112-116   TSEA: A SCIENCE CONFERENCE SIMULATION

OBJECTIVES

- To demonstrate your ability to integrate your knowledge and skills.
- To demonstrate your ability to solve problems and make correct decisions.

112A-116A

Conditioning Practice

Key each line twice daily.

alphabet	1	Zelda was quite naive to pack two big boxes with just fresh yams.
figures	2	Flight 4365 will leave Runway 28L at 10 p.m. with 297 passengers.
speed	3	Mandi kept the emblem and shamrock in the fir box in the cubicle.

| gwam | 1' | 1 | 2 | 3 | 4 | 5 | 6 | 7 | 8 | 9 | 10 | 11 | 12 | 13 |

CYCLE 2
Review

• To review Cycle 2 document processing, computer application, and straight-copy skills.

Conditioning Practice

Key each line twice.

alphabet	1	Carl asked to be given just a week to reply to the tax quiz form.
figures	2	Rooms 268 and 397 were cleaned for the 10:45 meetings last night.
speed	3	Vivian burns wood and a small bit of coal to make a dismal flame.

gwam 1' | 1 | 2 | 3 | 4 | 5 | 6 | 7 | 8 | 9 | 10 | 11 | 12 | 13 |

Activity 1 E-mail

Key the text at the right as an e-mail to your instructor. Send a Bcc notation to yourself and request a delivery receipt. Attach the *DF CR2 ACTIVITY1* file. Proofread and correct.

Save as: CR2 ACTIVITY1

Subject: Sales Report

The sales figures you requested are attached. This month's sales figures should be available on Friday. As soon as I receive them, I'll update the file to include those figures and e-mail them to you.

If there is any other information I can provide for the meeting next month, let me know. I'm looking forward to seeing you again in San Francisco.

Activity 2 Memo

Format and key the text at the right as a memo to **Investment Club Members** from **Gordon Chandler**. Date the memo **April 20, 20–** and use **Portfolio Update** for the subject line.

Save as: CR2 ACTIVITY2

The table below shows the current value of our portfolio. As you are well aware, market results have been mixed this year. The total value of the portfolio increased 12 percent since January 1. Most of this increase is due to additional contributions by members rather than increases in the value of stocks in the portfolio.

Insert table from file:
DF CR2 ACTIVITY2

Stock		Shares Owned	Price Per Share	Value of Stock
Company Name	Symbol			
Citigroup Inc.	C	200	26.03	$ 5,206.00
Coke	KO	250	59.25	14,812.50
Ford	F	100	6.08	608.00
Intel	INTC	175	20.27	3,574.25
J. P. Morgan	JPM	300	43.82	13,146.00
U.S. Bank	USB	200	32.40	6,480.00
Xcel Energy	XEL	250	20.61	5,152.50
Cash				23,495.77
Total Portfolio Value				$ 72,475.02

Our cash balance ($23,495.77) is quite large. We should decide at our next meeting what we want to do with this cash. As I recall, we are scheduled to meet on May 6 and will have potential investment opportunity reports from Catherine Cloninger and Mario Fernandez by then.

If you have questions about the report, please call me.

Activity 14

Timed Writings

Key two 5' writings on all ¶s combined; find *gwam* and errors.

 A all letters used MicroPace

| | gwam | 3' | 5' |

Many obvious steps should be taken when you search for a job. One step that is not so obvious and often is overlooked by applicants is reviewing the interview session. By taking the time and effort needed to accomplish this, you might give yourself the slight advantage you need to convince an employer that you are the person who should be hired. This critical step involves reviewing and analyzing all aspects of the interview to determine what went well and what did not. Your review should be completed as soon as the interview is over, and it should give you the information you need when you call or write the interviewer for the follow-up step.

Begin the survey by listing all the questions you were asked during the interview session and then examine your answers. Were they clear, complete, accurate, and to the point? Next, list your best qualities for the job, and relate them to what you studied. Did you stress your assets for the position? Last, try to figure how you could have presented yourself in a better way. Did you project interest and energy, use proper body language, and respond to every question properly? Jot down notes you acquired from the session that may help you if you are interviewed again for this job or contact another company.

3' column	5' column
4	2
8	5
13	8
17	10
21	13
26	16
30	18
35	21
39	24
44	26
48	29
52	31
57	34
61	37
65	39
70	42
74	44
79	47
83	50
85	51

gwam 3' | 1 | 2 | 3 | 4 | 5 |
5' | 1 | 2 | 3 |

Activity 3

Letter

Format and key the letter at the right.

Proofread your copy; correct all keying and format errors.

Save as: CR2 ACTIVITY3

January 16, 20-- | Mr. Caden O'Rourke | 278 Rangeview Drive | Littleton, CO 80120-7611 | Dear Mr. O'Rourke

It was fun visiting with you last week at the Colorado Historical Society's Annual Meeting. It seems impossible that ten years have passed since I was a student in your class.

As I recall, you always start each class off with a trivia question. Since the inauguration is next week, I thought you might like to use some of the following:

- Who was the first President inaugurated in Washington, D.C.? **(Thomas Jefferson in 1801.)**

- Who was the youngest President-elect at the time of his inauguration? **(John F. Kennedy at 43 years, 236 days.)**

- Who was the first inaugurated President to be born outside the original 13 states? **(Abraham Lincoln of Illinois.)**

- Who was the first President inaugurated for a term limited by the Constitution? **(Dwight D. Eisenhower in 1952. The 22nd amendment limits a president to two terms.)**

Thanks for the information on summer school. I'll reserve the week of June 15 for the workshop.

Sincerely | Justin C. Phipps

Report

Activity 4

Report

Format and key the copy below and on p. 224 as a bound report with footnotes.

Save as: CR2 ACTIVITY4

Activity 5

Report

Prepare a reference page from the footnotes shown below on a separate sheet. Refer to 174 for reference page formatting.

Save as: CR2 ACTIVITY5

Activity 6

Report

Prepare a title page for the report using a template included with your software. Include the name of the report, the author, and date.

Save as: CR2 ACTIVITY6

REVOLUTIONARY WAR
OPPOSING FORCES

By Logan Paul

The Battle of Bunker Hill vividly emphasized the stark contrast between the opposing forces of the Revolutionary War. The English displayed his majesty's finest—highly trained, professional, and obedient troops marching into battle, remaining cool, poised, and confident under fire, and relentlessly pushing forward. On the other hand, the American militia failed to conduct themselves like soldiers and demonstrated a complete lack of "soldiering skills."

American Soldiers

It seems the American militia had an extreme aversion to receiving commands from generals who were from a different colony, and thus not legally their general. This, along with other factors, led to the conspicuous lack of "a higher command structure."[1] This added to the chaos of the situation. An aversion to following orders and the overall fear of the bombardment of cannon fire that was perpetually barraging the Americans made being a general a difficult task.

At one point, a captain retreated from his duty to reinforce Prescott on Breed's Hill. Nothing short of General Putnam putting a pistol muzzle to his head

(continued on next page)

Activity 12

Open the *Route 153 Customer List* database table from *DF CA3 ACTIVITY12* and do the following:

- Using the *Subscription Data* form, enter the subscribers' type of service—**Daily** or **Weekend Only**. The new subscribers shown at the right are *Weekend Only*; all others are *Daily* subscribers.
- Sort the table by *Last Name* and then by *Type of Service*.
- Print a copy of the table.

Last Name	First Name	Courtesy Title	Address
Sherman	Stuart	Mr. and Mrs.	216 Lincoln Place
Furyk	Lindsey	Mrs.	228 Berkeley Place
Jackson	Duncan	Mr. and Mrs.	333 Flatbush Avenue
Monrow	Tyler	Mr. and Mrs.	318 Flatbush Avenue
Koszo	Miguel	Mr. and Mrs.	320 St. Johns
York	Kiesha	Ms.	1206 8th Avenue

Activity 13

Open the database file *DF CA3 ACTIVITY12*, and enter and verify the four new subscriptions shown at the right.

Also, make the following changes:

Chelsea Hathaway's address should be **210** rather than 220.

Natalie Madison has moved; delete her record from the file.

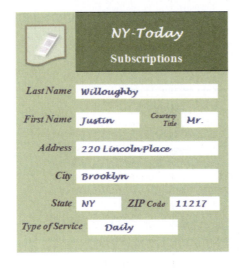

NY-Today
Subscriptions

Last Name: Willoughby
First Name: Justin   Courtesy Title: Mr.
Address: 220 Lincoln Place
City: Brooklyn
State: NY   ZIP Code: 11217
Type of Service: Daily

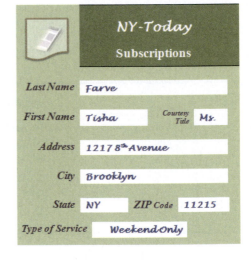

NY-Today
Subscriptions

Last Name: Farve
First Name: Tisha   Courtesy Title: Ms.
Address: 1217 8th Avenue
City: Brooklyn
State: NY   ZIP Code: 11215
Type of Service: Weekend Only

NY-Today
Subscriptions

Last Name: Biltmore
First Name: Jay   Courtesy Title: Mr. & Mrs.
Address: 321 Flatbush Avenue
City: Brooklyn
State: NY   ZIP Code: 11238
Type of Service: Daily

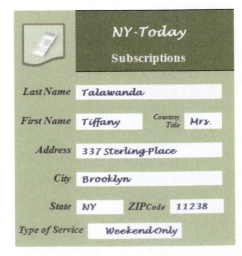

NY-Today
Subscriptions

Last Name: Talawanda
First Name: Tiffany   Courtesy Title: Mrs.
Address: 337 Sterling Place
City: Brooklyn
State: NY   ZIP Code: 11238
Type of Service: Weekend Only

could convince the shameful captain that "Breed's was a logical destination."[2] The performance of the officers at Bunker Hill left much to be desired. After Prescott had repealed the first couple of British attacks on Breed's Hill, his men were running low on ammunition. General Putnam headed over to Bunker Hill to procure reinforcements for the embattled men at Breed's Hill. Wood describes the chaos that was present at Bunker Hill, calling the sight "A disordered mass of milling men moving around the top of the hill . . . through incompetence or inexperience, (the officers) had given up any attempts at rallying and reorganizing their units."[3]

The British assumed, as one of their generals, John Burgoyne, put it, that no number of "untrained rabble" could ever stand up against "trained troops." Under General William Howe, British forces attempted a series of frontal assaults on the American position. These attacks were eventually successful, but only at the terrible cost of 1,000 British casualties.[4]

British Soldiers

Nothing could contrast the chaos on the side of the Americans more sharply than the stoicism of the average British soldiers. Wood explains, "British discipline held fast" even while "whole ranks of light infantry (were being leveled) as though a giant hand had swept them down to the sand."[5] Wave after wave of British soldiers obediently carried out their orders, each being met with the same deadly barrage of bullets the preceding wave had been cut down by. While the Americans were having difficulty maintaining order when they weren't even fighting, the British, like automatons, performed their duty under the harshest of conditions.

Summary

Though the colonists' spirits were buoyed by the massive casualties they inflicted on British forces at Bunker Hill, they could not always hope to have such favorable fighting conditions on their side. The British demonstrated such discipline, resilience, endurance, and indifference to casualties that the colonists surely knew they could not expect to win an easy victory.

When taking into consideration the complete lack of soldiering skills the colonists often demonstrated at Bunker Hill, the success of the battle for the colonists is significantly abated. Indeed, the series of losses the colonists suffered at the hands of the British in the following year made it clear that the initial success at Bunker Hill would not be easily replicated. A single victory under choice conditions is one thing, but to actually win a prolonged war against the mighty British Empire would be another. It speaks volumes of George Washington's leadership that he was able to hold such a force together for such a prolonged period and put together enough success in individual battles to win a war.

Footnotes

[1]W. J. Wood, *Battles of the Revolutionary War, 1775–1781* (Cambridge, MA: Da Capo Press, 2003), p. 33.

[2]Ibid., p. 16.

[3]Ibid., p. 27.

[4]Gordon S. Wood, *The American Revolution* (New York: Modern Library Paperback Edition, 2002), p. 54.

[5]Wood, W. J., op.cit., 20.

Activity 7

Electronic Presentations

Create the six slides as shown at the right and on page 221. Choose appropriate clip art if the art shown at the right isn't available with your software.

Include transitions between each slide. Use your choice of custom animations to create interest in your slide show.

Save as: CR2 ACTIVITY7

Slide 1

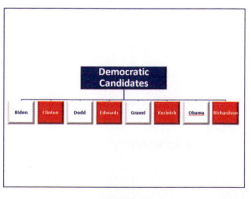

Slide 2

Activity 9

Worksheet

Document 1 (Worksheet)

1. Key the worksheet, formatting numbers with thousands separator as appropriate.

2. In row 15, calculate the Total Tons for each year.

3. In columns D, F, H, and J, calculate the percent of change (one decimal place) from year to year.

4. Add a column K with a heading, and calculate the yearly average for each item (to one decimal place).

5. Add the main title: **Harris County Recycling Statistics (in tons)**.

6. Apply cell styles and/or other formatting features to make the worksheet attractive and easy to read.

Save as: CA3 ACTIVITY9

	A	B	C	D	E	F	G	H	I	J
1	Item	2000	2002	% +/-	2004	% +/-	2006	% +/-	2008	% +/-
2	Aluminum cans	206	218		204		245		280	
3	Cardboard	780	820		923		1054		1229	
4	Steel cans	192	133		188		226		194	
5	Clear glass	466	483		406		422		464	
6	Mixed glass	158	152		110		142		231	
7	Green glass	0	38		48		55		61	
8	Brown glass	0	28		27		22		32	
9	Magazines	0	0		75		169		221	
10	Newsprint	294	376		282		321		389	
11	Mixed paper	0	0		29		20		41	
12	Office paper	30	51		37		88		131	
13	Phone books	0	6		9		18		24	
14	Leaf/yard waste	688	838		1000		1550		1663	
15	Total Tons									

Activity 10

Column Chart

1. Open *DF CA3 ACTIVITY10*.

2. Create a column chart to show the amount of trash produced by six countries. Use **Top Six Trash-Producing Nations** as the title and show a legend.

Save as: CA3 ACTIVITY10

Activity 11

Pie Chart

Convert CA3 ACTIVITY10 to a pie chart with a legend and data labels. Change the title to **kg of Waste per Person per Day**.

Save as: CA3 ACTIVITY11

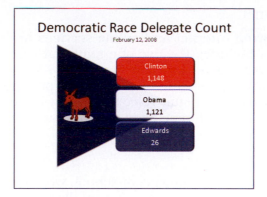

Slide 3

Slide 4

Slide 5

Slide 6

Activity 8

Skill Check

1. Key a 1' timing on each ¶; determine *gwam* and number of errors.

2. Take a 3' timing on ¶s 1–2 combined; determine *gwam* and number of errors.

A all letters used MicroPace   gwam 3'

Each President since George Washington has had a   4

cabinet.   The cabinet is a group of men and women selected   8

by the President.   The senate must approve them.   It is the   12

exception rather than the rule for the President's choice   15

to be rejected by this branch of the government.   In   19

keeping with tradition, most of the cabinet members belong   23

to the same political party as the President.   26

The purpose of the cabinet is to provide advice to the   30

President on matters pertaining to the job of President.   34

The person holding the office, of course, may or may not   38

follow the advice.   Some Presidents have frequently   41

utilized their cabinet.   Others have used it little or not   45

at all.   For example, President Wilson held no cabinet   49

meetings at all during World War I.   51

Citation 2 (Book)

Author: Fulton-Calkins, Patsy and Karin M. Stulz

Title: Procedures & Theory for Administrative Professionals

Year: 2004

City: Mason, OH

Publisher: South-Western Cengage Learning

Page: 250

Edition: 5th ed.

Citation 3 (Book)

Author: Odgers, Patty

Title: Administrative Office Management

Year: 2005

City: Mason, OH

Publisher: South-Western Cengage Learning

Page: 77

Edition: 13th ed.

3. Place the works cited on a separate page at the end of the report.

Save as: CA3 ACTIVITY8

Using the Internet

The following Internet and online services are used by millions of people each day. This includes the use of e-mail software to transmit messages and files, FTP software to upload and download files with other computers, chat rooms and instant messaging to exchange typewritten conversations, Internet telephone services to transmit voice messages, bulletin boards to read and post messages, and videoconferencing to conduct meetings among people at different locations.

Accessing the Internet

If you are using the Internet at school, work, or home, someone is paying a fee so you can access the Internet. School districts, businesses, and individuals pay a fee to an Internet Service Provider (ISP) to access the Internet.

An ISP is a business that sells access to its permanent Internet connection for a fee. Fees are usually based on a standard monthly charge, but may vary by hours of actual connection. Individuals should be aware of their Internet use and pick an ISP accordingly. (Fulton-Calkins and Stultz, 250)

The Intranet

An intranet is a private network within an organization. It belongs to the organization to be used by the organization's employees. Employees are typically required to enter a password to access information that is to be restricted to the employees and not made available to the public. Information that is commonly available on an intranet include such things as telephone directories, employee handbooks, policy and procedure manuals, employee benefit information, frequently used forms, calendars of events, and job postings.

The Extranet

An extranet operates much like an intranet in that it is a private network within an organization. The primary difference between an intranet and extranet is that an extranet makes selected parts of the information stored on the network available to people outside the organization (Odgers, 77). These people may include current customers, students, businesses, etc. Access to the selected information is gained by using a user name and password. Examples of extranets include banks, credit card companies, and investment organizations that provide their customers with access to their account information and to conduct business over the extranet. Colleges and universities often provide students access to their schedule of courses, grades, and financial accounts.

Activity 9

Table

Format the table at the right. Use the table formatting features you have learned to arrange the information attractively on the page. Include the following source note:

Source: *Fodor's 2000, San Francisco,* and *Fodor's 2000, USA.*

Save as: CR2 ACTIVITY9

Places to Explore in San Francisco

Places to Explore	Description	Major Attractions
Union Square	Heart of San Francisco's downtown, major shopping district	❑ Westin St. Francis Hotel ❑ Old San Francisco Mint
Chinatown	Home to one of the largest Chinese communities outside Asia	❑ Chinese Culture Center ❑ Old Chinese Telephone Exchange
Nob Hill	Home of the city's elite and some of its finest hotels	❑ Cable Car Museum ❑ Grace Cathedral ❑ Mark Hopkins Hotel
Civic Center	One of the country's great city, state, and federal building complexes	❑ City Hall ❑ Performing Arts Center ❑ War Memorial Opera House
The Embarcadero	Waterfront promenade great for walking and jogging	❑ Ferry Building ❑ Embarcadero Center ❑ Justin Herman Plaza
Fisherman's Wharf	Hyde cable-car line, waterfront, Ghirardelli Square, Piers 39 and 41	❑ Lombard Street ❑ National Maritime Museum ❑ Museum of the City of San Francisco
Financial District	Cluster of steel-and-glass high-rises and older, more decorative architectural monuments to commerce	❑ Transamerica Pyramid ❑ Bank of America ❑ Pacific Stock Exchange ❑ Stock Exchange Tower

Activity 10

Format the table at the right. Center the table horizontally and vertically. Use a row height of 0.4" for the heading and 0.3" for the body rows.

After you complete the table, shade in red the state where the attraction is located. For example, Arizona is shaded because Hoover Dam is located there.

Save as: CR2 ACTIVITY10

Activity 11

Skill Check

1. Key a 1' timing on each ¶ of Activity 7, p. 221; determine *gwam* and errors.
2. Take a 3' timing on ¶s 1–3 of Activity 8, p. 225; determine *gwam* and errors.

Name That State!

Attractions	A	B	C
Hoover Dam	**Arizona**	California	Colorado
Niagara Falls	Massachusetts	**New York**	Pennsylvania
Independence Hall	**Pennsylvania**	Virginia	Washington
Alamo	Arizona	New Mexico	**Texas**
Zion National Park	Nevada	California	**Utah**
Jamestown	North Carolina	South Carolina	**Virginia**
Harvard University	**Massachusetts**	New Jersey	New York
Mt. Rushmore	Montana	**South Dakota**	Wyoming
Kennedy Space Center	**Florida**	Ohio	Texas

Activity 6

Meeting Minutes with Template

1. Open the data file *DF CA3 ACTIVITY6*.
2. Using the template, format the meeting minutes at the right. The minutes were submitted by Sue Smedley.

Save as: CA3 ACTIVITY6

Activity 7

Meeting Minutes without Template

Format the meeting minutes at the right without using a template.

Save as: CA3 ACTIVITY7

GREENWOOD HIGH SCHOOL SCIENCE CLUB

Meeting Minutes

February 15, 20--

1. Call to order: President Dee McClinton called the meeting of the Greenwood High School Science Club to order at 2:15 p.m. on February 15, 20–in Room 107.

2. Attendance : Sue Smedley recorded the attendance. Fifteen members and Terry L. Gronbacher, Sponsor, were present.

3. Secretary Sue Smedley read the minutes, which were accepted.

4. Unfinished business

   a. President McClinton reported that the school science fair date has been set for April 23–25.
   b. The Science Club's request for a table to display promotional materials was approved by Principal Huerta.
   c. Awards have been decided. They will be given to first-, second-, and third-place winners by grade level in 12 different categories.
   d. Engineers from Greenwood Laboratories will serve as judges and assist in presenting the awards.

5. New business

   a. The Club approved the purchase of a microscope as the Science Club's gift to the Greenwood High School Science Department.
   b. The club officers will present the microscope to Principal Huerta at the March meeting of the Greenwood Board of Education.

6. Adjournment

   Dee McClinton adjourned the meeting at 3:10 p.m.

Activity 8

Report in MLA Format

1. Format in MLA style.
2. Use the Citations and Bibliography features to insert the citations and prepare the Works Cited page.

Citation 1 (Book)
Author: Oliverio, Mary Ellen, William E. Pasewark, and Bonnie R. White
Title: The Office, Procedures and Technology
Year: 2007
City: Mason, OH
Publisher: South-Western Cengage Learning
Page: 7
Edition: 5th ed.

Harry Zelasco
Ms. Li Pak
Computer Literacy

The Internet, Intranet, and Extranet

Anyone using computers for school, business, or personal use knows the difficulty of keeping up with changing technology. Computer users are demanding that microprocessors become faster and easier to use in order to keep up with the many software applications used today. Users also want Internet and intranet connections that upload and download information quickly.

The Internet

The Internet is "a public, world-wide computer network made up of smaller, interconnected networks that span the globe" (Oliverio, Pasewark, and White, 7). Internet users can generally make better decisions because they have instant and convenient access to information that is stored anywhere in the world. However, the Internet user must decide the quality of the information.

(continued on next page)

OBJECTIVE

- To assess Cycle 2 document processing, computer application, and straight-copy skills.

Conditioning Practice

Key each line twice.

alphabet	1	Bugs quickly explained why five of the zoo projects cost so much.
figures	2	Jo's office phone number is 632-0781; her home phone is 832-4859.
speed	3	Pamela may go with us to the city to do the work for the auditor.

gwam 1' | 1 | 2 | 3 | 4 | 5 | 6 | 7 | 8 | 9 | 10 | 11 | 12 | 13 |

Activity 1

Check Keying Skill

Key two 3' timings on ¶s 1–3 combined; determine *gwam* and errors.

A **all letters used** **MicroPace**

gwam 2' | 3'

The City of Philadelphia is where the roots of | 5 | 3
this nation were founded. Independence Hall, which | 10 | 7
is located in the center of the city, is often | 14 | 10
referred to as the place where the nation was born. | 20 | 13
It was here that they met to discuss and agree upon | 25 | 16
the Declaration of Independence and the United | 30 | 20
States Constitution. It was here that Ben Franklin | 35 | 23
said, "If we don't hang together, we shall assuredly | 40 | 27
hang separately!" | 41 | 27

An easily recognized symbol of our freedom, the | 46 | 31
Liberty Bell, can also be seen in the city which is | 51 | 34
often called "The City of Brotherly Love." Another | 56 | 37
distinction of the city is that it was the first | 61 | 41
capital of our new nation. The building where the | 66 | 44
Senate and the House met is located right next to | 71 | 47
Independence Hall. People can enjoy these and other | 76 | 51
exquisite landmarks by spending time in the city. | 81 | 54

gwam 2' | 1 | 2 | 3 | 4 | 5 | 6 |
3' | 1 | 2 | 3 | 4 |

Activity 4

Two-page Memo with Track Changes

1. Open *DF CA3 ACTIVITY4*.
2. Make the changes noted in the comments and then delete the comments.
3. Accept or reject the changes.
4. Key the information at the right to complete the two-page memo.
5. Use a 12-pt. font and 1.25" side margins.
6. Supply all missing memo parts.

Save as: CA3 ACTIVITY4

A comparison of the course placements reveals a steady decline in the percent and number of students needing to enter MATH 100 Pre-College Algebra and a steady increase in the percent and number of students entering MATH 180 College Algebra and MATH 250 Calculus I. This finding supports the contention that as SAT math scores increase, students will begin their college studies in higher-level courses.

This comparison will be reported to Dr. Theodore R. Ostrom, head of the Mathematics Department in SCAS. He and his faculty will then know that more and more arts and sciences students are enrolling in higher-level math courses and that the number needing MATH 100 is decreasing.

I will e-mail the comparison to all SCAS faculty so that they, too, will be aware of the increasing mathematical ability of the students entering SCAS programs.

Perhaps you would like to share this information with the dean of the School of Education since it provides further evidence of success in the education reform movement.

Activity 5

Outline

Format as an outline. Use a 2" top margin.

Save as: CA3 ACTIVITY5

LEADERSHIP SEMINAR PROGRESS REPORT

1) Introduction
2) Seminar presenter
   a) Selection–Jackson & Associates selected
   b) Reason–Jackson & Associates' definition of leadership
3) Seminar development
   a) Meeting #1–Review content of previous seminars
   b) Meeting #2–Decide content of seminars
4) Seminar dates and locations
   a) October 15–Coultersville
   b) October 22–North Irwin
   c) October 29–Port Washington
   d) November 5–Portersburg
5) Seminar content
   a) Leadership characteristics
      i) Social and environmental responsibility
      ii) International awareness
      iii) Honesty and consistency
   b) Leadership styles–from autocratic to democratic

Activity 2

Memo

Format the text at the right as a memo to **Kathleen Maloney** from **Miguel Gonzalez**. Date the memo **May 5, 20--**; use **Budget Request** for the subject line. Send a copy of the memo to **Sarah Cambridge** and **Ricardo Castello**.

Save as: CA2 ACTIVITY2

As I searched the Internet for teaching resources, I came across some audiocassettes that would be an excellent addition to my World History course. The audiocassette collection, *The World's 100 Greatest People*, currently sells for $295, plus sales tax and shipping and handling charges of $9.95.

According to the advertisement (http://www.4iq.com/iquest16.html), "The 50 tapes included in this collection represent an audio treasury of 100 biographies detailing the life, time, achievement, and impact of some of history's greatest personalities, including philosophers, explorers, inventors, scientists, writers, artists, composers, and religious, political, and military leaders." These tapes could be used in many classes outside the Social Studies Department. Perhaps some of the other departments would be willing to share the cost of the tapes.

When you have a few minutes, I would like to discuss how we should proceed to get these tapes in time for next year.

Activity 3

Letter

Format the text at the right as a letter. Leave 1.5" TM.

Save as: CA2 ACTIVITY3

March 3, 20-- | Mr. Michael Kent, President | Quote of the Month Club | 97 Liberty Square | Boston, MA 02109-3625 | Dear Michael

Arrangements for our April **Quote of the Month Club** meeting are progressing nicely. The meeting will be held at the Pilgrims' Inn in Plymouth on Saturday, the 15th.

Members didn't like the format of our last meeting, so I'm proposing this plan: Each person attending will be assigned to a team, and each team will be given four quotes. The team will select one quote and prepare a five-minute presentation explaining the meaning of the quote (their opinion). Each team will select a member to present to the entire group. These are the four quotations I selected:

Person	Quote
Walter Elias Disney	"Our greatest natural resource is the mind of our children."
Ayn Rand	"Throughout the centuries there were men who took first steps down new roads armed with nothing but their own vision."
Wendell Lewis Willkie	"Our way of living together in America is a strong but delicate fabric. It is made up of many threads. It has been woven over many centuries by the patience and sacrifice of countless liberty-loving men and women."
Althea Gibson	"No matter what accomplishments you make, somebody helps you."

These topics provide for excellent discussions leading up to the presentations. When you send the meeting notice, please send the quotes to give members time to think about them prior to the meeting.

Sincerely | Patricia Fermanich | xx | Enclosures

CYCLE 3
Assessment

- To assess Cycle 3 document processing, computer application, and straight-copy skills.

Conditioning Practice

Key each line twice daily.

alphabet	1	Jimmy wants seven pens and extra clips in a kit for the big quiz.
figures	2	I sold 56 advertisements for $6,738 between 9/12/04 and 12/19/05.
speed	3	A goal of the proficient tutor is to quantify the right problems.

gwam	1'	1	2	3	4	5	6	7	8	9	10	11	12	13

Activity 1

Letter

Key in modified block format using mixed punctuation and no ¶ indentations.

Save as: CA3 ACTIVITY1

Activity 2

Letter

Open CA3 ACTIVITY1 and format the letter in block style with open punctuation; delete the postscript. Use 1.25" side margins and a 12-pt. font.

Save as: CA3 ACTIVITY2

June 9, 20-- | Mrs. Vera L. Bowden | 3491 Rose Street | Minneapolis, MN 55441-5781 | Dear Mrs. Bowden | SUBJECT: YOUR DONATION What a pleasant surprise it was to find your $50 donation to Beta Xi in my mail this morning. I think it is great that you thought of Beta Xi and decided to help members of your local chapter serve those who are less fortunate.

Your contribution will be used to purchase food and clothing for young children in our community as part of Community Day. As you know, Beta Xi, Minnesota Epsilon Chapter, conducts a fall drive to support this event.

I have heard about the success you are having in microbiology. Perhaps you would return to speak to our Beta Xi members? Please let me know if you can.

Yours truly | Miss Amelia R. Carter | Beta Xi Sponsor | xx | Enclosure | c Thomas Turnball, Treasurer | A receipt is enclosed since your contribution is tax deductible.

Activity 3

Flyer

Design a flyer to present the information at the right. Use SmartArt or WordArt, shapes or text boxes, and clip art or pictures in your flyer. You decide other formatting features.

Save as: CA3 ACTIVITY3

Event:	Lifestyle Program for Young Adults
Description:	A one-hour presentation about a new program that will make it easier for you to lead a healthier life and offers financial incentives for your efforts!
When:	Friday, January 11
Time:	8:30 p.m.
Where:	Redbank High School Auditorium
Instructor:	Dr. Jerome T. Noseck, Certified Personal Trainer
Main Feature:	Participants will learn that the way we live has a real impact on how we feel. When we take care of ourselves, we have more drive and energy and better attitudes.

Activity 4

E-mail

Send the text at the right as an e-mail to your instructor. Send a Bcc notation to yourself and request a delivery receipt. Use **ANSWER TO YOUR QUESTION** for the subject line.

Save as: CA2 ACTIVITY4

Your question is a good one. Yes, Nellie Tayloe Ross of Wyoming and Miriam (Ma) Ferguson of Texas were elected on the same day, November 4, 1924. However, Ms. Ross took office 16 days before Ms. Ferguson; therefore, Ms. Ross is considered the first woman governor in the United States, and Ms. Ferguson is considered the second. It should also be noted that Ms. Ross completed her husband's term as governor of Wyoming prior to being elected in 1924.

If you have other questions before the exam on Friday, please let me know. I hope you do well on it.

Activity 5

Electronic Presentations

Create the slides as shown at the right. Use the Foundry design theme with Paper colors.

Slide 1: The picture is in data file *DF CA2 ACTIVITY5*.

Use SmartArt to create slides 2–4.

Slide 2: Vertical Box List—adjust to fit text.

Slide 3: Trapezoid List

Slide 4: Vertical Chevron List

Slide 5: Basic Block List—add two shapes to get the seven blocks.

Apply transitions of your choice between slides. Apply custom animation of your choice so that each shape on the slide comes in *one by one* using *very fast* speed for slides 2–5.

Save as: CA2 ACTIVITY5

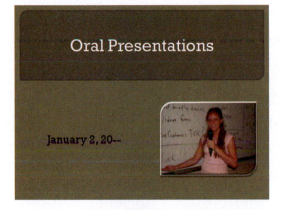

Slide 1

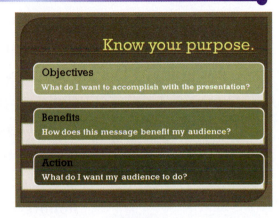

Slide 2

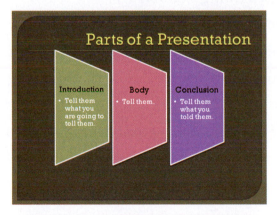

Slide 3

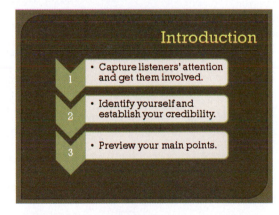

Slide 4

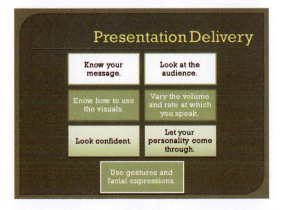

Slide 5

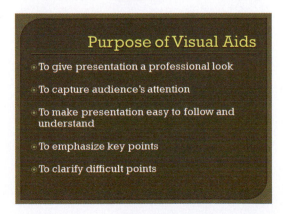

Slide 6

Activity 14

Timed Writings

Key two 5' writings on all ¶s combined; find *gwam* and errors.

  all letters used **MicroPace**

	3'	5'
Learning to prepare a good resume is an important	3	2
step in the process of searching for a job. The resume given	7	4
to a prospective employer is critical because the average	11	7
time an employer takes to review a resume is about one-third	15	9
of a minute, studies have shown. You have only about twenty	19	12
seconds, therefore, to make the impression that you have	23	14
something extra to offer and are worth more attention.	27	16
To make a good presentation, you should plan carefully	31	18
what you want to include in your resume. Begin by taking	34	21
time to prepare a list of your most important attributes.	38	23
The list may include many of the business courses you com-	42	25
pleted, the quality grade point average you attained, the	46	28
clubs you joined, the offices you held, and the awards and	50	30
honors you won. Also, remember to describe any jobs you	54	32
held while attending school.	56	33
After you have selected the content of your resume, you	59	36
should format it so that your strengths are emphasized early.	64	38
Make a point of explaining how your strengths relate to the	68	41
position for which you are applying. Most students find that	72	43
they prefer to list their educational experience at the top	76	45
of the resume because it is often the most valuable quality	80	48
being offered to the employer.	82	49

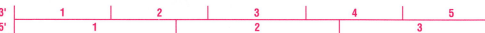

gwam | 3' | 1 | 2 | 3 | 4 | 5 |
| | 5' | 1 | 2 | 3 |

Activity 6

Report

Format the text at the right as a bound report with footnotes. Use **Four Outstanding Americans** for the title.

Footnotes

[1]**Susan Clinton,** The Story of Susan B. Anthony **(Chicago: Children's Press, 1986), p. 5.**

[2]**Jim Powell, "The Education of Thomas Edison,"** http://www.self-gov.org/freeman/9502powe.htm, **April 25, 2000.**

[3]**"An Overview of Abraham Lincoln's Life,"** http://home.att.net/~rjnorton/Lincoln77.html, **March 30, 2004.**

Save as: CA2 ACTIVITY6

Many outstanding Americans have influenced the past, and many more will impact the future. Choosing the "Four Greatest Americans" does injustice to the hundreds of others who left their mark on our country and diminishes their contributions. This report simply recognizes four great Americans who helped make America what it is today.

Without these four individuals, America perhaps would be quite different from the country we know. The four individuals included in this report are: Susan B. Anthony, Thomas A. Edison, Benjamin Franklin, and Abraham Lincoln.

Susan B. Anthony

Susan B. Anthony is noted for her advancement of women's rights. She and Elizabeth Cady Stanton organized the national woman suffrage association. The following quotation shows her commitment to the cause.

> At 7 a.m. on November 5, 1872, Susan B. Anthony broke the law by doing something she had never done before. After twenty years of working to win the vote for women, she marched to the polls in Rochester, New York, and voted. Her vote—for Ulysses S. Grant for president—was illegal. In New York state, only men were allowed to vote.[1]

Anthony continued to fight for women's rights, however, for the next 33 years of her life. Even though she died in 1906 and the amendment granting women the right to vote (nineteenth amendment) was not passed until 1920, that amendment is often called the "Susan B. Anthony Amendment" in honor of Anthony's efforts to advance women's rights.

Thomas Alva Edison

Imagine life without the incandescent light bulb, phonograph, kinetoscope (a small box for viewing moving films), or any of the other 1,090 inventions patented by Edison. Life certainly would be different without these inventions or later inventions that came as a result of Edison's work.

Activity 12

Open the database table in *DF CR3 ACTIVITY12* and do the following:

- A new field in the table called *Committee* has been added.
- Using the *FBLA Membership Data* form, enter the committee membership as shown at the right in blue. Note that some of the members have not been assigned to a committee.
- Sort the table by *Last Name* and then by *Committee*.
- Print a copy of the table.

	Last Name	Committee
1	McWilliams	Community Service
2	Sanchez	Membership
3	Radclif	Financial
4	Saxon	Program
5	Covington	Executive Committee
6	Williams	Social
7	Farina	Public Relations
8	Alexander	Community Service
9	Stewart	Newsletter
10	Taylor	Newsletter
11	Wickman	
12	Blair	Leadership Conference
13	Garland	
14	Loganberry	Leadership Conference
15	Martin	Public Relations
16	Foster	Executive Committee
17	Massena	Social
18	Devereaux	Program

	Last Name	Committee
19	Hemingway	Membership
20	Dickerson	Community Service
21	Moffet	Financial
22	Norton	Social
23	Hawthorne	Leadership Conference
24	Coolidge	Membership
25	Lockwood	Newsletter
26	Eastwick	Program
27	Gutierrez	Community Service
28	Fitzgerald	Membership
29	Saevig	
30	Covington	Financial
31	Foster	Social
32	Matsuzaka	Social
33	Pierzynski	Executive Committee
34	Cordova	
35	Van Buren	Newsletter
36	Rousseau	Executive Committee
37	Underwood	Public Relations

Activity 13

Open the DF Franklin High School FBLA database. Enter the two new members shown at the right; verify your entries.

Franklin High School FBLA

Last Name	Kennedy
First Name	Jamison
City	San Francisco
Street Address	538 Davis Street
State	CA ZIP 94111

Franklin High School FBLA

Last Name	Yamaguchi
First Name	Kijuro
City	San Francisco
Street Address	712 Hyde Street
State	CA ZIP 94109

Interestingly enough, most of Edison's learning *took* place at home under the guidance of his mother. "Nancy Edison's secret: she was more dedicated than any teacher was likely to be, and she had the flexibility to experiment with various ways of nurturing her son's live for learning."[2]

Benjamin Franklin

Benjamin Franklin was a man of many talents. He was an inventor, printer, diplomat, philosopher, author, postmaster, and leader. A few of his more noteworthy accomplishments included serving on the committee that created the Declaration of Independence; *publishing* Poor Richard's Almanac; and *inventing* the lightning rod, the Franklin stove, the odometer, and bifocal glasses.

Abraham Lincoln

For many Americans the impact of Abraham Lincoln is as great today as it was during his life time.

> Abraham Lincoln is remembered for his vital role as the leader in preserving the Union and beginning the process that led to the end of slavery in the United States. He is also remembered for his character, his speeches and letters, and as a man of humble origins whose determination and perseverance led him to the nation's highest office.[3]

DS Lincoln is a great example of one who dealt positively with adversity in his personal and professional life. His contributions towards the shaping of America will be long remembered.

Activity 7

References Page

Format a references page from the information shown at the right.

Save as: CA2 ACTIVITY7

Activity 8

Title Page

Format a title page for the report.

Save as: CA2 ACTIVITY8

"An Overview of Abraham Lincoln's Life." March 30, 2004. http://home.att.net/~rjnorton/Lincoln77.html.

Clinton, Susan. The Story of Susan B. Anthony. Chicago: Children's Press, 1986.

Powell, Jim. "The Education of Thomas Edison." April 25, 2000. http://www.self-gov.org/freeman/9502powe.htm.

Activity 9

Worksheet

1. Key the worksheet.
2. Calculate the Overtime Pay Rate at 1.5 times Regular Pay Rate.
3. Add a **Gross Pay** column to the right of Overtime Pay Rate, and calculate Gross Pay for each employee.
4. Add a **Net Pay** column to the right of Total Deductions, and calculate the Net Pay for each employee.
5. Calculate column totals and averages in unshaded cells. Round averages to two decimal places.
6. Format numbers in columns D, F, G, H, and I as Currency.
7. Delete the row for Everett.
8. Insert the information for Kennyman, Means, and Conway so the last names are in alphabetical order.
9. Add a title, **Jefferson Medical Association Payroll--Week 6**, in row 1.
10. Apply cell styles and/or other formatting features to make the worksheet attractive and easy to read.

Save as: **CR3 ACTIVITY9**

Employee	Employee Number	Regular Hours	Regular Pay Rate	Overtime Hours	Overtime Pay Rate	Total Deductions
Ronald Alvarez	101	40	9.97	2		65.45
Barry Barton	103	40	9.15	0		69.87
Harriet Demonti	106	38	10.52	0		61.86
Sylvester Everett	108	40	10.56	6		66.23
Maryanne Gigliotti	110	40	10.75	4		56.31
Kim Lu	115	36	9.99	0		51.78
Martin Menendez	123	40	9.99	0		66.56
Susan Tofflin	136	32	9.45	0		45.65
Beatrice Robertson	145	40	10.97	6		70.30
William Tellison	152	40	10.15	2		67.76
Totals						
Averages						
Tom Kennyman	112	36	8.	0		48.65
Margaret Means	119	40	9.25	2		65.43
Mario Conway	105	40	8.55	0		53.25

Activity 10

Pie Chart

1. Open *DF CR3 ACTIVITY10*.
2. Create a pie chart showing the percent of each investment category. Use **Investment Portfolio** as the title; show percents as data labels, and show a legend.

Save as: **CR3 ACTIVITY10**

Activity 11

Doughnut Chart

Convert the CR3 ACTIVITY10 pie chart to a doughnut chart. Remove the data labels.

Save as: **CR3 ACTIVITY11**

Activity 9

Table

Format the table at the right. Center the table horizontally and vertically. Key the main heading in 16-pt. font and the secondary headings in 13-pt. font. Make the main heading row height .5" and the rest of the rows .3"

Save as: CA2 ACTIVITY9

Major United States Rivers

River	Length	
	Miles	Kilometers
Arkansas	1,459	2,348
Colorado	1,450	2,333
Columbia	1,243	2,000
Mississippi	2,348	3,779
Missouri	2,315	3,726
Red	1,290	2,080
Rio Grande	1,900	3,060
Snake	1,038	1,670
Yukon	1,979	3,185

Source: *Time Almanac 2004*, pp. 500–501.

Activity 10

Table

Format the table at the right. Adjust column widths and heights to attractively arrange the text on the page. In cells, use bottom vertical alignment and the horizontal alignment shown. Apply shading in the *Dem.* and *Rep.* columns. Center the table horizontally and vertically.

Save as: CA2 ACTIVITY10

Note: Since 2000, many additional female governors have been elected.

United States Female Governors
1925–2000

Name		Party Affiliation		State	Years Served
Last	First	Dem.	Rep.		
Collins	Martha	X		Kentucky	1984–1987
Ferguson	Miriam	X		Texas	1925–1927 1933–1935
Finney	Joan	X		Kansas	1991–1995
Grasso	Ella	X		Connecticut	1975–1980
Hollister	Nancy		X	Ohio	1998–1999
Hull	Jane		X	Arizona	1997–2003
Kunin	Madeleine	X		Vermont	1985–1991
Mofford	Rose	X		Arizona	1988–1991
Orr	Kay		X	Nebraska	1987–1991
Ray	Dixy Lee	X		Washington	1977–1981
Richards	Ann	X		Texas	1991–1995
Roberts	Barbara	X		Oregon	1991–1995
Ross	Nellie	X		Wyoming	1925–1927
Shaheen	Jeanne	X		New Hampshire	1997–2003
Wallace	Lurleen	X		Alabama	1967–1968
Whitman	Christine		X	New Jersey	1994–2001

Source: http://www.cawp.rutgers.edu/Facts/Officeholders/govhistory.pdf, February 11, 2008.

Name of Web Page:
Occupational Outlook
Handbook

Name of Website:
United States Department of
Labor, Bureau of Statistics

Year: 2006–2007

Year Accessed: 2007

Month Accessed: August

Day Accessed: 27

URL: http://stats.bls.gov
/oco/ocos014.htm#outlook

Name of Web Page:
Medical and Health Services
Management Careers, Jobs,
and Training Information

Name of Website: Career
Overview

Year: 2004

Year Accessed: 2007

Month Accessed: August

Day Accessed: 27

URL: http://www
.careeroverview.com
/medical-health-manager-
careers.html

3. Place the works cited on a
   separate page at the end of
   the report.

Save as: **CR3 ACTIVITY8**

People who manage health services are needed in a wide variety of work settings. The most common place of employment for these individuals is hospitals, followed by the offices of physicians, dentists, and other health-related practitioners (Occupational Outlook Handbook).

Because of a growing health services industry, the employment of health services and medical managers is projected to expand more than the average occupation through 2012. Increasing opportunities will be found in outpatient care centers, health practitioners and doctor's offices, and in home healthcare services. Workers with good management and business skills and experience in the healthcare industry will have the greatest opportunities. (Medical and Health Services Management, Careers, Jobs, & Training Information)

Educational Opportunities

Bachelor's, master's, and doctoral degree programs in health administration are offered by colleges, universities, and schools of public health, medicine, allied health, public administration, and business administration. In 2005, 70 schools had accredited programs leading to the master's degree in health services administration. . . . (Occupational Outlook Handbook)

Health services managers are often recruited from the college or university they attend before they graduate. In larger hospitals, they are often recruited to fill assistant department head positions. In smaller hospitals, they may enter at the department head level.

Additional Information

The organizations listed below will be contacted to gather information about academic programs and employment opportunities in health services management.

- American College of Healthcare Executives, One North Franklin Street, Suite 1700, Chicago, IL 60606-3529

- Association of University Programs in Health Administration, 2000 14th Street North, Suite 780, Arlington, VA 22201

- Medical Group Management Association, 104 Inverness Terrace East, Englewood, CO 80112-5306

- American College of Health Care Administrators, 300 North Lee Street, Suite 301, Alexandria, VA 22314

Work Assignment

HPJ Communication Specialists prepares, organizes, and delivers communication training seminars. Three partners—Stewart **H**errick, Natasha **P**arker, and Spencer **J**orstad—founded the company in 1991. In 1998, Ms. Parker bought out the other two partners. Today the company has five branches located in Dallas, Denver, Minneapolis, New York, and San Francisco.

Because of your skills with *Word, Outlook,* and *PowerPoint,* you have been hired by HPJ to work part-time for the administrative assistant, Helen St. Claire. Ms. St. Claire processes documents for the President and CEO, Natasha S. Parker, as well as for Erika Thomas, the Minneapolis branch manager.

During your training program, you were instructed to use the unbound format for reports and block format for all company letters. Ms. Parker likes all her letters closed as follows:

Sincerely

Natasha S. Parker
President & CEO

When a document has more than one enclosure, format the enclosure notation as follows:

Enclosures: Agenda
              Hotel Confirmation

General processing instructions will be attached to each document you are given to process. Use the date included on the instructions for all documents requiring a date.

As with a real job, you will be expected to learn on your own (using resources that are available to you) how to do some things that you haven't previously been taught.

You will also be expected to use your decision-making skills to arrange documents attractively whenever specific instructions are not provided. Since HPJ has based its word processing manual on the *Century 21* textbook, you can refer to this text in making formatting decisions and learning how to do things that you haven't been taught. In addition to your textbook, you can use the Help feature of your software to review a feature you may have forgotten or to learn new features you may need.

You are expected to produce error-free documents, so check spelling, proofread, and correct your work carefully before presenting it for approval.

Contacts File

Use the Contacts feature of *Outlook* to create an HPJ Branch Managers contact folder with information for each of the branch managers.

HPJ Files and Website

Some jobs will require you to use documents stored in HPJ company files. Some documents will require you to gather information from the company's website at www.cengage.com/school/keyboarding/hpj. All files you create should be named with *HPJ,* followed by the job number (*HPJ JOB1, HPJ JOB2,* etc.).

HPJ Website

HPJ Headquarters

MATH DEPARTMENT MEETING MINUTES

November 12, 20--

1. Call to order: Department Head Michael Mariani called the Math Department meeting to order at 2:30 p.m. on November 12, 20-- in Room 410.

2. Attendance: Mary Johnson recorded the attendance. All department teachers were present except Norman Householder.

3. Minutes of the October 11 meeting were read and approved.

4. The unfinished business related to the procedure for identifying external factors likely to affect the math curriculum during the next five years was decided:

    a. Spend ten minutes writing external factors on small notepaper.

    b. Post written notes on the walls.

    c. Review all posted notes and group similar ones. Teachers will not talk to each other during this time.

    d. Discuss the groupings and attempt to label each group.

    e. Make needed revisions to the factors in each group.

5. This new business was decided:

    a. The math teachers identified 12 external factors grouped into four categories.

    b. The factors and categories will be presented to the curriculum director.

    c. The curriculum director will be invited to the December 14 meeting.

6. Adjournment

    Michael Mariani adjourned the meeting at 4:30 p.m.

Susan LeCartia
Ms. Julia Betters
Business Management
June 5, 20--

Health Services Management Program

This report gives information about opportunities in health services management, a program of study that several of my classmates and I are considering upon graduation from high school.

Employment Opportunities

Opportunities for employment in health services are numerous and growing "faster than the average for all occupations through the year 2014 as health services continue to expand and diversify" (Occupational Outlook Handbook).

(continued on next page)

OBJECTIVES
- To use your decision-making skills to process documents.
- To improve your ability to read and follow directions.

76–80A

Conditioning Practice

Key each line twice.

alphabet	1	Seven complete textbooks were required for the new zoology major.
figures	2	Shipping charges ($35.98) were included on the invoice (#426087).
speed	3	A sick dog slept on the oak chair in the dismal hall of the dorm.

gwam 1' | 1 | 2 | 3 | 4 | 5 | 6 | 7 | 8 | 9 | 10 | 11 | 12 | 13 |

76–80B

Work Assignment

Job 1

> **HPJ** From the Desk of
> **Helen St. Claire**
>
> You will be corresponding with the branch managers frequently. Create an HPJ Branch Managers contact folder and enter contact information for each of the branch managers as shown at the right. You will need to get the information for the other three managers from the company website.
>
> June 5   HSC

Job 2

> **HPJ** From the Desk of
> **Helen St. Claire**
>
> Ms. Parker wants the attached letter sent to each branch manager. Find mailing addresses from your contacts. Save each letter with the last name of the addressee, e.g., HPJ JOB2 CARTER.
>
> June 5   HSC

Dear

Each of you has indicated a need for additional personnel. I've heard your requests. With this quarter's increase in seminar revenues, I am now in a position to respond to them. Five new communication specialist positions, one for each branch, have been added.

Since training for the positions takes place here at the home office, it is more cost effective to hire communication specialists from this area. I will take care of recruitment and preliminary screening. However, since each of you will work closely with the individual hired, I think you should make the final selection.

When you are here for the annual meeting, I'll schedule time for you to interview eight individuals. If you are not satisfied with any of the eight, we will arrange additional interviews. I should have a job description created within the next week. When it is completed, I'll send it to you for your review.

Activity 4

Two-page Memo

1. Open *DF CR3 ACTIVITY4*.
2. Make the changes noted in the comments and then delete the comments.
3. Accept or reject the changes.
4. Key the information at the right to complete the two-page memo.
5. Use a 12-pt. font and 1.25" side margins.
6. Supply all missing memo parts.

Save as: CR3 ACTIVITY4

Screen incoming calls by determining who is calling and the purpose of the call. Thus, you can decide to process the call or transfer it to another person.

Whenever you transfer a call, be certain the caller speaks to the correct person on the first transfer.

Place calls on hold only when necessary, for short periods, and in a courteous manner. If calls need to be put on hold for more than a minute or two, give callers the option of being called back.

These techniques should be used to improve outgoing calls:

- Outline the major points, and gather needed materials before placing each call.
- Group calls and make them during set times each day.
- Place calls in order of importance.
- Identify yourself as soon as your call is answered.

Write down the name and extension number of the person with whom you are speaking, for when a follow-up call must be made.

Activity 5

Outline

Format as an outline. Use a 2" top margin.

Save as: CR3 ACTIVITY5

HIRING EMPLOYEES

1) Advertise the position
   a) Professional journals
   b) Area newspapers
     i) Daily papers
     ii) Sunday papers
   c) Personal calls
   d) Placement services
2) Hire the right person
   a) Evaluate applicants' resumes
   b) Identify top applicants
     i) Check references and credentials
     ii) Rank applicants
   c) Interview top three applicants
   d) Decide top applicant
   e) Make offer

Job 3

HPJ From the Desk of
Helen St. Claire

I've started the attached letter from Ms. Parker to the branch managers. It is saved as DF HPJ JOB3. Please finish the letter. You will need to use your textbook to see how to format the heading for the second page of a letter. Save each letter with the last name of the addressee, e.g., HPJ JOB3 CARTER.

June 6   *HSC*

Technology. The changed marketplace is demanding that we explore new ways of delivering our seminars. How can we better use technology to deliver our product? This may include putting selected seminars online, inter- and intra-company communication, etc.

Company growth. What steps can we take to increase company growth? Last year revenues grew by 15 percent; our expenses grew by 8 percent.

Employee incentives. Last year we implemented a branch manager profit-sharing plan. Some of you have indicated that we need to expand this profit-sharing plan to include our communication specialists.

Regional expansion. Some of the regions have been very successful. How do we capitalize on that success? Is it time to divide the successful regions?

International expansion. **HPJ** has put on several seminars overseas--at a very high cost. Is it time to start thinking about creating a branch of **HPJ** at a strategic overseas location?

I am proud of what we have been able to accomplish this year. The foundation is in place, and we are ready to grow. Each of you plays a critical role in the success of **HPJ**. Thank you for your dedication and commitment to making our company the "leader in providing corporate and individual communication training." Best wishes for continued success. I'm looking forward to discussing **HPJ**'s future at this year's annual meeting. If you have additional items that you would like included on the agenda, please get them to me before June 15.

Job 4

HPJ From the Desk of
Helen St. Claire

Format the attached Job Description. I've included some notes. In order to get the title on two lines, you need to key the entire title on one line and then go back and tap ENTER after Description.

June 6   *HSC*

> **2" TM—Use 12 pt. Calibri for body**
>
> # Job Description
> # HPJ Communication Specialist
>
> **HPJ Communication Specialists** work cooperatively with other branch members to develop and deliver communication seminars throughout the United States.
>
> ### Position Requirements
> a. College degree
> b. Excellent oral and written communication skills
> c. Excellent interpersonal skills
> d. Technology skills
> e. Knowledge of business concepts
>
> ### Duties and Responsibilities
> a. Research seminar topics
> b. Develop seminars
> c. Prepare electronic presentations for seminars
> d. Prepare seminar manual
> e. Present seminars

CYCLE 3
Review

• To prepare for assessment of Cycle 3 document processing, computer application, and straight-copy skills.

Conditioning Practice

Key each line twice daily.

alphabet	1	Sixty glazed rolls with jam were quickly baked and provided free.
figures	2	Ted was born 1/7/42, Mel was born 3/2/86, and I was born 5/18/90.
speed	3	The auditor cut by half the giant goal of the sorority endowment.

gwam 1' | 1 | 2 | 3 | 4 | 5 | 6 | 7 | 8 | 9 | 10 | 11 | 12 | 13 |

Activity 1

Letter

Key in modified block format using mixed punctuation and ¶ indentations.

Save as: CR3 ACTIVITY1

Activity 2

Letter

Open *CR3 ACTIVITY1* and format the letter in block style with open punctuation; delete the postscript. Use 1.25" side margins.

Save as: CR3 ACTIVITY2

September 5, 20-- | Dr. Louis L. Elmore | Medical Park Drive | Birmingham, AL 35213-2496 | Dear Dr. Elmore

The next meeting of the Longfellow Observatory Amateur Astronomers Club is scheduled for 7:30 p.m. on Friday, September 23, in Room 102 of the Longfellow Observatory.

As the enclosed agenda indicates, the primary purpose of the meeting is to plan next year's schedule of events. As usual, the events are likely to include a lecture series and one or two star parties. A project to involve high school students in astronomy needs to be planned and approved.

Please mark your calendar for this important meeting. If you are unable to attend, please call me at 555-0151.

Sincerely | Richard Clavijo | Assistant Director | RC:xx | Enclosure | I'm glad that you are bringing Aaron Lee to the meeting. Perhaps he will consider joining LOAAC.

Activity 3

Flyer

Design a flyer to present the information at the right. Use SmartArt or WordArt, shapes or text boxes, and clip art or pictures in your flyer. You decide other formatting features.

Save as: CR3 ACTIVITY3

Event:	CPR Instructions
Description:	Two-hour CPR (cardiopulmonary resuscitation) class for those interested in learning how to administer CPR to adults and infants.
When:	Wednesday, December 5
Time:	7:15 p.m.
Where:	River Valley Health and Fitness Club
Instructor:	Dr. Marilyn Guiterez, River Valley Hospital
Main Feature:	Participants will gain the confidence needed to respond in an emergency situation with skills that can save a life.

Job 5

HPJ From the Desk of
Helen St. Claire

Prepare (don't send) the attached message as an e-mail from Ms. Parker to the branch managers. Attach the job description that you created. Get e-mail addresses from your contacts file you created for Job 1.

June 7   HSC

Job 6

HPJ From the Desk of
Helen St. Claire

The New York Branch has moved into their new office located at 488 Broadway. The ZIP code is 10012-3871. Update your contact file information for Serena DeCosta to reflect this change.

June 7   HSC

Job 7

HPJ From the Desk of
Helen St. Claire

Create the attached New Seminar Descriptions table. You can copy and paste seminar descriptions from our website. Leave 1 blank line before and after each description.

June 7   HSC

SUBJECT: JOB DESCRIPTION FOR COMMUNICATION SPECIALISTS

I've attached a draft of the job description for the communication specialists that we will be hiring for each branch. I wanted to give each of you an opportunity to review it before we advertise for the positions in the newspaper.

If there are additional responsibilities that you would like to see included with the job description before we post it, please let me know by Friday. The advertisement will run in the _Star_ on Sunday and appear on its Job Board website next week. I'm confident that we will have an even greater interest in the positions than we had when we hired a couple of communication specialists last January.

New Seminar Descriptions

Seminar Title	Seminar Description	Cost per Person
Business Etiquette: You Cannot Not Communicate!		$99
Gender Communication: "He Says, She Says"		$75
International Communication		$75
Listen Up!		$99
Technology in the Workplace		$125

Illustration of an Advanced Filter/Sort

The illustration at right shows an advanced filter/sort on the *Eastwick Address* file. The file was first sorted (*primary sort*) by State in ascending order. This sort placed all the students with a Minnesota address together and all the students with a Wisconsin address together.

The second sort (*secondary sort*) was by City in ascending order. This sort put all the Minnesota cities in alphabetical order and all the Wisconsin cities in alphabetical order.

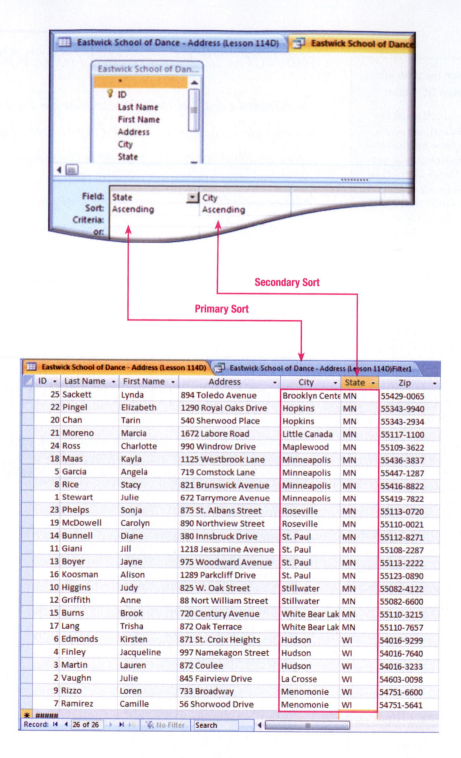

HPJ From the Desk of
Helen St. Claire

Format the attached agenda for the annual meeting. Use 12-pt. font for the text after the heading.

June 8   *HSC*

Agenda

I.   Greetings
II.   Overview of past year
III.   Seminars
     a. Enhancement
     b. Expansion
     c. Client base
IV.   Leadership
V.   Company growth
     a. Regional expansion
     b. International expansion
VI.   Employee Incentives
     a. Branch managers
     b. Communication specialists
VII.   Technology
VIII. Miscellaneous
IX.   Adjournment

Job 9

HPJ From the Desk of
Helen St. Claire

Ms. Parker would like the attached letter sent to the branch managers. Enclose a copy of the agenda and the hotel confirmation (when it's available) with the letter. Save each letter with the last name of the addressee, e.g., HPJ JOB9 CARTER

June 8   *HSC*

Attached is the agenda for the annual meeting. I didn't hear from any of you about additions to the agenda; so if you have items to discuss, we can include them under Miscellaneous.

Your accommodations have been made for the McIntyre Inn. Your confirmation is enclosed. A limousine will pick you up at the Inn at 8:30 a.m. on Monday. Activities have been planned for Monday and Wednesday evenings. Tuesday and Thursday mornings have been left open. You can arrange something on your own, or we can make group arrangements. We'll decide on Monday before adjourning for the day.

I'm looking forward to seeing you on the 26th.

Job 10

HPJ From the Desk of
Helen St. Claire

Create tables for each of the branch managers similar to the attached one for Carter. Save all five tables in one file in alphabetic order by last name, with each table on a separate page. The information for these tables is saved in the master interview schedule (DF HPJ JOB10). Copy and paste the information from the master to each individual table. Key the headings in 14 pt. and the body in 12 pt.

June 9   *HSC*

HPJ Communication Specialists
Interview Schedule for **Jamal Carter**
June 29, 20--, Room 101

Time	Name of Interviewee
1:00 – 1:15	Joan Langston
1:20 – 1:35	Tim Wohlers
1:40 – 1:55	Mark Enqvist
2:00 – 2:15	Stewart Peters
2:20 – 2:35	Felipe Valdez
2:40 – 2:55	Katarina Dent
3:00 – 3:15	Jennifer Kent
3:20 – 3:35	Sandra Baylor

Sort for Quick Answers

1. Open the *Sales Reps – District 13* table.
2. Run sorts to answer the questions at the right.
3. Open *DF 111E* and record your answers.

Save as: **111E Rockwell Technologies**

RT	ROCKWELL TECHNOLOGIES
No.	**Question**
1	How many Arizona sales reps are in District 13?
2	How many sales reps sold over $60,000 in July?
3	How many sales reps sold over $60,000 in August?
4	How many sales reps' last names start with **H**?
5	Do any of the sales reps have the same first name?
6	Do any of the sales reps have the same last name?
7	Which sales reps had less than $30,000 in sales in July?
8	Which sales reps had less than $30,000 in sales in August?

Sorting for Quick Answers

1. Open the *Eastwick School of Dance* database.
2. Run sorts to answer the questions at the right.
3. Open *DF 111F* and record your answers.

Save as: **111F Eastwick School of Dance**

Eastwick School of Dance	
No.	**Question**
1	How many of the students enrolled in Eastwick School of Dance are from Wisconsin?
2	How many of the students are from Minneapolis?
3	How many students are taking beginning jazz for their first class?
4	How many students are taking beginning jazz for their first or second class?
5	How many students have not paid their September fees?
6	How many students have not paid their October fees?
7	How many students are taking advanced ballet for their first or second class?

HPJ From the Desk of
Helen St. Claire

Prepare the Seminar Objectives list in final form for Erika Thomas. Key the entire heading on one line and then put in hard returns. Change the font size to 18 pt. for the first and third lines of the heading. Make the text 12 pt. after the heading.

June 9   HSC

Seminar Objectives for:
Technology in the Workplace
Minneapolis Branch

1. *Discuss the role of communication technology in today's business environment and how it has changed over the past ten years.*
2. *Inform participants of various technological communication tools presently available.*
3. *Highlight the advantages/disadvantages of these tools presently available.*
4. *Demonstrate:*
   - *Videoconferencing*
   - *Teleconferencing*
   - *Data conferencing*
   - *GroupSystems*
   - *Internet resources*
5. *Inform participants of various technological communication tools that are in development.*
6. *Discuss Internet resources available to participants.*
7. *Discuss how using high-speed communication in today's business environment can give a firm a competitive advantage in the global marketplace.*

Job 12

HPJ From the Desk of
Helen St. Claire

Prepare a final draft of the attached memo to Natasha from Erika Thomas. The subject is Monthly Progress Report. Be sure to include the attachment.

Use Heading 1 style for the headings in the body of the memo.

June 9   HSC

Here is an update on recent progress of the Minneapolis Branch.

Seminar Bookings

We are fully booked through April and May. Additional communication specialists are desperately needed if we are going to expand into other states in our region. Most of our current bookings are in Minnesota, Iowa, and Wisconsin. We will be presenting in Illinois for the first time in May. I anticipate this will lead to additional bookings that we won't be able to accommodate. This is a problem that I enjoy having. Michigan, Indiana, and Ohio provide ample opportunities for expansion, when resources are made available.

New Seminar

A lot of progress has been made on the new seminar we are developing, "Technology in the Workplace" (see attachment for seminar objectives). Our branch will be ready to preview the seminar at our annual meeting. Not only will the seminar be a great addition to our seminar offerings, but also I believe HPJ can use it to communicate better internally. I will present my ideas when I preview the seminar. The seminar covers:

- Videoconferencing
- Teleconferencing
- Data conferencing
- GroupSystems
- Internet resources

(Memo continued on next page)

OBJECTIVE

• To learn to create single and multiple data sorts.

111B

Use the Sort Feature

1. Read the text at the right.
2. Read and study the example of the multiple sort on p. 341.

The records of tables and forms can be arranged in a specific order by using the Sort feature. A sort can be done on one field or on multiple fields.

For example, the Eastwick Address table could be sorted by State in ascending order. A sort using the State field would group all students from Minnesota first, with all students from Wisconsin next. It would not, however, arrange the cities in each state alphabetically. A **multiple sort**, first by State and then by City, would be necessary to accomplish this arrangement.

111C

Create Single and Multiple Sorts

1. Open the *Franklin High School Membership* table file.
2. Perform the sorts at the right.
3. Print a copy of the single sort by Last Name in Descending order.
4. Save and close the database.

Single Sorts – Ascending Order

1. Last Name
2. ZIP Code

Single Sorts – Descending Order

1. Last Name
2. ZIP code

111D

Sort for Quick Answers

Learning Tip:
Sorts and queries can be used to arrange information to provide quick answers to questions. (Queries will be taught in a future lesson.)

1. Open the *Software Professionals* table.
2. Run sorts to answer the questions at the right.
3. Open *DF 111D* and record your answers.

Save as: **111D Software Professionals**

No.	Software Professionals
	Question
1	What were the top three software packages in terms of number of copies sold?
2	What were the two software packages with the lowest beginning inventory?
3	How many software packages were designed mainly for education?
4	How many software packages sell for more than $250?
5	How many software packages sell for less than $100?

Graphic Designer

A graphic artist has been hired to design all of the materials for the new seminar. He will design promotional items as well as content-related items. Currently he is working on the manual cover and divider pages. These items will be coordinated with the emblems used in the slide show portion of the presentation, along with name tags, promotional paraphernalia, and business cards. This should give our seminar a more professional appearance. If it works as well as I think it is going to, we will have the designer work on materials for our existing seminars to add the "professional" look.

Job 13

> **HPJ** From the Desk of
> **Helen St. Claire**
>
> *Format the text as an unbound report with foot-notes (shown at bottom of attached copy). The report will be a handout for the "Listen Up!" seminar.*
>
> *June 12*   *HSC*

LISTEN UP!

According to Raymond McNulty, "Everyone who expects to succeed in life should realize that success only will come if you give careful consideration to other people."[1] To accomplish this you must be an excellent listener. One of the most critical skills that an individual acquires is the ability to listen. studies indicate that a person spends 70 percent to 80 percent of his or her time communicating, of which 32.7% is spent listening. Adler and Elmhorst give the following breakdown for the average individual of an time spends communicating.[2]

- Writing 18.8%
- Reading 22.6%
- Speaking 25.8%
- Listening 32.7%

Since a great deal of the time spent communicating is spent listening, it is important to overcome any obstacles that obstruct our ability to listen and to learn new ways to improve our listening ability.

Barriers to Listening

Anything that interferes with our ability to listen is classi-fied as a barrier to listening. These Barriers that obstruct our ability to listen can be divided into two basic categories--external and internal barriers.

(Report continued on next page)

110D

Editing Records

1. Open the *Eastwick Fees* database table.
2. Make the changes at the right.
3. Save and close the database.

1. **Stacy Rice** is enrolled in Inter. Jazz and Inter. Ballet (Be sure to change fees.)
2. *Byrns* should be spelled **Burns**.
3. *Tasha Lang* should be **Trisha Lang**.
4. Diane Bunnell is enrolled in Adv. Ballet, not Inter. Make the necessary adjustments.
5. Lynda Sackett decided not to take Adv. Tap. Make the necessary adjustments to reflect this change. The September Fees will stay at $63.00; however, change the Monthly Fee to **$30.00** to reflect this change for future months.

110E

Editing Records

1. Open the *Eastwick Address* database table.
2. Make the changes given at the right.
3. Save and close the database.

1. Diane Bunnell has a new address and telephone number.

   380 Innsbruck Drive
   St. Paul, MN 55112-8271
   612-329-7621

2. Jackqueline Finley's name should be spelled **Jacqueline**. Her phone number should be **715-386-6764**.
3. Make sure you change the spelling of Brook Byrns (**Burns**) and Tasha Lang (**Trisha**).
4. Change Judy Higgin's mother's name to **Ms.** Erin **Schultz**.
5. Kayla Maas has a new address and telephone number.

   1125 Westbrook Lane
   Minneapolis, MN 55436-2837
   612-348-8211

110F

Editing Records

1. Open the *Sales Reps – District 13* table.
2. Make the changes given at the right.
3. Save and close the database.

1. Carrie Chi's first name should be spelled **Karrie**.
2. Jay Reese has moved; his new address is:

   1811 Olympic Way, N.
   Scottsdale, AZ 85268-8811

3. Devlin Tapani's July sales were incorrectly recorded. They should have been **$49,145**.
4. The ZIP code for Jason Henneman should be **59102-5624**.
5. Mary Carter would like her name recorded as **Mary Carter-Bond**.

110G

Editing Records

1. Open the *FHS FBLA Members* table to correct data entry errors.
2. Make the changes shown at the right to the table.
3. Save and close the database.

1. Ms. Radclif's first name should be spelled **Julia**, not Julie.
2. Ms. Sanchez moved to **748 Market Street**; the ZIP Code didn't change.
3. Ms. Hawthorne's address should be **874** Montgomery Street.
4. Mr. Lockwood's first name is **Greg**, not Gregg.
5. Mr. Fosters's address should be **874** Franklin Street.

Job 13 continued

Internal barriers. Internal barriers are those that deal with the mental or psychological aspects of listening. The perception of the importance of the message, the emotional state, and the tuning in and out of the speaker by the listener are examples of internal barriers.

External Barriers. External barriers are barriers other than those that deal with the mental and psychological makeup of the listener that tend to keep the listener from devoting full attention to what is being said. Telephone interruptions, uninvited visitors, noise, and the physical environment are examples of external barriers.

Ways to Improve Listening

Barriers to listening can be overcome. However, it does take a sincere effort on the part of the listener. Neher and Waite suggest the following ways to improve listening skills.[3]

- Be aware of the barriers that are especially troublesome for you. Listening difficulties are individualistic. Developing awareness is an important step in overcoming such barriers.

- Listen as though you will have to paraphrase what is being said. Listen for ideas rather than for facts.

- Expect to work at listening. Work at overcoming distractions, such as the speaker's delivery or nonverbal mannerisms.

- Concentrate on summarizing the presentation as you listen. If possible, think of additional supporting material that would fit with the point that the speaker is making. Avoid trying to refute the speaker. Try not to be turned off by remarks you disagree with.

---

[1]H. Dan O'Hair, James S. O'Rourke IV, and Mary John O'Hair, *Business Communication: A Framework for Success* (Cincinnati: South-Western Publishing, 2001), p. 211.

[2]Ronald B. Adler and Jeanne Marquardt Elmhorst, *Communicating at Work* (New York: The McGraw-Hill Companies, 2008), p. 77.

[3]William W. Neher and David H. Waite, *The Business and Professional Communicator* (Needham Heights, MA: Allyn and Bacon, 1993), p. 28.

OBJECTIVES

• To learn efficient ways to move around in a database.
• To edit records in a database table.

110B

Move Around in a Database

1. Read the text at the right.
2. Open the *Franklin High School FBLA* database membership table that you worked with in Lesson 108, and practice moving through it.
3. Open the *Franklin High School FBLA* database membership form file and practice moving through it.
   • Find Mitchell Wickman's record.
   • Go to Record 23.
   • Find all the records with a ZIP code of 94111 (key **94111** in the Search box at the bottom of the screen and tap ENTER until it remains on the same record after you tap ENTER.
4. Save and close the database.

There are several ways to move to a new location on the screen of a database table and a database form. Some methods take more keystrokes than others. Practicing the fastest methods, those using fewest keystrokes, until they feel automatic makes for efficient database work.

INSERTION POINT MOVES – TABLE

To move:	Keys
One field left	←
One field right	→
One line up	↑
One line down	↓
Leftmost field	HOME
Rightmost field	END
Down one window	PgDn
Up one window	PgUp
To first record	CTRL + HOME
To last record	CTRL + END

INSERTION POINT MOVES – FORM

To move:	Keys
Next field	↓
Previous field	↑
Top of form	HOME
Bottom of form	END
First record	CTRL + HOME
Last record	CTRL + END
Next record*	PgDn
Previous record*	PgUp

*In case the record has more than one screen, use CTRL + PgUp (PgDn).

110C

Editing Records

1. Read the text at the right.
2. Open the *Software Professionals Inventory* database table.
3. Make the changes at the right.
4. Save and close the database.

Editing existing database records is similar to editing word processing documents. Simply move the insertion point to the location where the change is to be made and use the INSERT, DELETE, or BACKSPACE keys to make changes.

1. Change the price of Computer Geography to **$279**.
2. Change the name of *Creative Business Letters* to **Creative Letters**.
3. Change the price of Basic Spreadsheets to **$159**.
4. The beginning inventory of Data Controller should have been **300**.
5. Change the name of *Language Arts Skills* to **Language Skills**.

Job 14 (shown below)   **Job 15** (shown right)

HPJ From the Desk of
Helen St. Claire

Here is the company organization chart we have on file (DF HPJ JOB14). Some of the information is missing or outdated. Each branch's website contains the most up-to-date information. Print a copy of the file; then verify the information against that on the website. Mark the changes on the printed copy; finally, make the changes to the master file. Be sure to change the date to today's date, June 12.

June 12   HSC

HPJ From the Desk of
Helen St. Claire

Prepare (don't send) this message as an e-mail to the communication specialists in the Minneapolis branch from Erika Thomas. You will need to get the e-mail addresses from their Web page. New Communication Specialist is the subject.

June 12   HSC

Stewart Peters will be joining our branch as a Communication Specialist on Monday, July 15.

Stewart grew up in New York, where he completed an undergraduate degree in organizational communication at New York University. He recently completed his master's degree at the University of Minnesota.

Stewart's thesis dealt with interpersonal conflict in the corporate environment. Since we intend to develop a seminar in this area, he will be able to make an immediate contribution.

Please welcome Stewart to HPJ and our branch when he arrives on the 15th.

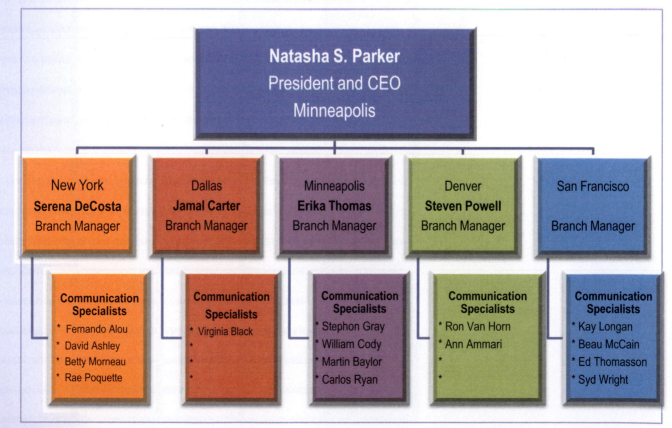

HPJ COMMUNICATION SPECIALISTS

Organizational Chart

January 2, 20--

Add New Table Fields and Data

Eastwick

1. Open the *Eastwick Fees* table.
2. Add the fields shown below.
   - **September Fees**
   - **October Fees**
   - **November Fees**
   - **December Fees**
3. Update the records in the database table to include the new information provided at the right.
4. Print a copy of the revised table in landscape orientation.
5. Save and close the database.

Eastwick School of Dance

Name	Sept. Fees	Oct. Fees	Nov. Fees	Dec. Fees
Stewart	55	55	55	
Vaughn				
Martin	53	53		
Finley				
Garcia	57	57		
Edmonds	59	59		
Ramirez	58	58		
Rice				
Rizzo				
Higgins	27			
Giani	28	28		
Griffith	59	59		
Boyer	52	52		
Bunnell				
Byrns	57	57	57	
Koosman	66	66		
Lang				
Maas	25	25	25	
McDowell	28	28		
Chan	62	62		
Moreno	29			
Pingel	25	25		
Phelps	62	62	62	
Ross	28	28		
Sackett	63			

HPJ From the Desk of
Helen St. Claire

I've started an electronic slide presentation for the annual meeting (DF HPJ Job16). Please insert slides 2–8. I've attached sketches of slides 2, 3, and 4. Slides 5–8 will be similar to slide 4, showing a description of each of the new seminars. Get the information for the slides from the New Seminar Descriptions table (Job 7) you formatted earlier. Add transitions for slides 2–9.

June 12   HSC

Slide 2

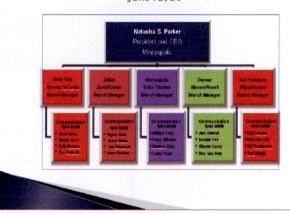

Slide 3

New Seminars

‣ Business Etiquette: You Cannot Not Communicate!

‣ Gender Communication: "He Says, She Says."

‣ International Communication

‣ Listen Up!

‣ Technology in the Workplace

Slide 4

Business Etiquette:
You Cannot Not Communicate!

‣ If business etiquette is important to you, don't miss this seminar. Learn what's acceptable—and what's not—in formal business settings.

Add New Table Fields and Data

1. Open the *Sales Reps – District 13* table.
2. Add the fields shown below.

   Territory
   ZIP
   July Sales
   August Sales
3. Update the records in the database table to include the new information provided at the right.
4. Add another new field with a field name of **Courtesy Title**. Use **Ms.** for all female reps except McRae, Donovan, and Finley. They prefer to use **Mrs.** for their courtesy title. Use **Mr.** for all male reps.
5. Print a copy of the revised table in landscape orientation.
6. Save and close the database.

SALES REPRESENTATIVES

Last Name	Territory	ZIP	July Sales	August Sales
Carter	Wyoming	82001-1837	45,351	37,951
Hull	Colorado	30233-0070	53,739	49,762
McRae	Utah	84404-2835	33,371	38,978
Hernandez	Utah	84057-1572	39,371	40,790
Camby	Idaho	83702-8312	42,173	65,386
Henneman	Montana	59102-6735	17,219	29,737
Reed	Wyoming	82607-9956	53,791	59,349
Logan	Montana	59404-3883	49,712	21,790
Cirillo	Idaho	83202-7523	29,731	37,956
LeClair	Colorado	81503-2270	63,212	40,321
Donovan	Colorado	80123-0091	37,198	45,865
Young	Utah	84118-0111	44,876	56,791
Tapani	South Dakota	57702-9932	59,145	39,645
Rivera	Colorado	81005-8376	55,400	37,751
Walker	Idaho	83402-3326	43,900	44,750
Wetteland	Montana	59803-8388	33,650	40,765
Chi	Arizona	85224-1157	39,750	48,621
Finley	Arizona	85711-5656	19,765	35,765
Reese	Arizona	85268-0012	67,890	45,780
Bell	Colorado	80401-7529	39,200	43,286
Doolittle	South Dakota	57106-7621	64,890	37,102
Butler	Arizona	85302-1300	35,975	46,873
Hulett	Arizona	85023-2766	56,730	46,720

CYCLE 3

As you think about shaping your future, you will want to add experiences and information in the areas of science and mathematics. With skills and knowledge in science and math, there are no limits to what you can achieve.

No matter what field you choose, you will be working on a computer without a doubt. In this cycle, you'll become a more effective communicator as you enhance documents with graphics, work with templates, and create a flyer. You'll discover how databases and spreadsheets can help you be more effective.

In addition, you'll learn special report formats, and you'll help coordinate a science conference. All the units in Cycle 3—plus special sections between units—can make you more marketable in any line of work.

Science & Math

• To add new fields to an existing database.

109B

Add New Fields to an Existing Database Table

1. Read the copy at the right.
2. Add the two new fields to the *Software Professionals Inventory* database table.

Database software lets you add additional fields to a database table after you have created it. *Software Professionals* would like you to add the fields shown at the right:

Purchases
Sales

109C

Update Records

1. Update the records in the *Software Professionals Inventory* database table to include the new information provided at the right.
2. Print a copy of the revised table in landscape orientation.
3. Save and close the database.

	Record 1	Record 2	Record 3
Software:	Basic Spreadsheets	Computer Geography	Computerized Reading
Purchases:	1200	400	500
Sales:	1578	850	674

	Record 4	Record 5	Record 6
Software:	Creative Bus. Letters	Data Controller	English Enhancement
Purchases:	250	0	1000
Sales:	400	240	1200

	Record 7	Record 8	Record 9
Software:	Financial Advisors	Graphics Designer	Keyboard Composition
Purchases:	1000	500	1000
Sales:	1987	437	1753

	Record 10	Record 11	Record 12
Software:	Language Arts Skills	Quick Key WP	Spelling Mastery
Purchases:	500	1000	0
Sales:	759	1378	300

	Record 13	Record 14	Record 15
Software:	Tax Assistant	Telephone Directory	Art Gallery
Purchases:	0	1000	500
Sales:	980	1873	673

	Record 16	Record 17	Record 18
Software:	Your Time Manager	Office Layout	Math Tutor
Purchases:	1000	300	0
Sales:	1379	475	39

Format Guides: Business Letters

A variation of the block format (see References, pp. R15–R16) is the modified block format. The following paragraphs contain information about this letter style and other letter and memo features.

Modified block format. In modified block format the block format is changed. (See model, p. 252.) The date and the closing lines (complimentary close, writer's name, and writer's title) begin at or near the horizontal center of the page instead of at the left margin. A tab nearest to center may be used to place the date and closing lines (usually 3"). The paragraphs of a letter in modified block format may be indented 0.5", or they may be blocked at the left margin.

Mailing and addressee notations. Mailing notations (such as REGISTERED, CERTIFIED, or FACSIMILE) and addressee notations (such as CONFIDENTIAL) may be included on a letter as well as on the envelope. Tap ENTER once after keying the date, key the notation, and tap ENTER once after keying the notation to key the letter address. On the envelope, key a mailing notation below the stamp, about 0.5" above the envelope address. Tap ENTER once to key an addressee notation at the left margin below the return address. (See model, p. 252.)

Attention line. Use an attention line to specify a department or job title (*Attention Human Resources Manager*) when the name of a specific person is not available. Key it as the first line of the letter address; use *Ladies and Gentlemen* as the salutation. (See model, p. 252.)

Open or mixed punctuation. Open or mixed punctuation may be used within a letter (block or modified block format).

Open punctuation has no punctuation mark after the salutation or complimentary close. Mixed punctuation uses a colon (**:**) after the salutation and a comma (**,**) after the complimentary close. (See model, p. 252.)

Subject line. A subject line provides the reader with a brief description of the purpose of the letter. If used, it is keyed in ALL CAPS or initial caps and lowercase between the salutation and the body of the letter. Tap ENTER once before and after keying the subject line. (See model, p. 252.)

Bulleted or numbered items. Using default line spacing and hanging indent format, align bulleted or numbered items with the beginning of the first word of a paragraph.

Tables in letters or memos. Format an inserted table even with the left and right margin of the document or centered between them. Tap ENTER once before inserting the table and once before the first line of text after the table. Gridlines may be used or omitted.

Postscript. A postscript is an optional message added to a letter as the last item on the page. A postscript may be used to emphasize information in the body or to add a personal message to a business letter. Tap ENTER once before keying the postscript. Block or indent the first line of the postscript to match paragraphs in the body. Omit the postscript abbreviation (P.S.). (See model, p. 252.)

Second-page heading. If a letter or memo is more than one page, a header is placed on all pages except the first using the Header feature. The header consists of three lines blocked at the left margin. Line 1 contains the addressee's name, line 2 contains the word *Page* and the page number, and line 3 contains the date.

Update a Database Table

1. Open the *Eastwick Fees* table.
2. Key the records information shown at the right in the table.
3. Save and close the database after you key the information.

Eastwick
School of Dance

Name	Dance Class 1	Dance Class 2	Monthly Fees
Tarin Chan	Inter. Ballet	Adv. Jazz	$62
Marcia Moreno	Inter. Jazz		$29
Elizabeth Pingel	Beg. Tap		$25
Sonja Phelps	Inter. Jazz	Adv. Tap	$62
Charlotte Ross	Beg. Ballet		$28
Lynda Sackett	Inter. Ballet	Adv. Tap	

Update a Database Table

1. Open the *Franklin HS FBLA* database.
2. Add the three new memberships shown at the right to the membership table.
3. Save and close the database.

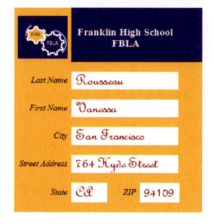

Franklin High School FBLA

Last Name: Van Buren
First Name: Dianna
City: San Francisco
Street Address: 773 Broadway Street
State: CA   ZIP: 94133

Franklin High School FBLA

Last Name: Rousseau
First Name: Vanessa
City: San Francisco
Street Address: 764 Hyde Street
State: CA   ZIP: 94109

Franklin High School FBLA

Last Name: Underwood
First Name: Katelin
City: San Francisco
Street Address: 834 Van Ness Avenue
State: CA   ZIP: 94109

Office Features 8

Activity 1

Find and Replace Text

WP • Home/Editing/Find or Replace

1. Key the ¶ at right.
2. Find and count each occurrence of *are* and *each month*.
3. Replace all occurrences of these words: *assessments* with *taxes*, *subtracted* with *deducted*, *month* with *pay period*.

Save as: OF8 ACTIVITY1

The **Find** feature is used to locate a specified keystroke, word, or phrase in a document. You can refine this feature to find only occurrences that match the specified case; to find only whole words containing the specified text; to find all forms of a specified word; and to find specified text involving the asterisk (*) and question mark (?) as wildcard (unspecified) characters. The **Replace** feature finds a specified keystroke, word, or phrase and then replaces it with another keystroke, word, or phrase. All occurrences of the specified text can be replaced at one time, or replacements can be made individually (selectively).

An individual has to pay a number of assessments. FICA assessments are the assessments that support the social security system and are subtracted from your pay each month. Federal income assessments are also subtracted from your check each month. Assessments that are not subtracted from your check each month include property assessments and sales assessments.

Activity 2

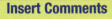

Insert Comments

WP • Review/Comments/New Comment

1. Open *DF OF8 ACTIVITY2*.
2. Key **Add text about keying and editing text in a balloon** as a comment after the word *icon* in ¶ 2, line 2.
3. Key **Add text about just clicking in a balloon to make it the active balloon** as a comment after the word "group" in ¶ 2, line 4.
4. Make the changes to the text that are indicated in the 1st, 4th, and 6th comments and then delete each of the comments.

Save as: OF8 ACTIVITY2

Comments can be inserted in a document with the **New Comment** feature. Comments are usually typed in balloons in the margin of a document, but they can be handwritten or spoken if a Tablet PC is being used. Comments are visible in Print Layout, Full Screen, Reading, and Web Layout views. Comments can be viewed in Outline and Draft views by moving the mouse over the text indicating that a comment was inserted. Comments can be edited, and they can be deleted individually or all at one time.

Comments

This text contains four comments. The first one, a formatting reminder, was inserted after the title. The second comment was inserted here and contains information about comment balloons. The third comment was inserted at the end of this sentence. The third and fourth comments contain information about the Comment feature—please read them carefully. You can edit the comment in the balloon by clicking in the balloon and using your word processor's editing features.

Comment [JAS1]: Format this report using the Word 2007 stlye set.

Comment [JAS2]: The balloon is color-coded and shaded. It contains the initials of the person inserting the comment and a number the software assigned to the comment.

Comment [JAS3]: A line from the insertion point to the balloon is shown.

Comment [JAS4]: You can move to the previous or next comment or delete by using the Previous, Next, and Delete features in the Comments group.

Lesson 108   ADD NEW RECORDS TO UPDATE A DATABASE

- To update an existing database.
- To add new records to a database table.

108B

Add New Records to an Existing Database Table

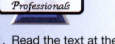
Software Professionals

1. Read the text at the right.
2. Open the *Software Professionals Inventory* table.
3. Add the records shown at the right to the table.
4. Save and close the database.

Database software lets you add records to update a database table at any time. Lynda Smoltz provided the information below to be added to the *Software Professionals* database table.

	Record 13	Record 14	Record 15
Stock No.:	B952	B658	B839
Software:	Tax Assistant	Telephone Directory	Art Gallery
Price:	$129	$119	$249
Beg. Invt.:	5000	5000	1000

	Record 16	Record 17	Record 18
Stock No.:	B794	B833	E910
Software:	Your Time Manager	Office Layout	Math Tutor
Price:	$69	$129	$59
Beg. Invt.:	2500	500	2000

108C

Update a Database Table

1. Read the text at the right.
2. Open the *Sales Reps – District 13* table.
3. Add the records shown at the right to the table.
4. Save and close the database.

Mr. Vermillion would like the information about the additional sales reps listed below added to the *Sales Reps – District 13* table.

	SALES REPRESENTATIVES			
Last Name	First Name	Address	City	State
Walker	Trent	872 Texas Avenue	Idaho Falls	ID
Wetteland	Cynthia	380 Clearview Drive	Missoula	MT
Chi	Carrie	310 Sagebrush Court	Chandler	AZ
Finley	Ann	388 Oxford Drive	Tucson	AZ
Reese	Jay	330 Shiloh Way	Scottsdale	AZ
Bell	Scott	7211 Larkspur Drive	Golden	CO
Doolittle	Lisa	872 Kingswood Way	Sioux Falls	SD
Butler	Warren	398 Navajo Drive	Glendale	AZ
Hulett	Sandra	450 La Paz Court	Phoenix	AZ

Activity 3

Displaying Tracked Changes

WP · Review/Tracking/Track Changes

1. Open *DF OF8 ACTIVITY3* and display the tracked changes.
2. Read the content of the file.
3. Change the way tracked changes are displayed by following the directions in the comment balloon and the last two ¶s.

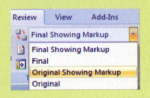

Save as: OF8 ACTIVITY3

When the **Track Changes** feature is active, each insertion, deletion, or formatting change made while editing a document is tracked. A mark is inserted where changes are made. By default, insertions are shown underlined in a colored text in the document, and deletions and formatting changes are shown in balloons in the right margin. Balloons showing editing changes are outlined in the same color as balloons used for comments, but they are not shaded (see illustration below).

Editing changes, like comments, are visible in Print Layout, Full Screen Reading, and Web Layout views. The changes can be viewed in Outline and Draft views by moving the mouse over the text, indicating that a change was made.

Editing changes can be displayed in reverse (insertions shown in balloons and deletions shown in the document) by changing the default display *Final Showing Markup* to *Original Showing Markup*. All changes, including comments, can be hidden by selecting *Final* or *Original*.

Display for Review Button

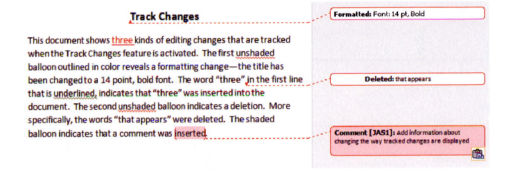

Activity 4

Using Track Changes

WP · Review/Tracking/Track Changes

Open *DF OF8 ACTIVITY4* and track the changes listed at the right.

Save as: OF8 ACTIVITY4

When the Track Changes feature is activated, you can make changes to your document without losing the original text. If desired, the Track Changes feature can be deactivated while editing a document.

a. Insert **WITH WORD 2007** at the end of the title and then format the title in 16 point, bold font.
b. Bold each occurrence of *Track Changes* in ¶ 1.
c. Insert **to revise** at the end of the 1st sentence in ¶ 1.
d. Delete **that you** *want* from the 1st sentence in ¶ 2.
e. Change *insertions that you make* to **text that you insert** in line 2 of ¶ 2 and then change the last word of that sentence from *text* to **document**.
f. Delete **that is displayed** in the 4th sentence of ¶ 2.

Lesson 107

CREATE A NEW TABLE IN AN EXISTING DATABASE

OBJECTIVES
- To create a new table in an existing database.
- To add records to a database.

107B

Create a New Table in an Existing Database

1. Read the text at the right.
2. Open the *DF Eastwick School of Dance* database and save it as **Eastwick School of Dance**.
3. Create and save a new table using the name **Eastwick Fees**.

The owner of Eastwick School of Dance, Ashley Eastwick, would like you to create another table (*Eastwick Fees*) in the *Eastwick School of Dance* database to keep track of student fees. She would like you to use the field names shown at the right.

Last Name
First Name
Dance Class 1
Dance Class 2
Monthly Fees

107C

Add Records to a Database File

1. Enter the records information given at the right into the *Eastwick Fees* database table.

   If the monthly fee is not given, use the following Fee Schedule information to calculate the fee.

Fee Schedule	
Beg. Ballet	$28
Beg. Tap	25
Beg. Jazz	27
Inter. Ballet	30
Inter. Tap	29
Inter. Jazz	29
Adv. Ballet	34
Adv. Tap	33
Adv. Jazz	32

2. Save and close the database.

Eastwick School of Dance

Name	Dance Class 1	Dance Class 2	Monthly Fees
Julie Stewart	Beg. Ballet	Beg. Jazz	$55
Julie Vaughn	Adv. Ballet		$34
Lauren Martin	Beg. Ballet	Beg. Tap	$53
Jacqueline Finley	Inter. Ballet		$30
Angela Garcia	Beg. Jazz	Inter. Ballet.	
Kirsten Edmonds	Beg. Tap	Adv. Ballet	
Camille Ramirez	Inter. Tap	Inter. Jazz	$58
Stacy Rice	Inter. Jazz		
Loren Rizzo	Beg. Ballet		$28
Judy Higgins	Beg. Jazz		
Jill Giani	Beg. Ballet		$28
Anne Griffith	Inter. Ballet	Inter. Jazz	$59
Jayne Boyer	Beg. Tap	Beg. Jazz	$52
Diane Bunnell	Inter. Ballet		
Brook Byrns	Beg. Jazz	Inter. Ballet	$57
Alison Koosman	Adv. Ballet	Adv. Jazz	$66
Tasha Lang	Beg. Ballet	Inter. Tap	$57
Kayla Maas	Beg. Tap		$25
Carolyn McDowell	Beg. Ballet		

Activity 5

Accept and Reject Tracked Changes

WP • Review/Changes/Accept or Reject

1. Open *DF OF8 ACTIVITY5* and read the document.
2. Accept or reject changes as directed.
   a. Make the formatting change suggested in the 1st comment and then delete the comment.
   b. Accept all changes related to text in ¶ 1.
   c. Reject the first change (*the*) in ¶ 2 and accept all others in this ¶.
   d. Accept each change in ¶ 3.
   e. Reject the change in ¶ 4.
   f. Accept the change in ¶ 5 and delete the comment at the end of the text.
   g. Use the Reviewing Pane to ensure no tracked changes or comments remain in the document.
   h. Deactivate the Track Changes feature.

Save as: OF8 ACTIVITY5

Tracked changes can be accepted or rejected in a variety of ways. One way is to review each change in sequence and accept or reject changes one at a time. Another way is to accept or reject all changes at one time. Rejecting all tracked changes at once will not delete comments. Comments need to be deleted individually.

Use the buttons and drop-down lists in the Changes group to accept or reject individual or all tracked changes and to move to the previous or next comment or tracked change (see illustration).

If you are going to share an electronic copy of your document with another person and don't want any tracked changes or comments to display, you can use the Reviewing Pane in the Tracking Group to verify that all changes have been accepted or rejected and that all comments have been deleted. The Reviewing Pane can be displayed vertically or horizontally.

Reviewing Pane with options

Activity 6

Printing Documents with Tracked Changes

1. Open *DF OF8 ACTIVITY6* and print the document showing the markups.
2. Print the document so the markups do not show.

Save as: OF8 ACTIVITY6

Before printing a document with tracked changes or comments (markups), decide if the markups are to show or not show on the printed copy. One way to select the desired option is to access the Print dialog box and select either *Document showing markup* or *Document* from the Print what list box. *Document showing markup* will print the changes and comments. *Document* will hide them.

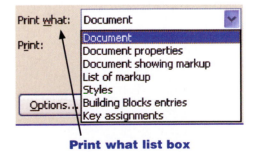

Print what list box

OBJECTIVES

- To create a database table.
- To add records to a database.

106B

Create a Database and Personnel Table

1. Read the text at the right.
2. Create a new database using the filename **Rockwell Technologies**.
3. Create and save a table in Design View with the filename **Sales Reps – District 13**.

Paul M. Vermillion, District 13 sales manager, would like you to create a database containing the names and addresses of all sales representatives in his district. He would like you to use the field names shown at the right.
Last Name

Last Name
First Name
Address
City
State

106C

Add Records to a Database

1. Enter the records given at the right into the *Sales Reps – District 13* database table.
2. Save and close the database table.

RT	SALES REPRESENTATIVES			
Last Name	**First Name**	**Address**	**City**	**State**
Carter	Mary	310 Old Trail Road	Cheyenne	WY
Hull	Dale	2710 Blue Jay Lane	Denver	CO
McRae	Jessica	475 Canyon Road	Ogden	UT
Hernandez	Erika	375 Highland Drive	Orem	UT
Camby	Sue	378 Ranchero Road	Boise	ID
Henneman	Jason	762 Nugget Drive	Billings	MT
Reed	Jessica	817 Herrington Drive	Casper	WY
Logan	Marsha	905 Chickadee Court	Great Falls	ID
Cirillo	Mathew	1208 Whitaker Road	Pocatello	ID
LeClair	Justin	830 Whitehead Drive	Grand Junction	CO
Donovan	Kellee	765 Coal Mine Avenue	Littleton	CO
Young	Marsha	7563 Ferncrest Circle	Salt Lake City	UT
Tapani	Devlin	543 Lookout Mountain	Rapid City	SD
Rivera	Jose	756 Royal Crest Drive	Pueblo	CO

Activity 7

Header and Footer

WP • Insert/Header & Footer/ Header or Footer

1. Open *DF OF8 ACTIVITY7* and complete the steps at the right.
2. View the pages to see the header and footer.

Save as: **OF8 ACTIVITY7**

A header is text (such as a title, name, page number, date, etc.) printed in the top margin of a page. Letters, memos, and reports that are longer than one page often contain a header.

A footer is similar to a header, except the information is placed at the bottom of the page.

Like the Page Number feature learned earlier, headers and footers are often omitted on page 1.

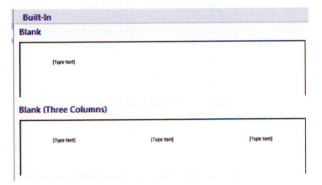

1. Insert a three-line header (blocked at the left margin) using the Built-In Blank style.

   Your name

   Page #

   Date

2. Insert a one-line footer using the Built-In Blank (Three Column) style. Use the same information as you used for the header.

- To create a new database and table.
- To add records to a new database.

105B

Create/Tables/Table Design

Create a Database and Table

Software Professionals

1. Study the text at the right.
2. Create a new database using the filename **Software Professionals**.
3. Create a table using Design Table (Design View).

Save as: Software Professionals Inventory

Information has always been critical to the successful operation of a business. In today's business environment, more and more information is being stored and accessed through the use of databases. As noted earlier, a database is a computerized filing system that is used to organize and maintain a collection of data. The data is stored in tables. A database may contain one table or any number of tables. A few examples of different types of databases include customers' names and addresses, personnel records, sales records, payroll records, telephone numbers, and investment records.

The database you worked with in Lesson 104 was a membership file that contained information about each member. In the remainder of this unit you will be creating and working with several different databases. The first database you will create is for *Software Professionals*. Lynda Smoltz, the manager, would like you to create a database for the software products they sell. She would like the database table to include the following field information:

Stock Number
Software
Price
Beginning Inventory

105C

Add Records to a Database

Software Professionals

1. Enter the records given at the right into the *Software Professionals Inventory* database table.
2. Save and close the database table.

	Record 1	Record 2	Record 3
Stock No.:	B929	E246	E786
Software:	Basic Spreadsheets	Computer Geography	Computerized Reading
Price:	$139	$259	$189
Beg. Invt.:	2000	2500	1000

	Record 4	Record 5	Record 6
Stock No.:	E561	B821	E320
Software:	Creative Bus. Letters	Data Controller	English Enhancement
Price:	$125	$309	$219
Beg. Invt.:	500	500	800

	Record 7	Record 8	Record 9
Stock No.:	B689	B586	E758
Software:	Financial Advisors	Graphic Designer	Keyboard Composition
Price:	$99	$165	$155
Beg. Invt.:	2500	400	3000

	Record 10	Record 11	Record 12
Stock No.:	B615	B731	E641
Software:	Language Arts Skills	Quick Key WP	Spelling Mastery
Price:	$139	$75	$139
Beg. Invt.:	1500	2500	2000

OBJECTIVES

- To review block letter format and letter parts.
- To edit a document using the Track Changes feature.

81A–85A

Conditioning Practice

Key each line twice daily.

alphabet 1 To what extent was Kazu involved with my project before quitting?

figures 2 A van with License No. B928-754 is parked in Space 103 in Lot 16.

speed 3 To my dismay, the official kept the fox by the dog in the kennel.

gwam 1' | 1 | 2 | 3 | 4 | 5 | 6 | 7 | 8 | 9 | 10 | 11 | 12 | 13 |

81B

Letters

Letter 1 (Personal-Business Letter)

1. Key in block format, using open punctuation and Times New Roman, 12 pt.
2. Use **207 Brainard Road, Hartford, CT 06114-2207** for the return address.
3. Bold the name of the program in ¶ 1.
4. Address an envelope with a return address.

Formatting: Place a copy notation (c) at the left margin one line below the preceding letter part.

Save as: 81B LETTER1

| Current date | Mr. Justin A. Alaron | Brighton Life Insurance Co. | I-84 & Rt. 322 | Milldale, CT 06467-9371 | Dear Mr. Alaron

As a senior at Milldale High School, I participate in the **Shadow Experience Program** (SEP). The enclosed resume indicates my career objective: to become an actuary for a large insurance company.

SEP encourages students to "shadow" a person who is working in their planned career field. I would like to shadow you to see firsthand what an actuary does. I can spend one or two days with you at your office during the coming month.

Please send your written response to me so that I can present it to Ms. Michelle Kish, SEP Coordinator. Thank you.

| Sincerely | Ms. Valerie E. Lopez | SEP Member | Enclosure | c Ms. Michelle Kish

Letter 2 (Business Letter)

Format in block style with open punctuation, using 12-pt. Calibri and 1.25" side margins.

Save as: 81B LETTER2

Formatting: If you make a copy of the letter, tap **ENTER** once and key a blind copy (bc) notation at the left margin below the last line. Do not key the bc notation on the copy of the letter sent to the person named in the letter address.

Formatting: When keying reference initials, the initials of the originator of the document may be keyed along with the initials of the keyboard operator. Use the format XX:xx, with the originator's initials in caps followed by a colon and the operator's initials in lowercase.

| Current Date | Dr. Diana Patsiga | Apartment 256 | 320 Fort Duquesne Road | Pittsburgh, PA 15222-0320

Dear Dr. Patsiga

After discussions with members of the Presidential Planning Council, I believe that Sundy Junior College should carefully review the curriculum for developing mathematical reasoning skills.

To do so, I am establishing a task force composed of faculty from various disciplines and my planning council. Dean Carolyn Pucevich will chair the task force.

The primary charge to the task force is to determine what mathematical content is to be learned and applied in required general education courses, including required math courses.

If you are interested in serving on this task force, please attend an informational meeting on June 2 at 2:30 p.m. in Carter Hall, Board Room C.

| Sincerely | Mary B. Trunno | President | MT:xx | bc Dean Carolyn Pucevich

Franklin High School
FBLA

Last Name   Pierzynski

First Name   Kim

City   San Francisco

Street Address   574 California Street

State   CA   ZIP   94108

Franklin High School
FBLA

Last Name   Cordova

First Name   Roberto

City   San Francisco

Street Address   38 Stockton Street

State   CA   ZIP   94108

104E

Print Table

Open the Franklin High
School database and print
a copy of the *FHS FBLA
Members* table file in landscape orientation.

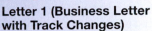
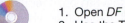

Letter with Tracked Changes

Letter 1 (Business Letter with Track Changes)

1. Open *DF 81C LETTER1*.
2. Use the Track Changes feature to edit (correct errors) and arrange the letter in block format with open punctuation.
3. Print the letter with the markups showing.
4. Save and close as *81C LETTER1*.
5. Exchange your *81C LETTER1* file with a classmate.
6. Open your classmate's file.
7. Accept or reject the changes your classmate made to the letter, and mark any additional changes you recommend.
8. Save as *81C LETTER1A* and return it to your classmate so he/she can see the changes you accepted and rejected.

Lesson 82   MEMOS WITH TRACKED CHANGES

OBJECTIVES

- To review memo format and memo parts.
- To edit a memo using the Track Changes feature.

82B

Memos

Memo 1

Format as a memo, supplying reference initials and enclosure notation.

Save as: 82B MEMO1

Memo 2

Open *82B MEMO1*; change all occurrences of Antech to AnTech by using the Replace feature.

Save as: 82B MEMO2

Memo 3

Format as a memo, supplying reference initials and enclosure notation.

Save as: 82B MEMO3

| TO: Mary Guerra, Science Department Chair | FROM: Jose L. Domingo, Principal | DATE: April 15, 20-- | SUBJECT: PHYSICS LABORATORY EQUIPMENT DONATION

Antech Laboratories has up-to-date physics laboratory furniture and equipment that it can donate to our high school. They are confident that our physics teacher and students will derive great benefits from what they are offering.

A list of the major items Antech can donate is enclosed. All items will be available before the end of July so they can be delivered and installed before school starts in late August.

Please let me know if you can attend a meeting with me at Antech next Tuesday at 3:15 p.m. The purpose of the meeting is to see the laboratory equipment. Antech will need a decision within ten days after the meeting.

| TO: All Intermediate and Senior High School Science Teachers | FROM: Mudi Mutubu, Department Head | DATE: April 15, 20-- | SUBJECT: LABORATORY RENOVATIONS

I've met several times with our school district architects and the science facility consultants they employed to plan the renovations needed for our biology, chemistry, and physics laboratories at the intermediate and senior high schools.

The architect is prepared to have us review and discuss the enclosed preliminary drawings that show the proposed changes to the facilities, including the preparatory rooms and laboratory furniture. I've scheduled a meeting for Wednesday, April 22, at 2:30 p.m. in the conference room near the Principal's Office.

Please arrange your schedules so you can attend this important meeting. The meeting should not last more than one hour, and we will then have ten days to make recommendations so the architect can prepare the second set of drawings.

Note that this is a database that includes very limited information about the Franklin High School FBLA members. As requests for additional information are made, the membership director will expand the database to provide the information that has been requested by adding new fields to the database. For example, the advisor may want to recognize all seniors who are members of FBLA. Or the president may want a report to show which members are serving on each of the organization's committees. Currently, the database wouldn't provide this information. You will learn how to make this information available before completing the database unit.

104C

Add Records to an Existing Database Table

1. Open the *DF Franklin HS FBLA* database and save it as Franklin HS FBLA. Open the *FHS FBLA Members* table.
2. Franklin High School FBLA had five more students join. Include them in the FBLA database. They are all from San Francisco. Key the membership information contained at the right directly into the database table.
3. Close the database file after entering the last record.

New Members
September 16–September 30, 20xx

First Name	Last Name	Address	ZIP
Michael	Gutierrez	635 California Street	94108
Karla	Fitzgerald	368 Mission Street	94105
Justin	Saevig	573 Annie Street	94105
Shannon	Covington	670 Stockton Street	94108
Cody	Foster	873 Franklin Street	94102

104D

Adding Records to an Existing Database Form File

1. Open the *FHS FBLA Members* form file in the *Franklin High School FBLA* database.
2. Key the information contained on the membership applications at the right into the database form.
3. After entering the last record, close the file.

Franklin High School FBLA

Last Name: *Matsuzaka*

First Name: *Vanessa*

City: *San Francisco*

Street Address: *773 Broadway Street*

State: *CA*   ZIP: *94133*

82C

Memo with Tracked Changes

Memo 1 (Memo and Track Changes)

1. Open *DF 82C MEMO1*.
2. Activate Track Changes feature, if needed.
3. Follow the directions in the comments, and then delete the comments.
4. Use the Track Changes feature to edit (correct errors).
5. Print the letter with the markups showing.

Save as: **82C MEMO1**

Optional steps

1. Exchange 82C MEMO1 files with a classmate.
2. Open your classmate's file.
3. Accept or reject the changes your classmate made to the letter and mark any additional changes you recommend.
4. Save as 82C MEMO1A and return it to your classmate so he/she can see the changes you accepted and rejected.

Lesson 83   MODIFIED BLOCK LETTERS

OBJECTIVES

- To learn modified block format.
- To learn mixed punctuation and additional letter parts.

83B

Modified Block Letters

Letter 1

1. Study the format guides on p. 244 and the model letter on p. 252.
2. Key the letter on p. 252.
3. Use the Print Preview feature to check the format.

Save as: **83B LETTER1**

Letter 3

1. Format the text at the right as a modified block letter with mixed punctuation and indented paragraphs.
2. Prepare a large envelope.

Save as: **83B LETTER3**

Letter 2

1. Open *83B LETTER1* and make these changes:
   a. Delete the subject line and mailing notation.
   b. Change the letter address to:
      Attention Office Manager
      Family Practice Associates
      875 Kenilworth Avenue
      Indianapolis, IN 46246-0087
   c. Use open punctuation.
   d. Indent first line of ¶s 0.5".
   e. Change wording of ¶s 2 and 3 to reflect changes in punctuation style and ¶ indentations.
   f. Use Times New Roman, 11-pt. font.

Save as: **83B LETTER2**

| April 17, 20-- | Ms. Kelly Zelasco | Public Relations | AnTech Laboratories | 8201 E. Skelly Drive | Tulsa, OK 74107-8201 | Dear Ms. Zelasco

SUBJECT: PHYSICS LABORATORY EQUIPMENT DONATION

This letter confirms East Tulsa High School's interest in the physics laboratory furniture and equipment that AnTech Laboratories is able to donate.

Ms. Mary Guerra, Science Department Head, and I would like to meet with you on April 24 at AnTech's offices at 3:15 p.m. There is a possibility that one or two of the physics teachers will join us. Please let me know if this date and time are good for you.

Support such as this from business and industry is needed for today's schools to prepare students for the changing world of work. Your generosity is greatly appreciated.

| Sincerely | Jose L. Domingo, Ph.D. | Principal | JLD:xx | c Dr. Randy DuPont, Superintendent | Mrs. Guerra is familiar with many AnTech laboratory employees since she worked in several of your labs as part of our Teachers in the Workplace program.

Lesson 104   ADDING RECORDS TO AN EXISTING DATABASE

OBJECTIVES

• To add records to an existing database.
• To print a database table.

104A–111A

Conditioning Practice

Key each line twice daily.

alphabet	1	Next week Zelda Jacks will become a night supervisor for quality.
figures	2	Scores of 94, 83, 72, 65, and 100 gave Rhonda an average of 82.8.
speed	3	Kay paid the maid for the work she did on the shanty by the lake.

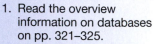

gwam   1' | 1 | 2 | 3 | 4 | 5 | 6 | 7 | 8 | 9 | 10 | 11 | 12 | 13 |

104B

Database Overview

1. Read the overview information on databases on pp. 321–325.
2. Read the information about adding records to an existing database at the right and on p. 327.

The membership director of FBLA at Franklin High School decided to use a database to keep track of membership records. Currently the membership director has the database set up to include the following information about each member:

- First Name
- Last Name
- Address
- City
- State
- Zip

Take a look at what the membership director has created. First open *Microsoft Office Access* and then open *DF Franklin HS FBLA* database.

There are currently four objects that appear when you open the database: Tables, Queries, Forms, and Reports. Click the down arrow to the right of *All Tables* and click *Object Type*. This puts labels to each of the icons at the right.

Currently in the database there is a table of FHS FBLA Members that displays all the member information. Double-click the first *FHS FBLA Members* table to view the information. How many members are currently listed in the database? (26)

The Queries object provides a table to view only the FHS FBLA Members who have a ZIP Code of 94111. Open the query by double-clicking on *94111 ZIP Code Members*. How many current members have a ZIP Code of 94111? (5)

The Forms object allows the viewer to see each member's data individually. Double-click *FHS FBLA Members* under the Forms object. Use the arrows to move from record to record. To find a specific piece of information, click Search and key the information you are looking for. Notice what happens when you click Search and key *Loganberry*. You are automatically taken to Judy Loganberry's membership record.

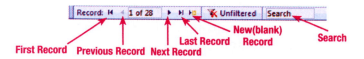

The last object shown on the left is the Reports object. Double-click *FHS FBLA Members* beneath the Reports object to open this file. This particular report shows all of the FBLA members grouped by ZIP Code. Notice that all members in each ZIP Code area are listed alphabetically by last name. You will learn how to make reports with such groupings in later lessons.

Begin Dateline, Complimentary Close,
Writer's name and title at same tab at
or near the center.

Date   September 15, 20-- ↓1

Mailing   FACSIMILE ↓1
notation

Attention line in   Attention Training and Development Department ↓1   }   Remove space after paragraph—
letter address   Science Technologies ↓1   use Shift Enter to insert Line Break
   3368 Bay Path Road ↓1   after first three lines.
   Miami, FL 33160-3368 ↓1

Salutation   Ladies and Gentlemen: ↓1

Subject line   MODIFIED BLOCK FORMAT ↓1

Body   This letter is arranged in modified block format. In this letter format the date and closing lines (complimentary close, name of the writer, and the writer's title) begin at or near horizontal center. In block format all letter parts begin at the left margin. ↓1

Default or 1.25"   Mixed punctuation (a colon after the salutation and a comma after the complimentary close) is used in
LM and RM   this example. Open punctuation (no mark after the salutation or complimentary close) may be used with the modified block format if you prefer. ↓1

The first line of each paragraph may be blocked as shown here or indented one-half inch. If paragraphs are indented, the optional subject line may be indented or centered. If paragraphs are blocked at the left margin, the subject line is blocked, too. ↓1

Complimentary   Sincerely, ↓2
close

Writer   Derek Alan ↓1   }   Remove space after paragraph—
Writer's title   Manager ↓1   use Shift Enter to insert Line Break
                                       after name.

Reference   DA:xx ↓1
initials

Enclosure   Enclosure ↓1
notation

Copy notation   c Kimberly Rodriquez-Duarte ↓1

Postscript   A block format letter is enclosed so that you can compare the two formats. As you can see, either format presents an attractive appearance.

At least 1" BM

Letter in Modified Block Format with Mixed Punctuation

Report Illustration

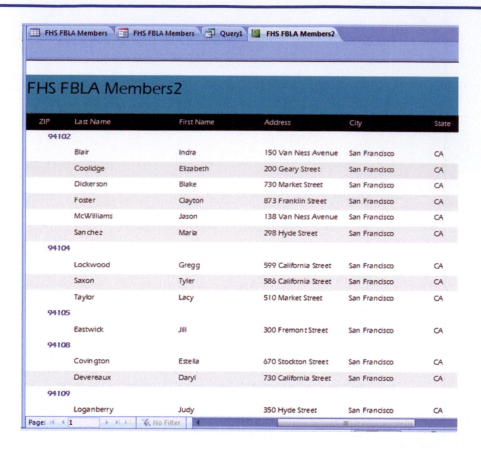

ZIP	Last Name	First Name	Address	City	State
94102					
	Blair	Indra	150 Van Ness Avenue	San Francisco	CA
	Coolidge	Elizabeth	200 Geary Street	San Francisco	CA
	Dickerson	Blake	730 Market Street	San Francisco	CA
	Foster	Clayton	873 Franklin Street	San Francisco	CA
	McWilliams	Jason	138 Van Ness Avenue	San Francisco	CA
	Sanchez	Maria	298 Hyde Street	San Francisco	CA
94104					
	Lockwood	Gregg	599 California Street	San Francisco	CA
	Saxon	Tyler	586 California Street	San Francisco	CA
	Taylor	Lacy	510 Market Street	San Francisco	CA
94105					
	Eastwick	Jill	300 Fremont Street	San Francisco	CA
94108					
	Covington	Estella	670 Stockton Street	San Francisco	CA
	Devereaux	Daryl	730 California Street	San Francisco	CA
94109					
	Loganberry	Judy	350 Hyde Street	San Francisco	CA

How Can Database Tables/Forms be Modified?

When necessary, database tables/forms can be modified. For example, if a new field is needed, it can be added and then the field information for each record can be entered. Also, it is possible to delete a field. When a field is deleted, *all* the information in that field is deleted.

What Is Sorting?

The **Sort** feature is responsible for controlling the sequence, or order, of the records. This feature allows sorts in ascending or descending order of words (alphabetically) or numbers (numerically). Ascending order is from A to Z and 0 to 9; descending order is from Z to A and 9 to 0.

Preview

In Units 27 and 34, you will have the opportunity to work with databases of several companies. There is **Franklin High School FBLA**, whose database contains student membership information. The **Software Professionals** database contains information about its software. **Rockwell Technologies** has a sales rep database; **Eastwick School of Dance** has a student information database. **Jaeger Enterprises** is an employee database you create.

Letter with Embedded Errors

Letter 1 (Modified Block Letter)

1. Open *DF 83C LETTER1*.
2. Format the letter in modified block format without paragraph indentions using open punctuation.

3. Set side margins at 1.25" and use a 12 pt. Calibri font.
4. Use **Sincerely** as the complimentary close.
5. Add *Gold* before *Instant Access* in ¶ 1. Change all instances of *automatic teller* to *ATM*.
6. Proofread the document carefully; identify and correct the 12 embedded errors in the letter body.

Save as: 83C LETTER1

Letter 2 (Blind Copy)

Open *83C LETTER1* and prepare it as a blind copy for Mr. Kerry Johnson.

Save as: 83C LETTER2

Lesson 84   TWO-PAGE LETTERS AND MEMOS

OBJECTIVE

- To learn to format second-page headings for letters and memos.

Second-Page Headings

Document 1 (Two-Page Memo)

1. Review the format guide for second-page headings on p. 244.
2. Read the text at the right.
3. Key the text in memo format using 1.25" side margins and a 12-pt. font.
4. Include any missing memo parts.
5. Proofread and make any necessary changes.
6. Insert a three-line second-page heading.

Save as: 84B MEMO1

Document 2 (Two-Page Letter)

1. Open *DF 84B LETTER1*.
2. Format the letter in modified block style with indented paragraphs and mixed punctuation.
3. Add this postscript: "Please say hello to Mr. Harold for me. He was my favorite math teacher when I attended your school."
4. Change the font size to 12 pt. and the side margins to 1.25".
5. Proofread then insert a second-page heading.

Save as: 84B LETTER1

| TO: All Employees | FROM: Melanie J. Kohl | DATE: May 12, 20-- | SUBJECT: SECOND-PAGE HEADINGS

This memo provides information about controlling line breaks when paragraphs are split between two pages and when side headings appear as the last line on a page. It also reviews how to format and insert headings in letters and memos that are longer than one page.

Controlling Line Breaks in a Paragraph

It is important to verify that a paragraph that continues from the bottom of one page to the top of the next page is divided appropriately. Paragraphs should always be divided so that at least two lines of the paragraph appear at the bottom of a page and at least two lines appear at the top of the next page. This means that a three-line paragraph should not be divided. If you have the Widow/Orphan control activated to control paragraph splits, the word processor will divide the paragraph correctly. If you do not have the Widow/Orphan control activated, you will need to insert manual page breaks as needed to format paragraph splits correctly.

To activate the "Widow/Orphan control," check the "Widow/Orphan control" box accessed by Page Layout/Paragraph group dialog box launcher/Line and Page Breaks tab.

Keeping Side Headings with Text

If your letter or memo contains a side heading and the word processor displays it at the bottom of a page by itself or with only one line of text following it, you need to move the heading (and single line, if applicable) to the next page. The "Keep with next" feature can be activated to control this type of line break. To activate "Keep with next," check the "Keep with next" box accessed by Page Layout/Paragraph group dialog box launcher/Line and Page Breaks tab.

Second-Page Heading Format and Contents

Since only page 1 contains all the information that is printed on the letterhead (business letters) or keyed in the return address (personal-business letters) or keyed beside guide words (memos), a heading must be included on all pages except page 1. The second-page heading can be inserted using the Header feature that was learned and practiced in Office Features 8. Since the header is not to appear on the first page of the letter or memo, be sure to check the Different First Page box in the Options

(continued on next page)

Query Illustration

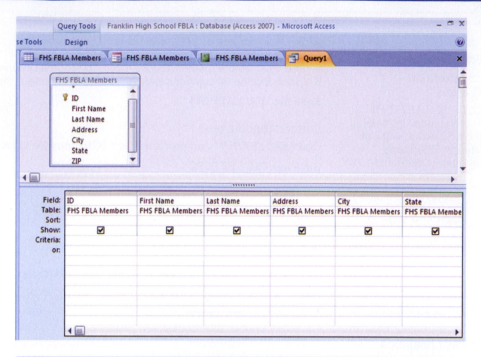

What Is a Database Query?

Database reports are created from database tables and queries. Reports are used for organizing, summarizing, and printing information. The easiest way to generate a report is by using the Report Wizard. The Report Wizard provides for grouping and sorting the data, as well as for designing various layouts and styles in which to present the data. Notice in the example report shown on the next page that the members are grouped by ZIP Code and sorted by last name.

group on the Design tab in the Headers & Footers Tools. As learned in Office Features 8, the text in the second-page heading may be blocked at the right margin using the Built-in Blank style. The heading may also be formatted across one line by using the Built-in Blank (Three Column) style. The heading should contain the name of the addressee(s), the page number, and the current date, keyed in that order. Use the Current Position feature to insert the page number (Header & Footer Tools, Design tab, Headers & Footer group, Page Number) at the proper position.

Inserting Second-Page Headings

If the second-page heading is inserted using the Header feature, it can be entered before final editing since additions or deletions made while editing will not affect the placement of the header. If you insert the second-page heading without using the Header feature, you should not insert it until final editing is completed and the document is to be printed or distributed electronically. The reason for this is that additions or deletions to the document's text can affect page breaks in your document and move the second-page heading to an incorrect position in your document.

Lesson 85 — LETTERS, MEMOS, AND TRACK CHANGES

OBJECTIVE

- To apply what you have learned in this unit.

85B

Letters and Memos

Letter (Modified Block)

Format the letter in modified block format with paragraph indentions. Use mixed punctuation.

Save as: 85B LETTER1

| *Current date* | Ms. Kelli Pardini | 598 S. Sundance Drive | Lake Mary, FL 32746-6355 | Dear Ms. Pardini:

Congratulations! You have been accepted into the School of Arts and Sciences at Duncan College for the semester that begins in September. Your major will be Mathematics.

You should schedule a placement examination to determine your beginning mathematics and English courses at Duncan. Choose a date from those listed on the enclosed card and return the card.

The courses you have completed, the grades you have earned, and your class rank indicate that you are eligible for a Presidential Scholarship. This is an academic scholarship awarded without regard to financial need to six outstanding freshmen. To be considered, you must schedule an interview with faculty. The interview dates and times are listed on the enclosed card. Indicate your first three choices, and return the card as soon as possible.

To reserve your spot in the September freshman class and the dormitory, you need to remit a $150 deposit. This deposit will be deducted from your tuition, fees, and room and board charges for the first semester.

We are glad that you chose Duncan College. We are committed to offering quality education in and out of the classroom.

| Sincerely | Gerri D. Rhodes | President | GDR:xx | Enclosures | I expect you to score high enough on the placement exam to earn at least six college credits for what you have learned in high school math and English.

What Is a Database Form?

Form

Database forms are created from database tables and queries. Forms are used for entering, viewing, and editing data.

Database forms are computerized versions of paper forms, such as a job application or a credit card application. On a printed form, you fill in the blanks with the information that is requested, such as your name and address. In a database form, the blanks in which information is entered are called **fields**. In the example above, *Last Name,*

First Name, Address, City, and *State* are field names. When the blanks are filled in, the form becomes a **record**. The form illustrated below is Record 14 from the table illustration on page 322.

Depending on the software used, a variety of different form formats are available. The form may show only one record (as shown below), or it may show multiple records in the database. Forms may be created manually or by using the software Wizard.

Form Illustration

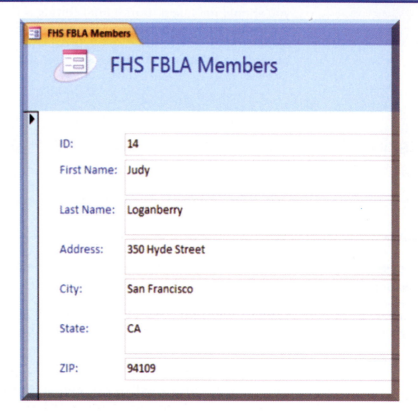

What Is a Database Query?

Query Wizard

Queries are questions. The Query feature of a database software program allows you to ask for specific information to be retrieved from tables that have been created. For example, the query shown on the next page is based on the table illustration on p. 322. The query answers the question, "Which members live in the 94111 ZIP Code area?" As shown in the query illustration below, there are currently five members living in the 94111 ZIP Code area.

When the membership table is expanded to include dues paid, a query could be made requesting a list of all members who have not paid their dues, thus allowing the membership chair to send reminders to only those who have not paid their dues. By using the query feature, you can answer a variety of questions that are based on the information contained in database tables.

Memo

Format as a memo.

Save as: 85B MEMO1

| TO: Katherine H. Holt, Dean | FROM: Connor Anthony, President | DATE: *Current date* | SUBJECT: MATHEMATICAL REASONING SKILLS TASK FORCE |

A meeting to discuss the formation of a Mathematical Reasoning Skills Task Force has been arranged for Tuesday, April 21, in my office at 2:30 p.m. Vice President Kyle Johns will join us. Purposes of the meeting are to finalize the project description and identify faculty and advisory committee members who might join the task force.

CA:xx | c Kyle Johns, Vice President |

85C

Editing Letter with Tracked Changes

Letter 1 (Modified Block Letter with Tracked Changes)

1. Open *DF 85C LETTER1*.
2. Format as modified block letter with mixed punctuation by accepting/rejecting tracked changes, following directions in the comments, and making any other changes necessary.
3. Proofread for unmarked errors.

Save as: 85C LETTER1

Letter 2 (Edit Letter using Track Changes)

1. Open *DF 85C LETTER2*.
2. Format in modified block style with mixed punctuation and no paragraph indentions.
3. Center the letter vertically.

4. Change all occurrences of *pamphlet* to *brochure*.
5. Change *Monday* in last line to *Friday*.
6. Change *Public Relations* in ¶ 2 to *The Public Relations Department*.
7. Use Track Changes to mark the remaining embedded errors.
8. Print the letter with markups showing.

Save as: 85C LETTER2

85D   Language Skills

Language Skills: Word Choice

Language Skills: Word Choic

1. Study the spelling and definitions of the words.
2. Key all *Learn* and *Apply* lines, choosing the correct word in the *Apply* lines.

Save as: 85D CHOICE

farther (adv) greater distance	**whose** (adj) of or to whom something belongs
farther (adv) in greater depth, extent, or importance; additional	**who's** (cont)) who is

Learn   1   The **farther** I drive, the **further** my mind wanders.

Apply   2   With (farther, further) effort, I ran (farther, further) ahead of the group.

Apply   3   Tom could see (farther, further) into the distance than Jane.

Apply   4   With (farther, further) practice, he threw the javelin (farther, further).

Learn   1   **Who's** to say **whose** fault it is that we scored only one touchdown?

Apply   2   (Whose, Who's) kite is it, and (whose, who's) going to fly it?

Apply   3   (Whose, Who's) going to accompany Mr. Smith to the store?

Apply   4   (Whose, Who's) knit sweater is hanging in the closet?

85E

INTERNET ACTIVITY

Explore space at the National Aeronautics and Space Administration.

1. Access NASA's home page through http://www.school.cengage.com/keyboarding/c21key

2. Explore links that interest you.

3. Write a letter to a friend describing what you located. Use the letter format of your

choice and supply all letter parts.

4. Print one or two pages from the website that relate to your letter to enclose with it.

Table Illustration

Field

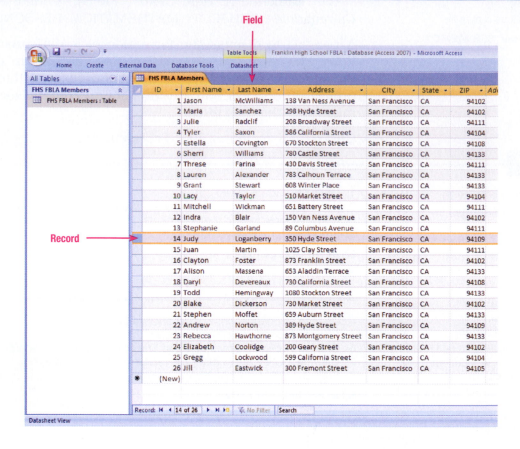

Record →

Defining and Sequencing Fields of Database Tables

Fields should be arranged in the same order as the data in the **source document** (paper form from which data is keyed). This sequence reduces the time needed to enter the field contents and to maintain the records. The illustration below shows the field definition and sequence for the table shown above. The **primary key** shown below is used to identify each record in the table with a number. In this case, a unique ID number would automatically be assigned each member's record.

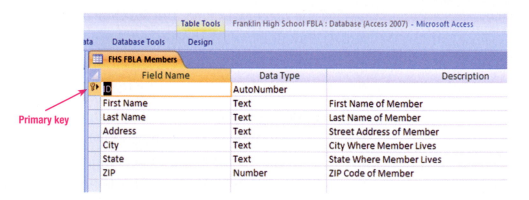

Primary key →

Skill 4 Builder

Alabama	Alaska	Arizona	Arkansas
Montgomery	Juneau	Phoenix	Little Rock
California	Colorado	Connecticut	Delaware
Sacramento	Denver	Hartford	Dover
Florida	Georgia	Hawaii	Idaho
Tallahassee	Atlanta	Honolulu	Boise
Illinois	Indiana	Iowa	Kansas
Springfield	Indianapolis	Des Moines	Topeka

Tabulation

1. Set tabs at 1.5", 3", and 4.5" from the left margin.
2. Key the text, using the TAB key to move from column to column.
3. Key three 1' writings.

Timed Writing

1. Take a 1' writing.
2. Add 5 *wam* to the rate attained in step 1.
3. Take four 1' writings, trying to achieve the rate set in step 2.

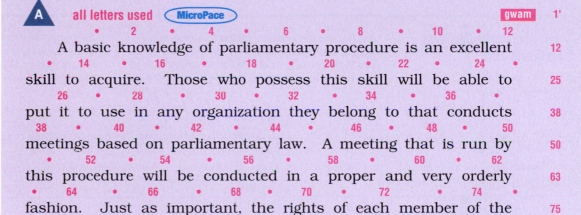

A   all letters used   (MicroPace)   gwam 1'

	1'
A basic knowledge of parliamentary procedure is an excellent	12
skill to acquire. Those who possess this skill will be able to	25
put it to use in any organization they belong to that conducts	38
meetings based on parliamentary law. A meeting that is run by	50
this procedure will be conducted in a proper and very orderly	63
fashion. Just as important, the rights of each member of the	75
group are protected at all times.	82

gwam 1' | 1 | 2 | 3 | 4 | 5 | 6 | 7 | 8 | 9 | 10 | 11 | 12 | 13 |

Reading/Keying Response Patterns

Key each line 3 times (slowly, faster, top speed).

Goal: To reduce time interval between keystrokes (read ahead to anticipate stroking pattern).

Emphasize curved, upright fingers; finger action keystroking.

1 car no cat inn fat ink ear beg verb sea lip oil tea pull see milk
2 acre pool rest link base lily seat lion vase noun dear junk barge

Emphasize independent finger action; stationary hands.

3 at my best|in my career|best dessert|my bad debts|my exact grades
4 only rebate|in my opinion|we deserve better|minimum grade average

Emphasize continuity; finger action with fingers close to keys.

5 Ada agreed on a minimum oil target after a decrease in oil taxes.
6 In my opinion, Edward Freeberg agreed on a greater water reserve.

gwam 1' | 1 | 2 | 3 | 4 | 5 | 6 | 7 | 8 | 9 | 10 | 11 | 12 | 13 |

UNIT 27
Lessons 104-111
Develop Database Skills

What Is a Database?

A database is an organized collection of facts and figures (information). The phone book, which includes names, addresses, and phone numbers, is an example of a database in printed form.

It is also quite common in today's environment to have databases stored in electronic form.

Names and addresses, inventories, sales records, and client information are just a few examples of information that is stored in a database. Having information in a database makes it easy to compile and arrange data to answer questions and make well-informed decisions.

What Are the Components of a Database?

A database may include **tables** for entering and storing information, **forms** for entering and displaying information, **reports** for summarizing and presenting information, and **queries** for drawing

information from one or more tables. The illustration below shows the components that can be created in a database. These components are accessed by clicking the Create tab in *Microsoft Access*.

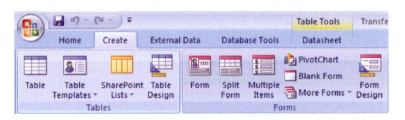

What Is a Database Table?

Database tables are created by the user in software programs such as *Access* for inputting, organizing, and storing information. The tables are set up to contain columns and rows of information. In a database table, the columns are called **fields** and the rows are called **records**.

The table illustration on the next page shows a table that contains five fields—*First Name,*

Last Name, Address, City, State, and ZIP Code (plus the ID number).

Record 14 is highlighted in the illustration and shows the information contained in each of the six fields for Record 14. The database table is the foundation from which forms, queries, and reports are created.

INTERNAL PUNCTUATION

ACTIVITY 1

Internal Punctuation: Comma and Colon

1. Study each of the six rules.
   a. Key the *Learn* line(s) beneath each rule, noting how the rule is applied.
   b. Key the *Apply* lines, using commas and colons correctly.

Internal Punctuation: Comma

Rule 1: Use a comma to separate the day from the year and the city from the state.

Learn 1 Lincoln delivered the Gettysburg Address on November 19, 1863.

Learn 2 The convention will be held at Cobo Hall in Detroit, Michigan.

Apply 3 Did you find this table in the March 17 2008, *USA Today*?

Apply 4 Are you on the history panel in San Antonio Texas?

Rule 2: Use a comma to separate two or more parallel adjectives (adjectives that could be separated by the word *and* instead of a comma).

Learn 5 The big, loud bully was ejected after he pushed the official.

Learn 6 Cynthia played a black lacquered grand piano at her concert.

Apply 7 The big powerful car zoomed past the cheering crowd.

Apply 8 A small red fox squeezed through the fence to avoid the hounds.

Rule 3: Use a comma to separate (a) unrelated groups of figures that occur together and (b) whole numbers into groups of three digits each. (Note: Policy, year, page, room, telephone, invoice, and most serial numbers are keyed without commas.)

Learn   9 By the year 2012, 1,100 more local students will be enrolled.

Learn 10 The supplies listed on Invoice #274068 are for Room 1953.

Apply 11 During 2008 2050 new graduates entered our job market.

Apply 12 See page 1069 of *Familiar Quotations*, Cat. Card No. 68-15664.

Internal Punctuation: Colon

Rule 4: Use a colon to introduce an enumeration or a listing.

Learn 13 These students are absent: Adam Bux, Todd Cody, and Sue Ott.

Apply 14 Add to the herb list parsley, rosemary, saffron, and thyme.

Apply 15 We must make these desserts a cake, two pies, and cookies.

Rule 5: Use a colon to introduce a question or a quotation.

Learn 16 Here's the real question: Who will pay for the "free" programs?

Learn 17 Who said: "Freedom is nothing else but a chance to be better"?

Apply 18 My question stands Who are we to pass judgment on them?

Apply 19 He quoted Browning "Good, to forgive; Best, to forget."

Rule 6: Use a colon between hours and minutes expressed in figures.

Learn 20 They give two performances: at 2:00 p.m. and at 8:00 p.m.

Apply 21 You have a choice of an 11 15 a.m. or a 2 30 p.m. appointment.

Apply 22 My workday begins at 8 15 a.m. and ends at 5 00 p.m.

(continued on next page)

CAREER Clusters

ACTIVITY 10

You must complete Career Exploration Activities 1–3 before completing this activity.

1. Retrieve your Career folder and the information in it that relates to the career cluster that is your first choice.

2. Use the Internet to search for the education that is recommended for occupations in this career cluster and then compose a paragraph or two explaining what you have learned. Print your file, save it as Career10, and keep it open.

3. Exchange papers with a classmate and have the classmate offer suggestions for improving the content and correcting any errors he or she finds in your paragraph(s). Make the changes that you agree with, and print a copy to turn in to your instructor. Save it as Career10 and close the file.

4. Return your folder to the storage area. When your instructor returns your paper, file it in your Career folder.

BLEND IMAGES/JUPITER IMAGES

Proofread & Correct

Rules		
1,3	1	The memorial was dedicated on November 13 1999--not 1,999.
1	2	We played in the Hoosier Dome in Indianapolis Indiana.
1	3	I cited an article in the May 20 2008, *Wall Street Journal*.
2	4	Carl sent Diana a dozen bright red, long-stem roses.
2	5	He buys most of his clothes at a store for big tall men.
3	6	Our enrollment for 2007, 1,884; for 2008 2040.
3	7	Where is the request for books and supplies for Room 1,004?
1,3	8	Policy #HP294,873 took effect on September 22 2008.
3	9	Della and Eldon Simms paid $129000 for their new condo.
4	10	Dry cleaning list 1 suit; 2 jackets; 3 pants; 2 sweaters.
5	11	Golden Rule Do unto others as you would have them do unto you.
5	12	I quote Jean Racine "Innocence has nothing to dread."
5	13	Glynda asked me to meet her 2 15 p.m. flight at JFK Airport.
6	14	Ten o'clock in the morning is the same as 10 00 a.m.

2. Key Proofread & Correct, inserting commas and colons correctly.

a. Check answers.

b. Using the rule number(s) at the left of each line, study the rule relating to each error you made.

c. Rekey each incorrect line, inserting commas and colons correctly.

Save as: CS8 ACTIVITY1

ACTIVITY 2

Listening

Complete as directed.

Save as: CS8 ACTIVITY2

1. You answered a telephone call from George Steward, your father's business associate. Mr. Steward asked you to take a message for your father.

2. Open sound file *DF CS8 ACTIVITY2*. As you listen to the message, take notes as needed.

3. Close the sound file.

4. Key the message—in complete sentences—for your father.

ACTIVITY 3

Composing

1. Key the ¶, correcting word-choice errors. (Every line contains at least one error.)

2. Compose a 2nd ¶ to accomplish these goals:
- Express your viewpoint about special treatment of "stars."
- State your view about whether the *same offense/same penalty* concept should apply to everyone alike.

3. Proofread, revise, and correct.

Save as: CS8 ACTIVITY3

Some people think that because their good at sum sport, music, or other activity, there entitled to respect and forgiveness for anything else they choose to do in the passed. Its not uncommon, than, when such people break the law or violate sum code of conduct, four them to expect such behavior to be overlooked buy those who's job it is to enforce the law or to uphold an established code of conduct. Sum parents, as well as others in hour society, think that a "star's" misbehavior ought too be treated less harshly because of that person's vary impressive "celebrity" status; but all people should be treated equally under and threw the law.

2. Key Proofread & Correct, using apostrophes correctly.
   a. Check answers.
   b. Using the rule number(s) at the left of each line, study the rule relating to each error you made.
   c. Rekey each incorrect line, using apostrophes correctly.

Save as: CS10 ACTIVITY1

Proofread & Correct

Rules

1	1	Jay Corbin played 12 min. 30 sec.; Jack Odom, 26 min. 20 sec.
1	2	My desk is 3 ft. x 5 ft. 6 in.; the credenza is 2 ft. x 6 ft.
2	3	Didnt O'Brien prepare a sales comparison for 06 and 07?
3	4	Major changes in technology occurred in the 1980's and 1990s.
3	5	Dr. Knox gave mostly As and Bs, but he gave a few Cs and Ds.
2,4	6	Didnt you go to the big sale on childrens items?
5	7	Tess escort gave her a wrist corsage of exquisite violets.
6	8	The boys and girls teams appreciated Dr. Morris compliments.
6	9	Do you know whether the ladies swim coach is in her office?
2,6	10	Didnt you ask if the cast is set for Miss Winters new play?

ACTIVITY 2

Composing

1. Read the case of the "extra change."
2. Considering the comments and suggestions, compose a ¶ to indicate what you would do in this situation, identifying how and why you made your choice.
3. Proofread, revise, and correct.

Save as: CS10 ACTIVITY2

You and your friends have arranged to go to dinner together before separating for other activities: a ball game, a movie, a "mixer." To pay for the dinner, you have collected money from each friend.

The restaurant is upscale, the food very good, and the service excellent. Your server has been friendly and has quickly met all your needs. Your server has not rushed you to finish, so you and your friends have enjoyed conversation and laughter long after the meal ended.

When it is time to go, you ask your server for the check and pay it. When you receive your change and are leaving a tip, you notice that your change is $10 more than you should have received.

A discussion takes place among the six of you regarding this error. Various comments and suggestions are made:

1. Keep the money; the server will never know to whom he gave the extra change.

2. Are you lucky! This never happens to me.

3. You have to return the money. If you don't, the server will have to make up the loss of money at the end of the evening.

Several thoughts go through your mind as you listen to the comments of your friends. You know it would be great to have ten extra dollars to share with your friends. What will my friends think if I return the money, or if I keep it? The server has been very pleasant and has worked hard this evening. If I keep the money, is it right to make the server pay for the error? How would I want to be treated if I made the same mistake at my job?

ACTIVITY 3

Math: Working with Measures of Central Tendency

1. Open *DF CS10 ACTIVITY3* and print the file.
2. Solve the problems as directed in the file.
3. Submit your answers.

1. Open *DF CS8 ACTIVITY4* and print the file.
2. Solve the problems as directed in the file.
3. Submit your answers.

CAREER Clusters

ACTIVITY 8

You must complete Career Exploration Activities 1–3 before completing this activity.

1. Retrieve your Career folder and the information in it that relates to the career cluster that is your second choice.

2. Reflect on the skills and knowledge you have gained in the courses you have taken and the extracurricular activities in which you are involved that will be beneficial in the career you selected as your second choice. Then compose a paragraph or two describing the connection between what you have learned and/or your activities and this career. Print your file and then save it as Career8 and keep the file open.

3. Exchange papers with a classmate and have the classmate offer suggestions for improving the content and correcting any errors he or she finds in your paragraph(s). Make the changes that you agree with, and print a copy to turn in to your instructor. Save it as Career8 and close the file.

4. Return your folder to the storage area. When your instructor returns your paper, file it in your Career folder.

Communication & Math
SKILLS10

ACTIVITY 1

Internal Punctuation: Apostrophe

1. Study each of the six rules.
   a. Key the *Learn* line(s) beneath each rule, noting how the rule is applied.
   b. Key the *Apply* lines, using apostrophes correctly.

Internal Punctuation: Apostrophe

Rule 1: Use an apostrophe as a symbol to represent feet or minutes. (Quotation marks may be used to signify inches or seconds.).

Learn 1 Floyd bought twenty-four 2" x 4" x 12' studs for the new deck.

Learn 2 Shawnelle scored the 3-pointer with only 1' 18" left to go.

Apply 3 The new computer lab at my school is 18 ft. 6 in. x 30 ft.

Apply 4 The students were told to print 3 min. writings on 8.5 in. x 11 in. paper.

Rule 2: Use an apostrophe as a symbol to indicate the omission of letters or figures (as in contractions).

Learn 5 Didn't you enjoy the "Spirit of '76" segment of the pageant?

Apply 6 I dont know why he doesnt take advantage of our new terms.

Apply 7 Last years reunion combined the classes of 97, 98, and 99.

Rule 3: Use an apostrophe plus *s* (*'s*) to form the plural of most figures, letters, and words used as words rather than for their meaning *(6's, A's, five's)*. In stock quotations and to refer to decades or centuries, form the plural of figures by adding *s* only.

Learn 8 She studied hard and earned A's throughout the early 2000s.

Learn 9 I sold Century As and 4s and bought Cosco 45s.

Apply 10 Correct the outline by changing the As, Bs, and Cs to CAPS.

Apply 11 My father's broker urged him to buy Apache 76's in the 1990's.

Rule 4: To show possession, use an apostrophe plus *s* after (1) a singular noun and (2) a plural noun that does not end in *s*.

Learn 12 Jerrod's store had a great sale on men's and women's apparel.

Apply 13 Ritas class ring was lost under the stands in the schools gym.

Apply 14 Our back-to-school sale on childrens clothes is in progress.

Rule 5: To show possession, use an apostrophe plus *s* (*'s*) after a proper name of one syllable that ends in *s*.

Learn 15 Jon Hess's next art exhibit will be held at the Aronoff Center.

Apply 16 Rena Haas new play will premiere at the Emery Theater.

Apply 17 Jo Parks ACT scores were superb; Ed Sims SAT scores, mediocre.

Rule 6: To show possession, use only an apostrophe after (1) plural nouns ending in *s* and (2) a proper name of more than one syllable that ends in *s* or *z*.

Learn 18 The girls' new coach will visit at the Duclos' home next week.

Apply 19 The new shipment of ladies sportswear will arrive on Friday.

Apply 20 Lt. Santos plan for the officers annual ball was outstanding.

(continued on next page)

Format Guides: MLA Style

The **Modern Language Association (MLA)** style is often used to document and format students' papers. The MLA documentation method, called *parenthetical reference*, is similar to the textual citation method. MLA reports have these distinctive format features (shown on pp. 266 and 267):

Margins. On all pages, the top, bottom, left, and right margins are 1".

Header and page number. A header contains the page number; the writer's last name may be included. The header is right-aligned. Every page is numbered, including the first.

Line spacing. The entire report is double-spaced, including long quotations, bulleted and numbered items, tables, and works cited. Before you begin to key, set Line Spacing to 2.0 with 0 points of spacing after paragraphs.

Report identification. The writer's name, instructor's name, course title, and date (day/month/year style) are keyed on separate lines at the top of p. 1 at the left margin. If a title (cover) page is used, the report identification information need not be repeated on p. 1.

Report title. The title is centered a DS below the date in title case. The body begins a DS below the title.

Indentations and long quotations. The first line of each paragraph is indented 0.5" (or at the first default tab setting). Long quotations (four or more lines) are indented 1" (or at the second default tab setting) from the left margin.

Inserted tables. Insert a table as near as possible to the text that it illustrates. Key a number (*Table 1*) and caption (title) above the table left-aligned in title case. DS above the table number, below the last line (or source note), and between lines *within* the table. Hide table gridlines. Adjust table width to fit within the left and right margins.

Works cited (references). Key the works cited on a separate page, using the same margins and header as the report body. Center *Works Cited* in title case at the top margin. A DS below the title, list the references in alphabetical order by authors' last names (or by title when a work has no author). DS the list and use hanging indent.

Binding. Staple or clip all pages of the report at the top-left corner.

Outline

Outlines, useful for planning and organizing reports, occasionally appear in a finished document—so readers can see the report structure. Unless otherwise directed, use one of the styles in the Multilevel List word processing feature (see p. 261) to show different topic levels. The margins and line spacing for an outline should match the report body. Use default tab settings to indent the outline levels unless otherwise instructed.

Title Page

Normally, a title page is not required with an MLA-style report since the report identification lines contain the information that is usually printed on the title page. However, if your instructor requires a title page, an appropriate format to use is a bold, 14-pt. font for all text. Center the title in ALL CAPS, about ten ENTERs from the TM. Center the writer's name about ten ENTERs below the title, and center the writer's organization a DS below the name (both in title case). Center the date about ten ENTERs below the organization name. The placement and size of the title page parts can be adjusted for borders and clip art as long as an attractive arrangement is maintained. If your instructor permits it, the report identification lines on p. 1 of the report can be omitted when a title page is prepared.

Skill 6 Builder

Tab Setting

1. Set left tabs at 1.5", 3", and 4.5" from the left margin.
2. Key the text, using the TAB key to move from column to column.
3. Key three 1' writings.

Keying Technique

1. Key each line once.
2. Key two 30" writings on each even-numbered line.

				words
North Carolina	North Dakota	Ohio	Oklahoma	8
Raleigh	Bismarck	Columbus	Oklahoma City	16
Oregon	Pennsylvania	Rhode Island	South Carolina	26
Salem	Harrisburg	Providence	Columbia	33
South Dakota	Tennessee	Texas	Utah	40
Pierre	Nashville	Austin	Salt Lake City	48
Vermont	Virginia	Washington	West Virginia	56
Montpelier	Richmond	Tacoma	Charleston	64
Wisconsin	Wyoming			67
Madison	Cheyenne			71

Alphabet

1 zebra extra vicious dozen happen just quick forgot way limp exact
2 Everyone except Meg and Joe passed the final weekly biology quiz.

Figure/Symbol

3 Account #2849 | 10% down | for $6,435.70 | Lots #8 & #9 | $250 deductible
4 The fax machine (#387-291) is on sale for $364.50 until March 21.

Bottom row

5 modern zebra extinct moving backbone moon vacate exam computerize
6 Zeno's vaccine injection for smallpox can be given in six months.

Third row

7 you tip rip terror yet peer quit were pet tire terrier pepper out
8 Our two terrier puppies were too little to take to your pet show.

Double letters

9 footnote scanner less process letters office cell suppress footer
10 Jill, my office assistant, will process the four letters by noon.

Balanced hands

11 wish then turn us auto big eight down city busy end firm it goals
12 If the firm pays for the social, the eight officials may also go.

Shift keys

13 The New York Times | Gone with the Wind | Chicago Tribune | WordPerfect
14 Alan L. Mari finished writing "Planning for Changing Technology."

Adjacent keys

15 were open top ask rest twenty point tree master merge option asks
16 The sort option was well received by all three new group members.

Space bar

17 it is fix and fox go key do by box men pen six so the to when big
18 Did they use the right audit form to check the new city bus line?

| gwam | 1' | 1 | 2 | 3 | 4 | 5 | 6 | 7 | 8 | 9 | 10 | 11 | 12 | 13 |

For each activity, read and learn the feature described, then follow instructions at the left.

Activity 1

Multilevel List and Increase and Decrease Indent

WP • Home/Paragraph/ Multilevel List

WP • Home/Paragraph/ Increase or Decrease Indent

Key the outline text (not the level numbers or letters) using the Multilevel List feature and Increase or Decrease Indent buttons to format the levels.

Save as: OF9 ACTIVITY1

TIP: The TAB SHIFT (tapped together) or the TAB key can be used to format the desired levels as well as the Increase Indent or Decrease Indent buttons.

Use the Multilevel List feature to key the main points and subpoints when preparing an outline. This feature labels each point with a number, letter, and/or symbol, depending on the numbered list style chosen. The Increase Indent or Decrease Indent feature can be used to format the desired levels.

The Multilevel List feature can be activated before text is keyed or applied to selected text after it has been keyed. In either method, you need not key the numbers, letters, or symbols used to label each point—as indents are increased or decreased, the software adjusts the labels automatically.

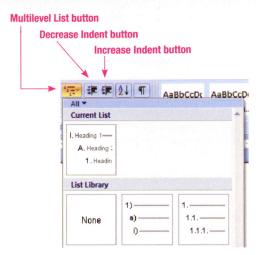

1) Breakfast
   a) Cereal
      i)   Rice
      ii) Skim Milk
      iii) No Sugar
   b) Toast
      i)   Jam
      ii) Butter
   c) Orange Juice
2) Lunch
   a) Sandwich
      i)   Wheat Bun
      ii) Meat
      iii) Cheese
      iv) Mustard
   b) Chicken Soup
   c) Apple

103C

Organization Chart 1

Using SmartArt, prepare an organization chart that is similar to the one at the right. Your chart should show that the Clerk, Treasurer, City Manager, and Attorney report directly to the Mayor and that the supervisors report to the City Manager.

Save as: **103C CHART1**

Organization Chart 2

Using flowchart shapes in Shapes, prepare an organization chart using the same information at the right.

Save as: **103C CHART2**

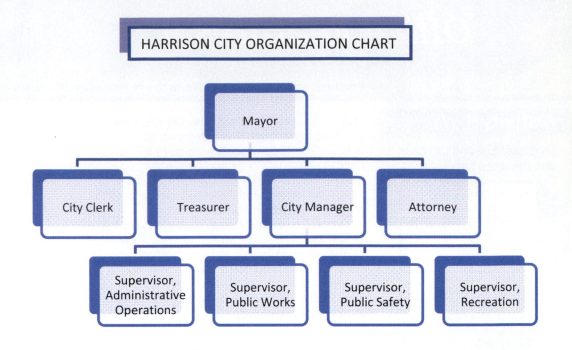

HARRISON CITY ORGANIZATION CHART

Mayor

City Clerk | Treasurer | City Manager | Attorney

Supervisor, Administrative Operations | Supervisor, Public Works | Supervisor, Public Safety | Supervisor, Recreation

103D

Word Choice

1. Study the spelling and definitions of the words.
2. Key the *Learn* and *Apply* lines, choosing the correct words in the *Apply* lines.

Save as: **103D CHOICE**

choose (vb) to select; to decide on	**than** (conj/prep) used in comparisons to show difference between items
chose (vb) the past tense of choose	**then** (n/adv) that time; at that time

Learn 1 Jane **chose** a Eureka computer; I may **choose** a Futura.

Apply 2 After he (choose/chose) a red cap, I told him to (choose/chose) blue.

Apply 3 Mae (choose/chose) you as a partner; Janice may (choose/chose) me.

Learn 4 If she is older **than** you, **then** I am older **than** you.

Apply 5 We (than/then) decided that two hours were more (than/then) enough.

Apply 6 Fewer (than/then) half the workers were (than/then) put on overtime.

103E

Internet Activity

1. Access the United States Environmental Protection Agency (EPA) website via http://school.cengage .com/keyboarding/ c21key.
2. Complete steps 1–2.

Save as: **103E INTERNET**

1. Click the link that gives basic information **About EPA** and follow at least one link of interest to you. Then write, using keyboard or speech recognition software, a brief ¶ describing what you have learned.
2. Click on the home page link to **Educational Resources**, select **High School**, and follow at least one link of interest to you. Then key one or more ¶s describing what you have learned. Print one page from the EPA website relating to the ¶ (s) you wrote.

Activity 2

Page and Paragraph Borders

WP • Page Layout/Page Background/Page Borders

1. Open *DF OF9 ACTIVITY2* and put shadow borders around the second and fourth ¶s.
2. Add a page border in the line style of your choice.

Save as: OF9 ACTIVITY2

Use the Border feature to add a border to any or all sides of a page, ¶, or column, as well as a table or cell within a table. Many line styles and colors are available. In addition, page border options include small graphics (pictures).

Borders not only enhance appearance; they also can make text easier to read by emphasizing certain passages. Borders are most effective when used sparingly, however.

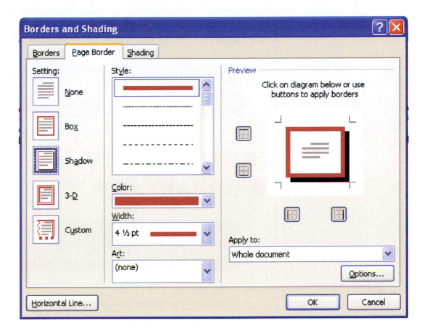

Activity 3

Insert Clip Art or Pictures

WP • Insert/Illustrations/ Picture or Clip Art

1. Open *DF OF9 ACTIVITY3*.
2. From Clip Art, search for and select a picture that represents a construction worker or one of the building trades named in ¶ 2.
3. Insert the picture into the middle of ¶ 2, wrapping text around it.
4. Select a picture of a building from Clip Art.
5. Insert the picture into the middle of ¶ 3 so it is behind the text.

Save as: OF9 ACTIVITY3

Using the Picture or Clip Art features, you can insert pictures, drawings and photographs, even sounds and video clips into documents. You can select from a collection of clip art files provided with your wp software or from files you add to the clip art or picture files. Most wp programs have a Search feature to help you locate the right clip art for your document.

When the picture or clip art is selected, options in the Size and Arrange groups in the Format tab of the Picture Tools ribbon can be used to size, crop, and position the picture in relation to the paper and text. Other options in the Adjust and Picture Styles groups on the Format tab can also be used to format your picture as desired.

- To prepare ads and organization charts using shapes, WordArt, SmartArt, clip art, and text box features.

103B

Advertisement

Design a one-page advertisement for these two businesses that is similar to the one at the right. If you want to use the clip art shown, insert file *DF 103B BASKET*.

Save as: **103B AD**

HUNT RUN RESTAURANT

435-555-0170
Ask for Nancy or Helen

HUNT RUN BED & BREAKFAST

435-555-0175
Ask for Chris or Martha

BANQUET ROOM

IDEAL FOR SHOWERS, RECEPTIONS, REUNIONS, ETC.

SEATING UP TO 120 PEOPLE

NO ROOM CHARGE

BED & BREAKFAST

PERFECT FOR YOUR OUT-OF-TOWN GUESTS

WE CAN ACCOMMODATE UP TO EIGHT PEOPLE IN FOUR ROOMS WITH PRIVATE BATHROOMS

http://www.huntrun.com

Hunt Run Restaurant and Bed & Breakfast are located on Hunt Run Road, one mile off Route 58 between Easton and Huntville at the Hunt Run Golf Course.

Activity 4

Insert Citations and Source Information

WP
- References/Citations & Bibliography/Insert Citation

1. Open *DF OF9 ACTIVITY4*. In this activity, you will choose MLA as the documentation style, and key information in a Create Source dialog box where each of the three textual citations is to appear in the text. The software will insert the citation in the text. In Activity 5, you will use the software to generate the bibliography page for these three sources.

2. Follow the directions in steps 1–10 in *DF OF9 ACTIVITY4* to complete Activity 4. Key the following information for each citation when directed:

In previous units, you keyed textual citations, footnotes, and endnotes in reports and then keyed the source information on a reference page.

In Unit 22, you will use features in the Citations & Bibliography group on the References ribbon to have the software create the textual citation and then the bibliography for a particular documentation style (MLA, APA, Chicago, etc.).

To use these features, you will click in the document where the citation is to appear, select the documentation style you want to use, and then key information about the source you are citing in a Create Source dialog box. The software uses the information you key in this box to create and insert the citation in the text where you have clicked. When you are ready to generate the bibliography, you will use the software to create the bibliography page by using the Bibliography feature. Remember that a bibliography is sometimes titled *References or Works Cited. Works Cited* is the title used with MLA-style reports you will learn about in Unit 22.

The Citations & Bibliography buttons

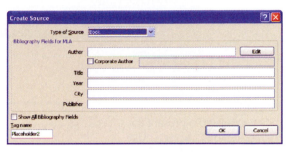

The Create Source dialog box

Citation 1 (Book)
Author: Pacella, Michael
Title: History of Word Processors
Year: 2008
City: Chicago
Publisher: Technology Experts

Citation 2 (Journal Article)
Author: Hoffner, Mary and Helen Salitros
Title: Communicating with Confidence
Journal Name: Workplace News
Year: 2007
Pages: 15–18

Citation 3 (Document from Web Site)
Name of Web Page: Math for Young Children
Name of Web Site: Advocates for Early Math
Year: 2008
Year Accessed: 2008
Month Accessed: September
Day Accessed: 14
URL: http://www.afem.org/article1035

Save as: OF9 ACTIVITY4

Flyer 2

Design a flyer to present the information at the left. You decide the use of WordArt, SmartArt, shapes, clip art, pictures, and/or text boxes and all other formatting features.

Save as: 102B FLYER2

Event:	The Dangers of Drinking and Driving
Sponsored by:	Students Against DUI
When:	Friday, May 3, at 3:30 p.m.
Where:	Gymnasium B, Welton High School
Cost:	Free admission with school ID card
Guest speaker:	Sgt. Terry Hollinsworth State Trooper Welton South Barracks
Main feature:	Students will use a simulator to observe the effects of DUI.

Flyer 3

Design a flyer to present the information at the right. Use SmartArt as directed. You decide the use of WordArt, shapes, clip art, pictures, and/or text boxes and all other formatting features.

Save as: 102B FLYER3

Sponsoring instructor:	Mrs. Porterfield
When:	Wednesday, October 3, Periods 1, 2, 5, 6, and 7
Where:	Classroom 222
Guest speaker:	Dr. Ida Meinert Nutritionist, Blair Hospital
Topic:	Recognizing Eating Disorders
Excuse form:	Use the Vertical Chevron list in SmartArt for the form. Key **Student's name** in the first chevron, **Course and period missed** in the second chevron, and **Teacher's signature** in the third chevron. Do not key any text to the right of the chevrons.

Flyer 4

1. Design a flyer your instructor can use to inform others of the value of the course in which you are using this textbook.
2. You decide all formatting features.

Save as: 102B FLYER4

1. Key the name of the course.
2. Identify some course activities you enjoy.
3. Describe the important things you have learned.
4. Specify reasons why others should take this course.
5. Identify the hardware and software that you use.
6. Explain how this course helps you in other classes or at work.

Activity 5

Create a Bibliography Page

WP
- References/Citations & Bibliography/Bibliography

1. Open *OF9 ACTIVITY4*.
2. Follow the directions in steps 10–14 to create and format a Works Cited page.

Save as: **OF9 ACTIVITY5**

Once you have entered the source information for each of the citations included in a document and have completed keying your document, you can have the software create a bibliography page by using the Bibliography feature in the Citations & Bibliography group. You can choose to have the page titled Bibliography or Works Cited (see illustration).

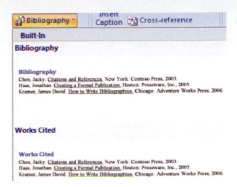

Options in the Bibliography feature

Activity 6

Manage Sources

WP
- References/Citations & Bibliography/Manage Sources

1. Open *OF9 ACTIVITY5*.
2. Change Hoffner to Hoffman in the existing book source and update it so it is the same in the Current and Master lists.
3. Close the Source Manager and go to the Hoffner citation at the end of step 4 in *OF9 ACTIVITY5*.
4. Update the Hoffner citation and bibliography entry to Hoffman.
5. Verify that the Hoffner entry has been changed to Hoffman in the text and Works Cited page.

Save as: **OF9 ACTIVITY6**

The Manage Sources feature contains a list of all the sources you have used; therefore, previously used sources are available for you to use if you write a paper on a related topic. Previously used sources are listed in a Master List on the left side of the Source Manager dialog box. Sources that you have cited in the current paper are listed in the Current List on the right side. When you enter a source in the Current List, it automatically is stored in the Master List and available for later use.

You can use the Source Manager to move sources from the Master List to the Current List or vice versa. You can enter information for new sources before you write your paper, and then cite them as you write your paper. You can also edit sources if you find they must be changed or delete sources you no longer need.

As you work in the Source Manager, a preview for the documentation style you have chosen is provided for the citation and the bibliography entry in the lower portion of the dialog box.

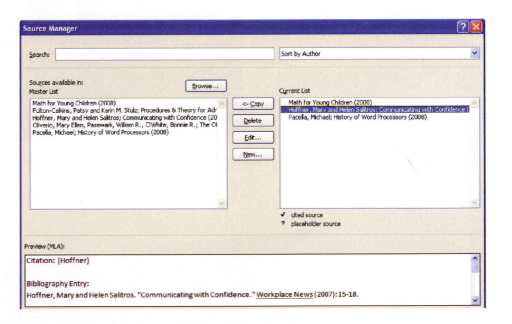

Diagram

1. Open *DF 101D DIAGRAM* and resize it so it is a 2" square.
2. Using shapes and text box features, prepare a copy of the diagram at the right. You decide the size and position of the components of the diagram.

Save as: **101D DIAGRAM**

The Shadow Effects Group on the Format Ribbon

Click here to select and insert a shadow for a shape

Click one of the four outside boxes to nudge the shadow in the direction of the arrow

Click here to turn the shadow on or off

Lesson 102   FLYERS

OBJECTIVE

• To prepare flyers using shapes, WordArt, and text box features.

Flyers

Flyer 1

1. Prepare a one-page flyer, using shapes, WordArt, and text boxes as shown.
2. You decide the size, color, and format of the shapes and the placement of all information.

Save as: **102B FLYER1**

5K Run or Walk

Join RT Alumni

on

Saturday, August 14, 20--

at 9 a.m.

in East Park

$12 ENTRANCE FEE INCLUDES T-SHIRT, PRIZES, AND REFRESHMENTS

CALL (422) 555-0192 TO REGISTER

PRIZES WILL BE AWARDED TO TOP THREE MEN AND WOMEN FINISHERS IN THREE AGE GROUPS

See our website at http:www. pphs org/5k

OBJECTIVES

- To format an outline.
- To format reports in MLA style.

86A–89A

Conditioning Practice

Key each line twice daily.

alphabet	1	Jake will buy very good quality zinc from experts at the auction.
fig/sym	2	Al's gas bill was $89.35 (-6%); his office bill was $40.17 (-2%).
speed	3	Nancy may go with me to visit them by the cornfield and big lake.

gwam 1' | 1 | 2 | 3 | 4 | 5 | 6 | 7 | 8 | 9 | 10 | 11 | 12 | 13 |

86B

Outline and MLA-Style Report

Document 1 (Outline)

1. Read the format guides for outlines on p. 260.
2. Prepare the outline DS.

Save as: 86B OUTLINE1

Document 2 (Report)

1. Read about MLA style on p. 260; study the models on pp. 266 and 267.
2. Key the MLA-style report on pp. 266 and 267.

Save as: 86B MLA1

Earth's Nearest Neighbor in Space

1) Introduction
   a) Moon's size
   b) Moon's reflection
   c) Moon's atmosphere
2) Moon's Surface
   a) Lowlands (called *maria*) and highlands
   b) Craters
      i) Ray craters
      ii) Secondary craters
3) Moon's Composition
   a) Soil
      i) Color is dark gray to brownish gray
      ii) Consists of ground-up rock and bits of glass
      iii) Depth of soil varies
   b) Rocks
      i) Minerals in the rock
      ii) Basalt and breccia rocks
4) Moon's Orbit
   a) Time to revolve around Earth
   b) Shape of its orbit
   c) Phases of the moon
      i) New moon
      ii) First quarter
      iii) Full moon
      iv) Last quarter
5) Eclipses
   a) Lunar eclipse
   b) Solar eclipse
6) Tides
   a) Caused by the moon's gravity
   b) Frequency of daily high and low tides

OBJECTIVE

• To prepare documents using shapes, WordArt, clip art, and text box features.

101A–103A

Conditioning Practice

Key each line twice daily.

alphabet	1	Zack told Peg to be quiet and enjoy the first extra cowboy movie.
fig/sym	2	Ho's expenses are taxi--$59; airline--$260; car--$37 (148 miles).
speed	3	Claudia is to land the giant dirigible by the busy downtown mall.

gwam   1' | 1 | 2 | 3 | 4 | 5 | 6 | 7 | 8 | 9 | 10 | 11 | 12 | 13 |

101B

Letterhead

Using the information at the right, create a header that serves as letterhead for the company. Use WordArt within a text box to display the company name. You decide all other format features.

Save as:
101B LETTERHEAD

Paragon Group

Specialists in Actuarial Recruiting

22 East Ohio Street
Chicago, IL 60613

Phone: 312.555-0100
Fax: 312.555-0130
Email: actuarialrecruits@group-paragon.com
www.group-paragon.com

101C

Business Card

1. In a new document, draw a text box 2" high and 3.5" wide.

2. Within that text box, design a business card using black and shades of gray and the information at the right. Use WordArt to display the owner's name and title. You may choose a different logo and decide all other formatting features.

Save as: 101C CARD

 Tri-County Science Supplies

Deanne A. Gardner, Owner
6010 N. Scottsdale Road
Scottsdale, AZ 85253-6000
480.555.0110
480.555.0111
gardner@az-tcss.com

1" TM

DS I.D. Information

James Henderson

Professor Lewis

HC101 Composition

15 February 20--

Career Planning

Indent ¶ 0.5" and DS ¶s

Career planning is an important, ongoing process. It is important because the career you choose will affect your quality of life.

One important step in career planning is to define your career goals.

Indent long quotes 1" from LM and DS

Whatever your present plans for employment or further education, you should consider your long-term career goals. You might wonder why someone who is considering a first job should be thinking beyond that job. Thinking ahead may help you choose a first job that is closely related to long-term interests. . . . With a career goal in mind, you can evaluate beginning job offers in relation to that goal.

(Oliverio, Pasewark, and White 516)

1" LM and RM   1" LM and RM

Another useful step in career planning is to develop a personal profile of your skills, interests, and values.

An analysis of your skills is likely to reveal that you have many different kinds: (1) functional skills that determine how well you manage time, communicate, and motivate people; (2) adaptive skills that determine your efficiency, flexibility, reliability, and enthusiasm; and (3) technical skills such as keyboarding, computer, and language skills that are required for many jobs.

Values are "principles that guide a person's life" (Fulton-Calkins and Stulz 543), and you should identify them early so that you can pursue a career that will improve your chances to acquire them. Values include the importance you place on family, security, wealth, prestige, creativity, power, and independence.

At least 1" BM

MLA Report, page 1

(continued on next page)

Activity 5

SmartArt Organization Chart

WP • Insert/Illustrations/ SmartArt/Hierarchy

Complete steps 1–5.

Save as: OF11 ACTIVITY5

You can use SmartArt to create an organization chart to show the relationship between individuals in an organization. Boxes can be added and positioned as needed.

1. Open a new document.
2. Use the Organization Chart SmartArt in the Hierarchy category to create the following organization chart by adding/deleting and positioning the boxes as needed.

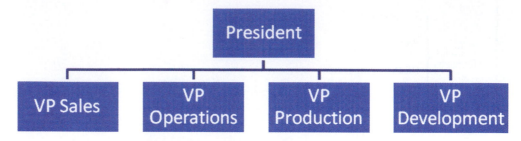

3. Change the SmartArt style to a red Flat Screen.
4. Arrange the VP titles in alphabetic order, left to right.
5. Change width of the SmartArt to 6" and center-align all the titles if needed.

Activity 6

Wrap Text Around Graphics

WP • Page Layout/Arrange/ Text Wrapping

Complete steps 1–2.

Save as: OF11 ACTIVITY6

You can choose how text is to appear near a graphic. Text near a graphic object can be **wrapped** (positioned) so it is above and below the object only, surrounds the object, or appears to be keyed behind or in front of the object. You can also position the graphic so it "moves along" with the text.

In this example, the word processing operator selected the option to place the text around the object. Other options are available and can be tried to give the desired result.

1. Open *DF OF11 ACTIVITY6*.
2. Choose an appropriate shape or clip art image (approx 0.5" high) to insert in each ¶. In ¶ 1, position the object near the center and place it behind the text. In ¶ 2, position the object at the right margin and wrap the text squarely around it. In ¶ 3, position the object at the left margin and wrap the text squarely around it.

1" TM

Interests are best described as activities you like and enthusiastically pursue. By listing and analyzing your interests, you should be able to identify a desirable work environment. For example, your list is likely to reveal if you like to work with things or people, work alone or with others, lead or follow others, or be indoors or outdoors.

MLA Report, page 2

1" TM

Works Cited

Fulton-Calkins, Patsy and Karin M. Stulz. *Procedures & Theory for Administrative*

Hanging indent with 0.5" indentation ──→ *Professionals*. 5th ed. Cincinnati: South-Western, 2004.

Oliverio, Mary Ellen, William R. Pasewark, and Bonnie R. White. *The Office: Procedures and*

Technology. 4th ed. Cincinnati: South-Western, 2003.

Works Cited Page for MLA Report

Lesson 87 MLA-STYLE REPORT WITH TABLE

OBJECTIVES

- To practice MLA-style report formatting skills.
- To insert a table in an MLA-style report.

87B

MLA Report with Tracked Changes

1. Open *DF 87B MLA1*.
2. Insert a header that contains your last name and the page number.

3. Insert the following for the report identification:
   - Your name
   - Your instructor's name
   - The course title
   - The current date (day/month/year)
4. Accept or reject the tracked changes in the document and follow directions in the comments.

(continued on next page)

Activity 3

Drawing Shapes

WP • Insert/Illustrations/Shapes

1. Study the illustration below.

This shape has text inserted.

2. Complete steps 1–2.

Save as: OF11 ACTIVITY3

Office provides a variety of ready-made shapes (lines; basic shapes for squares, circles, triangles, braces, brackets, etc.; arrows; flowchart symbols; callouts; stars; and banners) that you can add to a document. A freeform (a shape within the Lines category in the list of shapes) can be used to create a customized shape by using your mouse as a pen.

Once a drawing shape is added, features on the Drawing Tools Format ribbon can be used to insert a shape or text within a shape; edit the shape size and form; apply shape styles, shadow, and 3-D effects; and specify the position and size of the shape. The illustration at the left shows Cloud Callout that has been inserted, sized, shaped, and shaded. Text has been added, and the outside border and text have been colored blue.

Shapes can be quickly deleted by selecting the shape and then tapping DELETE. Perfect squares or circles can be drawn by selecting the Oval or Rectangle button on the Shapes gallery and then pressing and holding the SHIFT key as you drag.

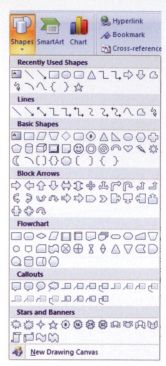

Shapes Gallery

1. Open a new document. Select a star shape. Draw a 2.5" star near the horizontal center at the top of the page, and insert your name using a 14-pt. bold font for the text. Resize the star as needed to attractively display your name on one or two lines.

2. Near the center of the page, draw a shape of your choice. Using WordArt, key your school name in the shape. Format the shape and WordArt as you think appropriate, using 3-D or shadow effects for the shape.

Activity 4

SmartArt

WP • Insert/Illustrations/SmartArt

1. Open a new document and insert the Continuous Block Process SmartArt from the Process category.

2. Key the following text in the Smart Art:

   Warm up, Work out, Cool down

Save as: OF11 ACTIVITY4

Office provides a variety of built-in diagrams that convey processes or relationships in a SmartArt gallery. Using a SmartArt graphic makes it easy to create and modify charts without having to create them from scratch. SmartArt in *Word* is used in much the same way as it is used in PowerPoint. Once a graphic is added, you can use features on the SmartArt Tools Format and Design ribbons to insert text; add or delete portions of the graphic; change the shape style, WordArt style, format, layout, and orientation of the flow; and specify the position and size of the graphic.

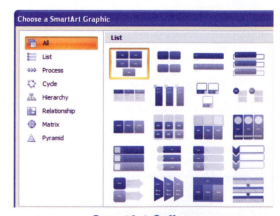

SmartArt Gallery

5. Use the Insert Citation feature to insert the citations and add the books at the right as new sources to the Master Source List where indicated in the text.

6. Key the text at the right following the table.

7. Use the Bibliography feature to generate a Works Cited page that is formatted correctly. Make any changes necessary to ensure that hanging indent style and DS are used for works cited, the title is formatted correctly, no punctuation is underlined, and the edition information is not underlined.

8. Proofread carefully and check for formatting errors, especially widow/orphan lines and side headings not with the text that follows them.

Save as: **87B MLA1**

Schultheis, Robert A. and Raymond M. Kaczmarski. *Business Math.* 16th ed. Mason, OH: Thomson South-Western, 2006.

The World Almanac and Book of Facts, 2007. New York: World Almanac Books, 2007.

The table can be used several ways to accomplish the instructional objectives.

1. The first column can be used for an oral exercise in which students pronounce each unit of measure.

2. The second column can be used to show students the abbreviations for metric units, which are always shown in lowercase letters, without punctuation.

3. The third column can be used to explain that the meter is the basic unit used for measuring length and that other units are parts or multiples of a meter. The table lists the units of measurement from the smallest to the largest.

4. The third column can also be used to show students how to convert from one metric unit to another. Moving the decimal point in the meter measurement to the left converts it to smaller units; moving the decimal point to the right converts it to larger units.

5. The last column of the table can be used to establish the relationship between selected metric and English measurement units.

Summary

The metric system of measurement must be taught along with the English system. Metrics can be presented in an understandable manner if the teacher establishes goals and uses good examples, illustrations, and applications. The table in this report can be used easily to enhance learning.

87C

MLA-Style Report and Proofreading

1. Format the report below in MLA style, correcting the unmarked errors (about 12).

2. Insert your last name and the page number as a header.

3. Insert the following report identification:
   - Your name
   - Your instructor's name
   - The course title
   - The current date

Save as: **87C MLA**

The Importance of Saving Money

Open savings account early, financial planners say, so you get into the habit of saving. Later, you may chose higher-yielding and higher-risk investments such as stocks and bonds; but opening an savings account (in your teens or earlier) is a critical first step to a secure future.

A good financial plan is one that makes you feel good now in anticipation of what your will be able to do with your savings in the future.

One of the best ways to save is to have money deducted from earnings before receiving you're paycheck. The idea is this: You wont miss what you dont receive.

Experts agree that saving is simpler when your set financial goals. The goals may relate to a major purchase like a house or car, a college education for yourself or some one else, or retirement.

By saving regularly and allowing the interest to accumulate, you earn interest on the original investment *and* on the interest earned. This is known as *compounding*, and it is a important part of any savings plan.

Besides helping you reach goals for the future, saving also helps the economy, as you savings increase money flow. Thus, your savings may help build a house or school or office building that, in turn, helps other industry's prosper.

Activity 2

Text Boxes

WP
• Insert/Illustrations/ Text Box

1. Study the text box below.

> This is a shaded text box without a border that illustrates reverse type (white letters on green background) using Calibri 12-pt. font. The text is center-aligned.

2. Complete steps 1–3.

Save as: OF11 ACTIVITY2

Text boxes are frequently used for labels or callouts in a document. You can use a built-in text box that has pre-designed information and formats, or you can draw a blank text box to hold you information and format as desired.

Once a text box is inserted in your document, you can edit it by using available features on the Text Box Tools Format ribbon that appears when a text box is selected. You can use the features within the groups on this ribbon to change the text or text box style, change shadow or 3-D effects, and specify the position and size of your text box as you did with WordArt.

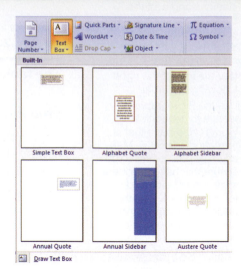

Text box options

1. Open a new document. Draw a text box that is 1" high × 2" wide and is near the horizontal center and the top margin of the page. Key the following information in the text box, using a 12-pt. Arial italic font. Change the shape outline to a 3-pt. solid, red line, and then resize the text box to fit the text on two lines, using center alignment.

This text box uses Arial 12-pt. italic font for the letters.

2. Near the horizontal and vertical center of the page, draw a text box that is about 1" high × 3" wide. Shade the text box with a dark color and remove the shape outline. Using center alignment and bold, white 12-pt. Arial font, key the following copy in the text box. Resize the text box to fit the text on one line.

> This is centered text in a shaded text box that has no shape outline.

3. Near the bottom right corner of the page, insert the built-in Braces Quote and key your first and last name, your school name, and the current date inside the box on three lines. Change the font color of the text and braces to a dark burgundy and adjust the lines so there is about the same space between the text and the braces. If needed, position the text box near the bottom right corner.

• To practice MLA-style report formatting skills.

88B

MLA-Style Report

1. Key the report on this and the next page.
2. Insert a header that has your last name and the page number.
3. Insert the following report identification:
   • Your name
   • Your instructor's name
   • The course title
   • The current date
4. Use the Insert Citation and Bibliography features to insert citations and bibliography.
5. Eliminate any widow or orphan lines and keep all headings with the text that follows them.

Save as: 88B MLA

Works Cited

"Algebra." *Encyclopaedia Britannica*. 2007. Encyclopaedia Britannica Online. 14 July 2007 <http://search.eb.com/eb/article-9111000>.

"Calculus." *Encyclopaedia Britannica*. 2007. Encyclopaedia Britannica Online. 14 July 2007 <http://search.eb.com/eb/article-9018631>.

"Geometry." *Encyclopaedia Britannica*. 2007. Encyclopaedia Britannica Online. 14 July 2007 <http://search.eb.com/eb /article-9126112>.

"Statistics." *Encyclopaedia Britannica*. 2007. Encyclopaedia Britannica Online. 14 July 2007 <http://search.eb.com/eb/article-9108592>.

Mathematics

Most high school students study several types of mathematics. In college, they complete additional math courses, some of which prepare them to study even more kinds of mathematics. You may think of math as one subject; in fact, there are many types of mathematics. This report describes seven kinds.

Arithmetic

Arithmetic is the first branch of mathematics that you studied in elementary and middle school. It deals with the study of numbers and the use of the four fundamental processes:

• Addition
• Subtraction
• Multiplication
• Division

Arithmetic is everyday math. You use it daily in your personal affairs, and arithmetic is the basis for most other branches of mathematics.

Algebra

Algebra is used widely to solve problems in business, industry, and science by using symbols, such as x and y, to represent unknown values (Algebra). The power of algebra is that it enables us to create, write, and rewrite problem-solving formulas. Without algebra, we would not have many of the items we use on a daily basis: television, radio, telephone, microwave oven, etc.

Geometry

Geometry is the branch of mathematics that deals with shapes. More specifically, geometry is the study of relations, properties, and measurements of solids, surfaces, lines, and angles (Geometry). It is most useful in building or measuring things. Architects, astronomers, construction engineers, navigators, and surveyors are just a few professionals who rely on geometry.

Trigonometry

Trigonometry is mathematics that deals with triangular measurements. Plane trigonometry computes the relationships between the sides of triangles on level surfaces called planes. Spherical trigonometry studies the triangles on the surface of a sphere.

Calculus

Calculus is high-level mathematics dealing with rates of change (Calculus). It has many practical applications in engineering, physics, and other branches of science. Using calculus, we understand and explain how water flows, the sun shines, the wind blows, and the planets cycle through the heavens. Differential calculus determines the rate at which an object's speed changes. Integral calculus determines the object's speed when the rate of change is known.

(continued on next page)

Office Features 11

Activity 1

Create WordArt

WP
• Insert/Illustrations/WordArt

1. Study the illustration below.

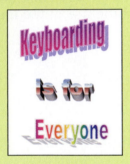

2. Complete steps 1–2.

Save as: OF11 ACTIVITY1

You can change text into a graphic by using the WordArt feature. When you use WordArt, you can choose from a variety of styles in the WordArt gallery. After you choose a style from the gallery, you can change the font, font size, and font style while keying before or after replacing the placeholder text in the Edit WordArt Text dialog box. Once your text has been converted to the WordArt style you chose, you can edit it by using features on the WordArt Tools Format ribbon that appears when the WordArt is selected. You can use the features within the groups on this ribbon to change the text or WordArt style, change shadow or 3-D effects, and specify the position and size of your WordArt.

WordArt should be used sparingly for a word or short phrase and should be surrounded by white space so it appears uncluttered.

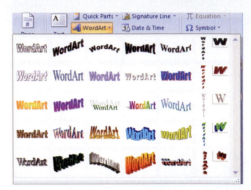

Word Art Option and Word Art Gallery

WordArt Tools Format Ribbon

1. Open a new document and use Word Art to insert your first and last name across the top of the page. Center-align your name; size, shape, and format it as you like.
2. In the same document, use Word Art to insert the name of your school as a footer. Center the text in the text box; size, shape, and format it as you want, using one or more of your school colors.

Probability

Probability is the study of the likelihood of an event's occurrence. It is useful in predicting the outcomes of future events. Probability originated from the study of games of chance. It is now used for other purposes, including to (1) control the flow of traffic through a highway system; (2) predict the number of accidents people of various ages will have; (3) estimate the spread of rumors; (4) predict the outcome of elections; and (5) predict the rate of return in risky investments.

Statistics

Statistics is the branch of mathematics that helps mathematicians organize and find meaning in data. Statistics is

> . . . the science of collecting, analyzing, presenting, and interpreting data. Governmental needs for census data as well as information about a variety of economic activities provided much of the early impetus for the field of statistics. Currently the need to turn the large amounts of data available in many applied fields into useful information has stimulated both theoretical and practical developments in statistics. (Statistics)

88C

MLA-Style Report with Embedded Errors

1. Open file *DF 88C REPORT* and format it in MLA style using Times New Roman 12-pt. font. Include your name, instructor's name, course title, and date to identify the report, and add a header.

2. Change all occurrences of *unit* to *department* and *teachers* to *instructors*.

3. The report contains 20 errors in capitalization, grammar, punctuation, word choice, etc. Correct them.

4. Reverse the order of the Advisory Boards and Awards and Recognition sections.

Save as: 88C MLA

Lesson 89 — UNBOUND AND BOUND REPORTS

OBJECTIVES

- To format title pages.
- To apply report formatting skills.

89B

Document 1 (Unbound Report with Textual Citations)

1. Review the format guides for unbound reports on p. 86 and the model report on p. 87.

2. Key the text as an unbound report using Word 2007 Style.

3. Format the references as a separate page.

Save as: 89B REPORT

The Great Lakes

The five Great Lakes (Lake Erie, Lake Huron, Lake Michigan, Lake Ontario, and Lake Superior) in North America are the largest group of freshwater lakes in the world.

The present configuration of the Great Lakes basin is the result of the movement of massive glaciers through the mid-continent, a process that began about one million years ago. . . . Studies in the Lake Superior region indicate that a river system and valleys formed by water erosion existed before the Ice Age. The glaciers undoubtedly scoured these valleys, widening and deepening them and radically changing the drainage of the area. (Great Lakes, 2007)

Physical Features

The Great Lakes have a combined area of 94,510 square miles (244,780 square kilometers). Although the Great Lakes were all formed by glacial activity during the same period, they are quite different from one another. The irregular movement of the glacier created variation in the size, elevation, and depth of the lakes.

(continued on next page)

Document Design

In this unit, you will learn desktop publishing skills to design flyers, posters, announcements, circulars, charts, etc. that contain graphics. The graphics will include pictures, clip art, WordArt, SmartArt, text boxes, and/or shapes. You can give your documents a professional appearance and make them easy to read and understand by following these basic document design guidelines.

Font size. Headlines, headings, and titles in flyers, posters, announcements, brochures, advertisements, newsletters, etc. may be in a large font to capture the reader's attention. Use an 11- or 12-point font size for most of the text in a document since it is a notably readable size, preferred by most readers. A font that is too small strains the reader's eye and makes the document look crammed and difficult to read. A font that is too large uses more space than is necessary and causes readers to read slowly (letter by letter rather than whole words and phrases).

Fonts. Use only a few fonts (Calibri, Arial, Times New Roman, Comic Sans MS, etc.) in a document. The variety of sizes and the available variations (styles and effects) within the font provide for sufficient emphasis and contrast and lessen the need to use many different fonts.

Underlining and ALL CAPS. Use **bold**, *italic*, and variations in font size rather than underlining and ALL CAPS to emphasize text. Underlining and ALL CAPS, especially in large blocks of text, can make words harder to read.

Typographic elements. Use boxes, borders, bullets, special characters, etc. in consistent styles and sizes throughout a document to improve overall appearance.

Lists. Use numbers and/or letters in outlines to show different levels and when sequencing, cross-referencing, and quantity are important. If listing alone is the goal, bullets (or appropriate special characters) are sufficient.

Side margins. Use margins of 1" to 2". Long lines tend to tire the eye quickly, and short lines cause the eye to jump back and forth too often. The use of a few long or short lines in a document is not likely to cause readers problems, however.

Justification. With normal-length lines, use a ragged right margin. Varying the line endings of normal-length lines is easier to read than justified text, where the lines end evenly and there is inconsistent spacing between words. Justified text is permissible in documents like newsletters that use shorter lines in narrow columns.

White space. Use white space in the margins to keep a document from looking crowded. Use white space between document parts to inform the reader where one part ends and another part begins.

Emphasis. Use **bold**, *italic*, and effects (underlining, shadow, outline, emboss, engrave, SMALL CAPS, etc.) in small amounts to call attention to some parts of a document. Avoid overusing one technique or using too many different techniques in a document. When too many parts of a document are emphasized, no one part will seem especially important. When too many different techniques are used, the document will appear cluttered.

Color. Use color to enhance the message or appearance of the document. Generally, use dark shades of color for fonts and lighter shades of color for highlights and fills. Select contrasting font colors to improve readability when different colors are used near each other. Built-in Themes provide acceptable color combinations, fonts, and effects.

Graphics. Place graphics (clip art, pictures, charts, shapes, text boxes, etc.) near the text they enhance or as close as possible to their references in the text. Keep the size of the graphic in proportion to the text, column width, and space available.

References

"Great Lakes." *Ency-clopædia Britannica.* <http://search.eb.com/eb /article-39973> (14 July 2007).

The New York Times Almanac. "Great Lakes and St. Lawrence Sea-way." New York: Penguin Books, 2007.

The World Almanac and Book of Facts. "The Great Lakes." New York: World Almanac Books, 2007

Document 2 (Title Page)

1. Prepare a title page for the Great Lakes report.

2. Use your name, your school's name, and the current date.

3. Insert an appropriate page border. Insert clip art appropriately on the page.

Save as: 89B TITLE PAGE

Lake Superior, the largest of the lakes, is only slightly smaller than Maine; and Lake Ontario, the smallest of the lakes, is about the size of New Jersey.

The lakes vary greatly in elevation. Lake Superior, the highest, lies 600 feet (183 meters) above sea level, while Lake Ontario, the lowest, lies just 245 feet (75 meters) above sea level. There is a 325-foot difference in elevation between Lakes Erie and Ontario. Most of the water from the lakes drains into the St. Lawrence River, which flows into the Atlantic Ocean (*The World Almanac and Book of Facts*, 2007, p. 707).

The depth of the Great Lakes varies greatly, too. The deepest, Lake Superior, is 1,333 feet (406 meters) deep. Lake Erie, the shallowest, is only 210 feet (64 meters) deep (*New York Times Almanac*, 2007, p. 64).

Connecting Waterways

Three sets of locks and canals make it possible for ships to sail from one Great Lake to another and from Lake Ontario to the Atlantic Ocean, from which they can sail to any port in the world. The canal and the bodies of water they connect are listed here.

1. Welland Canal--connects Lake Erie and Lake Ontario.
2. Soo Canal--connects Lake Superior and Lake Huron.
3. St. Lawrence Seaway--connects Lake Ontario with the Atlantic Ocean.

Significance of the Lakes

The five Great Lakes and the canals that link them together make up the most important inland waterway in North America. They provide the inexpensive transportation system needed to make the Great Lakes region one of the most important industrial areas in the United States.

89c

Report with Endnotes

Document 1 (Bound Report with Endnotes)

Formatting: Review Bound Reports and Endnotes on pp. 173–174.

1. Open *DF 89C REPORT*.
2. Proofread the text carefully. Correct any errors you detect.
3. Format the text as a bound report with endnotes using Word 2007 Style.
4. Insert the following three citations as endnotes where indicated by the comments.

   1 Pattie Odgers, *Administrative Office Management*. 13e (Cincinnati: South-Western, 2005), p. 74.

   2 Russell, Robert F., and A. Gregory Stone, "A Review of Servant Leadership Attributes: Developing a Practical Model," *Leadership & Organizational Development Journal*, Bradford, Vol. 23, Iss. 3/4, 2002, pp. 145–158.

   3 Fulton-Calkins, Patsy, and Karin M. Stulz. *Procedures & Theory for Administrative Professionals*. 5th ed. (Cincinnati: South-Western, 2004), 483.

Save as: 89C REPORT

Document 2 (Title Page)

Prepare a title page for the leadership report (*89C REPORT*) as directed.

1. Use **LEADERSHIP SEMINAR PROGRESS REPORT** as the title.
2. Use **Kimberly Jurgaitis** as the writer, **The Kemp Group** as the organization, and **August 15, 20--** as the date.
3. Insert an appropriate page border.
4. Insert clip art appropriately on the page.

Save as: 89C TITLE PAGE

Skill Check

1. Key three 1' writings on each ¶ for speed; determine *gwam*.
2. Key two 3' writings on all ¶s combined for control; circle errors.
3. Key two 5' writings on all ¶s combined. Record and retain your better 5' *gwam* and error count, and compare it to the score you received in 99D.

A   all letters used   MicroPace   gwam   3' | 5'

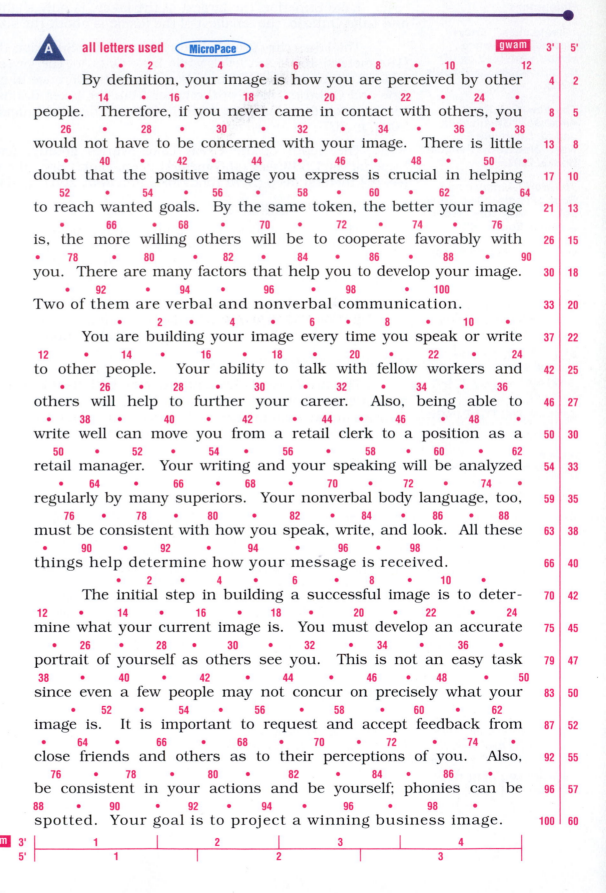

	gwam 3'		5'
By definition, your image is how you are perceived by other	4		2
people. Therefore, if you never came in contact with others, you	8		5
would not have to be concerned with your image. There is little	13		8
doubt that the positive image you express is crucial in helping	17		10
to reach wanted goals. By the same token, the better your image	21		13
is, the more willing others will be to cooperate favorably with	26		15
you. There are many factors that help you to develop your image.	30		18
Two of them are verbal and nonverbal communication.	33		20
You are building your image every time you speak or write	37		22
to other people. Your ability to talk with fellow workers and	42		25
others will help to further your career. Also, being able to	46		27
write well can move you from a retail clerk to a position as a	50		30
retail manager. Your writing and your speaking will be analyzed	54		33
regularly by many superiors. Your nonverbal body language, too,	59		35
must be consistent with how you speak, write, and look. All these	63		38
things help determine how your message is received.	66		40
The initial step in building a successful image is to deter-	70		42
mine what your current image is. You must develop an accurate	75		45
portrait of yourself as others see you. This is not an easy task	79		47
since even a few people may not concur on precisely what your	83		50
image is. It is important to request and accept feedback from	87		52
close friends and others as to their perceptions of you. Also,	92		55
be consistent in your actions and be yourself; phonies can be	96		57
spotted. Your goal is to project a winning business image.	100		60

gwam   3' | 1   2   3   4
      5' | 1   2   3

Language Skills: Word Choice

1. Study the spelling and definitions of the words.
2. Key all *Learn* and *Apply* lines, choosing the correct word in the *Apply* lines.

Save as: 89D CHOICE

---

affect (vb) to influence
effect (n) result; consequence; (vb) to cause; to accomplish

complement (n) something that completes or makes up a whole
compliment (n) an expression of praise or congratulation

Learn 1 The **effect** of the recent change will **affect** our annual profit.

Apply 2 Will cutting the staff 25 percent (affect/effect) worker morale?

Apply 3 What (affect/effect) will new equipment have on productivity?

Learn 1 Jo's **compliment** to Dan was that his tie **complemented** his suit.

Apply 2 The laser printer is a (complement/compliment) to the system.

Apply 3 Gloria accepted Kevin's (complement/compliment) with a smile.

89E

INTERNET ACTIVITY

1. Access the National Air and Space Museum at http://www.school.cengage.com/keyboarding/c21key
2. Find answers to the questions at the right.
3. Key your answers in sentence form.

Save as: 89E INTERNET

1. How long and how far did Orville Wright fly during the Kitty Hawk's first flight (12/17/1903)? How much did the Kitty Hawk weigh?

2. What was the name of the Apollo 11 Command Module (first manned flight to land on the moon)? How much did Apollo 11 weigh?

3. How many miles did the Breitling Orbiter 3 Gondola fly during the first nonstop balloon flight around the world (March 1999)? How much did the gondola weigh?

Courtesy of NASA

- To improve keyboarding techniques and straight-copy speed and control.
- To improve language skills.

100B

Word Choice

1. Study the spelling and definitions of the words.
2. Key all *Learn* and *Apply* lines, choosing the correct words in the *Apply* lines.

Save as: 100B CHOICE

> **poor** (adj) having little wealth or value
> **pore** (vb/n) to study carefully; a tiny opening in a surface, such as skin
> **pour** (vb) to make flow or stream; to rain hard
>
> **right** (adj) factual; true; correct
> **rite** (n) customary form of ceremony; ritual
> **write** (vb) to form letters or symbols; to compose and set down in words, numbers, or symbols

Learn 1 **Pour** the fertilizer over the **poor** soil before you till it.

Learn 2 As we **pore** over these formulas, others are playing football.

Apply 3 You can (poor/pore/pour) the soup for the (poor/pore/pour) men.

Apply 4 (Poor/pore/pour) over the fine print before you buy the policy.

Learn 5 I may **write** a paper on the tribal **rite** of passage into manhood.

Learn 6 You have a **right** to participate in the **rite** of graduation.

Apply 7 To succeed, (right/rite/write) in the (right/rite/write) way.

Apply 8 The processional is just one (right/rite/write) in the ceremony.

100C   Skill Building

Technique: Response Patterns

Key each line twice.

Technique: Reach with the fingers; keep hands still.

One-hand words

1 are ace ill bar lip cat mom dad nil ear oil fad pop cab were upon

2 beg rag hip sat hop sew ink tag joy tea mop wax pin web noun seat

3 cab area hook beef join drab jump edge look fact moon nylon gates

4 egg rare imply saga jolly star onion tear phony weave union zebra

gwam 1' | 1 | 2 | 3 | 4 | 5 | 6 | 7 | 8 | 9 | 10 | 11 | 12 | 13 |

Balanced-hand words

5 aid bug cob cut dig elf fit got ham iris jams kept lake meld name

6 owl own pro pay quay roam sick soap than curl vial wish yang meld

7 rue also body city disk envy foam goal half idle jape kale laughs

8 oak usual mantle naught orient papaya quench enrich social theory

gwam 1' | 1 | 2 | 3 | 4 | 5 | 6 | 7 | 8 | 9 | 10 | 11 | 12 | 13 |

Format Guides for Special Documents

Agenda. An agenda is a list of things to be done or actions to be taken, usually at a meeting. An agenda is prepared using margins and page numbering for an unbound report and 1.15 line spacing with 10-pt. spacing after paragraphs. If desired, an agenda may be centered vertically.

Key the name of the group holding the meeting in Title style on the first line. In Subtitle style, key the word *Agenda*, the meeting date, and the time and location on three separate lines at the left margin beneath the name of the group.

In Normal style, key the information about the type of meeting, the meeting facilitator, the invitees, etc., on separate lines, each beginning at the left margin.

The agenda items can be keyed using the Multilevel List feature with default tab settings.

Meeting minutes. Use margins and page numbering for an unbound report and 1.15 line spacing with 10 pt. spacing after paragraphs.

Key the name of the group that met in Title style on the first line. Key the words *Meeting Minutes* and the meeting date on separate lines in Subtitle style, each beginning at the left margin.

Use the Numbered List feature with a 0.25" hanging indentation to format the items in the minutes.

After the last item, indicate the name of the person who submitted the minutes, blocked at the left margin.

News release. Use margins and page numbering for an unbound report and 1.15 line spacing with 10 pt. spacing after paragraphs.

Key the words **News Release** on line 1 in Title Style. On the next line at the left margin, key the words *For Release: . . .* in Subtitle style.

On the next line, key *Contact: . . .* in Subtitle style at the left margin. Tap ENTER once; begin the news release body. Key the body using 1.15 line spacing. Center the symbols ### below the last line of the news release.

Itinerary. An itinerary is an outline of a person's travel plans. For business travel involving air travel, the itinerary typically contains information about flights, transportation at the destination site, hotel lodging, and the travel agency used. Itineraries may also include information about specific activities (meetings, presentations, conferences, etc.) while at the destination.

An itinerary can be prepared as an attractively formatted table with or without gridlines.

Templates

Many business and personal documents are keyed using a template. The business documents include news releases, meeting minutes, itineraries, agendas, purchase orders, and invoices. Templates can also be used for documents such as greeting cards, invitations, and certificates.

A template is a master copy of a set of predefined styles for a particular type of document. The template may contain text and formatting for margins, line spacing, colors, borders, styles, themes, etc.

The use of a template saves you time since you use it as a starting point rather than creating every document from scratch. For example, if you have weekly meetings and have to create a similar agenda for each meeting, starting out with a template that is formatted and has a lot of the repetitive information already in place will save time, since you will need to change only the details that differ from week to week.

Word response

6 by to do or it am bus key off cog cod rot hep make clap bury risk
7 of so is if me cot sit fig zoo jam yang zori thru make wick virus
8 to roam rush it six pair sight land may mend cozy flame the forks
9 Dirk is due to dismantle the worn antique chair in the dorm hall.
10 My busy neighbor is to go downtown to the giant mall to visit me.

gwam 1' | 1 | 2 | 3 | 4 | 5 | 6 | 7 | 8 | 9 | 10 | 11 | 12 | 13 |

Combination

11 xi mu pi nu eta xi psi beta phi psi beta zeta kappa sigma phi eta
12 see far eye him jump fast hand held save both they fish do it kin
13 dials six queue up right hand look at him men and girls profit by
14 The six beggars deserved a better neighbor than the neurotic man.
15 As a visitor, you may see my hilly island area better by bicycle.

gwam 1' | 1 | 2 | 3 | 4 | 5 | 6 | 7 | 8 | 9 | 10 | 11 | 12 | 13 |

99D

Skill Check

1. Key three 1' writings on each ¶ for speed; determine *gwam*. Count errors. If the number of errors is two or fewer on any writing, set a goal to increase speed one or two *gwam* in step 2. If the number of errors on any writing is more than two, set a goal to increase control (0–2 errors) in step 2.

2. Key two 3' writings on all ¶s combined; determine *gwam* and count errors.

3. Key two 5' writings on all ¶s combined; determine *gwam* and count errors. Record and retain your better 5' *gwam* and error count for use in 133D.

A all letters used (MicroPace)   gwam 3' | 5'

	3'	5'
Character is often described as a person's combined moral	4	2	43
and ethical strength. Most people think it is like integrity,	8	5	46
which is thought to be a person's ability to adhere to a code or	12	7	48
a set standard of values. If an individual's values are accepted	17	10	51
by society, others are likely to view her or him as having a some-	21	13	53
what high degree of integrity.	23	14	55
You need to know that character is a trait that everyone	27	16	57
possesses and that it is formed over time. A person's character	31	19	59
reflects his or her definition of what is good or just. Most	35	21	62
children and teenagers model their character after the words and	40	24	65
deeds of parents, teachers, and other adults with whom they have	44	26	67
regular contact.	45	27	68
Existing character helps mold future character. It is impor-	49	29	70
tant to realize that today's actions can have a lasting effect.	53	32	73
For that reason, there is no better time than now to make all your	58	32	73
words and deeds speak favorably. You want them to portray the	62	37	78
things others require of people who are thought to possess a high	67	40	80
degree of character.	68	41	81

gwam 3' | 1 | 2 | 3 | 4 |
      5' | 1 | 2 | 3 |

For each activity, read and learn the feature described, then follow instructions at the left.

Activity 1

Create Templates

WP
- Office Button/New/ Templates

1. Read the text about templates on p. 273 and at the right.
2. Open the Fax template, *DF OF10 ACTIVITY1* (or the Equity Fax template that is installed on your computer).
3. Replace the text in the template with that shown in italics in the fax transmittal sheet at the right to create a new fax transmittal sheet that is based on the template.

Save as: OF10 ACTIVITY1

TIP: If you need to delete a template item that has been keyed using a content control, click the item to select it, click the content control handle that appears, and tap DELETE.

[Type the recipient name]

↑

Content control handle

You can use the Template feature to create a document. When you open a template, a new document opens that's based on the template you selected. That is, you're really opening a copy of the template, not the template itself. You work in that new document, using what was built into the template and adding or deleting as necessary. Because the new document is not the template itself, your changes are saved to the copy of the template, and the template is left in its original state. Therefore, one template can be the basis for an unlimited number of documents.

Normally, you select templates from those that are installed on your computer. You can also download templates from Microsoft Office Online, or you can use a template that you have saved. In this unit, you will mostly use *Word* templates that have been saved to your computer.

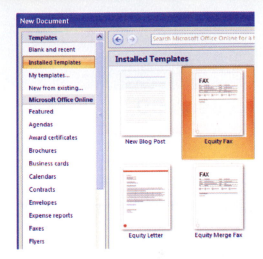

FAX

To:	Mr. Harold Robelen	**From:**	[Your Name]
Fax:	213-555-0181	**Pages:**	Six
Phone:	213-555-0180	**Date:**	[Pick the date]
Re:	Newtown Project Proposal	**CC:**	None

[ ] Urgent   [x] For Review   [ ] Please Comment   [ ] Please Reply   [ ] Please Recycle

Comments:
I'll call you on Thursday to set up an appointment to discuss the proposal.

UNIT 25
Lessons 99-100
Build Keyboarding Skill

KEYBOARDING SKILLS

OBJECTIVES
- To improve keyboarding techniques and language skills.
- To improve straight-copy speed and control.

99A-100A

Conditioning Practice

Key each line twice daily.

alphabet	1	Tezz quickly indexed jokes for a public performance he will give.
fig/sym	2	Sales discounts (15%) amount to $134,682, an increase of $21,790.
speed	3	The eight busy men may do the work for us if he pays for the ivy.

gwam 1' | 1 | 2 | 3 | 4 | 5 | 6 | 7 | 8 | 9 | 10 | 11 | 12 | 13 |

99B

Word Choice

1. Study the spelling and definitions of the words.
2. Key all *Learn* and *Apply* lines, choosing the correct word(s) in the *Apply* lines.

Save as: 99B CHOICE

> **desert** (n) a region rendered barren by environmental extremes
> **dessert** (n) the last course of a lunch or dinner
>
> **miner** (n) one who removes minerals/ore from the earth; machine used for that purpose
> **minor** (adj/n) lesser/smaller in amount, extent, or size; under legal age

Learn   1 The diner will keep the **dessert** to eat as a snack in the **desert**.
Apply   2 April is planning to serve apple pie for (desert/dessert) today.
Apply   3 The men filled six water bottles for the (desert/dessert) trip.

Learn   4 The injury to the copper **miner** is no **minor** legal matter.
Apply   5 The law states that a (miner/minor) can't work as a (miner/minor).
Apply   6 This is a (miner/minor) point, but the (miner/minor) will retire soon.

99C

Technique: Response Patterns

Key each line twice.

Technique Cue

Letter response—Key these one-hand words with a continuous pace.

Letter response

1 at ad be ho we him age ill awe pop cabs hull deaf junk mill areas
2 as we up in be at pin up see him look upon were traded phony beef
3 my ink red car pink nylon sets free join union fast reader awards
4 Extra reserved seats set up in my area at noon served only a few.
5 Rebecca served a plump, sweet plum dessert on my terrace at noon.

gwam 1' | 1 | 2 | 3 | 4 | 5 | 6 | 7 | 8 | 9 | 10 | 11 | 12 | 13 |

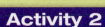

Activity 2

Create a Building Block (Quick Part)

 WP • Insert/Text/Quick Parts

1. Read the text at the right.
2. Learn to create and save a building block that can be reused via the Quick Parts tool.
3. Use the information at the right to create a heading for meeting minutes as a building block. You choose the clip art and format.
4. Save the information as a building block to the Quick Parts Gallery, using **BCIT Advisory Committee** as the name.

In previous units, you used existing building blocks in the Quick Parts tool to insert reusable pieces of content to prepare cover pages for your reports. In this activity, you will save text to use as a building block, using the Quick Parts tool. The content you save can include text, images, and special formats. Whatever you select to save as a building block will be placed in the new document. A building block can be used as is, edited, or deleted using the Building Blocks Organizer in the Quick Parts drop-down list.

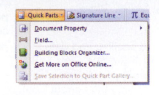

Central Morris School District

Business, Computer, and Information Technology Studies

Advisory Committee Meeting Minutes

Month Day, Year

Activity 3

Use a Building Block (Quick Part)

1. Open a blank document.
2. Insert the BCIT Advisory Committee Quick Part.
3. Replace the date placeholder with the current date.
4. Key the text at the right.

Save as: OF10 ACTIVITY3

Committee members present: Robert Dry-Kenich, Deborah Edington, Amy Lovetro, Ray Meucci, Kenneth Ryave, and Leo Yazzani

District employees present: Mary Araral, Drew Bowen, Larry Kauffman, Fed Niklas, and Carla Nilson

Recorder of minutes: Joseph Gloss

Activity 4

Apply Templates

1. Open *DF OF10 ACTIVITY1* (fax transmittal sheet template).
2. Key the information at the right into the template.

Save as: OF10 ACTIVITY4

To:	Ms. Mary Gettens	From:	Carita Menendez
Fax:	718-555-0108	Pages:	Five
Phone:	718-555-0107	Date:	[Pick the date]
Re:	Investment Portfolio Allocations	CC:	Mr. Jim Holden

☐ Urgent   ☒ For Review   ☐ Please Comment   ☐ Please Reply   ☐ Please Recycle

Comments:

Please review the allocations I suggest for your investment portfolio. The weights for the mutual fund categories are appropriate for variables we discussed at our preliminary consultation. Based on past performance, this mix of assets should return 10-12 percent annually with a risk level suitable for your age, goals, and risk tolerance.

Language Skills: Word Choice

1. Study the spelling and definitions of the words.
2. Key all *Learn* and *Apply* lines, choosing the correct word in the *Apply* lines.

Save as: **98D CHOICE**

principal (n/adj) a person in authority; a capital sum; main, primary	**stationary** (adj) fixed in position, course, or mode; unchanging in condition
principle (n) a rule	**stationery** (n) paper and envelopes used for processing personal and business documents

Learn 1 The new **principal** is guided by the **principle** of fairness.

Apply 2 The (principal/principle) reason I'm here is to record the talk.

Apply 3 What (principal/principle) of law was applied in the case?

Learn 1 We store **stationery** on **stationary** shelves in the supply room.

Apply 2 Desks remain (stationary/stationery), but we'll shift the files.

Apply 3 Were you able to get a good discount on (stationary/stationery)?

INTERNET ACTIVITY

Follow the directions at the right to learn about a math or science course.

Save as: **98E INTERNET**

1. From http://school.cengage.com/keyboarding/c21key, search the World Wide Web, using the Web address for one or more of the search engines listed below. Enter the name of a math or science course you are taking (or plan to take) as the keyword(s).

   Google, Yahoo, and/or one suggested by your teacher

2. Find a link that interests you and go to that site.

3. Identify the link by its URL (Web address). Then key a ¶ or two describing information at the site and how you can use it.

Lesson 90   AGENDAS, MEETING MINUTES, AND TEMPLATES

OBJECTIVES

- To format an agenda and meeting minutes.
- To use templates to prepare an agenda and meeting minutes.

90A–92A

Conditioning Practice

Key each line twice daily.

alphabet   1   June quickly wraps the five dozen macaroons and six big cupcakes.

fig/sym   2   I got 25% off on orders over $83,900 because of contract #41-6-7.

speed   3   If I go to the city to visit them, I may go to the spa and dorms.

gwam   1' | 1 | 2 | 3 | 4 | 5 | 6 | 7 | 8 | 9 | 10 | 11 | 12 | 13 |

90B

Agenda

Agenda 1

1. Read the format guides for preparing agendas on p. 273.
2. Key the agenda at the right.

Save as: 90B AGENDA1

Agenda 2 (Using Template)

1. Open *DF 90B AGENDA2* (a template file).
2. Key the information at the right using the template settings for font, font size, font style, line spacing, etc. Add to and delete from the template content as needed.

Save as: 90B AGENDA2

WOODWARD HIGH SCHOOL BIOLOGY CLUB
March 2, 20-- Meeting Agenda

2:45 p.m. in Room 214
Type of Meeting: Regular meeting
Meeting Facilitator: Marcie Holmquist, President
Invitees: All members and faculty sponsor

1) Call to order
2) Roll call
3) Approval of minutes from last meeting
4) Unfinished business
    a) Finalize team assignments for candy sale that begins May 1
    b) Plan approved community service project to care for one mile of State Route 163
    c) Discuss recommendation that the Club help support an international student
5) New business
    a) Appoint nominating committee
    b) Discuss plans for regional leadership conference on April 12
    c) Discuss annual give-back gift to Woodward High
6) Adjournment

90C

Meeting Minutes

Meeting Minutes 1

1. Read the format guides for preparing meeting minutes on p. 273.
2. Key the minutes at the right.

Save as: 90C MINUTES1

WOODWARD HIGH SCHOOL BIOLOGY CLUB
March 2, 20-- Meeting Minutes

1. Call to order: President Marcie Holmquist called the Biology Club meeting to order at 2:45 p.m. on March 2, 20-- in Room 214.
2. Attendance: Jerry Finley, Secretary, recorded the attendance. All officers, 23 members, and the faculty sponsor were present.
3. Approval of minutes: The minutes were approved as read by Jerry Finley.
4. This unfinished business was acted upon:
    A. There will be five teams of four members each for the candy sale that begins on May 1. Team captains are Bruce Holstein, Anita Jones, Roberto Nuez, Ty Billops, and Gracie Walton. Each captain will select three members for his/her team.

(continued on next page)

Lesson 98   WORKSHEETS

OBJECTIVE

• To apply what you have learned to prepare worksheets and charts.

98B

Charts

Chart 1: Pie

1. Key the worksheet.
2. Create a pie chart, using **BUDGET** as the title.
3. Select a chart layout and chart style to show the data.

	A	B
1	CATEGORY	PERCENT
2	Savings	10%
3	Food	20%
4	Clothing	15%
5	Shelter	40%
6	Transportation	15%

Save as: 98B WORKSHEET1

Chart 2

1. Key the worksheet.
2. Create a column chart to display the data.
3. Choose an appropriate chart layout to show **PARTICIPANTS** as the title and the number of participants in each column.
4. Choose an appropriate chart style.

	A	B
1	Area	Number
2	Northeast	155
3	Midwest	145
4	Southeast	175
5	West	135
6	Southwest	75

Save as: 98B WORKSHEET2

98C

Worksheets

Worksheet 1

1. Key the worksheet, keying column A as labels.
2. Use center alignment; Number format; adjust column width to fit contents.
3. Change row height to 24 pts.
4. Complete steps 1 and 2.
5. Apply desired cell styles.

Save as: 98C WORKSHEET1

	A	B	C	D	E	F	G	H	I
1	Ages	1950	1960	1970	1980	1993	2000	2010	2020
2	1-18	47.3	64.5	69.8	63.7	64.2	72.4	74.4	80.3
3	0-5	19.1	24.3	20.9	19.6	22.5	23.2	25.6	27.5
4	6-11	15.3	21.8	24.6	20.8	21.6	25.0	24.4	26.9
5	12-18	12.9	18.4	24.3	23.3	20.1	24.2	24.4	26.0

1. In cell A1, key **MILLIONS OF U.S. CHILDREN UNDER AGE 18** using bold, ALL CAPS 12-pt. font for the title.
2. In cell A7, key **Source:** http://www.childstats.gov/ in italic.

Worksheet 2

1. Open *DF 98C WORKSHEET2*.
2. In column G, calculate a total of all the test scores for each student.
3. In column H, calculate an average score (one decimal place) for each student.
4. In row 25, calculate an average class score (one decimal place) for each test.
5. In row 26, display the lowest score for each test.
6. Complete steps 1–8.

Save as: 98C WORKSHEET2

1. Insert these rows in alphabetic order:
   MACY | 80 | 75 | 83 | 93 | 95 |
   WEHNER | 67 | 72 | 85 | 92 | 88 |
2. Delete the Como, Rogers, and Stoehr rows.
3. Center-align all numbers.
4. Shade every other row from Briggs to Zigerell, using the same color.
5. Copy row 2 to the row after MINIMUM; delete contents in cell A26.
6. Change Gordon's score for Test 2 to **88** and for Test 5 to **78**.
7. Bold all cells in the TOTAL, MINIMUM, and AVERAGE columns and rows.
8. Apply appropriate cell styles to rows 1, 2, 24, 25, and 26.

Lesson 98   Worksheets   301

1. Open *DF 90C MINUTES2* (a template file).

2. Using the same information that you used to prepare 90C MINUTES1 and the template file above, prepare another set of meeting minutes. Use the template settings for font, font size, font style, line spacing, etc. Add to and delete from the template content as needed.

Save as: 90C MINUTES2

B. Bill Eaton will organize a team of volunteers for the Route 163 project. He will try to get at least 15 members to clean up the litter on May 15. The Chamber of Commerce will provide adult supervision, safety vests and gloves, road signs, and collection bags. The volunteers will begin at 9:15 a.m. and work until about 11:30 a.m. They are to meet at the Carriage Inn parking lot at 8:45 a.m.

C. The officers recommended that the Club not provide financial support for an international student this coming year since all members who attend the Fall Regional Leadership Conference will need financial assistance for travel, food, and lodging. The officers' recommendation was approved.

5. This new business was discussed and acted upon:

A. President Holmquist appointed the Nominating Committee (Sissy Erwin, Roberta Shaw, and Jim Vance), and they are to present a slate of officers at the April meeting.

B. The membership approved officers to attend the Spring Regional Leadership Conference at Great Valley Resort and Conference Center on April 12. Their expenses for travel and meals will be reimbursed.

C. Three suggestions for a give-back were discussed. The possibilities include planting a tree near the student parking lot, donating one or more biology reference books to the school library, and purchasing a banner that can be used to welcome students back to school each fall. The Give-Back Committee, chaired by Annie Sexton, will study all three options and report back at the April meeting.

6. The next meeting is April 3 at 2:45 p.m. in Room 103. The meeting was adjourned at 3:35 p.m. by Marcie Holmquist.

Minutes submitted by Jerry Finley, Secretary

Lesson 91 — NEWS RELEASES, ITINERARIES, AND TEMPLATES

OBJECTIVES

- To format a news release and an itinerary.
- To use templates to prepare a news release and an itinerary.

91B

News Releases

News Release 1

1. Read the format guide for news releases on p. 273.

2. Key the text at the right as a news release.

Save as: 91B NEWS RELEASE1

News Release   **For Release: Immediate**
                                                          Contact: Heidi Zemack

CLEVELAND, OH, May 25, 20--. Science teachers from school districts in six counties are eligible for this year's Teacher Excellence awards funded by The Society for Environmental Engineers.

Nominations can be submitted through Friday, July 31, by students, parents, residents, and other educators. Nomination forms are available from the participating school districts or on the Society's website at http://www.tsee.webhost.com.

An anonymous committee reviews the nominations and selects ten finalists. From that group, seven "teachers of distinction" and three award winners

Change Chart Layout and Styles

1. Read the text.
2. Learn to change chart layout and chart styles.
3. Open *97B WORKSHEET1*.
4. Change chart layout to Layout 9.
5. Key **February Sales** as the title; **Salesperson** for the X-axis title; **Sales and Returns** for the Y-axis title.
6. Use Chart Style 42 to change the appearance of the chart.

Save as: **97D WORKSHEET**

Once a chart has been created, you can change the Chart Layout to display or not display such chart parts as:

Titles—Headings that identify chart contents and the X-axis and/or Y-axis. To key your chart titles, click the default title names and key the names you want.

Data labels—Numbers or words that identify values displayed in the chart.

Gridlines—Lines through a chart that identify intervals on the axes.

Legend—A key (usually with different colors or patterns) used to identify the chart's data categories.

Chart Styles has several options that enable you to change the overall visual appearance of your chart, including the color of the bars, lines, pie slices, etc.

Column Chart with Layout 9 and Chart Style 42

Charts

Chart 1: Bar

1. Key the worksheet.
2. Create a bar chart.
3. Choose an appropriate chart layout to show **PATIENT REPORT** as the title and **Month** and **Number of Patients** for the axis titles.
4. Select an appropriate chart style.

Save as: **97E WORKSHEET1**

	A	B	C
1	Month	In Patient	Out Patient
2	APRIL	350	725
3	MAY	365	752
4	JUNE	290	645

Chart 2: Column

1. Key the worksheet.
2. Create a column chart, using **PROM ATTENDANCE** as the title and **Students** and **Number Attending** for the axis titles.

Save as: **97E WORKSHEET2**

	A	B	C
1		THIS	LAST
2	CLASS	YEAR	YEAR
3	Seniors	132	89
4	Juniors	154	144
5	Sophomores	66	54
6	Freshmen	12	18

1. Open *DF 91B NEWS RELEASE2* (a template file).
2. Use the information for *91B NEWS RELEASE1* to prepare a news release. Use the template settings for font, line spacing, etc. Add to and delete from the template content as needed.

Save as: 91B NEWS RELEASE2

are selected. The top award winner receives $5,000, the second receives $2,500, and the third receives $1,500. Each teacher of distinction receives $500. The teachers of distinction and the award winners will be announced on September 5 at a dinner at the Cleveland Inn.

School districts participating in the program include those in these counties: Cuyahoga, Lorain, Medina, Summit, Lake, and Geauga.

###

News Release 3

Format the text at the right as a news release. If desired, you may use the template, *DF 91B NEWS RELEASE2*.

Save as: 91B NEWS RELEASE3

News Release

For Release: Upon Receipt
Contact: Guy Madison

LORAIN, OH, March 24, 20--. Three East Lorain County High School students, members of the ELCHS Science Club, have been invited to exhibit their projects at the Eastern Ohio Academy for Science Fair on April 21-24. The fair will be held in the Stern Exhibit Hall at the Erie Civic Center.

Susan Marks, Juanita Perez, and John Lavic earned this honor by placing first in their respective categories at the Lorain County Academy for Science Fair on March 15. Marks competed in microbiology, Perez in chemistry, and Lavic in physical science. Ms. Kelly Wyatt, ELCHS physics teacher, is the club's sponsor.

###

91C

Quick Part

Create a Quick Part named PEROTTA for use in *91D Itinerary 1* and *Itinerary 3*. Use an 11 pt. font.

TRAVEL ITINERARY FOR LISA PEROTTA

222 Pine View Drive

Coraopolis, PA 15108

(412) 555-0120

perotta@fastnet.com

OBJECTIVE

• To prepare embedded column, bar, and pie charts using worksheet information.

97B

Charts

SS • Insert/Charts

1. Read the text.
2. Learn to construct column, bar, and pie charts.
3. Open *DF 97B WORKSHEET1* and create an embedded column chart.

Save as: 97B WORKSHEET1

4. Open *DF 97B WORKSHEET2* and create an embedded bar chart.

Save as: 97B WORKSHEET2

5. Open *DF 97B WORKSHEET3* and create an embedded pie chart.

Save as: 97B WORKSHEET3

Spreadsheet software provides options to create a variety of charts including **column, bar, line,** and **pie** charts. Usually, charts can be created as (1) an **embedded chart** that appears as an object in the worksheet with the chart data or (2) a **chart sheet** where the chart appears on a separate worksheet.

In this activity, you will create simple embedded column, bar, and pie charts using the default chart layout.

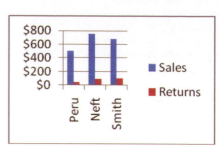

Column Chart

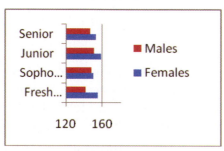

Bar Chart

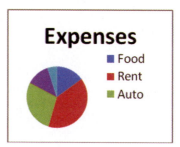

Pie Chart

97C

Change Chart Type

SS • Insert/Charts

1. Read the text.
2. Learn to change chart types.
3. Open *97B WORKSHEET1* and change the column chart to an embedded line chart.

Save as: 97C WORKSHEET1

4. Open *97B WORKSHEET2* and change the bar chart to an embedded area chart.

Save as: 97C WORKSHEET2

5. Open *97B WORKSHEET3* and change the pie chart to an embedded doughnut chart.

Save as: 97C WORKSHEET3

There are several types of charts that you can select. In addition to bar, column, and pie charts, there are line, area, scatter, and doughnut charts. The chart you initially select to display your data can be changed to other chart types to help you decide which type best presents your data.

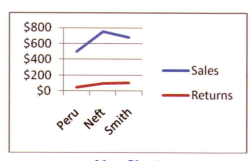

Line Chart

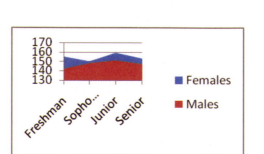

Area Chart

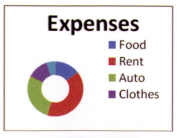

Doughnut Chart

Itineraries

Itinerary 1

1. Read the format guide for itineraries on p. 273.
2. Format the itinerary as a table. You decide format. Insert the PEROTTA Quick Part as directed.
3. Center the itinerary on the page.

Save as: 91D ITINERARY1

Itinerary 2 (Using Template)

1. Open *DF 91D ITINERARY2* (a template file).
2. Use the information for *91D* to prepare an itinerary. Use the template settings for font, line spacing, etc. Add to and delete from the template content as needed.

Save as: 91D ITINERARY2

Itinerary 3

1. Format using these features:
   a. Use small caps for rows 3 and 6.
   b. Horizontally center all lines.
   c. Use a 2" top margin.
2. Insert the PEROTTA Quick Part as directed.
3. You decide other formatting features.

Save as: 91D ITINERARY3

TRAVEL ITINERARY FOR LISA PEROTTA
222 Pine View Drive
Coraopolis, PA 15108
(412) 555-0120
perotta@fastnet.com
Pittsburgh, PA to Santa Ana, CA—April 18-22, 20--

Date	Time	Activity	Comments
Tuesday April 18	3:30 p.m. (ET)	Depart **Pittsburgh International Airport** (PIT) for Santa Ana, CA Airport (SNA) on **USEast Flight 146**. *Arrival time is 5:01 p.m. (PT).*	The flight is non-stop on an Airbus A319, and you are assigned seat 22E.
	5:30 p.m. (PT)	Reservation with **Star Car Rental** (714-555-0190). Return by 12 noon (PT) on April 22.	Confirmation No.: 33-345. Telephone: (714) 555-0130.
	6:00 p.m. (PT)	Reservations at the Hannah Hotel, 421 Race Avenue, Santa Ana for April 18 to April 22 for a single, non-smoking room at $145 plus tax. Telephone: (714) 490-1200.	Confirmation No.: 632A-04/18. Check-in after 6 p.m. is guaranteed. Check out by 11 a.m.
Saturday April 22	1:25 p.m. (PT)	Depart **Santa Ana Airport** (SNA) for Pittsburgh International Airport (PIT) on **USEast Flight 148**. *Arrival time is 8:52 p.m. (ET).*	The flight is non-stop on an Airbus A319, and you are assigned seat 16A.

Travel Agency Contact Information—Agent is Mary Grecco; 444 Grant Street, Pittsburgh, PA 15219; Telephone: (412) 555-0187; Fax: (412) 555-0188; E-mail: greccom@netway.com

---

TRAVEL ITINERARY FOR LISA PEROTTA
222 Pine View Drive
Coraopolis, PA 15108
(412) 555-0120
perotta@fastnet.com
Roundtrip Between Indianapolis, IN, and Shreveport, LA
August 18 and August 20, 20--

Flight	Departure	Arrival	Equipment
SEGMENT ONE--AUGUST 18--INDIANAPOLIS TO SHREVEPORT			
Amerifast #1233	8:38 a.m. Indianapolis	11:04 a.m. Houston, TX	Boeing 737-300
Amerifast #3482	1:10 p.m Houston, TX	2:15 p.m. shreveport	Aerospatiale ATR
SEGMENT TWO--AUGUST 20--SHREVEPORT TO INDIANAPOLIS			
Southern #3416	5:55 p.m. Shreveport	7:20 p.m. Memphis, TN	Saab-Fairchild 340
Southern #1706	8:30 p.m. Memphis, TN	9:48 p.m. Indianapolis	Boeing 737-300

Worksheets

Worksheet 1

1. Key the worksheet.
2. Enter a formula in column F (cells F1:F10) to calculate the individual batting averages (Hits/At Bats) to three decimal places.
3. In row 10 (cells B10:E10), use the SUM function to calculate the team totals.
4. In row 11 (cells B11:F11), use the MIN function to calculate the team lows.
5. In row 12 (cells B10:F10), use the MAX function to calculate the team highs.
6. Use Cell Styles as desired.
7. Adjust column 1 width to fit cell contents.
8. In cell A13, key **BASE-BALL TEAM STATIS-TICS**, using a 14-pt. font.

Save as: 96D WORKSHEET1

	A	B	C	D	E	F
1	PLAYER	AT BATS	HITS	HOMERS	RBI	AVG
2	Roberto Orlando	700	225	23	45	
3	Bill York	423	134	2	14	
4	Ernie Hack	590	176	15	35	
5	Joe Dimperio	805	256	33	102	
6	Jose Carlos	476	175	12	31	
7	Hector Avila	365	75	2	5	
8	George Barnes	402	99	16	45	
9	Harry Bell	575	158	17	55	
10	TOTAL					
11	MINIMUM					
12	MAXIMUM					

Worksheet 2

Using *96D WORKSHEET1*, insert the rows at the right after Harry Bell. Delete the Carlos row. Make format changes as desired.

Save as: 96D WORKSHEET2

PLAYER	AT BATS	HITS	HOMERS	RBI
Pat Ortega	25	8	1	2
Brett Peterson	45	14	3	7

Worksheet 3

1. Open *DF 96D WORKSHEET3*.
2. Use the information at the right to construct formulas or functions in the column or row indicated or perform stated action.

- Col E=col C amount *2
- Col F=col B *col C amounts
- Col G=col D *col E amounts
- Col H=col F+col G amounts

- Row 13: SUM(row 4:row 12)
- Clear the contents in cells C13 and E13.
- Row 14: AVERAGE(row 4:row 12); two decimal places

3. Adjust column widths.
4. In cell A16, key **RADIOL-OGY PAYROLL**.
5. In cell B21, calculate the days in the pay period.
6. Format worksheet as desired.

Save as: 96D WORKSHEET3

- To use purchase order and invoice templates to prepare business documents.
- To use card, certificate, and invitation templates to prepare personal documents.

92B

Business Documents

Purchase Order

1. Open *DF 92B PURCHASE ORDER1* (a template file).
2. Use the information at the right to prepare a purchase order.

Save as: 92B PURCHASE ORDER1

Your Company Info:	Vendor Info:
Name: Alpha Mortgage, Inc.	**Name:** Janet McDougal, Manager
Street: 1590 Clifton Avenue	**Company name:** Webster's Office Supply
City, State, ZIP: Columbus, OH 43202-1704	**Street:** 4646 West Broad Street
Phone: (614) 555-0001	**City, State, ZIP:** Columbus, OH 43228-1687
Fax: (614) 555-0002	**Phone:** (614) 555-0149
E-mail: purdir@alpha.com	**Customer ID:** W-1567
P.O. #: AQ-4931	
Date: July 25, 20--	

Ship To Info:

Name: Ned Thomas	**City, State, ZIP:** Columbus, OH 43202-1704
Company name: Alpha Mortgage, Inc.	**Phone:** (614) 555-0112
Street Address: 1590 Clifton Avenue	**Customer ID:** A-2612

Qty	Item #	Description	Unit Price	Line Total
6	F5-16	Computer Printers	119.95	719.70
24	E4-501	8" Book Display Stands	3.95	94.80
24	B5-12	Three-ring binders (3" burgundy)	3.45	82.80
			Subtotal	897.30
			Sales Tax	53.84
			Total	951.14

Invoice

1. Open *DF 92B INVOICE1* (a template file).
2. Use the information at the right to prepare an invoice.

Save as: 92B INVOICE1

Your company name: Park's Office Depot	To Info:
Street: 5704 Hollis Street	**Name:** Margaret Stiddard
City, State, ZIP: Oakland, CA 94608-2514	**Company name:** Century Publishing, Inc.
Phone: (415) 555-0101	**Street:** 1661 East 32nd Street
Fax: (415) 555-0102	**City, State, ZIP:** Long Beach, CA 90807-5291
E-mail: acctpay@parks.com	**Phone:** (462) 555-0150
Invoice #: AP-1659-T	**Customer ID:** C-12-98
Date: October 21, 20--	

Qty	Item #	Description	Unit Price	Line Total
1	PS2PR	Electronic Postage Scale	179.95	179.95
2	KP33-BG	Electronic Sharpener	24.95	49.90
5	N1-502	Double Pen Desk Set	57.00	285.00
10	P2-S52	Box of #10 Envelopes	7.05	70.50
			Subtotal	585.35
			Tax	40.98
			Shipping	10.45
			Total	636.78

96C

Functions

SS • Formulas/Function Library/
AutoSum or Date & Time

1. Read the text.
2. Learn about and how to enter functions.
3. Complete steps 1–8.

Save as: 96C WORKSHEET

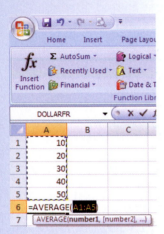

Spreadsheet software has built-in predefined formulas called functions. Functions have three parts: an equals sign to signal the beginning of the mathematical operation; the function name (SUM, COUNT, etc.) to identify the operation; and an argument (usually the cell range) that defines the numbers to be used in the calculation. Commonly used functions, their meaning, and examples are given in the chart below.

Function	Meaning	Examples
SUM	Adds the numbers in specified cells	=SUM(A1:A10) adds cells A1 through A10 =SUM(A1,A10) adds cells A1 and A10
AVERAGE	Averages all values in specified cells	=AVERAGE(A1:A10) averages cells A1 through A10 =AVERAGE(A1,A10) averages cells A1 and A10
COUNT	Counts the number of cells that contain numbers in specified cells	=COUNT(A1:A10) counts cells A1 through A10 =COUNT(A1,A10) counts cells A1 and A10
MIN	Identifies and prints the smallest number in specified cells	=MIN(A1:A10) finds smallest number in cells A1 through A10 =MIN(A1,A10) finds smallest number in cells A1 and A10
MAX	Identifies and prints the largest number in specified cells	=MAX(A1:A10) finds largest number in cells A1 through A10 =MAX(A1,A10) finds largest number in cells A1 and A10
DAYS360	Counts the number of days between two dates based on a 360-day year (twelve 30-day months)	=DAYS360(A1,A2) finds the number of days between A1 (the start date) and A2 (the end date)

1. Open *DF 96C WORKSHEET*.

2. Use the SUM function to add the numbers in cells A1:F1 and cells A2:F2, placing the answers in column G; add the numbers in cells A1:A6 and cells B1:B6, placing the answers in row 7.

3. Use the AVERAGE function to average the numbers in cells A3:F3 and cells A4:F4, placing the answers in column G; average the numbers in cells C1:C6 and cells D1:D6, placing the answers in row 7.

4. In cell G5, use the MIN function to find the lowest number in cells A5:F5; in cell E7, display the lowest number in cells E1:E6.

5. In cell G6, use the MAX function to find the highest number in cells A6:F6; in cell F7, display the highest number in cells F1:F6.

6. Format all numbers in cell range A1:G7 as Accounting with no decimal places.

7. In cell C8, find the number of days between the date in cell A8 and the date in cell B8 based on a 360-day year. Format as General.

8. Print gridlines and column/row headings.

Lesson 96 Worksheets with Formulas and Functions **297**

Personal Documents

Invitation

1. Open *DF 92C INVITA-TION1* (a template file).
2. Use the information at the right to prepare a party invitation.

Save as: 92C INVITATION1

Thank-You Card

1. Open *DF 92C THANKS1* (a template file).
2. Revise the message on the inside of the card, using the information at the right. Use that information to prepare a thank-you card. Key the president's name and title on a separate line(s) in the box.

Save as: 92C THANKS1

Certificate

1. Open *DF 92C CERTIFICATE1* (a template file).
2. Use the information at the right to prepare a certificate.

Save as: 92C CERTIFICATE1

Internet Activity

1. Read the text.
2. Access Nutrition.gov at http://www.school.cengage.com/keyboarding/c21key
3. Follow a link about nutrition that interests you.
4. Compose 2–3 ¶s describing what you learned from this site and print 1–2 pages from the site that relate to what you wrote.

Save as 92D INTERNET

Date: September 15, 20--

Time: 7:30 p.m.

Location: 527 Longview Drive

RSVP: (724) 555-0129

Your hosts: Don and Sharon

. . . with your generous support, the Woodward High School Biology Club was able to raise $1,515 to help pay for the medical costs of our member, Jane Wilhelm.

Marci Holmquist, President

School name: Wilson High School

Student name: Mary Killiany

Nutrition is the science that pertains to foods and the way our bodies use them. Our bodies use the nutrients in food for energy so all of our body functions can be maintained. The energy in food is measured in calories. One food calorie equals the amount of energy required to raise the temperature of 1,000 grams of water one degree Celsius.

The amount of energy needed varies from person to person. Have you ever wondered how much energy you need to maintain your weight, lose weight, or gain weight? How many carbohydrates, fats, proteins, minerals, and vitamins should you have each day to get the energy you need? Perhaps you can get the answers to these or other questions you have at the Nutrition.gov website.

Worksheet 3

1. Open *95F WORK-SHEET2*.
2. Complete steps 1–4, using Cell Styles and other format options.

Save as: **95F WORKSHEET3**

1. Insert the two rows below in the proper places.

2001	$147,800	7.03%	$789	18.4%
2006	$227,500	6.63%	$1,166	23.6%

2. Make formatting adjustments.
3. Change the font to 12-pt. Times New Roman, and bold and center all the headings.
4. Adjust column widths.

Lesson 96 WORKSHEETS WITH FORMULAS AND FUNCTIONS

OBJECTIVE

• To perform worksheet calculations using formulas and functions.

96B

Enter Formulas

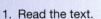

1. Read the text.
2. Learn how to enter formulas.
3. Complete steps 1 and 2.

Save as: **96B WORKSHEET**

Spreadsheet software can add, subtract, multiply, and divide numbers keyed into the cells. To perform calculations, activate the cell in which the results of the calculation are to appear and then enter a formula in the formula bar. Formulas typically begin with an equals sign (=).

The ss software interprets the formula, following this order of operations: (1) Calculations inside parentheses are performed first before those outside parentheses. (2) Multiplication and division are performed next in the order that they occur in the formula. (3) Addition and subtraction are performed last in their order of occurrence.

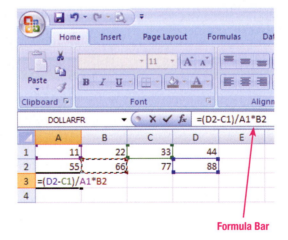

Formula Bar

1. Open *DF 96B WORKSHEET* and enter these formulas in the specified cell.

   a. A1+B1 in cell A3

   b. D2-C1+B2 in cell B4

   c. A1*B2+E1-D2 in cell C5

   d. C2*B1/C2+A2-B2 in cell D6

   e. (C1+D2)+(D1/A1)+E2 in cell E7

   f. (D1+A1*B2)-(E2/C2-B1*A1)+E1 in cell F8

   g. In cell G9, write and enter a formula to add cells C2, D1, and E2; divide that answer by cell B1; and then subtract cell D2.

2. Format the answers for steps 1a–1g above as Currency with two decimal places.

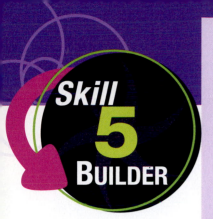

Technique: Keystroking Patterns

Key each line twice.

Adjacent key

1 are ire err her cash said riot lion soil join went wean news
2 pew art sort try tree post upon copy opera three maker waste
3 sat riot coil were renew forth trade power grope score owner

One hand

4 ad bar car deed ever feed hill jump look null noon poll upon
5 him joy age kiln noun loop moon bear casts deter edges facet
6 get are save taste versa wedge hilly imply phony union yummy

Balanced hand

7 go aid bid dish elan fury glen half idle jamb lend make name
8 oak pay hen quay rush such urus vial works yamen amble blame
9 cot duty goal envy focus handy ivory lapel oriel prowl queue

gwam 1' | 1 | 2 | 3 | 4 | 5 | 6 | 7 | 8 | 9 | 10 | 11 | 12 |

Timed Writings: Straight Copy

1. Key three 1' writings on each ¶; determine *gwam*. Count errors. If errors are two or fewer on any writing, goal is to increase speed by one or two words on next writing. If errors on any writing are more than 2, goal is control on next writing.

2. Key two 3' writings on ¶s 1–3 combined; determine *gwam* and count errors.

3. Key a 5' writing on ¶s 1–3 combined; determine *gwam* and count errors.

A all letters used MicroPace

	gwam	3'	5'

There are many opportunities for jobs in the physical | 4 | 2
fitness industry. The first step for many people is to be a | 8 | 5
fitness instructor in a fitness center or program. A genuine | 12 | 7
interest in the field as well as evidence of a personal com- | 16 | 9
mitment to good fitness are frequently the major things needed | 20 | 12
to land a job as a fitness instructor. | 22 | 13

Another opportunity in the fitness industry is to become | 26 | 16
a strength coach for an athletic team. This person works to | 30 | 18
make the team members fit and strong at the same time the | 34 | 21
athletic coach works to maximize their skills. A college | 38 | 23
degree in physical education or a related field is usually | 42 | 25
needed for this kind of job. | 44 | 26

Others in the fitness field often get a job in a big | 47 | 28
company or hospital as a fitness program director. These | 51 | 31
directors run programs that improve the fitness and overall | 55 | 33
health of the people who work in the hospital or company. | 59 | 36
Directors usually need a college degree and a lot of training | 63 | 38
in fitness skills, health promotion, and business. | 67 | 40

gwam 3' | 1 | 2 | 3 | 4 |
5' | 1 | 2 | 3 |

Format Cell Content

SS • Home/Font or Home/Styles/Cell Styles

1. Read the text.
2. Learn to format text.
3. Complete steps 1–10.

Save as: 95E WORKSHEET

The contents of cells (both numbers and text) can be formatted in much the same way as text is formatted using word processing software. A **font** and **font style, size, color** and **effect, underline, border, shading,** etc., can be selected and applied to a cell, a cell range, or one or more rows and/or columns.

If desired, you can use the Cell Styles feature to format cell content. A cell style is a defined collection of formats for font, font size, font color, font attributes, numeric formats, shading, borders, etc. You can use built-in cell styles or create new ones.

1. Open *DF 94C WORKSHEET*.
2. Format row 1 using Heading 1 Cell Style.
3. Format cells A2:A10 using Blue 60% Accent 1 Cell Style.
4. Format cell ranges B2:B10, D2:D10, and F2:F10 using Neutral Cell Style.
5. Format cell ranges C2:C10 and E2:E10 using Good Cell Style.
6. Bold and italicize cell range A2:A10.
7. Key **Wednesday** in cell D1.
8. Key [1] in superscript position to the right of *Hector* in cell C10.
9. Double underline *Bonita* in cell D7.
10. Adjust column width to fit contents and center-align all cells.

Worksheets

Worksheet 1

1. Key the worksheet.
2. Insert a row between rows 5 and 6; key **Lunch** in A6, **5** in B6, and **Cafeteria** in C6.
3. Format the worksheet using Cell Styles and other format options.
4. Adjust the column widths to fit the contents.
5. Center-align cells B3:B10.

Save as: 95F WORKSHEET1

Worksheet 2

1. Key the worksheet at the right.
2. Set column widths at 16 pts.
3. Center-align cells A1:E6.
4. Format using Cell Styles and other format options.

Save as: 95F WORKSHEET2

	A	B	C
1	TOM HALL'S SCHEDULE		
2	COURSE	PERIOD	ROOM
3	Applied Mathematics I	1	134-E
4	Consumer Economics	2	114-S
5	Sophomore English	3	210-E
6	Physical Education	4	Gym-N
7	Computer Applications	6	104-S
8	Principles of Technology	7	101-W
9	World Cultures	8	205-S

	A	B	C	D	E
1	YEAR	MEDIAN	LOAN	MONTHLY	% OF
2		PRICE	RATE	PAYMENT	INCOME
3	2002	$158,000	6.55%	$804	18.3%
4	2003	$180,200	5.74%	$840	19.1%
5	2004	$195,200	5.73%	$909	20.2%
6	2005	$219,000	5.91%	$1,040	21.8%
7	Source: *The World Almanac,* 2007.				

Communication & Math
SKILLS 9

SEMICOLON AND UNDERLINE USAGE

Internal Punctuation: Semicolon and Underline

1. Study each of the six rules.
   a. Key the *Learn* line beneath each rule, noting how the rule is applied.
   b. Key the *Apply* lines, using semicolons and underlines correctly.

Internal Punctuation: Semicolon

Rule 1: Use a semicolon to separate two or more independent clauses in a compound sentence when the conjunction is omitted.

Learn 1 Ms. Willis is a superb manager; she can really motivate workers.

Apply 2 His dad is a corporate lawyer his law degree is from Columbia.

Apply 3 Orin is at the Air Force Academy Margo is at the Naval Academy.

Rule 2: Use a semicolon to separate independent clauses when they are joined by a conjunctive adverb (*however, therefore, consequently*, etc.).

Learn 4 Patricia lives in Minneapolis; however, she works in St. Paul.

Apply 5 No discounts are available now consequently, I'll buy in July.

Apply 6 I work mornings therefore, I prefer an afternoon interview.

Rule 3: Use a semicolon to separate a series of phrases or clauses (especially if they contain commas) that are introduced by a colon.

Learn 7 Al spoke in these cities: Denver, CO; Erie, PA; and Troy, NY.

Apply 8 Overdue accounts follow: Ayn, 30 days. Lowe, 60 days. Shu, 90 days.

Apply 9 I paid these amounts: April, $375 May, $250 and June, $195.

Rule 4: Place the semicolon outside the closing quotation mark. (A period and a comma are placed inside the closing quotation mark.)

Learn 10 Miss Trent spoke about "leaders"; Mr. Sanyo, about "followers."

Apply 11 The coach said, "Do your very best" Paula said, "I'll try"

Apply 12 He said, "It's your own fault" she said, "With your help"

Internal Punctuation: Underline

Rule 5: Use an underline to indicate titles of books and names of magazines and newspapers. (Titles may be keyed in ALL CAPS or italic without the underline.)

Learn 13 The <u>World Almanac</u> lists <u>Reader's Digest</u> as the top seller.

Apply 14 I read the review of Runaway Jury in the New York Times.

Apply 15 He quoted from an article in Newsweek or the Chicago Sun-Times.

Rule 6: Use an underline to call attention to words or phrases (or use quotation marks). *Note:* Use a continuous underline (see line 13 above) unless each word is to be considered separately as shown below. Do not underline punctuation marks (commas, for example) between separately underlined words.

Learn 16 Students often use <u>then</u> for <u>than</u> and <u>its</u> for <u>it's</u>.

Apply 17 I had to select the correct word from their, there, and they're.

Apply 18 He emphasized that we should stand up, speak up, then sit down.

(continued on next page)

Format Numbers

SS
• Home/Number

1. Read the text at the right and the chart on the next page.
2. Learn to format numbers.
3. Complete steps 1–12 below.

When numbers are keyed into a worksheet, ss software formats them as General, the default format. If another format (Currency, Percentage, numbers with commas or a fixed number of decimal places, Date, etc.) is preferred, the number(s) can be formatted accordingly. The chart below provides information about commonly used number formats.

Buttons in the Number group or options in the Format Cells dialog (accessed via the Number dialog box launcher) can be used to make further changes to number formats or to select other number formats like those listed in the Special row in the chart below.

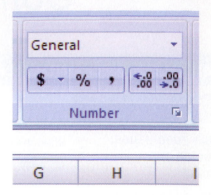

Format	Description	Example
General	The default; displays value as keyed	2010.503
Number	Displays value with a fixed number of decimal places	2010.50
Currency	Displays value with $, two default decimal places, and comma separators	$2,010.50
Accounting	Same as currency except $ sign and decimal point are aligned vertically in the column	$2,010.50
Short Date	Displays value in the xx/xx/xxxx date format	5/12/2007
Long Date	Displays value in the Day, Month xx, xxxx date format	Saturday, May 12, 2007
Date	Provides a list of date formats that can be selected for the day and month, with or without the year and time (accessed by selecting More Number Formats from the Number Format drop-down list).	5/12 May 12, 2007, etc.
Time	Displays value in the xx:xx:xx X.M. time format	10:04:33 P.M.
Percentage	Multiplies value in cell by 100 and displays value and two default decimal places with percent sign	201050.30%
Fraction	Displays a value in its equivalent fraction format	¼
Scientific	Display a value in exponential notation	1.23+02
Text	Displays the number as a left-aligned label	1234
Special	Provides a list to format number as ZIP Code, ZIP Code + 4, telephone number, or social security number	12345 12345-6789 (123) 456-7893 123-45-6789

1. Open *DF 95D WORKSHEET*.
2. Format cells A1:A7 using Number format, two decimal places, and no comma separators.
3. Format cells B1:B7 using Currency format with two decimal places.
4. Format cells C1:C7 using Accounting format with two decimal places.
5. Format cells D1:D7 using Percentage format with two decimal places.
6. Copy D1:D7 to E1:E7 and apply Percentage format with no decimal places.
7. Format cells A9:D9 using Special, Type: Phone Number.
8. Format cells A10:D10 using Special, Type: Social Security Number.
9. Format cells A11:D11 using Short Date format.
10. Format cells A12:D12 using Long Date format.
11. Format cells A13:D13 using Date, Type: March 14, 2001.
12. Adjust column widths to fit longest entry.

Save as: **95D WORKSHEET**

2. Key Proofread & Correct, using semicolons and underlines correctly.
   a. Check answers.
   b. Using the rule number(s) at the left of each line, study the rule relating to each error you made.
   c. Rekey each incorrect line, using semicolons and underlines correctly.

Save as: CS9-ACTIVITY1

ACTIVITY 2

Listening

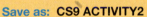

Complete as directed.

Save as: CS9 ACTIVITY2

ACTIVITY 3

Write to Learn

Complete as directed.

Save as: CS9 ACTIVITY3

ACTIVITY 4

Composing

1. Key the ¶, correcting errors.
2. Compose a second ¶, including the information below:
   - The level of your self-image: high, low, or in-between.
   - Factors that make your self-esteem what it is.
   - Factors you think could improve your self-esteem.
   - Plans you have to raise your self-esteem.
3. Proofread, revise, and correct.

Save as: CS9 ACTIVITY4

Proofread & Correct

Rules

1	1	Ms. Barbour is a great coach she is honest and fair.
1	2	Joe Chin won a scholastic award Bill Ott, an athletic one.
1	3	Maxine works from 4 to 8 p.m. she studies after 7:30 p.m.
3	4	The cities are as follows: Ames, IA Provo, UT and Waco, TX.
2	5	The play starts at 8 p.m. therefore, you should be ready by 7:30 p.m.
3	6	They hired 11 new workers in 2006 6, in 2007 and 8, in 2008.
1,4	7	Troy said, "You can do it" Janelle said, "You're kidding."
1,4	8	Rona sang "Colors of the Wind" Cory sang "Power of the Dream."
5	9	TV Guide ranks No. 2 according to Information Please Almanac.
6	10	"Why," she asked, "can't people use affect and effect properly?"

1. Open *DF CS9 ACTIVITY2*. It contains three mental math problems.
2. Each problem starts with a number, followed by several addition and subtraction steps. Key or handwrite the new answer after each step, *but* compute the answer mentally.
3. Record the last answer for each problem.
4. After the third problem, close the sound file.

1. Using word processing or voice recognition software, write a ¶ explaining how you insert a dot leader tab in a table of contents.
2. Write a second ¶ explaining how you add a light red shaded row in a table.

Narcissus, a mythical young man saw his image reflected in a pool of water fell in love with his image, and starved to death admiring himself. Unlike Narcissus, our self-esteem or self-image should come not threw mirror reflections but buy analysis of what we are—inside. Farther, it is dependent upon weather others who's opinions we value see us as strong or week, good or bad positive or negative. No one is perfect, of course; but those, who develop a positive self-image, wait the factors that affect others views of them and work to improve those factors. Its time to start.

Worksheet 3

1. Key worksheet at the right, using the Copy feature as much as possible.
2. Print with gridlines and row and column headings.

Save as: 94F WORKSHEET3

	A	B	C	D	E	F	G
1	NAME	QUIZ 1	QUIZ 2	QUIZ 3	QUIZ 4	QUIZ 5	QUIZ 6
2	JOE	90	90	90	100	90	90
3	MARY	90	90	90	80	90	90
4	PAUL	100	100	100	100	100	100
5	CARL	100	80	90	100	90	90
6	SUE	90	100	100	100	100	80
7	TWILA	90	90	90	80	80	80

Lesson 95   FORMATTING WORKSHEETS

OBJECTIVE

• To format cell contents, adjust column width, and insert/delete columns and rows.

95B

Adjust Column and Row Height and Width

SS • Home/Cells/Format

1. Read the text.
2. Learn to size columns and rows.
3. Complete steps 1–7.

You can narrow or widen column and/or row width and/or height to accommodate the contents of your worksheet cells. The column/row width/height can be changed by using the mouse, specifying the desired width/height in a dialog box, or AutoFit. Row height will change automatically as the font size is increased for one or more cells in that row.

1. Open *DF 94C WORKSHEET* and edit cell D1 so *Wednesday* is spelled out.
2. Change the size of the text in row 1 to 18 pt.
3. Resize the columns so each is as wide as its longest entry.
4. Change height of rows 2–10 to exactly 18 pts.

Save as: 95B WORKSHEET1

5. Open *DF 94B WORKSHEET* and designate that gridlines and column and row headings should print.
6. Adjust the width of each column so it is as wide as the longest entry in the column.
7. Change height of rows 1, 2, 4, 5, 7, and 8 to 26 pts.

Save as: 95B WORKSHEET2

95C

Insert and Delete Rows and Columns

SS • Home/Cells/Insert or Delete

1. Read the text.
2. Learn to insert/delete rows and columns.
3. Complete steps 1–9.

Save as: 95C WORKSHEET

Rows and columns can be inserted and deleted. One or more rows or columns can be inserted at a time. Columns may be added at the left or within worksheets; rows may be added at the top or within worksheets.

1. Open *DF 94C WORKSHEET* and insert two rows at the top.
2. Insert one column between Monday and Tuesday, one column between Tuesday and Wednesday, and two columns between Wednesday and Thursday. Delete the Friday column.
3. Key **Murphy** in cells D2 and I2; **Shandry** in cells C2, E2, and G2; and **Lawler** in cell H2.
4. Key **Monday** in C3; **Tuesday** in E3; **Wednesday** in F3:H3.
5. Insert a row between 2 p.m. and 3 p.m. and key **2:30 p.m.** in cell A11.
6. Insert three rows between 3 p.m. and 4 p.m.; key **3:15 p.m.** in A13, **3:30 p.m.** in A14, and **3:45 p.m.** in A15.
7. Clear contents of cells B3:I3.
8. Adjust all column widths to fit the cell contents.
9. Key **APPOINTMENT SCHEDULE** in cell A1.

Working with Simple Interest

1. Open *DF CS9 ACTIVITY5* and print the file.
2. Solve the problems as directed in the file.
3. Submit your answers.

 CAREER **Clusters**

ACTIVITY 9

You must complete Career Exploration Activities 1–3 before completing this activity.

1. Retrieve your Career folder and the information in it that relates to the career cluster that is your third choice.

2. Reflect on the skills and knowledge you have gained in the courses you have taken and the extracurricular activities in which you are involved that will be beneficial in the career you selected as your third choice. Then compose a paragraph or two describing the connection between what you have learned and/or your activities and this career. Print your file and then save it as Career9 and keep it open.

3. Exchange papers with a classmate and have the classmate offer suggestions for improving the content and correcting any errors he or she finds in your paragraph(s). Make the changes that you agree with and print a copy to turn in to your instructor. Save it as Career9 and close the file.

4. Return your folder to the storage area. When your instructor returns your paper, file it in your Career folder.

94D

Select a Range of Cells

1. Read the text.
2. Learn to select a range of cells.
3. Complete steps 1–3.

Save as: 94D WORKSHEET

A range of cells may be selected to perform an operation (move, copy, cut, clear, format, print, etc.) on more than one cell at a time. A range is identified by the cell in the upper-left corner and the cell in the lower-right corner, usually separated by a colon (for example, A5:C10). To select a range of cells, highlight the cell in one corner. Hold down the left mouse button and drag to the cell in the opposite corner. The number of rows and columns in the range is typically shown in the Name box as you drag the mouse. When you release the mouse button, the left-top cell is the active cell and its name appears in the Name box.

1. Open *DF 94C WORKSHEET*.
2. Select the range of cells B1:F1, and bold the text in the cells.
3. Select the range of cells A1:F6, and print the text in the cells.

94E

Cut, Copy, and Move

SS • Home/Clipboard/Cut, Copy, or Paste

1. Read the text.
2. Learn to cut, copy, and paste.
3. Complete steps 1–7.

Save as: 94E WORKSHEET

The contents of a cell or range of cells can be cut (moved) and copied to save time and improve accuracy. Select the cell or range of cells to be cut or copied; select the operation (*Cut* or *Copy*); select the cell (or first cell in the range) where the information is to be copied or moved; and finally, click Paste to copy or move the information.

1. Open *DF 94C WORKSHEET*.
2. Clear the contents of cells B6:F6.
3. Move the data in cells in B2:F3 to a range beginning in cell B11.
4. Copy the data in cells in A2:A10 to a range beginning in cell A11.
5. Copy the data in cells in A1:F1 to a range beginning in cell A20.
6. Copy C5 to C6, E5 to E6, B4 to D3, and F4 to F3.
7. Move D12 to B3, C12 to E3, B12 to D6, and F11 to B6.

94F

Worksheets

Worksheet 1

Key the worksheet and then print with gridlines and row and column headings.

Save as: 94F WORKSHEET1

Worksheet 2

Using *94F WORKSHEET1*, make the following changes:

1. Edit cell A1 to read: **BUDGET AND MONTHLY EXPENSES**
2. Move row 18 to row 3.
3. Copy column B to column F.
4. Clear rows 16 and 17.
5. Edit cell E15 to 95.
6. Copy B3 to C3:E3 and B4 to C4:E4.
7. Copy B10 to C10:E10.
8. Print without gridlines and row and column headings.

Save as: 94F WORKSHEET2

	A	B	C	D	E
1	BUDGET				
2	ITEM	BUDGET	JAN	FEB	MAR
3					
4	Rent	400			
5	Electric	44	46	43	42
6	Oil	110	115	90	72
7	Water	20		60	
8	Sewage	22			67
9	Telephone	35	32	38	45
10	Cable TV	35			
11	Insurance	80	120		95
12	Food	315	305	302	325
13	Clothing	75	60	90	55
14	Leisure	75	55	80	60
15	Personal	90	90	85	100
16	Auto Loan	425			
17	Auto Exp.	80	80	95	110
18	Savings	185			

Communicating
YOUR PERSPECTIVE | 4

The 190 independent states of the world are becoming increasingly inter-dependent. One reason that countries work together is to promote peace and to help people live better lives. The United Nations, originally an alliance of 51 countries, was formed for that reason at the end of World War II. The United Nations now includes nearly every country and has expanded its mission to include promoting human rights, improving the quality of human life, protecting the environment, and fostering development.

A second reason that countries depend on one another is economics. Internal changes like the collapse of the Soviet government in 1991 have lowered trade barriers and opened new markets. Growing economies in some developing countries have improved trade. Trade agreements and groups such as the North American Free Trade Agreement, the European Union, and the World Trade Organization have also increased commerce among nations.

Our culture is changed by each new invention. Imagine how the culture in the place you live was changed by the invention of the telephone. How was it changed by the invention of the television? You grandparents or great grand-parents may remember how some inventions that happened before your time changed their lives. In some countries many of the inventions that are readily available to you are not available.

What would you do for three months without the Internet? a CD player? How about electricity or an indoor toilet? A television station in the United Kingdom took a suburban London row house—and modern British family—back in time 100 years to answer questions like these.

The house was stripped of modern conveniences and restored to what it would have been like at the end of the nineteenth century. The Bowler family lived, for three months, exactly like a London family in 1900, and their experiences were the subject of a TV series.

Each person in the family—two parents and four children—had three outfits and three sets of underwear, all that a middle-class Victorian family could have afforded. Washing clothes took 12 hours, with the two younger girls staying home from school to help. No pizza or fast-food burgers were allowed. The family ate food that would have been served in Victorian England and brushed their teeth with hog-bristle brushes dipped in bicarbonate of soda. They had no telephones, but the mail arrived three times a day.

The Bowlers could ride bikes and swim. The children played cards, took old-time photographs, wrote and acted a play, and read. The pace of life slowed down. When the series was over, the Bowlers returned to modern life with a new appreciation of some of their things—and the knowledge that they could do fine without some things.

Global Awareness

ACTIVITIES

1. Form a group with three other students. Choose a country that you would like to learn more about.

2. Assign each person in the group to research one of the following topics: economics, geography, history, culture (how are the customs in this country different than those of your country), or recent events.

3. Outline, compose, format, and key your section of the report in bound report format.

4. Combine your section with the sections written by other members of your group. Prepare a references page and title page for the report.

Cultural Diversity

ACTIVITIES

1. Read the material at the left.

2. Key a list of items invented in the last 100 years that you use daily.

3. Compare lists as a class activity. Make a list that represents the best thinking of the group.

4. Talk to your parents and/or grandparents to see how many of the items on your list were invented during their lifetime. Ask them what it was like living without some of the items.

5. Try to spend one day without some of the items on your list. What was most difficult to live without? What was the easiest? Key a ¶ about your experiences. Be prepared to share your experience and what you learned from your relatives with the class.

Lesson 94   EDIT WORKSHEETS

OBJECTIVE

• To select a range of cells and edit, clear, copy, and move information in a worksheet.

94B

Select and Edit Cell Content

1. Read the text.
2. Learn to edit cell content.
3. Complete steps 1–4.

Save as: **94B WORKSHEET**

To select (activate) a cell, click the cell. The Edit feature enables you to change information already entered in a cell. To edit, double click the desired cell and then use the mouse, navigation keys, **Font** group buttons, etc., as you would with wp software to make the changes in the cell. When finished, tap ENTER or click the Enter button (checkmark) on the formula bar.

Alternatively, cell contents can be edited by clicking the desired cell once and then making the changes in the formula bar.

If the entire contents of a cell are to be changed, click the desired cell once and then enter the correct information. The new information will replace the old information.

1. Open *DF 94B WORKSHEET*.

2. **Edit** existing cell content to what is given below:

   A1: **charge**   B1: **care**   C1: **butler**   D1: **compost**
   A2: **whether**   B2: **flew**   C2: **except**   D2: **personal**

3. **Change** the cell contents to what is given below:

   A4: **54321**   B4: **20202**   C4: **four**   D4: **shirt**
   A5: **98765**   B5: **stars**   C5: **herd**   D5: **college**

4. Edit or change the cell contents to what is given below:

   A7: **4567**   B7: **Jeanne**   C7: **Kristine** D7: **8614**
   A8: **Dormont** B8: **Sandra**   C8: **Hutton**   D8: **Blue**

94C

Clear and Delete Cell Content and Format

SS • Home/Editing/Clear & Home/Cells/Delete

1. Read the text.
2. Learn to clear cell contents and formats.
3. Complete steps 1–5.

Save as: **94C WORKSHEET**

Most ss software has a Clear command that enables you to clear the contents *or* format of a cell *or both* without shifting the surrounding cells to replace the cell you cleared.

The Delete command (not the DELETE key) deletes the contents *and* format of the cell, and surrounding cells are shifted to replace the deleted cell.

1. Open *DF 94C WORKSHEET* and specify that gridlines and row and column headings are to be printed.

2. Make these changes without having surrounding cells shift:

   a. Clear contents in cells B2, C4, D6, E8, and F10.

   b. Clear format (bold) in cells B4, B6, D4, D8, F6, and F8.

   c. Clear contents and formats in cells B8, B10, D2, D5, F2, and F4.

3. Delete cell B3 and have cells C3 through F3 shift to the left.

4. Delete cell C5 and have cells C6 through C10 shift up.

5. Key **Susan** in cell F4.

What Is Spreadsheet Software?

Spreadsheet software. Spreadsheet software is a computer program used to record, report, and analyze information, especially information that relates to numbers. Many different types of employees in business, education, and government use spreadsheet software in a variety of ways. Spreadsheet software is especially useful when you need to make repetitive calculations accurately, quickly, and easily. It works equally well with simple and complex calculations.

Numbers can be added, subtracted, multiplied, and divided in a worksheet, and formulas are used to perform calculations quickly and accurately. Additionally, charts can be constructed to present the worksheet information graphically.

One big advantage of spreadsheet software is that when a number is changed, all related "answers" are automatically recalculated. For example, you can use spreadsheet software to quickly calculate how money saved today will grow at various interest rates over various periods of time by changing the values for the rate and time.

What Are Worksheets and Workbooks?

Worksheet. A worksheet is one spreadsheet computer file—it is where you enter information.

Workbook. A workbook contains one or more worksheets, usually related. When spreadsheet software is opened, a worksheet will appear on the screen. Other worksheets in the workbook appear as sheet tabs at the bottom of the screen. If needed, additional worksheets can be inserted into the workbook.

What Are the Basic Parts of a Worksheet?

Cells. A worksheet contains cells where information is keyed. The cells are arranged in rows and columns.

Columns. Columns run vertically in a worksheet. Each column has a heading (letters from A to Z, AA to AZ, etc.) running left to right across the worksheet.

Rows. Rows run horizontally in a worksheet. Each row has a heading (a number) running up and down the left side of the worksheet.

Refer to the illustration on the next page to learn the basic parts of a worksheet screen.

Lesson 93   WORKSHEETS

OBJECTIVE

• To enter data, move around in a worksheet, and print a worksheet.

93A–98A

Conditioning Practice
Key each line twice daily.

alphabet	1	Many plaques were just the right sizes for various duck exhibits.
fig/sym	2	The ski outfit costs $358.41 (20% off), and she has only $297.60.
speed	3	Claudia did lay the world map and rifle by the end of the mantle.

gwam	1'	1	2	3	4	5	6	7	8	9	10	11	12	13

View and Print Gridlines and Column and Row Headings

SS
• Page Layout/Sheet Options/Gridlines or Headings/View or Print

1. Read the text.
2. Learn to view or print (or not view or not print) gridlines and row and column headings.
3. Complete steps 1–2.

Save as: 93E WORKSHEET

Gridlines and row and column headings may or may not be viewed on the screen or printed on a worksheet. If the default setting is to *not view or print* gridlines and/or row and column headings, you must select the desired features if they are to be printed or viewed (see illustration below).

1. Open *DF 93E WORKSHEET* and use Print Preview to determine if the worksheet will be printed with gridlines and column/row headings.
2. Change the default setting as follows:
   a. If the worksheet *does not* have gridlines and column/row headings, specify that they print and then print the worksheet.
   b. If the worksheet *has* gridlines and column/row headings, specify that they not print and then print the worksheet.

If the default setting is to *view or print* gridlines and/or row and column headings, you must choose not to print or view any or all of these features if they are not to be printed.

Worksheets

Worksheet 1

1. Key the worksheet.
2. View and print the gridlines but not the headings.

Save as: 93F WORKSHEET1

	A	B	C	D	E	F
1	MONTH	JOHN	MARY	LUIZ	PEDRO	SARA
2	January	5567	6623	7359	4986	6902
3	February	2457	7654	3569	2093	6432
4	March	6930	3096	5792	4607	7908
5	April	4783	6212	4390	5934	5402
6	May	5042	5092	4500	9453	5321
7	June	5430	6098	5781	5009	6023

Worksheet 2

1. Key the worksheet while viewing the gridlines and headings.
2. Print without gridlines but with headings.

Save as: 93F WORKSHEET2

	A	B	C	D	E
1	PLAYER	SINGLES	DOUBLES	TRIPLES	HOMERS
2	Bosco	65	13	3	1
3	Elliot	54	14	8	4
4	Horan	58	19	10	5
5	Huang	64	22	9	14
6	Myers	52	21	4	9
7	Pasco	49	14	3	4
8	Cordero	25	7	2	2
9	Paulie	27	2	4	0

93B

Learn About Spreadsheets, Workbooks, and Worksheets

1. Read about spreadsheet software (ss) on p. 287.
2. Access your ss software and learn the parts of the program window and worksheet by referring to the illustration.
3. Open wp file *DF 93B LEARN* and complete the activity.

Save as: **93B LEARN**

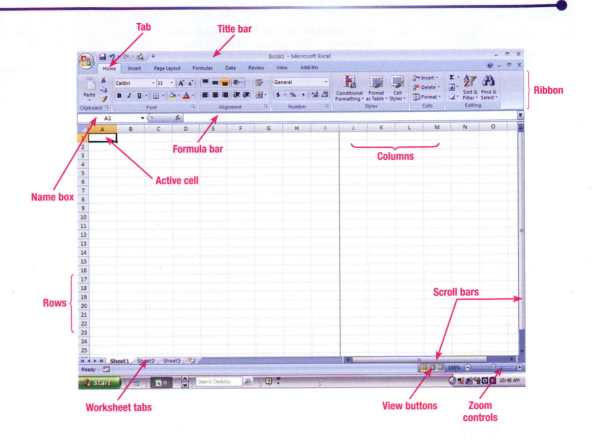

Title bar: Displays the current worksheet and application names.

Ribbon: Contains the commands and tools grouped by category on different tabs.

Tabs: Click to access tools and commands related to the name of the tab.

Name box: Identifies the active cell by the letter of the column and the number of the row that it intersects. The Name box also identifies the range of cells being selected.

Formula bar: Displays the contents of the active cell and is used to create or edit text or values. It may be expanded or contracted by clicking the double arrows at the right edge of the bar.

Active cell: Highlighted with a thick border; stores information that is entered while it is active.

Columns: Identified by **letters** that run horizontally.

Rows: Identified by **numbers** that run vertically.

Worksheet tabs: Identify the active worksheet in the workbook.

View buttons: Click to display the worksheet in Normal, Page Layout, or Page Break View.

Zoom controls: Click the buttons or move the slide to zoom in or out.

Scroll bars: Used to move horizontally or vertically within a worksheet.

Move Around in a Worksheet

1. Read the text and study the illustration below.
2. Learn how to move around in a worksheet.
3. Open a new blank worksheet and complete steps 1–9.

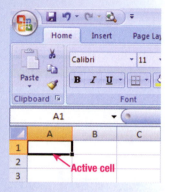

Active cell

Information is entered in the **active cell** of a worksheet. The active cell is the one with the thick border around it (see illustration at the left). Cells can be activated with the mouse, the arrow keys, or keyboard shortcuts.

To activate a cell with the mouse, move the pointer to the desired cell and click the mouse.

To move the active cell one or more cells to the left, right, up, or down, use the arrow keys.

To move the active cell from one spot to another quickly, use the keyboard shortcuts. For example, to make the first cell in a row active, tap HOME; to activate cell A1, press CTRL + HOME; to move the active cell up one page, tap PgUp, etc.

1. Use the mouse to make cell G4 active.
2. Use the mouse to make cell B24 active.
3. Use the mouse to make cell A12 active.
4. Use the arrow keys to make cell D11 active.
5. Use the arrow keys to make cell F30 active.
6. Use the arrow keys to make cell P30 active.
7. Use PgDn and arrow keys to make J100 active.
8. Use PgUp and the mouse to make L40 active.
9. Press CTRL + HOME to make cell A1 active.

Enter Labels and Values

1. Study the text at right and the illustration below.

Labels align at left   Values align at right

	A	B	C	D
1	text is		1234	
2	left		567	
3	aligned		89	
4				

2. Learn how to enter data and how to format numbers as labels.
3. Complete steps 1–4.

Save as: 93D WORKSHEET

Data entered into a cell is automatically assigned either a label or value status. Data that is to be used in calculations must be entered as a value, since labels cannot be used in calculations. When only numbers are entered into a cell, the value status is assigned and the data are right-aligned. When letters and/or symbols (with or without numbers) are entered into a cell, the label status is assigned and the data are left-aligned. Numbers that *will not be used* in calculations (such as house or room numbers, years, course or invoice numbers, etc.) can be entered as labels by preceding the cell entry with an apostrophe.

1. Key the following names as labels, each in a separate cell, in column A, beginning with row 1: **Mary**, **Henry**, **Pablo**, **Susan**, **Helen**, **John**, **James**, **Paul**, and **Sandy**.
2. Enter the following numbers as values, each in a separate cell, in row 15, beginning with column A: **135793**, **673455**, **439321**, **93888**, **569321**, **102938**, **547612**, **102938**, and **601925**.
3. Key the following invoice numbers as labels, each in a separate cell, in column I, beginning with row 11: **514620**, **687691**, and **432987**.
4. Check that data entered as labels are left-aligned and data entered as values are right-aligned.

Resources

© ARNE TRAUTMANN 2008/USED UNDER LICENSE FROM SHUTTERSTOCK.COM

Electronic Resume (Resume 1)

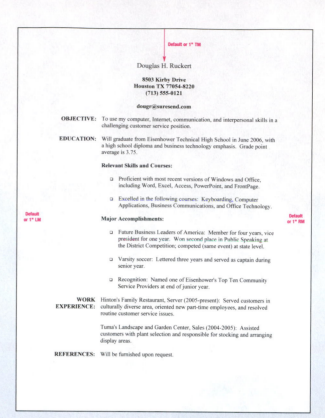

Print Resume (Resume 2)

Employment Application Form

Application for Employment			An Equal Opportunity Employer
Regency Insurance Company			

PERSONAL INFORMATION

NAME (LAST FIRST): *Ruckert, Douglas H.*	SOCIAL SECURITY NO. *368-56-1890*	CURRENT DATE *5/22/06*	PHONE NUMBER *(713) 555-0121*
ADDRESS (NUMBER, STREET, CITY, STATE, ZIP CODE): *8503 Kirby Dr., Houston, TX 77054-8220*		US CITIZEN ☒ YES ☐ NO	DATE YOU CAN START *6/10/06*
ARE YOU EMPLOYED NOW? ☒ YES ☐ NO	IF YES, MAY WE INQUIRE OF YOUR PRESENT EMPLOYER? ☒ YES ☐ NO	IF YES, GIVE NAME AND NUMBER OF PERSON TO CALL: *James Veloski, Manager (713) 555-0182*	
POSITION DESIRED *Customer Service*	SALARY DESIRED *Open*	STATE HOW YOU LEARNED OF POSITION *From Ms. Anne D. Salgado, Eisenhower Business Technology Instructor*	
HAVE YOU EVER BEEN CONVICTED OF A FELONY? ☐ YES ☒ NO IF YES, EXPLAIN			

EDUCATION

	NAME AND LOCATION OF SCHOOL	YEARS ATTENDED	DID YOU GRADUATE?	SUBJECTS STUDIED
COLLEGE				
HIGH SCHOOL	*Eisenhower Technical High School Houston, TX*	*2002 to 2006*	*Will graduate 06/06*	*Business Technology*
GRADE SCHOOL				
OTHER				

SUBJECTS OF SPECIAL STUDY/RESEARCH WORK OR SPECIAL TRAINING/SKILLS DIRECTLY RELATED TO POSITION DESIRED

Windows and Office Suite, including Word, Excel, Access, PowerPoint, and FrontPage

Office Procedures course with telephone training and interpersonal skills role playing

FORMER EMPLOYERS (LIST LAST POSITION FIRST)

FROM - TO (MTH & YEAR)	NAME AND ADDRESS	SALARY	POSITION	REASON FOR LEAVING
9/05 to present	*Hinton's Family Restaurant, 1204 S. Manfield Avenue, Houston, TX 77023-8846*	*$6.85/hr.*	*Server*	*Want full-time position in my field*
6/04 to 9/05	*Tuma's Landscape and Garden Center, 10155 East Freeway, Houston, TX 77029-6619*	*$5.75/hr.*	*Sales*	*Employed at Hinton's*

REFERENCES (LIST THREE PERSONS NOT RELATED TO YOU, WHOM YOU HAVE KNOWN AT LEAST ONE YEAR)

NAME	BUSINESS ADDRESS	PHONE NUMBER	TITLE	YEARS KNOWN
Ms. Anne D. Salgado	*Eisenhower Technical High School, 100 W. Cavalcade, Houston, TX 77009-8457*	*(713) 555-0134*	*Business Technology Instructor*	*Four*
Mr. James R. Veloski	*Hinton's Family Restaurant, 1204 S. Manfield Avenue, Houston, TX 77023-8846*	*(713) 555-0182*	*Manager*	*One*
Mrs. Helen T. Landis	*Tuma's Landscape and Garden Center, 10155 East Freeway, Houston, TX 77029-6619*	*(713) 555-0149*	*Owner*	*Three*

I UNDERSTAND THAT I SHALL NOT BECOME AN EMPLOYEE UNTIL I HAVE SIGNED AN EMPLOYMENT AGREEMENT WITH THE FINAL APPROVAL OF THE EMPLOYER AND THAT SUCH EMPLOYMENT WILL BE SUBJECT TO VERIFICATION OF PREVIOUS EMPLOYMENT DATA PROVIDED IN THIS APPLICATION, ANY RELATED DOCUMENTS, OR DATA SHEET. I KNOW THAT A REPORT MAY BE MADE THAT WILL INCLUDE INFORMATION CONCERNING ANY FACTOR THE EMPLOYER MIGHT FIND RELEVANT TO THE POSITION FOR WHICH I AM APPLYING, AND THAT I CAN MAKE A WRITTEN REQUEST FOR ADDITIONAL INFORMATION AS TO THE NATURE AND SCOPE OF THE REPORT IF ONE IS MADE.

Douglas H. Ruckert
SIGNATURE OF APPLICANT

Employment Application Letter

8503 Kirby Drive
Houston, TX 77054-8220

May 10, 2009

Ms. Jenna St. John
Personnel Director
Regency Insurance Company
219 West Greene Road
Houston, TX 77067-4219

Dear Ms. St. John:

Ms. Anne D. Salgado, my business technology instructor, informed me of the customer service position with your company that will be available June 15. She speaks very highly of your organization. After learning more about the position, I am confident that I am qualified and would like to be considered for the position.

Currently I am completing my senior year at Eisenhower Technical High School. All of my elective courses have been computer and business-related courses. I have completed the advanced computer application class where we integrated word processing, spreadsheet, database, presentation, and Web page documents by using the latest suite software. I have also taken an office technology course that included practice in using the telephone and applying interpersonal skills.

My work experience and school activities have given me the opportunity to work with people to achieve group goals. Participating in FBLA has given me an appreciation of the business world.

The opportunity to interview with you for this position will be greatly appreciated. You can call me at (713) 555-0121 or e-mail me at dougr@suresend.com to arrange an interview.

Sincerely,

Douglas H. Ruckert

Enclosure

Know Your Computer

The numbered parts are found on most computers. The location of some parts will vary.

1. **CPU (Central Processing Unit):** Internal operating unit or "brain" of computer.
2. **CD-ROM drive:** Reads data from and writes data to a CD.
3. **Monitor:** Displays text and graphics on a screen.
4. **Mouse:** Used to input commands.
5. **Keyboard:** An arrangement of letter, figure, symbol, control, function, and editing keys and a numeric keypad.

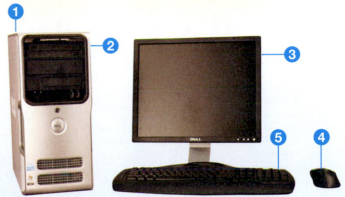

© FRANKSITEMAN.COM 2007

KEYBOARD ARRANGEMENT

© FRANKSITEMAN.COM 2007

1. **Alphanumeric keys:** Letters, numbers, and symbols.
2. **Numeric keypad:** Keys at the right side of the keyboard used to enter numeric copy and perform calculations.
3. **Function (F) keys:** Used to execute commands, sometimes with other keys. Commands vary with software.
4. **Arrow keys:** Move insertion point up, down, left, or right.

5. ESC **(Escape):** Closes a software menu or dialog box.
6. TAB: Moves the insertion point to a preset position.
7. CAPS LOCK: Used to make all capital letters.
8. SHIFT: Makes capital letters and symbols shown at tops of number keys.
9. CTRL **(Control):** With other key(s), executes commands. Commands may vary with software.

10. ALT **(Alternate):** With other key(s), executes commands. Commands may vary with software.
11. **Space Bar:** Inserts a space in text.
12. ENTER **(RETURN):** Moves insertion point to margin and down to next line. Also used to execute commands.
13. DELETE: Removes text to the right of insertion point.

14. NUM LOCK: Activates/deactivates numeric keypad.
15. INSERT: Activates insert or typeover.
16. BACKSPACE: Deletes text to the left of insertion point.

WOODWARD HIGH SCHOOL BIOLOGY CLUB

AGENDA

March 2, 20--

2:45 p.m. in Room 214

Type of Meeting: Regular meeting

Meeting Facilitator: Marcie Holmquist, President

Invitees: All members and faculty sponsor

1) Call to order

2) Roll call

3) Approval of minutes from last meeting

4) Unfinished business

    a) Finalize team assignments for candy sale that begins May 1

    b) Plan approved community service project to care for one mile of State Route 163

    c) Discuss recommendation that the Club help support an international student

5) New business

    a) Appoint nominating committee

    b) Discuss plans for regional leadership conference on April 12

    c) Discuss annual give-back gift to Woodward High

6) Adjournment

Agenda

TRAVEL ITINERARY FOR LISA PEROTTA
222 Pine View Drive
Coraopolis, PA 15108
(412) 555-1320
perotta@fastnet.com
Pittsburgh, PA to Santa Ana, CA—April 18-22, 20--

Date	Time	Activity	Comments
Tuesday April 18	3:30 p.m. (ET)	Depart **Pittsburgh International Airport** (PIT) for Santa Ana, CA Airport (SNA) on **USEast Flight 146**. *Arrival time is 5:01 p.m.(PT).*	The flight is non-stop on an Airbus A319, and you are assigned seat 22E.
	5:30 p.m. (PT)	Reservation with **Star Car Rental** (714-555-0190). Return by 12 noon (PT) on April 22.	Confirmation No.: 33-345. Telephone: 714-555-1030.
	6:00 p.m. (PT)	Reservations at the Hannah Hotel, 421 Race Avenue, Santa Ana for April 18 to April 22 for a single, non-smoking room at $145 plus tax. Telephone: 714-555-0200.	Confirmation No.: 632A-04/18. Check-in after 6 p.m. is guaranteed. Check out by 11 a.m.
Saturday April 22	1:25 p.m. (PT)	Depart **Santa Ana Airport** (SNA) for Pittsburgh International Airport (PIT) on **USEast Flight 148**. *Arrival time is 8:52 p.m. (ET).*	The flight is non-stop on an Airbus A319, and you are assigned seat 16A.
Travel Agency Contact Information—Agent is Mary Grecco; 444 Grant Street, Pittsburgh, PA 15219; Telephone: 412-555-0087; Fax: 412-555-0088; E-Mail: greccom@netway.com			

Itinerary

WOODWARD HIGH SCHOOL BIOLOGY CLUB

MEETING MINUTES

March 2, 20--

1. Call to order: President Marcie Holmquist called the Biology Club meeting to order at 2:45 p.m. on March 2, 20-- in Room 214.

2. Attendance: Jerry Finley, Secretary, recorded the attendance. All officers, 23 members, and the faculty sponsor were present.

3. Approval of minutes: The minutes were approved as read by Jerry Finley.

4. This unfinished business was acted upon:

    a. There will be five teams of four members each for the candy sale that begins on May 1. Team captains are Bruce Holstein, Anita Jones, Roberto Nuez, Ty Billops, and Gracie Walton. Each captain will select three members for his/her team.

    b. Bill Eaton will organize a team of volunteers for the Route 163 project. He will try to get at least 15 members to clean up the litter on May 15. The Chamber of Commerce will provide adult supervision, safety vests and gloves, road signs, and collection bags. The volunteers will begin at 9:15 a.m. and work until about 11:30 a.m. They are to meet at the Carriage Inn parking lot at 8:45 a.m.

    c. The officers recommended that the Club not provide financial support for an international student this coming year since all members who attend the Fall Regional Leadership Conference will need financial assistance for travel, food, and lodging. The officers' recommendation was approved.

5. This new business was discussed and acted upon:

    a. President Holmquist appointed the Nominating Committee (Sissy Erwin, Roberta Shaw, and Jim Vance), and they are to present a slate of officers at the April meeting.

    b. The membership approved officers to attend the Spring Regional Leadership Conference at Great Valley Resort and Conference Center on April 12. Their expenses for travel and meals will be reimbursed.

6. The next meeting is April 3 at 2:45 p.m. in Room 103. The meeting was adjourned at 3:35 p.m. by Marcie Holmquist.

Minutes submitted by Jerry Finley, Secretary

Meeting Minutes

News Release

For Release: Immediate
Contact: Heidi Zemack

    CLEVELAND, OH, May 25, 20--. Science teachers from school districts in six counties are eligible for this year's Teacher Excellence awards funded by The Society for Environmental Engineers.

    Nominations can be submitted through Friday, July 31, by students, parents, residents, and other educators. Nomination forms are available from the participating school districts or on the Society's website at http://www.tsee.webhost.com.

    An anonymous committee reviews the nominations and selects ten finalists. From that group, seven "teachers of distinction" and three award winners are selected. The top award winner receives $5,000, the second receives $2,500, and the third receives $1,500. Each teacher of distinction receives $500. The teachers of distinction and the award winners will be announced on September 5 at a dinner at the Cleveland Inn.

    School districts participating in the program include those in these counties: Cuyahoga, Lorain, Medina, Summit, Lake, and Geauga.

###

News Release

Windows® Tutorial

Microsoft® Windows® is an **operating system**, a program that manages all the other programs on a computer. Like other operating systems, *Windows®* provides a **graphical user interface** (**GUI**, pronounced "gooey") of **icons** (picture symbols) and **menus** (lists of commands).

Currently, the newest version of *Windows®* is called *Windows® Vista*. The version before *Vista* was called *Windows® XP*. This tutorial will show you how to use basic *Windows®* features. A few features may look, work, or be named slightly differently on your computer, depending on your operating system version and setup.

THE DESKTOP

After you turn on your computer and it has powered up, it will display the **desktop**, your main working area. The first illustration below shows a *Windows® Vista* desktop.[1] The second illustration shows the *Windows® XP* desktop. Your desktop will have many of the same features; but because the desktop is easy to customize, some items will be different.

Desktop icons   Sidebar

Start button   Quick Launch toolbar   Taskbar   Background   Gadget

***Windows® Vista* desktop**

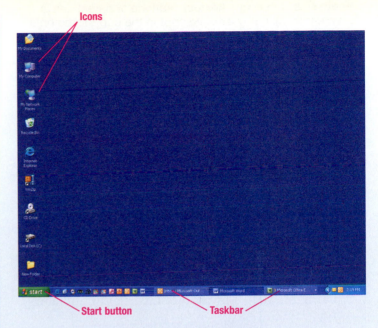

Icons

Start button   Taskbar

***Windows® XP* desktop**

On the desktop, you will see icons and a **taskbar** (a tool for opening programs and navigating on your computer). Icons provide an easy way to access programs and documents that you use frequently. Double-click an icon to open the program, document, or **folder** (storage place for files and other folders) that it represents. (If the single-click option is selected on your computer, you will find that you can click an icon once instead of double-clicking. For more information about this option, open the Help Index—click *Help and Support* on the Start menu—and key **single-click**.)

On the right side of the *Vista* desktop, the Sidebar contains small programs called gadgets. *Vista* ships with several interesting gadgets including a clock, a calculator, and news headlines. You can add or remove gadgets from the Sidebar, and additional gadgets are available online.

---

[1]Microsoft® and Windows® are registered trademarks of Microsoft Corporation in the United States and/or other countries.

REPORT DOCUMENTATION

Good report writing includes proof that the reported statements are sound. The process is called **documenting.**

Most school reports are documented in the body and in a list. A reference in the body shows the source of a quotation or paraphrase. A list shows all references alphabetically.

In the report body, references may be noted (1) in parentheses in the copy (textual citations or parenthetical documentation); (2) by a superscript in the copy, listed on a separate page (endnotes); or (3) by a superscript in the copy, listed at the bottom of the text page (footnotes). A list may contain only the sources noted in the body (REFERENCES or Works Cited) or include related materials (BIBLIOGRAPHY).

Two popular documenting styles are shown: *Century 21* and MLA (Modern Language Association).

Century 21

Examples are listed in this order: (1) textual citation, (2) endnote/footnote, and (3) References/Bibliography page.

Book, One Author

(Schaeffer, 1997, 1)

[1]Robert K. Schaeffer, *Understanding Globalization,* (Lanham, MD: Rowman & Littlefield Publishers, Inc., 1997), p. 1.

Schaeffer, Robert K. *Understanding Globalization* (Lanham, MD: Rowman & Littlefield Publishers, Inc., 1997).

Book, Two or Three Authors

(Prince and Jackson, 1997, 35)

[2]Nancy Prince and Jeanie Jackson, *Exploring Theater* (Minneapolis/St. Paul: West Publishing Company, 1997), p. 35.

Prince, Nancy, and Jeanie Jackson. *Exploring Theater.* Minneapolis/St. Paul: West Publishing Company, 1997.

Book, Four or More Authors

(Gwartney, et al., 2009, 9)

[3]James D. Gwartney, et al., *Economics: Private and Public Choice* (Cincinnati: South-Western, Cengage Learning, 2009), p. 9.

Gwartney, James D., et al. *Economics: Private and Public Choice.* Cincinnati: South-Western, Cengage Learning, 2009.

Encyclopedia or Reference Book

(*Encyclopedia Americana*, 2008, Vol. 25, p. 637)

[4]*Encyclopedia Americana*, Vol. 25 (Danbury, CT: Grolier Incorporated, 2008), p. 637.

Encyclopedia Americana, Vol. 25. "Statue of Liberty." Danbury, CT: Grolier Incorporated, 2008.

Journal or Magazine Article

(Harris, 1993, 755)

[5]Richard G. Harris, "Globalization, Trade, and Income," *Canadian Journal of Economics*, November 1993, p. 755.

Harris, Richard G. "Globalization, Trade, and Income." *Canadian Journal of Economics*, November 1993, 755–776.

Web Site

(Railton, 1999)

[6]Stephen Railton, "Your Mark Twain," http://www.etext.lib.virginia.edu/railton/sc_as_mt/yourmt13.html (September 24, 1999).

Railton, Stephen. "Your Mark Twain." http://www.etext.lib.virginia.edu/railton/sc_as_mt/yourmt13.html (24 September 1999).

Modern Language Association

Examples include reference (1) in parenthetical documentation and (2) on Works Cited page.

Book, One Author

(Schaeffer 1)

Schaeffer, Robert K. *Understanding Globalization.* Lanham, MD: Rowman & Littlefield, 1997.

Book, Two or Three Authors

(Prince and Jackson 35)

Prince, Nancy, and Jeanie Jackson. *Exploring Theater.* Minneapolis/St. Paul: West Publishing, 1997.

Book, Four or More Authors or Editors

(Gwartney et al. 9)

Gwartney, James D., et al. *Economics: Private and Public Choice.* Cincinnati: South-Western, Cengage Learning, 2009.

Encyclopedia or Reference Book

(*Encyclopedia Americana* 637)

Encyclopedia Americana. "Statue of Liberty." Danbury, CT: Grolier, 2008.

Journal or Magazine Article

(Harris 755)

Harris, Richard G. "Globalization, Trade, and Income," *Canadian Journal of Economics.* Nov. 1993: 755–776.

Web Site

(Railton)

Railton, Stephen. *Your Mark Twain Page.* (24 Sept. 1999) http://www.etext.lib.virginia.edu/railton/sc_as_mt/yourmt13.html.

COMMON DESKTOP ICONS

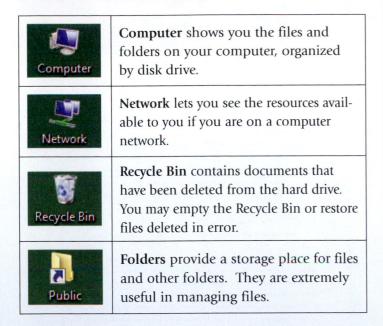 Computer	**Computer** shows you the files and folders on your computer, organized by disk drive.
Network	**Network** lets you see the resources available to you if you are on a computer network.
Recycle Bin	**Recycle Bin** contains documents that have been deleted from the hard drive. You may empty the Recycle Bin or restore files deleted in error.
Public	**Folders** provide a storage place for files and other folders. They are extremely useful in managing files.

The taskbar usually appears at the bottom of the screen. The standard *Windows®* taskbar consists of the Start button, a button for each program or document that you have open, and an icon for your computer's internal clock. Your taskbar may have additional icons.

The **Start button** opens the **Start menu**, shown on p. R6. Like a restaurant menu, a software menu offers you choices—commands you can choose. You can accomplish almost any task in *Windows®* from the Start menu.

The left pane of the Start menu shows the pinned program list and the Search results box. Pinned programs are programs that you use regularly, so *Vista* creates a shortcut to them. You can pin or unpin an icon by right-clicking it and then choosing *Pin to Start Menu* or *Remove from this list*. The right side of the Start menu contains shortcuts to many predefined folders. Quick access to features such as Search, Control Panel, and Help are available here. You can install updates, lock the computer, restart it, shut it down, or switch users from here as well.

> **Note:** The *Windows®* operating system requires a mouse or other pointing device. For help with using a mouse, see the Computer Concepts section at the front of this text.

START MENU

Pinned programs
Frequently used programs
Commonly used folders
Help
Switch users, log off, restart, shut down
Search
Install updates
Lock computer

BASIC FEATURES OF WINDOWS

Microsoft® Windows® displays folders, applications, and individual documents in **windows**. The basic features of all windows are the same.

The **title bar** lists the name of the window.

From the **Ribbon**, you can access all the commands available in the software. Ribbon names are similar in application programs that run under the *Microsoft® Windows®* operating system (as are icons and other features).

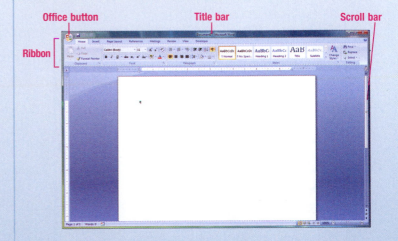

Office button
Title bar
Scroll bar
Ribbon

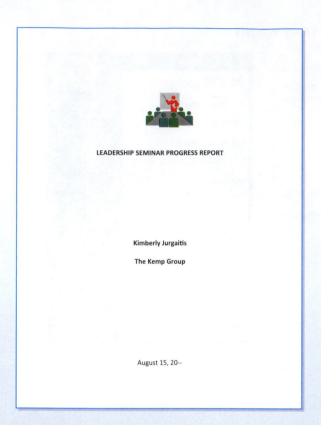

Title Page

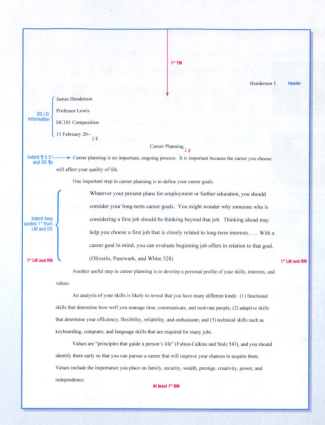

MLA Report, page 1

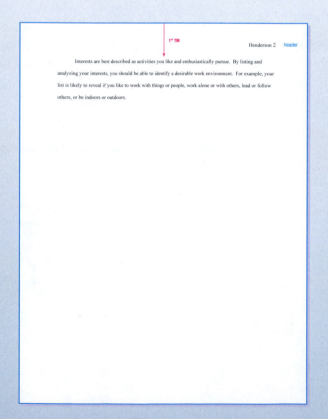

MLA Report, page 2

Works Cited Page for MLA Report

For more information on Windows programs, see the section on Computer Concepts at the front of this text.

If the window contains more material than you can see at once, **scroll bars** may appear at the right and/or bottom. Clicking a scroll bar arrow moves the document in small increments. Clicking the empty area of a scroll bar moves the document in larger increments. Dragging the bar portion of a scroll bar moves the document exactly as much and as fast as you want.

At the right end of the title or menu bar are the Minimize, Maximize, and Close buttons. Clicking the **Minimize button** reduces a window to a button on the taskbar. This is useful when you want to **multitask** (perform more than one task at a time) and do not want to exit a program. To restore the window, click the button on the taskbar.

Clicking the **Maximize button** enlarges a window to take up almost the entire screen. Many people like to maximize application documents to have more room to work.

Minimize   Maximize   Close   Restore

After you have maximized a window, the **Restore button** will replace the Maximize button. Clicking this button restores the window to its original size and location.

Clicking the **Close button** closes a window.

To move a window, drag it by the title bar. To resize a window, move the mouse pointer to a side or corner of the window. The pointer will become a double-headed arrow (↔). Drag until the window is the size you want.

When more than one window is displayed at a time, clicking a window makes it the **active window**—the one you can work in. The other window(s) will have a gray title bar to indicate that it is **inactive**.

DIALOG BOXES

A **dialog box** displays when software needs more information to carry out a task. The illustrations at the right show how to choose common dialog box options. Clicking OK executes the selected option; clicking Cancel closes the dialog box.

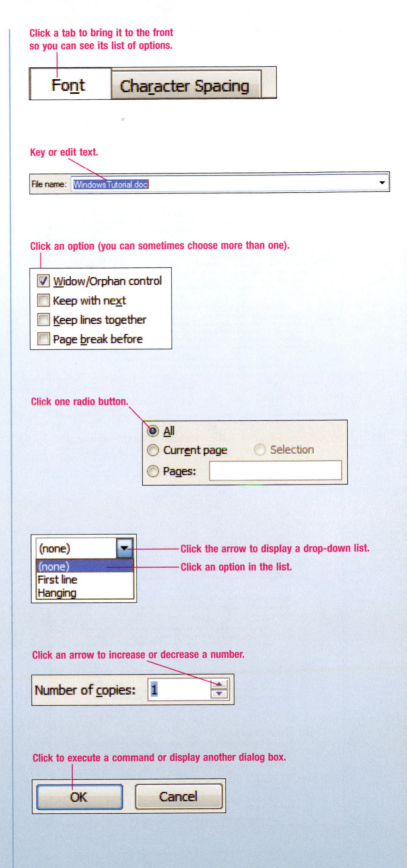

Click a tab to bring it to the front so you can see its list of options.

Key or edit text.

Click an option (you can sometimes choose more than one).

Click one radio button.

Click the arrow to display a drop-down list.

Click an option in the list.

Click an arrow to increase or decrease a number.

Click to execute a command or display another dialog box.

2" TM

Title # Samuel Clemens ("Mark Twain")

Report body Samuel Clemens was one of America's most renowned authors. The colorful life he led was the basis for his writing. Although his formal education ended when he was 12 years old with the death of his father, his varied career interests provided an informal education, not unlike many others of his generation. Clemens brings these rich experiences to life in his writing.

Textual citation Sam Clemens was recognized for his fiction as well as for his humor. It has been said that " . . . next to sunshine and fresh air Mark Twain's humor has done more for the welfare of mankind than any other agency" (Railton, "Your Mark Twain," 2003). By cleverly weaving fiction and humor, he developed many literary masterpieces. Some say his greatest masterpiece was "Mark Twain," a pen name (pseudonym)

Textual citation Clemens first used in the Nevada Territory in 1863. This fictitious name became a kind of mythic hero to the American public (Railton, "Sam Clemens as Mark Twain," 2003).

Mark Twain was brought to national prominence when his first book, *The Celebrated Jumping Frog of Calaveras County and other Sketches*, was published in 1867. The book was comprised of 27 sketches,

1" SM some of which had previously been published in newspapers. Some of his masterpieces that are among his most widely read books are *The Adventures of Tom Sawyer, Adventures of Huckleberry Finn*, and *The Prince and the Pauper*.

Side heading **The Adventures of Tom Sawyer**

The Adventures of Tom Sawyer was first published in 1876. Such characters as Tom Sawyer, Aunt Polly, Becky Thatcher, and Huck Finn have captured the attention of readers for generations. Boys and girls, young and old, enjoy Tom Sawyer's mischievousness. Who can forget how Tom shared the privilege of whitewashing Aunt Polly's fence? What child isn't fascinated by the episode of Tom and Becky lost in the cave?

Side heading **Adventures of Huckleberry Finn**

Adventures of Huckleberry Finn, the story about a boy who runs away from home and lives in the wild, has appealed to young and old alike since it was first published in 1885. Many of the characters included in *The Adventures of Tom Sawyer* surface again in *Huckleberry Finn*. The widow Douglas and the widow's sister, Miss Watson, provide formidable foes for Huckleberry despite their good intentions.

Children are able to live vicariously through Huck. What child hasn't dreamed of sneaking out of the house at night and running away to live a lifestyle of their own making?

About 1" BM

Unbound Report with Textual Citations, page 1

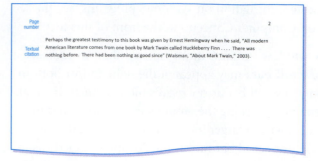

Page number 2

Textual citation Perhaps the greatest testimony to this book was given by Ernest Hemingway when he said, "All modern American literature comes from one book by Mark Twain called Huckleberry Finn . . . . There was nothing before. There had been nothing as good since" (Waisman, "About Mark Twain," 2003).

Unbound Report with Textual Citations, page 2

3

Title ## References

List of references Railton, Stephen. "Your Mark Twain." http://etext.lib.virginia.edu/railton/sc_as_mt/yourmt13.html (accessed October 23, 2007).

Railton, Stephen. "Sam Clemens as Mark Twain." http://etext.virginia.edu/railton/sc_as_mt/cathompg.html (accessed October 14, 2007).

Waisman, Michael. "About Mark Twain." http://www.geocities.com/swaisman/huckfinn.htm (accessed October 18, 2007).

References Page

2" TM

Title ## Globalization

Footnote Superscript We live in a time of worldwide change. What happens in one part of the world impacts people on the other side of the world. People around the world are influenced by common develop- ments.[1]

The term "globalization" is used to describe this phenomenon. According to Harris, the term is being used in a variety of contexts.[2] However, in the broadest context globalization can be de- fined as:

Long Quote . . . a process of interaction and integration among the people, companies, and govern- ments of different nations, a process driven by international trade and investment and aided by information technology. This process has effects on the environment, on cul- ture, on political systems, on economic development and prosperity, and on human physical well-being in societies around the world.[3]

1.5" LM The business world uses this term in a narrower context to refer to the production, distribution, and marketing of goods and services at an international level. Everyone is impacted by the con- tinued increase of globalization in a variety of ways. The types of food we eat, the kinds of clothes we wear, the variety of technologies we utilize, the modes of transportation available to us, and the types of jobs we pursue are directly linked to globalization. Globalization is changing the world we live in. **1.0" RM**

Side Heading **Causes of Globalization**

Harris indicates that there are three main factors contributing to globalization. These factors include:

Footnotes [1] Robert K. Schaeffer, *Understanding Globalization* (Lanham, MD: Rowman & Littlefield Publishers, Inc., 1977), p. 1.

[2] Richard G. Harris, "Globalization, Trade, and Income," *Canadian Journal of Economics*, November 1993, p. 755.

[3] "Globalization 101.org," http://www.globalization101.org/What_is_Globalization.html (accessed November 1, 2007).

Bound Report with Long Quotation and Footnotes

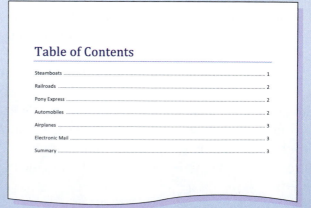

Table of Contents

Table of Contents

File Management in Windows®

Establishing a logical and easy-to-use file management system will help you organize files efficiently and find them quickly and easily. You can manage files on the desktop or in your file management program, *Windows Explorer*. This feature may be somewhat different on your computer, depending on your *Windows*® version and setup.

NAMING FILES AND FOLDERS

Good file organization begins with giving your files and folders names that are logical, relevant, and easy to understand. For example, you might create a folder for your English assignments called *English*. In this folder, you might have a journal that you add to each day (called *Journal*); monthly compositions (e.g., *Comp10-09, Comp3-10*); and occasional essays (such as *EssaySports* or *EssayEthics*). A system like this would make finding files simple.

UNDERSTANDING THE FILE SYSTEM

You can use *Windows Explorer* to see how files and folders are organized on your computer. *Windows Explorer* shows files and folders in a **hierarchical** or **tree** view. At the top is Desktop. Desktop contains all the items that appear on the desktop of your computer. The first item in Desktop, My Computer, contains the files and folders on your computer, organized by drives.

Drill 1: Navigate the File System

1. Click the *Start* button, point to *All Programs* (then to *Accessories*, if you have the *Windows® XP* operating system), and click *Windows Explorer*.
2. Click a plus sign beside a drive or folder to display below it a list of any folders that it contains. Click the minus sign to close the folder.
3. Click a folder (icon or name) in the left pane. All its contents (files and/or folders) will be displayed in the right pane.
4. Double-click a folder with a plus sign (double-click the icon or name, not the plus sign). Any folders inside the folder will be listed below, and all the contents of the folder (files and/or folders) will be displayed in the right pane.
5. Practice Steps 2–4 with other folders.

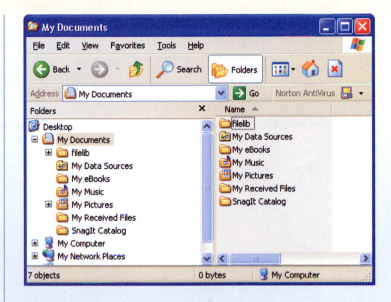

You do not have to be in *Windows Explorer* to locate a file or folder. You can use the My Computer icon on the desktop, the Search option on the Start menu, or the Address box (if available) in a drive or folder window.

CREATING FOLDERS

You will want to create folders to store files. You can do so using *Windows Explorer* or the desktop. In addition to putting files in your folders, you can create folders within folders if you need to.

- In *Windows Explorer*, click the drive or folder that will contain the new folder, click the *File* menu, point to *New*, and click *Folder*.
- On the desktop, double-click the drive or folder that will contain the new folder (if the drive or folder is not on the desktop, you can access it by double-clicking *My Computer*). In the window that opens, click the *File* menu, point to *New*, and click *Folder*. To create a folder on the desktop itself, right-click in a blank area of the desktop, point to *New*, and click *Folder*.

ENVELOPE GUIDES

Return Address

Use block style, SS, and Initial Caps or ALL CAPS. If not using the Envelopes feature, begin as near to the top and left edge of the envelope as possible—TM and LM about 0.25".

Receiver's Delivery Address

Use block style, SS, and Initial Caps. If desired, use ALL CAPS instead of initial caps and omit the punctuation. Place city name, two-letter state abbreviation, and ZIP Code +4 on last address line. One space precedes the ZIP Code.

If not using the Envelopes feature, tab over 2.5" for the small envelope and 4" for the large envelope. Insert hard returns to place the first line about 2" from the top.

Mailing Notations

Key mailing and addressee notations in ALL CAPS.

Key mailing notations, such as SPECIAL DELIVERY and REGISTERED, below the stamp and at least three lines above the envelope address.

Key addressee notations, such as HOLD FOR ARRIVAL or PERSONAL, a DS below the return address and about three spaces from the left edge of the envelope.

If an attention line is used, key it as the first line of the envelope address.

Standard Abbreviations

Use USPS standard abbreviations for states (see list below) and street suffix names, such as AVE and BLVD. Never abbreviate the name of a city or country.

International Addresses

Omit postal (ZIP) codes from the last line of addresses outside the U.S. Show only the name of the country on the last line. Examples:

```
Mr. Hiram Sanders
2121 Clearwater St.
Ottawa, Onkia  OB1
CANADA

Ms. Inge D. Fischer
Hartmannstrasse 7
4209 Bonn 5
FEDERAL REPUBLIC OF GERMANY
```

Folding Procedures

Small Envelopes (Nos. 6¾, 6¼)

1. With page face up, fold bottom up to 0.5" from top.
2. Fold right third to left.
3. Fold left third to 0.5" from last crease.
4. Insert last creased edge first.

Large Envelopes (Nos. 10, 9, 7¾)

1. With page face up, fold slightly less than one-third of sheet up toward top.
2. Fold down top of sheet to within 0.5" of bottom fold.
3. Insert last creased edge first.

Window Envelopes (Letter)

1. With page face down, top toward you, fold upper third down.
2. Fold lower third up so address is showing.
3. Insert sheet into envelope with last crease at bottom.
4. Check that address shows through window.

State and Territory Abbreviations

Alabama	AL	Illinois	IL	Nebraska	NE	South Carolina	SC
Alaska	AK	Indiana	IN	Nevada	NV	South Dakota	SD
Arizona	AZ	Iowa	IA	New Hampshire	NH	Tennessee	TN
Arkansas	AR	Kansas	KS	New Jersey	NJ	Texas	TX
California	CA	Kentucky	KY	New Mexico	NM	Utah	UT
Colorado	CO	Louisiana	LA	New York	NY	Vermont	VT
Connecticut	CT	Maine	ME	North Carolina	NC	Virgin Islands	VI
Delaware	DE	Maryland	MD	North Dakota	ND	Virginia	VA
District of Columbia	DC	Massachusetts	MA	Ohio	OH	Washington	WA
Florida	FL	Michigan	MI	Oklahoma	OK	West Virginia	WV
Georgia	GA	Minnesota	MN	Oregon	OR	Wisconsin	WI
Guam	GU	Mississippi	MS	Pennsylvania	PA	Wyoming	WY
Hawaii	HI	Missouri	MO	Puerto Rico	PR		
Idaho	ID	Montana	MT	Rhode Island	RI		

Drill 2: Create Folders

1. In the left pane of *Windows Explorer*, click *Desktop* (you may need to scroll up a little to find it).
2. Click the *File* menu, point to *New,* and click *Folder*. A new folder called *New Folder* will appear in both panes of the window. In the right pane, the name will be highlighted.
3. Key a name for the folder (**Century21**) and tap ENTER.
4. Minimize *Windows Explorer* (click the minus sign at the upper right of the window). Right-click in a blank area of the desktop, point to *New,* and click *Folder*.
5. Key a name for the folder (**Compositions**) and tap ENTER.

RENAMING FILES AND FOLDERS

You can rename a file or folder in one of these ways:

- In *Windows Explorer* or in a window opened by double-clicking a drive or folder, click the file or folder, choose *Rename* from the File menu, key the new name, and tap ENTER.
- Right-click the file or folder, choose *Rename*, key the new name, and tap ENTER.

In the filename *Lesson1.wpd*, the *wpd* **extension** indicates that the file is a *Corel® WordPerfect®* document. When you rename a file, be sure to include the extension that is recognized by your software program, or you may not be able to open the file.

Drill 3: Rename Folders

1. Right-click the *Century21* folder on the desktop, choose *Rename*, key **Keyboarding**, and tap ENTER.
2. Bring up *Windows Explorer*. If necessary, click the *Compositions* folder. Choose *Rename* from the File menu, key **English**, and tap ENTER.

MOVING AND COPYING FILES AND FOLDERS

You can move or copy files or folders in *Windows Explorer* or on the desktop.

- To move a file or folder, drag it to its new location.
- To copy a file or folder, hold down the CTRL key while dragging. The pointer icon will change to include a plus sign to indicate that you are copying.

Drag your file or folder on top of the destination drive or folder. You will know you are doing it correctly if the destination drive or folder is darkened, just as when you click it. If you are moving or copying to the open window for a drive or folder (as you will in Drill 5), drag the item anywhere inside the window.

When you are moving or copying files or folders, **selecting** (clicking) several items at once can save time.

- To select consecutive items, click the first item, hold down the SHIFT key, and click the last item.
- To select items in different places, hold down the CTRL key while you click each item.

Drill 4: Copy Files

1. In the left pane of *Windows Explorer*, locate and click the drive or folder from which you retrieve data files for this text. The files will be displayed in the right pane.
2. If necessary, scroll in the left pane until you can see the *English* folder.
3. Hold down CTRL and drag one of your data files to the *English* folder.
4. Select a block of data files to copy by selecting the first file and pressing SHIFT as you select the last file. Hold down CTRL and drag the files to the *English* folder.
5. Select several separate data files to copy from your student disk by pressing CTRL as you select each file. Hold down CTRL and drag these files to the *English* folder.
6. Close *Windows Explorer* (click the *X* at the upper right of the window).

Oops! We put keyboarding files in the *English* folder. Now we'll use the desktop to move the files to the *Keyboarding* folder.

Letter in Modified Block Format with Postscript

Approximately 2" TM or Center Vertically

Begin Dateline, Complimentary Close, Writer's name and title at same tab at or near the center.

Date — September 15, 20-- ↓1

Mailing notation — FACSIMILE ↓1

Attention line in letter address —
Attention Training and Development Department ↓1 **Remove space after paragraph—use Shift Enter to insert Line Break after first three lines.**
Science Technologies
3368 Bay Path Road
Miami, FL 33160-3368 ↓1

Salutation — Ladies and Gentlemen: ↓1

Subject line — MODIFIED BLOCK FORMAT ↓1

Body — This letter is arranged in modified block format. In this letter format the date and closing lines (complimentary close, name of the writer, and the writer's title) begin at or near horizontal center. In block format all letter parts begin at the left margin. ↓1

Default or 1.25" LM and RM — Mixed punctuation (a colon after the salutation and a comma after the complimentary close) is used in this example. Open punctuation (no mark after the salutation or complimentary close) may be used with the modified block format if you prefer. ↓1

The first line of each paragraph may be blocked as shown here or indented one-half inch. If paragraphs are indented, the optional subject line may be indented or centered. If paragraphs are blocked at the left margin, the subject line is blocked, too. ↓1

Complimentary close — Sincerely, ↓2

Writer / Writer's title —
Derek Alan ↓1 **Remove space after paragraph—use Shift Enter to insert Line Break after name.**
Manager ↓1

Reference initials — DA:xx ↓1

Enclosure notation — Enclosure ↓1

Copy notation — c Kimberly Rodriquez-Duarte ↓1

Postscript — A block format letter is enclosed so that you can compare the two formats. As you can see, either format presents an attractive appearance.

At least 1" BM

Memo with Special Features

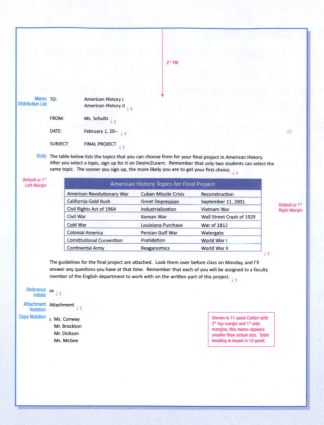

2" TM

Memo Distribution List —
TO: American History I
              American History II ↓1

FROM: Ms. Schultz ↓1

DATE: February 1, 20-- ↓1

SUBJECT: FINAL PROJECT ↓1

Body — The table below lists the topics that you can choose from for your final project in American History. After you select a topic, sign up for it on Desire2Learn. Remember that only two students can select the same topic. The sooner you sign up, the more likely you are to get your first choice. ↓1

Default or 1" Left Margin

American History Topics for Final Project		
American Revolutionary War	Cuban Missile Crisis	Reconstruction
California Gold Rush	Great Depression	September 11, 2001
Civil Rights Act of 1964	Industrialization	Vietnam War
Civil War	Korean War	Wall Street Crash of 1929
Cold War	Louisiana Purchase	War of 1812
Colonial America	Persian Gulf War	Watergate
Constitutional Convention	Prohibition	World War I
Continental Army	Reaganomics	World War II

Default or 1" Right Margin

The guidelines for the final project are attached. Look them over before class on Monday, and I'll answer any questions you have at that time. Remember that each of you will be assigned to a faculty member of the English department to work with on the written part of this project. ↓1

Reference Initials — xx ↓1

Attachment Notation — Attachment ↓1

Copy Notation —
c Ms. Conway
   Mr. Brockton
   Mr. Dickson
   Ms. McGee

Shown in 11-point Calibri with 2" top margin and 1" side margins, this memo appears smaller than actual size. Table heading is keyed in 13-point.

Letter in Modified Block Format with Paragraph Indentations and List

Current date

Ms. Valerie E. Lopez
207 Brainard Road
Hartford, CT 06114-2207

Dear Ms. Lopez:

SHADOWING AT BRIGHTON LIFE INSURANCE CO.

I'm pleased that you have chosen Brighton Life Insurance Co. as the place where you want to complete your shadow experience. I believe that you will learn a great deal about being an actuary by spending two days at Brighton with me.

To help you prepare for your visit, I have listed some of the things you should know about actuaries:

- Gather and analyze statistics to determine probabilities of death, sickness, injury, disability, unemployment, retirement, and property loss.

- Specialize in either life and health insurance or property and casualty insurance; or specialize in pension plans or employee benefits.

- Hold a bachelor's degree in mathematics or a business area, such as actuarial science, finance, or accounting.

- Possess excellent communication and interpersonal skills.

Also, I have enclosed actuarial career information published by the Society of Actuaries (life and health insurance), Casualty Actuarial Society (property and casualty insurance), and American Society of Pension Actuaries (pensions). These three associations offer actuaries professional certification through a series of examinations. We can discuss the societies and the importance of obtaining the professional designations they offer.

Letter (p. 2) Showing Second-Page Heading

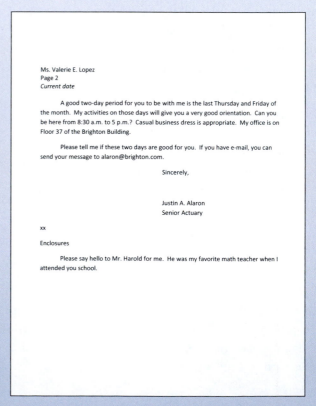

Ms. Valerie E. Lopez
Page 2
Current date

A good two-day period for you to be with me is the last Thursday and Friday of the month. My activities on those days will give you a very good orientation. Can you be here from 8:30 a.m. to 5 p.m.? Casual business dress is appropriate. My office is on Floor 37 of the Brighton Building.

Please tell me if these two days are good for you. If you have e-mail, you can send your message to alaron@brighton.com.

Sincerely,

Justin A. Alaron
Senior Actuary

xx

Enclosures

Please say hello to Mr. Harold for me. He was my favorite math teacher when I attended you school.

Drill 5: Move Files

1. Double-click the *English* folder on the desktop to open the *English* window. Move the window, if necessary (drag it by its title bar), so you can see the *Keyboarding* folder on the desktop.
2. Drag the first file from the *English* window to the *Keyboarding* folder.
3. Double-click the *Keyboarding* folder on the desktop to open the *Keyboarding* window. You need to be able to see all of the *English* window and at least part of the *Keyboarding* window. If you cannot, move the window(s) until you can see them.
4. If the *English* window has a gray title bar, select it to make it the **active window** (the window in which you can work).
5. Select a group of files in the *English* window and move them anywhere inside the *Keyboarding* window. Continue until all the files have been moved. Do not worry if the files are not neatly arranged. You will organize them in the next drill.
6. Close the *English* window.

ARRANGING FILES AND GETTING DATA

You can arrange the icons in a window by name, type, size, or date modified. You can also get details about files such as the file size and the date the file was last modified. In Drill 6, you will organize the file folders in the *Keyboarding* window, then look at details of these files.

Drill 6: Arrange Files and Get Data

1. In the *Keyboarding* window, click the *View* menu, point to *Arrange Icons by*, and select *Name*.
2. With no files selected, note (between the window and the taskbar) how many files the *Keyboarding* window contains and the total file size.
3. Select one file. What does the window tell you about it? What does it tell you about a group of selected files?
4. Select *Details* from the View menu. If necessary, scroll to see the information this view provides.
5. Click the *View* menu, point to *Arrange Icons by*, and choose *Modified*. When might this view be useful?

DELETING FILES AND FOLDERS

You can select and delete several files and folders at once, just as you selected several items to move or copy. If you delete a folder, you automatically delete any files and folders inside it. Here are two ways to delete a file or folder:

- In *Windows Explorer* or in a drive or folder window, select the file or folder and choose *Delete* from the File menu. Answer *Yes* to the question about sending the item to the Recycle Bin.
- Right-click the file or folder and choose *Delete*. Answer *Yes* to the question about sending the item to the Recycle Bin.

Drill 7: Delete Files

1. In the *Keyboarding* window, right-click a file, choose *Delete*, and answer *Yes* to send the file to the Recycle Bin.
2. Select several files in the *Keyboarding* window, choose *Delete* from the File menu, and answer *Yes* to send the files to the Recycle Bin.

RESTORING DELETED FILES AND FOLDERS

Assume that there was one file you didn't mean to delete from the *Keyboarding* window. When you delete a file or folder, the item goes to the Recycle Bin. You can restore files and folders from the Recycle Bin.

Drill 8: Restore a Deleted File

1. Minimize the *Keyboarding* window. Double-click the *Recycle Bin* icon on the desktop to open the Recycle Bin window.
2. Select one of the files you just deleted and click *Restore this item* (you may need to scroll down in the left pane to see the option). Or select *Restore* from the File menu, depending on your *Windows*® operating system version.
3. Close the Recycle Bin window. Click the *Keyboarding* button on the taskbar to bring up the *Keyboarding* window. It should contain the file you just restored.
4. Close the *Keyboarding* window and delete the *Keyboarding* and *English* folders from your desktop.

Format References

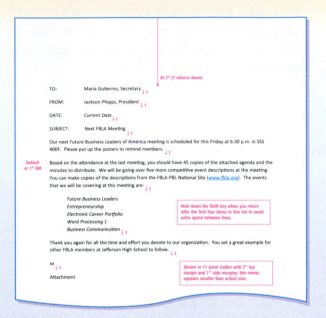

At 2" (3 returns down)

TO: Maria Gutierrez, Secretary ↓1

FROM: Jackson Phipps, President ↓1

DATE: *Current Date* ↓1

SUBJECT: Next FBLA Meeting ↓1

Our next Future Business Leaders of America meeting is scheduled for this Friday at 6:30 p.m. in SSS 400F. Please put up the posters to remind members.

Default or 1" SM

Based on the attendance at the last meeting, you should have 45 copies of the attached agenda and the minutes to distribute. We will be going over five more competitive event descriptions at the meeting. You can make copies of the descriptions from the FBLA-PBL National Site (www.fbla.org). The events that we will be covering at this meeting are: ↓1

> *Future Business Leaders*
> *Entrepreneurship*
> *Electronic Career Portfolio*
> *Word Processing 1*
> *Business Communication* ↓1

Hold down the Shift key when you return after the first four items in this list to avoid extra space between lines.

Thank you again for all the time and effort you devote to our organization. You set a great example for other FBLA members at Jefferson High School to follow. ↓1

xx ↓1

Attachment

Shown in 11-point Calibri with 2" top margin and 1" side margins, this memo appears smaller than actual size.

Interoffice Memo

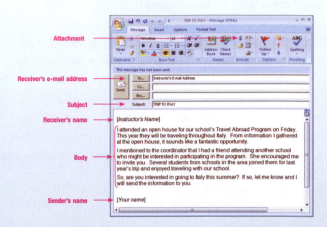

Attachment

Receiver's e-mail address → To... [Instructor's E-mail Address]

Subject → Subject: TRIP TO ITALY

Receiver's name → [*Instructor's Name*]

Body → I attended an open house for our school's Travel Abroad Program on Friday. This year they will be traveling throughout Italy. From information I gathered at the open house, it sounds like a fantastic opportunity.

I mentioned to the coordinator that I had a friend attending another school who might be interested in participating in the program. She encouraged me to invite you. Several students from schools in the area joined them for last year's trip and enjoyed traveling with our school.

So, are you interested in going to Italy this summer? If so, let me know and I will send the information to you.

Sender's name → [*Your name*]

E-mail Message

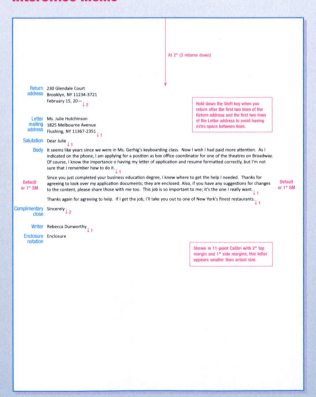

At 2" (3 returns down)

Return address   230 Glendale Court
Brooklyn, NY 11234-3721
February 15, 20— ↓2

Hold down the Shift key when you return after the first two lines of the Return address and the first two lines of the Letter address to avoid having extra space between lines.

Letter mailing address   Ms. Julie Hutchinson
1825 Melbourne Avenue
Flushing, NY 11367-2351 ↓1

Salutation   Dear Julie ↓1

Body   It seems like years since we were in Ms. Gerhig's keyboarding class. Now I wish I had paid more attention. As I indicated on the phone, I am applying for a position as box office coordinator for one of the theatres on Broadway. Of course, I know the importance o having my letter of application and resume formatted correctly, but I'm not sure that I remember how to do it.

Default or 1" SM   Since you just completed your business education degree, I knew where to get the help I needed. Thanks for agreeing to look over my application documents; they are enclosed. Also, if you have any suggestions for changes to the content, please share those with me too. This job is so important to me; it's the one I really want. ↓1   **Default or 1" SM**

Thanks again for agreeing to help. If I get the job, I'll take you out to one of New York's finest restaurants. ↓1

Complimentary close   Sincerely ↓2

Writer   Rebecca Dunworthy ↓1

Enclosure notation   Enclosure

Shown in 11-point Calibri with 2" top margin and 1" side margins, this letter appears smaller than actual size.

Personal-Business Letter in Block Format with Open Punctuation

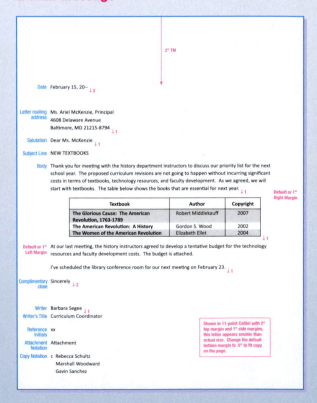

2" TM

Date   February 15, 20— ↓2

Letter mailing address   Ms. Ariel McKenzie, Principal
4608 Delaware Avenue
Baltimore, MD 21215-8794 ↓1

Salutation   Dear Ms. McKenzie ↓1

Subject Line   NEW TEXTBOOKS

Body   Thank you for meeting with the history department instructors to discuss our priority list for the next school year. The proposed curriculum revisions are not going to happen without incurring significant costs in terms of textbooks, technology resources, and faculty development. As we agreed, we will start with textbooks. The table below shows the books that are essential for next year.   **Default or 1" Right Margin**

Textbook	Author	Copyright
The Glorious Cause: The American Revolution, 1763-1789	Robert Middlekauff	2007
The American Revolution: A History	Gordon S. Wood	2002
The Women of the American Revolution	Elizabeth Eliet	2004

↓1

Default or 1" Left Margin   At our last meeting, the history instructors agreed to develop a tentative budget for the technology resources and faculty development costs. The budget is attached.

I've scheduled the library conference room for our next meeting on February 23. ↓1

Complimentary close   Sincerely ↓2

Writer   Barbara Segee ↓1
Writer's Title   Curriculum Coordinator

Reference Initials   xx

Attachment Notation   Attachment

Shown in 11-point Calibri with 2" top margin and 1" side margins, this letter appears smaller than actual size. Change the default bottom margin to .5" to fit copy on the page.

Copy Notation   c Rebecca Schultz
Marshall Woodward
Gavin Sanchez

Business Letter in Block Format with Special Features

Language and Writing References

CAPITALIZATION GUIDES

Capitalize

1. The first word of every sentence and complete quotation. Do not capitalize (a) fragments of quotations or (b) a quotation resumed within a sentence.

    Crazy Horse said, "I will return to you in stone."
    Gandhi's teaching inspired "nonviolent revolutions."
    "It is . . . fitting and proper," Lincoln said, "that we . . . do this."

2. The first word after a colon if that word begins a complete sentence.

    Remember: Keep the action in your fingers.
    These sizes were in stock: small, medium, and extra large.

3. First, last, and all other words in titles except articles, conjunctions, or prepositions of four or fewer letters.

    The Beak of the Finch
    Raleigh News and Observer
    "The Phantom of the Opera"

4. An official title when it precedes a name or when used elsewhere if it is a title of distinction.

    In what year did Juan Carlos become King of Spain?
    Masami Chou, our class president, met Senator Thurmond.

5. Personal titles and names of people and places.

    Did you see Mrs. Watts and Gloria while in Miami?

6. All proper nouns and their derivatives.

    Mexico   Mexican border   Uganda   Ugandan economy

7. Days of the week, months of the year, holidays, periods of history, and historic events.

    Friday   July   Labor Day
    Middle Ages   Vietnam War   Woodstock

8. Geographic regions, localities, and names.

    the East Coast   Upper Peninsula Michigan
    Ohio River   the Deep South

9. Street, avenue, company, etc., when used with a proper noun.

    Fifth Avenue   Wall Street   Monsanto Company

10. Names of organizations, clubs, and buildings.

    National Hockey League   Four-H Club
    Biltmore House   Omni Hotel

11. A noun preceding a figure except for common nouns, such as line, page, and sentence.

    Review Rules 1 to 18 in Chapter 5, page 149.

12. Seasons of the year only when they are personified.

    the soft kiss of Spring   the icy fingers of Winter

NUMBER EXPRESSION GUIDES

Use words for

1. Numbers from one to ten except when used with numbers above ten, which are keyed as figures. Common business practice is to use figures for all numbers except those that begin a sentence.

    Did you visit all eight Web sites, or only four?
    Buy 15 textbooks and 8 workbooks.

2. A number beginning a sentence.

    Twelve of the new shrubs have died; 48 are doing well.

3. The shorter of two numbers used together.

    fifty 33-cent stamps   150 twenty-cent stamps

4. Isolated fractions or indefinite numbers in a sentence.

    Nearly seventy members voted, which is almost one-fourth.

5. Names of small-numbered streets and avenues (ten and under).

    The theater is at the corner of Third Avenue and 54th Street.

Use figures for

1. Dates and times except in very formal writing.

    The flight will arrive at 9:48 a.m. on March 14.
    The ceremony took place the fifth of June at eleven o'clock.

2. A series of fractions and/or mixed numbers.

    Key 1/4, 1/2, 5/6, and 7 3/4.

3. Numbers following nouns.

    Case 1849 is reviewed in Volume 5, page 9.

4. Measures, weights, and dimensions.

    6 feet 9 inches   7 pounds 4 ounces
    8.5 inches by 11 inches

5. Definite numbers used with percent (%), but use words for indefinite percentages.

    The late fee is 15 percent of the overdue payment.
    The brothers put in nearly fifty percent of the start-up capital.

6. House numbers except house number *One*.

    My home is at 8 Weber Drive; my office is at One Weber Plaza.

7. Amounts of money except when spelled for emphasis (as in legal documents). Even amounts are keyed without the decimal. Large amounts (a million or more) are keyed as shown.

    $17.75   75 cents $775
    seven hundred dollars ($700)
    $7,500 $7 million $7.2 million $7 billion

Proofreaders' Marks

Proofreaders' marks are used to mark corrections in keyed or printed text that contains problems and/or errors. As a keyboard user, you should be able to read these marks accurately when revising or editing a rough draft. You also should be able to write these symbols to correct the rough drafts that you and others key. The most-used proofreaders' marks are shown below.

Mark	Meaning
‖	Align copy; also, make these items parallel
¶	Begin a new paragraph
Cap ≡	Capitalize
◡	Close up
ℓ	Delete
<#	Delete space
No¶	Do not begin a new paragraph
∧	Insert
⌄	Insert comma
⊙	Insert period
∨∨	Insert quotation marks
#>	Insert space
∨	Insert apostrophe
stet	Let it stand; ignore correction
lc	Lowercase
⌐⌐	Move down; lower
⌐	Move left
⌐	Move right
⌐	Move up; raise
sp	Spell out
∩ tr	Transpose
—	Underline or italic

E-MAIL FORMAT AND SOFTWARE FEATURES

E-mail format varies slightly, depending on the software used to create and send it.

E-mail Heading
Most e-mail software includes these features:

Attachment: line for attaching files to an e-mail message

Bcc: line for sending copy of a message to someone without the receiver knowing

Cc: line for sending copy of a message to additional receivers

Date: month, day, and year message is sent; often includes precise time of transmittal; usually is inserted automatically

From: name and/or e-mail address of sender; usually is inserted automatically

Subject: line for very brief description of message content

To: line for name and/or e-mail address of receiver

E-mail Body
The message box on the e-mail screen may contain these elements or only the message paragraphs (SS with DS between paragraphs).
- Informal salutation and/or receiver's name (a DS above the message)
- Informal closing (e.g., "Regards," "Thanks") and/or the sender's name (a DS below the message). Additional identification (e.g., telephone number) may be included.

Special E-mail Features
Several e-mail features make communicating through e-mail fast and efficient.

Address list/book: collection of names and e-mail addresses of correspondents from which an address can be entered on the To: line by selecting it, instead of keying it.

Distribution list: series of names and/or e-mail addresses, separated by commas, on the To: line.

Forward: feature that allows an e-mail user to send a copy of a received e-mail message to others.

Recipient list (Group): feature that allows an e-mail user to send mail to a group of recipients by selecting the name of the group (e.g., All Teachers).

Reply: feature used to respond to an incoming message.

Reply all: feature used to respond to all copy recipients as well as the sender of an incoming message.

Signature: feature for storing and inserting the closing lines of messages (e.g., informal closing, sender's name, telephone number, address, fax number).

PUNCTUATION GUIDES

Use an apostrophe

1. As a symbol for *feet* in charts, forms, and tables or as a symbol for *minutes*. (The quotation mark may be used as a symbol for *seconds* and *inches*.)

   12' x 16'   3' 54"   8' 6" x 10' 8"

2. As a symbol to indicate the omission of letters or figures (as in contractions).

   can't   do's and don'ts   Class of '02

3. To form the plural of most figures, letters, and words used as words rather than for their meaning: Add the apostrophe and *s*. In market quotations and decades, form the plural of figures by the addition of *s* only.

   7's   ten's   ABC's   Century 4s   1960s

4. To show possession: Add the apostrophe and *s* to (a) a singular noun and (b) a plural noun that does not end in *s*.

   a woman's watch   men's shoes   girl's bicycle

   Add the apostrophe and *s* to a proper name of one syllable that ends in *s*.

   Bess's Cafeteria   James's hat   Jones's bill

   Add the apostrophe only after (a) plural nouns ending in *s* and (b) a proper name of more than one syllable that ends in *s* or *z*.

   girls' camp   Adams' home   Martinez' report

   Add the apostrophe (and *s*) after the last noun in a series to indicate joint or common possession by two or more persons; however, add the possessive to each of the nouns to show separate possession by two or more persons.

   Lewis and Clark's expedition
   the secretary's and the treasurer's reports

Use a colon

1. To introduce a listing.

   These poets are my favorites: Shelley, Keats, and Frost.

2. To introduce a question or a long direct quotation.

   The question is this: Did you study for the test?

3. Between hours and minutes expressed in figures.

   10:15 a.m.   4:30 p.m.   12:00 midnight

Use a comma (or commas)

1. After (a) introductory phrases or clauses and (b) words in a series.

   When you finish keying the report, please give it to Mr. Kent.
   We will play the Mets, Expos, and Cubs in our next home stand.

2. To set off short direct quotations.

   Mrs. Ramirez replied, "No, the report is not finished."

3. Before and after (a) appositives—words that come together and refer to the same person, thing, or idea—and (b) words of direct address.

   Colette, the assistant manager, will chair the next meeting.
   Please call me, Erika, if I can be of further assistance.

4. To set off nonrestrictive clauses (not necessary to meaning of sentence), but not restrictive clauses (necessary to meaning).

   Your report, which deals with that issue, raised many questions.
   The man who organized the conference is my teacher.

5. To separate the day from the year in dates and the city from the state in addresses.

   July 4, 2005   St. Joseph, Missouri   Moose Point, AK

6. To separate two or more parallel adjectives (adjectives that modify the noun separately and that could be separated by the word *and* instead of the comma).

   The big, loud bully was ejected after he pushed the coach.
   The big, powerful car zoomed past the cheering crowd.
   Cynthia played a black lacquered grand piano at her concert.
   A small red fox squeezed through the fence to avoid the hounds.

7. To separate (a) unrelated groups of figures that occur together and (b) whole numbers into groups of three digits each. (Omit commas from years and page, policy, room, serial, and telephone numbers.)

   By the year 2005, 1,200 more local students will be enrolled.
   The supplies listed on Invoice #274068 are for Room 1953.

Use a dash

Create a dash by keying two hyphens or one em-dash.

1. For emphasis.

   The skater—in a clown costume—dazzled with fancy footwork.

2. To indicate a change of thought.

   We may tour the Orient—but I'm getting ahead of my story.

3. To emphasize the name of an author when it follows a direct quotation.

   "All the world's a stage. . . ."—Shakespeare

4. To set off expressions that break off or interrupt speech.

   "Jay, don't get too close to the—." I spoke too late.
   "Today—er—uh," the anxious presenter began.

CONFUSING WORDS

accept (vb) to receive; to approve; to take

except (prep/vb) with the exclusion of; leave out

affect (vb) to produce a change in or have an effect on

effect (n) result; something produced by an agent or a cause

buy (n/vb) to purchase; to acquire; a bargain

by (prep/adv) close to; via; according to; close at hand

choose (vb) to select; to decide

chose (vb) past tense of "choose"

cite (vb) use as support; commend; summon

sight (n/vb) ability to see; something seen; a device to improve aim

site (n) location

complement (n) something that fills, completes, or makes perfect

compliment (n/vb) a formal expression of respect or admiration; to pay respect or admiration

do (vb) to bring about; to carry out

due (adj) owed or owing as a debt; having reached the date for payment

farther (adv) greater distance

further (adv) additional; in greater depth; to greater extent

for (prep/conj) indicates purpose on behalf of; because of

four (n) two plus two in number

hear (vb) to gain knowledge of by the ear

here (adv) in or at this place; at or on this point; in this case

hole (n) opening in or through something

whole (adj/n) having all its proper parts; a complete amount

hour (n) the 24th part of a day; a particular time

our (adj) possessive form of "we"; of or relating to us

knew (vb) past tense of "know"; understood; recognized truth or nature of

new (adj) novel; fresh; existing for a short time

know (vb) to be aware of the truth or nature of; to have an understanding of

no (adv/adj/n) not in any respect or degree; not so; indicates denial or refusal

lessen (vb) to cause to decrease; to make less

lesson (n) something to be learned; period of instruction; a class period

lie (n/vb) an untrue or inaccurate statement; to tell an untrue story; to rest or recline

lye (n) a strong alkaline substance or solution

one (adj/pron) a single unit or thing

won (vb) past tense of win; gained a victory as in a game or contest; got by effort or work

passed (vb) past tense of "pass"; already occurred; moved by; gave an item to someone

past (adv/adj/prep/n) gone or elapsed; time gone by

personal (adj) of, relating to, or affecting a person; done in person

personnel (n) a staff or persons making up a workforce in an organization

plain (adj/n) with little decoration; a large flat area of land

plane (n) an airplane or hydroplane

pole (n) a long, slender, rounded piece of wood or other material

poll (n) a survey of people to analyze public opinion

principal (n/adj) a chief or leader; capital (money) amount placed at interest; of or relating to the most important thing or matter or persons

principle (n) a central rule, law, or doctrine

right (adj) factual; true; correct

rite (n) customary form of ceremony; ritual

write (v) to form letters or symbols; to compose and set down in words, numbers, or symbols

some (n/adv) unknown or unspecified unit or thing; to a degree or extent

sum (n/vb) total; to find a total; to summarize

stationary (adj) fixed in a position, course, or mode; unchanging in condition

stationery (n) paper and envelopes used for processing personal and business documents

than (conj/prep) used in comparisons to show differences between items

then (n/adv) that time; at that time; next

to (prep/adj) indicates action, relation, distance, direction

too (adv) besides; also; to excessive degree

two (n/adj) one plus one

vary (vb) change; make different; diverge

very (adv/adj) real; mere; truly; to high degree

waist (n) narrowed part of the body between chest and hips; middle of something

waste (n/vb/adj) useless things; rubbish; spend or use carelessly; nonproductive

weak (adj) lacking strength, skill, or proficiency

week (n) a series of seven days; Monday through Sunday

wear (vb/n) to bear or have on the person; diminish by use; clothing

where (adv/conj/n) at, in, or to what degree; what place, source, or cause

your (adj) of or relating to you as possessor

you're (contraction) you are

PUNCTUATION GUIDES (continued)

Use an exclamation point

1. After emphatic interjections.
   Wow!   Hey there!   What a day!

2. After sentences that are clearly exclamatory.
   "I won't go!" she said with determination.
   How good it was to see you in New Orleans last week!

Use a hyphen

1. To join parts of compound words expressing the numbers twenty-one through ninety-nine.
   Thirty-five delegates attended the national convention.

2. To join compound adjectives preceding a noun they modify as a unit.
   End-of-term grades will be posted on the classroom door.

3. After each word or figure in a series of words or figures that modify the same noun (suspended hyphenation).
   Meeting planners made first-, second-, and third-class reservations.

4. To spell out a word.
   The sign read, "For your c-o-n-v-i-e-n-c-e." Of course, the correct word is c-o-n-v-e-n-i-e-n-c-e.

5. To form certain compound nouns.
   WGAL-TV   spin-off   teacher-counselor   AFL-CIO

Use italic

To indicate titles of books, plays, movies, magazines, and newspapers. (Titles may be keyed in ALL CAPS or underlined.)
A review of *Runaway Jury* appeared in *The New York Times*.

Use parentheses

1. To enclose parenthetical or explanatory matter and added information.
   Amendments to the bylaws (Exhibit A) are enclosed.

2. To enclose identifying letters or figures in a series.
   Check these factors: (1) period of time, (2) rate of pay, and (3) nature of duties.

3. To enclose figures that follow spelled-out amounts to give added clarity or emphasis.
   The total award is fifteen hundred dollars ($1,500).

Use a question mark

At the end of a sentence that is a direct question. But use a period after requests in the form of a question (whenever the expected answer is action, not words).
What has been the impact of the Information Superhighway?
Will you complete the enclosed form and return it to me.

Use quotation marks

1. To enclose direct quotations.
   Professor Dye asked, "Are you spending the summer in Europe?"
   Was it Emerson who said, "To have a friend is to be one"?

2. To enclose titles of articles, poems, songs, television programs, and unpublished works, such as theses and dissertations.
   "Talk of the Town" in the *New Yorker*   "Fog" by Sandburg
   "Survivor" in prime time   "Memory" from *Cats*

3. To enclose special words or phrases or coined words (words not in dictionary usage).
   The words "phony" and "braggart" describe him, according to coworkers.
   The presenter annoyed the audience with phrases like "uh" and "you know."

Use a semicolon

1. To separate two or more independent clauses in a compound sentence when the conjunction is omitted.
   Being critical is easy; being constructive is not so easy.

2. To separate independent clauses when they are joined by a conjunctive adverb, such as *consequently* or *therefore*.
   I work mornings; therefore, I prefer an afternoon interview.

3. To separate a series of phrases or clauses (especially if they contain commas) that are introduced by a colon.
   Al spoke in these cities: Denver, CO; Erie, PA; and Troy, NY.

4. To precede an abbreviation or word that introduces an explanatory statement.
   She organized her work; for example, naming folders and files to indicate degrees or urgency.

Use an underline

To call attention to words or phrases (or use quotation marks or italic).
Take the presenter's advice: <u>Stand</u> up, <u>speak</u> up, and then <u>sit</u> down.
Students often confuse <u>its</u> and <u>it's</u>.

BASIC GRAMMAR GUIDES

Use a singular verb

1. With a singular subject.

   Dr. Cho was to give the lecture, but he is ill.

2. With indefinite pronouns (*each, every, any, either, neither, one,* etc.)

   Each of these girls has an important role in the class play.

   Neither of them is well enough to start the game.

3. With singular subjects linked by *or* or *nor*; but if one subject is singular and the other is plural, the verb agrees with the nearer subject.

   Neither Ms. Moss nor Mr. Katz was invited to speak.

   Either the manager or his assistants are to participate.

4. With a collective noun (*class, committee, family, team,* etc.) if the collective noun acts as a unit.

   The committee has completed its study and filed a report.

   The jury has returned to the courtroom to give its verdict.

5. With the pronouns *all* and *some* (as well as fractions and percentages) when used as subjects if their modifiers are singular. Use a plural verb if their modifiers are plural.

   Some of the new paint is already cracking and peeling.

   All of the workers are to be paid for the special holiday.

   Historically, about 40 percent has voted.

6. When *number* is used as the subject and is preceded by *the*; use a plural verb if *number* is the subject and is preceded by *a*.

   The number of voters has increased again this year.

   A number of workers are on vacation this week.

Use a plural verb

1. With a plural subject.

   The players were all here, and they were getting restless.

2. With a compound subject joined by *and*.

   Mrs. Samoa and her son are to be on a local talk show.

Negative forms of verbs

1. Use the plural verb *do not* or *don't* with pronoun subjects *I, we, you,* and *they* as well as with plural nouns.

   I do not find this report believable; you don't either.

2. Use the singular verb *does not* or *doesn't* with pronouns *he, she,* and *it* as well as with singular nouns.

   Though she doesn't accept the board's offer, the board doesn't have to offer more.

Pronoun agreement with antecedents

1. A personal pronoun (*I, we, you, he, she, it, their,* etc.) agrees in person (first, second, or third) with the noun or other pronoun it represents.

   We can win the game if we all give each play our best effort.

   You may play softball after you finish your homework.

   Andrea said that she will drive her car to the shopping mall.

2. A personal pronoun agrees in gender (feminine, masculine, or neuter) with the noun or other pronoun it represents.

   Each winner will get a corsage as she receives her award.

   Mr. Kimoto will give his talk after the announcements.

   The small boat lost its way in the dense fog.

3. A personal pronoun agrees in number (singular or plural) with the noun or other pronoun it represents.

   Celine drove her new car to Del Rio, Texas, last week.

   The club officers made careful plans for their next meeting.

4. A personal pronoun that represents a collective noun (*team, committee, family,* etc.) may be singular or plural, depending on the meaning of the collective noun.

   Our women's soccer team played its fifth game today.

   The vice squad took their positions in the square.

Commonly confused pronouns

it's (contraction): it is; it has
its (pronoun): possessive form of *it*

It's good to get your e-mail; it's been a long time.
The puppy wagged its tail in welcome.

their (pronoun): possessive form of *they*
there (adverb/pronoun): at or in that place; sometimes used to introduce a sentence
they're (contraction): they are

The hikers all wore their parkas.
Will they be there during our presentation?
They're likely to be late because of rush-hour traffic.

who's (contraction): who is; who has
whose (pronoun): possessive form of *who*

Who's seen the movie? Who's going now?
I chose the one whose skills are best.

NOTE: See p. R13 for other confusing word groups.

Documentation in reports: Century 21 style, R20; Modern Language Association style, R20

Dollar sign ($) key, 47

Double letters, 22, 36, 54, 317

Drop cap, office features, 414

E key, control of, 5, 512

E-mail messages, 76–77, 161–169, R14, R15; address list, 161, R14; assessment, 132, 220; attachments, 76, 162–163; blind copy notation (Bcc), R14; body, 76, R14; copies being sent, 76, 161; copy notation (Cc), R14; delay delivery, 161, 168; distribution list, 161–162, 164; formatting, 80, 165–168; guidelines, 571–572; heading, 76, R14; inbox, 77; out of office assistant, 163–164, 168; in personal information management, 77; reply and forward, 161; request delivery receipt, 161; request read receipt, 168; review, 127, 222; searches and sorts, 77; signature, 161, 169, R14; special features, 161–164, R14

Electronic postage software, 59

Electronic presentations, 110–125, 212–221; add notes, 216–217; aspect design theme, 115; assessment, 136–137, 229; bar graph, 121; basic shapes, 117; block arrows, 117; bulleted list with clip art, 116; bulleted list with photo, 116; choice diagram, 118; clip art, 116; concourse design theme, 115; defined, 110; deliver a slide presentation, 125, 220–221; design themes, 110–111, 115; design tips, 221; equation shapes, 117; evaluation of a slide presentation, 125; features of, 110; flowchart, 120; flowchart shapes, 117; graphics, 215–217; graphs and charts, 121–123; hyperlinks, 212; line and area graph, 121, 122; lines, 117; normal view, 113; opulent design theme, 115; photos, 116; pictures, 212; pie chart, 121, 123; review, 130–131, 224–225; section header layout, 111; shapes, 117; slide animations, 212, 215; slide layouts, 111; slide presentation, 124, 213–214; slide show view, 113; slide sorter view, 113; slide transitions, 212, 215; slide with clip art, 118; slide with shapes, 117; SmartArt graphics, 212; solstice design theme, 115; sound, 212, 217–219; stair steps diagram, 119; stars, banners, and callouts, 117; tables, 120; template design, 115; timing, 212; title and content bulleted list, 115; title and content layout, 111; title slide, 114; title slide layout, 111; view options, 112–113; view presentation, 114

Electronic reports, 380

Electronic resumes, 560, 561, R22

Embed a file, spreadsheets, 452

Emoticons, 572

Emphasis, in document design, 307

Employment application form, R22

Employment documents, 559–564, R22

End key, office features, 149

End key in document navigation, 149

End-of-lesson routine, 509

Endnotes: in bound reports, 174, 181–184; in MLA-style reports, 271; office features, 171

Energy-saving tips, 422

Enter formulas, spreadsheets, 296

Enter key, 3, 4, 6, 8, 10, 12, 16, 19, 59, 508, 510, 515, 521, 522, 527, 533, R2

Enumerated items, in bound reports, 173

Envelopes, 59, 69, R17; delivery address, 59, R17; electronic postage software, 59; in mail merge, 436; office features, 59, 148; in personal-business letter, block style, 69; return address, 59, R17; size of, 59, R17

Environmental Protection Agency (EPA), 316

Equal sign (=) key, 50

Equation shapes, in electronic presentations, 117

Esc key, R2

Ethics, 75, 188; assumptions, 75; in computer use, 570–571; consequences, 75; decision making, 75; facts, 75; personal values, 75; and your career, 556

Excel, 455, 461

Excel spreadsheet in a *Word* document, 384

Exclamation point, 186, R11

Exclamation point (!) key, 50

Exercise methods, 375

Extranet, 352

F key, control of, 3

Facts in ethics, 75

Fax template, 274

Fields: adding new to database, 334–336; database, 321, 322, 438

Figure-key mastery, 29–32

Figures: apostrophes to indicate omission of, 318

See also Number expressions; Numbers

File management, R6–R8

Files, in mail merge, 369

Fill feature, spreadsheets, 401

Find and replace text, office features, 245

Finger gymnastics, RSI-3

First Amendment vs. libel, slander, aspersion, harassment, and defamation, 571

Flowchart, in electronic presentations, 117, 120

Flyers, document design for, 313–314, 342, 349

Fonts: color of, 56; in document design, 307; office features, 56, 59; size in document design, 307; size of, 56

Footers: in business plans, 380; office features, 248; spreadsheets, 396

Footnotes: in bound reports, 174, 178–181; office features, 171

Format painter, office features, 82, 147

Format references, R15–R22; agenda, R21; bound report with long quotation and footnotes, R18; business letter in block format with specialized features, R15; business letter in modified block format with list, R16; business letter in modified block format with postscript, R16; business letter showing second-page heading, R16; e-mail message, R15; electronic resume, R22; employment application form, R22; employment application letter, R22; envelope guides, R17; interoffice memo, R15; interoffice memo with special features, R16; itinerary, R21; meeting minutes, R21; MLA report, R19; MLA report with works cited page, R19; news release, R21; personal business letter in block format with open punctuation, R15; print resume, R22; reference pages, R18; report documentation, R20; table of contents, 418; title page, R19; unbound report with textual citations, R18

Forms, database, 321, 323, 325, 327–328, 428–429, 437

Formula bar, spreadsheets, 288

Fractions, 74

Freeze/unfreeze columns and rows, spreadsheets, 403

Function keys, R2

Functions, spreadsheets, 297

G key, control of, 8, 518

Getting ready to key, 511

Global awareness, 138, 286, 504

Go to, office features, 381

Grammar Check, office features, 57

Grammar guides, R12

Graphical user interface (GUI), R3

Graphics: in document design, 307, 312–313; in electronic presentations, 215–217

Graphs and charts, 121–123; bar graph, 121; in electronic presentations, 121–123; grids, 121; labels, 121; legend, 121; line and area graphs, 121, 122; pie charts, 121, 123; scale, 121; tick marks, 121; X-axis, 121; Y-axis, 121

Greater than sign (>) key, 51

Gridlines: office features, 195; spreadsheets, 290

Grids, in graphs and charts, 121

Guided timings, 22, 37, 49

Guided writing, 26, 35, 53

Microsoft Office® programs, 455
Microsoft Windows® tutorial: basic features of, R4–R5; desktop, R3; dialog boxes, R5; file management in, R6–R8; graphical user interface (GUI), R3; icons, R3, R4; menus, R3; minimize and maximize buttons, R5; ribbon, R4; scroll bars, R5; sidebar, R3; start button, R3, R4; start menu, R4; taskbar, R3; title bar, R4
Microsoft Word, 455, 461
Microsoft Word 2003, 60, 65, 67, 93–94
Microsoft Word 2007, 60, 66, 87, 89–90
Minimize and maximize buttons, R5
Mixed cell referencing, spreadsheets, 443
MLA-style reports, 260–271, R19, R20; assessment, 351–352; binding, 260; with endnotes, 271; formatting, 269–271; header and page number, 260; indentations and long quotations, 260; inserted table, 260; line spacing, 260; margins, 260; model, 266–267; outline, 260, 265, 343, 350; and proofreading, 268; report identification, 260; report title, 260; review, 344–345; title page, 260; with tracked changes, 267–268; unbound and bound, 270–271; works cited (references), 260, R19
Modern Language Association (MLA) style of report documentation, R20
Monitor, R2
Monthly expenses table, 557
Mouse, R2, R4
Multilevel list feature, office features, 261
Multiple-column documents, office features, 415
Multiple worksheets and 3-D references, 454
Multiplying numbers, 46

N **key**, control of, 8, 418
Name badges, 374
Name box, spreadsheets, 288
Name of writer, in personal-business letter, block style, 60
National Air and Space Museum, 272
Navigate a document, office features, 149
Negative forms of verbs, R12
Netiquette, 572
New comment feature, office features, 245
News release, 273, R21
Newsletters, 415, 417–420, 422; assessment, 474
Normal view, of electronic presentations, 113
Notes: in electronic presentations, 216–217; in personal information management, 77, 79, 81
Num Lock key, R2
Num (number) lock, 546
Number expressions, 73–74, 411, R9; spell a number that begins a sentence, 73; spell and capitalize names of streets numbered ten and under, 73; spell indefinite numbers, 73; use figures for house numbers except house number One, 73; use figures for numbers above ten, 73; use figures for numbers following nouns, 73; use figures to express date and time unless followed by o'clock, 73; use figures to express measures and weights, 73
Number keys, 140, 142, 143
Number/pounds (#) key, 48
Numbering, office features, 172
Numbers, spreadsheets, 294
Numeric keypad, 29–32, 546–551, 547, R2; addition, 547–550; division, 551; math calculations, 551; multiplication, 550; subtraction, 550
Nutrition, 281

O **key**, control of, 7, 516
Occupations, top 30 fastest-growing, 554
Office documents as Web pages, 456
Office features: AutoComplete, 149; AutoCorrect, 38; AutoFit contents, 193; AutoFit window, 193; bibliography page (reference list or works cited), 264; bold, 38, 40,
147; book marks and hyperlinks, 383; borders feature, 195; borders for page and paragraph, 262; building block, 275; bullets, 172; cell size and alignment, 97; cells, 95; center alignment, 58; center page, 82; change styles, 382; citation insert, 263; clip art insert, 262; column lengths, 416; column number and width, 415; column width, 96; columns, 95; copy, 39, 40, 148; cover page, 171; Ctrl key, 149; cut, 39; decimal tabs, 58, 148; drawing shapes, 310; drop cap, 414; end key, 149; endnotes, 171; envelopes, 59, 148; *Excel* spreadsheet in a *Word* document, 384; find and replace text, 245; fonts, 56, 59; footers, 248; footnotes, 171; format painter, 82, 147; go to, 381; Grammar Check, 57; gridlines, 195; hanging indent, 84, 170; hard page break, 83; headers, 248; heading style, 84; home key, 149; horizontal alignment, 58; hyphenation, 57; indent increase or decrease, 261; indentations, 84; insert, 38, 40; insert and delete rows and columns, 95; insert table, 95; inserting the date, 149; italicize, 38, 147; justify alignment, 58, 59; landscape orientation, 193; leader (……) feature, 172; left alignment, 58; left indent (paragraph), 84, 170; left tabs, 58, 148; line spacing, 56; margins, 56, 59, 170; merge cells table feature, 194; merging cells, 96; multilevel list feature, 261; multiple-column documents, 415; navigate a document, 149; new comment feature, 245; numbering, 172; orphan, 83; page number locations, 84, 170; paste, 39, 40, 148, 170; PgDn key, 149; PgUp key, 149; picture insert, 262; portrait orientation, 193; print, 57; print preview, 39, 57, 59; quick parts tool, 275; quick print, 57; redo, 39; references, 85, 170; right alignment, 58; right tabs, 58, 148; rows, 95; select all, 38; select text, 38, 40; shaded paragraphs, 414; show/hide, 382; SmartArt, 310; SmartArt organization chart, 311; soft page break, 83; sort feature, 82; source information insert, 263; source management, 264; Spelling Check, 57; split cells table feature, 194; split window, 381; status bar, 40; styles feature, 84; subtitle style, 84; superscript, 171; table centering, 97; table converting to text, 98; table formatting changes, 97; table formatting features, 193–195; table of contents, 383–384; table sort, 98; table tools design, 96; table tools layout tab, 95; tabs, 58, 148; templates, 274, 275; text boxes, 309; text from file, 172; text wrapping break, 59; thesaurus, 83; title style, 84, 170, 171; tracked changes, 246–247; typeover, 38; underline, 38, 147; undo, 39; vertical lines between columns, 416; watermarks, 41; widow, 83; WordArt feature, 308; wrap text around graphics, 311; zoom, 39
One-hand words, 20, 26, 282, 305, 376
Online training, in Help, 44
Open a Web page, 467
Opulent design theme, in electronic presentations, 115
Organization charts, document design for, 316
Orientation, 43
Orphans, office features, 83
Out of office assistant, in personal information management, 163–164, 168
Outlines, of MLA-style reports, 260, 265, 343, 350

P **key**, control of, 14, 532
Page breaks, spreadsheets, 399
Page numbering: in bound reports, 173; in business plans, 380; MLA-style reports, 260; office features, 84, 170; in unbound reports, 86
Page setup and print, spreadsheets, 396–398
Paper size, spreadsheets, 399
Pamphlets, 415
Paragraph headings, in bound reports, 173
Paragraphs, block, 16
Parentheses, 391–392, R11; for a name and date used as a reference, 391; for identifying letters or figures of lists within a sentence, 391; for parenthetical or explanatory matter and added information, 391
Parts of a whole, 109
Paste, office features, 39, 40, 148, 170
Paste special command, spreadsheets, 448
Percent sign key, 47
Percentage, 74, 145, 211
Period key, control of, 9, 520